Contents

5 Repetition Structures: Looping   255

In the Everyday World: Doing the Same Thing Over and Over and Knowing When to Stop   256

Preface

Prelude to Programming: Concepts & Design provides a language-independent introduction to programming concepts that helps students learn the following:

- General programming topics, such as data types, control structures, arrays, files, functions, and subprograms
- Structured programming principles, such as modular design, proper program documentation and style, and event-driven and object-oriented program design
- Basic tools and algorithms, such as data validation, defensive programming, sums and averages computation, and searching and sorting algorithms
- Real programming experience through the optional use of RAPTOR, a free flowchart-based programming environment
- Data representation of integer and floating point numbers

No prior computer or programming experience is necessary.

Changes to the Sixth Edition

There are significant and exciting changes in this edition. The text continues to strive to enhance learning programming concepts and to provide students with an enriched experience. Throughout the text, concepts build from clear and simple introductory explanations to complex and challenging Examples and Review Exercises. Major improvements include the following:

- Rather than relegating the material on data representation to Appendices, an entire chapter is devoted to these concepts. This chapter is completely independent of the rest of the content and can be skipped with no loss of continuity. However, instructors who want to include the material now have more examples and end-of-chapter Review Exercises.
- Chapter 0 has been revised with up-to-date content relating to new technologies.
- Chapter 1 has been revised and now includes information on the Boolean data type.
- The material on arrays, searching, and sorting has been divided into two chapters. Chapter 7 focuses on creating and using both one- and

two-dimensional arrays. Chapter 8 presents algorithms with extensive examples for searching and sorting.

- The text uses RAPTOR, a free flowcharting software application that allows students to create and run programs without focusing on syntax. Each chapter, from Chapter 3 on, includes an optional section devoted to learning RAPTOR and using RAPTOR to develop interesting, executable programs.
- Throughout the text Examples, Self Checks, and Review Exercises have been redesigned when necessary to ensure that they can be worked with or without RAPTOR.
- The Review Exercises in each chapter contain Multiple Choice, True/False, Short Answer, and a Programming Challenges section. All Challenge problems are suitable for RAPTOR.
- When real code is given throughout the text, JavaScript code has been added.
- More built-in functions and properties are introduced including Length_Of(), To_ASCII(), To_Character(), Indexing[], and more.
- The content in Chapter 11 on object-oriented programming has been thoroughly revised and simplified.
- New material on event-driven programming has been added to Chapter 11.

Organization of the Text

The text is written and organized to allow flexibility in covering topics. Material is presented in such a way that it can be used in any introductory programming course at any level. Each concept is presented in a clear, easily understood manner and the level of difficulty builds slowly. The **What & Why** sidebars give students the opportunity to think above and beyond the material in the Examples and encourage discussion and student interaction. The **Making it Work** sidebars demonstrate how concepts are applied in the real world. **Examples, Self Checks,** and **Review Exercises** increase in difficulty from most basic to very challenging. The **Programming Challenges** sections at the end of each chapter give students a chance to create longer, comprehensive programs from scratch and, if RAPTOR is used, they can run the programs and see the results.

The text has been designed so that instructors can use it for students at various levels. The core of the text consists of Chapter 1 and Chapters 3–7. Chapters 0 and 2 are optional; Chapter 2 in particular covers material that is relatively complex and may be skipped without consequence. Chapters 8–11 are independent of one another except that some material in Chapter 9 is required to understand Chapter 11. Thus, the text lends itself to a custom book adoption.

Chapter Summaries

- Chapter 0 provides an overview of general computer concepts.
- Chapter 1 discusses basic problem solving strategy and the essential components of a computer program (input, processing, and output). A section on data types introduces students to numeric, string, and Boolean types.

- Chapter 2 is dedicated to data representation. Students learn to convert decimal numbers to binary and hexadecimal. The various ways to represent integers (unsigned, signed, two's complement) as well as floating point numbers are covered. IEEE standards are used to represent floating point numbers in single- and double-precision. The material in this chapter is completely independent from the rest of the book.

- Chapter 3 introduces the program development process, the principles of modular design, pseudocode, and flowcharts. Documentation, testing, syntax and logic errors, and an overview of the basic control structures are covered.

- Chapter 4 covers decision (selection) structures including single-, dual- and multiple-alternative structures, relational and logical operators, the ASCII coding scheme, defensive programming, and menu-driven programs.

- Chapters 5 and 6 present a complete coverage of repetition structures (loops). Chapter 5 focuses on the basic loop structures: pre- and post-test loops, sentinel-controlled loops, counter-controlled loops, and loops for data input, data validation, and computing sums and averages. Chapter 6 builds on the basics from the previous chapters to create programs that use repetition structures in combination with decision structures, nested loops, and random numbers.

- Chapter 7 covers one-dimensional, two-dimensional, and parallel arrays. Representation of character strings as arrays is also discussed. The material in this chapter has been expanded from the previous edition, including more examples to assist students in understanding this difficult material.

- Chapter 8 covers searching and sorting. Two search techniques (serial and binary searches) and two sort techniques (bubble and selection sorts) are included with expanded coverage.

- Chapter 9 covers functions and modules, including the use of arguments and parameters, value and reference parameters, passing by reference versus passing by value, and the scope of a variable. Built-in and user-defined functions are covered. Recursion—an advanced topic—is discussed in some depth but can be skipped if desired.

- Chapter 10 is about sequential data files. The discussion covers records and fields and how to create, write, and read from sequential files. Topics also include how to delete, modify, and insert records, and how to merge files. Arrays are used in conjunction with data files for file maintenance. The control break processing technique is demonstrated in a longer program.

- Chapter 11 is an introduction to the concepts of object-oriented programming and event-driven programming. The object-oriented material in this chapter has been revised for better understandability. The material on event-driven programming is new to this edition. A short introduction to modeling languages, including UML is given. Object-oriented design topics include classes (parent and child), objects, inheritance, polymorphism, public versus private attributes and methods, and the use of constructors. The material on event-driven programming includes the graphical user interface and window components. Properties and methods for various window controls are also covered.

Many sections throughout the text are devoted to more advanced applications and are optional. In particular, the Focus on Problem Solving sections develop relatively complex program designs, which some instructors may find useful to illustrate the chapter material and others may elect to skip to save time. RAPTOR can be used as a tool to illustrate concepts by creating examples throughout the text in RAPTOR but can also be used to create longer and more challenging, creative programs.

Running With RAPTOR: A Flowcharting Environment

In this edition, each chapter from Chapter 3 onward contains an optional section entitled **Running With RAPTOR**. The section describes how to use RAPTOR for that chapter's material with screenshots and step-by-step instructions. Short examples demonstrate how RAPTOR is used to work with the chapter's content and a longer program is developed. In many chapters the RAPTOR program is an implementation of the long program developed in the Focus on Problem Solving section. The Running With RAPTOR sections can be skipped with no loss of continuity. However, if used, the longer RAPTOR programs give students a real-life experience by creating interesting, running programs including games, encryption, and more.

Features of the Text

In the Everyday World

Beginning with Chapter 1, each chapter starts with a discussion of how the material in that chapter relates to familiar things (for example, "Arrays in the Everyday World") This material provides an introduction to the programming logic used in that chapter through an ordinary and easily understood topic, and establishes a foundation upon which programming concepts are presented.

Making It Work

The **Making It Work** sidebars provide information about how to implement concepts in an actual high-level language, such as C++, Java, JavaScript, or Visual Basic. These boxed sidebars appear throughout the text and are self-contained and optional.

What & Why

Often we conclude an Example with a short discussion about what would happen if the program were run, or what would happen if something in the program were changed. These **What & Why** sidebars help students deepen their understanding of how programs run. They are useful in initiating classroom discussion.

Pointers and Style Pointers

The concepts of programming style and documentation are introduced in Chapter 3 and emphasized throughout. Other **Pointers** appear periodically throughout the text. These short notes provide insight into the subject or specialized knowledge about the topic at hand.

Examples

There are more than 200 numbered worked Examples in the text. The pseudocode in the Examples includes line numbers for easy reference. Detailed line-by-line discussions follow the code with sections entitled **What Happened?**

Focus on Problem Solving

Each chapter from Chapter 4 to the end includes a **Focus on Problem Solving** section which presents a real-life programming problem, analyzes it, designs a program to solve it, discusses appropriate coding considerations, and indicates how the program can be tested. In the process, students not only see a review of the chapter material, but also work through a programming problem of significant difficulty. These sections are particularly useful to prepare students for a language-specific programming course. For selected programs there are real code implementations in C++, Java, Visual Basic, and Python available on the Pearson website which can be used to demonstrate how the concepts learned in the text apply to real-life programs. The program code illustrates the congruence between the pseudocode taught in this book and the code in a specific programming language. Executable files are also included so the actual programs can be run, even if the code is not used pedagogically.

Exercises

Many new exercises have been added to this edition to correspond with new material. Many exercises have been revised to permit them to be implemented with RAPTOR. The text contains the following diverse selection:

- **Self Checks** at the end of each section include items that test students' understanding of the material covered in that section (answers to Self Checks are in Appendix C)
- **Review Questions** at the end of each chapter include questions of various types that provide further review of the chapter material (Answers to the odd-numbered questions are available on the student support website; answers to the even-numbered questions are on the instructor support web site).
- **Programming Challenges** at the end of each chapter require students to design programs using the material learned in that chapter and earlier chapters. All Programming Challenges can be implemented with RAPTOR. Solutions to all Programming Challenges in RAPTOR are available on the instructor support web site.

Supplements

Student Support Web Site

A variety of resources are available with this book. Students may access them at www.pearsonhighered.com/venit-drake.

Instructor's Supplements

Supplemental materials are available to qualified instructors at www.pearsonhighered .com/irc, including the following:

- PowerPoint Presentations for all Chapters
- Solutions to all Self Checks including RAPTOR implementations of select problems
- Solutions to all Review Exercises including corresponding RAPTOR programs
- RAPTOR programs corresponding to all Programming Challenges
- Testbank

For further information about obtaining instructor supplements, contact your campus Pearson Education sales representative.

Acknowledgments

The **In the Everyday World** essays, a unique feature of this book, were envisioned and drafted by Bill Hammerschlag of Brookhaven College for the second edition, and are expanded and revised in this edition.

The implementations of the code in C++, Visual Basic, Java, and Python from the **Focus on Problem Solving** sections were created by Anton Drake from the University of Florida, presently a software developer at OPIE Technologies.

A special thanks to Martin Carlisle who created RAPTOR and remains eager and generous with his support.

We want to extend our thanks to Matt Goldstein, our most supportive and caring Editor; to Marilyn Lloyd, the most patient and understanding Production Manager ever; to Haseen Khan, the Project Manager at Laserwords who works on the other side of the world but feels like my next-door neighbor; and to the entire team at Pearson Education, including Kayla Smith-Tarbox and Yez Alayan. We also want to extend a special thank you to Michael Hirsch who initially brought us together on this project; without Michael, none of this would have been possible.

—Elizabeth Drake
and Stewart Venit

I want to thank my coauthor, Stewart Venit. It's a pleasure to work with him. Marilyn Lloyd and Haseen Khan are very special people; they answer my questions with unfailing patience. I also want to thank my children, Anton and Severia, who have always encouraged my desire—my need—to write. My grandsons, Justy and Jacob, make me smile by being impressed by my work.

—Elizabeth Drake

I would like to thank my coauthor, Elizabeth Drake, for greatly enhancing and improving this book in each of the last four editions. I am grateful to my wife Corinne, who, over the course of my 35 year writing career, never complained about the countless hours I spent camped in front of a computer screen. I also want to thank the rest of my family for being my family: daughter Tamara, son-in-law Cameron, and grandchildren Evelyn and Damian.

—Stewart Venit

Introduction

0

In this introduction, we will discuss the history of computers and computer **hardware** and **software**—the devices and programs that make a computer work.

After reading this introduction, you will be able to do the following:

- Understand the evolution of computing devices from ancient Babylonia to the twenty-first century
- Understand the components that make up a typical computer system: the central processing unit, internal memory, mass storage, and input and output devices
- Know the types of internal memory—RAM and ROM—and understand their functions
- Know the types of mass storage: magnetic, optical, solid state, and online storage
- Know the types of software used by a modern computer: application software and system software
- Know the levels of programming languages: machine language, assembly language, and high-level language
- Know the types of programming and scripting languages used to create software
- Understand the distinction between programming and scripting languages

In the Everyday World

Computers Everywhere

A century ago, a child would listen in wonder as his parents described what life was like before cars, electricity, and telephones. Today, a child listens in wonder as his parents describe what life was like without video games, smart phones, GPS systems, and computers. Seventy years ago, electronic computers didn't exist. Now, we use computers daily. Computers are in homes, schools, and offices; in supermarkets and fast food restaurants; on airplanes and submarines. Computers are in our phones, kitchen appliances, and cars. We carry them in our backpacks, pockets, and purses. They are used by the young and old, filmmakers and farmers, bankers and baseball managers. By taking advantage of a wealth of diverse and sophisticated software (programs and apps), we are able to use computers almost limitlessly for education, communication, entertainment, money management, product design and manufacture, and business and institutional processes.

0.1 A Brief History of Computers

Calculators, devices used to increase the speed and accuracy of numerical computations, have been around for a long time. For example, the abacus, which uses rows of sliding beads to perform arithmetic operations, has roots that date back more than 5,000 years to ancient Babylonia. More modern mechanical calculators, using gears and rods, have been in use for almost 400 years. In fact, by the late nineteenth century, calculators of one sort or another were relatively commonplace. However, these machines were by no means *computers* as we use the word today.

What Is a Computer?

A **computer** is a mechanical or an electronic device that can efficiently store, retrieve, and manipulate large amounts of information at high speed and with great accuracy. Moreover, it can execute tasks and act upon intermediate results without human intervention by carrying out a list of instructions called a **program**.

Although we tend to think of the computer as a recent development, Charles Babbage, an Englishman, designed and partially built a true computer in the mid-1800s. Babbage's machine, which he called an *Analytical Engine*, contained hundreds of axles and gears and could store and process 40-digit numbers. Babbage was assisted in his work by Ada Augusta Byron, the daughter of the poet Lord Byron. Ada Byron grasped the importance of the invention and helped to publicize the project. A major programming language (Ada) was named after her. Unfortunately, Babbage never finished his Analytical Engine. His ideas were too advanced for the existing technology, and he could not obtain enough financial backing to complete the project.

Serious attempts to build a computer were not renewed until nearly 70 years after Babbage's death. Around 1940, Howard Aiken at Harvard University, John Atanasoff, and Clifford Berry at Iowa State University built machines that came close to being true computers. However, Aiken's Mark I could not act independently on its intermediate results, and the Atanasoff-Berry computer required the frequent intervention of an operator during its computations.

Just a few years later in 1945, a team at the University of Pennsylvania, led by John Mauchly and J. Presper Eckert, completed work on the world's first fully operable electronic computer. Mauchly and Eckert named it ENIAC, an acronym for Electronic Numerical Integrator and Computer. ENIAC (see Figure 0.1) was a huge machine. It was 80 feet long, 8 feet high, weighed 33 tons, contained over 17,000 vacuum tubes in its electronic circuits, and consumed 175,000 watts of electricity. For its time, ENIAC was a truly amazing machine because it could accurately perform up to 5,000 additions per second. However, by current standards, it was exceedingly slow. A modern run-of-the-mill personal computer can exceed 100 million operations per second!

For the next decade or so, all electronic computers used **vacuum tubes** (see Figure 0.2) to do the internal switching necessary to perform computations. These machines, which we now refer to as first-generation computers, were large by modern standards, although not as large as ENIAC. They required a climate-controlled environment and a lot of tender love and care to keep them operating. By 1955, about 300 computers—built mostly by IBM and Remington Rand—were being used, primarily by large businesses, universities, and government agencies.

Figure 0.1 The ENIAC computer

Source: U.S. Army

Figure 0.2 A vacuum tube

By the late 1950s, computers had become much faster and more reliable. The most significant change at this time was that the large, heat-producing vacuum tubes were replaced by relatively small transistors. The **transistor** (see Figure 0.3) is one of the most important inventions of the twentieth century. It was developed at Bell Labs in the late 1940s by William Shockley, John Bardeen, and Walter Brattain, who later shared a Nobel Prize for their achievement. Transistors are small and require very little energy, especially compared to vacuum tubes. Therefore, many transistors can be packed close together in a compact enclosure.

In the early 1960s, Digital Equipment Corporation (DEC) took advantage of small, efficient packages of transistors called **integrated circuits** to create the **minicomputer,** a machine roughly the size of a four-drawer filing cabinet. Because these computers not only were smaller but also less expensive than their predecessors, they were an immediate success. Nevertheless, sales of larger computers, now called **mainframes**, also rapidly increased. The computer age had clearly arrived and the industry leader was the IBM innovative System 360.

Personal Computers

Despite the increasing popularity of computers, it was not until the late 1970s that the computer became a household appliance. This development was made possible by the invention of the **microchip** (see Figure 0.4) in the 1960s. A microchip is a piece of silicon about the size of a postage stamp, packed with thousands of electronic components. The microchip and its more advanced cousin, the **microprocessor,** led to the creation of the world's first **personal computer (PC)** in 1974. The PC

Figure 0.3 An early transistor

Figure 0.4 The microchip

was relatively inexpensive compared to its predecessors and was small enough to fit on a desktop. This landmark computer, the Altair 8800 microcomputer, was unveiled in 1975. Although it was a primitive and not a very useful machine, the Altair inspired thousands of people, both hobbyists and professionals to become interested in PCs. Among these pioneers were Bill Gates and Paul Allen, who later founded Microsoft Corporation, now one of the world's largest companies.

Apple Computers and the IBM PC

The Altair also captured the imagination of two young Californians, Stephen Wozniak and Steven Jobs. They were determined to build a better, more useful computer. They founded Apple Computer, Inc., and in 1977 they introduced the Apple II, which was an immediate hit. With the overwhelming success of this machine and Tandy Corporation's TRS-80, companies that were manufacturing larger minicomputers and mainframes began to notice. In 1981, IBM introduced the popular IBM PC (see Figure 0.5), and the future of the PC was assured.

Figure 0.5 The IBM PC, introduced in 1981, is an antique now!

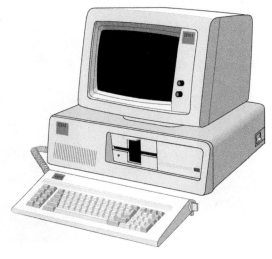

Many companies hoping to benefit from the success of the IBM PC, introduced computers that could run the same programs as the IBM, and these "IBM compatibles" soon dominated the market. Even the introduction of Apple's innovative and easy-to-use Macintosh in 1984 could not stem the tide of the IBM compatibles. These computers, virtually all of which make use of Microsoft's Windows operating system, have also spawned a huge array of software (computer programs) never dreamed of by the manufacturers of the original mainframes. This software includes word processors, photo editing programs, Web browsers, spreadsheet programs, database systems, presentation graphics programs, and a seemingly infinite variety of computer games. However, while in 2000 the Windows operating system commanded more than 95% of the market share, today's mobile devices, such as smart phones and tablets, have reduced Microsoft's domination drastically with Google's Android operating system and the Apple operating system providing strong competition.

Today's Computers

Today the computer market comprises a vast array of machines. Personal computers are everywhere and range in price from a few hundred to a few thousand dollars. For the most part, their manufacturers are billion dollar companies like IBM, Dell, Hewlett-Packard, and Apple. Although PCs are small and inexpensive, they produce a remarkable amount of computing power. Today's tablets, which can weigh less than a pound and fit into a handbag, are far more powerful than the most advanced mainframes of the mid-1970s (see Figure 0.6).

Minicomputers have also found their niche. Unlike PCs, these machines can be used by a number of people (typically 16 or more) working simultaneously at separate and remote **terminals**. Each terminal consists of a keyboard and a display screen. Minicomputers have become the mainstay of many small businesses and universities, but mainframe computers are by no means dinosaurs. These relatively large and costly machines supply users with tremendous power to manipulate information. **Supercomputers** (see Figure 0.7) are even more powerful than mainframes and can process well over 1 billion instructions per second. For a special effects company like Industrial Light and Magic or a government agency like the Internal Revenue Service, there is no substitute for a large mainframe or supercomputer.

Figure 0.6 Today's laptop and tablet computers

Figure 0.7 The Jaguar/Cray XT5—a modern supercomputer

The Internet

Despite the recent advances in computer technology, arguably the most significant development in the last 15 years has been the phenomenal rise in popularity of the **Internet**—a worldwide collection of *networks*. A **network** consists of two or more linked computers that are able to share resources and data wirelessly or via cable or phone lines. The Internet has roots that date back to a relatively small U.S. Defense Department project in the late 1960s. Since then, the Internet has grown from a small collection of mainframe computers used by universities and the military to more than 2.5 billion users worldwide who range in age from preschoolers to centenarians. Before the advent of smart phones, the two main attractions of the Internet were email and the World Wide Web. **Email**, which is short for *electronic mail*, allows anyone with access to the Internet to use his or her computer to exchange messages with another Internet user anywhere in the world almost instantaneously and at little or no cost. The **World Wide Web** (more simply called the **Web**) originated in 1989. It is a vast collection of linked documents (web pages) created by Internet users and stored on thousands of Internet-connected computers.

Today social networking sites have rivaled the popularity of email. These sites are part of Web2.0, the next generation of the World Wide Web. **Web2.0** consists of web applications that facilitate information sharing, user-centered design, and collaboration. While the term suggests a new version of the Web, it is not an update or change in technical specifications, but rather a change in the way people use the Web. Web2.0 generally refers to Web-based communities (such as Second Life), wikis (such as the online encyclopedia, Wikipedia), social-networking sites (such as Facebook), video-sharing sites (like YouTube), and more.

Self Check for Section 0.1

0.1 What characteristics of a computer distinguish it from the following?
   a. A simple (non-programmable) calculator
   b. A programmable calculator

0.2 Complete each of the following statements:
 a. A _____ is a list of instructions to be carried out by the computer.
 b. The first fully operative electronic computer was called _____.
 c. The fastest computers in use today are called _____.
 d. The _____ is a worldwide collection of interlinked networks.

0.3 True or false? The first personal computers were produced in the 1970s.

0.4 True or false? Transistors, which eventually replaced the vacuum tubes of early computers, were invented in the 1940s.

0.5 True or false? Minicomputers and mainframe computers have become obsolete; they are no longer in use.

0.6 True or false? Web2.0 is a new version of the World Wide Web, including updated technical specifications.

0.7 Match the people listed in the first column with the corresponding computer from the second column.
 1. Charles Babbage and Ada Byron   ___   a. ENIAC
 2. J. Presper Eckert and John Mauchly   ___   b. Apple II
 3. Steven Jobs and Stephen Wozniak   ___   c. Analytical Engine

0.2 Computer Basics

In Section 0.1 we defined a computer as a mechanical or an electronic device that can efficiently store, retrieve, and manipulate large amounts of information at high speed and with great accuracy. Regardless of the type of computer—from the original desktop machine with a separate tower, monitor, keyboard, and mouse to the smallest, thinnest smart phone to the elaborate digital display on a car's dashboard—a computer consists of the same basic components. As the definition implies, a computer must have the ability to input, store, manipulate, and output data. These functions are carried out by the following five main components of a computer system:

 1. The central processing unit (CPU)
 2. Internal memory (consisting of RAM and ROM)
 3. Mass storage devices (magnetic, optical, and solid state) and the Cloud
 4. Input devices (primarily the keyboard and mouse)
 5. Output devices (primarily the monitor and printer)

In this section, we will describe these components as they are implemented on a modern personal computer.

In a desktop PC, the CPU, internal memory, and most mass storage devices are located in the **system unit**. The input and output devices are housed in their own enclosures and are connected to the system unit by cables, or more recently, by wireless transmitters. Components like these, which are used by a computer but located outside the system unit, are sometimes referred to as **peripherals**. Laptop and tablet computers house the CPU, internal memory, mass storage devices, a monitor, and a keyboard, all in one relatively small package. The physical equipment that makes up the computer system is known as hardware.

The Central Processing Unit

The **central processing unit** (also called the **processor** or **CPU**) is the brain of the computer. It receives the program instructions, performs the arithmetic and logical operations necessary to execute them, and controls the other computer components. In a PC, the processor consists of millions of transistors that reside on a single microchip about the size of a postage stamp and plug into the computer's main circuit board, the **motherboard**.

More than any other component, the CPU distinguishes one computer from another. A primary factor in determining the power of a processor is its speed, measured in *gigahertz* (GHz). For example, the Pentium IV microprocessor, produced by Intel Corporation for use in PCs, is a chip that is produced in several variations that run at speeds up to 4 GHz. However, due to various factors, some processors are more powerful than others running at the same speed.

Internal Memory

A computer uses its **internal memory** to store instructions and data to be processed by the CPU. In a PC, memory resides on a series of chips either plugged directly into the motherboard or into one or more smaller circuit boards connected to the motherboard. There are two types of internal memory: **read-only memory (ROM)** and **random-access memory (RAM)**.

ROM contains an unalterable set of instructions that the computer uses during its start-up process and for certain other basic operations. RAM on the other hand, can be read from and written to. It's used by the computer to hold program instructions and data. You can think of ROM as a reference sheet, and RAM as a scratchpad, albeit a very large scratchpad. ROM is an integrated circuit programmed with specific data when it is manufactured. This information cannot be altered by the user; therefore, ROM is a permanent form of memory storage while RAM is the memory used by the computer to hold the data you are working on at any given time. For example, if you are writing an English essay with a word processor, as you write the essay you see it on your monitor, but it is also being held in RAM. When you close the word processing program or turn off the computer, all the information stored in RAM is lost. That's why it's important to save your work to some permanent storage medium—as most of us have learned at one time or another, to our dismay!

The smallest unit of memory is the **bit**. A bit can store only two different values—a zero or a one. It takes eight bits—one byte—to store a single character in memory. (Loosely speaking, a *character* is any symbol you can type, such as a letter, digit, or a punctuation mark.) Storing an instruction usually takes sixteen or more bits.

It would be impractical to talk about the size of a file in bits when just a single line of text might use hundreds of bits. Instead, the basic unit of memory is a **byte**. Memory is measured in **kilobytes (KB)**, **megabytes (MB)**, or **gigabytes (GB)**. One kilobyte is 1,024 ($1{,}024 = 2^{10}$) bytes and one megabyte is 1,024 kilobytes. A gigabyte is 1,073,741,824 ($1{,}024^9$ or 2^{30}) bytes. For example, 128 MB of RAM can store 134,217,728 characters of information at one time because, mathematically, the number of characters equals the number of bytes as follows:

$$128 \text{ MB} \times \frac{1{,}024 \text{ KB}}{\text{MB}} \times \frac{1{,}024 \text{ bytes}}{\text{KB}} = 134{,}217{,}728 \text{ bytes}$$

Mass Storage Devices

In addition to ROM and RAM, a computer needs **mass storage**, another form of memory, which stores programs and data semi-permanently. The data you store on a mass storage device remains on that device until *you* decide to erase or delete it. However, to make use of any information stored on a mass storage device, the computer must first *load* (copy) that information into RAM. In other words, when you begin to type your English essay, first the computer loads the word processing program into RAM. Then, as you type, your essay is also stored in RAM. When you finish your essay or stop for a snack, you save the essay to a storage device and close the word processing program. Both the essay and the word processing program disappear from RAM. But the word processing program still exists on your hard drive, and the essay is saved on whatever storage device you used.

There are many different types of mass storage and all of these devices fall into one of the following four categories:

1. **Magnetic storage** such as hard disks
2. **Optical storage** such as CDs and DVDs
3. **Solid-state storage** such as flash drives
4. **Cloud storage** where data is backed up on servers hosted by companies and accessed by users from the Internet

On PCs, the primary type of mass storage device is the *disk drive*. Most PCs are equipped with a **hard disk drive** and some other forms of storage. Modern removable storage devices offer many options. Storage capacity of some flash drives can be as much as 30 GB or more.

Magnetic Storage

The most common and enduring form of mass storage technology is magnetic storage, which is implemented on modern computers by a device called a hard disk drive. Hard disks are packaged with all PCs (including laptops) sold today. These devices have enormous capacities. As of this writing, the largest hard disk drives exceed several terabytes. One **terabyte** (TB) is 1,000 gigabytes or about 1 trillion bytes. Data can be read from and written to a hard disk at a high rate of speed; therefore, the hard drive is the primary mass storage device. It holds the operating system (see Section 0.3) and most of the applications and data used by the computer. Additionally, users normally store any other software they purchase, such as games, money managers, and so forth on the hard drive.

Optical Storage

You are undoubtedly familiar with **CDs** and **DVDs**. CDs (compact discs) are sometimes used to store music, and DVDs (digital versatile discs) do the same for video. Both types of discs are also used to provide a storage medium for use in PCs. We refer to this type of storage as optical because the data is read by a laser within the CD or DVD drive. CDs and DVDs are great storage mediums for prepackaged software or for storing a presentation file you may use for a class project or demonstration. The **DVD-ROM** discs have a capacity of almost 5 GB, more than seven times the storage capacity of a CD. Because this kind of drive can also read CDs, it is often packaged with a computer system.

Solid-State Storage

Flash memory, a type of solid-state technology, is a popular type of removable storage. Many people use flash drives to transport files or as backup, but the Cloud (see below) has become a much more popular way to store and backup one's personal data. A solid-state device is especially reliable because it has no moving parts. Flash drives are popular with computer users because they can be plugged into any USB port on any computer, and virtually all computers have USB ports. Therefore, you can be fairly sure that you will be able to access your files from a flash drive regardless of what computer you use. Flash drives come in many sizes from 2 MB to 256 GB and possibly more as new products are being introduced all the time.

Cloud Computing

Cloud computing is a general term that encompasses a way to deliver computer services over the Internet. A host is a third-party company that provides various services, which normally are of three types: infrastructure, platform, and software.

Infrastructure as a service refers to storage, hardware, servers, and networking components. A host that provides this service owns the equipment and is responsible for housing, running, and maintaining it, while the client, normally a business or an organization, pays the host for use of the services.

Platform as a service offers a client a way to rent hardware, operating systems, storage and networking capacity over the Internet. It is defined as a set of software and product development tools hosted by the provider.

Software as a service is a model where a client uses the software applications provided by the host for a fee. This model is rapidly becoming popular with individual users as well as with businesses and large organizations. With this type of service an individual user can have access to many different software packages as needed at a reasonable "rental" fee. It also ensures that the user has access to the latest and newest versions of software without worrying about upgrade installations or fees. For example, a web development student might need to use a graphics software program for one web authoring course but, since the student plans to become a developer and not a graphics designer, there is no reason to purchase an expensive graphics program. By using a cloud-based host, the student can pay for the use of the program that is needed for a single semester. This is, normally, far less than the cost of purchasing the entire program.

A cloud service is normally provided on demand, usually by the minute or hour, which allows a user the flexibility to have as much of the service wanted or needed at any time. It gives the user access to more software options that would be possible if each software item had to be purchased individually.

Cloud computing allows the user to access his or her own data from any computer with an Internet connection from anywhere in the world at any time. As anyone who has arrived at a meeting or a presentation only to realize the file he meant to bring was on a different flash drive or the application needed to open a file was not available on the computer to be used can attest—cloud computing can be a life saver.

Input Devices

The computer uses its **input devices** to receive data from the outside world. For this purpose, every PC includes a **keyboard** and a pointing device such as a **mouse** to allow you to enter information into a program. All tablets and most smart phones include a "virtual" keyboard, a keyboard that the user can display on-screen and type in by touching the keys.

Keyboard

Computer keyboards contain keys for alphanumeric characters, punctuation marks, and special keys. On PCs these special keys include *function keys*, which perform special tasks that vary from program to program, *cursor control keys*, which allow you to move the *cursor* (which indicates the current typing position) around the screen, and other specialized keys.

Mouse

Another standard input device is the mouse, a hand-held object containing one, two, or three buttons. A computer mouse, together with the cable that connects it to the computer, vaguely resembles a long-tailed rodent, which may explain where it got its name. When you roll the mouse around on your desktop, a pointer moves correspondingly on the screen. In fact, everything that you can do with a mouse you can do with a keyboard. However, few people know the keystrokes that correspond to most mouse movements. The mouse can speed up many input operations, but it lacks the versatility of the keyboard. Nowadays, many users are proficient in using a **touchpad** (also called a **trackpad**) and their fingers, thus eliminating the need for a mouse.

The keyboard and mouse are not the only devices that input data to a computer. Computers receive input from phone and cable lines as well as wireless Internet connections. Whenever you surf the Internet, your computer receives input. A tablet computer, which allows people to write directly on a screen with a digital pen, is another form of input. In fact, when you initiate an action by touching the screen of a tablet or a smart phone with your finger, your finger becomes an input device!

Voice Command

A **voice command device** (VCD) is a device controlled by means of human voice. By removing the need to use buttons, dials and switches, consumers can operate devices while doing other tasks. Some of the earliest types of VCDs were in various home appliances, but nowadays consumers expect smart phones to come equipped with voice activation. VCDs are now found in computer operating systems, commercial software for computers, smart phones, cars, and more. Technology today advances so rapidly that it's impossible to predict what the newest input device might be by the time you read this book!

Output Devices

Input devices allow us to communicate with the computer; **output devices** make it possible for the computer to communicate with us. The most common output devices are **display screens**, **speakers**, and **printers**.

Display Screens

Display screens, as the name suggests, display images (text and graphics) on a screen. They include the following basic types:

- A CRT (cathode ray tube) monitor resembles an old-fashioned television. CRTs are only used with older desktop PCs.
- A flat-panel display consists of a thin piece of glass or plastic together with electronic components that display the image. The electronics usually makes use of either LCD (liquid crystal display) or LED (light-emitting diode) technology. Nowadays, flat panel displays are used on virtually all computers, whether they be PCs, smart phones, tablets, or any other computing device.

For all displays, screen size is measured along the diagonal, just as it is with televisions. Another characteristic that affects the quality and cost of a monitor is its **resolution**—the number of **pixels** (tiny dots of light) used to create images.

Printers

Output to the screen is impermanent; it disappears when new information is displayed or if the power to the computer is turned off. If you want to make a permanent copy (a *hard copy*) of a program's output on a paper, you need to use a printer.

The text and pictures produced by all printers comprise tiny dots of ink or an ink-like substance. The size of these dots and how closely they are packed together determine the quality of the output. Currently, the following types of printers dominate the market:

- *Laser printers* have become the standard for business use. They produce excellent quality text and graphics at a high rate of speed and are remarkably reliable. Black and white laser printers cost relatively little to buy, operate, and maintain. Color laser printers are relatively expensive, and their photo output quality may not be as good as ink jet printers.
- *Ink jet printers* spray tiny drops of ink on the paper to create surprisingly clear images. Most ink jet printers produce excellent color output as well. Generally speaking, ink jet printers are less expensive than laser printers, but they are slower and have a higher cost of operation, making them more common in homes than in offices.

Although display screens and printers immediately come to mind when we think of output, there are many other types of output devices. Some fall into the category of input *and* output devices. For example, when you connect to the Internet, your connection is both an input and an output device. When you listen to a radio station on your computer, the speakers are an output device.

Self Check for Section 0.2

0.8 Name the five basic components that make up a typical computer system.

0.9 Describe the function of each of the following:
   a. The central processing unit (CPU)
   b. Mass storage devices

0.10 True or false? The speed of a processor is usually measured in *gigahertz*.

0.11 True or false? A *bit* is another name for one byte of memory.

0.12 True or false? If a computer has sufficient input devices, it doesn't need output devices.

0.13 Name two of each of the following:
   a. input device
   b. output device

0.14 Give one advantage and one disadvantage of cloud computing. (There are no right and wrong answers to this question.)

0.3 Software and Programming Languages

The most powerful hardware cannot accomplish anything by itself; it needs software to bring it to life. Software consists of computer programs that provide instructions for the CPU, and in so doing, allows the user to send email, calculate loan balances, edit photos, play games, share with friends and family on social networks, and perform countless other tasks. In this section, we will describe some types of software and discuss the means by which software is created.

Types of Software

Software can be divided into two general categories: application software and system software.

Application Software

Applications, which are called **apps** on tablets and smart phones, are programs you use to enhance your productivity, solve problems, supply information, or provide recreation. The following are some of the more popular kinds of applications:

- *Word processors* help you create, modify, and print documents such as letters, reports, and memos.

- *Database managers* allow you to enter, organize, and access large quantities of data. You might use a database program to create a personal phone directory. A business can use this kind of application to maintain customer lists and employee records.

- *Spreadsheet programs* simplify the manipulation and calculation of large amounts of tabular data (spreadsheets). These programs are often used by businesses to predict the effects of different strategies on their bottom line.

- *Photo editors* allow you to download photographs to your computer from a digital camera, modify, and print them. Audio and video editors, such as Camtasia or Jing, do the same thing for audio and video files.

- *Web browsers* and *email programs* allow you to make use of the Internet to view an incredible variety of electronic documents and to communicate with others around the world.

Applications are developed and published by many different companies and sold in retail stores, by mail order firms, and over the Internet. A software package contains one or more CDs or DVDs, which store the application files or it may simply contain a Web address and an access code, which will allow you to download the application directly from the Internet. The files contain the programs, data, and documents needed by the application. Before you can use a piece of software, it must be *installed* on your computer, which means the computer must copy files from the CDs or from the website to your computer's hard disk or flash memory and supply certain information about the application to the operating system.

System Software

System software consists of programs used by the computer to control and maintain its hardware and to communicate with the user. The most important piece of system software is the **operating system (OS)**, which is the computer's master control program. A computer must use an operating system written especially for that type of device. Some examples of operating systems are Windows 8 (for Windows-based computers), Apple iOS (for iPhones), and Android Jelly Bean (for Android-based tablets and smart phones).

Without an operating system, the computer would be useless. The operating system has two essential functions as follows:

1. It helps applications communicate with the computer hardware. Applications are written to run under a specific operating system; they need to access the computer's disk drives, memory, and so forth. There are many different operating systems, so you should check before you buy application software to be sure it runs with the type and version of the operating system on your computer.

2. It provides an interface between you and the computer so that you can install and start applications, manipulate files, and perform many other tasks.

Types of Programming and Scripting Languages

Just as a book must be written in a particular language such as English, Chinese, or French, programs must be written in a particular programming language. A **programming language** is a set of symbols and rules governing their use that are used in constructing programs.

There are four fundamental types of programming languages as follows:

1. Machine languages
2. Assembly languages
3. High-level languages
4. Scripting languages

Machine Language

A **machine language** program consists of a sequence of bits that are all zeros and ones. Each combination of zeros and ones is an instruction to the computer about something. Machine language is the only language the computer can understand directly. However, as you might imagine, it is very difficult for humans to read or write machine language programs. For this reason, **programmers** normally use either assembly or **high-level languages**.

Assembly Language

Assembly language is a symbolic representation of machine language. There is usually a one-to-one correspondence between the two; each assembly language instruction translates into one machine language instruction. However, assembly language uses easily recognizable codes, which make it a lot easier for people to understand. Before a computer can carry out an assembly language program, the computer must translate it into a machine language. This is done by a special program called an *assembler*.

Making It Work

Comparing Machine Language and Assembly Language

The following instruction adds two numbers on a certain minicomputer:

Machine Language Instruction:

    0110110111110111 0000000100000000 0000000100000000

Assembly Language Equivalent:

    ADD A, B

Of course the computer is not adding the letter A and the letter B. What this instruction actually means to the computer is to add the values that are stored in the spaces in the computer's memory, designated by A and B.

High-Level Languages

High-level languages usually contain English words and phrases. Their symbols and structure are far removed from those of machine language. High-level languages have several advantages over machine or assembly languages; they are easier to learn and use, and the resulting programs are easier to read and modify. A single instruction in a high-level language usually translates into many instructions in machine language. Moreover, a given high-level language does not differ much from one type of computer to another; a program written on one type of machine can usually be modified relatively easily for use on another. On the negative side, high-level languages are usually less powerful and produce less efficient programs than their assembly language counterparts. High-level languages, like assembly languages, must be translated into machine language before they can be understood by the computer.

FORTRAN (FORmula TRANslator), the first high-level language, was developed in the mid-1950s, primarily for engineering and scientific applications. Since then, there has been a flood of high-level languages. The following list includes a few of them:

- C++ is currently one of the most popular languages. It is used for efficient programming of many different types of applications.
- COBOL (COmmon Business Oriented Language) was once the most popular language for business-related programming applications. Although

it is not often taught or used to create new programs, many old COBOL programs exist and are in use in their original forms.

- Java is another very popular modern language, especially for web applications.
- Visual Basic is a new version of BASIC, an older very popular language. Visual Basic is well suited for software that runs on graphical user interfaces (GUIs), such as those on Windows and Macintosh computers.

High-level languages are continually changing. For example, C++ evolved from a language called C. C++ is still an important high-level language, but there are other versions of this C-based language as well, such as the dot-Net version, C# (C-sharp), and Objective C.

It may seem overwhelming that there are so many languages. If each programming language were as different as English is from Chinese then this would be true. However, basic programming logic applies to all programming languages. Once you have mastered one language, it is relatively easy to learn the rules and structures that govern another language.

Scripting Languages

It is difficult to characterize definitvely the differences between scripting languages like JavaScript and high-level programming languages. However, one important difference between the two types of languages has to do with what happens when a program is run. It may be more accurate to call a programming language a **compiled language**. When the code is run, it is translated into a machine-readable code. This process is called compilation. Compilation occurs before a program is executed. A scripting language is not compiled. The computer, of course, still needs to have the code translated to bits and bytes for understanding. But rather than completing this process before the program is run, scripting language code is interpreted "on the fly"—that is, as each line of code is executed, it is translated by an interpreter to the computer. Therefore, a scripting language may also be termed as an **interpreted language**.

Another characteristic of scripting languages refers to where the language is interpreted. Some languages, such as Active Server Pages (ASP), PHP, and Java Server Pages (JSP) are run on a user's **server**. These are **server-side** languages. Other scripting languages, such as the most popular one, JavaScript, are run on the user's own computer. This is called the **client** and these types of languages are **client-side** languages.

However, most scripting languages contain most of the same structures and use the same logic as the older programming languages and, therefore, a study of programming logic is equally valuable, regardless of what language you eventually use as a programmer. Further, in the past companies hired programmers based on which language that company used for its development. Thus, regardless of the task, the programmer wrote code in this preferred language. Today, it is more likely that a programmer will choose a language that fits the job rather than force a given language to do a job. A software developer must be fluent in several languages and understand how to quickly adapt to any new language. Therefore, it has become far more important to know the logic of writing code in any language than to focus on a specific language.

Writing Programs

To write a program in a high-level language, first you must have access to the appropriate software on your computer. This software usually consists of several programs that work together to help you create the finished product, including a **text editor** in which you type and edit (modify) the program statements (instructions); a **debugger** that helps you find errors in your program; and a **compiler** or an **interpreter** that translates your program into machine language. This software is readily available for many programming languages; it's sold in most campus bookstores, retail stores, and over the Internet, and many languages have free software.

To use a programming language software package, first you install it on your computer and start it as you would do for any application. Then you type the program statements and run the program. This executes the program statements and you can see if your program is working properly. If not, it's necessary to revise the program until it runs properly.

Of course, writing a suitable program to solve a specific problem requires a good deal of knowledge about programming concepts in general and a specific language in particular. The purpose of this book is to present the relevant general programming concepts. Once you have mastered the logic and structures of programming, learning a specific programming language should prove to be relatively easy.

Self Check for Section 0.3

0.15 What is the difference between application software and system software?

0.16 Briefly describe three types of applications.

0.17 Name the four basic types of programming languages.

0.18 High-level languages are easier to use, so why would a programmer want to write a program in assembly language?

0.19 What is the difference between a compiled language and an interpreted language?

0.20 Why do you think that there are so many different kinds of programming languages?

Key Terms

applications
apps
assembly language
bit
byte
calculators
CD-ROM
CD
central processing unit (CPU)
client
client-side
cloud computing
cloud storage
compilation
compiler
compiled language
computer
debugger
display screens
DVD-ROM drive
email
flash memory
gigabyte (GB)
hard disk drive
hardware
high-level languages
Infrastructure as a service
input devices
integrated circuits
internal memory
Internet
interpreted language
interpreter
keyboard
kilobyte (KB)
machine language
magnetic storage
mainframe
mass storage
megabyte (MB)
microchip

microprocessor
minicomputer
motherboard
mouse
network
operating system (OS)
optical storage
output device
peripherals
personal computer (PC)
pixels
platform as a service
printers
processor
program
programmer
programming language
random-access memory (RAM)
read-only memory (ROM)
resolution
scripting languages
server
server-side
software
software as a service
solid-state storage
speakers
supercomputers
system software
system unit
terabyte (TB)
terminal
text editor
touchpad
trackpad
transistor
vacuum tubes
voice command devices (VCDs)
Web2.0
World Wide Web (Web)

Chapter Summary

In this introduction, we discussed the following topics:

1. The history of computers, including the following:
   - Early computers, from the Analytical Engine in the mid-1800s, through the development of ENIAC, a century later
   - The significance of the use of transistors to replace vacuum tubes
   - The development of mainframe, minicomputer, and personal computer
   - The rise of the personal computer—the Altair 8800, Apple II, IBM PC, and Macintosh
   - The emergence of the Internet
2. The following basic hardware components that make up a typical computer system:
   - The central processing unit—the brain of the computer
   - Internal memory—RAM and ROM
   - The four types of mass storage devices—magnetic, optical, solid state, and the Cloud
   - Cloud computing
   - Input devices, such as a keyboard or a mouse
   - Output devices, such as a monitor or a printer
3. The following types of software (computer programs):
   - Applications, such as word processors, spreadsheet programs, database managers, photo editors, and web browsers
   - System software and the functions of the computer's operating system, which is the master control program
   - Programming languages for creating applications—machine language, assembly languages, high-level languages, scripting languages

Review Exercises

Fill in the Blank

1. A nineteenth-century computing pioneer named _____ designed a computer called the Analytical Engine.
2. The first fully operable electronic computer was named _____.
3. The invention of the _____ helped to make computers smaller by replacing the larger, less efficient vacuum tubes in the electronic circuits.
4. Until the appearance of the _____ in the mid-1960s, only large mainframe computers were available.
5. _____ allows someone with access to the Internet to exchange messages with other Internet users around the world.
6. The World Wide Web provides access to a huge number of electronic documents known as _____.

7. The physical components of a computer system are referred to as its
_____.

8. A personal computer's main circuit board is called its _____.

9. One byte of memory consists of _____ bits.

10. One kilobyte is equal to _____ bytes.

11. The hard drive is an example of _____ mass storage.

12. _____ allows a user access to software and the user's files from any computer connected to the Internet.

13. Solid-state mass storage like a flash drive is plugged into a computer through a(n) _____ port.

14. The operating system developed by Google is the _____ system.

15. Software is divided into two broad categories: _____ software and system software.

16. The master control program that oversees a computer's operations is called its _____.

17. High-level programming languages are translated into machine language by means of a(n) _____.

18. The first high-level programming language was known as _____, which stands for "formula translator."

Multiple Choice

19. Which of the following pairs were the founders of Microsoft Corporation?
a. John Mauchly and J. Presper Eckert
b. Steven Jobs and Stephen Wozniak
c. Bill Gates and Paul Allen
d. Richard Rodgers and Oscar Hammerstein

20. Which operating system is now used by almost all IBM compatible computers?
a. DOS
b. Microsoft Windows
c. Linux
d. Macintosh OS

21. Which of the following components is *not* contained within the system unit of a typical PC?
a. The motherboard
b. The monitor
c. Random-access memory (RAM)
d. None of the above

22. Which of the following is done by the computer's central processing unit?
a. Processing program instructions
b. Performing arithmetic and logical operations

    c. Controlling the other components of the computer

    d. All of the above

23. Which of the following is an input device?

    a. printer

    b. Keyboard

    c. CPU

    d. Read-only memory (ROM)

24. Which of the following is an output device?

    a. Display screen

    b. Keyboard

    c. CPU

    d. Read-only memory (ROM)

25. Which of the following is an advantage of cloud computing over purchasing all software you need separately?

    a. You have access to a large range of software products

    b. You only pay for a product if you use it

    c. The software you need is available to you from any computer connected to the Internet

    d. All of the above

26. Which of the following is an advantage of a flash drive over a hard disk drive?

    a. It uses removable media

    b. It holds more data

    c. It retrieves data more quickly

    d. None of the above

27. Which of the following is an example of application software?

    a. The computer's RAM

    b. The computer's operating system

    c. A programmable calculator

    d. A word processor

28. Which of the following is an example of system software?

    a. The computer's RAM

    b. The computer's operating system

    c. A programmable calculator

    d. A word processor

29. Which of the following is *not* a type of a programming language?

    a. Natural language

    b. Assembly language

    c. Machine language

    d. High-level language

30. Which of the following is *not* an example of a high-level language?

    a. C++

    b. FORTRAN

    c. Babbage

    d. Java

True or False

31. T F The Internet is a worldwide collection of networks.

32. T F The Internet's origins date back to the early 1990s.

33. T F Computer components housed outside the system unit are called peripherals.

34. T F The contents of a computer's ROM are lost when the power is turned off.

35. T F RAM stands for Remote Acccess Memory.

36. T F A scripting language is compiled before the code is executed.

37. T F Computer keyboards contain fewer keys than a standard typewriter.

38. T F Cloud computing is only available to large businesses and organizations.

Short Answer

39. Number the following personal computers in order of introduction (from earliest to most recent):

    a. Apple II   ____

    b. Altair 8800   ____

    c. Apple Macintosh   ____

    d. IBM PC   ____

40. Number the following types of computers in order of increasing size and power:

    a. Mainframes   ____

    b. Minicomputers   ____

    c. Personal computers ____

    d. Supercomputers   ____

In order to develop a program to solve a specific problem, you must know and understand programming concepts in general and a specific language in particular. In this book, we will concentrate on the first two steps of the program development cycle—especially, the program design phase. Our goal is to introduce programming concepts and program design generically, without referring to a specific language. We will present some short examples in several programming languages (C++, Java, Visual Basic, or JavaScript); these examples are for illustration purposes only. The text focuses on the programming concepts and logic that are relevant to all programming languages.

One of the best things about learning to program is that even though there are many different programming languages, the basic concepts of programming are the same regardless of what language you use. In fact, once you understand these programming concepts and learn one programming language, it is fairly easy to learn a new language. But first things first. Here, we concentrate on the basic building blocks of programming—the concepts. After you have learned these general ideas, it will be easy to implement them and the entire program development process using a particular computer language.

Self Check for Section 1.1

1.1 List the steps in the general problem-solving strategy described in this section.

1.2 Provide a precise list of instructions for traveling from your school to your home.

1.3 List the steps in the program development cycle.

1.4 What is the significance of the word *cycle* in the term *program development cycle*?

1.2 Basic Programming Concepts

In the previous section, you planned a trip to Paris. One of the most important things you need to do is prepare for a very long plane ride. You want to be sure you have a lot of good music to listen to, so you decide to download music from iTunes. But your funds are limited so you need to figure out how many songs you can buy with your limited resources. We will use this project as the basis for solving a simple programming problem and we will refer to this sample problem throughout the remainder of this chapter. First we will use this problem to illustrate the notions of data **input**, **constants**, and **variables**. Then we will return to this same problem when we discuss the concepts of **processing**, **output**, and types of **data**.

A Simple Program

You want to develop a program that will help you quickly see how much money you are spending as you download music. Today, the price of downloading one song is 99 cents ($0.99). You need a program that will tell you how much the price of 8 or 10 or any number of songs will be. You know how to do this calculation by hand with pencil and paper or with a calculator. To prepare to write the computer program, you write down the following instructions for using a calculator to perform the computation:

- Enter the number of songs to be purchased into the calculator.
- Press the multiply (×) key.
- Enter 0.99.
- Press the equals (=) key.
- The total cost will appear on the display.

This calculation will only be valid if a song costs 99 cents. However, if the price changes, the steps needed to find the total cost of one or more songs remain the same. The only thing that would need to change would be the cost of one song.

The Music Purchase Program

The instructions shown here are not very different from those in a computer program designed to perform this task. The Music Purchase program instructions, or **statements**, might look like the following:

```
Input the number of songs you wish to download today: Songs
Compute the cost of the purchase: Set DollarPrice = 0.99 * Songs
Display the value of DollarPrice
```

The asterisk (*) in the next-to-last line represents multiplication.

In this book, we will refer to a list of instructions like the one shown above as a *program*, but it is not a computer program in the strict sense of the word. Computer programs are written in programming languages and follow an exact **syntax**. The syntax of a computer language is its rules of usage. If you don't use correct syntax, your program won't work. For example, some computer languages use a semicolon (;) to tell the computer that a statement is ended. If you type a comma (,) or a colon (:) in that language by accident, you will get an error message or the program may not work at all. However, the semicolon may not be the end of statement indicator in another language. Each language has its own syntax and you must learn the syntax in order to write programs in a specific language.

The list of statements shown in the Music Purchase program is referred to as **pseudocode**. The prefix *pseudo* (pronounced *sue-dough*) means not real. Example 1.1 shows actual computer programs in Java, C++, and JavaScript that would solve the Music Purchase problem.

Example 1.1 Using Java, C++, and JavaScript to Code the Music Purchase Program

(a) Java Program Code

```
1   public static void main(String[] args)
2   {
3     int Songs = 0;
4     float DollarPrice = 0.0;
5     Scanner scanner = New Scanner(System.in);
```

```
6          println("Enter the number of songs you wish to purchase
                   today.");
7        Songs = scanner.nextInt();
8        DollarPrice = 0.99 * Songs;
9        println(DollarPrice);
10   }
```

(b) C++ Program Code

```
1   void main(void)
2   {
3     int Songs;
4     float DollarPrice;
5     cout << "Enter the number of songs you wish to purchase
                today.";
6     cin >> Songs;
7     DollarPrice = 0.99 * Songs;
8     cout << DollarPrice;
9     return;
10     }
```

(c) JavaScript Program Code (HTML page not included)

```
1   function getMusic()
2   {
3     var Songs = 0;
4     var DollarPrice = 0;
5     Songs = parseInt(prompt("Enter the number of songs you wish
                      to purchase today."));
6     DollarPrice = 0.99 * Songs;
7     document.write(DollarPrice);
8   }
```

Let's compare the three languages:

- The three programs differ in the way each starts a program (line 1 in each code snippet).
- However, all three languages use curly braces ({ }) to open and close a program. The opening curly brace immediately follows the start lines in all three languages (line 2).
- All three languages then set up the variables that will be used to store information. While the names chosen for variables are created by the programmer, in these examples the same names have been used in all three languages for simplicity and ease of comparison. Lines 3 and 4 in each example create two variables—Songs and DollarPrice—which will hold the value input by the user (Songs) and the resulting cost (DollarPrice). Both Java and C++ must specify the type of data that will be held by each variable. In both languages, the keywords int and float mean that a variable will be either an integer or a floating point number. This distinction is discussed in depth later in the chapter. JavaScript, however, does not require the

distinction between integers and floating point numbers at this time. The JavaScript keyword var indicates that this is a new variable.

- The next thing the program does is to prompt the user to enter the number of songs to be purchased and to store that number in the variable Songs. The syntax required for this task is somewhat different in each of the languages, but the end result is the same. After lines 5, 6, and 7 in the Java code or lines 5 and 6 in the C++ code, or line 5 in the JavaScript code are executed, Songs now holds whatever integer the user has entered.

- The "meat" of this program is the cost calculation. The cost, regardless of the language, is the number of songs to buy multiplied by 0.99. The syntax for this processing statement is identical in the three languages and occurs on line 8 in the Java code, line 7 in the C++ code, and line 6 in the JavaScript code:

```
DollarPrice = 0.99 * Songs;
```

- Finally, the result must be output to the user. Output syntax, like input, differs from one language to another but the result is the same; the user sees the result of the program. This occurs on line 9 in the Java code, line 8 in the C++ code, and line 7 in the JavaScript code.

- The last line of all three programs is a closing curly brace (}). Only C++ requires, for this program, a return; statement prior to closing the program.

Our simple program illustrates the basic structure of most computer programs. They input data, process it, and output the results. Here, the word *data* refers to the numbers, words, or more generally, any collection of symbols that is manipulated by a program.

Data Input

The input operation in a program transmits data from an outside source to the program. Often this data is typed at the computer keyboard by the person using the program. For example, the cout << statement of the C++ program shown in Example 1.1 causes execution of this program to pause and displays the text Enter the number of songs you wish to purchase today: on the screen. The program waits until the user types something. In computer lingo, the program **prompts** the user to enter a value. Different programming languages have different prompts—symbols or methods of telling the user to enter data. At this point, for example, the user might type 78, indicating that he wants to buy 78 songs. In the C++ program, the cin >> statement causes the program execution to resume, and Songs takes on the value 78. These actions are referred to as entering data from the keyboard.

The Input and Write Statements

In the pseudocode that is used in this book, we will use a statement that begins with the word Write to display messages and other information on the screen. We will use a statement that begins with the word Input to allow the user to enter data from the keyboard. If we follow the word Input with a variable, then it will be assumed that the value the user types will be stored in that variable. Therefore, although each language has its specific rules and instructions, we will use a general form. Our Music Purchase program, written in our own general pseudocode, is shown in Example 1.2.

Example 1.2 **Music Purchase Program Pseudocode**

```
Write "Enter the number of songs you wish to purchase: "
Input Songs
Set DollarPrice = 0.99 * Songs
Write DollarPrice
```

The first statement (Write) causes the message within the quotation marks to appear on the screen. The second statement (Input) causes execution to pause. Now the user clearly understands what data must be entered. When execution resumes, the Input statement also causes Songs to take on the value entered. After the calculation is completed, the next Write statement will cause the result to be displayed on the screen.

The last Write statement in Example 1.2 says Write DollarPrice. What will be displayed? The word DollarPrice won't be displayed, but the *value* of DollarPrice will be.

In other words, if the user wanted to download three songs, he would enter 3 after the Write prompt. The calculation would multiply 3 by 0.99 and the result would be 2.97. Three songs downloaded from iTunes will cost $2.97. So DollarPrice now has the value 2.97. The statement Write DollarPrice will cause 2.97 to be displayed on the screen.   ●

Use Input Prompts

When you want the user to input data to a program, you should always provide a prompt, indicating that data is needed and you should explain what kind of data is required. If you don't use a prompt, then the user will not know what kind of data to enter or even be aware, in most cases, that execution has paused!

If you want the user to enter several data items, you can use several Input statements, each preceded by a prompt. In some cases, however, a single input is enough. For example, suppose that at some point in a program you want the user to enter three numbers. This can be done by the following pair of statements:

```
Write "Enter three numbers."
Input Number1, Number2, Number3
```

In this case, Number1 takes on the first value entered, Number2 the second value, and Number3 the third value.   ●

Other Forms of Input

Input from the keyboard is very common, but data may be input into a program by other means as well. In some programs, the user inputs information by clicking or moving the mouse. For example, to draw a straight line in a graphics program, the user might click a symbol representing a line and then click the locations of the line's endpoints. Another common form of input doesn't involve the user at all—data can be transmitted to a program from a data file stored on a drive or server (discussed in Chapter 10).

Program Variables and Constants

We have been using variables in all the examples up to now, but it's important to discuss variables—what they are, how to use them, and how to name them—in more detail. Variables are such an integral part of all computer programs; it's impossible to describe a sample program without referring to one, as we have seen in the previous examples. On the other hand, it's almost impossible to talk about a variable without putting it in some context—in this case, a bit of program code. So you know something about variables already.

Let's return to our little Music Purchase program for a moment. If we had not used a variable, we still could have written a program to calculate the cost of three songs at $0.99 per song. A computer can do this conversion for us—a calculator does it all the time. We enter 3 into a calculator, press the multiplication sign, enter 0.99, press the = key, and get 2.97 as the result. If we wanted to buy 46 songs, we could do the same thing with our calculator. Because 46 * 0.99 = 45.54, we would know that it would cost $45.54 to download 46 songs from iTunes at $0.99 per song. But that's not what programming is all about. A computer program should be written so that the user doesn't have to reenter all the steps to get another result. The Music Purchase program we wrote will find the price of 1 song, 12 songs, 836 songs, or however many songs we decide to buy because we use variables instead of actual values.

When we write a program, most of the time we don't know the actual numbers or other data that the user will enter while running (executing) the program. Therefore, we assign the input data to a program variable. A variable is called a variable because it can vary! It is a quantity that can change value during the execution of a program. Whenever we need to refer to that data in a subsequent program statement, we simply refer to its variable name. At this point, the *value* of the variable—the number or other data value it represents—will be used in this statement.

In the Music Purchase program, the input variable is Songs. If in running the program the user enters 100, this value is assigned to Songs. Then if later in the program the expression 0.99 * Songs occurs, the computer will multiply 0.99 by 100. Note that in the expression above, the number 0.99 cannot be changed during program execution; it is referred to as a program constant.

Sometimes you may want to give a constant a name. When you do, it is called a **named constant**. Let's say you are writing a program to calculate the total cost of purchases made by customers for a small online business. First your program will add the purchases and then it will calculate the sales tax. Your program might use this tax rate value in several places. You might want to display a subtotal, the tax rate, and tax amount on a shopping cart page and later, display these amounts along with the shipping cost.

If you enter the value of the tax as a number (a constant) and the tax rate changes, you would have to go through your program code and change it each time that constant appears in the code. On the other hand, if you give the tax rate a variable name and use this variable name wherever you need to use the tax rate in a calculation, when the tax rate changes you would only have to change the value in one place. You would simply change the one line in the code where you assigned the constant value to the variable name and everywhere in the code where that variable was used, the new value would be in effect.

Variables Names

As a programmer, you choose the name of the variable. However, you need to know what types of names are acceptable and what types are unacceptable. The rules are different for different languages, but the following rules are the same for all:

- All variable names must be one word. In computer lingo, a "word" is any sequence of characters of text and can consist of one or more characters.
- Underscores are allowed and hyphens may be allowed, but spaces are never allowed.
  - `Miles_traveled` is fine but `Miles traveled` is not
  - `Cost-per-gallon` is fine but `cost per gallon` is not
- Variable names can be long; in fact, many languages allow more than 200 characters. But remember, you will have to type the variable name throughout the program. If you make the name too long or too complicated, you are asking for another reason to make an error. The variable name `the_Tax_Rate_On_Clothing_Bought_for_Children_under_Six` is a lot harder to remember than `tax_Rate_1`.
- Variable names can also be short; a single character is an acceptable variable name. There are many situations in a program where a variable name that is a single character is appropriate but in most cases, since one letter rarely indicates what the variable represents, it is best to reserve this type of variable name for specific circumstances, as we will see later in the text.
  - `A`, `x`, or `J` are all acceptable variable names
  - digits (0 to 9) are not valid variable names
  - special characters such as `#` or `$` are not valid variable names
- Many programmers use uppercase letters to distinguish one word from another within a single name. This is sometimes referred to as **CamelBack** (or CamelCase) notation.
  - `MilesTraveled` works as well as `Miles_Traveled` and may be easier to type
  - `CostPerGallon` works as well as `Cost_Per_Gallon` and may be easier to type
- Most languages allow numbers to be part of variable names, but variable names may never start with a number.
  - `TaxRate_1` is fine but `1_TaxRate` is not
  - `Destination2` is fine but `2Destination` is not

Variable Names Should Be Meaningful!

Style Pointer

If you name your variables the perfectly acceptable names of `variableNumber_1`, `variableNumber_2`, `variableNumber_3`, and so forth, you will soon find that you are spending most of your time trying to remember what each variable represents, instead of fine-tuning your program.

It's best to name variables with the shortest possible name that allows you some meaningful representation and does not conflict with any of the rules stated here or any of the rules of your specific programming language. For example, we could have used `X` or `PP` or even `George` to represent the number of songs to be purchased in

Music Purchase program. However, to minimize confusion, you should give meaningful names to variables. So instead of Songs, we might have used NumberOfSongs or perhaps MySongs. But we must be consistent! If you use NumberOfSongs in the input statement, then the name of this variable in the next statement, currently

```
Set DollarPrice = 0.99 * Songs
```

must also be changed to

```
Set DollarPrice = 0.99 * NumberOfSongs
```

What's Really Going On with Variables in the Computer?

Technically, a program variable is the name for a storage location in the computer's internal memory, and the **value of a variable** is the contents of that location. It might help to think of the storage locations as mailboxes. Each variable can be thought of as the name printed on a certain mailbox, and the value of a variable as its contents. For example, the following is a picture of what the computer's memory might look like after the Input statement in the Music Purchase program is executed and the user wants to download 78 songs:

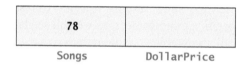

Notice that the DollarPrice mailbox is empty, indicating that at this point in the program DollarPrice has not yet been assigned a value. At the end of the program, after the conversion has been made, the picture would look like the following:

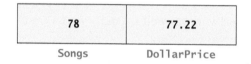

If you run the program a second time to purchase a different number of songs, the picture will change. The contents of the Songs mailbox will be replaced by the new number of songs to be purchased, and after the calculation is made, the contents of the DollarPrice mailbox will be replaced by the new value. This process is discussed in more detail later in the next section.

Self Check for Section 1.2

1.5 What are the three components that make up the basic structure of most computer programs?

1.6 Write a pair of statements, the first of which is an appropriate prompt to input a temperature in degrees Fahrenheit (use Temperature for the name of the variable) and the second statement should assign the value entered by the user to the variable.

1.7 Suppose a program is to calculate the final (maturity) value of an investment. You will be given the amount invested, the rate of interest, and the length of time that the money is invested.

    a. What data must be input to this program?

    b. Give reasonable names for each of the input variables.

    c. Give `Write` and `Input` statements that prompt for and input the data for this problem.

1.8 What (if anything) is wrong with each of the following variable names?

    a. `Sales Tax`

    b. `1_2_3`

    c. `TheCowJumpedOverTheMoon`

    d. `OneName`

    e. `G`

1.3 Data Processing and Output

In this section, we will continue the discussion of the fundamental building blocks that make up a program: input, processing, and output. In Section 1.2, we concentrated on data input; here, we will discuss the concepts of processing and output.

Processing Data

Let's return to the current version of the Music Purchase program, which was introduced in Section 1.2:

```
Write "Enter the number of songs you wish to purchase: "
Input Songs
Set DollarPrice = 0.99 * Songs
Write DollarPrice
```

The Set Statement

After the user has input the value of Songs, the instruction

```
Set DollarPrice = 0.99 * Songs
```

is executed. This statement comprises the processing part of the program. It accomplishes two things as follows:

1. It multiplies the value of Songs (the number of songs the user wishes to buy) by 0.99 (the cost of one song). Notice that we use the asterisk (*) for the multiplication symbol.

2. It *assigns* the resulting value of the expression on the right of the equals sign to the variable, DollarPrice, on the left. The value of Songs does *not* change. For this reason, it is called an **assignment statement**. For example, if the value of Songs is 100 when this statement is executed, then the expression on the right side is computed to be 99.00 and is assigned to the variable DollarPrice.

Assigning and Reassigning Values to Variables

What happens if a variable that already has a value is assigned a new one? For example, suppose a program has a variable named `NumberX` and contains the following statements:

```
Set NumberX = 45
Set NumberX = 97
```

In such a case, `NumberX` first contains the value of 45, and in the next statement, the value of 45 is replaced by 97. `NumberX` will keep the value of 97 until something else in the program reassigns it a new value. In terms of storage locations, when the second of the two assignment statements is executed, the value currently stored in location `NumberX` (45) is erased and the new value (97) is stored in its place.

Assignment statements can sometimes look a little strange. For example, a common program statement looks as follows:

```
Set Counter = Counter + 1
```

Although this looks confusing, if you look carefully, it's easy to see what happens here. First the right side is evaluated, and 1 is added to the current value of the variable `Counter`. Then this new value is assigned to the variable on the left, `Counter`. The net result is to add one to the previous value of `Counter`. So if the value of `Counter` were equal to 23 prior to execution of this statement, its value would be 24 afterward. Using a variable in this manner is very common in programs; therefore, it's very important to understand this kind of statement.

Operations on Data

The `*` symbol used to denote multiplication is an example of an **arithmetic operator**. Almost all programming languages use at least four basic arithmetic operators—addition, subtraction, multiplication, and division. Some languages contain other arithmetic operators, such as exponentiation (taking a number to a power) and modulus.

The modulus operator may seem odd at first, but as you start to write programs you will see its many uses. The **modulus operator** acts on two integers and returns the remainder after dividing one integer by another. The symbol commonly used to denote the modulus operator is the percent sign (%) or the abbreviation `MOD`. We will use the `%` to designate the modulus operator in this text. Some examples using the modulus operator appear in Example 1.3.

Example 1.3 **The Modulus Operator**

1. What is `15 % 2`?
    ⇨ 15 divided by 2 `= 7` with a remainder of 1 so `15 % 2 = 1`
2. What is `39 % 4`?
    ⇨ 39 divided by 4 `= 9` with a remainder of 3 so `39 % 4 = 3`
3. What is `21 % 7`?
    ⇨ 21 divided by 7 is 3 with no remainder so `21 % 7 = 0`

Table 1.1 gives examples of the six arithmetic operators.

Table 1.1 Arithmetic Operators

Operator	Computer Symbol	Example
Addition	+	2 + 3 = 5
Subtraction	−	7 − 3 = 4
Multiplication	*	5 * 4 = 20
Division	/	12 / 3 = 4
Exponentiation	^	2 ^ 3 = 8
Modulus	%	14 % 4 = 2

For example, to convert a temperature in degrees Fahrenheit to degrees Celsius, we use the following formula:

$$C = \frac{5(F - 32)}{9}$$

However, in a programming language (and in this book), the formula is written as follows:

```
C = 5 * (F - 32) / 9
```

In this example, C is the variable name that represents the number of degrees in Celsius, and F is the variable name that represents the number of degrees in Fahrenheit. To determine the value assigned to the variable C when the value of F is 77, we proceed as follows, substituting the value 77 for F:

```
C = 5 * (77 - 32) / 9
  = 5 * (45) / 9
  = 225 / 9
  = 25
```

Hierarchy of Operations

Notice that if the parentheses were missing in the last example, we would get a different result:

```
5 * 77 - 32 / 9 = 385 - 32 / 9, which is approximately 381.4.
```

The reason the two answers differ is due to the **hierarchy of operations**. This is also called **operator precedence**. The rules of arithmetic tell us that the order in which arithmetic operations is performed (i.e., their *hierarchy*) is as follows:

1. Perform the operations in parentheses (from the inside out, if there are parentheses within parentheses)
2. Perform exponentiations
3. Do multiplications, divisions, and modulus (from left to right if there is more than one)
4. Do additions and subtractions (from left to right if there is more than one)

Unless you specify something different, the computer will apply the hierarchy of operations to any mathematical expression in a program. The best way to write a mathematical expression is to put parentheses around parts of the expression that you want evaluated together. You will never get an error if you use a set of parentheses where none is needed, but you may get an error if you omit parentheses when a set should be included. Examples 1.4 and 1.5 demonstrate how parentheses can make a big difference in the answer to even the simplest mathematical calculations.

Example 1.4 **Using the Hierarchy of Operations**

Given the following arithmetic expression: 6 + 8 / 2 * 2^2

a. Evaluate without any parentheses:

```
6 + 8/2 * 2^2 = 6 + 4 * 4
              = 6 + 16
              = 22
```

b. Evaluate with parentheses:

```
6 + 8/(2 * 2^2) = 6 + 8/8
                = 6 + 1
                = 7
```

c. Evaluate with different parentheses:

```
(6 + 8)/2 * 2^2 = 14/2 * 4
                = 7 * 4
                = 28
```

d. Evaluate with two sets of parentheses:

```
(6 + 8)/(2 * 2^2) = 14/8
                  = 1⁶/₈
                  = 1.75
```

It's obvious that parentheses can make quite a difference in your results!

Example 1.5 **One More Example for Emphasis**

Given the following arithmetic expression: 20/5 + 5 * 4 − 3

a. Evaluate without parentheses:

```
20/5 + 5 * 4 − 3 = 4 + 20 − 3
                 = 21
```

b. Evaluate with parentheses:

```
20/(5 + 5) * 4 − 3 = 20/10 * 4 − 3
                   = 2 * 4 − 3
                   = 8 − 3
                   = 5
```

c. Evaluate with more parentheses:

$$(20/(5 + 5 * 4)) - 3 = (20/(5 + 20)) - 3$$
$$= 20/25 - 3$$
$$= 0.8 - 3$$
$$= -2.2$$

d. Evaluate with different parentheses:

$$(20/(5 + 5 * 4 - 3) = 20/(5 + 20 - 3)$$
$$= 20/22$$
$$= 0.909$$

By now you should understand why it's important to know the hierarchy of operations and write arithmetic expressions in your programs with great care.

Computers Have Limits

It's generally accepted that computers can do calculations very quickly, very accurately, and normally without complaint. But it's also important to realize that computers can only handle a finite range of numbers and a finite amount of data. The actual range of values that a computer can process varies from computer to computer, from language to language, and from programmer to programmer (depending on how variables are declared). But even the biggest, fastest computer cannot process any and all numbers. For example, in C++ the largest value a 10-byte number can take on is 10^{4932}. This is 10 multiplied by itself 4,932 times. It is certainly an enormous number, but it's smaller than 10^{5000}.

We will discuss the exact ways the computer stores numbers in Chapter 2. You should know, without going into too much detail, that the computer can process a finite range of numbers and therefore, is only as precise as its range allows. This is not a problem for most normal uses, but care must be taken in high-level computations.

Data Output

A program's output is data sent by the program to the screen, printer, or another destination such as a file. The output normally consists, at least in part, of the results of the program's processing component.

The Write Statement Revisited

Recall from Section 1.2 that we used a Write statement to display messages on the screen. We will also use this statement to display the values of variables on the screen. So from now on, we will use a statement like the following to display the value of a variable:

```
Write DollarPrice
```

When this statement is executed, the current value of the variable DollarPrice is displayed and then the cursor moves to the beginning of the next line on the screen.

For example, if the values of `DollarPrice` and `Songs` are 9.90 and 10, respectively, then the following pair of statements:

```
Write DollarPrice
Write Songs
```

produces the output

```
9.90
10
```

on the screen.

When outputting the values of variables, it is often useful to display text on the same screen line. For example, if the user inputs 10 for the number of songs he wishes to buy in the Music Purchase program as we have written it so far, the only output that would appear on the screen would be 9.90. It would be more informative to display the following:

```
The cost of your purchase is 9.90
```

We will accomplish this by using the following statement:

```
Write "The cost of your purchase is " + DollarPrice
```

This statement displays the text included between the quotation marks followed by the value of the variable. As an alternative, we could use the following statement:

```
Write "The cost of your purchase is " + DollarPrice + "dollars."
```

to produce the following output:

```
The cost of your purchase is 9.90 dollars.
```

Notice that the text to appear on the screen is enclosed in quotes. In this book, text and variables are separated by + symbols, which are not displayed as part of the output. Each programming language has its own special statements to create the kinds of screen output described above.

Annotate Your Output

If the output of your program consists of numbers, you should also include explanatory text as output. In other words, **annotate** your output as demonstrated in Example 1.6 so that the user will understand the significance of these numbers.   ●

Example 1.6 **Annotating Your Output**

Let's assume that you have written a program to compute the temperature in degrees Celsius when degrees Fahrenheit is input. In very general terms, your program would follow the following logic:

```
Write "Enter temperature in degrees Fahrenheit to convert to Celsius:"
Input DegreesFahrenheit                              (get degrees to be converted)
DegreesCelsius = 5*(DegreesFahrenheit - 32)/9                        (calculate)
Write DegreesCelsius                                              (output result)
```

If a user inputs 77 degrees Fahrenheit, the answer would be 25 degrees Celsius. The following shows the screen output:

```
25
```

It would be far better to explain to the user what the result means by outputting some explanatory text. The improved program would look as follows:

```
Write "Enter temperature in degrees Fahrenheit to convert to Celsius:"
Input DegreesFahrenheit                          (get degrees to be converted)
Set DegreesCelsius = 5*(DegreesFahrenheit - 32)/9        (calculate)
Write DegreesFahrenheit + " degrees Fahrenheit"          (output)
Write "converts to " + DegreesCelsius + " degrees Celsius"   (output)
```

Now the output would look like the following and would make more sense to the user:

```
77 degrees Fahrenheit
converts to 25 degrees Celsius.
```

Example 1.7 uses all the ideas presented so far in this chapter.

Example 1.7 **Putting It All Together**

We will input two numbers and store their values in variables named Number1 and Number2. Then we will display the average of the two numbers. This calculation is done by adding the numbers and dividing the sum by two.

```
1  Write "Enter two numbers."
2  Input Number1
3  Input Number2
4  Set Average = (Number1 + Number2)/2
5  Write "The average of"
6  Write Number1 + " and " + Number2
7  Write "is " + Average
```

The following shows what happens in this program:

- Line 1 contains the Write statement, which is a prompt for the Input statements that follow.
- Lines 2 and 3 are the Input statements. When the user types in the first number, its value is stored in the variable named Number1. When the user types in the second number, its value is stored in the variable named Number2.
- Line 4 now calculates and stores the value of the variable named Average. The value of Average is set to be the sum of the values of Number1 and Number2 divided by 2. Note the use of parentheses here. If for example, Number1 = 10 and Number2 = 12, then Average = (10 + 12)/2, which is 11. But without the parentheses, the computer would follow the hierarchy of operations and do the division before the sum. Then we would have Average = 10 + 12/2, which would be 10 + 6 or 16. To get the result we want—the average of the two numbers—we must use parentheses to show that we want the addition to be done before the division.
- Lines 5, 6, and 7 produce the output. Line 5 outputs straight text. The words "The average of" are displayed on one line of the screen. Lines 6 and 7 each output a mixture of text and variable values. Let's examine line 6.

The first thing that is shown on the screen is the value of Number1. The next thing output is the word "and". But there is also a space before and after the word "and". Then the value of Number2 is output. Without the spaces included inside the quote marks, the computer would not know to leave a space between the value of a variable and the text. When you write something you want to show on the screen you have to take into account the formatting of what shows up as well as the content.

If the user enters the numbers 8 and 6 as Number1 and Number2, the output would look like the following (with and without formatting for spaces where needed):

Formatted with spaces between values and text:	Unformatted output:
The average of	The average of
8 and 6	8and6
is 7	is7

Self Check for Section 1.3

1.9 If the temperature is 95 degrees Fahrenheit, use the formula in this section to find the resulting temperature in degrees Celsius.

1.10 If X = 2 and Y = 3, give the value of each of the following expressions:

a. (2 * X - 1) ^ 2 + Y

b. X * Y + 10 * X / (7 - Y)

c. (4 + (2 ^ Y)) * (X + 1) / Y

d. (19 % 5) * Y / X * 2

1.11 If Number is a variable and has the value 5 before the execution of the following statement:

Set Number = Number + 2

what is the value of Number after the execution of this statement?

1.12 If Songs = 100 and DollarPrice = 99.00, write statements that use these variables to produce the following output on the screen:

a. 100 songs will cost $ 99.00

b. The number of songs to be downloaded is 100
   The cost for this purchase in dollars is 99.00

1.13 Write a program (like the Music Purchase program of this section) that inputs a temperature in degrees Fahrenheit and outputs the corresponding temperature in degrees Celsius. Use DegreesF and DegreesC for your variable names. (*Hint*: use the formula given earlier in this section.)

1.4 Data Types

We have discussed the way a computer stores the value of a variable in a memory location. The same is true of all data stored in a computer. Each piece of data, be it a single letter, a number, or a paragraph of text, is stored in at least one memory location. The computer allocates a certain amount of space in its memory for data. But some data requires more space than other data. For example, a single alphanumeric character (the letters A through Z, a through z, and the digits 0 through 9) requires eight bits of space, while a floating point number (such as 3.7, −43.9825, or 126,854,927.38726) requires much more space in memory. Chapter 2 discusses these concepts in greater detail; for now, we simply need to know that all data requires memory space and the type of data determines how much memory is needed.

For this reason, when we write programs, we must tell the computer what type of data we are dealing with. In other words, we must define the **data type** of the variables we use.

Computer languages make use of two fundamental data types: **numeric data** and **character string** (or **alphanumeric**) **data**. Numeric data can be further divided into two major types—integer and floating point—and both of these are discussed in Chapter 2. In some languages, data that consists of text is divided into two types: character data that consists of a single alphanumeric character and string data that consists of as much text as desired. In this chapter, we will define what is meant by each of these types and also introduce another data type—the Boolean type.

The Declare Statement

As you have learned, a variable is a name for a storage location in the computer's memory. For example, if your program contains a variable named Color (that you plan to use to store the user's favorite color), there will be a storage location inside the computer set aside to hold its value. When you ask the user to type in his or her favorite color, that information is stored in the location which you have named Color. Therefore, before you begin to use a variable, you must explain to the computer that you want a storage location set aside and you want to give that location a name. In other words, you must **declare** your variable.

Different programming languages use different syntax to declare variables. In this text, we use the word Declare. Before using any variables in our pseudocode, they must be declared with a statement that includes the keyword Declare, the variable name, and the variable type.

A Declare statement, in this text, takes the following form:

```
Declare VariableName As DataType
```

Character and String Data

Loosely speaking, a character is any symbol that can be typed at the keyboard. This includes the letters of the alphabet, both uppercase and lowercase, numbers, punctuation marks, spaces, and some of the extra characters that a computer keyboard contains, such as the pipe key (|), the various types of brackets (curly brackets {} or square brackets []), and other special characters like $, &, <, >, and so forth. A string is a sequence of characters. In most programming languages, strings are enclosed in quotation marks. We will follow this practice in this book—in fact, we already have. For example, the Music Purchase program contains the following statement:

```
Write "Enter the number of songs you wish to purchase:"
```

A single character is also considered to be a string, so "B" and "g" are strings. But a string may be void of *any* characters; if this is the case, it's called the **null string** (or empty string) and is represented by two consecutive quotation marks (""). The length of a string is simply the number of characters in it. For example, the string "B$? 12" has length 6 because the space between the ? and 1 counts as a character. A single character, such as "Y", has length 1 and the null string has length 0.

Many programming languages contain a **Character data type**. A single character takes little storage space in the computer's memory and characters are easy to manipulate. There are some times when it is most efficient to store a variable as a Character data type, but you must be certain that only a single character will be stored in that variable. For example, if a user is required to type in either the letter Y or the letter N in response to a yes-or-no question, then the Character data type is most appropriate. However, some languages, such as JavaScript, contain only a String data type which is used for all text, including a single character. More often in this text, we will use the String data type for nonnumeric data. However, to declare a variable to hold only a single character, we can use a statement such as

```
Declare Response As Character
```

to declare a variable (in this case the variable is named Response) to be of Character type.

Most programming languages contain a String data type. In these languages, we can declare variables to be of String type in an appropriate statement within the program. In some older languages, strings are constructed as arrays of characters. In this book, to define a string variable, we will use a statement such as the following, in which the variable is UserName:

```
Declare UserName As String
```

Operating on Strings

Like numbers, strings can be input, processed, and output. We will use Input and Write statements to input and display the values of character and string variables in Example 1.8.

Example 1.8 **Using String Variables**

If UserName is declared to be a String variable, then the statement

```
Input UserName
```

allows the user to enter a string at the keyboard and then assigns that string to the variable UserName.

The statement

```
Write UserName
```

displays the value of UserName on the screen.

Any data stored in a string variable is treated as text. Therefore, if you declare a variable named `ItemNumber` as a `String` variable and then assign `ItemNumber = "12"`, you cannot do any mathematical operations on the variable.

In Section 1.3, we introduced six arithmetic operators: addition, subtraction, multiplication, division, modulus, and exponentiation. Each of these operators acts on two given numbers to produce a numeric result. Many programming languages include at least one string operator, **concatenation**, which takes two strings and joins them to produce a string result. The symbol that is often used to concatenate two strings is the plus sign, +. For example, if `String1 = "Part"` and `String2 = "Time"`, then the statement

```
Set NewString = String1 + String2
```

assigns the string `"PartTime"` to the string variable `NewString`. In other words, the value stored in the variable `String1` is *concatenated* with the value stored in `String2` to form the new string, which is now stored in the variable named `NewString`.

The + sign is used to represent both addition and concatenation in a computer program. However, the computer will never be confused by this. If the variables in a statement are numeric, the + sign will signify addition. If the variables are `String` data, the + sign will represent concatenation. In the concatenation operation, the values of the items that are concatenated are simply joined together.

What do you think the computer would display if you used the + operator on a string variable and a numeric variable? For example, let's assume that `ItemName` and `TextString` are declared as `String` variables, `ItemCost` is a number, and the following values are inputted for these variables:

? **What & Why**

```
ItemName = "Cashmere sweater "
TextString = "will cost $ "
ItemCost = 125
```

Then the output, given the following statement that uses the concatenation operator twice, would be as shown:

Statement: `Write ItemName + TextString + ItemCost`

Display on Screen: `Cashmere sweater will cost $ 125`   ●

The program shown in Example 1.9 illustrates concatenating string variables.

Example 1.9 **Concatenating String Variables**

The program below inputs a first and last name from the user as `String` variables, makes use of the concatenation operator to create a string of the form `Last name, First name`, and then displays this string.

```
1 Declare FirstName As String
2 Declare LastName As String
3 Declare FullName As String
4 Write "Enter the person's first name: "
5 Input FirstName
```

```
6 Write "Enter the person's last name: "
7 Input LastName
8 Set FullName = LastName + ", " + FirstName
9 Write "The person's full name is: " FullName
```

Let's run through the execution of the program:

- Lines 1, 2, and 3 declare our three variables, FirstName, LastName, and FullName, to be of the String data type.
- Line 4 contains the first Write statement, which is an input prompt. It displays a message on the screen asking the user to input a first name.
- Line 5 is the first Input statement, which assigns the text (the string) entered by the user to the variable FirstName.
- Lines 6 and 7 contain the next Write and Input statements, which prompt for and assign the value of the variable LastName.
- In line 8, when the assignment (Set) statement is executed, two things happen. First, the right side is evaluated. The value of LastName (a string input by the user) is concatenated with the string consisting of a comma and a blank space. Then, that string is concatenated with the first name entered by the user. Second, this new string is assigned to the variable FullName.
- Finally, in line 9, the value of the string variable FullName is displayed on the screen. Note that the quotation marks surrounding the text are not displayed. To display quotation marks on the screen, you must use the rules specific to each programming language to do this.

If the user entered FirstName = "Sam" and LastName = "Smith", the result is FullName = "Smith, Sam" and the characters shown on the screen are:

```
The person's full name is: Smith, Sam
```

1.5 Integer Data

Most programming languages allow at least two types of numeric data to be used in programs: **integers** and **floating point numbers**. These types of data are stored differently and they take up different amounts of space in the computer's memory. Integer data consists of all the whole numbers, negative, zero, and positive. Floating point data consists of all numbers that include a decimal part. First we will discuss integer data and then we will discuss floating point data.

In programming, an integer is a positive, negative, or zero whole number written without using a decimal point. For example, the numbers 430, –17, and 0 are integers. While the number 8 is an integer, the number 8.0 is not considered as an integer in programming. It has a decimal part, even though the value of the decimal part is 0. Because they are relatively simple numbers, integers take up relatively little storage space in the computer's memory.

As we have seen, before a variable is used in a program, it should be declared to be of a particular type, which in this text book is accomplished by using the Declare statement. Specifically, to declare the variable Number to be of type Integer, we will use the following statement:

```
Declare Number As Integer
```

Declaring Data Types in C++, Visual Basic, and JavaScript

In most programming languages, a variable can or must be declared (defined) to be of a particular type by placing the proper statement within the program. For example, to declare the variable Number to be of Integer type in C++, we use the following statement:

```
int Number;
```

and in Visual Basic the statement

```
Dim Number As Integer
```

does the same thing. When the program is run, this statement tells the computer to set aside a storage location of the proper size for the integer variable Number.

In some languages, a variable can simultaneously be declared as Integer type and assigned a value. When we assign a variable an initial value, we say that we **initialize** the variable. For example, in C++, to declare Number to be an integer and assign it an initial value of 50, we use the following:

```
int Number = 50;
```

However, some languages do not require a data type to be specified when the variable is created. In JavaScript, a variable's data type is defined by its initial value. For example, the following creates a perfectly acceptable variable named Number in JavaScript:

```
var Number;
```

To make Number into a variable with the integer data type, it is simply given an initial integer value:

```
var Number = 0;
```

Operations on Integers

The six arithmetic operators (+, -, *, /, %, ^) discussed in Section 1.3 may be used on calculations with integers. The result of adding, subtracting, multiplying, or taking the modulus of a pair of integers is another integer. The result of exponentiation (when we raise an integer to a power that is a positive integer) is also an integer. However, dividing one integer by another may result in a noninteger value as the following shows:

- The results of these five operators performed on two integers will always be another integer:

  ```
  5 + 2 = 7     5 - 2 = 3     5 * 2 = 10     5^2 = 25     5 % 2 = 1
  ```

- The result of the division operator on two integers is not *normally* an integer:

  ```
  5 / 2 = 2.5
  ```

Next, we will explain why we say that the results of the division operator on two integers are not *normally* an integer. When you divide two integers, the result may or may not be an integer. For example, $24 \div 8 = 3$ and 3, of course, is an integer.

But 22 ÷ 8 = 2.75 and 2.75 is not an integer. Computer programming languages have their own ways of dealing with this situation. When the division operator (/) is applied to two integers, and the result is not mathematically an integer, the language may treat the result as an integer or not, depending on the language. Some languages will **truncate** the fractional part, which means that the fractional part is simply discarded. This is demonstrated in Example 1.10.

Example 1.10 **The Result of Integer Division**

Suppose that `Number1` and `Number2` have been declared to be integers and assigned the values 22 and 8, respectively. Then we have the following:

- In Visual Basic, the result of computing `Number1/Number2` is 2.75.
- In C++ and Java, `Number1/Number2` is the integer 2. In these languages, the result of dividing 22 by 8—2.75—is *truncated* to the integer 2. Its fractional part, .75, is discarded.
- The issue is a bit more complicated in JavaScript. If the user does not specify that an integer result is required, the result of `Number1/Number2` will be 2.75. However, if an integer value is specified, the program will truncate the value, as with C++ and Java, and the result will be 2.

In this book, we take the approach of C-based languages, so that 22/8 = 2.

1.6 **Floating Point Data**

In programming, a floating point number is, roughly speaking, any number that is not of integer type. This includes all numbers with fractional parts, such as 4.6, –34.876, 6⅓ and 7.0. A floating point number differs from an integer because all floating point numbers have both an integer part and a fractional part.

When you begin programming, you will see that, for most languages, you must declare your numbers as either integers or floating point numbers. This is because the computer both stores and manipulates integers in a different manner from floating point numbers.

You might wonder why we can't simply represent all numbers as floating point and leave the fractional part as zero for integers. There are many reasons why programs use both integer and floating point numbers. Probably the most important reason is time and space. The range of possible representations changes dramatically with the size of memory allotted to store a number. For example, a 16-bit memory location can store positive integers up to +65,535. If signed integers (negative and positive) must be used, the range of positive integers is reduced by half. Since a floating point number must have two parts, the integer part and the decimal part, some memory bits would have to be reserved for the decimal part (even if they were all zero), further reducing the range. Thus, it would not be practical to store any usable range of floating point numbers in a 16-bit location. For applications that do not require the use of numbers with decimal parts, integer representations take up a lot less space in the computer's memory. If the computer does not have to deal with a large memory space, it will work faster. So integer representations allow the computer to save time and space. ●

There are many types of applications done by a computer that only need integers. For these, it would be inefficient to use floating points. For example, many websites count the number of "hits" (the number of times people access the site). This example, and numerous other types of counting applications, uses integers. Assigning numerical identification to customers in a database, to students in a university, or to serial numbers on products are all examples of where integer representation makes sense.

Of course, there are many more instances where integers simply won't do the job. Most scientific calculations require floating point numbers. Any financial application requires floating point numbers to store dollar amounts. When you begin to write computer programs, you will find that you use both integers and floating points in most programs.

The Declare Statement Revisited

In this text, when we declare variables in our programs we will use statements like the following:

```
Declare Price As Float
Declare Counter As Integer
Declare Color As String
```

Many programming languages also allow you to declare several variables in one statement, so long as all the variables in that statement have the same data type. To declare several variables of the same data type at once, we will use the following:

```
Declare Number1, Number2 As Integer
Declare FirstName, LastName, FullName As String
Declare Price, DiscountRate As Float
```

Be Careful with Data Type Declarations

Making It Work

In the Music Purchase program, the value of DollarPrice might be an integer, but it might not, so we should declare this variable to be of type Float. This can be done by placing the statement

```
Declare DollarPrice As Float
```

at the beginning of the program.

There may be times when you are not sure what data type your variable is. For example, say you want to declare a variable named Age that will hold the value of a user's age. Should this variable be declared as Integer or as Float? If you are absolutely sure that your program will require the age input to be a whole number and that no internal computations within the program will cause that variable to become a number with a decimal part, then you may want to declare Age as Integer. After all, as we have learned, integers take up less room in the computer's memory.

However, if there is a possibility that some computation could result in the value of Age becoming a floating point number, then it is always safer to declare Age as Float. Saving a little space by using Integers where Floats are needed is not worth the risk of errors in your program.

Naming Conventions for Variables

We have said that the programmer decides how to name the variables in a program, within the parameters allowed. Although this is true, there are naming conventions that are used by many programmers. Some naming conventions may be common in one language and not in another; yet there are conventions that are common to all. Some programmers like to identify the data type in variable names. For example, instead of using `Number1` as the name of an integer variable, `intNumber1` might be used, where the first three characters of the variable's name (`int` in this case) indicates that this variable is of type `Integer`. Other examples might be as follows:

- `strName` for a string variable, where the identifier `str` indicates that this variable is of type `String`
- `fltPrice` for a floating point variable, where `flt` indicates that this is of type `Float`

Regardless of what you name your variables or what convention you follow, you still must declare the type if required by the language, as in the following:

- `Declare Number1 As Integer`
- `Declare Name As String`
- `Declare Price As Float`

Some programs use what is often termed CamelBack (or sometimes CamelCase) notation as a naming convention. In **CamelBack** notation, the first letter of the variable name is either upper or lowercase, depending on the programmer's preference. But if a variable consists of two or more words, such as `DollarPrice`, the first letter of each subsequent word is uppercase. Some examples of variables declared with CamelBack notation are as follows:

- `Declare NumberOne As Integer`
- `Declare FirstName As String`
- `Declare StateTaxRate As Float`

A variation of this type of notation uses underscores to separate words in a variable name. The variables used to demonstrate CamelBack notation might then be as follows:

- `Declare Number_one As Integer`
- `Declare First_name As String`
- `Declare State_tax_rate As Float`

In this text, we use CamelBack notation as our naming convention for variables, but that is simply the author's preference. No one way is better or more preferable to another. ●

The Last Word on the Music Purchase Program

Now we have all the tools we need to present the final version of the Music Purchase program that was introduced in Section 1.2. This version makes use of our `Declare`, `Input`, `Set`, and `Write` statements, and looks as follows:

```
Declare Songs As Integer
Declare DollarPrice As Float
```

```
Write "Enter the number of songs you wish to purchase: "
Input Songs
Set DollarPrice = 0.99 * Songs
Write "The price of your purchase is " + DollarPrice + dollars.
```

Types of Floating Point Numbers

Floating point numbers are represented in a completely different manner from integers in a computer's memory. In Chapter 2, you will learn how this is done. Now we begin with a short review of the types of floating point numbers. There are two types of numbers that can be represented by floating point. The first is the set of **rational numbers**. A rational number is any number that can be written as an integer divided by another integer. Example 1.11 shows some rational numbers.

Example 1.11 Some Rational Numbers

$5\frac{1}{2} = \frac{11}{2}$	$207.42 = \frac{20742}{100}$	$0.5 = \frac{1}{2}$
$4\frac{3}{4} = = \frac{19}{4}$	$8.6 = \frac{86}{10}$	$0.0 = \frac{0}{anything\ but\ zero}$
$2.0 = \frac{20}{10} = \frac{2}{1}$	$0.8754 = \frac{8754}{10,000}$	$.333333\ldots = \frac{1}{3}$

A number whose decimal representation eventually becomes periodic (i.e., the same sequence of digits repeats indefinitely) is called a **repeating decimal**. Therefore, the number 1/3 is a repeating decimal. If you try to write 1/3 as a decimal, the 3s will repeat indefinitely. Another example is 1/11. If you convert this to a decimal representation, you get 0.09090909... and the sequence, 09, repeats indefinitely. All rational numbers have either finite decimal expansions (like $5\frac{1}{2} = 11/2 = 5.5$) or repeating decimals (like $1/11 = 0.09090909$)

The second type of floating point number is the set of irrational numbers. An **irrational number** is a number that cannot be expressed as a fraction because the fractional part would go on forever without ever repeating a sequence. A repeating sequence is called a period. Irrational numbers have decimal expansions that neither terminate nor become periodic. Example 1.12 shows some irrational numbers.

Example 1.12 Some Irrational Numbers

$$\sqrt{2} = 1.4142135\ldots \quad \pi = 3.1415926535\ldots$$

In programming, all rational and irrational numbers are represented as floating point numbers.

Making It Work

A Word about Accuracy

If you were asked to divide $9.00 evenly between three people, it is clear that each person would get $3.00. But if you were asked to evenly divide $10.00 among the same three people, it would be impossible. Two people would get $3.33 and one would have to get $3.34. There is no way to evenly divide any number that is not a multiple of 3 by 3. That is because $1/_3$ is a repeating decimal. If you needed to represent $1/_3$ in a computer, you could not keep repeating 3s forever; the computer's memory contains a finite number of storage locations. Let's say you were allowed four places to represent the decimal part of a number. Then $1/_3$ would be represented as 0.3333. This number has the exact same value as 0.33330. But $1/_3$ does not equal 0.33330. Computer programs do not always calculate with complete accuracy!

Example 1.13 Your Computer May Not Be as Accurate as You Think!

a. Calculate the circumference of a circle with a radius of 10 inches, using four places in the representation of π:
   - The formula for the circumference of a circle is C = 2 * π * R, where C is the circumference and R is the radius of the circle.
   - Using four places to represent the fractional part of a number, $\pi = 3.1416$. This is because the first five digits of the fractional part of π are 14159 and, when using only four digits, we round up to 1416.
   - So C = 2 * 3.1416 * 10 = 62.8320.

b. Calculate the circumference of a circle with a radius of 10 inches, using six places in the representation of π:
   - Using six places to represent the fractional part of a number, $\pi = 3.141592$.
   - So C = 2 * 3.1416 * 10 = 62.831840.

And 62.831840 does not equal 62.8320.

We can see from Example 1.13 that a computer is not always accurate. In fact, sometimes the computer may not be accurate when doing relatively simple calculations. Depending on various factors, a number as simple as 2.0 may actually be stored in the computer as 1.99999999 or 2.00000001. (The material in Chapter 2 can help you understand how this might happen.) This difference may not affect the results in most cases, but it is important to realize that a computer is not always 100% accurate!

What & Why

The fact that a computer may not be perfectly accurate is no reason to stop trusting computers. In the real world, we can never measure anything with absolute accuracy. For example, if you weigh yourself on a digital scale, the reading is only as accurate as the number of fractional digits your scale allows. With a scale that is advertised to display accurately to half-pounds, a display of 134.5 pounds means you may actually weigh between $134^1/_4$ and $134^3/_4$ pounds. Anything less than $134^1/_4$ would round down to 134.0 and anything greater than $134\tfrac{3}{4}$ would round up to 135.0 on the scale. For a given weight, the difference between the lowest and highest possible readings on such a scale is $\tfrac{1}{2}$ pound. So your scale actually weighs with accuracy of $\pm\tfrac{1}{2}$ pound. A computer that stores the number 2.0 as 1.99999999 or 2.00000001 is accurate to within ± 0.00000002. And that's a lot more accurate than your bathroom scale! ●

Integers versus Floating Point Numbers

The number 7.0 is a floating point number. The number 7 is an integer. These numbers have exactly the same value, but they are stored differently in the computer and are treated differently within a program. Just something to keep in mind...

Although variables declared to be of type Integer cannot take on noninteger values (such as 2.75), variables declared to be of type Float *can* take on integer values. For example, if NumberFloat is of type Float and NumberInt is of type Integer, then the following statements apply:

- Set NumberFloat = 5.5 is *valid* (that is, correct)
- Set NumberInt = 5.5 is *invalid* (incorrect since 5.5 is not an integer)
- Set NumberFloat = 5 may result in an error. In some languages this statement would be acceptable and NumberFloat would be stored at 5.0. In other languages if you do not specify the decimal part, even if that part is 0, you will get an error.

In most programming languages, a variable is declared to be of type Float by using the proper statement within the program. For example, to declare the variable Number to be of type Float in C++ and Java, we use the following statement:

```
float Number;
```

but in Visual Basic, we use the following statement:

```
Dim Number As Double
or
Dim Number As Decimal
```

These statements cause the computer to allocate the amount of memory needed to store the floating point variable named Number. Typically, this is twice as much memory as needed for an integer variable.

Boolean Data

The last type of data we will discuss in this chapter is the Boolean data type. A Boolean variable can only have a value of either **true** or **false**. This probably sounds odd to people who are new at programming. We have consistently emphasized the importance of using variables because a variable can take on many different values and in this way make programs functional in a wide array of situations. What use, therefore, is a variable that can only have two specific values? You will see.

What's in a Name? Who is George Boole?

George Boole was an English mathematician, philosopher, and logician who lived in the mid-1800s. He worked in the fields of differential equations and algebraic logic and helped establish modern symbolic logic. He developed the algebra of logic, which is now called Boolean algebra and is basic for the design of digital computer circuits. As the inventor of the prototype of what is now called **Boolean logic** and is the basis of the modern digital computer, Boole may be regarded as a founder of the field of computer science. Students of computer hardware and digital circuits know that a computer consists of millions of switches, which are only either on or off. The vast number of possible combinations of these switches, in one of these two possible conditions, is, in essence, how a computer works.

A switch that is "on" is also referred to as having high voltage or can be identified as a "1" or a true value. A switch that is "off" can be thought of as having low voltage or "0" or "false". As the father of the logic created by various combinations of on/off, high/low, 1/0, or true/false, it is only fitting that a data type that takes one of these two values be named after George Boole.

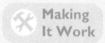
Making It Work

Using Boolean variables

In our earliest and simplest programs, we will not have any use of Boolean variables. However, as programs become more complex, programmers come to depend on Booleans.

For example, imagine you are creating a game program. You want your player to be allowed to continue at a certain level, through a multitude of scenarios, until the player reaches some specified point. At that time, the player can move to the next level. If you set a variable to be false throughout the game until a condition is met, at which time the variable becomes true, you can use this to check throughout the player's gaming session, whether he or she is ready to move on.

You might also create a program for a large business that searches an enormous database of customers for one specific customer. As soon as that customer is found, a variable (often called a flag and initially set to false) might be set to true, allowing the program to exit the search and save a lot of time.

Creating **Boolean** Variables

We will find many uses for Boolean variables in later chapters. For now, it is enough to understand that this type exists and see how to declare it in this text. Most programming languages have a data type that allows for either true or false as the only options. The name of this type may differ slightly from one language to another but they all perform the same way. Some names of this data type are Boolean, boolean, or bool. In this text, we will use the following syntax to declare a Boolean variable named Flag:

```
Declare Flag As Boolean
```

With a Boolean variable, it is always a good idea to give the variable an initial value. In most languages, if an initial value is not set, a Boolean variable will default to a value. In many languages, the default is false but not always. Therefore, it is best to be sure and give your variable your own initial value. Example 1.14 shows how a Boolean variable might be used in our Music Purchase Program.

Example 1.14 Using a `Boolean` Flag in the Music Purchase Program Pseudocode

```
Declare Flag As Boolean
Set Flag = false
Write "Enter the number of songs you wish to purchase: "
Input Songs
If Songs < 0 The
   Set Flag = true
If Flag is true Then
   Write "You cannot order a negative number of songs"
If Flag is false Then
   Set DollarPrice = 0.99 * Songs
   Write DollarPrice
```

This program uses some programming logic (decisions) that will be covered in Chapter 4, but it gives you the general idea of how a `Boolean` variable can be used.

Self Check for Section 1.4

1.14 What is the difference between the `Character` data type and the `String` data type?

1.15 What would be the result of the following operation, given that the variables named `JackOne` and `JillTwo` are of `String` type?

```
Set JackOne = "3"
Set JillTwo = "5"
Write JackOne + JillTwo
```

1.16 What would be the result of the following operation, given that the variable named `JackOne` is of `String` type and `JillTwo` is of `Character` type?

```
Set JackOne = "Jackie"
Set JillTwo = "J"
Write JackOne + JillTwo
```

1.17 True or False? The + operator is used to mean either addition or concatenation.

1.18 Suppose `GetThere` and `String1` are string variables with `String1 = "Step"`. What would be displayed if the following program were run?

```
Set GetThere = String1 + "-by-" + String1
Write GetThere
```

1.19 Which of the following is not considered an integer in programming?

    a. `6`

    b. `0`

    c. `-53`

    d. `2.0`

1.20 Which of the following is not a floating point number?

    a. `6`

    b. `0.0`

    c. `-0.53`

    d. `125,467,987.8792`

1.21 Which of the following is not a rational number?

    a. $\sqrt{2}$

    b. $^{567}/_{32}$

    c. $^{1}/_{3}$

    d. `7.623623623623623623`

1.22 The following data will be used in a program. Create appropriate variable names and declare these variables with the data type needed for their use:

    a. the number of batteries needed to operate a flashlight

    b. the price of filling up a car's gas tank

    c. the area of a circle, given the radius

1.23 True or False? Declaring a variable as type `Float` is efficient because the `Float` data type uses less memory than the `Integer` type.

1.24 List two possible situations that might use a `Boolean` variable in a program.

1.25 True or False? George Boole invented the `Boolean` data type?

1.7 Running With RAPTOR (Optional)

Introducing RAPTOR

We have stated that today's programmers must not only be fluent in several programming languages but—and this is even more important than knowing specific languages—a good programmer must be able to learn new languages quickly. A software developer may be given a task that can only be implemented in a language that developer has never seen. For experienced programmers, this is rarely a problem because all programming languages depend on the same logic. Learning specific syntax rules for a new language will hardly slow down a developer who knows programming logic well.

The logic of a program is what allows a program to produce the intended results. For example, if you want a program to average the sum of four numbers, your code must first add the four numbers and then divide by 4. If the logic is incorrect, the results will be incorrect, as shown in Example 1.15:

Example 1.15 **Using Correct Logic to Achieve Intended Results**

Given the four numbers: 70, 76, 80, 84

    a. average = 70 + 76 + 80 + 84 ÷ 4

    b. average = (70 + 76 + 80 + 84) ÷ 4

The result of part (a) is 247, while the true average, 77.5, is the result of part (b). Part (a) uses faulty programming logic but, if coded with correct syntax, would run without error. The programmer must be sure that not only will a program run without errors, but that the logic is such that the results are the ones actually desired.

This textbook will teach you the logic of writing program code. But because we do not use a specific language, you would not be able to test to see if your logic gives the correct results without a way to run the programs you create and see the results. For this reason, we include a free software program called RAPTOR.

RAPTOR allows you to create a program without using the syntax of any specific language, run that program, and view the results. It provides a way for people who are new to programming to focus on the logic of the code without becoming bogged down in the minutiae of syntax rules.

At the end of each chapter in this book, beginning with Chapter 3, there is a section called Running With RAPTOR. The section will demonstrate how to use the features of RAPTOR that correspond to that chapter's material and will walk you through creating relevant RAPTOR programs. Your instructor may or may not choose to use RAPTOR as part of your course but, regardless of your course requirements, the RAPTOR program is free, open-source software which anyone can use. When you see the RAPTOR icon, you will know that the pseudocode given can be used with the RAPTOR program. A copy of RAPTOR is available in the Student Data Files on the website or can be obtained by going to the RAPTOR website at http://raptor.martincarlisle.com/.

Chapter Review and Exercises

Key Terms

+
−
*
/
^
%
alphanumeric data
annotate
arithmetic operators
assignment statement
binary system
Boolean data type
Boolean logic
CamelBack notation
Character data type
character string
concatenation
constant (in program)
cyclic process
data
data types
declare (variables)
false
Float data type
floating point number
George Boole

hierarchy of operations
initialize
input (to program)
Integer data type
irrational number
modulus operator
named constant
null string
numeric data
operator precedence
output (of program)
processing
program development cycle
prompt
pseudocode
RAPTOR
repeating decimal
rational number
statement (in program)
String data type
syntax
true
truncate
value of a variable
variable (in program)

Chapter Summary

In this chapter, we discussed the following topics:

1. The nature of programs both in everyday life and for the computer as follows:
   - A general problem-solving strategy—understand the problem, devise a plan, carry out the plan, and review the results
   - The program development cycle—analyze the problem, design a program, code the program, and test the program
2. The following basic building blocks of a computer program:
   - Input statements transmit data to the program from an outside source
   - Processing manipulates data to obtain the desired results
   - Output statements display the results on the screen, printer, or another device

3. Pseudocode statements introduced in this chapter as follows:
   - `Input`, `Declare`, `Set` (assignment), and `Write`
4. The use of input prompts in a program
5. The use of variables in a program such as the following:
   - Variable names
   - Constants and named constants
   - How the computer processes variables
6. Basic arithmetic operations (addition, subtraction, multiplication, division, modulus, and exponentiation) as follows:
   - How arithmetic operators are represented in a programming language
   - The order in which arithmetic operations are performed (hierarchy of operations)
7. `Character` and `String` data types as follows:
   - The definition of a character string
   - Declaring `Character` and `String` variables
   - The concatenation operator (+) for joining strings
8. Other data types:
   - Declaring integer variables
   - How `Float` numbers differ from `Integers`
   - Rational and irrational numbers
   - The limits of computer accuracy
   - `Boolean` variables

Review Exercises

Fill in the Blank

1. A computer _____ is a list of instructions to be executed by the computer to accomplish a certain task.

2. The general process of designing a suitable computer program to solve a given problem is known as the _____.

3. The three basic building blocks of a program are input, _____, and output.

4. The term _____ refers to the numbers, text, and other symbols that are manipulated by a program.

5. The first of the following statements
   ```
   Write "Enter your weight in pounds:"
   Input Weight
   ```
   provides a(n) _____ for the input.

6. The `Input` statement in the previous exercise (Review Exercise 5) assigns the number entered by the user to the variable _____.

7. The two basic types of numeric data are _____ data and _____ data.

8. In most programming languages, variables that represent numbers must be _____, or defined, prior to their use.

9. The data type that gives a variable only one of two possible values is the _____ data type.

10. A(n) _____ statement is displayed on the screen to explain to the user what to enter.

11. A floating point variable requires _____ (more/less) storage space in the computer's memory than an integer variable.

12. Roughly speaking, a(n) _____ is any symbol that can be typed at the keyboard.

13. A character _____ is any sequence of characters.

Multiple Choice

14. Which of the following is the first step in the general problem-solving strategy?
    a. Devise a plan to solve the problem
    b. Make sure that you completely understand the problem
    c. Make a list of possible solutions to the problem
    d. Make a list of what is needed to review the results

15. After coding a computer program, you should do which of the following?
    a. Analyze the problem that led to that program
    b. Devise a plan for using the code to solve the given problem
    c. Run the program to see if it works
    d. Move on to the next problem

16. Which of the following is *not* an integer?
    a. 4
    b. 28754901
    c. –17
    d. 3.0

17. Which of the following is *not* a floating point number?
    a. 236,895.34766
    b. –236,895.34766
    c. 0
    d. $^6/_{18}$

18. Which of the following is *not* a rational number?
    a. $\sqrt{3}$
    b. 0.873
    c. $^1/_3$
    d. $^{22}/_5$

True or False

19. T F In everyday life, a program is a plan of action to attain a certain end.

20. T F Problem solving is a cyclic process, often requiring you to return to a previous step before you find a satisfactory solution.

21. T F After devising and carrying out a plan of action to solve a problem, you should review your results to see if the plan has worked.

22. T F As you develop a computer program, you should code the program before designing it.

23. T F A variable may be considered the name for a certain storage location in the computer's memory.

24. T F Since integers can only be positive numbers, it is always best to declare all numbers as floating point numbers.

25. T F A rational number is any number that can be represented as an integer divided by another integer.

26. T F A number stored as an integer takes up less space in the computer's memory than a floating point number.

27. T F If the value of the variable MyAge is 3, then the statement

    ```
    Set MyAge = 4
    ```
    assigns the value 7 to MyAge.

Short Answer

28. Suppose X = 3 and Y = 4. Give the value of each of the following expressions:

    a. X * Y ^ 2 / 12
    b. ((X + Y) * 2 - (Y - X) * 4) ^ 2

29. What are the two possible values (depending on the programming language that is being used) of the expression 7/2?

30. Suppose X = 3 and Y = 4. If all parentheses were omitted from the expression in Exercise 28b, what would be its value?

31. Suppose X = 14. Give the value of each of the following expressions:

    a. X % 5
    b. X % 7

32. Suppose X = 12, Y = 6, and Z = 5. Give the value of each of the following expressions:

    a. X % Z + Y
    b. X % (Y + Z)

33. What is the difference between the following two variables?

    ```
    Number1 = 65
    Number2 = 65.0
    ```

34. Given that the variable named Boy = "Joey" and the variable named Age = 6, create statements that will output the following message. Use a variable named Message to store the message.

    Congratulations, Joey! Today you are 6 years old.

35. If Name1 = "John" and Name2 = "Smith", what string results from each of the following operations?

    a. Name1 + Name2

    b. Name2 + ", " + Name1

36. Write a pair of statements that prompts for and inputs the user's age.

37. Write a pair of statements that prompts for and inputs an item's price.

38. Write a series of statements that does the following:
    - Inputs the user's age (including a suitable prompt).
    - Subtracts 5 from the number entered by the user.
    - Displays the message "You don't look a day over" followed by the number computed in the previous step.

39. Write a series of statements that does the following:

    Step 1   Inputs the price of an item, in dollars, from the user (including a suitable prompt).

    Step 2   Divides the number entered in Step 1 by 1.62.

    Step 3   Displays the message "That's only", followed by the number computed in Step 2, followed by the message "in British pounds."

40. Suppose that Number1 = 15 and Number2 = 12 are both of Integer type. Give the two possible values (depending on the programming language in use) of Number1/Number2.

41. If Name1 = "Marcy", Text1 = "is now", Text2 = " years old.", and Age = 24, what will be output after the following operation:

    Name1 + Text1 + Age + Text2

42. If Character1 and Character2 are single characters, is Character1 + Character2 also a single character?

Exercises 43–50 refer to the following program:

```
Set Number1 = 4
Set Number1 = Number1 + 1
Set Number2 = 3
Set Number2 = Number1 * Number2
Write Number2
```

43. List the variables in the program.

44. What are the program's
    a. Input statements?
    b. Assignment statements?
    c. Output statements?

45. What number is displayed by this program?

46. Replace each of the first and third statements of this program by a statement that inputs a number from the user.

47. Write a statement that supplies a suitable input prompt for the Input statements in Exercise 46.

48. Suppose we want to precede the last statement in this program by a statement that displays the following message:

    The result of the computation is:

    Write such a statement.

49. What are the possible data types for Number1 and Number2 in this program?

50. Write statements that declare the variables used in this program.

Programming Challenges

1. Write a list of instructions (like those that appear in Section 1.1) so that someone can perform each of the following tasks:

   a. Do one load of laundry

   b. Use an ATM machine to withdraw money

   c. Make a sandwich (you choose the type of sandwich)

In Programming Challenges 2–6, write a program (like the programs in this chapter) to solve the given problem. Include appropriate input prompts and annotate output.

2. Write a program that computes and displays a 15 percent tip when the price of a meal is input by the user. (*Hint*: the tip is computed by multiplying the price of the meal by 0.15.) You will need the following variables:

   MealPrice (a Float)   Tip (a Float)

3. Write a program that converts a temperature input in degrees Celsius into degrees Fahrenheit and displays both temperatures. You will need the following variables:

   Celsius (a Float)   Fahrenheit (a Float)

   You will need the following formula:

   Fahrenheit = (9/5) * Celsius + 32

4. Write a program that computes and displays the batting average for a baseball player when the user inputs the number of hits and at-bats for that player. Batting average is computed by dividing the number of hits by the number of at-bats. You will need the following variables:

   Hits (an Integer)   AtBats (an Integer)   BatAvg (a Float)

5. Write a program to compute and display an investment's total interest and final value when the user inputs the original amount invested, rate of

interest (as a decimal), and number of years invested. You will need the following variables:

```
Interest (a Float)      Principal (a Float)      Rate (a Float)
FinalValue (a Float)    Time (an Integer)
```

You will need the following formulas:

```
Interest = Principal * Rate * Time
FinalValue = Principal + Interest
```

6. Write a program that inputs the first name, middle initial (without the period), and last name of a user and displays that person's name with the first name first, middle initial followed by a period, and last name last. You will need the following variables:

```
FirstName (a String)    MiddleInitial (a String)
LastName (a String)
```

Data Representation

This chapter is different from the rest of the chapters in the textbook. It can be skipped (if your instructor does not wish to cover this material) and will not affect the understanding of future chapters. It does not include any computer programs or any further information on how to write programs. No new pseudocode is presented. However, all programs depend on data. It is data, in the form of numbers and text, that is input, processed, and the results created and output. Thus, it is imperative to understand how a computer stores and manipulates data and that is what this chapter is about. Here, you will learn how various types of data are represented in a computer.

After reading this chapter, you will be able to do the following:

- Convert a decimal integer in base 10 to a binary integer in base 2 and do the reverse (convert binary numbers to decimal)
- Convert decimal integers and binary integers to hexadecimal (base 16) integers and do the reverse
- Understand the difference between signed and unsigned integer representation
- Convert decimal integers to sign-and-magnitude binary integers and do the reverse
- Convert decimal integers to binary using one's complement and two's complement formats and do the reverse
- Convert decimal floating point numbers to binary and do the reverse
- Use scientific and exponential notation
- Create normalized floating point binary numbers using the Excess_127 system
- Create single- and double-precision binary floating point numbers
- Represent floating point normalized binary numbers in the hexadecimal system

It Isn't Magic—It's Just Computer Code

This chapter is about how data is represented inside a computer's memory. While different types of data (whole numbers, fractions, text, and more) are represented differently, as you will see, each piece of data is stored as a long (or very long or exceedingly long) series of 0s and 1s. It's hard to imagine any real-life situation where you might encounter a series of thousands of 0s and 1s in long lines. But have you ever wondered what the self-proclaimed geeks, nerds, and IT people of the twenty-first century movies and television cop shows are doing when they scroll through screens full of 0s and 1s? After working through the material in this chapter, you still will not be able to read a screenful of machine language code, but you will know that it is just data and you will know that, given the right software to translate all those binary digits to some semblance of English, you too could decipher the material on those screens. It isn't magic; it's just computer code, written by ordinary people who learned to be programmers, as you are doing right now.

2.1 Decimal and Binary Representation

The number system we all use in everyday life is the decimal number system. It most likely developed from the fact that we have ten fingers so it is natural for us to count by tens. As you will soon see, 10 is a key number in the decimal system, and we refer to this system as a **base 10 system**. The number 23, for example, is 2 tens and 3 ones (2*10 + 3*1). The number 4,657 is 4 thousands, 6 hundreds, 5 tens, and 7 ones (4*1000 + 6*100 + 5*10 + 7*1).

Bases and Exponents

The **decimal system** uses a base of 10. This is the system we normally use for all our mathematical operations but it is just one system out of innumerable possibilities. Before we go further into this definition, we need to understand bases and exponents.

The **base** is the number we are acting on, and the **exponent** (the number written, usually, as a superscript) tells the reader what to do with the base. In the expression 3^5, we call 3 the base and 5 the exponent. Example 2.1 demonstrates bases and exponents.

Example 2.1 **Bases and Exponents**

- Any number squared means that number times itself. In the following example, 10 is the base and 2 is the exponent:

    10^2 = 10*10 = 100

- A number that is cubed means that the number is multiplied by itself 3 times. Here, 4 is the base and 3 is the exponent:

    4^3 = 4*4*4 = 64

- When a number is raised to a positive integer power, it is multiplied by itself that number of times. In the following, the base is 5 and the exponent is 6:

    5^6 = 5*5*5*5*5*5 = 15,625

- In the following, the base is 8 and the exponent is 1:

    8^1 = 8

Note: When a nonzero number is raised to the power of 0, the result is always 1. This is true no matter what the number is. As you can see from the following examples, bases change but the exponents are all zero.

- $5,345^0$ = 1
- 4^0 = 1
- $(-31)^0$ = 1
- 0^0, however, is undefined

Note: Any number raised to a power can be written as X^a, where X is the base and a is the exponent. However, in computer programming, a base with an exponent is represented as X^a where X is the base, the carat (^) indicates raising a number to an exponent, and a is the exponent.

All of this relates directly to our decimal number system. Later, we will see how the same concepts apply to the binary and hexadecimal systems. As we said earlier, in a number like 4,657, we say there are 4 thousands, 6 hundreds, 5 tens, and 7 ones. In other words, we can express the number in terms of the 1's column, the 10's column, the 100's column, and the 1,000's column. There is a reason for these specific columns. Each column represents the base of the system (10) raised to a power. The one's column represents 10 raised to the 0th power, the 10's column represents 10 raised to the 1st power. The 100's column represents 10 raised to the 2nd power, the 1,000's column represents 10 raised to the 3rd power, and so forth. Table 2.1 shows the first eight columns of the decimal system.

Table 2.1 The decimal system

The first eight columns of the decimal system							
10^7	10^6	10^5	10^4	10^3	10^2	10^1	10^0
10,000,000	1,000,000	100,000	10,000	1,000	100	10	1
ten millions	millions	hundred thousands	ten thousands	thousands	hundreds	tens	ones

Expanded Notation

The ten digits that are used in the decimal system are 0, 1, 2, 3, 4, 5, 6, 7, 8, and 9. This is because the system uses the base of 10. Any number in the decimal system can be written as a sum of each digit multiplied by the value of its column. This is called **expanded notation**. Example 2.2 shows how expanded notation works.

Example 2.2 Using Expanded Notation

The number 23 in the decimal system actually means the following:

$$
\begin{array}{lll}
& 3*10^0 = 3*1 & = & 3 \\
+ & 2*10^1 = 2*10 & = & 20 \\
\hline
& & & 23
\end{array}
$$

Therefore, 23 can be expressed as $2*10^1 + 3*10^0$.

The number 6,825 in the decimal system actually means the following:

$$
\begin{array}{lll}
& 5*10^0 = 5*1 & = & 5 \\
+ & 2*10^1 = 2*10 & = & 20 \\
+ & 8*10^2 = 8*100 & = & 800 \\
+ & 6*10^3 = 6*1,000 & = & 6,000 \\
\hline
& & & 6,825
\end{array}
$$

Therefore, 6,825 can be expressed as $6*10^3 + 8*10^2 + 2*10^1 + 5*10^0$.

In the decimal system, to express a number in expanded notation, you multiply each digit by the power of 10 in its place value. The decimal number 78,902 in expanded notation is written as follows:

$$(7*10^4) + (8*10^3) + (9*10^2) + (0*10^1) + (2*10^0)$$

The Binary System

The binary system follows the same rules as the decimal system. The difference is that while the decimal system uses a base of 10 and has ten digits (0 through 9), the **binary system** uses a base of 2 and has two digits (0 and 1). The rightmost column of the binary system is the one's column (2^0). It can contain a 0 or a 1. The next number after one is two, but in binary, a two is represented by a 1 in the two's column (2^1), just as 10 in decimal is represented by a 1 in the 10's column (10^1). One hundred in decimal is represented by a 1 in the 100's (10^2) column and in binary, a 1 in the 2^2's column represents the number 4.

Through examples, we will show how to convert numbers from decimal to binary and back again. Before we do, we need a convention to tell us if the number in question is a decimal number or a binary number. For example, the number 10 is ten in decimal but two in binary. We will use subscripts to indicate whether a number is a decimal or a binary number. Thus, 10_{10} indicates the number ten, base 10 but 10_2 indicates the number two, base 2.

The easiest way to convert a decimal number to binary is to create a little chart with the values of the columns as shown in Table 2.2 and, as you work through a problem, you can fill in the bottom row.

Look at the decimal number you are given. Then find the largest decimal number in the chart that is less than or equal to the given number. Next, in the row for the binary number you are creating, put a 1 in the column corresponding to the number you found in the chart. For example, suppose the given number is 11. The largest number in the chart that is less than or equal to 11_{10} is 8_{10}, which is 2^3. So, put a 1 in the 2^3 column. Now, subtract the decimal number you've found in the chart from the given number. In this example, 11 - 8 = 3. Then repeat the process, finding the largest number in the chart that is less than or equal to 3. This is 2, so we put a 1 in the 2^1 column of the binary number we are creating. However, we must also put a 0 in the 2^2 column. Now, subtract 2 from 3, getting 1. Put a 1 in the 2^0 column. The result, in binary, is 1011_2.

Table 2.2 Chart to use to convert a decimal number to binary

	The first eight columns of the binary system							
Power of 2	2^7	2^6	2^5	2^4	2^3	2^2	2^1	2^0
Decimal value	128	64	32	16	8	4	2	1
Binary representation								

Example 2.3 **Convert the Decimal Number 7_{10} to Binary**

- 7 is less than 8 but greater than 4 so put a 1 in the four's (2^2) column.
- 7 – 4 = 3
- 3 is less than 4 but greater than 2 so put a 1 in the two's (2^1) column.
- 3 – 2 = 1
- You have 1 left so put a 1 in the one's (2^0) column.

Power of 2	2^5	2^4	2^3	2^2	2^1	2^0
Decimal value	32	16	8	4	2	1
Binary representation	0	0	0	1	1	1

- Therefore, $7_{10} = 111_2$.

Example 2.4 **Convert the Decimal Number 29_{10} to Binary**

- 29 is less than 32 but greater than 16 so put a 1 in the 16's (2^4) column
- 29 – 16 = 13
- 13 is less than 16 but greater than 8 so put a 1 in the eight's (2^3) column
- 13 – 8 = 5
- 5 is less than 8 but greater than 4 so put a 1 in the four's (2^2) column
- 5 – 4 = 1
- 1 is less than 2 so there is nothing in the two's (2^1) column
- Put a 0 in the two's column
- You have 1 left so put a 1 in the one's (2^0) column

Power of 2	2^5	2^4	2^3	2^2	2^1	2^0
Decimal value	32	16	8	4	2	1
Binary representation	0	1	1	1	0	1

- Therefore, $29_{10} = 11101_2$.

Example 2.5 **Convert the Decimal Number 172_{10} to Binary**

- There is one 128 in 172 so put a 1 in the 128's (2^7) column.
- $172 - 128 = 44$
- 44 is less than 64 so put a 0 in the 64's (2^6) column.
- 44 is less than 64 but greater than 32 so put a 1 in the 32's (2^5) column.
- $44 - 32 = 12$
- 12 is less than 16 but greater than 8 so put a 0 in the 16's (2^4) column and a 1 in the eight's (2^3) column.
- $12 - 8 = 4$
- Put a 1 in the four's (2^2) column.
- $4 - 4 = 0$
- Put 0s in the last two columns.

Power of 2	2^7	2^6	2^5	2^4	2^3	2^2	2^1	2^0
Decimal value	128	64	32	16	8	4	2	1
Binary representation	1	0	1	0	1	1	0	0

- Therefore, $172_{10} = 10101100_2$.

Note: To convert numbers larger than 255, we need to add additional columns ($2^8 = 256$, $2^9 = 512$, and so on) to the chart.

Converting Binary to Decimal

To convert a binary number back to a decimal number, just add the value of each column in which a 1 is displayed. The binary number 10_2 has nothing in the one's column and a 1 in the two's column. The value of the number is $0 + 2 = 2_{10}$. Examples 2.6 and 2.7 show how it's done.

Example 2.6 **Convert the Binary Number 1011_2 to Decimal**

- There is a 1 in the one's column.
- There is a 1 in the two's column so the value of that column is 2.
- There is a 0 in the four's column so the value of that is 0.
- There is a 1 in the eight's column so the value of that column is 8.
- $1 + 2 + 0 + 8 = 11$
- Therefore, $1011_2 = 11_{10}$.

Example 2.7 **Convert the Binary Number 10101010_2 to Decimal**

- There is a 0 in the one's column.
- There is a 1 in the two's column so the value of that column is 2.
- There is a 0 in the four's column so the value of that is 0.
- There is a 1 in the eight's column so the value of that column is 8.
- There is a 0 in the 16's column.

- There is a 1 in the 32's column so the value of that column is 32.
- There is a 0 in the 64's column.
- There is a 1 in the 128's column so the value of that column is 128.
- 0 + 2 + 0 + 8 + 0 + 32 + 0 + 128 = 170
- Therefore, 10101010_2 = 170_{10}.

Self Check for Section 2.1

2.1 Given the decimal number 5^7, identify the base and the exponent.

2.2 What is the value of 482^0?

2.3 Convert the following decimal numbers to binary:

    a. 6_{10}

    b. 38_{10}

    c. 189_{10}

2.4 Convert the following binary numbers to decimal:

    a. 0010_2

    b. 101010_2

    c. 11111111_2

2.2 The Hexadecimal System

Before a computer can execute any of the instructions it receives, it must translate those instructions into a language it understands. Computers only understand the binary system. But it would be almost impossible for a human being to read or write in binary code. It's hard enough to keep track of a series of eight 0s and 1s. Imagine trying to write hundreds of lines of code if it was all 0s and 1s. One way to make reading and writing code easier is to use a shorthand for binary code. This is why we use the hexadecimal system.

The **hexadecimal system** uses a base of 16. This means there is a one's column (16^0), a 16s column (16^1), a 256s column (16^2), a 4,096s column (16^3), a 65,536s column (16^4), and so forth. We rarely need to deal with anything larger than the 16^4 column. Table 2.3 shows the first few columns of the hexadecimal system.

Table 2.3 The first five columns of the hexadecimal system

16^4	16^3	16^2	16^1	16^0
16*16*16*16	16*16*16	16*16	16	1
65,536	4,096	256	16	1

Hexadecimal Digits

The decimal system uses 10 digits (0 through 9) in each column because the base is 10. The binary system uses two digits (0 and 1) in each column because the base is 2. The hexadecimal system uses 16 digits in each column because the base is 16. However, it would make no sense to write 10 in the one's column to represent the number ten because there would be no way to distinguish "ten" (written as 10) from "sixteen" (also written as 10 → a one in the 16's column and a zero in the one's column). So we need another way to write the number 10 in the hexadecimal system. We use uppercase letters to represent the digits 10 through 15. Therefore, the **hexadecimal digits** are 0 through 9 and A through F.

In hexadecimal:

- 10_{10} is represented as A_{16}
- 11_{10} is represented as B_{16}
- 12_{10} is represented as C_{16}
- 13_{10} is represented as D_{16}
- 14_{10} is represented as E_{16}
- 15_{10} is represented as F_{16}

Note: To avoid confusion, numbers in systems other than decimal are read digit by digit. For example, the number 283 in decimal is read "two hundred eighty-three." But the binary number 1011 is read "one-zero-one-one" and the hexadecimal number 28A is read "two-eight-A."

Converting Decimal to Hexadecimal

Decimal numbers can be converted to hexadecimal in the same manner as we converted decimal to binary in the previous section. You can use Table 2.4 to see the hexadecimal values of some binary and decimal numbers. Example 2.8 provides examples.

Table 2.4 Sample hexadecimal values and their decimal equivalents

Decimal	Hex	Decimal	Hex	Decimal	Hex	...	Decimal	Hex	Decimal	Hex
0	0	16	10	32	20	...	160	A0	256	100
1	1	17	11	33	21	...	161	A1	257	101
2	2	18	12	34	22	...	162	A2	258	102
3	3	19	13	35	23	...	163	A3	259	103
4	4	20	14	36	24	...	164	A4	260	104
5	5	21	15	37	25	...	165	A5	261	105
6	6	22	16	38	26	...	166	A6	262	106
7	7	23	17	39	27	...	167	A7	263	107
8	8	24	18	40	28	...	168	A8	264	108
9	9	25	19	41	29	...	169	A9	265	109
10	A	26	1A	42	2A	...	170	AA	266	10A
11	B	27	1B	43	2B	...	171	AB	267	10B
12	C	28	1C	44	2C	...	172	AC	268	10C
13	D	29	1D	45	2D	...	173	AD	269	10D
14	E	30	1E	46	2E	...	174	AE	270	10E
15	F	31	1F	47	2F	...	175	AF	271	10F

Example 2.8(a) **Convert a Decimal Number to Hexadecimal**

Convert 9_{10} to hexadecimal.

- $9_{10} = 9_{16}$ because the one's column in hexadecimal takes all digits up to 15

Example 2.8(b) **Convert Another Decimal Number to Hexadecimal**

Convert 23_{10} to hexadecimal.

- Refer to Table 2.3 to see the columns in the hexadecimal system
- There is one 16 in 23_{10} so put a 1 in the 16's column
- $23 - 16 = 7$ so put a 7 in the one's column
- Therefore, $23_{10} = 17_{16}$

Before we convert a larger decimal number to hexadecimal notation, we include a brief math refresher.

A Little Math Lesson

Making It Work

We have seen how to convert large decimal numbers to binary and this was relatively easy because for each column in the binary system, the decimal number contains either one or none of the value of that column. But it is a little harder to convert a large decimal number to hexadecimal. The following example demonstrates how to do it.

Convert $89,468_{10}$ to hexadecimal.

The necessary columns in the hexadecimal system for this number are as follows:

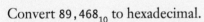

16^4	16^3	16^2	16^1	16^0
65,536	4,096	256	16	1

- Look at the number: $89,468_{10}$.
- There is one $65,536$ in 89468 so we put a 1 in the 16^4 column. (Use the table below, which is already filled in but you will fill in the bottom row yourself as you work through subsequent problems.
- Subtract: $89468 - 65536 = 23932$.
- Now, we must find out how many 4096s are there in 23932.
- Divide: $23932 \div 4096 = 5.8427\ldots$ This means there are five 4096s in 23932 with some left over. Put a 5 in the 16^3 column.
- What is left over? In other words, what does the fractional part of $5.8427\ldots$ represent? To do this:
  - Multiply 4096 by 5: $4096 * 5 = 20480$. This is what was used by putting 5 in the 16^3 column.
  - Subtract 20480 from 23932: $23932 - 20480 = 3452$. So 3452 is the amount left (the remainder after using five 4096s).

- Now, go through a similar process to fill in the rest of the columns:
- The 16^2 column: $3452 \div 256 = 13.48437\ldots$ There are thirteen 256s so put a D in the 16^2 column.
- $13 * 256 = 3328$
- $3452 - 3328 = 124$ (This is the remainder.)
- To fill in the 16^1 column, find how many 16s are there in 124: $124 \div 16 = 7.75$ so put a 7 in the 16^1 column.
- What is left over goes in the 16^0 column:
  - $7 * 16 = 112$
  - $124 - 112 = 12$ (the remainder)
- There are twelve 1s so put a C in the 16^0 column to represent 12.

16^4	16^4	16^3	16^2	16^1	16^0
1,048,576	65,536	4,096	256	16	1
	1	5	D	7	C

Now we know that $89,468_{10} = 15D7C_{16}$.

Example 2.8(c) One More Conversion

Convert 875_{10} to hexadecimal.

- Refer to Table 2.3 to see the columns in the hexadecimal system.
- 875 is less than 4,096 but greater than 256 so there is nothing in the 4,096's (16^3) column.
- Divide 875 by 256 to see how many 256s are there.
- $875 \div 256 = 3$ with a remainder of 107. (Refer to the previous Making It Work section to see how this remainder is obtained.)
- Put a 3 in the 256's column.
- $107 \div 16 = 6$ with a remainder of 11.
- Put a 6 in the 16's column.
- 11 in decimal notation $=$ B in hexadecimal notation.
- Put a B in the one's column.
- Therefore, $875_{10} = 36B_{16}$.

You can use expanded notation to check your work!

Check your answer by writing $36B_{16}$ in expanded notation:

$(3*256) + (6*16) + (11*1) = 768 + 96 + 11 = 875$

Converting Hexadecimal to Decimal

To convert a hexadecimal number to decimal, find the decimal value of each digit in the hexadecimal number and add the values.

Example 2.9(a) **Convert a Hexadecimal Number to Decimal**

Convert $A2_{16}$ to decimal.

- In expanded notation, this hexadecimal number is $A*16 + 2*1$.
- The digit A in hexadecimal means 10 in decimal. The A in this number is in the 16^1s column.
- $A*16 = 10*16 = 160$.
- $2*1 = 2$.
- Add these decimal values: $160 + 2 = 162$.
- Therefore, $A2_{16} = 162_{10}$.

Example 2.9(b) **Convert Another Hexadecimal Number to Decimal**

Convert $123D_{16}$ to decimal.

- In expanded notation, this hexadecimal number is: $(1*4,096) + (2*256) + (3*16) + (D*1)$
- D in hexadecimal is 13 in decimal, so $4,096 + 512 + 48 + 13 = 4,669$
- Therefore, $123D_{16} = 4,669_{10}$.

Using Hexadecimal Notation

A computer has no problem dealing with **binary notation**. It handles enormous strings of data, all represented as 0s and 1s (binary notation) with ease. But, unless you are a truly unusual human being, it would be difficult for you to do the following computation:

0101110010011101 + 1111111110010101 + 1000000101011001 + 0001111100101010

Imagine working with hundreds of such long strings of binary numbers! But computers store data in groups of binary numbers. Each binary digit is called a **bit**. Four bits can represent the decimal numbers 0 through 15. This makes **hexadecimal notation** a natural choice for a shorthand representation of long binary numbers. Each hexadecimal digit can represent the numbers 0 through 15 in binary. For example, $3_{10} = 3_{16} = 0011_2$ and $14_{10} = E_{16} = 1110_2$. Table 2.5 shows the conversions for numbers 0 through 15 in decimal, hexadecimal, and binary.

Frequently, binary data is written in hexadecimal. For example, when creating a graphic for a website, colors are represented by six hexadecimal digits. Each hexadecimal digit represents an amount of a color. So white is represented by FFFFFF and black is 000000. Red is FF0000, blue is 0000FF, and green is 00FF00 in the red–green–blue (RGB) system.

Table 2.5 Decimal, hexadecimal, and binary equivalents

Decimal	Hexadecimal	Binary	Decimal	Hexadecimal	Binary
0	0	0000	8	8	1000
1	1	0001	9	9	1001
2	2	0010	10	A	1010
3	3	0011	11	B	1011
4	4	0100	12	C	1100
5	5	0101	13	D	1101
6	6	0110	14	E	1110
7	7	0111	15	F	1111

Converting Binary to Hexadecimal

It is common to write a long binary number in hexadecimal notation. Example 2.10 shows how this is done.

Example 2.10(a) **Convert a Binary Number to Hexadecimal**

Convert the following binary number to hexadecimal notation: 10010011_2.

- First, separate the binary number into sets of 4 digits: 1001 0011.
- If necessary, refer to Table 2.5 to make the conversions:
  $1001_2 = 9_{16}$ and $0011_2 = 3_{16}$
- Therefore, 10010011_2 is 93_{16}.

Example 2.10(b) **Convert Another Binary Number to Hexadecimal**

Convert the following binary number to hexadecimal notation: 100011110111_2.

- First, separate the binary number into sets of 4 digits:
  1000 1111 0111
- Refer to Table 2.5, if necessary, to make the conversions:
  $1000_2 = 8_{16}$ and $1111_2 = F_{16}$ and $0111_2 = 7_{16}$.
- Therefore, 100011110111_2 is $8F7_{16}$.

Example 2.10(c) **One More Conversion**

Convert the following binary number to hexadecimal notation: 1110101000001111_2.

- First, separate the binary number into sets of 4 digits:
  1110 1010 0000 1111
- Refer to Table 2.5, if necessary, to make the conversions:
  $1110_2 = E_{16}$ and $1010_2 = A_{16}$ and $0000_2 = 0_{16}$ and $1111_2 = F_{16}$
- Therefore, 1110101000001111_2 is $EA0F_{16}$.

Any Base Will Do, If You're a Mathematician Looking to Have Fun

We suggested that our "normal" number system uses 10 as the base because human beings have ten fingers and ten toes so it might have seemed natural to count to ten and then start over. This may or may not be true but it does seem logical. We do know, however, that the computer uses the binary system because of the structure of a computer. All processes in a computer are a product of combining switches that are either on or off or, as we have seen in Chapter 1, represented as either true or false or 0 or 1. This makes the binary system a necessity for computer programming. The hexadecimal system was chosen for use with many programming languages because, as we have just seen, a single hexadecimal digit represents four bits.

But a number system can be constructed with any base. If an alien species arrives on planet Earth tomorrow with five legs and five arms, they might use a base 5 number system. It is easy, now that you know how to convert decimal to base 2 and base 16, to convert our number system to a system with any base. Let's take base 5 as an example.

In base 5, the only available digits would be 0, 1, 2, 3, and 4. The first five columns in base 5 would look as follows:

The first five columns of a base 5 system				
5^4	5^3	5^2	5^1	5^0
5*5*5*5	5*5*5	5*5	5	1
625	125	25	5	1

Some conversions from decimal to base 5 would look like this:

$$3_{10} = 3_5 \qquad 5_{10} = 10_5 \qquad 27_{10} = 102_5 \qquad 2131_{10} = 32011_5$$

Can you see why?

- There are three 1s in 3_{10} so $3_{10} = 3_5$
- There is one 5 and no 1s in 5_{10} so $5_{10} = 10_5$
- There is one 25, no 5s, and two 1s in 27_{10} so $27_{10} = 102_5$
- There are three 625s, two 125s, no 25s, one 5 and one 1 in 2131_{10} so $2131_{10} = 32011_5$

Self Check for Section 2.2

2.5 Explain why a system with base 16 needs to use letters to represent some digits.

2.6 What are the hexadecimal values of the following numbers:

   a. 10_2

   b. 10_{10}

2.7 Convert the following decimal numbers to hexadecimal notation:

a. 64_{10}

b. 159_{10}

c. $76,458_{10}$

2.8 Convert the following binary numbers to hexadecimal notation:

a. 1110_2

b. 1111111101000110_2

c. 0100101000110100_2

2.9 Explain why hexadecimal notation is often used to represent binary numbers.

2.3 Integer Representation

The manner in which computers process numbers depends on each number's type. Integers are stored and processed in quite a different manner from floating point numbers. But even within the broad categories of integers and floating point numbers, there are more distinctions. Integers can be stored as unsigned numbers (all nonnegative) or as signed numbers (positive, negative, and zero). Floating point numbers also have several variations. This section will give a general overview of the various ways integers can be stored and processed by a computer. Floating point numbers are discussed later in this chapter.

Unsigned Integer Format

In the previous section, we saw how to convert a decimal number to binary form. The number 2_{10} in decimal is 10_2 in binary and the number 101101_2 is 45_{10}. Notice that 10_2 uses two binary digits and 101101_2 uses six binary digits. However, a computer stores information in memory locations that are normally sixteen to sixty-four bits in length. To store the numbers 10_2 and 101101_2 in a computer, both of these numbers must have the same length as a storage location. We do this by adding 0s to the left of the number to fill up as many places as needed for a memory location. This is called the **unsigned form of an integer**. When a decimal number is converted to an unsigned binary format, the integer value of the number in binary must be calculated and it must also match the number of bits it takes up in the computer's memory. Therefore, after you change the number to binary, if the result has fewer bits than the number allocated by that computer for integer representation, you need to add 0s to the left of the number. Following are a few examples:

- Store the decimal integer 6_{10} in a 4-bit memory location:
  - Convert 6_{10} to binary: 110_2.
  - Add a 0 to the left to make 4 bits: 0110_2.
- Store the decimal integer 5_{10} in an 8-bit memory location:
  - Convert 5_{10} to binary: 101_2.
  - Add five 0s to the left to make 8 bits: 00000101_2.
- Store the decimal integer 928_{10} in a 16-bit memory location:
  - Convert 928_{10} to binary: 1110100000_2.
  - Add six 0s to the left to make 16 bits: 0000001110100000_2.

Overflow

If you try to store an unsigned integer that is bigger than the maximum unsigned value that can be handled by that computer, you get a condition called **overflow**. This kind of error occurs in programming frequently and you need to be aware of it. If overflow occurs in your programming, you will have to find another way to write that part of the code. Following are a few examples of overflow:

- Store the decimal integer 23_{10} in a 4-bit memory location:
  - The range of integers available in a 4-bit location is 0_{10} through 15_{10}. Therefore, attempting to store 23_{10} in a 4-bit location will give you an overflow.
- Store the decimal integer $65,537_{10}$ in a 16-bit memory location:
  - The range of integers available in a 16-bit location is 0_{10} through $65,535_{10}$. Therefore, attempting to store this number in a 16-bit location will give you an overflow.

Unsigned integers are the easiest to convert from decimal and also take up the least amount of room in the computer's memory. However, they do not allow for much flexibility because they are limited in how many numbers can be represented. The **range** of a given method, with a specific number of bits allowed, is the span of numbers—from the smallest to the largest—that can be represented. Table 2.6 provides sample ranges of unsigned integers.

Table 2.6 Sample ranges of unsigned integers

Number of Bits	Range
8	0...255
16	0...65,535
32	0...4,294,967,295
64	0...18,446,740,000,000,000,000 approximately

Sign-and-Magnitude Format

The simple unsigned integer method of converting a decimal integer to binary works well to represent positive integers and zero. However, we need a way to represent negative integers. The **sign-and-magnitude format** provides one way. In sign-and-magnitude format, the leftmost bit is reserved to represent the sign. The other bits represent the magnitude (or the absolute value) of the integer. Table 2.7 shows sample ranges of sign-and-magnitude integers.

Table 2.7 Sample ranges of sign-and-magnitude integers

Number of Bits	Range
8	-127...+127
16	-32,767...+32.767
32	-2,147,483,647...+2,147,483,647

The **absolute value** of a number is its value, ignoring the sign. The **magnitude** of a number is its absolute value. For example, the absolute value of -3 is 3, the absolute value of 5 is 5, and the absolute value of 0 is 0.

Representation of Sign-and-Magnitude Integers

In this format, if the leftmost bit is 0, the number is positive and if the leftmost bit is 1, the number is negative. The rest of the bits give the magnitude of the number, as in unsigned integer format. So the sign-and-magnitude number 0111_2 represents $+7_{10}$ and the number 1111_2 represents -7_{10}. To convert a decimal integer to sign-and-magnitude number, you need to know both the sign of the number and the number of bits allocated for storing integers. In an N-bit allocation, N-1 bits are used to store the magnitude of the number and the Nth bit is used to represent the sign. Examples 2.11 and 2.12 show how this works.

Example 2.11(a) Convert a Decimal Number to Sign-and-Magnitude Binary Format

Store the decimal integer $+23_{10}$ in an 8-bit memory location using sign-and-magnitude format:

- Convert 23_{10} to binary: 10111_2.
- Since this is an 8-bit memory location, 7 bits are used for storing the magnitude of the number.
- The number 10111_2 uses 5 bits so add two 0s to the left to make up 7 bits: 0010111_2.
- Finally, look at the sign. This number is positive so add a 0 in the leftmost place to show the positive sign.
- Therefore, $+23_{10}$ in sign-and-magnitude format in an 8-bit location is 00010111_2.

Example 2.11(b) Convert Another Decimal Number to Sign-and-Magnitude Binary Format

Store the decimal integer -19_{10} in an 8-bit memory location using sign-and-magnitude format:

- Convert 19_{10} to binary: 10011_2.
- Since this is an 8-bit memory location, 7 bits are used for storing the magnitude of the number.
- The number 10011_2 uses 5 bits so add two 0's to the left to make up 7 bits: 0010011_2.
- Finally, look at the sign. This number is negative so add a 1 in the leftmost place to show the negative sign.
- Therefore, -19_{10} in sign-and-magnitude format in an 8-bit location is 10010011_2.

Example 2.12(a) Convert a Sign-and-Magnitude Binary Number to Decimal

a. Given that 00110111_2 is an 8-bit binary integer in sign-and-magnitude format, what is its decimal equivalent?
   - First convert the rightmost 7 bits to decimal to get 55_{10}.
   - Look at the leftmost bit; it is a 0. That means this number is positive.
   - Therefore, 00110111_2 represents the decimal integer $+55_{10}$.

Example 2.12(b) Convert Another Sign-and-Magnitude Binary Number to Decimal

Given that 10001110_2 is an 8-bit binary integer in sign-and-magnitude format, what is its decimal equivalent?
   - First convert the rightmost 7 bits to decimal to get 14_{10}.
   - Look at the leftmost bit; it is a 1. That means this number is negative.
   - Therefore, 10001110_2 represents the decimal integer -14_{10}.

The Zero

One serious problem faced by programmers is how to represent zero in binary. As you will see, by the following examples, the sign-and-magnitude form has two ways to represent zero.

Example 2.13 Two Ways to Represent Zero in Sign-and-Magnitude Format

(a) Store the decimal integer 0_{10} in an 8-bit memory location using sign-and-magnitude format:
   - Convert 0_{10} to binary: 0_2.
   - Since this is an 8-bit memory location, 7 bits are used for storing the magnitude of the number.
   - The number 0_2 uses 1 bit so add six 0s to the left to make up 7 bits: 0000000_2.
   - Finally, look at the sign. Zero is considered a non-negative number so you should add a 0 in the leftmost place to show that it is not negative.
   - Therefore, 0_{10} in sign-and-magnitude in an 8-bit location is 00000000_2.

(b) ... but ... given that 10000000_2 is an 8-bit binary integer in sign-and-magnitude form, find its decimal value:
   - First convert the rightmost 7 bits to decimal to get 0_{10}.
   - Look at the leftmost bit; it is a 1. That means this number is negative.
   - Therefore, 10000000_2 represents the decimal integer -0_{10}.

We see, then, that using sign-and-magnitude format allows both 00000000_2 and 10000000_2 to represent the same number. This can wreak havoc in a computer program.

One's Complement Format

The fact that 0 has two possible representations in sign-and-magnitude format is one of the main reasons why computers usually use a different method to represent signed integers. There are two other formats that may be used to store signed integers. The one's complement method is not often used; but it is explained here because it helps to understand the most common format: two's complement.

In sign-and-magnitude format, the number $+6_{10}$, in a 4-bit allocation, is written as 0110_2. The leftmost bit is reserved for the sign of the number. So the 0 on the left here represents a positive sign. The number -6_{10}, in a 4-bit allocation, is written as 1110_2 where the leftmost bit, a 1, represents a negative sign. The one's complement method is slightly different.

To **complement** a binary digit, you simply change a 1 to a 0 or a 0 to a 1. In the **one's complement** method, positive integers are represented as they would be in sign-and-magnitude format. The leftmost bit is still reserved as the sign bit. So $+6_{10}$, in a 4-bit allocation, is still 0110_2. But in one's complement, -6_{10} is just the complement of $+6_{10}$. So -6_{10} becomes 1001_2. This means that the range of one's complement integers is the same as the range of sign-and-magnitude integers. It also means that there are still two ways to represent the zero. Following are a few examples of how decimal numbers are converted to signed binary integers using the one's complement method.

Example 2.14(a) Convert a Decimal Number With One's Complement Format

Store the decimal integer $+78_{10}$ in an 8-bit memory location using one's complement format:

- Convert 78_{10} to binary: 1001110_2.
- Since this is an 8-bit memory location, 7 bits are used for storing the magnitude of the number.
- The number 1001110_2 uses all 7 bits.
- Finally, look at the sign. This number is positive so add a zero in the leftmost place to show the positive sign.
- Therefore, $+78_{10}$ in one's complement in an 8-bit location is 01001110_2.

Example 2.14(b) Convert Another Decimal Number With One's Complement Format

Store the decimal integer -37_{10} in an 8-bit memory location using one's complement format:

- Convert 37_{10} to binary: 100101_2.
- Since this is an 8-bit memory location, 7 bits are used for storing the magnitude of the number.
- The number 100101_2 uses 6 bits so add one 0 to the left to make up 7 bits: 0100101_2.
- Now, look at the sign. This number is negative.
- Complement all the digits by changing all the 0s to 1s and all the 1s to 0s.
- Add a 1 in the 8th bit location because the number is negative.
- Therefore, -37_{10} in one's complement in an 8-bit location is 11011010_2.

Example 2.14(c) Another Conversion

Store the decimal integer $+139_{10}$ in an 8-bit memory location using one's complement format:

- Convert 139_{10} to binary: 10001011_2.
- Since this is an 8-bit memory location, only 7 bits may be used for storing the magnitude of the number.
- The magnitude of this number requires 8 bits.
- Therefore, 139_{10} cannot be represented in an 8-bit memory location in one's complement format.

To convert a one's complement number back to decimal, simply look at the leftmost bit to determine the sign. If the leftmost bit is 0, the number is positive and can be converted back to decimal immediately. If the leftmost bit is a 1, the number is negative. Uncomplement the other bits (change all the 0s to 1s and all the 1s to 0s) and then convert the binary bits back to decimal. Remember to include the negative sign when displaying the result!

The Zero Again

Unfortunately, the one's complement method does not solve the problem of a dual representation for zero. With one's complement, as shown in the following, there are still two representations for zero.

Example 2.15 Representing Zero With One's Complement Format

(a) Store the decimal integer 0_{10} in an 8-bit memory location using one's complement format:
  - Convert 0_{10} to binary: 0_2.
  - Since this is an 8-bit memory location, 7 bits are used for storing the magnitude of the number.
  - The number 0_2 uses 1 bit so add six 0's to the left to make up 7 bits: 0000000_2.
  - Now, look at the sign. Zero is considered a non-negative number so you probably should add a zero in the leftmost place to show that it is not negative.
  - Therefore, 0_{10} in one's complement in an 8-bit location is 00000000_2.

(b) but . . . given that 11111111_2 is a binary number in one's complement form, find its decimal value:
  - First look at the leftmost bit. It is a 1 so you know the number is negative.
  - Since the leftmost bit is 1, you also know that all the other bits have been complemented. You need to "un-complement" them to find the magnitude of the number.
  - When you un-complement 1111111_2, you get 0000000_2.
  - Therefore, 11111111_2 in one's complement represents the decimal integer -0_{10}.

Why So Much Fuss About Nothing?

You may wonder why there is so much fuss about the zero. Why not just define zero in binary as 0000_2 (or 00000000_2 or 0000000000000000_2, depending on how many bits you are using) and be done with it? However, in, for example, a 4-bit allocation, the bit-pattern 1111_2 still exists. When calculations are performed, this number could be the result. Unless the computer knows what to do with it, the program will get an error. It might even not work at all. Here's one possible scenario: If the result of a calculation using one's complement was 1111_2, the computer would read this as -0, as we have seen in Example 2.15, part (b). If you then try to add 1 to it, what would the answer be? The number that follows 1111_2 in a 4-bit allocation is 0000_2. (We will learn later how to add binary integers.) So that would mean, using one's complement, that -0 + 1 = +0. This certainly would not be an irrelevant issue! ●

To avoid the complications caused by two representations of zero, programmers usually use a slightly more complicated but more accurate form called **two's complement** to represent integers.

Two's Complement Format

In the one's complement method, positive integers are represented as they would be in sign-and-magnitude format. The leftmost bit is reserved as the sign bit. A negative integer is just the complement of the positive integer, with a 1 in the leftmost spot to represent the negative sign. We have seen that this creates some problems, especially in the case of zero. The two's complement solves the problem of the zero.

The following is how to find the two's complement of an X-bit number:

1. If the number is positive, just convert the decimal integer to binary and you are finished.
2. If the number is negative, convert the number to binary and find the one's complement.
3. Add a binary 1 to the one's complement of the number.
4. If this results in an extra bit (more than X bits), discard the leftmost bit.

Binary Addition

To do the addition (Step 3), we need to learn to add in binary. Binary arithmetic operations are a bit more complicated than what we show here, but this brief explanation is enough for the purpose of finding the two's complement of a number.

- In binary, adding 1 to 0 results in 1, adding 0 to 1 also results in 1, and adding 0 to 0 results in 0 (as you might expect).
- In the decimal system, if you add 1 to 9, you put a zero in the one's column and carry a 1 to the 10's column. In the binary system, you do virtually the same thing. If you add 1 to 1 in binary, you put a zero in that column and carry a 1 to the next column. This is because 1 + 1 in binary = 2 but there is no digit "2" in binary. Instead, you must carry a 2 to the next column.
- To complete the addition you need for two's complement, you need to remember two rules of binary addition, as shown in Table 2.8. Examples 2.16–2.18 provide examples.

Table 2.8 The two rules of binary addition

Rule	1 + 0 = 1	1 + 1 = 10
Example 1	$\begin{array}{r} 1\ 0 \\ +\quad 1 \\ \hline 1\ 1 \end{array}$	$\begin{array}{r} 1 \\ +\quad 1 \\ \hline 1\ 0 \end{array}$
Example 2	$\begin{array}{r} 1\ 0\ 1 \\ +\ 1\ 0 \\ \hline 1\ 1\ 1 \end{array}$	$\begin{array}{r} 1\ 1 \\ +\quad 1 \\ \hline 1\ 0\ 0 \end{array}$
Example 3	$\begin{array}{r} 1\ 0\ 0 \\ +\quad 1 \\ \hline 1\ 0\ 1 \end{array}$	$\begin{array}{r} 1\ 0\ 1 \\ +\quad 1 \\ \hline 1\ 1\ 0 \end{array}$

Example 2.16(a) Finding the Two's Complement of a 4-bit Binary Integer

Find the two's complement of $+2_{10}$ as a 4-bit binary integer.

- Convert 2_{10} to binary: 10_2.
- Add zeros to the left to complete 4 bits: 0010.
- Since this is already a positive integer, you are finished.

Example 2.16(b) Finding the Two's Complement of Another 4-bit Binary Integer

Find the two's complement of -2_{10} as a 4-bit binary integer:

- Convert 2_{10} to binary: 10_2.
- Add zeros to the left to complete 4 bits: 0010.
- Since the number is negative, do the one's complement to get: 1101.
- Now add binary 1 to this number:

$$\begin{array}{r} 1101 \\ +\ \ 1 \\ \hline 1110 \end{array}$$

- Therefore, -2_{10} in two's complement in a 4-bit location is 1110.

Example 2.17(a) Finding the Two's Complement of an 8-bit Binary Integer

Find the two's complement of $+43_{10}$ as an 8-bit binary integer:

- Convert 43_{10} to binary: 101011_2.
- Add zeros to the left to complete 7 bits: 00101011.
- Since this is already a positive integer, you are finished.

Example 2.17(b) Finding the Two's Complement of Another 8-bit Binary Integer

Find the twos complement of -43_{10} as an 8-bit binary integer:
- Convert 43_{10} to binary: 101011_2.
- Add zero's to the left to complete 8 bits: 00101011.
- Since the number is negative, do the one's complement to get: 11010100.
- Now add binary 1 to this number:

```
    11010100
+          1
    11010101
```

- Therefore, -43_{10} in two's complement in an 8-bit location is 11010101.

Example 2.18 Carrying 1s with Binary Addition

Find the two's complement of -24_{10} as an 8-bit binary integer:
- Convert 24_{10} to binary: 11000_2.
- Add zeros to the left to complete 7 bits: 00011000.
- Since the number is negative, do the one's complement to get: 11100111.
- Now add binary 1 to this number:

```
    11100111
+          1
    11101000
```

- Therefore, -24_{10} in two's complement in an 8-bit location is 11101000.

Pay close attention to the math in Example 2.18. Starting at the rightmost column, you add a 1 to the 1 in the one's column: 1 + 1 = 0 with a carry. When you carry the 1 to the two's column, you also get 1 + 1 = 0 with another carry. You carry this 1 to the four's column where you also get 1 + 1 = 0 with another carry. But in the eight's column, you add 1 + 0 so the result in the eight's column is a 1 with no carry.

But what happens when the two's complement cannot be done? This is shown in Example 2.19.

Example 2.19 When the Two's Complement Cannot Be Done

Find the two's complement of -159_{10} as an 8-bit binary integer:
- Convert 159_{10} to binary: 10011111_2.
- 10011111 already takes up 8 bits so there is nothing left for the sign bit.
- Therefore, -159_{10} cannot be represented as a two's complement binary number in an 8-bit location.

We will leave the process of converting from a two's complemented number back to binary for a more advanced course.

The Two's Complement Zero

You will recall that, in both sign-and-magnitude and in one's complement representation, there are two ways to represent binary 0. This problem is solved by using two's complement. You will see why in Example 2.20, which shows how to represent +0 and -0 in two's complement.

Example 2.20 **The Solution to the Problem of Zero!**

(a) Find the two's complement of $+0_{10}$ as an 8-bit binary integer:
   - Convert 0_{10} to 8-bit binary: 00000000_2.
   - The number is positive, so nothing more needs to be done.
   - Therefore, +0 in two's complement in an 8-bit location is 00000000.

(b) Find the two's complement of -0_{10} as an 8-bit binary integer:
   - Convert 0_{10} to 7-bit binary: 0000000_2.
   - Since the number is negative, do the one's complement, including a 1 as the eighth bit, to get: 11111111_2.
   - Now add binary 1 to this number:

$$
\begin{array}{r}
11111111 \\
+ \qquad 1 \\
\hline
100000000
\end{array}
$$

   - Recall that Step 4 in the rules for converting to two's complement states that, after the addition of 1 to the one's complement, any digits to the left of the maximum number of bits (here, 8 bits) should be discarded.
   - Discard the leftmost 1.
   - Therefore, -0_{10} in two's complement in an 8-bit location is 00000000 which is exactly the same as $+0_{10}$.

The problem of representing zero in two ways is solved by the two's complement method!

Why the Two's Complement Works

We have seen how complementing all the bits turns a positive integer into a negative one using one's complement. The two's complement may seem even more confusing. How in the world does flipping digits and then adding 1 somehow end up with the negative of the number you started with? But it does make mathematical sense, especially if you think like a computer. That means you must think in the binary system.

We will use a 4-bit allocation for our example, since this is easiest to manage. A 4-bit allocation allows for 16 binary numbers ranging from 0000 to 1111 or 0_{10} to $15_{10.}$ In this situation, we define the "flip side" of any number between 0 and 16 to be 16 minus that number. On the other hand, if we had 8 bits available, there would be 256 possible numbers (0_{10} to 255_{10}), so the flip side of a number between 0 and 256 would be 256 minus that number. For example, the flip side of 4 is 16 - 4 = 12. In two's complement, the negative of a number is represented as the flip side of its positive value. Thus, using two's complement notation, a -3_{10} is represented as the flip side of $+3_{10}$. In a 4-bit location, this would be $16 - 3 = 13$. In an 8-bit location, this would be $256 - 3 = 253$ because $2^8 = 256$.

In mathematical terms, this can be expressed as follows: Assume you are working with an X-bit memory allocation. Then, for a number, N, the two's complement is $2^X - |N|$, where $|N|$ denotes the absolute value of the given number, N.   ●

The following example illustrates how to use this formula.

Example 2.21 Using a Formula to Find the Two's Complement

Use the formula:

$$2^X - |N|$$

to find the two's complement of -37_{10}, stored in an 8-bit memory location.

By the formula shown above, the answer should be as follows:

- $-37 = (2^8 - |37|) = 256 - 37 = 219$ (since, in this example, $N = -37$)
- 219_{10}, converted to binary, is 11011011_2.

Check, using the first method described earlier:

- Convert 37_{10} to 8-bit binary to get 00100101_2.
- Since this is a negative number, complement each bit to get 11011010.
- Add a binary 1 to this number to get 11011011.
- $11011011_2 = 219_{10}$

The two's complement is the standard representation for storing positive, zero, and negative integers in computers today. We have already discussed (in depth!) how important this method is when it comes to representing the zero.

Self Check for Section 2.3

2.10 Convert the following decimal numbers to binary using the sign-and-magnitude format, using 8 bits:

a. 48_{10}

b. -39_{10}

c. -284_{10}

d. 0_{10}

2.11 Convert the following decimal numbers to binary using the one's complement format, using 8 bits:

a. 48_{10}

b. -39_{10}

c. -284_{10}

d. 0_{10}

2.12 Convert the following decimal numbers to binary using the two's complement format, using 8 bits:

   a. 48_{10}

   b. -39_{10}

   c. -284_{10}

   d. 0_{10}

2.13 Briefly explain why two's complement is the best format for representing signed integers in a computer.

2.4 Floating Point Representation

A **floating point number** differs from an integer because all floating point numbers have both an integer part and a fractional part, even if that fractional part is 0. For example, the number 8 is an integer but the number 8.0 is a floating point number. To a computer, this distinction is extremely significant.

To represent a floating point number in binary, you divide the number into its two parts: the whole number (integer) part and the fractional part. First, we will convert simple decimal numbers to binary floating point numbers. Then, we will learn to convert the larger numbers that computers deal with to floating point using a process called normalization. This requires knowledge of scientific and exponential notation as well as the Excess_127 system.

Floating Point Numbers: the Integer Part

A floating point number always has three parts: the sign, the whole number (integer) part, and the fractional part. A specific bit is set aside to denote the sign so we do not need to worry about the sign at first. To convert the integer part to binary, simply convert in the same way you convert positive integers to binary as discussed in Section 2.1.

Floating Point Numbers: the Fractional Part

As with decimal numbers, the integer part of a floating point binary number is separated from the fractional part. The dot (or period) between the integer and the fractional parts of a binary number will be referred to as a **point** from now on. The point is, in effect, a **binary point** and does the same thing as a decimal point in the decimal system. In this section, we will learn to convert the fractional part of a number to binary. This is a little more difficult than converting the integer part.

We know that the columns in the integer part of a binary number represent powers of 2. The first column, 2^0 is the one's column; the second column, 2^1 is the two's column; the third column, 2^2 is the four's column; and so on. We can think of the fractional part in similar terms. The decimal number 0.1_{10} represents 1/10. The decimal number 0.01_{10} represents 1/100 and the decimal number 0.001_{10} represents 1/1,000. The first place to the right of the decimal point, in decimal notation, is $1/10^1$. The next place is $1/10^2$, the next is $1/10^3$, and so on.

Note: The rule governing exponents is that an exponent in the denominator is the same as a **negative exponent**. In mathematical terms, this says: $1 \div X^a = X^{-a}$ or $\frac{1}{X^a} = X^{-a}$. Table 2.9 shows the values, in the exponential form, of the first six places of the fractional part of a decimal number.

Table 2.9 First six columns of the fractional part of the decimal system (base 10)

The first six columns of the fractional part of a number in the decimal system					
0.1	0.01	0.001	0.0001	0.00001	0.000001
$1/10^1 = 10^{-1}$	$1/10^2 = 10^{-2}$	$1/10^3 = 10^{-3}$	$1/10^4 = 10^{-4}$	$1/10^5 = 10^{-5}$	$1/10^6 = 10^{-6}$
tenths	hundredths	thousandths	ten-thousandths	hundred-thousandths	millionths

We use the same method to define the fractional columns in the binary system. However, we replace 10 with 2. Table 2.10 shows what the first six columns of the fractional part of a binary number look like.

Table 2.10 First six columns of the fractional part of the binary system (base 2)

The first six columns of the fractional part of a number in the binary system					
0.1	0.01	0.001	0.0001	0.00001	0.000001
$1/2^1 = 2^{-1}$	$1/2^2 = 2^{-2}$	$1/2^3 = 2^{-3}$	$1/2^4 = 2^{-4}$	$1/2^5 = 2^{-5}$	$1/2^6 = 2^{-6}$
halves	fourths	eighths	sixteenths	thirty-seconds	sixty-fourths

To convert a decimal integer to an 8-bit binary, we have to see if there are any 128's in the number, any 64's in the number, any 32's in the number, all the way down to 1's. We do almost the same thing when we convert a decimal fraction to binary. First, we have to see if there are any 1/2's in the number. Then we have to see if there are any 1/4's in the number, any 1/8's in the number, and so forth. Example 2.22 demonstrates the conversion process.

Example 2.22 Convert the Decimal Fractions 0.5 and 0.75 to Binary

(a) It is easy to see that $0.5_{10} = 1/2$ so the binary conversion is simply 0.1_2

(b) $0.75_{10} = 3/4 = 1/2 + 1/4$
  - This means that there is a 1 in the 1/2's column and a 1 in the 1/4's column.
  - Therefore, 0.75_{10} in decimal is 0.11_2 in binary.

But how would you convert a much more complicated fraction like 0.98213_{10} or 0.8887_{10}? Guessing or just eyeballing the number will only work for easy fractions. A procedure that can be applied to all fractions is necessary.

Converting a Decimal Fraction to Binary

1. First, you need to know how many bits are allowed for the fractional part of a given number. Some fractions will convert easily, like those shown in Example 2.22, but most will not. As we have seen in Example 2.22, 0.5_{10} = 0.1_2. If you were to store this in 4 bits, then the conversion would be 0.5_{10} = $.1000_2$. Often, decimal fractions require many place values in binary to convert evenly and some will never convert evenly to a binary number (as, for example, 1/3 which can never be converted to an exact decimal number). When converting a decimal fraction to binary, the conversion ends either when the last result is 0 or when you have filled in all the bits required.

2. Next, create a little chart with the decimal values of the binary fractional columns as follows:

Binary	2^{-1}	2^{-2}	2^{-3}	2^{-4}	2^{-5}	2^{-6}
Decimal	0.5	0.25	0.125	0.0625	0.03125	0.015625
Conversion						

3. As you work, you can fill in the boxes in the third row.

4. If the number is equal to or greater than 0.5, put a 1 in the 2^{-1} column. Otherwise, put a 0 in the 2^{-1} column. Then subtract 0.5 from the decimal number. If the result is 0, you are done.

5. If the result is equal to or greater than 0.25, put a 1 in the 2^{-2} column. Then, subtract 0.25 from the decimal number. If the result is 0, you are done.

6. If the result of your subtraction is less than 0.25, put a 0 in the 2^{-2} column. Look at the next column. If your number is less than 0.125, put a 0 in the 2^{-3} column.

7. Repeat with each subsequent column until the subtraction either gives a result of 0 or until you reach the end of the bits required. Put 0s in every column until you either get to a column with a value greater than the number you have (and enter a 1 in that column) or until you reach the end of the number of bits required.

Example 2.23 demonstrates the conversion process from a decimal fraction to a binary.

Example 2.23 **Convert the Decimal Fraction** 0.875 **to Binary**
- This number is greater than 0.5, so put a 1 in the 2^{-1} column.
- Subtract: $0.875 - 0.5 = 0.375$.
- 0.375 is greater than the next column, 0.25, so put a 1 in the 2^{-2} column.
- Subtract: $0.375 - 0.25 = 0.125$.
- 0.125 equals the value of the 2^{-3} column, so put a 1 in that column.

- $0.125 - 0.125 = 0$ so you are done.

Binary	2^{-1}	2^{-2}	2^{-3}	2^{-4}	2^{-5}	2^{-6}
Decimal	0.5	0.25	0.125	0.0625	0.03125	0.015625
Conversion	1	1	1			

- Therefore, 0.875 in decimal is 0.111 in binary.

For some decimal fractions, the conversion ends because, after converting a few place values, the result of the final subtraction is 0. However, there are many fractions that require many place values before the result of the final subtraction is 0. And, of course, just as there are repeating decimal numbers (such as $2/3 = 0.66666\overline{6}$), there are some fractional numbers that may never convert to binary completely. For this reason, you need to know the decimal fraction to be converted as well as the number of bits to be allocated to that conversion. Example 2.24 shows how to convert a decimal fraction to a 6-bit binary number. While the resulting fraction is not exactly the same as the decimal fraction, it is acceptable for our purposes.

Example 2.24 Convert the Decimal Number 0.4 to a 6-Bit Binary Number

- This number is less than 0.5, so put a 0 in the 2^{-1} column.
- The number is greater than 0.25, so put a 1 in the 2^{-2} column.
- Subtract: $0.4 - 0.25 = 0.15$.
- 0.15 is greater than the next column, 0.125, so put a 1 in the 2^{-3} column.
- Subtract: $0.15 - 0.125 = 0.025$.
- 0.025 is less than the next column, 0.0625, so put a 0 in the 2^{-4} column.
- 0.025 is less than the next column, 0.03125, so put a 0 in the 2^{-5} column.
- 0.025 is greater than the next column, 0.015625, so put a 1 in the 2^{-6} column.
- Even though there is a remainder when you subtract ($0.025 - 0.015625 = 0.009375$), you do not need to do anything more because the problem specified that only 6 bits are needed.

Binary	2^{-1}	2^{-2}	2^{-3}	2^{-4}	2^{-5}	2^{-6}
Decimal	0.5	0.25	0.125	0.0625	0.03125	0.015625
Conversion	0	1	1	0	0	1

- Therefore, 0.4 in decimal = 0.011001 in a 6-bit binary representation.

Example 2.25 is an interesting example of what can happen with a decimal fraction when the conversion uses too few bits to be significant.

Example 2.25 Convert Decimal Number 0.009 to Binary Using 6 and 8 Bits

(a) Using 6 bits
   - This number is less than 0.5, so put a 0 in the 2^{-1} column.
   - The number is less than 0.25, so put a 0 in the 2^{-2} column.
   - In fact, this number is less than all the first six columns shown, so put 0s in all 6 places.

Binary	2^{-1}	2^{-2}	2^{-3}	2^{-4}	2^{-5}	2^{-6}
Decimal	0.5	0.25	0.125	0.0625	0.03125	0.015625
Conversion	0	0	0	0	0	0

   - Therefore, 0.009_{10} = 0.000000_2 in a 6-bit binary representation.

(b) Using 8 bits
   - Now, we will continue the conversion for an 8-bit representation. We know that the first six digits of this number, from left to right, are 0s.
   - However, the number is greater than 2^{-7} (0.0078125 rounded up to 0.007813), so put a 1 in the 2^{-7} column.
   - Subtract: 0.009 - 0.007813 = 0.001188.
   - 0.001188 is less than the next column, 0.003906 (0.00390625, rounded), so put a 0 in the 2^{-8} column.
   - You do not need to do anything more because only 8 bits are needed.

Binary	2^{-1}	2^{-2}	2^{-3}	2^{-4}	2^{-5}	2^{-6}	2^{-7}	2^{-8}
Decimal	0.5	0.25	0.125	0.0625	0.03125	0.015625	0.007813	0.003906
Conversion	0	0	0	0	0	0	1	0

   - Therefore, 0.009_{10} is 0.000000_2 if only 6 bits are used, but is 0.00000010_2 if 8 bits are used.

How Accurate Should It Be?

It is interesting to note, from Example 2.25, that some numbers may look like 0 when they actually have a much greater value. The number 0.009_{10} may seem small, but it would depend on what it represents. For example, 0.009 centimeters is 9/100,000 of a meter, but 0.009 kilometers is 9 meters. To confuse 9 meters with 0 meters might be a significant error . . . or it might not, depending on what is being measured. If a computer program were written to calculate the distance between the sun and the earth, 9 meters might not be significant, but the difference would matter a great deal if the program was written to calculate the dimensions of a room.

Putting the Two Parts Together

To represent the whole floating point number, simply put a point between the integer part and the fractional part. In Example 2.26, we put the parts together.

Example 2.26 Store the Decimal Floating Point Number 75.804 as a Binary Number

Convert 75.804 to binary using 4 bits for the fractional part.

- Convert 75 to binary: 1001011.
- Convert 0.804 to binary:
  - Put a 1 in the 2^{-1} column and subtract: 0.804 - 0.5 = 0.304.
  - Put a 1 in the 2^{-2} column and subtract: 0.304 - 0.25 = 0.054.
  - Put a 0 in the 2^{-3} column.
  - Put a 0 in the 2^{-4} column.
  - You do not need to do anything more because the problem specified that only 4 bits are needed for the fractional part.

Binary	2^{-1}	2^{-2}	2^{-3}	2^{-4}	2^{-5}	2^{-6}
Decimal	0.5	0.25	0.125	0.0625	0.03125	0.015625
Conversion	1	1	0	0		

- Therefore, 75.804 in decimal is 1001011.1100 in binary.

Self Check for Section 2.4

2.14 Convert the following decimal fractions to binary floating point representation, using 4 bits:
a. 0.5625
b. 0.3125
c. 5/8

2.15 Convert the following binary fractions to decimal representations:
a. 0.101
b. 0.11111
c. 0.00001

2.16 Convert the following decimal fractions to binary floating point representation, using 6 bits:
a. 0.515625
b. 0.125
c. 3/32

2.17 Convert the following decimal numbers to binary floating point representation, using 4 bits for the fractional part:

a. 68.5

b. 125.44

c. 99.99

2.5 **Putting it All Together**

There are several concepts we need to cover before showing how a floating point number is actually represented inside the computer. Today, it is the rare programmer who will have to convert decimal numbers to binary floating point numbers. Most calculators, nowadays, can do basic conversions for you. However, it is valuable to understand the process and will prove helpful when writing programs. Therefore, we will go through the steps in detail.

Scientific Notation

Computers are used for many scientific applications, which often use very large or very small numbers. For example, the distance from the Earth to Proxima Centauri, the nearest star that is not our Sun, is 4.2 light years. A light year is the distance light travels in a year: 5,880,500,000,000 miles. So we are 24,698,100,000,000 miles from Proxima Centauri. To represent this distance as a binary number, even with only four place values for the fractional part, we would need 49 places. A 49-digit binary number, using the conversion process we have just learned, might look something like this:

1111000111010011100000000110111110100111100011.0000

Computers also deal with very, very small numbers. For example, an atom is one of the basic units of matter. It is a million times smaller than the thickest human hair. The diameter of an atom ranges from about 0.1 to 0.5 nanometers. Therefore, the diameter of an average atom (if there can be such a thing as an average atom!) is 0.25 nanometers or 0.000000025 meters. In binary, this would require at least 30 places to the right of the point or more, depending on the accuracy required, and might look something like this:

0.000000000000000000000000000000001011

It is clear that a better way to represent floating point numbers is necessary if human programmers are to work with them.

Scientific notation allows us to represent very large and very small numbers in a way that is easy to read and relatively easy to work with. In **scientific notation**, a given number is written as a number between 1 and 9 multiplied by the appropriate power of 10. The number 200 is the same as 2×100. But 100 is also 10×10 or 10^2. So we can write the number 200 as 2×10^2. This same reasoning can be applied to very, very large numbers. The following are a few more examples:

Example 2.27 **Using Scientific Notation for Very Large Numbers**

- $680,000 = 6.8 \times 10^5$
- $1,502,000,000 = 1.502 \times 10^9$
- $8,938,000,000,000 = 8.938 \times 10^{12}$

The same principle applies when we deal with numbers that are less than 1. We write the number as a number between 1 and 9 multiplied by the appropriate power of 10. With numbers that are less than 1, the power of 10 needed will be negative. Remember that one-tenth(1/10) is the same as 10^{-1} and the number 0.2 is the same as 2.0 × 1/10 or 2.0 × 10^{-1}. Therefore, we can write the number 0.2 as 2.0 × 10^{-1}. This same reasoning can be applied to very, very small numbers. For example, 0.000002 is the same as 2.0 × 1/1,000,000, which is the same as 2.0 × 10^{-6}. Following are a few illustrations of this concept.

Example 2.28 Using Scientific Notation for Very Small Numbers

- 0.068 = 6.8 × 10^{-2}
- 0.00001502 = 1.502 × 10^{-5}
- 0.000000000008938 = 8.938 × 10^{-12}

Note that when you use scientific notation for numbers that are less than 1, the power of 10 will always be a negative power.

Exponential Notation

The computer equivalent of scientific notation is known as **exponential notation**. In programming, instead of writing 10^{power}, we use the letter E followed by the required power. Therefore, 2,000,000 is written as 2.0 × 10^6 in scientific notation, and it is written as 2.0E+6 in exponential notation. Similarly, 0.000002 is written as 2.0 × 10^{-6} in scientific notation, and it is written as 2.0E-6 in exponential notation. Following are a few illustrations of how very large and very small numbers are written in exponential notation:

Example 2.29 Using Exponential Notation

- 680,000 = 6.8E+5
- 1,502,000,000 = 1.502E+9
- 8,938,000,000,000 = 8.938E+12
- 0.068 = 6.8E-2
- 0.00001502 = 1.502E-5
- 0.000000000008938 = 8.938E-12

If a number is displayed in exponential notation, you can convert it into ordinary notation by simply moving the decimal point the number of places indicated by the integer following E. If this integer is positive, move the decimal point to the right and you will get a number that is greater than 1. If the integer to the right of E is negative, move the decimal point to the left and you will get a number that is less than 1. Example 2.30 demonstrates how to do this.

Example 2.30 Converting Exponential Notation to Ordinary Representation

- Given 1.67E-4, we write 1.67 and move the decimal point four places to the left, filling in three zeros before 1 to make this possible. This gives us 0.000167.
- To convert 4.2E+6, we move the decimal point six places to the right, filling in five zeros to the right of 2, to get 4200000, or as it is usually written, 4,200,000.

What would happen if you had a number that had a whole number part and a fractional part but you still wanted to convert it to exponential notation? Can you convert the number 689,000.45 to exponential notation? If you multiply 6.8900045 by 100,000, you will get 689,000.45. Therefore, you can just write 689,000.45 as 6.8900045E+5.

What if you want to convert a negative number to exponential notation? The same rules hold. For example, -2,000 is the same as -2 × 1,000, so -2,000 = -2E+3 and -689,000.45 = -6.8900045E+5. Note that the sign of the number stays with the number to the left of E. The sign of the number to the right of E simply indicates if the number is between 0 and 1 (indicating that the number is a fraction) or greater than 1.

Base 10 Normalization

We have seen that there are many different ways to represent a single number. For example, the number 28 can be represented as 28_{10} or 11100_2 or $1C_{16}$ or any of a very long list of ways. The quantity, 28, is represented in several different ways here, but, to a person who has only $28 when he wants to buy something that costs $35, it all means the same thing; he doesn't have enough money. To the computer, all of these representations also mean the same thing. Internally, the values are all in what we call normalized form. We shall first discuss how to normalize a number in decimal (base 10) and then consider binary (base 2) and hexadecimal (base 16) normalization.

Normalized form is a lot like scientific notation. Each normalized number has two parts. The first part is called the **scaled portion** and the second part is the **exponential portion**. In scientific notation, the decimal point is moved to the right of the first nonzero digit. In normalized form, the decimal point is moved to the left of the first nonzero digit. Of course, the value of the number is always maintained. To normalize a decimal number, after moving the decimal point, the number is multiplied by 10 raised to whatever power is necessary to return the number to its original value. Table 2.11 shows some normalized decimal numbers.

Table 2.11 Normalized decimal numbers (base 10)

Number	Scaled Portion	Exponential Portion	Normalized Form
371.2	0.3712	10^3	0.3712×10^3
40.0	0.4	10^2	0.4×10^2
0.000038754	0.38754	10^{-4}	0.38754×10^{-4}
-52389.37	-0.5238937	10^5	-0.5238937×10^5

Normalizing Binary Floating Point Numbers

The **IEEE Standard** is the most widely accepted standard for representation of floating point numbers and it uses normalized binary numbers. IEEE was originally an acronym for the Institute of Electrical and Electronic Engineers, Inc. However, the organization's scope of interest has expanded into so many related fields that it is simply referred to by the letters I-E-E-E, pronounced eye-triple-e.

A normalized binary number consists of three parts: the sign part, the exponential part, and the mantissa. The **mantissa** is the binary equivalent to the scaled portion discussed in the previous section. Before we start to normalize binary numbers, we need to learn the Excess_127 system, which is used to represent the exponential portion of a normalized binary number.

The Excess_127 System

The Excess_127 system may seem, at first, to be a sort of sleight-of-hand magic trick. It is used to store the exponential value of a normalized binary number. There are two forms, Excess_127 and Excess_128, but we will use the more common one, the Excess_127. Since the Excess_127 system is used to store the exponential part of a number, an 8-bit allocation is all that is needed. This gives a range of values from -127 to +127 and it is extremely doubtful that a computer (or anyone!) will, under ordinary circumstances, need to work with a number greater than 2^{127} or less than 2^{-127}.

To represent an 8-bit number in the Excess_127 system:

- Add 127 to the number
- Change the result to binary
- Add zeros to the left to make up 8 bits

Example 2.31 shows how to represent binary numbers using Excess_127.

Example 2.31 **Representing Binary Numbers With Excess_127**

a. To represent $+9_{10}$ in Excess_127, add $9 + 127 = 136$
  - Convert 136 to binary: 10001000.
  - Therefore, $+9_{10}$ in Excess_127 is 10001000.

b. To represent -13_{10} in Excess_127, add $(-13) + 127 = 114$.
  - Convert 114 to binary: 01110010.
  - Therefore, -13_{10} in Excess_127 is 01110010.

Base 2 Normalization

To normalize a binary number, we go through a process similar to the one we followed to normalize a decimal number. The point is moved so it is directly to the right of the first nonzero bit. Normalizing a binary number, therefore, is more similar, in process, to representing a binary number with scientific notation. Then, we multiply the number by the power of 2 needed to express the original value of the number. It is not necessary to worry about the sign of the number since, in normalized form, the sign bit will take care of this. Examples 2.32–2.34 will make the process clearer.

Example 2.32 **Normalize the Binary Number +10110$_2$**

- Move the point to the left 4 places to get 1.0110.
- Since the point was moved 4 places to the left, the number needs to be multiplied by 2^4 to get the original number.
- Therefore, +10110 in normalized form is $2^4 \times 1.0110$

Example 2.33 **Normalize the Binary Number -101101.01010$_2$**

- Move the point to the left 5 places to get 1.0110101010.
- Since the point was moved 5 places to the left, the number needs to be multiplied by 2^5 to get the original number.
- Therefore, -101101.01010 in normalized form is $-2^5 \times 1.0110101010$.

Example 2.34 **Normalize the Binary Number +0.11110011$_2$**

- Move the point to the right 1 place to get 1.1110011.
- Since the point was moved 1 place to the right, the number needs to be multiplied by 2^{-1} to get the original number.
- Therefore, +0.11110011 in normalized form is $2^{-1} \times 1.1110011$.

There are a few things to notice about this process:

- The sign is ignored. It will be taken into account by the sign bit in the final form.
- The sign of the exponent is positive if the number is greater than 1.0.
- The point is moved to the left if the number is greater than 1.0.
- The sign of the exponent is negative if the number is less than 1.0.
- The point is moved to the right if the number if less than 1.0.

Single- and Double-Precision Floating Point Numbers

We will now bring together the concepts you have just learned to show how decimal floating point numbers are stored in a computer. The IEEE has defined three standards for storing floating point numbers. We will use their standard for what is called a **single precision** floating point. In single-precision format, a normalized floating point number has three parts. The sign is stored as a single bit, the exponent is stored in 8 bits, and the mantissa is stored in the rest of the bits. A single-precision floating point number always uses 32 bits. The first 9 bits are used for the sign and exponent. The remaining 23 bits are used for the mantissa.

To convert one decimal number to this representation requires several steps. While you may never need to do this conversion, the following explanations and accompanying examples will help you understand exactly what is going on inside the computer when you use floating point numbers in your programs.

The process to convert a decimal number to single-precision floating point follows:

1. The **sign bit**: If the number is positive, put a 0 in the leftmost bit. If it is negative, put a 1 in the leftmost bit.
2. Convert the number to binary. If there is an integer and a fractional part, convert the entire number to binary, as you have learned.
3. Normalize the number; that is, move the point so it is directly to the right of the first nonzero bit.
4. Count the number of places you moved the point. This is your exponent.
5. If you moved the point to the right, your exponent is negative. If you moved the point to the left, your exponent is positive.
6. The exponential portion: Convert your exponent to a binary number, using the Excess_127 system. Store this number in the 8 bits to the right of the sign bit.
7. The mantissa: The number you have from Step 3 is your mantissa. But there is one more piece of "magic" involved. When you store the normalized part of the number, you discard (yes, throw it out!) the 1 to the left of the point. Then everything to the right of the point is called the mantissa.

Examples 2.35–2.38 demonstrate how to convert numbers to a single-precision floating point, using the IEEE Standards.

Example 2.35 Represent the Following Normalized Number as a Single-Precision Floating Point Number

$$+2^5 \times 1.1101001101$$

- The sign is positive so the leftmost bit is a zero.
- The exponent is 5. Use the process described earlier to convert this to Excess_127.
  - Add: (+5) + 127 = 132
  - Convert 132 to binary to get 10000100.
  - Store this number in the next 8 bits.
- The rest of the number is 1.1101001101.
- Discard the leftmost 1 (the one to the left of the point) and store the remainder of the number in the last 23 bits.

- This number takes up 10 bits. But, in single-precision floating point, the mantissa is 23 bits long. You *must* add 13 0s at the end to complete 23 bits.
- Therefore, $+2^5 \times 1.1101001101$ as a single-precision floating point number is

0	10000100	11010011010000000000000
sign	exponent	mantissa

Example 2.36 Represent the Following Normalized Number as a Single-Precision Floating Point Number

$$-2^{-9} \times 1.00001011$$

- The sign is negative so the leftmost bit is a 1.
- The exponent is -9. Use the process described earlier to convert this to Excess_127:
  - Add: $(-9) + 127 = 118$.
  - Convert 118 to binary: 01110110.
  - Store this number in the next 8 bits.
- The rest of the number is 1.00001011.
- Discard the leftmost 1 (the one to the left of the point) and store the remainder of the number in the last 23 bits.
- This number takes up 8 bits while, in single-precision floating point, the mantissa is 23 bits long. You *must* add 15 0's at the end to complete 23 bits.
- Therefore, $-2^{-9} \times 1.00001011$ as a single-precision floating point number is

1	01110110	00001011000000000000000
sign	exponent	mantissa

The last two examples will take a decimal number and convert it to single-precision floating point but the steps will be listed without explanation. Refer to previous sections of this chapter for explanations, if necessary.

Example 2.37 Represent the Following Decimal Number as a Single-Precision Floating Point Number

$$-2651.578125_{10}$$

- The sign is negative so the sign bit is a 1.
- Convert to binary: 101001011011.100101.
- Normalize: $1.01001011011100101 \times 2^{11}$.
- Represent the exponent with Excess_127: 10001010.
- Store the number as a floating point single-precision number.
- Therefore, -2651.578125 as a single-precision floating point number is

1	10001010	01001011011100101000000
sign	exponent	mantissa

Example 2.38 **Represent the Following Decimal Number as a Single-Precision Floating Point Number**

$$+0.046875_{10}$$

- The sign is positive so the sign bit is 0.
- Convert to binary: 0.000011.
- Normalize: 1.1×2^{-5}
- Represent the exponent with Excess_127: 01111010.
- Store the number as a floating point single-precision number.
- Therefore, +0.046875 as a single-precision floating point number is

0	01111010	10000000000000000000000
sign	exponent	mantissa

There is also a double-precision representation of floating point numbers. **Double precision** allows for a much larger range of numbers. In double precision, the sign of the number still uses one bit, but the exponent uses 11 bits and the mantissa uses 52 bits. An 11-bit exponent uses the Excess_1023 system and can handle exponents up to ±1023. Imagine the size of a number multiplied by 2^{1023}! Since the sign takes one bit, the exponent takes 11 bits, and the mantissa uses 52 bits, a double-precision number requires 64 bits to store each number. Although it would be very tedious for people to manipulate numbers that are 64 bits, it hardly strains a computer's brain. This allows for much greater accuracy than single precision but, as you remember, nothing is ever 100% accurate. However, we will leave that representation to a computer.

Hexadecimal Representation

We have seen that it is much easier to read a hexadecimal number than to read a long string of 0s and 1s. It's easy to convert binary to hexadecimal and that's why single-precision floating point numbers are sometimes changed to hexadecimal. All you need to do is divide the binary number into groups of four digits and convert each group to a single hexadecimal number, which is the same technique we used to convert binary integers to hexadecimal earlier in this Chapter. The examples that follow simply show how to convert the binary single-precision floating point numbers we got from Examples 2.35–2.38 to hexadecimal.

From Example 2.35:

0 10000100 11010011010000000000000

Rewrite the binary number in groups of 4 binary digits and convert each group to hex.

0100	0010	0110	1001	1010	0000	0000	0000
4	2	6	9	A	0	0	0

Therefore, 0 10000100 11010011010000000000000 is $4269A000_{16}$.

From Example 2.36:

    1 01110110 00001011000000000000000

Rewrite the binary number in groups of 4 binary digits and convert each group to hex:

1011	1011	0000	0101	1000	0000	0000	0000
B	B	0	5	8	0	0	0

Therefore, 1 01110110 00001011000000000000000 is $BB058000_{16}$.

From Example 2.37:

    1 10001010 01001011011100101000000

Rewrite the binary number in groups of 4 binary digits and convert each group to hex:

1100	0101	0010	0101	1011	1001	0100	0000
C	5	2	5	B	9	4	0

Therefore, 1 10001010 01001011011100101000000 is $C525B940_{16}$.

From Example 2.38:

    0 01111010 10000000000000000000000

Rewrite the binary number in groups of 4 binary digits and convert each group to hex:

0011	1101	0100	0000	0000	0000	0000	0000
3	D	4	0	0	0	0	0

Therefore, 0 01111010 10000000000000000000000 is $3D400000_{16}$.

Self Check for Section 2.5

2.18 Convert the following decimal numbers to scientific notation:
  a. $450,000_{10}$
  b. 0.000456789_{10}
  c. $3,400,004,000_{10}$

2.19 Convert the following decimal numbers to exponential notation:

    a. $123{,}000{,}000_{10}$

    b. 0.0000003_{10}

    c. 600_{10}

2.20 Normalize the following decimal numbers using base 10 normalizarion:

    a. $456{,}000_{10}$

    b. 0.000456789_{10}

    c. $3{,}400{,}004{,}000_{10}$

2.21 Normalize the following binary numbers:

    a. $+11100_2$

    b. -1010101.0101_2

    c. -101.101_2

2.22 Represent, as a single-precision floating point number, the following normalized binary numbers:

    a. $+2^3 \times 1.100100111$

    b. $-2^{-12} \times 1.010101$

2.23 Represent the single-precision numbers you got from Self Check 2.22 in hexadecimal notation.

Chapter Review and Exercises

Key Terms

$A_{16}, B_{16}, C_{16}, D_{16}, E_{16}, F_{16}$

absolute value

base

base 10 system

binary digit

binary notation

binary point

binary system

bit

byte

complement (a binary digit)

decimal system

double precision

Excess_127 system

expanded notation

exponent

exponential notation

exponential portion (of a normalized number)

floating point number

hexadecimal digits

hexadecimal notation

hexadecimal system

IEEE Standard

magnitude

mantissa

negative exponent

normalized form

one's complement

overflow

point

range (of integers)

scaled portion (of a normalized number)

scientific notation

sign-and-magnitude format

sign bit

single precision

two's complement

unsigned integers

Chapter Summary

In this chapter, we have discussed the following topics:

1. Number systems, including representing numbers in expanded notation
2. The binary system uses base 2 and consists of two digits only: 0 and 1
   - Converting decimal (base 10) numbers to binary (base 2)
   - Converting binary (base 2) numbers to decimal (base 10)
3. The hexadecimal system is base 16 and consists of 16 digits including 0-9 plus A, B, C, D, E, and F
   - Converting decimal (base 10) numbers to hexadecimal (base 16)
   - Using hexadecimal notation to facilitate reading long binary numbers
4. There are various ways to store integers in a computer's memory:
   - unsigned
   - sign-and-magnitude
   - one's complement
   - two's complement
5. The problem of representing zero as an integer is best solved by using two's complement representation
6. Floating point decimal numbers can be converted to binary, but special attention must be paid to the fractional part of the number
7. The number of bits allocated to store a number may significantly affect the range of numbers allowed and the accuracy of the representation
8. Scientific notation, exponential notation, and normalization are methods used to represent very large and very small numbers
9. Single-precision floating point numbers require three parts when stored in binary in a computer:
   - the sign bit
   - the 8-bit exponent, converted to the Excess_127 representation
   - the 23-bit mantissa, which is the magnitude of the binary number in normalized form

Review Exercises

Fill in the Blank

1. Given the number 10^8, _____ is the base.
2. Given the number 7^5, _____ is the exponent.
3. When a base is raised to a power of _____, the result is 1.
4. There are _____ digits in the decimal system.
5. There are _____ digits in the hexadecimal system.
6. The smallest unsigned integer is _____.
7. A floating point number has a(n) _____ part and a(n) _____ part.

8. The two parts of a normalized number are the _____ portion and the _____ portion.

9. To convert the number 8.396052×10^6 to regular notation, you multiply 8.396052 by _____.

10. Using exponents, the number 1/1000 is _____.

Multiple Choice

11. What is the decimal value of the B in the hexadecimal number $3AB4_{16}$?
    a. 11_{10}
    b. 16_{10}
    c. 176_{10}
    d. 256_{10}

12. What is the decimal value of the 2 in the hexadecimal number $F42AC_{16}$?
    a. 4096_{10}
    b. 512_{10}
    c. 256_{10}
    d. 2_{10}

13. Imagine you are creating a new number system that uses 12 as the base. How many digits would be in your system?
    a. 11
    b. 12
    c. 13
    d. This cannot be done

14. Which of the following is not an integer?
    a. -5
    b. 0
    c. 95842213
    d. 6.0

15. Which of the following is not an integer?
    a. 5
    b. -4
    c. 0
    d. 2.8

16. What is the largest integer that can be represented in 4 bits in sign-and-magnitude format?
    a. 7
    b. 15
    c. 8
    d. none of these

17. What is the smallest integer that can be represented in 8 bits in sign-and-magnitude format?
  a. 0
  b. -255
  c. -127
  d. -128

18. Which of the following is the correct representation of -780,030,000 in exponential notation?
  a. -7.8003×10^8
  b. 7.8003E-8
  c. -7.8E+8
  d. -7.8003E+8

19. Which type of integer representation would have a range of 0 - 255?
  a. unsigned
  b. sign-and-magnitude
  c. one's complement
  d. two's complement

20. In binary representation, $1_2 + 1_2 =$
  a. 1_2
  b. 10_2
  c. 11_2
  d. cannot be done

True or False

21. T F In a storage location of 4 bits, a sign-and-magnitude integer could be any integer from 0 to 15, inclusive.

22. T F To make it easier for a human to read a binary floating point number, the number may be converted to hexadecimal notation.

23. T F A double-precision floating point number has twice the range of a single-precision floating point number.

24. T F The biggest problem with using the two's complement method to store signed integers is that the zero is represented in two ways.

25. T F The fraction ¾ when converted to binary and stored in a 4-bit location is represented as 0.0011_2.

26. T F To store the binary number 110_2 in an 8-bit location, simply add five zeros to get 11000000_2.

27. T F The smallest unsigned integer that can be represented in a 16-bit memory location is 0_2.

28. T F A number system that uses 7 as a base would be impossible to devise since only even numbers can be used as bases.

29. T F To convert a negative integer to binary using one's complement format, you convert the integer to binary and "flip" all the digits.

30. T F In sign-and-magnitude format, the leftmost bit is saved for the sign where 1 indicated a negative number and 0 indicates a positive number.

Short Answer

31. Write the binary representation of the following:
    a. 7_{10}
    b. 34_{10}
    c. 63_{10}
    d. 157_{10}

32. Write the binary representation of the following:
    a. 14_{10}
    b. 62_{10}
    c. 986_{10}
    d. 5824_{10}

33. Write the decimal value of the following binary numbers:
    a. 11_2
    b. 1011_2

34. Write the decimal value of the following binary numbers:
    a. 101010_2
    b. 1000011_2

35. Write the decimal value of the following hexadecimal numbers:
    a. 64_{16}
    b. $9F_{16}$

36. Write the decimal value of the following hexadecimal numbers:
    a. 234_{16}
    b. $112D_{16}$

37. Write the hexadecimal representation of the following decimal numbers:
    a. 12_{10}
    b. 160_{10}

38. Write the hexdecimal representation of the following decimal numbers:
    a. 303_{10}
    b. 4111_{10}

39. Convert the value of the following binary numbers to hexadecimal notation:
    a. 1101_2
    b. 11101110_2

40. Convert the following binary numbers to easily readable hexadecimal notation (i.e., convert each four binary digits to a hexadecimal digit):
    a. 101010101010_2
    b. 00001111110011010110_2

41. What is wrong with the following binary number: 011001120110_2

42. What hexadecimal number immediately precedes the following:

   a. $E9_{16}$

   b. 200_{16}

43. What binary number immediately follows the following:

   a. 10101_2

   b. 10111100_2

44. Convert the following decimal integers to 8-bit unsigned binary integers or indicate if an overflow condition occurs:

   a. 10_{10}

   b. 43_{10}

45. Convert the following decimal integers to 8-bit unsigned binary integers or indicate if an overflow condition occurs:

   a. 129_{10}

   b. 304_{10}

46. Convert the following decimal integers to 8-bit sign-and-magnitude binary integers or indicate if an overflow condition occurs:

   a. $+34_{10}$

   b. -39_{10}

47. Convert the following decimal integers to 8-bit sign-and-magnitude binary integers or indicate if an overflow condition occurs:

   a. -112_{10}

   b. $+342_{10}$

48. Find the two's complement of the following decimal integers using an 8-bit memory location or indicate if an overflow condition occurs:

   a. $+23_{10}$

   b. -23_{10}

49. Find the two's complement of the following decimal integers using an 8-bit memory location or indicate if an overflow condition occurs:

   a. $+52_{10}$

   b. -59_{10}

50. Convert the following decimal fractions to 4-bit binary numbers:

   a. 0.6875_{10}

   b. 0.0625_{10}

51. Convert the following decimal fractions to 6-bit binary numbers:

   a. $3/16_{10}$

   b. $8/9_{10}$

52. Represent the following decimal numbers as floating point binary numbers. Take each fractional part out to to 4 bits.

   a. 32.375_{10}

   b. 543.025_{10}

53. Represent the following decimal numbers as floating point binary numbers. Take each fractional part out to to 4 bits.
    a. 1248.6875_{10}
    b. 94.03125_{10}

54. Represent the following numbers in Excess_127:
    a. $+9_{10}$
    b. -4_{10}

55. Represent the following numbers in Excess_127:
    a. $+121_{10}$
    b. -121_{10}

56. Normalize the following binary number: 10101010.1101_2

57. Normalize the following binary number: 11110011.0110_2

58. Given the following single-precision floating point binary number:

    0   10000110   11110010100000000000000
    a. Convert the number to hexadecimal notation
    b. Convert the number to decimal

Programming Challenges

1. Convert the following decimal numbers to base 3:
   a. 5_{10}
   b. 9_{10}
   c. 126_{10}

2. Convert the following decimal numbers to base 12, using X, Y, and Z for the extra digits:
   a. 23_{10}
   b. 563_{10}
   c. $2,832_{10}$

3. Given the decimal number -1659_{10}, convert the number to a 16-bit memory location in binary:
   a. using two's complement
   b. using the formula $(2^x - |N|)$ where x is the number of bits and N is the decimal number

4. Given the decimal number -9546_{10}. Convert the number to a 16-bit memory location in binary:
   a. using two's complement
   b. using the formula $(2^x - |N|)$ where x is the number of bits and N is the decimal number

5. Briefly describe the difference between a single-precision and a double-precision floating point number. Then describe one possible scenario where double precision would be required.

Developing a Program

3

In Chapter 1, we introduced some basic programming concepts and examined a few examples of very simple programs. In this chapter, we will discuss the process of developing a program at length.

After reading this chapter, you will be able to do the following:

- Explain the general program development process of problem analysis, program design, coding and documenting, and testing
- Use pseudocode to design a program
- Use the principles of modular program design
- Use hierarchy charts to depict a modular design
- Use internal documentation in program code
- Identify the two types of program errors encountered in program code: syntax errors and logic errors
- Understand and distinguish between the types of external documentation
- Use flowchart symbols to design a short program segment
- Understand the three fundamental control structures: sequential, selection, and repetition—and how to represent them using flowcharts

Planning to Program? You Need a Plan

As you know, a computer program is nothing more than a list of instructions. It may be long, complex, and hard to read for a beginner, but it's still just a list of instructions. The basic structure is no different from the instructions for assembling a bicycle, building a bookshelf, or baking a cake.

Unfortunately, the world is chock-full of poorly written and hard-to-use instructions. The clocks in many household appliances continually flash 12:00 because their owners can't understand the manual. *Some assembly required* strikes fear into the hearts of many parents shopping for gifts for their children because they know how difficult it can be to follow the directions. Writing good instructions takes time, patience, discipline, and organization, and it's something you must learn before you dive into the details of programming.

Consider a person writing a cookbook that you will use to bake a cake. Initially, you might suspect that the author simply wrote down some recipes and sent them to a publisher. If you give this a little more thought, you will see that this is a poor way to solve the "write a cookbook" problem. The potential for trouble is just too great, and there is a real risk that the organization of the cookbook would be haphazard. Rather than just sit down and write recipe after recipe, a much better approach for the writer would be to do the following:

- Spend a good deal of time thinking about the book and the recipes it will contain. Look at some other cookbooks and talk to some cooks.
- Write down a plan for the basic organization of the chapters in the book. Should the book be organized by food groups, by ease-of-preparation, or by alphabetical order? Then write the recipes that will go into each chapter.
- Try all the recipes. Then have several other people do the same thing to get results that are independent of any bias.
- Taste all the food and determine which recipes work and which need to be fixed, either because there are errors, the process is confusing, or the end result doesn't taste very good.

It's natural and normal to encounter some mistakes. If you want to write a cookbook that people will buy, recommend to friends, and use for many years, the errors must be corrected—even if it means a lot of rewriting and further testing in the kitchen.

The basic process of thinking about a solution to a given problem, composing a solution, trying the solution, and checking the results works very well and is a natural way of proceeding, whether you are baking a cake or writing a computer program. Be warned though, that you may sometimes be tempted to take shortcuts in carrying out this process, which can leave you with a cake that would taste like a cardboard or a program that doesn't work properly—and who wants that?

3.1 The Program Development Cycle

In Chapter 1 we gave an example of a very simple computer program—first generically and then by supplying the corresponding Java, C++, and JavaScript code. Once you gain some experience at programming, you will find writing this type of program may be relatively easy. However, most real-world programs are considerably more complicated. In this section, we will describe a general systematic approach to programming that works well regardless of the complexity of the given problem.

The Process of Developing a Program

In Chapter 1 we described a time-honored strategy for solving problems. The four steps to this plan are as follows:

1. Completely understand the problem
2. Devise a plan to solve it
3. Carry out the plan
4. Review the results

We also pointed out that when this strategy is applied to program writing, it provides a framework for creating a suitable program to solve a given problem. This framework is known as the **program development cycle**. Recall that there are four basic steps in this process.

Analyze the Problem

In general terms, this step entails identifying the desired results (output), determining what information (input) is needed to produce these results, and figuring out what must be done to proceed from the known data to the desired output (processing). Although this step is described in one sentence, actually it may be the hardest part. And it is certainly the most important part! When you **analyze** the problem, as shown in Example 3.1, you determine what the result will be. If you don't do this correctly, all the elegant code in the world, written and executed flawlessly, will not solve your problem.

Example 3.1 **Playing the Lottery**

Now that you are taking a programming course, your friend asks you to write a program to generate six numbers to play the lottery every week. First you analyze the problem.

Let's take a closer look at the kinds of numbers this program should output. Could your friend play the following six numbers: −2, 3, 3, 984, 0, 7.436? Would your friend be happy if the computer outputs the same six numbers every week? While generating six numbers that include negative numbers, very large numbers, fractional numbers, or even six identical numbers certainly does what you have been asked to do, it would not accomplish the required task. The computer would generate six numbers every time the program is run. But a person cannot play the lottery with duplicate numbers, negative numbers, numbers outside a given range, or numbers that include fractions. An analysis of the problem demonstrates that what you actually want is for the computer to generate six different integers within a given range.

The required result drives the creation of a program that is very different from the problem that was initially stated as "create a program to generate six numbers." As a programmer, it is up to you to analyze the requirement "to play the lottery" and to realize what this means to the program design. Assuming you know that the lottery in question selects numbers between 1 and 45, the problem can now be defined as "create a program that will generate six different whole numbers between 1 and 45." Now you are ready to move to Step 2.

Design the Program

To **design** a program means to create a detailed description, using relatively ordinary language or special diagrams of the program to be created. Typically, this description is created in stages, proceeding from simple to more complex, and consists of a number of step-by-step procedures (algorithms) that combine to solve the given problem.

An **algorithm** is like a recipe. It is a step-by-step method for solving a problem or doing a task. Algorithms abound in programming, mathematics, and sciences and are common in everyday life as well. For example, you are making use of an algorithm when you follow a recipe to bake a cake or go through the process of using an ATM machine.

However, an algorithm to be used in a computer program is not like a recipe for making a cake. A cake recipe would, in all probability, contain some instructions that are not specific enough for a computer, such as "mix baking soda and cream in a bowl." This instruction would confuse a computer, possibly resulting in slow stirring of the ingredients, which would produce a batter full of lumps of baking soda floating in cream, or quickly whipping the ingredients, which would produce foam.

Similarly, a line in a cake recipe might say "sift flour with baking powder and spices." A computer program with this line of code would not work. A program is a list of instructions that a computer does in sequence. If we want the computer to bake a cake, the sequence of ingredients to be added to the flour mixture has to be specified.

Therefore, an algorithm used in a computer program must be *well defined* and *well ordered*, with no gap in instructions. And a programming algorithm must contain clear, unambiguous, step-by-step instructions. No step, not even the most basic and elementary, can be left out.

But there is more to a programming algorithm. An algorithm must *produce some result.* The actual result does not have to be earth shaking, or even delicious (as with a cake), but there must be some result. The result can be as simple as returning a value of `true` or `false` or as impressive as creating a new adventure game. And finally, an algorithm must *terminate in a finite time*. If it doesn't terminate, it's called an infinite loop—not an algorithm.

When we design a program, we do not completely define the algorithms all at once. As we develop the program and break down major components into smaller pieces, the algorithms for each task become more complex and detailed.

Code the Program

Once you have designed a suitable program to solve a given problem, you must translate that design into **program code**; that is, you must write statements (instructions) in a particular programming language such as Visual Basic, C++, or JavaScript to put the design into a usable form. Additional statements are included at this point to **document** the program. Documentation is a way to provide additional explanation in plain English that the computer ignores but which makes it easier for others to understand the program code. Normally, a programmer provides **internal** and **external documentation**. Internal documentation exists within the code and explains it. Internal documentation is discussed in detail in Section 3.3. External documentation is provided separate from the program in a user's guide or maintenance manual.

Coding the program entails using the programming language software to enter the program statements into the computer's memory (and ordinarily, to save them to a storage medium). This book doesn't make use of a specific programming language, so our comments about coding programs are usually general in nature. This is possible because the logic of computer programming remains constant, even though the actual words and symbols used in code may differ from one programming language to another. The ways that specific words and symbols are used by each language is called its **syntax**.

The actual code—the exact words and symbols used to write the code—depends on what language you are using. As explained in Example 3.2, every language (computer and otherwise) has its specific syntax—the rules that govern the structure of the language.

Example 3.2 **Using Correct Syntax**

The correct syntax for telling your friend where you put a cheese sandwich is:

"I have put it on the table."

It is an incorrect use of English syntax to say:

"I have it on the table put."

All the right words are there but without proper syntax; the sentence is gibberish in English. However, translated word for word, the second sentence is correct syntax in German. What is correct syntax in one computer language may be incorrect in another, just as is the case with spoken languages.

Test the Program

Testing the program ensures that it is free of errors and that it does indeed solve the given problem. At this point you run the program—have the computer execute its statements—using various sets of input data to determine if the program is working properly. However, running the whole program is really just the final test. Testing (or checking) should take place throughout the development process. This is means:

- When analyzing the problem, continually ask yourself questions: Have I interpreted the known data correctly? Have I used the correct formulas or procedures for what I'm trying to accomplish? Have I fulfilled the program requirements? And so on.

- In the design phase, imagine that you are the computer and run through the algorithm using simple input data to see if you get the expected results. This is sometimes referred to as **desk-checking** or walking through a program.

- While you are coding the program, the programming language software may do some checking to verify that each statement has the proper syntax, and you are alerted if a statement has not been properly phrased.

Program Development as a Cyclical Process

Figure 3.1 gives a schematic diagram of the program development cycle, as we have described it so far. However, this diagram is overly simplistic because it implies that once you have completed a step, you never return to the previous one. In fact, in real-world program development the following is true:

- The design process often uncovers flaws or inadequacies in the analysis of the problem and may necessitate a return to this phase.

- In coding the program certain problems may be encountered that may lead to the need for modifications or additions to the program design.

- The final testing phase, which can last for months for complex programs, inevitably uncovers problems with the coding, design, and analysis phases.

The need to return to the previous steps in the process of completing a program is why we refer to it as the program development cycle. The word *cycle* implies that you may have to repeat previous steps, perhaps over and over, until the program works correctly. In fact, in commercial programs (those written for profit), the cycle is rarely ever complete. These programs are continually evaluated and modified to meet changing demands or increasing competition.

Figure 3.1 The program development process

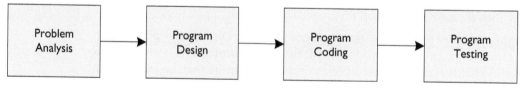

Additional Steps in the Cycle

We have described the program development cycle by relating it to the four steps in the general problem-solving strategy. Yet, this is another simplification; the process often involves additional steps. For example, the design phase can be broken into two major parts.

1. Create an outline of the program so that it is apparent what major tasks and subtasks have to be accomplished and the relationships among these tasks.
2. Describe in detail how each of these tasks is to be carried out.

Depending on the complexity of the program, there may be other aspects to the design phase. For example, the programmer or the programming team may have to design a user interface for the program. The user interface is a collection of displays, menus, and other features that provide an efficient way for the user to input data and view results.

Moreover, after the program has been thoroughly tested, an additional step in the process is to "put it into production." For the programs you write initially, this may simply mean that you save the final version to a storage medium, perhaps print a copy, or submit it to your instructor. To put a commercial program, produced by a software publishing company, into production may entail any or all of the following:

- Creating a user's guide to accompany the software so that users can understand the intricacies of the program
- Creating comprehensive help files that are installed with the software so that users can obtain on-screen help as problems arise
- Training employees to provide telephone or web-based customer support for the software
- Duplicating thousands of disks and accompanying materials for distribution to retailers or directly to users
- Advertising the program to attract buyers

Example 3.3 examines the phases of the program development cycle in greater detail and illustrates each step.

Example 3.3 Finding the Sale Price of Items in a Department Store

A local department store needs to develop a program, which when given an item's original price and the percentage it has been discounted, will compute the total price (including sales tax) of items that are on sale.

Analyzing the Problem

First, we must analyze the given problem, which means that we will study it until we fully understand it. To a large extent, this step entails acquiring all the necessary facts about the problem. In doing so, we ask ourselves the following important questions:

- What results are we trying to obtain—what is the required output?
- What data needs to be given—what is the necessary input?
- How will we obtain the required output from the given input?

Notice that these questions are directly related to the three main building blocks of most programs—input/process/output—but they are considered in a different order. When we analyze a problem, we usually begin by considering the desired output.

At this stage in the program development process, we choose variables to represent the given input and the required output. We also start to think about what formulas we will have to use and what processes we will have to carry out in order to get the desired results. Therefore, the analysis of the problem leads us naturally into the second step of the cycle, that of designing the program.

For the Sale Price problem, we need to output the values of the following variables:

- The name of the item being discounted, ItemName (a String variable)
- The discounted price of this item, SalePrice (a Float variable)
- The amount of sales tax on the sale price, Tax (a Float variable)
- The total price (including tax) of the item, TotalPrice (a Float variable)

We consider the necessary input to the program and see the following:

- In order to output the item's name (ItemName), the program must know what it is, so the String ItemName must be input by the user.
- To compute the item's sale price, the program must know the original price of the item and the percentage it is being discounted. We have learned that we need two more variables. We will call these variables OriginalPrice and DiscountRate and note that they are both Float variables and are also input data.

No additional data needs to be input. The remainder of the output data is calculated within the program, specifically as follows:

- To compute the sales tax (Tax), we need to know the item's sale price (SalePrice) and the sales tax rate in effect for this location. The tax rate will not change from run to run so it can be taken to be a program constant and therefore, it doesn't need to be input by the user. We will suppose in this example that the sales tax rate is 6.5 percent (0.065).
- The total price of the item (TotalPrice) is obtained from its sale price and the tax on that amount, both of which are computed within the program.

Obtaining the Necessary Formulas

Notice that in determining the necessary input, we have begun to think about what formulas we need to produce the desired output. In particular, we need formulas to calculate SalePrice, Tax, and TotalPrice. Perhaps the best way to determine these formulas is to imagine that you are buying an item that was originally at a specific price and that was discounted at a specific percentage. Then go through the calculations you would do to find the item's new cost by hand. Once you have done this, apply the same operations to the general case.

Suppose an item originally costs $50 and is on sale for 20 percent off. This means that you save $10 on the price of the item because 20 percent of $50 is $10.

$$\$50 \times 20\% = \$50 \times 20/100 = \$10$$

Thus, the discounted cost (the sale price) is $40.00 because the sale price is the original price minus the savings from the discount.

$$\$50 - \$10 = \$40.$$

We generalize these computations by using variables instead of numbers. This is shown as follows:

```
SalePrice = OriginalPrice - AmountSaved
```

where

```
AmountSaved = OriginalPrice * (DiscountRate/100)
```

We notice that we need another variable in this process, so we introduce the new variable, AmountSaved. It is neither an input nor output variable but is used solely in processing the data. This variable is of type Float.

The sales tax is figured on the sale price by multiplying the sale price by the tax rate, 6.5 percent. In our specific example, the sale price is $40.00, so the tax is $2.60.

$$\$40 \times 6.5\% = \$40 \times (6.5/100) = \$2.60$$

The total price is the sale price plus the tax, which turns out to be $42.60.

$$\$40 + \$2.60 = \$42.60$$

Our calculations suggest that the formulas we need are as follows:

```
Tax = SalePrice * .065
TotalPrice = SalePrice + Tax
```

Program Design, Coding, and Testing

As we progress through this chapter, we will discuss the remaining steps in the program development cycle in detail, using the Sale Price problem as an example. This is listed as follows:

- Program design is covered in Section 3.2.
- Program coding is covered in Section 3.3.
- Program testing is covered in Section 3.3.

Self Check for Section 3.1

3.1 Name the four fundamental phases of the program development cycle.

3.2 In one sentence each, describe what takes place during each phase of the program development cycle.

3.3 Indicate whether each of the following statements is true or false.
   a. If you completely understand a given problem, you should skip the design phase of the program development cycle.
   b. Program design provides an outline for the program code.
   c. Testing a program is only necessary for very complex programs.

3.4 Suppose you want to write a program that will input a person's weight in pounds and output that weight in kilograms. Analyze this problem: give the input and output variables, as well as the formula that will produce the required output from the given input. (*Hint*: the necessary formula is P = 2.2046 * K, where P is the number of pounds and K is kilograms.)

3.2 Program Design

The design phase of the program development cycle is often the most important aspect of developing a program, especially in the case of complex problems. A good, detailed design makes it much easier to write good, usable program code. Rushing into coding too quickly is like trying to build a house without a complete set of plans and may result in needing to redo a lot of hard work.

Modular Programming

A good way to begin the job of designing a program to solve a particular problem is to identify the major tasks that the program must accomplish. In designing the program, each of these tasks becomes a **program module**. Then if needed, we can break each of these fundamental "high-level" tasks into subtasks. The latter are called **submodules** of the original, or *parent*, module. Some of these submodules might be divided into submodules of their own, and this division process can be continued as long as necessary to identify the tasks needed to solve the given problem. Identifying the tasks and various subtasks involved in the program design is called **modular programming**. To illustrate the modular approach, Example 3.4 returns to the Sale Price problem discussed in Section 3.1.

Example 3.4 **The Sale Price Program Continued**

For the sake of convenience, we restate the original problem here.

A local department store needs to develop a program, which when given an item's original price and the percentage it has been discounted, will compute the total price, including sales tax, of that item.

Recall that in Section 3.1 we analyzed this problem. We described the data that had to be input and output by the program, and we found the formulas needed to compute the output. In particular, we defined the following variables:

- `ItemName`—the name of the item on sale
- `OriginalPrice`—the presale price of the item
- `DiscountRate`—the percentage that the item has been discounted
- `AmountSaved`—the dollar amount of the discount
- `SalePrice`—the price of the item after the discount
- `Tax`—the sales tax on the sale price
- `TotalPrice`—the total price of the item, including tax

Also, recall that we have taken the sales tax rate to be 6.5 percent.

The three fundamental tasks that we must perform to solve this problem are as follows:

1. **Input data:** Input the variables `ItemName`, `DiscountRate`, and `OriginalPrice`
2. **Perform calculations:** Compute the sale price, tax, and total price using the following formulas, which were derived in Section 3.1:

   `SalePrice = OriginalPrice - AmountSaved`

   where `AmountSaved = OriginalPrice * (DiscountRate/100)`

and `TotalPrice = SalePrice + Tax`

where `Tax = SalePrice * .065`

3. **Output results:** Display the total price (`TotalPrice`) of the item

Using Modules and Submodules

If we wanted, we could further divide the second task of the Sale Price program into two subtasks, computing the `SalePrice` in one and the `TotalPrice` in the other. How do we know when to stop breaking the submodules into more submodules? There is no definite answer to this question. The number and types of modules used in a program design are partly a matter of style. However, we can provide some general guidelines by listing the following characteristics of a program module:

- A module performs a single task. For example, an input module prompts for and then inputs data from the user.
- A module is self-contained and independent of other modules.
- A module is relatively short. Ideally, its statements should not exceed one page. This makes it easier to understand the way the module works.

Benefits of Modular Programming

So far our discussion has concentrated on what a program module is. Before we proceed to the next topic, let's talk about why the modular approach to program design is important. It has the following benefits:

- The program is easier to read. This in turn, reduces the time needed to locate errors in a program or make modifications to it.
- It's easier to design, code, and test the program one module at a time rather than all at once. This increases the productivity of the programmer or programmers involved in a project.
- Different program modules can be designed and/or coded by different programmers. This feature is essential when creating large, complex programs.
- In some cases a single module can be used in more than one place in the program. This reduces the amount of code in the program.
- Modules performing common programming tasks (such as sorting data in order) can be used in more than one program. Creating a library of such modules reduces design, coding, and testing time.

Pseudocode

Once we have identified the various tasks our program needs to accomplish, we must fill in the details of the program design. For each module, we must provide specific instructions to perform that task. We supply this detail using pseudocode. We have used pseudocode in Chapter 1, without explicitly defining it.

Pseudocode uses short, English-like phrases to describe the outline of a program. It's not actual code from any specific programming language, but sometimes it strongly resembles the actual code. We often start with a rough pseudocode outline for each module and then, as shown in Example 3.5, we refine the pseudocode to provide more and more detail. Depending on the complexity of a program module, little or no refinement of its initial pseudocode may be necessary, or we may go through several versions, adding detail each time until it becomes clear how the corresponding code should look.

Example 3.5 Pseudocode for the Sale Price Program

The initial pseudocode for the Sale Price program might look as follows:

```
Input Data module
    Input ItemName, OriginalPrice, DiscountRate
Perform Calculations module
    Compute SalePrice
    Compute TotalPrice
Output Results module
    Output the input data and TotalPrice
```

Then, we refine and add detail to each module, which gives us the following version of the pseudocode:

```
Input Data module
    Prompt for ItemName, OriginalPrice, DiscountRate
    Input ItemName, OriginalPrice, DiscountRate
Perform Calculations module
    Set AmountSaved = OriginalPrice * (DiscountRate/100)
    Set SalePrice = OriginalPrice - AmountSaved
    Set Tax = SalePrice * .065
    Set TotalPrice = SalePrice + Tax
Output Results module
    Write ItemName
    Write OriginalPrice
    Write DiscountRate
    Write SalePrice
    Write Tax
    Write TotalPrice
```

Recall from Chapter 1 the following concerning this pseudocode:

- The term **prompt** means to display a message on the screen that tells the user (the person running the program) what kind of data to input.
- When an Input statement is executed, program execution pauses to allow the user to enter data (numbers or characters) from the keyboard. This data is assigned to the listed variables.
- When a Set (assignment) statement is executed, the expression on the right of the equals sign is evaluated and assigned to the variable on the left.
- When a Write statement is executed, the text in quotation marks (if any) and the values of the listed variables (if any) are displayed on the screen and the cursor moves to the beginning of the next line.

At this point, we can still refine and provide more detail for the Input Data and Output Results modules. We can be more specific about how the data is to be entered and displayed. As it stands now, the Perform Calculations module contains sufficient detail. The following is the refined pseudocode for the input and output modules:

```
Input Data module
    Write "What is the item's name?"
    Input ItemName
    Write "What is its price and the percentage discounted?"
    Input OriginalPrice
    Input DiscountRate
Output Results module
    Write "The item is: " + ItemName
    Write "Pre-sale price was: " + OriginalPrice
    Write "Percentage discounted was: " + DiscountRate + "%"
    Write "Sale price: " + SalePrice
    Write "Sales tax: " + Tax
    Write "Total: $" + TotalPrice
```

Echo Print the Input Variables

Notice that in the Output Results module not only do we display the values of variables that were computed in the program (SalePrice, Tax, and TotalPrice), but also we display the values of all input variables. This is called **echo printing** the input. It's a good programming practice because it reminds the user what data has been entered and allows the user to check it for mistakes.

Calling Modules into Action

So far, we have described the modules in the Sale Price program, but we have not indicated how their execution is initiated—how they are called into action. To execute a particular program submodule, we place a statement in the parent module that **calls** the submodule. In other words, a **call statement** causes a submodule to be executed. Sometimes, we describe this action by saying that the call transfers program control to the beginning of the submodule. Then, when the submodule has completed its task, execution returns to the calling (parent) module. Note that execution returns specifically to the statement *after* the one that caused the transfer of control. Figure 3.2 shows a picture of this situation. The arrows indicate the flow of execution between the parent module and the submodule.

Figure 3.2 Calling a module

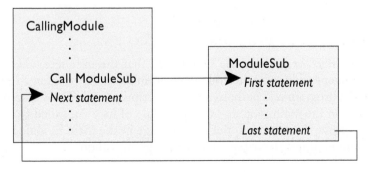

The Main Module

Every program has one special module, called its **main module**, which is where program execution begins and normally ends. The main module is the only program module that is not a submodule of another, and it is the parent module of the program's highest-level modules—those that perform the most fundamental of tasks. Consequently, these highest-level modules are called into action by the main module. When the program is coded, the main module becomes the main program, and all other modules are known as (depending upon the programming language) subprograms, procedures, subroutines, and/or functions. The main module may also be called the **driver**.

To illustrate how the call and transfer of control work in a particular example, we'll return again to the Sale Price problem, adding a Main module as the parent of the three existing modules: Input Data, Perform Calculations, and Output Results. The main module has to call these submodules. Thus, it takes the following form:

```
Main module
    Call Input Data module
    Call Perform Calculations module
    Call Output Results module
End Program
```

Notice that we have used Call, followed by the name of a module, to call that module into action. This kind of statement causes the named module to be executed, after which control returns to the next statement in the calling module. Thus, the flow of execution in this program proceeds as follows:

1. The statement Call Input Data module is executed, transferring control to the first statement in the Input Data module.

2. All statements in the Input Data module are executed and then control transfers to the next statement (Call Perform Calculations module) in the Main module, which transfers control to the first statement in the Perform Calculations module.

3. After the last statement in Perform Calculations is executed, control transfers to the statement Call Output Results module in the Main module, which in turn transfers control to the first statement in the Output Results module.

4. After the last statement in Output Results is executed, control transfers to the End Program statement in the Main module and execution terminates.

Before displaying the entire Sale Price program design, we will add one more feature to the program.

Making It Work

Provide a Welcome Message at the Beginning of Your Program

The first few lines, or perhaps the first screen that the user sees when running a program should provide some general information about the program. This includes the title of the program and perhaps a brief description of it. The welcome message can be placed in the main module or in a module of its own, called from the main module. In Example 3.6, we will put our message in the main module because it is short and simple. It just describes what the program will do.

The following example uses the Declare statement extensively. Recall that this statement defines a variable and sets its data type.

Example 3.6 **The Complete Sale Price Program Design**

```
1   Main module
2     Declare ItemName As String
3     Declare OriginalPrice As Float
4     Declare DiscountRate As Float
5     Declare SalePrice As Float
6     Declare TotalPrice As Float
7     Write "Sale Price Program"
8     Write "This program computes the total price, including ↵
             tax, of an item that has been discounted a ↵
             certain percentage."
9     Call Input Data module
10    Call Perform Calculations module
11    Call Output Results module
12  End Program
13  Input Data module
14    Write "What is the item's name?"
15    Input ItemName
16    Write "What is its price and the percentage discounted?"
17    Input OriginalPrice
18    Input DiscountRate
19  End Input Data Module
20  Perform Calculations module
21    Declare AmountSaved As Float
22    Set AmountSaved = OriginalPrice * (DiscountRate/100)
23    Set SalePrice = OriginalPrice - AmountSaved
24    Set Tax = SalePrice * .065
25    Set TotalPrice = SalePrice + Tax
26  End Perform Calculations Module
27  Output Results module
28    Write "The item is: " + ItemName
29    Write "Pre-sale price was: " + OriginalPrice
30    Write "Percentage discounted was: " + DiscountRate + "%"
31    Write "Sale price: " + SalePrice
32    Write "Sales tax: " + Tax
33    Write "Total: $" + TotalPrice
34  End Output Results Module
```

Notice that we have declared variables in two places in this program, as follows:

- The variables ItemName, OriginalPrice, DiscountRate, SalePrice, Tax, and TotalPrice, which are used in more than one module, are declared in the Main module.

- The variable AmountSaved, which is only used in the Perform Calculations module, is declared in that module.

- The concatenation operator (+) is used in the output statements to join together (concatenate) text (the words inside the quotation marks) with the value of a variable. For example, if the value of the variable `ItemName` is `basketball`, the result of the statement

  ```
  Write "The item is: " + ItemName
  ```

  will be:

  ```
  The item is: basketball
  ```

Making It Work

Code *vs* Output

Look at line 8 of Example 3.6. In your textbook, it spans two lines. At the end of the first line of the text is the symbol " ↵ ". When coding in a specific language, unless otherwise specified, text that is output to the screen will all be placed on one line and will wrap (i.e., move to the next line) around the screen only when the number of characters exceeds the number allowed for a computer monitor. Thus, programmers must tell the computer where to place line breaks when outputting text. This may take the form of a specific symbol or set of characters. In some languages just beginning a new statement will indicate that the text in that statement should be on a new line. In our pseudocode each `Write` statement will indicate a new line of text or text and variables should be output to the screen. Sometimes we may want a single line output without specific line breaks but the page of this textbook cannot handle all that text on one line. When you see the symbol " ↵ ", this indicates that everything following the symbol, until the next pseudocode instruction (such as a `Write` or `Set` or `Input` instruction) should be output without specific line breaks. The text may need more than one line on a user's screen for all the text but exactly where one line ends and a new one begins is simply a matter of the user's screen size. Thus, a statement like the one on line 8 of Example 3.6 might display as:

```
This program computes the total price, including tax, of an item
that has been discounted a certain percentage.
```

if the user's preferences are for one font size and his monitor is of a certain size or, if the user's monitor and font size are completely different, this line of text might display as:

```
This program computes the total price, including tax, of an item that has been
discounted a certain percentage.
```

or even:

```
This program computes the total price, including
tax, of an item that has been discounted a certain
percentage.
```

Style Pointer

Format Output for Readability

Sometimes, program output can be improved by skipping a line in certain places. For example, the first two `Write` statements in the main module of the Sale Price program produce the following output:

```
Sale Price Program
This program computes the total price, including tax, of
an item that has been discounted a certain percentage.
```

The output would look nicer if there were a blank line after the title. We accomplish this by using a statement that simply codes for a blank line. In the pseudocode used in this book, as well as in some programming languages, the statement Write (just the word Write, nothing else) will give us the blank line we want. For example, if we insert this statement after the first Write statement in the main module, then the output will look as follows:

```
Sale Price Program

This program computes the total price, including tax, of
an item that has been discounted a certain percentage.
```

Hierarchy Charts

In a complex program, there might be dozens of program modules and submodules. We can keep track of a program's modules and the relationships among them in a visual way through the use of a **hierarchy chart**, which describes these relationships in the same way that an organization chart determines who is responsible to whom in a business firm.

Figure 3.3 shows a typical hierarchy chart. Notice that the main module, which is where program execution begins, sits at the top of this chart. Think of the main module as the CEO of the code. Below the main module are the highest-level submodules (labeled A, B, and C, in Figure 3.3), those that perform the most fundamental of program tasks. Finally, the modules B1 and B2 are submodules of their parent module B. In other words, a line connecting a higher module to a lower one indicates that the former is the parent; it calls the latter into action. A hierarchy chart for the Sale Price program is shown in Figure 3.4.

Figure 3.3 A typical hierarchy chart

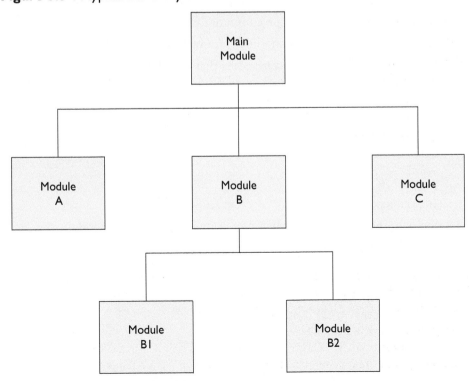

Figure 3.4 Hierarchy chart for the Sale Price program

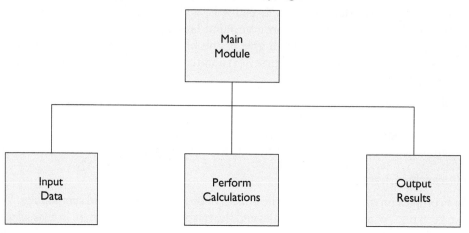

The Value of Modular Programming

When we first begin to write programs, they are normally short and simple. For most beginning programs, we do not break up the code into modules. As programs become longer and more complex, using modules (or subprograms, procedures, subroutines, or functions, as they may be called) becomes much more important. ●

Self Check for Section 3.2

3.5 List the characteristics of a program module.

3.6 What are three benefits of modular program design?

3.7 Write a sequence of Write statements that will display the following output with a blank line between each value. (Expressions like xxxx represent values of the corresponding variables.)

```
Item: xxxxxxxxx
OriginalPrice: xxx.xx
RateOfDiscount: xx.x%
SalePrice: xxx.xx
Tax: x.x%
Total: xxx.xx
```

3.8 Suppose that the following statements appear in the main module of a certain program:

```
Call Cancer Cure module
   Write "My job here is done!"
Cancer Cure module
   Set Doctor = "Dr. Miracle"
   Set Cure = "100%"
```

What statement is executed immediately after the following?

a. The Call statement

b. The last statement in the Cancer Cure module

3.9 Suppose that the Perform Calculations module in the Sale Price program is broken into two submodules, Compute Sale Price and Compute Total Price. Construct the corresponding hierarchy chart.

3.3 Coding, Documenting, and Testing a Program

In this section, we will discuss the last two steps of the program development cycle—*coding* the program and *testing* the program. We will also introduce the notion of documenting a program. We first discuss internal documentation and then discuss external documentation.

Coding and Documenting a Program

Once a suitable program design has been created to solve a given problem, it's time to **code** the program. This is where we translate the pseudocode of the design into the corresponding statements in a particular programming language. The result is a program that can be run (executed) on a computer. Of course, in order to carry out this phase of the program development cycle, you must be familiar with the syntax and structure of a programming language such as Visual Basic, C++, or JavaScript and also have access to any software you may need to work with this language. Although this is obviously a crucial step in developing a program, since this book presents programming concepts in a language-free environment we will have little to say about the translation of the design into actual code.

One aspect of the coding process is of importance regardless of the language used. All programs should include annotation that explains the purpose of portions of code within the program itself. This kind of annotation is known as internal documentation and is made up of *comments*. A **comment** is text inserted into the program for explanatory purposes but ignored by the computer when the program is run. Comments are not seen by the program's user; they are intended solely for those reading the code itself.

How Can a Computer Know What to Ignore?

In processing the program statements, how does the computer know what comments to ignore? The answer is simple. A special symbol or combination of symbols, depending on which programming language you use, indicates to the computer that what follows, or what lies between specific symbols, is a comment and not code to be processed. The following are the examples:

- In Visual Basic, an apostrophe (') anywhere on a line, or the letters REM at the beginning of a line, indicates that all text on that line is to be ignored by the computer. As you might guess, REM stands for remark.

- In C++, Java, and JavaScript two consecutive forward slashes (//) anywhere on a line indicate that all text following these symbols is to be ignored. All text contained between the symbols/* and */is ignored as well. These comment symbols are used to enclose comments that continue for more than one line in a program. This convention, as shown in Example 3.7, is what we will use throughout this textbook when we include comments in our pseudocode.

Example 3.7 **Commenting on the Sale Price Program Design**

A C++ program to solve the Sale Price problem of Sections 3.1 and 3.2 might begin as follows:

```
// Sale Price Computation
// Programmers: S. Venit, California State University
// E. Drake, Santa Fe College
// Version 6.0 - January 1, 2015
// This program computes the total price, including tax, of
// an item that has been placed on sale.
// Variables used:
// DiscountRate - Percentage of the discount
// ItemName - Name of the item on sale
... and so on.
```

There are two basic types of comments that have two distinct purposes.

1. **Header comments**, which appear at the beginning of a program or a program module, provide general information about that program or module. The comments in Example 3.7 are typical program header comments.

2. **Step comments**, also referred to as in-line comments, are shown in Example 3.8. Step comments appear throughout the program to explain the purpose of specific portions of code. For example, if your program includes code that finds the average of the numbers input, a step comment might precede this code that reads:

```
// Find the average of numbers input.
```

Example 3.8 **Using Step Comments in a Short Program**

Dexter Dinkels is buying a rug for his bedroom. He knows the dimensions of his room in inches but he needs to know the square footage so he can buy a rug that fits the whole room exactly. A short program to solve this problem, including step comments, might look like the following:

```
// Declare the variables
Declare WidthInches As Float
Declare LengthInches As Float
Declare WidthFeet As Float
Declare LengthFeet As Float
Declare SquareFeet As Float
```

```
// Get the values of the dimensions
Write "What are the length and width of the room in inches?"
Input LengthInches
Input WidthInches
// Convert dimensions from inches to feet
Set LengthFeet = LengthInches/12
Set WidthFeet = WidthInches/12
// Calculate square footage
Set SquareFeet = WidthFeet * LengthFeet
// Output the result
Write "Your room is " + SquareFeet + "square feet."
```

Include Comments in Your Program

Since comments are not processed by the computer and are not seen by users of the program, they don't affect the way the program runs. However, good comments make it easier for another programmer to understand your code. Nonetheless, don't over comment—in particular, don't explain every line of code. A good rule of thumb is to write enough step comments so that you will be able to easily read your program a year after you have written it. ●

Testing a Program

As we have said, it is necessary to test a program (or program-to-be) at every stage of the program development cycle to ensure that it is free of errors. The final and most important testing takes place when the code has been completed. At this point the program is run with simple input data (**test data**), and if it runs successfully, we compare its output to the results obtained by hand computation. If they agree, we try other sets of input data and recheck the results. Although program testing of this sort, as shown in Example 3.9, does not *guarantee* that a program is error free, it gives us some confidence that this is indeed the case.

Example 3.9 **Displaying a Test Run of the Sale Price Program**

Once the Sale Price program has been coded, the screen display for a test run might look like the following (user input is in blue):

```
Sale Price Program
This program computes the total price, including tax, of
an item that has been discounted a certain percentage.
What is the item's name?
Beach ball
What are its price and the percentage discounted?
60
20
The item is: Beach ball
Pre-sale price was: 60
Percentage discounted was: 20%
Sale price: 48
```

```
Sales tax: 3.12
Total: $ 51.12
```

If we check these results with those obtained by hand, we see that for this set of input data, the program has produced the correct result. A few more successful runs with different input data would convince us that the program is working properly.

Types of Errors

If a test run turns up problems with the program, we must **debug** it, which means we must locate and eliminate the errors. This may be relatively easy or very difficult, depending on the type of error and the debugging skill of the programmer. The two fundamental types of errors that can arise in coding a program are syntax errors and logic errors.

Syntax Errors

A **syntax error** is the violation of the programming language's rules for creating valid statements. It can be caused, for example, by misspelling a keyword or by omitting a required punctuation mark. Syntax errors are normally detected by the language software, either when the invalid statement is typed or when the program is translated by the computer into machine language. When the software detects a syntax error, normally it issues a message and highlights the offending statement. Therefore, syntax errors are often easy to find and correct. Sometimes, however, the software finds an error in one place that actually was caused by another type of error somewhere else in the code. In this case, it takes programming skill to analyze the error message, find the place where the error originates, and correct it.

Logic Errors

A **logic error** results from failing to use the proper combination of statements to accomplish a certain task. It may occur due to faulty analysis, faulty design, or failure to code the program properly. The following are a few kinds of logic errors:

- Use of an incorrect formula to produce a desired result
- Use of an incorrect sequence of statements to carry out an algorithm
- Failure to predict some input data that may lead to an illegal operation (such as division by zero) when the program is run—this kind of bug is sometimes called a **runtime error**

Logic errors often cause the program to fail to proceed beyond a certain point (i.e., to crash or hang or freeze) or to give incorrect results. Unlike syntax errors, logic errors are not detected by the programming language software. Usually they can be found only by running the program with a sufficient variety of test data. Extensive testing is the best way to ensure that a program's logic is sound.

3.10 Briefly describe the two basic types of comments that are used for internal documentation.

3.11 Fill in the blank: After a program is coded, it must be _____.

3.12 Briefly describe the difference between syntax errors and logic errors.

3.13 Imagine that you are writing a program to calculate how long it takes to get from one place to another. You want the user to be able to input a distance traveled and how fast he or she goes. The formula for this is simply:

```
Time = DistanceTraveled/RateOfSpeed
```

For example, if Ricardo drove his car 300 miles at 50 miles per hour, it would take him 6 hours to arrive at his destination, and if Marcy walked 8 miles at 2 miles per hour, it would take her 4 hours to arrive at her destination. List three good sets of test data you might use to test your program after it was written.

3.4 Commercial Programs: Testing and Documenting

Would you buy a new smart phone or a new car without a user's manual? There might be a few hardy souls reading this book who would like to press buttons until they stumble on how to set preferences or make their newest technology gadgets behave as they want. But most of us want each new product we buy—especially those run by software—to come with a user's manual, online help, or available phone assistance. Consumers spend a lot of money to buy products, but those products aren't useful if consumers can't figure out how to use them. On the commercial level, the programmer (or programming team) explains the software to the consumer by means of external documentation.

If you wrote a program for a friend to help him calculate how much he will pay for items on sale and your program worked only if your friend entered one item each time he ran the program, he might not love your program, but the tragedy would end there. However, if you bought a software program to help you with your budget and then discovered it only worked correctly for a maximum of three expenses per month, you would probably be pretty angry. Companies whose business is to create and sell software will only succeed if their programs work dependably and can be used by many users in a variety of ways. Therefore, commercial software undergoes a long and rigorous testing process, which rarely ends with the release of one version of the software.

In Section 3.3, we introduced the notions of testing and documenting within a program. In this section, we will expand upon these concepts and concentrate on how they apply to commercial programs—software that is sold for profit.

The Testing Phase Revisited

We have already discussed the need to test your programs and the kinds of errors—or **bugs**—that might creep into them. If you submit a program that does not work to your instructor in a programming course, you might get a zero on the project. More likely, you will receive feedback on how to correct the errors and get another chance to improve or just get a low grade. Unfortunately, the stakes are higher for a commercial project. A program that does not work is simply not marketable. In industry there's no partial credit for trying!

Testing commercial software is extremely important. Obviously, if the program doesn't work, it's of no use at all. But if a program works only sometimes, is error prone, or does not operate as easily and efficiently as it should, then consumers may buy a competitor's product instead. That's why commercial software must be tested again and again. Professional programmers try everything they can think of to test the software under all conditions. Testing commercial software is a process that often takes as long as the rest of the program's development and is a part of every phase of the development cycle.

Commercial programs are often so complex that the testing phase lasts for several months or more. For example, when Microsoft develops a new version of its Windows operating system, testing the software is a major project in itself that may take more than a year to complete. The code is tested, module by module, by Microsoft employees. Then the completed software is put through its paces, running on a wide range of different computers using different peripherals, in-house and at selected non-Microsoft sites. This phase of the process is known as **alpha testing**. Once the software is reasonably reliable, it is sent to thousands of **beta test** sites. In alpha and beta testing, users report problems to Microsoft, and the necessary changes are made to the code. During alpha and early beta testing, features are added and/or revised. Finally, when all reported problems are fixed, the code is finalized and the software is put into production.

External Documentation

As we mentioned in Section 3.3, every program benefits from good internal documentation—the proper use of comments to explain what the code does. Commercial programs also require extensive external documentation. External documentation serves two purposes. This is listed as follows:

1. Documentation found in a user's guide or an on-screen help system provides information about the program for its **end users**—people who will apply the software at work or in their everyday lives.
2. Documentation found in a program maintenance manual provides information about how the program code accomplishes its purposes. This kind of external documentation is written for the benefit of programmers who may have to modify the software in the future to correct bugs or add features.

The User's Guide

The **user's guide** and on-screen help documents are usually written once the program development cycle is well underway, often when the software is undergoing alpha or beta testing. Because this documentation is used by nonexperts—by people who know little about computers and often nothing about programming—the manner in which it is presented is very important. Most documentation prepared for a lay person is written by a **technical writer**. A technical writer must be experienced with computers and must be able to explain instructions so that they are clear, concise, and easily understood by consumers. The technical writer works closely with members of the programming team to ensure that the ins and outs of the software are well documented.

A user's guide may come in one or several forms. It can be a printed document, a file on a CD, an entire CD with tutorial exercises, a link to a website that provides information about using the software, or any combination of these forms.

The Program Maintenance Manual

It comes as no surprise to anyone who has recently purchased a digital camera, installed a computer game, or tried to get a new DVD player to work that a user's guide is necessary to explain the workings of a sophisticated piece of software. On the other hand, it may surprise you that programming experts also need documentation to help them fix or enhance the code that has been written by other programming experts. A **maintenance manual** may contain several different topics that pertain to the software and that are helpful to programming experts.

Design Documentation

Design documentation focuses more on the *why* than the *how*. In design documentation, the programmer might explain the rationale behind why certain data was organized in a particular way or why certain methods were used. The document might explain why one module was constructed in a particular way and might even suggest ways that an incoming programmer might improve the software.

You might wonder why a programmer would write a document that suggests how another programmer could improve his program. You might be thinking, "If he knew how to do it better, why didn't he do it better in the first place?" The information technology field is fast paced and competitive; programming new software is not done by an individual. A team of programmers is given a problem to solve and a deadline in which to do it. Sometimes, time is of the essence and the problem can be solved one way in the given time frame, but other, perhaps better, ways can be envisioned. New versions of software are continually being developed. The suggestions in the design documentation may make the next version of the software a much better product and might even reward the first programmers with a bonus!

Trade Study Documentation

Trade study documentation is another type of documentation with a somewhat surprising purpose. It is a comparison document, which focuses on one specific aspect of the system and suggests alternate approaches. It might outline what the situation is, describe alternatives, and explain the pros and cons of each. Good trade study documentation is heavy on research, expresses its idea clearly, and is impartial. A trade study is an attempt to find the best solution, rather than to push one point of view. It should be prepared as a scientific document and not as a marketing technique.

3.14 What is the main purpose of a user's guide? What is its target audience?

3.15 What is the main purpose of a maintenance manual? What is its target audience?

3.16 What are the qualifications of a technical writer? What does a technical writer do?

3.17 What is the difference between design documentation and trade documentation?

3.5 Structured Programming

Structured programming is a method used to design and code programs in a systematic and organized manner. In this chapter, we have already discussed some structured programming principles: follow the steps of the program development cycle; design a program in a modular fashion; and use comments to document a program. In this section, we introduce two more aspects of structured programming: designing each module as a sequence of control structures and using good programming style. We begin by discussing the use of flowcharts in program design.

Flowcharts

We have discussed two devices to aid in the design of a program: hierarchy charts and pseudocode. Each of these techniques has its place in program design. Hierarchy charts identify the program modules and show the relationships among them. Pseudocode fills in the details of how the modules are to be coded.

Another common program design tool is the **flowchart**, which is a diagram that uses special symbols to display pictorially the flow of execution within a program or a program module. It is a formalized graphic representation of a program's logic sequence, a work or manufacturing process, or any similar structure. While we will use flowcharts to help develop computer programs, flowcharts are also used in many other fields. Businesses use flowcharts to represent manufacturing processes and other industry operations pictorially. They are commonly used by industry to help people visualize content better or to find flaws in a process. Herman Goldstine, one of the original developers of ENIAC, first developed flowcharts with John von Neumann at Princeton University in the late 1946 and early 1947.

A flowchart provides an easy, clear way to see which pieces of your code follow the various programming structures that all programs are constructed from. These structures are discussed in detail in this section.

Creating Flowcharts

You can purchase inexpensive plastic templates in an office supply store to help you draw, by hand, the proper shapes for each type of process. Or you can simply draw the shapes by hand. Also, there are many software applications that will assist you with creating flowcharts on your computer. In fact, Microsoft's Word has a flowchart template built into its word processor.

Originally, a flowchart was a static image. A programmer would create a flow-chart to aid in understanding the flow of a program. Then, the programmer would write code, in a specific programming language, following the logic that he had created in the flowchart. However, recently, interactive flowcharting programs have become available, which add a great deal of functionality to a flowchart. Some of these programs are free, while others are available for purchase. These programs allow a programmer to create a flowchart, enter values into that flowchart, and see the execution of the program or program segment before writing the actual code. This can be extremely helpful, especially to a new programmer (or a new student of programming) because the focus is on a specific piece of the logic, outside of the formatting concerns and all the other details of a large program.

Using RAPTOR to Create Flowcharts That Run Your Programs

Making It Work

One of the resources available with this textbook is RAPTOR, a free flowcharting program. Many of the programming problems in the text and Review Exercises can be created, in a simplified form, and run through RAPTOR or other interactive flowcharting software. (See Section 3.6 for the beginning RAPTOR tutorial.)

Each chapter from now on will include a section at the end of each chapter, Running With RAPTOR, which will add to your abilities to work with RAPTOR and will allow you to create programs that can run and produce visible results. This will help you understand how creating "real" code works but in an environment that is nonlanguage based and removes the need to learn and use intricate syntax rules that are part and parcel of programming languages. RAPTOR allows you to focus specifically on the logic of creating programs.

As you learn to write programs, you will begin with short program segments. It may seem tedious to translate a very simple programming problem into a flowchart, but in fact, it is a valuable exercise. This is one of the most important practices that you can develop as a programmer. You will find that following the steps to creating a program carefully and precisely, even if these steps seem redundant in the beginning, will save you countless hours as your programs become longer and more difficult to manage.

Flowchart Symbols

Flowcharts are created from a specific number of standard symbols. This standardization ensures that anyone who knows programming can read and follow any flowchart. A typical flowchart will include some or all of the following symbols, which are shown in Figure 3.5:

- Start and End symbols are represented as ovals or rounded rectangles, usually containing the word Start or End or other phrases, such as Enter and Exit, to indicate the start and end of a program segment.

Figure 3.5 Basic flowcharting symbols

Symbol	Name	Description
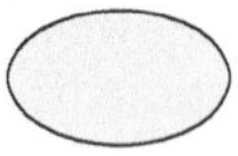 (oval)	Terminator	Represents the start or end of a program or module
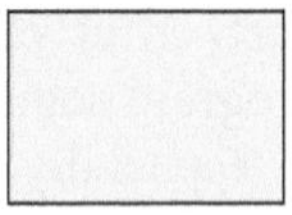 (rectangle)	Process	Represents any kind of processing function; for example, a computation
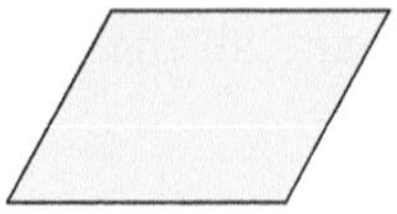 (parallelogram)	Input/output	Represents an input or output operation
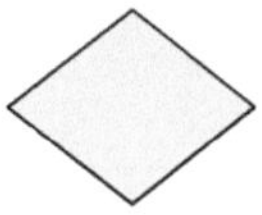 (diamond)	Decision	Represents a program branch point
(circle)	Connector	Indicates an entry to, or exit from, a program segment

- `Arrows` show the flow of control. An arrow coming from one symbol and ending at another symbol represents that control passes to the symbol to which the arrow points.
- `Processing` steps are represented as rectangles. For example, doing a calculation such as computing the sale price of an item, the sales tax of an item, or the total new price (from the Sale Price problem) are examples of processing steps.
- `Input/Output` steps are represented as parallelograms. In the Sale Price program, input steps are those that require the user to input the name of an item, its original price, and how much the item is discounted. Displaying the results of the computations, including the item's name, its sale price, the tax, and the new price, are examples of output steps.
- `Conditional` (or `decision` or `selection`) segments are represented as diamond shapes. These typically contain a `Yes/No` question or a `True/False` test. This symbol has two arrows coming out of it. One arrow corresponds to what happens in the program if the answer to the question is `Yes` or `True`, and the other arrow corresponds to what happens next if the answer to the question is `No` or `False`. The arrows should always be labeled. We will learn more about selection statements later in this chapter.
- `Connectors` are represented as circles. These are used to connect one program segment to another.

There are other symbols that are used less frequently but, for all basic programming logic, the symbols listed above are sufficient.

A flowchart for the Sale Price program is shown in Figure 3.6. To read it (or any flowchart), start at the top and follow the arrows. Example 3.10 compares pseudocode and flowcharts.

Figure 3.6 Flowchart for the Sale Price program

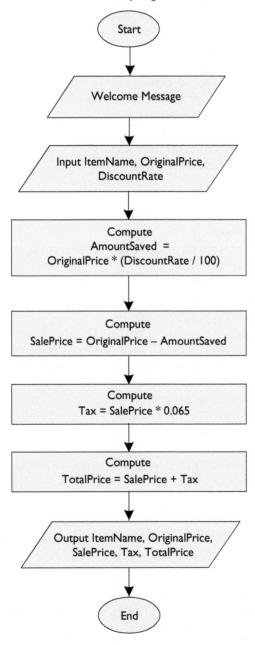

Example 3.10 **Comparing Pseudocode and Flowcharts**

You may notice that the pseudocode that was created for the Sale Price program of Section 3.2 had more detail than the flowchart. That pseudocode is repeated here for convenience:

```
1   Main module
2       Declare ItemName As String
3       Declare OriginalPrice As Float
4       Declare DiscountRate As Float
5       Declare SalePrice As Float
6       Declare TotalPrice As Float
7       Write "Sale Price Program"
8       Write "This program computes the total price, including ↵
              tax, of an item that has been discounted a ↵
              certain percentage."
9       Call Input Data module
10      Call Perform Calculations module
11      Call Output Results module
12  End Program
13  Input Data module
14      Write "What is the item's name?"
15      Input ItemName
16      Write "What is its price and the percentage discounted?"
17      Input OriginalPrice
18      Input DiscountRate
19  End Input Data Module
20  Perform Calculations module
21      Declare AmountSaved As Float
22      Set AmountSaved = OriginalPrice * (DiscountRate/100)
23      Set SalePrice = OriginalPrice - AmountSaved
24      Set Tax = SalePrice * .065
25      Set TotalPrice = SalePrice + Tax
26  End Perform Calculations Module
27  Output Results module
28      Write "The item is: " + ItemName
29      Write "Pre-sale price was: " + OriginalPrice
30      Write "Percentage discounted was: " + DiscountRate + "%"
31      Write "Sale price: " + SalePrice
32      Write "Sales tax: " + Tax
33      Write "Total: $" + TotalPrice
34  End Output Results Module
```

Compare this pseudocode to the flowchart shown in Figure 3.6. The `Input Data Module` (lines 13–19) of the pseudocode corresponds to the first `Input` box in the flowchart but does not include the specific wording of all the input prompts. It simply states the variables that will need to be inputted for the program to work. The four `Processing` rectangles in the flowchart correspond to the variable declaration (line 21) and the four computations (lines 22–25) in the

`Perform Calculations Module` of the pseudocode. These computations are the kernel of the program. This is where the computer takes the data that is input by the user and turns it into the desired output. The last `Output` parallelogram of the flowchart corresponds to the `Output Results Module` (lines 27–34) but it is in an abbreviated form.

As a programmer checks the logic of his or her program, the most important aspects are the internal logic and the flow of control from one statement to another. With a flowchart, the focus is specifically on this logic and flow. If you create careful flowcharts before you begin to enter program code, you will be able to trace the flow of the program and find errors quite easily. However, pseudocode is also a useful tool when designing programs. Pseudocode can be created and edited easily and, if written carefully and with detail, can make entering the actual program code relatively simple. While some programmers prefer to use pseudocode exclusively in the design of their programs, others prefer to use only flowcharts, and still others use a combination of flowcharts and pseudocode. As you learn more about writing a program code, you will find that there is almost always more than one way to code any programming problem. By the same token, there is almost always more than one way to design a program. Pseudocode and flowcharts are two excellent design tools for programmers.

Control Structures

To help create a well-structured program design, each module should consist of a series of properly organized groups of statements known as **control structures**. In fact, in the 1960s computer scientists showed that only three basic control structures (or constructs) are needed to create any program or algorithm. Pretty amazing, right? The three basic types of control structures are as follows:

1. The sequential (or sequence) structure
2. The decision (or selection) structure
3. The loop (or repetition) structure

The Sequential Structure

A **sequential structure** consists of a series of consecutive statements, executed in the order in which they appear. In other words, none of the statements in this kind of structure causes a *branch*—a jump in the flow of execution—to another part of the program module. The general form of a sequential structure is as follows:

```
Statement
Statement
 .
 .
 .
Statement
```

All the program modules you've seen so far consist of a single sequential structure. The flowchart for the Sale Price program, Figure 3.6, is an example of a sequential structure.

Decision or Selection Structures

Unlike sequential structures, loop and decision structures contain branch points or statements that cause a branch to take place. As shown in Example 3.11, in a **decision structure** (also known as a **selection structure**) there is a branch forward at some point, which causes a portion of the program to be skipped. Thus, depending upon a given condition at the branch point, a certain block of statements will be executed while another is skipped. The flowchart for a typical decision structure is shown in Figure 3.7.

Figure 3.7 Flowchart for a typical decision structure

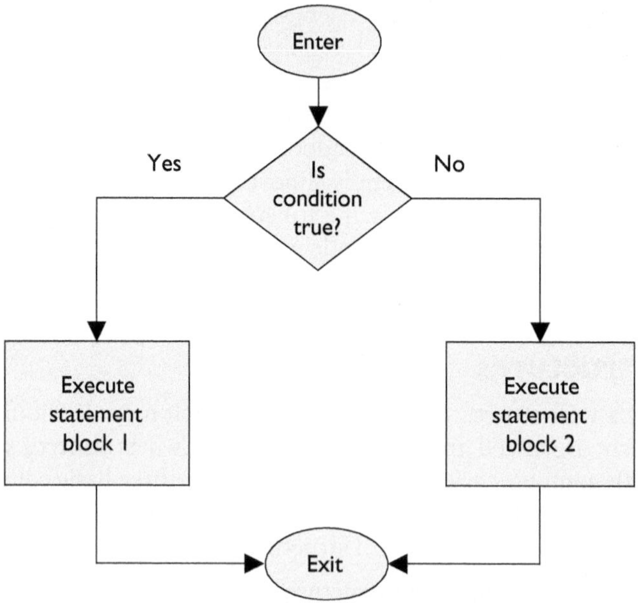

Example 3.11 **A Flowchart with a Decision Structure**

Joey and Janey Jimenez want to know what they will do on a Saturday. Their mother tells them to check the weather. If it is raining, they will go to a movie. If not, they will go to the park. The flowchart shown in Figure 3.8 shows this decision structure. The decision symbol in the flowchart branches off in two ways. If it is raining, the answer will be yes and the option, "Go to the movies" will be taken. If the answer is no, the option, "Go to the park" will be taken.

Loop or Repetition Structures

A **loop structure** (also known as a **repetition structure**) contains a branch which results in a block of statements that can be executed many times. It will be repeated as long as a given condition within the loop structure causes the branch to be taken. A flowchart of a typical loop structure is shown in Figure 3.9. Notice that the diamond-shaped decision symbol is used to indicate a branch point. If the condition within the diamond is true, follow the Yes arrow; if not, follow the No arrow. Example 3.12 provides an example of a flowchart with a loop structure.

Figure 3.8 Flowchart for Example 3.11

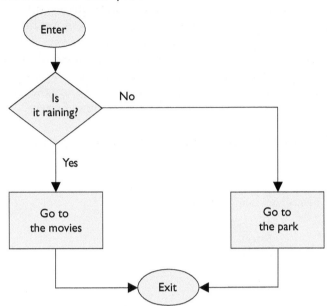

Figure 3.9 Flowchart for a typical loop structure

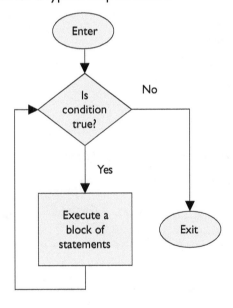

Example 3.12 **A Flowchart with a Loop Structure**

Joey and Janey Jimenez (the children who were deciding how to spend a free Saturday, thus demonstrating the decision structure in Example 3.11) have ascertained that it will rain all day so they will go to the movies. Their mother insists that they pick a G-rated movie. Each time they suggest a movie title, she asks them if it is G-rated. If the answer is No, they must go back to the list of movies and pick another one. They are inside the "pick a movie" loop until they find one that is G-rated.

This loop might last for one turn through the loop, if the first movie they select is G-rated or it might last for three turns or thirty-three turns—until they finally find a G-rated movie. The flowchart shown in Figure 3.10 shows this loop structure. The decision symbol in this flowchart branches off in two ways. If the answer to the question, "Is it a G-rated movie?" is Yes, the loop ends and the Jimenez family goes to the movies. But if the answer is No, the loop begins again, at the top of the decision symbol. Note also that a new movie is selected before the loop begins again. If a new movie was not selected, the loop would continue forever.

We will discuss decision structures in Chapter 4 and loop structures in Chapters 5 and 6.

Figure 3.10 Flowchart using a loop structure

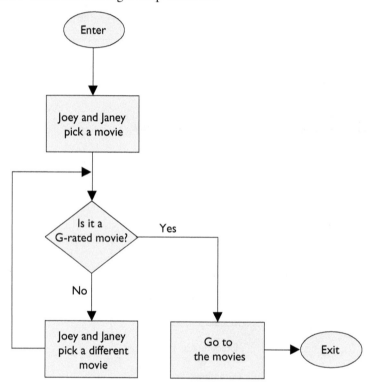

Programming Style

Most of the structured programming principles we've discussed so far have dealt with the design of a program. A well-structured design leads, in a natural way, to a well-structured, easy-to-read code. In fact, one of the goals of structured programming is to create a program that is easy for programmers to read and understand and for users to run. The elements of a program that affect its readability and ease of use are grouped together under the general heading of **programming style**. Some of the guidelines for developing a good programming style have already been discussed, and the following Pointers provide a summary of those guidelines.

Write Modular Programs. Design a program as a collection of modules. The more complex your program is, the greater will be the benefit of modular programming.

Use Descriptive Variable Names. To improve program readability, a variable name should remind anyone who reads the code what that variable represents. For example, `TotalPrice` is a better name than `T` or `Total` or `Price`.

Provide a Welcome Message for the User. The first few lines, or the first screen, displayed by your program should contain a welcome message, which typically contains the program title, programmer's name and affiliation, date, and possibly a brief description of the program.

Use a Prompt Before an Input. Before requesting input data from the user, display a message on the screen that states the type of the input desired. If you don't issue a prompt, in most programming languages, the user will not even be aware of the fact that execution has paused for an input.

Identify Program Output. The output produced by your program should stand on its own; it should make sense to someone who has no knowledge whatsoever of the code that produced it. In particular, never output numbers without an explanation of what they represent.

Document Your Programs. Use internal documentation (comments) in your program. Header comments should be used to provide general information about a program or a program module, and step comments should be used to explain the purpose of blocks of code.

Self Check for Section 3.5

3.18 List three principles of structured programming.

3.19 Draw and label the following flowchart symbols:
  a. Process
  b. Decision
  c. Input/output

3.20 What are the three basic control structures?

3.21 In one sentence, explain why using a good programming style is important.

3.22 List four principles of good programming style.

3.6 Running With RAPTOR (Optional)

RAPTOR is a visual programming environment based on flowcharts that are created to solve particular programming problems. Normally, programmers use flowcharts to design a program or part of a program before writing the actual code. RAPTOR allows you to take flowcharting one step further by allowing you to test (run) your program design and to confirm that your logic works correctly to solve your problem.

In a programming logic course, RAPTOR is useful for several reasons. Compared with other programming languages, the RAPTOR language has minimal syntax (grammar), which means you spend less time debugging syntax errors. You can concentrate on the most important aspect of programming: developing good logic and design. Also, the RAPTOR program is visual because it uses diagrams that allow you to understand the flow of control of the statements in your program.

Getting Started

Several versions of RAPTOR are available. This text will describe the Spring 2012 version, which can be obtained from the Student Data Files website or from the RAPTOR website at http://raptor.martincarlisle.com/.

After you download and install RAPTOR, you can open the program by locating the little RAPTOR icon ⟿ on your computer. You will see two screens: the RAPTOR work area screen and the MasterConsole screen (see Figure 3.11). When you first open RAPTOR your MasterConsole may be shrunk or hidden behind the main screen and you may have to click it to reveal it. You can resize the screens as you wish; it's convenient to view them side-by-side.

When you execute a RAPTOR program, the program begins at the Start symbol at the top and follows the arrows to the End symbol. The smallest RAPTOR program

Figure 3.11 RAPTOR screens

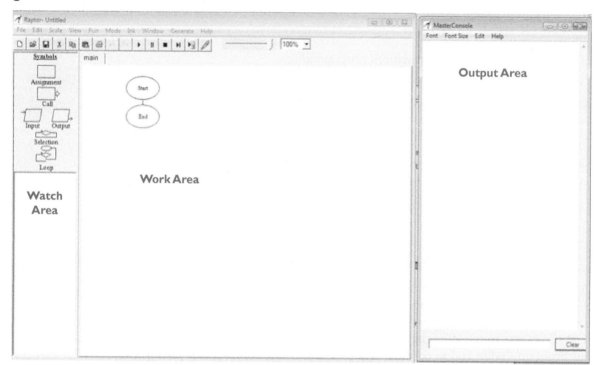

(which does nothing) is shown at the right. By placing additional RAPTOR state-ments between the Start and End symbols you create more meaningful RAPTOR programs.

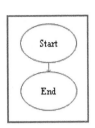

To create a RAPTOR program, you drag instances of each flowcharting symbol from the left side to the middle area of the screen, as shown in Figure 3.12.

RAPTOR will prompt you to save your file as soon as you drag one symbol onto the screen. Then you can begin to create your program. To enter information into a symbol that you have dragged to the screen, double-click it. A dialog box (a small window) will open, which allows you to enter the information that is possible or required for that symbol. For an Assignment box, as shown in Figure 3.12, double-clicking the box will open the dialog box as shown in Figure 3.13. Assignment boxes allow you to enter information about variables.

Introduction to RAPTOR Symbols

RAPTOR has six basic symbols; each symbol represents a specific type of program-ming statement or construct. The basic symbols are shown at the right. In this sec-tion, we will cover the use of the Input, Assignment, and Output symbols. We will discuss other symbols (Call, Selection, and Loop) in later chapters, as those topics are covered in the text.

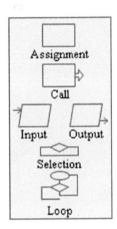

A typical computer program has three basic components:

- Input: Gets the data needed to accomplish the task.
- Processing: Manipulates the data to accomplish the task.
- Output: Displays (or saves) the solution to the task.

These components are directly correlated to RAPTOR symbols, as shown in Table 3.1.

Figure 3.12 Dragging flowchart symbols to the screen

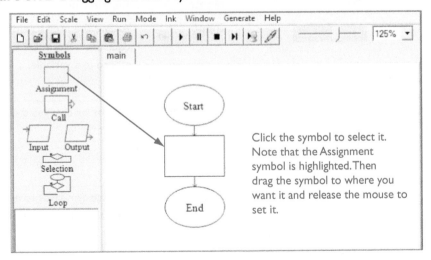

Figure 3.13 Entering information into a dialog box

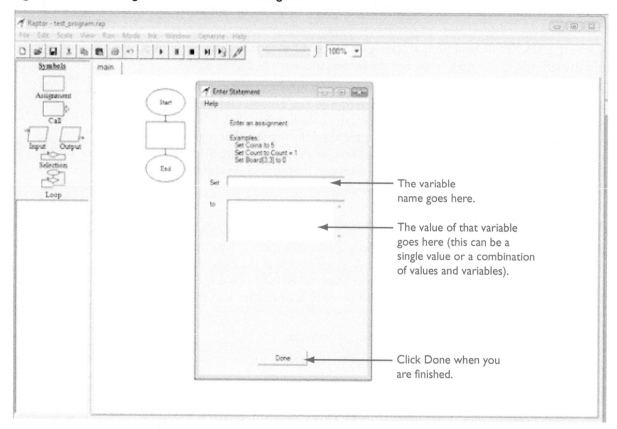

Table 3.1 RAPTOR symbols and instructions

Purpose	Symbol	Name	Instruction
Input		Input	Allows the user to enter data. Each data value is stored in a variable.
Processing		Assignment	Assigns or changes the value of a variable.
Output		Output	Displays (or saves to a file) the value of text and/or variables

Variables

In this text, the statement Set X = 32 assigns the value of 32 to the variable named X. In RAPTOR, an arrow pointing left ($\leftarrow$) assigns the value on the right-hand side to the variable named on the left-hand side. Therefore, X $\leftarrow$ 32 assigns the value of 32 to the variable named X.

In Figure 3.14, the box directly under the Start symbol (X $\leftarrow$ 32) assigns the value 32 to the variable X. The next statement, X $\leftarrow$ X + 1 says "X now is assigned the value it has (32) plus 1." So, after that statement executes, the previous value of X is replaced by the value 33.

Figure 3.14 Assigning a value to a variable

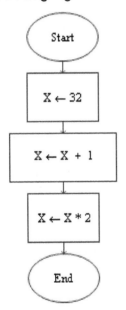

The next statement, X $\leftarrow$ X * 2 says "assign to the variable X the present value of X multiplied by 2." In this case, X had the value 33 and, after the statement is executed, it contains the value 66.

RAPTOR variables do not need to be declared in a separate section of the program; they may be declared at the same time as they are first used. However, in many programming languages, variables are declared before they are used, so it's strongly recommended that you do this in RAPTOR. It's good programming practice and will help you prepare to write program code in other languages.

All RAPTOR variables are of type Number or String. A Number can be either a whole number (an integer) or a decimal number (a floating point number). RAPTOR does not distinguish between number types. A String is a text value like "Hello, friend" or "pony" or a single character like "e" or "W" or even a number, as long as the number is not used for any computations. For example, a telephone number such as "352-381-3829" is a String.

A variable can have its value set or changed in RAPTOR by one of the three ways:

- The value can be entered from an Input statement
- The value can be calculated from an equation in an Assignment statement
- The value can be returned from a procedure Call (more on this later)

In this text, as in most languages, it's necessary to associate several things with a new variable. A variable must be given a name, a data type, and often an initial value.

Declaring variables

When a RAPTOR program begins its execution, no variables exist. The first time RAPTOR encounters a new variable name, it automatically creates a new memory location and associates this variable name with the new memory. Therefore, in RAPTOR you don't need to declare variables explicitly, as we do in the text with Declare statements. The variable will exist from the point at which it is created in the program execution until the program terminates.

Initializing variables

When a new variable is created in RAPTOR, it *must* be given an initial value. This is slightly different from other languages where it is possible to declare a variable without giving it a value at that time. The initial value in RAPTOR determines the variable's type. If the value is a number, the variable is of type Number. If the initial value is text, the variable is of type String. Note that any initial value that is enclosed in quotes is considered text:

- If the variable myNum is set to 34, it is stored with the Number type.
- If the variable myWord is set to "34", it is stored with the String type.
- A variable's data type cannot change during the execution of a program.

Beware! While a variable in RAPTOR can be created "on the fly" (i.e., by simply entering a variable name and giving it a value), a variable cannot be used until it has been created. Examples 3.13 and 3.14 demonstrate this distinction.

Example 3.13 **Declaring Variables in RAPTOR Correctly**

The following snippet of a RAPTOR program shows how to correctly declare a variable named jellybeans, give it an initial value of 8, and multiply the number of jellybeans by 2.

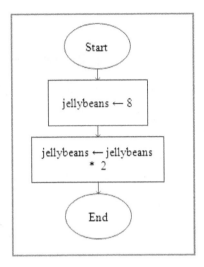

Example 3.14 Declaring Variables in RAPTOR Incorrectly

The following snippet of a RAPTOR program shows what happens when one attempts to use a variable named `jellybeans` before it is created.

What happened? In this program the `Assignment` statement attempted to use the value of `jellybeans` (on the right side of the ← symbol) before `jellybeans` had been assigned any value.

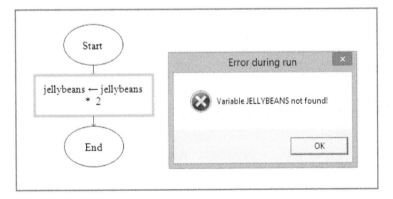

Common Errors and Their Causes

Error 1: `Variable ____ doesn't have a value.`

There are two common reasons for this error:

    1. The variable has not been given a value.

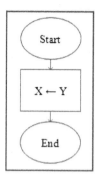

2. The variable name is misspelled.

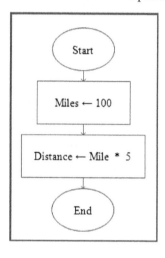

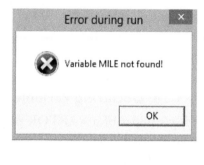

Error 2: `Variable ___ not found!`

This error means you have tried to use a variable before you have declared it or assigned it an initial value.

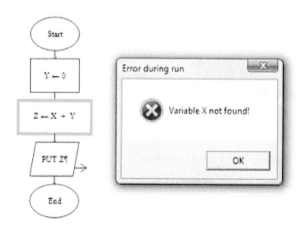

Error 3: `Can't assign string to numeric variable _____.`
`Can't assign numeric to string variable _____.`

This error occurs if your statements attempt to change the data type of a variable. In newer versions of RAPTOR, you may be allowed to change a data type "on the fly" but this is never a good programming practice.

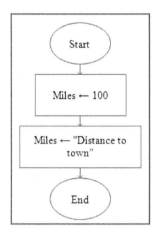

RAPTOR Symbols

The following sections provide details about each of the basic symbols: `Input`, `Assignment`, and `Output`. The other symbols will be covered later.

Input Symbol

Every programming language has statements that enable the program to get information from the user via the keyboard or mouse and display that information on the computer screen. This allows the user to enter instructions to the program or supply the program with necessary information.

In RAPTOR, when an `Input` **symbol** is executed, a prompt is displayed (prompting the user to enter some value); the user then enters a value which is stored in a given variable. The `Enter Input` dialog box (see Figure 3.15) shows what is displayed when you drag an `Input` symbol onto your flowchart and double-click in the symbol. In the `Enter Prompt Here` box at the top, you enter the text you want the user to see. The text typed in this box will be displayed to the user when the program is run and, therefore, should explain what information needs to be input. This text must be enclosed in quotes. Make sure your prompt is clear and complete. The `Enter Variable Here` box holds the name of the variable where the information the user enters will be stored. You can enter the name of a variable you have previously declared or you can declare a new variable and enter it here.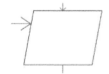

- The information entered will be stored in a variable and used later in the program. For example, if you are calculating the cost of buying widgets and the user enters `$1.50` for the price of one widget, this will be stored in a `String` variable called `Price`; the dollar sign (`$`) prevents it from being considered a `Number`. This will give you an error when you use `Price` in a calculation.

Figure 3.15 The Enter Input dialog box

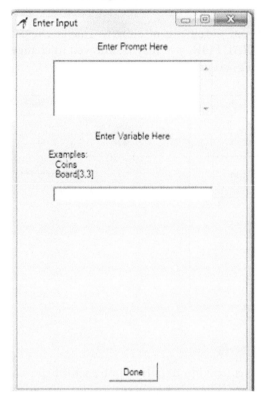

Since Price must be a Number, the dollar sign cannot be part of the user's entry. Be sure to tell the user not to include units when entering numbers. For example, a good prompt might read, "Enter the price of a widget, without the $ (i.e., 1.50 for a widget that costs $1.50)."

- If you are asking the user to enter a text response, you must be specific. For example, if you want the user to choose yes or no, you must tell the user what to type because, to a computer, "yes" is not the same as "y" or "YES". A good prompt for this example might read, "Do you want to continue? Type 'y' for yes or 'n' for no."

Making It Work

Nested Quotes

At this point it is helpful to point out a situation that occurs frequently when coding an output text. Imagine you want the following output to explain to the user how to enter a choice:

Do you want to play the game again? Type "y" for yes, "n" for no.

Often the output includes some text that needs to be wrapped in quotes. However, a String, to the computer, is any text enclosed in quotes. The computer understands that the beginning of a String starts with the first quote symbol (") and ends when it encounters a second quote symbol ("). If the output text shown above was to be stored in a variable named YourChoice and was coded as follows:

```
YourChoice = "Do you want to play the game again? Type "y" for yes,
  "n" for no."
```

the computer would process "Do you want to play the game again? Type " as the String to be stored in YourChoice and then display an error because the next character, y, is unintelligible to a computer interpreter or compiler.

That is why we must nest quotes within a String. We must use a different symbol for internal quotes (those that are part of the String text) than the outer quotes, which mark the beginning and end of the String. In this case, a single quote (') indicates that we are still inside the original text String. In some languages, the outer quotes must be double quotes ("), while in other languages double quotes can be nested inside single quotes as well as the other way around.

The correct way to write the code for the YourChoice variable, then is:

```
YourChoice = "Do you want to play the game again? Type 'y' for yes,
  'n' for no."
```

Figure 3.16 The Input prompt

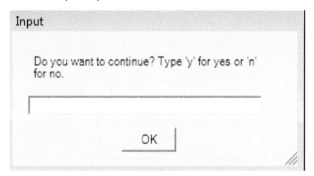

At runtime, an Input statement will display an Input prompt box, as shown in Figure 3.16. After a user enters a value and clicks OK, the value entered by the user is assigned to the Input statement's variable.

Examples 3.15 and 3.16 demonstrate the use of the Input box.

Example 3.15 Using the Input Box to Change the Value of a Declared Variable

The following snippet of a RAPTOR program shows how to correctly declare a variable named jellybeans and change its value with user input, through an Input box prompt. When this program is run, the initial value of jellybeans will be 0. If the user enters 15 at the prompt, the value of jellybeans will become 15.

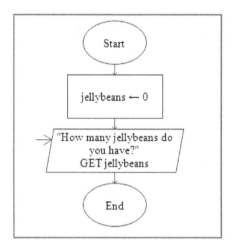

Example 3.16 Using the Input Box to Declare and Initialize a Variable

The following snippet of a RAPTOR program shows how, by using an Input box prompt, a variable named `jellybeans` can be declared and given an initial value at the same time. If the user enters 15 at the prompt, the value of `jellybeans` will become 15.

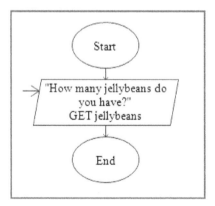

Assignment Symbol

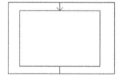

The **Assignment symbol** is used to set the value of a variable or to perform a computation and then store the results in a variable. The value stored in the variable can be retrieved and used in a statement later in the program.

The dialog box shown in Figure 3.17 is used to enter the name of the variable being assigned and its value. The variable name is entered in the small text box: Set _____. The value is entered in the large text box: to _____. This value can

Figure 3.17 The Enter Statement dialog box

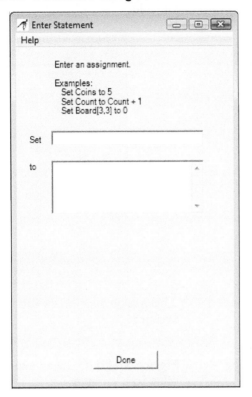

be a number, character, or a string of text. If this is the first time the variable has been used, its type is set by the value you enter. If you type a number, the variable becomes a Number type.

You can also type in a computation for the value of a variable. The result will be assigned to the variable. The different ways to use Assignment statements are shown in Figure 3.18.

Assignment statement syntax

An Assignment statement is displayed inside its RAPTOR symbol using the following syntax:

```
Variable  ←  Expression
```

An Assignment statement can only change the value of a single variable; that is, the variable on the left-hand side of the arrow. No variables on the right-hand side of the arrow (i.e., the expression) are ever changed by the Assignment statement.

Figure 3.18a Assigning a number value to a variable

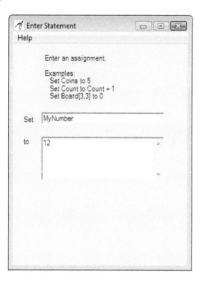

This Assignment sets a variable named MyNumber to 12.

Figure 3.18b Assigning a text value to a variable

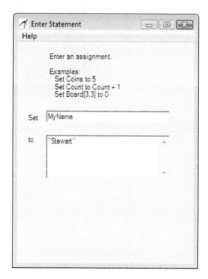

This Assignment sets a variable named MyName to Stewart.

Figure 3.18c Assigning a text value consisting of numbers to a variable

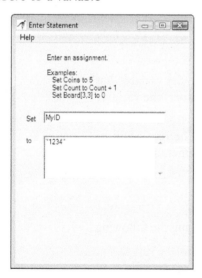

This Assignment sets a variable named MyID to 1234. Note: since "1234" is in quotes, it is a String variable and no computations can be done with this number. It is stored as text.

Figure 3.18d Using an expression to assign a value to a variable

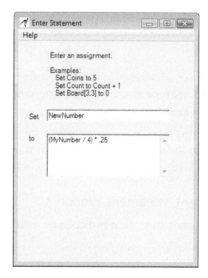

Here, we have a variable, NewNumber, that initially has the value of 12. This Assignment sets the variable NewNumber to 0.75
Note: The following computation is done first: MyNumber (which originally was 12) is divided by 4. The result is multiplied by 0.25. The final result, 0.75, is stored in NewNumber.

The following is an example of an `Assignment` statement:

```
Cost ← (Tax_Rate * Non_Food_Total) + Food_Total
```
        ↖— [Assignment]

Here is how RAPTOR processes an `Assignment` statement:

- First, the expression on the right-hand side of the `Assignment` operator is evaluated.
- Then, that value is placed in the memory location associated with the variable on the left side, replacing whatever data value had been stored there previously.

Expressions

The **expression** (or computation) of an `Assignment` statement can be any simple or complex equation that results in a single value. An expression is a combination of values (either constants or variables) and operators. A computer can perform only one operation at a time. RAPTOR follows the same mathematical order of preference as discussed in this text.

An operator or function directs the computer to perform some computation on data. Operators are placed between the data being operated on (e.g., X + 3), whereas functions use parentheses to indicate the data they are operating on (e.g., sqrt(4.7)). When executed, operators and functions perform their computation and return their result. We will learn more about functions later in the text.

The result of evaluating an expression in an `Assignment` statement must be either a single number or a single string of text. While many expressions will compute numbers, you can also perform simple text manipulation in RAPTOR by using a plus sign (+) to join (concatenate) two or more strings of text into a single string. You can also join numerical values with strings to create a single string. The following `Assignment` statement demonstrates string manipulation:

```
Full_name ← "Joe " + "Alexander" + "Smith"
```

The value of `Full_name`, after this `Assignment` statement, is `Joe Alexander Smith`.

`Output` Symbol

In RAPTOR, an **`Output` statement** displays a value to the `MasterConsole` screen when it is executed. When you define an `Output` statement by clicking on the `Output` symbol in your flowchart, the `Enter Output` dialog box (shown in Figure 3.19) asks you to specify the text or expression to display and whether or not the output should be terminated by a newline character. If you check the `End current line` box, any future output will start on a new line below the displayed text.

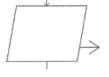

You can output text, the value of a variable, or any combination of text and variables. Examples of various output displays are shown in Figure 3.20, assuming the variables have already been declared and contain the values noted below:

- `MyName` is a `String` variable and has the value `Maurice Jones`.
- `Price` is a `Number` variable and has the value `5`.
- `Number` is a `Number` variable and has the value `8`.

Figure 3.19 The Enter Output dialog box

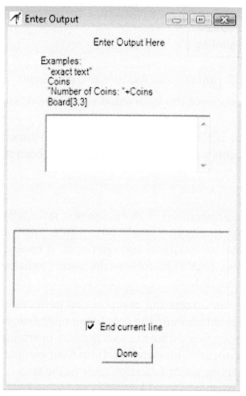

Figure 3.20a The Output is Set to simple text by enclosing the text in quotes. The output is displayed without the quotes.

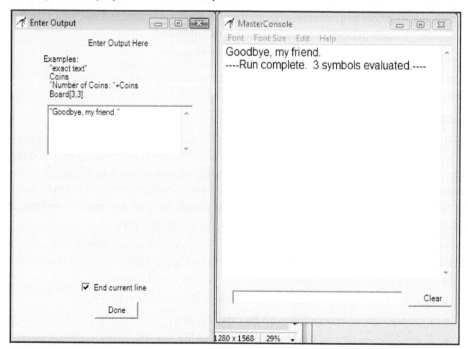

Figure 3.20b In this case, the variable `MyName` has previously been `Set` to "Maurice Jones" so the output concatenates the text "Goodbye, " with the value of `MyName` and the text "!". The output displays without any quotes. If you want a space after the comma and before the name `Maurice`, you must include a space before the ending quotes of "Goodbye, ". This is because a space, to the computer, is considered a character. Without the space, the output would look, unfortunately, like this: `Goodbye,Maurice Jones!`

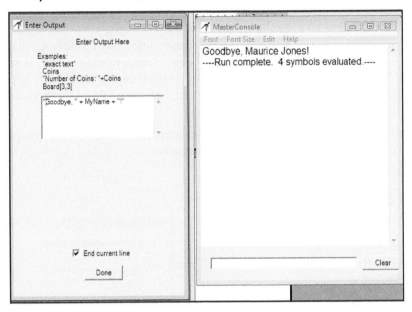

Figure 3.20c In this case, the variable `Number` has previously been `Set` to 8 and the variable `Price` has been `Set` to 5. The output concatenates the text in quotes with the values of the variables. It also does the computation (multiplying `Number` * `Price`) before outputting the result, 40, of this computation.

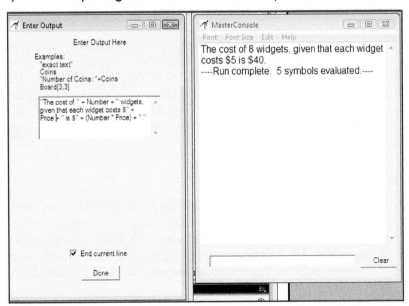

Comments

The RAPTOR development environment, like many programming languages, allows comments to be added to your program. All good programs include comments if the code itself is not self-explanatory. While in the beginning, comments often seem redundant or even downright silly since beginning programs are small and not particularly complex, it is a good idea to get into the habit of including comments.

To add a comment to a symbol in your flowchart, right-click the mouse button on the statement symbol and select the Comment line before releasing the button. Then, enter the comment text into the Enter Comment dialog box, as shown in Figure 3.21. The resulting comment can be moved in the RAPTOR window by dragging it, but normally you would not need to move the default location of a comment.

Typically, you should not comment every statement in a program but should include comments before each new section of a program.

Figure 3.21 The Enter Comment dialog box

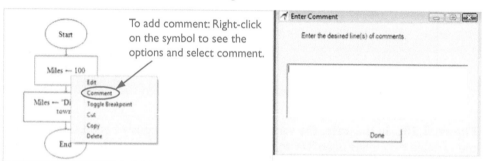

Backups

RAPTOR makes backup files of your programs automatically. After you work on a program for some time, if you look in Windows Explorer or MyComputer, you will see a group of files under your RAPTOR file. The RAPTOR file has the extension .rap and is identified by the RAPTOR icon. The backup files are named with the same name as your program but include .backup0, .backup1, and so on. These files can be ignored and, when you are finished creating your program, can be deleted.

Run It: The Sign-In Program

In each chapter of this text that has a Running With RAPTOR section, we will develop a longer program that, while demonstrating the concepts of the chapter and allowing you to practice using those concepts with RAPTOR, will also give you a chance to see a "real-life" application of programming skills. In this section, the program we develop will not be particularly exciting because we don't have enough programming tools yet but will show how to use the tools we have discussed so far. We will walk through creating a sign-in screen that a student might encounter when signing in to his or her school's website. The school uses the student's name to create a college email address for each student. The program will consist of Input, Assignment, and Output symbols.

In this program, the user will enter a first name, a last name, a desired username, and a student ID number. The program will concatenate the first and last name to form the user's full name and then use the same information (first and last name) to create a college email address. The results will be displayed for the student on the MasterConsole.

Developing the Program

When developing a program, it is essential to plan out the program, normally using pseudocode. Since this program uses only sequential statements, the plan is straight-forward and is as follows:

- Prompt for first name
- Prompt for last name
- Prompt for username
- Prompt for ID number
- Create full name by joining first and last names with a space between them
- Create email address by joining first name and last name with a dot between them and appending the college domain; we will use @mycollege.edu
- Display results

Next, it is time to decide on the variables needed. In this case, we need the following String variables: First, Last, Full, Username, Email. We will use one Number variable to store the ID number, which we will call IDnum. Since the ID number is not used in any computation, it could be stored as a String. However, in another program, ID numbers might be assigned to students by adding 1 to the last number used and, in that program, the ID number would have to be of the Number data type.

Creating the Program in RAPTOR: Input

To create this program, open RAPTOR and set up the screens so the work area and the MasterConsole are side by side. Save the program with the filename signIn.rap.

In this program, we will prompt for three String variables and one Number variable. Begin by dragging four Input symbols to the work area. Double-click in an Input symbol and enter your prompt in the Enter Prompt Here area when the Enter Input box appears. Then enter your variable name in the Enter Variable Here area below. Figure 3.22 shows what RAPTOR will look like when the first three Input boxes have been filled in and the fourth is in progress.

When you finish creating the Input statements, you can run this program. It will run and do exactly what you asked it to do: it will prompt the user for the information and

Figure 3.22 Input symbols for the Sign-In program

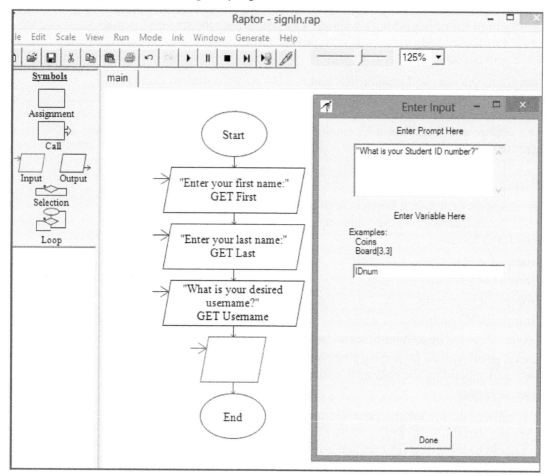

store that information in the variables you specified. To run the program, click on the Run button at the top of the screen and, for now, select Execute to Completion, as shown in Figure 3.23.

As the program runs, you will get a prompt for each Input symbol, as shown in Figure 3.24.

After the program runs, look at the Watch Window, which is the white space on the far left, just under the Symbols. You can see the variables you created and the values that are stored in them. At this time, nothing will show up in the MasterConsole because you have not programmed any Output. If you enter the following information, your Watch Window will look as shown in Figure 3.25.

First: Lizzy, Last: Lizardo, Username: lizard, IDnum: 1234

Figure 3.23 Run the program

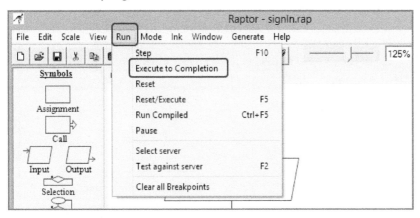

Figure 3.24 The first Prompt

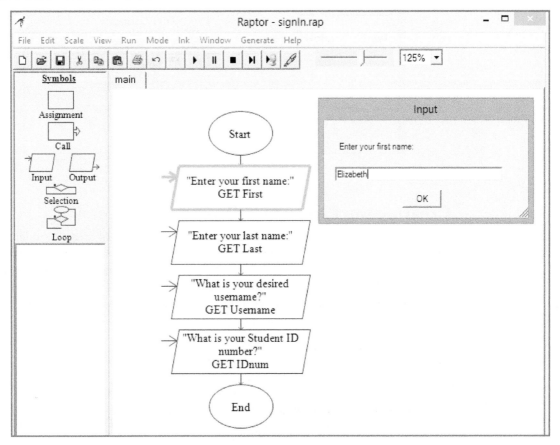

Figure 3.25 The Watch Window

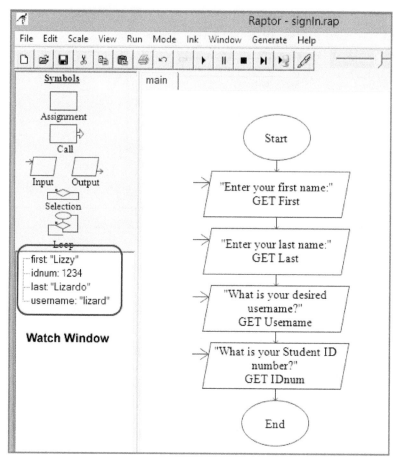

Creating the Program in RAPTOR: Processing

Now the program must process the variables First and Last to create a student's full name, to be stored in the variable Full, and the student's new college email address, to be stored in the variable Email. We will use two Assignment symbols to do this. For both of these operations, we must concatenate the values in variables with other text. Remember that text includes any ASCII character, even a blank space. The pseudocode to create the full name is:

```
Set Full = First + " " + Last
```

and the pseudocode to create the email address is:

```
Set Email = First + "." + Last + "@mycollege.edu"
```

To do this in RAPTOR, drag two Assignment symbols to the work area, directly under the last Input symbol and double-click on a symbol. The variable that will be assigned a value goes in the Set box in the Enter Statement pop-up window and the value (which includes any variables, text, or numbers you want) goes in the to box, as shown in Figure 3.26.

Figure 3.26 Using An Assignment Statement

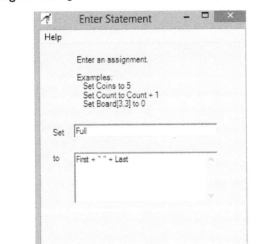

After completing both Assignment statements and running your program with the values entered previously, your program will look as the one shown in Figure 3.27, with the Watch Window filled with information for the two new variables, Full and Email. The MasterConsole has been shown in this Figure, although, at this time, it contains no output.

Creating the Program in RAPTOR: Output

We can finish our program now by creating the output we want the student to see after he or she uses the program. We need to spend some time considering how we want the output displayed. We want to show the student what was entered. Eventually, as you learn more programming logic, you could revise this program to allow the student to check the entries and make corrections in case something was entered incorrectly. For now, though, we will simply display the information entered. But we cannot just list the values of the variables; we need to add some explanation of what these values represent. One possible output display might look like this:

```
Hello, [Username]!
You entered the following information:
Your name: [Full]
Your student ID Number: [IDnum]
You have been assigned a college email address:
[Email]
```

Figure 3.27 Processing Variables and the `MasterConsole`

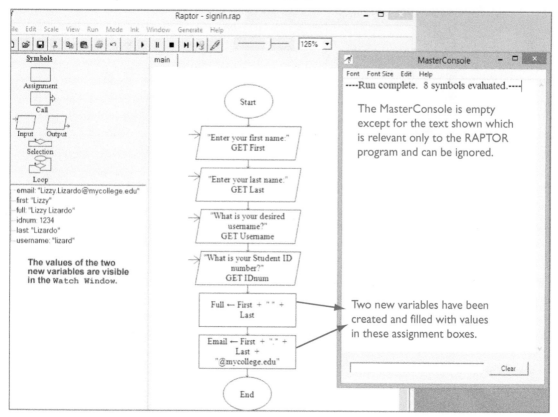

Notice that not all the information entered is used. The student entered values for `First` and `Last` but we used those values internally to output `Full` and `Email`.

To create this output, drag five `Output` symbols to the work area and enter the following in each `Enter Output` box. Be sure to put the text you want displayed inside quotes and use the concatenation operator (+) to join this text with the value of a variable. Remember to include spaces within the quotes if you do not want the value of the variable to be squashed up right next to the text.

- Output box 1: `"Hello, " + Username + "!"`
- Output box 2: `"You entered the following information:"`
- Output box 3: `"Your name: " + Full`
- Output box 4: `"Your student ID Number: " + IDnum`
- Output box 5: `"You have been assigned a college email address: "`
- Output box 6: `Email`

Figure 3.28 shows what the RAPTOR work area looks like after these `Output` boxes have been created.

Check It Out

Finally we can run the program and view the output. In Figure 3.29, the font face of the `MasterConsole` has been changed to `Courier` font. The information entered is the same as previously noted.

Figure 3.28 Using Output boxes

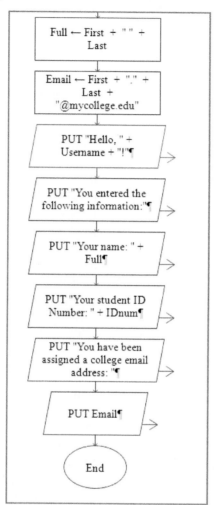

Figure 3.29 The Final Output

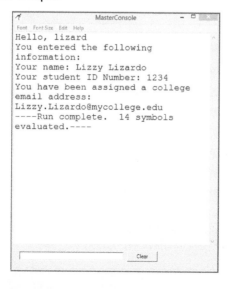

Chapter Review and Exercises

Key Terms

algorithm
alpha testing
analyze (a problem)
Assignment symbol
beta testing
bugs
call (a module)
call statement
code
comment
control structure
debug
decision structure
design (a program)
design documentation
desk-checking
document (a program)
driver
echo printing
end users
expression
external documentation
flowchart
header comments
hierarchy chart
Input symbol
internal documentation
logic error

loop structure
main module
maintenance manual
MasterConsole
modular programming
Output symbol
program code
program development cycle
program module
programming style
prompt
pseudocode
repetition structure
runtime error
selection structure
sequential structure
step comments
structured programming
submodule
syntax
syntax error
technical writer
test (a program)
test data
top-down design
trade study documentation
user's guide
watch window

Chapter Summary

In this chapter, we have discussed the following topics:

1. The program development cycle consists of the four phases:
   - Analyze the problem
   - Design the program
   - Code the program
   - Test the program

2. The modular programming approach to program a design consists of the following:
   - Break a program into modules and submodules that perform the basic tasks that the program must carry out

- Provide a pictorial representation of the modules using hierarchy charts
- Use pseudocode to fill in the details of each module and if necessary, repeatedly refine the pseudocode

3. Other aspects of modular programming include:
   - The Call statement is used to call a module into action, which means that the statements in the called module are executed and then the program execution returns to the calling module
   - The characteristics of a module: a module is self-contained, compact, and performs a single task
   - The benefits of modular programming: program readability is improved and programmer productivity is increased

4. It is important to include program documentation such as:
   - Internal documentation (comments) benefits another programmer who needs to revise, edit, or use the program code
     - header comments appear at the beginning of a program or program module and provide general information about it
     - step comments appear throughout the program to explain (annotate) portions of code
   - External documentation benefits someone using the program; it consists of on-screen help or a printed user's guide

5. To test a program, the program is run with various sets of input data (test data) to check it for errors:
   - Syntax errors are caused by violations of the programming language's rules for statement structure
   - Logic errors are caused by combinations of statements that fail to carry out the desired task

6. The following are structured programming principles:
   - Solve a problem by following the steps of the program development cycle
   - Design the program in a modular fashion
   - Design and code each module as a series of control structures
   - Use good programming style—code the program in a way that enhances readability and ease of use, including the appropriate use of internal and if necessary, external documentation
   - Test the program systematically to ensure that it is error free

7. Flowcharts and control structures are used as follows:
   - Flowchart symbols include the terminator, process, input/output, decision, and connector
   - Flowcharts are used to describe the three basic control structures: sequence, decision (selection), and loop (repetition)
   - Flowcharts are tools used by programmers to design programs, to help follow program logic and flow of control, and to facilitate debugging
   - Interactive flowchart software, such as RAPTOR can be used to help design and test program segments

Review Exercises

Fill in the Blank

1. The process of solving a problem by analyzing it, designing an appropriate program, coding the design, and testing the code is known as the _____.

2. When analyzing a problem, we usually start by identifying the results we want the program to produce; that is, the program's _____.

3. The _____ is the generic name for the module in which program execution begins.

4. To _____ a module (or subprogram) into action means to cause execution to transfer to that module.

5. A(n) _____ is a pictorial representation of a program's modules and the relationships among them.

6. _____ makes use of short, English-like phrases to describe the design of a program.

7. A(n) _____ comment provides a general description of a program or program module.

8. A(n) _____ comment provides an explanation of a portion of code.

9. A(n) _____ error is a violation of a programming language's rules for the structure of statements.

10. A(n) _____ error results from statements that do not properly perform their intended task.

11. The two types of testing done on commercial software are _____ testing and _____ testing.

12. The type of external documentation that is written mainly for the benefit of programmers is a(n) _____.

Multiple Choice

13. Which of the following is not necessarily a characteristic of a program module?
    a. It performs a single task
    b. It contains several submodules
    c. It is self-contained
    d. It is relatively small in size

14. Which of the following is *not* a benefit of modular programming?
    a. It increases program readability
    b. It increases programmer productivity
    c. It allows for the creation of a "library" of common programming tasks
    d. It allows one programmer to do the job of many in the same amount of time

15. The main module of a program contains the following statements:

```
Call ModuleA
Call ModuleB
Call ModuleC
```

Which of the following statements is executed *after* Call ModuleB ?

a. Call ModuleA

b. Call ModuleC

c. The first statement in ModuleB

d. None of the above

16. The main module of a program contains the following statements:

```
Call ModuleA
Call ModuleB
Call ModuleC
```

Which of the following statements is executed after all statements in ModuleB have been carried out?

a. Call ModuleA

b. Call ModuleC

c. The first statement in ModuleC

d. None of the above

17. Which of the following is *not* a principle of structured programming?

a. Design the program in a modular fashion

b. Write each program module as a series of control structures

c. Code the program so that it runs correctly without testing

d. Use good programming style

18. The flowchart symbol shown at the right is a(n)

a. Process symbol

b. Input/output symbol

c. Decision symbol

d. Terminator symbol

19. The flowchart symbol shown at the right is a(n)

a. Process symbol

b. Input/output symbol

c. Decision symbol

d. Terminator symbol

20. The flowchart symbol shown at the right is a(n)

a. Process symbol

b. Input/output symbol

c. Decision symbol

d. Terminator symbol

21. Which of the following is *not* a basic control structure?
    a. The process structure
    b. The loop structure
    c. The decision structure
    d. The sequential structure

22. Which of the following is *not* a principle of good programming style?
    a. Use descriptive variable names
    b. Provide a welcome message
    c. Identify, using text, the numbers that are output
    d. Test the program

True or False

23. T F Before we code a program, we should design it.

24. T F A logic error is a violation of the programming language's rules for creating valid statements.

25. T F A program's welcome message consists of a series of comments.

26. T F The contents of comments are ignored by the computer while running a program.

27. T F Program comments are also known as external documentation.

28. T F Step comments are intended to be read by someone using the program.

29. T F If you are sure that you have coded a program correctly, then there is no need to test it.

30. T F Commercial programs, like those developed by Microsoft, do not normally require testing.

31. T F To debug a program means to correct its errors.

32. T F Structured programming is a method for designing and coding programs effectively.

33. T F A control structure is a means by which programmers control the user's input.

34. T F If you don't use good programming style, then your programs will not run.

Short Answer

In Exercises 35–40, suppose that you are asked to write a program that computes the average (mean) of three numbers entered by the user.

35. Give the input and output variables for this program.

36. Draw a hierarchy chart for this program that reflects the following basic tasks:

```
Display Welcome Message
Input Data
Calculate Average
Output Results
```

37. Write pseudocode for the main module and `Display Welcome Message` module. You do not have to write pseudocode for the other three modules.

38. Add pseudocode for the `Input Data`, `Calculate Average`, and `Output Results` modules to the pseudocode created in Review Exercise 37.

39. Construct a flowchart for this program (viewing it as a single module).

40. Give three examples of reasonable input data for testing this program.

Programming Challenges

Each of the following Programming Challenges can be solved by a program that performs three basic tasks—Input Data, Process Data, and Output Results. For each problem, use pseudocode to design a suitable program to solve it. Be sure to identify the data type of each variable used.

1. Prompt for and input a saleswoman's sales for the month (in dollars) and her commission rate (as a percentage). Output her commission for that month. Note that you will need to convert the percentage to a decimal. You will need the following variables:

    SalesAmount   CommissionRate   CommissionEarned

   You will need the following formula:

   `CommissionEarned = SalesAmount * (CommissionRate/100)`

2. The manager of the Super Supermarket would like to be able to compute the unit price for products sold there. To do this, the program should input the name and price of an item per pound and its weight in pounds and ounces. Then it should determine and display the unit price (the price per ounce) of that item and the total cost of the amount purchased. You will need the following variables:

ItemName	Pounds	Ounces
PoundPrice	TotalPrice	UnitPrice

   You will need the following formulas:

   ```
   UnitPrice = PoundPrice/16
   TotalPrice = PoundPrice * (Pounds + Ounces/16)
   ```

3. The owners of the Super Supermarket would like to have a program that computes the monthly gross pay of their employees as well as the employee's net pay. The input for this program is an employee ID number, hourly rate of pay, and number of regular and overtime hours worked. Gross pay is the sum of the wages earned from regular hours and overtime hours; overtime is paid at 1.5 times the regular rate. Net pay is gross pay minus deductions. Assume that deductions are taken for tax withholding (30 percent of gross pay) and parking ($10 per month). You will need the following variables:

EmployeeID	HourlyRate	RegHours	OvertimeHours
GrossPay	Tax	Parking	NetPay

You will need the following formulas:

```
GrossPay = (RegularHours * HourlyRate) +
           (OvertimeHours * (HourlyRate * 1.5))
NetPay = GrossPay - (GrossPay * Tax) - Parking
```

4. Shannon and Jasmine bowl as a team. Each of them bowls three games in a tournament. They would like to know their individual averages for their three games and the team average. Allow the user to input the scores for each player. Output Shannon's average, Jasmine's average, and the team's average. You will need the following variables:

```
Score1        Score2        Score3        avgJasmine
sumShannon    sumJasmine    avgShannon    teamAvg
```

You will need the following formulas:

```
teamAvg = (avgShannon + avgJasmine)/2
```

5. Kim wants to buy a car. Help Kim compute the monthly payment on a loan, given the loan amount, the annual percentage rate of interest, and the number of monthly payments. The program should allow Kim to input the loan amount, interest rate, and how many payments she wants to make. It should then compute and display the monthly payment.

You will need the following variables:

```
Payment       LoanAmt       InterestRate
MonthlyRate   NumberMonths
```

You will need the following formulas:

```
MonthlyRate = InterestRate/1200
```

Note: when the user enters InterestRate as a percentage, it must be divided by 100 to make it a decimal (i.e., 18% = 18/100 = 0.18). The InterestRate offered by car dealers is an annual rate so this must be divided by 12 to get the MonthlyRate. The formula given above combines the two steps (i.e., annual rate of 18% = 18/100 = 0.18 and the monthly rate is 0.18/12 = 0.015 or 18/(100*12) = 18/1200.

```
Payment = LoanAmt * MonthlyRate * (1 +
          MonthlyRate)^NumberMonths ÷ ((1 +
          MonthlyRate)^NumberMonths - 1)
```

Note: The formula must be entered carefully, exactly as shown.

Selection Structures: Making Decisions

4

One of a computer's characteristic qualities is its ability to make decisions—to select one of several alternative groups of statements. These groups of statements, together with the condition that determines which of them is to be executed, make up a **selection (or decision) control structure**. In this chapter, we will discuss the various types of selection structures as well as some of their applications.

After reading this chapter, you will be able to do the following:

- Construct single- and dual-alternative selection structures
- Identify and apply relational and logical operators in program segments
- Use the ASCII coding scheme for associating a number with each character
- Use the relational operators <, !=, ==, <=, >, and >= with arbitrary character strings
- Construct multiple-alternative selection structures
- Use different types of selection structures to solve different programming problems
- Use defensive programming to avoid program crashes, such as division by zero and taking the square root of a negative number
- Identify and write program segments that use menu-driven programs
- Use the built-in square root function in your programs

Decisions, Decisions, Decisions . . .

When was the last time you made a decision? A few seconds ago? A few minutes ago? Probably not longer than that because the capability to choose a course of action is a built-in part of being human. It's a good thing too because it gives us the adaptability we need to survive in an ever-changing world. Examples of decisions you make on a daily basis are plentiful. Some examples are as follows:

- IF it's the end of the month, THEN pay the rent.
- IF the alarm clock rings, THEN get up.
- IF you're driving AND it's nighttime OR it's raining, THEN turn on the headlights.
- IF the cat is chewing on the furniture, THEN chase him away, OR ELSE give him a treat.
- IF the boss is approaching, THEN resume work, OR ELSE continue playing computer games.

One type of decision is called a *simple* decision. A simple decision is both straightforward and limited. The action you take is based on whether a condition is true or false. You won't feed the dog if you don't have a dog. However, you may base your decision about what action to take on more than one condition. For example, you will turn on your car headlights if it is nighttime *or* if it is raining or if it is nighttime *and* raining. The decision to turn on your headlights is based on whether one or both of these two conditions are true. If neither is true, you keep your headlights off.

One of the differences between humans and computers is that the human brain can handle much more complicated decisions and can deal with vague or indefinite outcomes like "maybe" or "a little."

It is certain that if you didn't have the ability to make decisions, you probably wouldn't get very far in this world. And if a computer program was written without any decision-making ability, it would probably be pretty useless. After all, we want computers to solve our problems, and our situations are usually far from simple. For example, if you were writing a payroll processing program for a large company, you would quickly discover that there are many different types of employees. Each worker type (salaried, hourly, temporary) might have his or her pay calculated by a different method. Without writing code to allow the computer to make choices, your program would only be able to process paychecks one way and you would need many different programs to process the payroll. Some would be used for people who worked overtime, some for people who didn't, some for employees due bonuses, and even more programs for individuals with different tax rates. Not only is this approach tedious and inefficient, but you would also need to employ a person to decide which program to use for each employee. Instead, you can use decisions such as IF the employee worked overtime, THEN add extra pay to create one efficient and flexible program.

Read on—because IF you master the concepts of this chapter, THEN you will open the door to a very powerful programming technique!

4.1 An Introduction to Selection Structures

In this section, we introduce the three basic types of selection structures and discuss two of them in detail. The third type is presented in Section 4.4. Selection structures may also be referred to as decision structures—the names are interchangeable.

Types of Selection Structures

A selection structure consists of a **test condition** together with one or more groups (or *blocks*) of statements. The result of the test determines which of these blocks is executed. The following are the three types of selection structures:

1. A **single-alternative** (or If-Then) **structure** contains only a single block of statements. If the test condition is met, the statements are executed. If the test condition is not met, the statements are skipped.

2. A **dual-alternative** (or If-Then-Else) **structure** contains two blocks of statements. If the test condition is met, the first block is executed and the program skips over the second block. If the test condition is not met, the first block of statements is skipped and the second block is executed.

3. A **multiple-alternative structure** contains more than two blocks of statements. The program is written so that when the test condition is met, the block of statements that goes with that condition is executed and all the other blocks are skipped.

Figures 4.1 and 4.2 show the flow of execution in each of the three types of selection structures. Note that in Figure 4.1, the blocks of statements to be executed or skipped are referred to as the **Then** and **Else clauses**, respectively.

Figure 4.1 Flowcharts for single- and dual-alternative selection structures

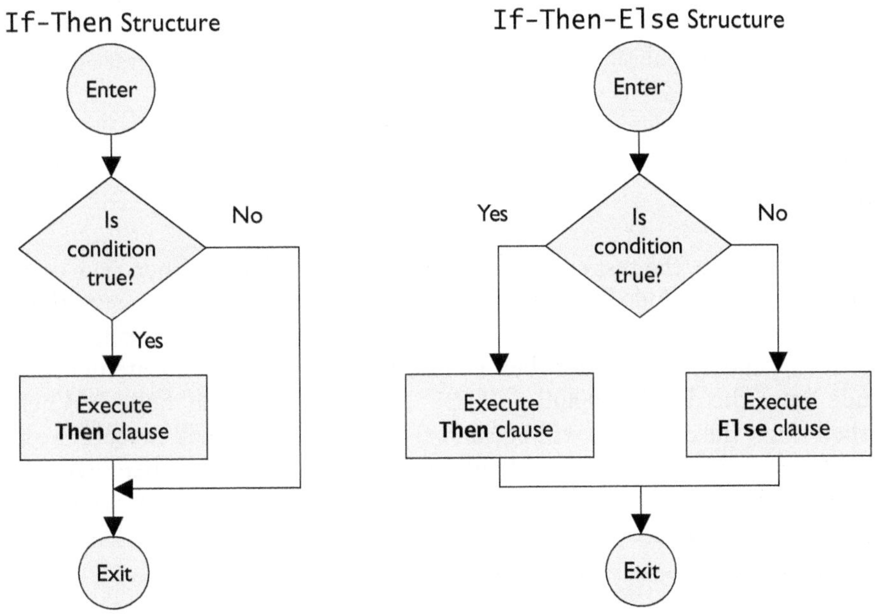

Figure 4.2 Flowchart for a multiple-alternative selection structure

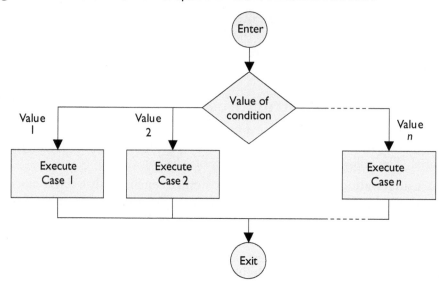

Single- and Dual-Alternative Structures

In this section, we will consider single- and dual-alternative selection structures. These are more commonly called If-Then and If-Then-Else structures.

Single-Alternative Structure: The **If-Then** Structure

The simplest type of selection structure is the If-Then, or single-alternative, structure. The general form of this selection structure is as follows:

```
If test condition Then
    Statement
    Statement
      .
      .
      .
    Statement
End If
```

In this pseudocode, the test condition is an expression that is either true or false at the time of execution. For example, if you wanted a robot to answer the door for you, you would program it to open the door when the doorbell rings. The test condition would be "Is the doorbell ringing?" and the block of statements might include "turn the doorknob and pull open the door" and "say hello." When the doorbell rings, the condition will become true and the robot will execute the statements by turning the doorknob and pulling to open the door and then saying hello. As long as the test condition is not met (the doorbell does not ring), the robot will sit quietly.

```
If doorbell rings Then
   Turn doorknob and pull door open
   Say hello
End If
```

In the pseudocode used in this book, we indicate the beginning of a selection structure with an `If` statement. The end of the structure is indicated by `End If`. In many programs, a typical test condition is `"Is Number equal to 0?"` which is `true` if the value of `Number` is `0` and is `false` otherwise. The execution would flow as follows:

- If `Number` is equal to `0`, then the test condition is `true` and the block of statements between the `If` statement and the `End If` statement (the `Then` clause) is executed.
- If the value of `Number` is anything else besides `0`, then the test condition is `false` and the block of statements between the `If` statement and the `End If` statement is skipped.

In either case, execution proceeds to the program statement following `End If`. Example 4.1 provides an illustration of the `If-Then` structure.

Example 4.1 If You Have Children, Say Yes ... If Not, Say No

Suppose you are writing a program to collect information about employees in a firm. You would like each employee to enter his/her name, address, and other personal data such as marital status, number of children, and so forth. The pseudocode for part of this program might look as follows:

```
Write "Do you have any children? Type Y for yes, N for no"
Input Response
If Response is "Y" Then
   Write "How many?"
   Input NumberChildren
End If
Write "Questionnaire is complete. Thank you."
```

What Happened?

The first two lines of this program segment ask an employee to state whether he has any children. If the response is `"yes"`, the program will ask the next question. If the response is `"no"`, there is no point in asking how many, so this question is skipped. To accomplish this, we use the `If-Then` structure.

If the test condition (`Response is "Y"`) is `true`, the `Then` clause—the statements between `If` and `End If`—is executed. If the `Response` is anything but `"Y"`, the condition is `false`, the `Then` clause is skipped, and the next statement executed is the last `Write` statement in this program segment. The flowchart shown on the left of Figure 4.1 illustrates this logic.

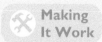

Making It Work

You might wonder why this program asks for the specific response of N if the answer is "no" since any response, other than Y will give the same result—the statements inside the If–End If block would still be skipped. Programmers always consider the users when they write programs. In this case, many users would be confused if they were asked to type Y for "yes" and any other key for "no". It makes more sense to the user to type N for "no" if Y is typed for "yes".

Making It Work

A note about writing test conditions in decision structures: Test conditions can always be written in more than one way. For example, the following program segment gives the same result as the one in Example 4.1:

```
Write "Do you have any children? Type Y for yes, N for no"
Input Response
If Response is not "N" Then
   Write "How many?"
   Input NumberChildren
End If
Write "Questionnaire is complete. Thank you."
```

It is up to the programmer to decide how to write a test condition. In many cases, it is simply a matter of personal preference, but in some situations there may be valid reasons for writing a condition in one specific way. In the example shown here, the If clause is executed if the user enters anything *except* N. In the original Example 4.1, the If clause is executed *only* if the user enters Y. Which of these two test conditions do you think is better? Why do you think so? Considerations like this often drive the way a test condition is written.

Dual-Alternative Structure: The If-Then-Else Structure

The If-Then-Else, or dual-alternative, structure has the following general form:

```
If test condition Then
   Statement
   .
   .
   .
   Statement
Else
   Statement
   .
   .
   .
   Statement
End If
```

Here's how this structure works.

- If the test condition is true, then the block of statements between the If statement and the word Else (the Then clause) is executed.
- If the test condition is false, then the block of statements between Else and End If (the Else clause) is executed.

In either case, execution proceeds to the program statement following End If. Example 4.2 provides an illustration of the If-Then-Else structure.

Example 4.2 **Profit or Loss: An If-Then-Else Structure**

As an example of an If-Then-Else structure, suppose that part of a program is to input the costs incurred and revenue earned from producing and selling a certain product and then display the resulting profit or loss. To do this, we need statements that do the following:

- Compute the difference between revenue and cost, which gives us the profit or loss
- Describe this quantity as a profit if revenue is greater than cost (i.e., if the difference is positive) and as a loss, otherwise

The following pseudocode does the job. The flowchart shown in Figure 4.3 is the graphical representation of this example.

```
 1  Write "Enter total cost:"
 2  Input Cost
 3  Write "Enter total revenue:"
 4  Input Revenue
 5  Set Amount = Revenue - Cost
 6  If Amount > 0 Then
 7     Set Profit = Amount
 8     Write "The profit is $" + Profit
 9  Else
10     Set Loss = -Amount
11     Write "The loss is $" + Loss
12  End If
```

What Happened?

The first four statements in this program segment (lines 1–4) prompt for and input the total cost and revenue for the product. We compute the difference between these quantities and store the result in Amount (line 5). The result will be a profit if Amount is a positive number and a loss otherwise. So we want to check to see if the value of Amount is positive, in which case we can proudly display a profit, or if it is negative and we are forced to report a loss. Our test condition, Amount > 0, in the If statement (line 6) is evaluated as follows:

- If this condition is true, the Then clause

```
Set Profit = Amount
Write "The profit is $" + Profit
```

is executed and the profit is displayed.

- If this condition is `false`, the `Else` clause

```
Set Loss = -Amount
Write "The loss is $" + Loss
```

    is executed.

Why is `Loss = -Amount`? `Loss` is set equal to the negative of `Amount` (so `Loss` becomes a positive number) and then this amount is displayed. The following examples illustrate what would happen in two instances of input values to this little program:

- If the input values are `Cost = 3000` and `Revenue = 4000`, then `Amount = 1000` and the output is as follows: `The profit is $1000`.
- However, if the input values are `Cost = 5000` and `Revenue = 2000`, then `Amount = -3000`. The line that sets `Loss = -Amount` simply changes the sign of `Amount` and stores that value (now a positive number) in `Loss`. If we did not change the sign of `Amount`, the output would read: `The loss is $-3000`. A loss is already a negative number so a loss of a negative number would make no sense. By changing the value of `Amount` from a negative value to a positive value, our output now makes sense: `The loss is $3000`.

Figure 4.3 Flowchart for profit or loss program shown in Example 4.2

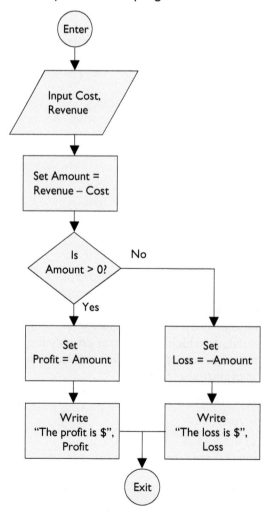

What would happen if Amount was exactly zero? For example, if the input values are Cost = 3000 and Revenue = 3000, then Amount = 0. In this example, our test condition ensures that there is profit if Amount > 0 and that there is a loss in any other case. But this is clearly not true if Amount = 0 exactly. The display should say something like "You broke even this year." We could deal with this possibility with a multiple-alternative structure. Multiple-alternative structures are discussed later in this chapter.

●

Format If-Then and If-Then-Else Structures for Easy Readability

To make it easier to read the pseudocode (or code) for an If-Then or If-Then-Else structure, indent the statements that make up the Then and Else clauses. Moreover, in the program code, it is always a good idea to precede the structure with a step comment that explains its purpose. ●

Self Check for Section 4.1

4.1 Name the three types of selection structures.

4.2 What is the output of code corresponding to the following pseudocode if
   a. Amount = 5?
   b. Amount = -1?
```
If Amount > 0 Then
   Write Amount
End If
   Write Amount
```

4.3 What is the output of code corresponding to the following pseudocode if
   a. Amount = 5?
   b. Amount = -1?
```
If Amount > 0 Then
   Write Amount
Else
   Set Amount = -Amount
   Write Amount
End If
```

4.4 For the following pseudocode:
```
If Number > 0 Then
   Write "Yes"
End If
If Number = 0 Then
   Write "No"
End If
If Number < 0 Then
   Write "No"
End If
```
   a. What is the output of the corresponding code if Number = 10? If Number = -10?

      b. Write a single `If-Then-Else` structure that has the same effect as the given pseudocode.

      c. Create a flowchart for the given pseudocode.

4.2 Relational and Logical Operators

As you have seen in Section 4.1, decision making involves testing a condition. To help construct these conditions, we use relational and logical operators. In this section, we will discuss these operators.

Relational Operators

Previously, we gave examples of selection structures that included conditions such as `Amount < 0` and `Amount > 0`. The symbols that appear in these conditions are known as **relational operators**. There are six standard relational operators, as shown in Table 4.1, together with the symbols we use to represent them.

Table 4.1 Relational operators

Operator	Description
<	is less than
<=	is less than or equal to
>	is greater than
>=	is greater than or equal to
==	is equal to (is same as)
!=	is not equal to

A Little More Explanation About Relational Operators

At this point, we should pause and examine these relational operators for a moment. Several of them are clear and uncomplicated, but some of them are either specific to programming or have notation that may be new to you. You are probably familiar with the greater than symbol (>) and the less than symbol (<) from math classes, but the other symbols deserve some comment.

There is no single symbol to represent the concepts *less than or equal to* or *greater than or equal to* on a keyboard. These concepts are represented by a combination of symbols. That's why <= represents *less than or equal to* and >= represents *greater than or equal to*. This notation will be used in pseudocode throughout this text.

Similarly, there is no single symbol to represent the concept *not equal to*, so again, a combination of two symbols is used. In this textbook, following the lead of many programming languages, we will use the symbol != to represent the not equal operator.

Finally, special attention needs to be paid to the *equals sign.* In programming, there is a distinction between setting one thing equal to the value of another and asking the question, "Is this thing equal to this other thing?" When we assign the value of one variable to something else, we use the equals sign (=). In this case, the equals sign is used as an **assignment operator**. When we compare the value of one thing with another, we mean "is the value of the thing on the left the same as the value of the thing on the right?" This is called a **comparison operator**. In our pseudocode, as in many programming languages, we use the symbol == (a double equals sign) when comparing the value of a variable with another variable, value, or expression.

The Comparison Operator versus the Assignment Operator

In pseudocode, when we write Set Variable1 = Variable2, we are actually putting the value of Variable2 into Variable1. For example, if Cost contains the value 50 and SalePrice contains the value 30, after the statement Cost = SalePrice, both Cost and SalePrice will contain the value 30. The value of 50 is gone.

However, if we want to check to see if the value of Cost is the same as the value of SalePrice, we use the comparison operator. In some programming languages (as in this textbook's pseudocode), we would write Cost == SalePrice. To the computer program, this would translate as, "Is the value of Cost the same as the value of SalePrice?" In this case, if Cost is 50 and SalePrice is 30, the answer is no. The two variables, Cost and SalePrice retain their initial values. *Note:* if you use RAPTOR, refer to Section 4.7 to see how RAPTOR handles the comparison operator.

This distinction may not have serious consequences as you continue through this text and write pseudocode, but it can wreak havoc on a program when you begin to write a code in a specific programming language. Be aware of this important distinction as you go through the examples.

The relational operators <, >, <=, >=, ==, and != can be used to compare numeric data as well as string data. We will describe how these operators are used with strings in Section 4.3. Examples 4.3 and 4.4 illustrate the use of relational operators with numbers.

Example 4.3 **Using Relational Operators on Numbers**

Let Number1 = 3, Number2 = -1, Number3 = 3, and Number4 = 26. Then, all of the following expressions are true:

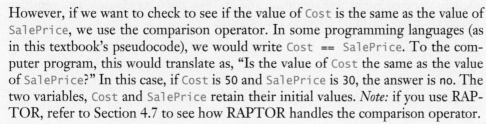

(a) Number1 != Number2   (b) Number2 < Number1

(c) Number3 == Number1   (d) Number2 < Number4

(e) Number4 >= Number1   (f) Number3 <= Number1

What Happened?

- To see that the conditions in (a) and (b) are true, substitute 3 for Number1 and -1 for Number2.
- In (c), since Number3 has the value of 3 and Number1 has the value of 3, these two variables are the same.

- In (d) it is true that the value of Number2 (-1) is less than 26, the value of Number4.
- Both (e) and (f) are true. Number4 has the value of 26, which is definitely greater than Number1 (3). The relational operator, >=, asks, "is the value of Number4 greater than *or* equal to the value of Number1?" It is true if *either* Number4 is greater than Number1 *or* if Number4 is the same as Number1. Example (f) illustrates this; this condition is also true since Number3 and Number1 have the same value.

Example 4.4 Two Ways to Obtain a Positive Result

The program segment below on the right-hand side was obtained from the one on the left by reversing its test condition and its Then and Else clauses. The resulting pseudocode has the same effect as the original.

```
If Number >= 0 Then                    If Number < 0 Then
   Write Number                           Set PositiveNumber = -Number
Else                                      Write PositiveNumber
   Set PositiveNumber = -Number        Else
   Write PositiveNumber                   Write Number
End If                                  End If
```

What Happened?

What do both these program segments do? In the program segment on the left, the first line asks, "Is Number greater than or equal to zero?" If this condition is true, then the number is displayed as is. If this condition is not true, then the program continues to the Else clause. If the condition is not true, it means that Number must be less than zero (a negative number). The statements that are then executed (the Else clause) change Number (a negative number) to a positive number by setting PositiveNumber equal to the negative of a negative number. Then the new value, a positive number, is displayed.

In the program segment on the right, the first line tests the opposite condition. It asks if Number is negative (less than zero). If this is true, then Number is converted to a positive number in the same way as in the example on the left. If Number is not less than zero, then it can only be either zero or greater than zero. So the program skips to the Else clause and displays the number as is.

Both program segments take a number and display the magnitude (or absolute value) of that number. It does not matter which condition we test for first in this example.

Documentation Is Always Important

Often a program can achieve the desired results in one of several ways. The decision about which code to use is up to you, the programmer. While many of our examples are short and simple, real programs may be much longer and more complicated. Professional programmers often work on code written by other people. It is easier for a programmer to edit someone else's code if the programmer knows what the segment is designed to do. This is one reason why it is so important to use documentation in the form of comments to explain what your code is doing.   ●

Logical Operators

Logical operators are used to create compound conditions from given simple conditions. This is illustrated in Examples 4.5 and 4.6, which introduce the most important logical operators—OR, AND, and NOT.

Example 4.5 **Save Time and Space with the OR Operator**

The following program segments are equivalent; each displays the message OK if the number input is either less than 5 or greater than 10. The segment on the right uses the logical operator OR to help perform this task.

```
Input Number                    Input Number
If Number < 5 Then              If (Number < 5) OR (Number > 10) Then
  Write "OK"                       Write "OK"
End If                          End If
If Number > 10 Then
  Write "OK"
End If
```

In the second program segment, the compound condition (Number < 5) OR (Number > 10) is true if either the simple condition, Number < 5 or the other simple condition, Number > 10, is true. It is false if and only if both simple conditions are false.

The AND operator also creates a compound condition from two simple ones. Here, however, the compound condition is true if and only if *both* simple conditions are true. For example, the expression (A > B) AND (Response == "Y") is true if and only if A is greater than B *and* Response is equal to "Y". If A is not greater than B *or* if Response is not equal to "Y", then the compound condition is false.

The NOT operator, unlike OR and AND, acts upon a single given condition. The resulting condition formed by using NOT is true if and only if the given condition is false. For example, NOT(A < 6) is true if A is not less than 6; it is false if A is less than 6. Thus, NOT(A < 6) is equivalent to the condition A >= 6.

Example 4.6 **Compounding Conditions with Logical Operators**

Suppose Number = 1. Is each of the following expressions true or false?

(a) ((2 * Number) + 1 == 3) AND (Number > 2)

(b) NOT (2 * Number == 0)

- In (a) the first simple condition is true, but the second is false (Number is not greater than 2). Hence, the compound AND condition is false.
- In (b) since 2 * Number = 2, 2 * Number is not equal to 0. Thus, the condition 2 * Number == 0 is false, and the given condition is true.

Truth Tables for the **OR**, **AND**, and **NOT** Operators

The action of the operators OR, AND, and NOT can be summarized by the use of **truth tables**. Let X and Y represent simple conditions. Then for the values of X and Y given on each line (`true` or `false`) on the two leftmost columns of the following table, the resulting truth values of X OR Y, X AND Y, and NOT X are as listed on the right.

Table 4.2 Truth Tables for the OR, AND, and NOT operators

X	Y	X OR Y	X AND Y	NOT X
true	true	true	true	false
true	false	true	false	false
false	true	true	false	true
false	false	false	false	true

Example 4.7 illustrates how logical operators can be useful in programming.

Example 4.7 **Working Overtime ... or Maybe Not**

In a certain firm suppose that the following is true:

- Workers who earn less than $10 per hour are paid "time-and-a-half" (i.e., 1.5 times their normal rate of pay) for overtime hours worked.
- Workers who earn $10 or more per hour are paid their regular hourly rate regardless of the number of hours they work.
- In this firm, working more than 40 hours per week is considered overtime.

The following program segment computes a worker's weekly earnings (TotalPay) based on his or her hourly wage (PayRate) and number of hours worked (Hours).

```
1  If (PayRate < 10) AND (Hours > 40) Then
2     Set OvertimeHours = Hours - 40
3     Set OvertimePay = OvertimeHours * 1.5 * PayRate
4     Set TotalPay = 40 * PayRate + OvertimePay
5  Else
6     Set TotalPay = Hours * PayRate
7  End If
```

What Happened?

To see that this program segment works correctly, we need to try it out using sample values as follows:

- Suppose that a worker earns $8 per hour and works 50 hours. Then PayRate = 8 and Hours = 50, so both conditions in the If statement are `true`, and thus the compound AND condition is `true` as well. As a result, the Then clause is executed (and the Else clause is skipped), setting the following:

```
OvertimeHours = 50 - 40 = 10
OvertimePay = 10 * 1.5 * 8 = 120
TotalPay = 40 * 8 + 120 = 440
```

- However, if a worker earns more than $10 per hour or works less than 40 hours per week, then at least one of the conditions in the `If` statement is `false`, and thus the compound `AND` condition is `false`. In this case, the `Then` clause is skipped and the `Else` clause is executed, which computes the employee pay in the usual way, ignoring overtime pay.

Compounding the Compound Condition Issue

As you begin to understand more about programming, you will find that, while each language has specific and strict syntax rules, not every aspect of writing programs is strictly defined. There is almost always more than one way to solve a programming problem. This is especially true when writing compound conditions, as we have seen for conditional statements using relational operators as follows:

```
10 < 12 is the same as 12 >= 10
6,895 >= 0 is the same as 0 <= 6,895
```

And the same can be true of compound conditions. For example,

Let A = 1 and let B = 2, then
```
    If A == 1 AND B == 2 Then
      Execute Task 1
    Else
      Execute Task 2
    End If
```

will produce the same result as

```
    If A != 1 OR B != 2 Then
      Execute Task 2
    Else
      Execute Task 1
    End If
```

Example 4.8 demonstrates how we can get the same result as in Example 4.7, using an alternate version.

Example 4.8 Overtime or No Overtime, Revisited

In this example, the `If` statement checks to see if the employee is eligible for over-time pay, as it did in Example 4.7. However, this time, if either part of the compound condition is `true` (i.e., if the employee's pay rate is greater than $10 per hour or the employee has worked fewer than 40 hours), then a calculation of pay is made without overtime.

This compound condition uses an `OR` operator. Therefore, the only way it will fail is if both parts are `false`. This means an employee would have to both make less than $10 per hour and work more than 40 hours. In that case—and only in that case—would the `Else` clause be executed and pay be calculated with overtime.

From the pseudocode you can see that this accomplishes the same thing as Example 4.7 but uses a different test condition.

```
1  If (PayRate >= 10) OR (Hours <= 40) Then
2    Set TotalPay = Hours * PayRate
3  Else
```

```
4      Set OvertimeHours = Hours - 40
5      Set OvertimePay = OvertimeHours * 1.5 * PayRate
6      Set TotalPay = 40 * PayRate + OvertimePay
7   End If
```

Figure 4.4 shows the flowcharts for Examples 4.7 and 4.8. These flowcharts demonstrate how it's possible to use different compound conditions to accomplish the same programming task.

Before we move to the next section, we will use Example 4.7 once more to illustrate the differences and similarities among programming languages. The pseudocode shown in Example 4.7 will be used to develop true program code for four popular

Figure 4.4 Flowcharts for two versions of the overtime pay calculation problem

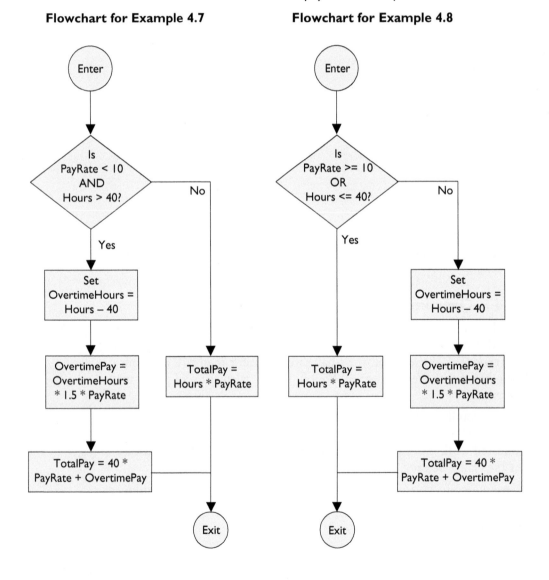

programming languages—C++, Java, Visual Basic, and JavaScript. In all the code samples, the variable names have been kept exactly the same as the pseudocode. It should be noted that different programming languages have specific conventions for variable names, but for the purposes of comparison, and to enable you to see the similarities and differences more clearly, all variable names remain the same here.

Calculating a Paycheck in C++ and Java

Making It Work

The following code demonstrates the use of the If-Then-Else structure in both C++ and Java. It corresponds to the pseudocode shown in Example 4.7. While there are syntactical and other differences between C++ and Java, the code for this program segment is identical. This code segment presumes that the following variables have been declared as floating point numbers (type double in C++ and Java): PayRate, Hours, OvertimeHours, OvertimePay, and TotalPay. It also presumes that values have been input for PayRate and Hours.

```
1   if(PayRate < 10 && Hours > 40)
2   {
3      OvertimeHours = Hours - 40;
4      OvertimePay = OvertimeHours * (1.5 * PayRate);
5      TotalPay = (40 * PayRate) + OvertimePay;
6   }
7   else
8   {
9      TotalPay = Hours * PayRate;
10  }
```

The following things can be noted about this C++ and Java code:

- Each executable statement ends with a semicolon
- The symbol for the AND operator is &&
- The compound condition is enclosed in parentheses

Calculating a Paycheck in Visual Basic

Making It Work

The following code demonstrates the use of the If-Then-Else structure in Visual Basic. It corresponds to the pseudocode shown in Example 4.7. This code segment presumes that the following variables have been declared as floating point numbers (type single in Visual Basic): PayRate, Hours, OvertimeHours, OvertimePay, and TotalPay. It also presumes that values have been input for PayRate and Hours.

```
1   If PayRate < 10 AND Hours > 40 Then
2      OvertimeHours = Hours - 40
3      OvertimePay = OvertimeHours * 1.5 * PayRate
4      TotalPay = 40 * PayRate + OvertimePay
5   Else
6      TotalPay = Hours * PayRate
7   End If
```

The following things can be noted about this Visual Basic code:

- Semicolons are not needed at the end of executable statements.
- The If-Then-Else structure must have an End If statement.
- The compound condition does not need to be enclosed in parentheses.

 **Making It Work**

Calculating a Paycheck in JavaScript

The following code demonstrates the use of the If-Then-Else structure in JavaScript. It would probably be called from a web page and the results displayed on the web page. It corresponds to the pseudocode shown in Example 4.7. This code segment presumes that the following variables have been declared as floating point numbers, which require the use of the parseFloat() JavaScript function (not shown): PayRate, Hours, OvertimeHours, OvertimePay, and TotalPay. It also presumes that values have been input for PayRate and Hours.

```
1  if(PayRate < 10 && Hours > 40)
2  {
3     OvertimeHours = Hours - 40;
4     OvertimePay = OvertimeHours * (1.5 * PayRate);
5     TotalPay = (40 * PayRate) + OvertimePay;
6  }
7  else
8  {
9     TotalPay = Hours * PayRate;
10 }
```

You may note that this code is virtually identical to both C++ and Java. The differences would become apparent when each code snippet is utilized in a larger program. The JavaScript code would probably be executed by clicking on a button on a web page. You may also notice that Visual Basic code is the most different from the other three. JavaScript, Java, and C++ descended from the same original language, while Visual Basic was developed independently.

Hierarchy of Operations

In a single given condition, there may be arithmetic, relational, and logical operators. If parentheses are present, we perform the operations within parentheses first. In the absence of parentheses, the arithmetic operations are done first (in their usual order), then any relational operation, and finally, NOT, AND, and OR, in that order. This hierarchy of operations is summarized in Table 4.3 and is illustrated in Example 4.9.

Table 4.3 Hierarchy of order of operations

Description	Symbol
Arithmetic Operators are evaluated first in the order listed	
First: Parentheses	( )
Second: Exponents	∧
Third: Multiplication/Division/Modulus	*, /, %
Fourth: Addition/Subtraction	+ -
Relational Operators are evaluated second, and all relational operators have the same precedence	
Less than	<
Less than or equal to	<=
Greater than	>
Greater than or equal to	>=
The same as, equal to	==
Not the same as	!=
Logical Operators are evaluated last in the order listed	
First: NOT	! or NOT or not
Second: AND	&& or AND or and
Third: OR	|| or OR or or

More Symbols

In this text, we will use the short words, OR, AND, and NOT to represent the three logical operators. However, some programming languages use symbols to represent these operators. The corresponding symbols are shown in Table 4.3.

Example 4.9 **Combining Logical and Relational Operators**

Let Q = 3 and let R = 5. Is the following expression true or false?

```
NOT Q > 3 OR R < 3 AND Q - R <= 0
```

Keeping in mind the hierarchy of operations, in particular, the fact that among logical operators, NOT is performed first, AND is second, and OR is last, let's insert parentheses to explicitly show the order in which the operations are to be performed:

```
(NOT(Q > 3)) OR ((R < 3) AND ((Q - R) <= 0))
```

We evaluate the simple conditions first and find that Q > 3 is false, R < 3 is false, and (Q - R) <= 0 is true. Then, by substituting these values (true or false) into the given expression and performing the logical operations, we arrive at the answer. We can show this is by means of an evaluation chart as follows:

```
Given:    (NOT(Q > 3))    OR    ((R < 3)    AND    ((Q - R) <= 0))
Step 1:   (NOT(false))    OR    ((false)    AND    (true))
Step 2:   (true)          OR    (false)
Step 3:   true
```

Thus, the given relational expression is `true`.

Making It Work

The Boolean Type

Most programming languages allow variables to be of logical (also called `Boolean`) type. Such a variable may only take one of two values, `true` or `false`. For example, we can declare a variable, say `Answer`, to be of `Boolean` type and then use it in a statement anywhere that a value of `true` or `false` is valid, such as the following C++ snippet:

```
bool Answer;
Answer = true;
if(Answer) cout << "Congratulations!";
```

This statement means: If the value of `Answer` is true, then write `"Congratulations!"` on the screen. The following C++ statement is equivalent to the `if` statement shown above and may be clearer:

```
if (Answer == "true") cout << "Congratulations!";
```

Self Check for Section 4.2

4.5 Replace the blank by one of the words: *arithmetic, relational,* or *logical.*

a. `<=` is a(n) _____ operator.

b. `+` is a(n) _____ operator.

c. `OR` is a(n) _____ operator.

4.6 Indicate whether each of the following expressions is `true` or `false`.

a. `8 <= 8`

b. `8 != 8`

4.7 Indicate whether each of the following expressions is `true` or `false`.

a. `8 = 9 OR 8 < 9`

b. `3 < 5 AND 5 > 7`

c. `4 != 6 AND 4 != 7`

d. `6 == 6 OR 6 != 6`

4.8 Let `X = 1` and let `Y = 2`. Indicate whether each of the following expressions is `true` or `false`

a. `X >= X OR Y >= X`

b. `X > X AND Y > X`

c. X > Y OR X > 0 AND Y < 0

d. NOT(NOT X == 0 AND NOT Y == 0)

4.9 Write a program segment that inputs a number `Number` and displays the word `Correct` if `Number` is between 0 and 100. This means `Number` must be both greater than 0 and less than 100.

4.3 ASCII Code and Comparing Strings

In Chapter 1, we loosely defined a character as any symbol that can be typed on the keyboard. These symbols include special characters like asterisks (*), ampersands (&), @ signs and the like, as well as letters, digits, punctuation marks, and blank spaces. In this section, we give a more precise definition of a character and discuss how characters are represented in a computer's memory. We also describe how the relational operators <, <=, >, !=, ==, and >= can be applied to any string of characters.

Representing Characters With Numbers

Strictly speaking, a **character** is any symbol that is recognized as valid by the programming language you are using. Consequently, what constitutes a character varies from language to language. Nevertheless, most programming languages recognize a common core of about 100 basic characters including all those that can be typed on the keyboard.

All data, including characters, are stored in the computer's memory in a binary form—as bit patterns; that is, as sequences of zeros and ones. Thus, to make use of character and string variables, a programming language must use a scheme to associate each character with a number. The standard correspondence for a basic set of 128 characters is given by the **American Standard Code for Information Interchange (ASCII code)**. The acronym ASCII is pronounced "askey."

Under this coding scheme, each character is associated with a number from 0 to 127. For example, the uppercase (capital) letters have ASCII codes from 65 ("A") to 90 ("Z"); the digits have codes from 48 ("0") to 57 ("9"), and the ASCII code for the blank (the character that results from pressing the keyboard's spacebar) is 32. Table 4.4 lists the characters corresponding to ASCII codes from 32 to 127; codes 0 to 31 represent special symbols or actions, such as sounding a beep (ASCII 7) or issuing a carriage return (ASCII 13) and are not shown here.

Thus, to store a character string in the computer's internal memory, the programming language software can simply place the ASCII codes for its individual characters in successive memory locations. For example, when program code corresponding to the following pseudocode:

```
Set Name = "Sam"
```

is executed, the ASCII codes for S, a, and m (83, 97, and 109, respectively) are stored in consecutive memory locations. These numbers, as you recall, are stored in binary, as a series of zeros and ones. Each location uses 1 byte—8 bits—of memory. Then, when the string variable `Name` is referenced in the program, the programming language interprets the memory contents as ASCII codes and displays the string properly.

Table 4.4 The ASCII codes from 32 to 127

Code	Character	Code	Character	Code	Character	Code	Character	Code	Character	Code	Character
32	[blank]	48	0	64	@	80	P	96	`	112	p
33	!	49	1	65	A	81	Q	97	a	113	q
34	"	50	2	66	B	82	R	98	b	114	r
35	#	51	3	67	C	83	S	99	c	115	s
36	$	52	4	68	D	84	T	100	d	116	t
37	%	53	5	69	E	85	U	101	e	117	u
38	&	54	6	70	F	86	V	102	f	118	v
39	'	55	7	71	G	87	W	103	g	119	w
40	(	56	8	72	H	88	X	104	h	120	x
41	)	57	9	73	I	89	Y	105	i	121	y
42	*	58	:	74	J	90	Z	106	j	122	z
43	+	59	;	75	K	91	[	107	k	123	{
44	,	60	<	76	L	92	\	108	l	124	|
45	–	61	=	77	M	93	]	109	m	125	}
46	.	62	>	78	N	94	^	110	n	126	~
47	/	63	?	79	O	95	_	111	o	127	[delete]

Consider the string "31.5" and the floating point number 31.5. These expressions look similar, but from a programming standpoint they are quite different.

- The number 31.5 is stored in memory as the binary equivalent of 31.5. Moreover, since it is a number, it can be added to, subtracted from, divided by, or multiplied by another number.
- The string "31.5" is stored in memory by placing the ASCII codes for 3, 1, ., and 5 in consecutive storage locations. Since "31.5" is a string, we cannot perform arithmetic operations on it, but we can concatenate it with another string.

Now you understand why it is necessary to declare a variable with a data type!

Ordering Arbitrary Strings

We have seen how to use the relational operators, equal to (==) and not equal to (!=). With the aid of the ASCII code, all six relational operators may be applied to arbitrary strings of characters.

Notice that we can order the set of characters based on the numerical order of their ASCII codes. For example, "*" < "3" because the ASCII codes for these characters are 42 and 51, and 42 < 51, respectively. Similarly, "8" < "h" and "A" > " " (the blank). Therefore, under the ASCII code ordering, the following is true:

- Letters are in alphabetical order and all uppercase letters precede all lower-case letters.
- Digits (viewed as characters) retain their natural order. For example, "1" < "2", "2" < "3", and so forth.
- The blank precedes all digits and letters.

Examples 4.10 and 4.11 illustrate how ASCII codes are used to compare string data.

Example 4.10 **Comparing Characters**

All of the following conditions are true:

(a) "a" > "B"

(b) "1" <= "}"

(c) "1" >= ")"

To check that each condition holds, just find the ASCII codes for the two characters involved (Table 4.4) and verify that the ASCII codes are in the proper order.

Two strings, S1 and S2, are equal (S1 == S2) if they have exactly the same characters in exactly the same order; they are not equal (S1 != S2) otherwise. To determine which of the two unequal strings comes first, use the following procedure:

1. Scan the strings from left to right, stopping at the first position for which the corresponding characters differ or when one of the strings ends.
2. If two corresponding characters differ before either string ends, the ordering of these characters determines the ordering of the given strings.
3. If one string ends before any pair of corresponding characters differ, then the shorter string precedes the longer one.

When applying this procedure, the following is true:

- If string S1 precedes string S2, then S1 < S2.
- If string S1 follows string S2, then S1 > S2.

Example 4.11 **True (or False) Comparisons**

Is each of the following expressions true or false?

(a) "Word" != "word"

(b) "Ann" == "Ann "

(c) "*?/!" < "*?,3"

(d) "Ann" <= "Anne"

- In (a) the two strings do not consist of the same characters. The first contains an uppercase W, which is a different character from the lowercase w. Hence, the strings are not equal, and this expression is true.
- In (b) again the strings do not consist of the same characters. The second string contains a blank at the end, while the first does not. Hence, this expression is false.
- For (c) the first pair of characters that differ occurs in the third position. Since "/" has ASCII code 47 and "," has code 44, the first string is greater than the second. Therefore, this expression is false.
- For (d) the first string ends before any pair of characters differ. Hence, the first string is less than the second, and this expression is true.

Beware of Strings of Digits

A character string may consist solely of digits, say "123", in which case it looks like a number. However, "123" is *not* the same as 123. The first is a string constant, while the second is a numeric constant. Remember: The numeric constant is stored in memory by storing the binary equivalent of 123, but the string constant is stored in memory by successively storing the ASCII codes for 1, 2, and 3. Moreover, since we have no mechanism for comparing numbers with strings, if the variable (Num) is a numeric variable, statements like the following:

```
Num == "123"
```

make no sense and will lead to an error message if used in a program.

There is another, more subtle, problem that occurs when we compare strings of digits. Following the procedure given above for ordering strings, we see that the following statements:

```
"123" < "25"    and    "24.0" != "24"
```

are true statements (check for yourself!), even though, on the surface, neither inequality seems reasonable.

Self Check for Section 4.3

4.10 Indicate whether each of the following statements is true or false.
   a. Two characters are equal if their ASCII codes are equal.
   b. If string A is longer than string B, then A is always greater than B.

4.11 Indicate whether each of the following statements is true or false.
   a. "m" <= "M"
   b. "*" > "?"

4.12 Indicate whether each of the following statements is true or false.
   a. "John" < "John "
   b. "???" <= "??"

4.13 Write a program segment that inputs two strings and displays the one that comes first under the ASCII code ordering.

4.4 **Selecting from Several Alternatives**

The If-Then-Else (dual-alternative) structure selects, based on the value of its test condition, one of the two alternative blocks of statements. Sometimes, however, a program must handle decisions having more than two options. In these cases, we use a multiple-alternative selection structure. As you will see, this structure can be implemented in several different ways. To contrast the different methods, we will use each method to solve the same problem. The problem involves a selection structure with four alternatives.

Imagine that you were recently hired as a Mystery Shopper and your task is to rate products. You test each product and assign it a score, from 1 to 10, based on your opinion of the product. But the report you are required to submit to your employer states that you must give each product a letter grade. So you decide to develop a program that will change your number rating into a letter grade and will display the new ratings. We will write a program segment that translates your numerical score (an integer from 1 to 10) into a letter grade according to the following rules:

- If the score is 10, the rating is "A."
- If the score is 8 or 9, the rating is "B."
- If the score is 6 or 7, the rating is "C."
- If the score is below 6, the rating is "D."

Using If Structures

You could implement a multiple-alternative structure by using several applications of If-Then or If-Then-Else statements. The simplest technique makes use of a sequence of If-Then statements in which each test condition corresponds to one of the alternatives. Example 4.12 illustrates this technique.

Example 4.12 **Assigning Ratings—the Long Way**

```
1   Declare Score As Integer
2   Declare Rating As Character
3   Write "Enter score: "
4   Input Score
5   If Score == 10 Then
6      Set Rating = "A"
7   End If
8   If (Score == 8) OR (Score == 9) Then
9      Set Rating = "B"
10  End If
11  If (Score == 6) OR (Score == 7) Then
12     Set Rating = "C"
13  End If
14  If (Score >= 1) AND (Score <= 5) Then
15     Set Rating = "D"
16  End If
```

This technique is straightforward and involves pseudocode (and corresponding program code) that is easy to understand. However, it is tedious to write and is inefficient. Regardless of the value of Score, the program must evaluate all four test conditions. Figure 4.5 contains a flowchart showing the flow of execution in this example.

Figure 4.5 Using a sequence of If-Then statements

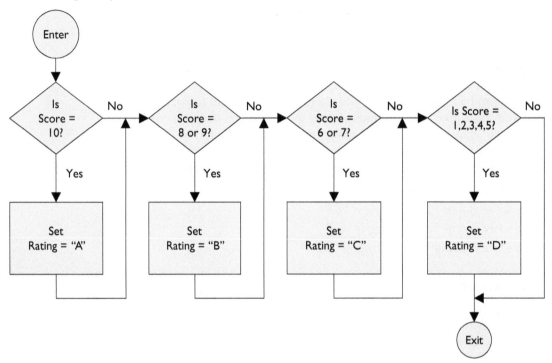

Another way to implement a multiple-alternative structure is to **nest** If-Then-Else structures. When one structure is nested in another, this means the entire inner structure occurs within an outer structure. This technique is illustrated in Example 4.13.

Example 4.13 **Assigning Ratings, the Nested If-Then-Else Way**

This program segment uses nested If-Then-Else structures to solve the rating assignment problem. Although the resulting code will be more efficient than that shown in Example 4.12, it's still long and tedious and is also more difficult to follow. The flowchart shown in Figure 4.6 should help you untangle the flow of execution in the following pseudocode:

```
1  Declare Score As Integer
2  Declare Rating As Character
3  Write "Enter score: "
4  Input Score
5  If Score == 10 Then
6     Set Rating = "A"
7  Else
```

```
8     If (Score == 8) OR (Score == 9) Then
9        Set Rating = "B"
10    Else
11       If (Score == 6) OR (Score == 7) Then
12          Set Rating = "C"
13       Else
14          Set Rating = "D"
15       End If
16    End If
17  End If
```

What Happened?

Let's take a test value of Score and see how this pseudocode works. You have just tried out a new coffee pot and given it a rating of 8. The value of Score is now equal to 8. Since Score is not 10, the first statement (Set Rating = "A") is skipped and the first Else clause is executed. The test condition (Score == 8) OR (Score == 9)

Figure 4.6 Using a nested If-Then-Else structure

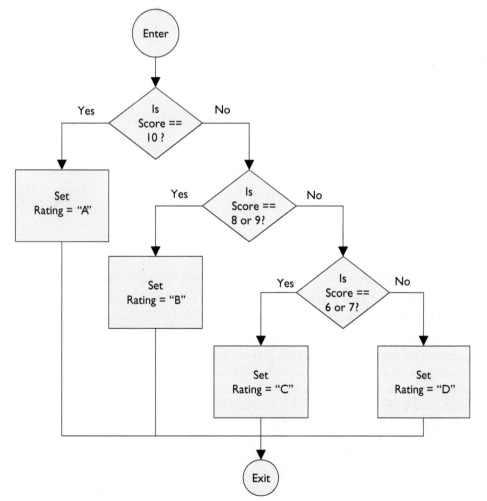

is evaluated and found to be true. Thus, the Then clause of this particular structure is executed, Rating is set equal to "B", the next two Else clauses are skipped, and execution of all If-Then-Else structures is complete. Notice that unlike the technique used in Example 4.12, this program does not always have to evaluate all test conditions to accomplish the rating assignment.

Using Case-Like Statements

So far, we have demonstrated two ways (both using If structures) to create a multiple-alternative selection structure. To make it easier to code multiple-alternative structures, many programming languages contain a statement, usually called **Case** or **Switch**, specifically designed for this purpose. This statement contains a single test expression that determines which block of code is to be executed. A typical Case statement looks as follows:

```
Select Case Of    test expression to be evaluated
   Case 1st value:

        Statements
        Break out of Cases
   Case 2nd value:

        Statements
        Break out of Cases
   Case 3rd value:

        Statements
        Break out of Cases

    .
    .        All the rest of the values that can be chosen
    .

   Case nth value:

        Statements
        Break out of Cases
   Default:

        Statements    to execute if test expression does not match any of the above
   End Case
```

The Action of a **Case** Statement

Here's how this statement works: The test expression is evaluated and its value is compared with the first Case value. If there is a match, the first block of statements is executed and the structure is exited. If there is no match, the value of the test expression is compared with the second value. If there is a match here, the second block of statements is executed and the structure is exited. This process continues until either a match for the test expression value is found or until the end of the Cases is encountered. The programmer can either write a Default statement—something that will happen if the test expression does not match with any of the Cases, or the programmer can allow no action to be taken. After either the Default or the end of all the Cases, the structure is exited. The Case statement works only when the test expression is an integer or a single character. Use of the Case statement is illustrated in Examples 4.14 and 4.15.

Example 4.14 **Assigning Ratings, Using a Case Statement**

Let's return to the rating assignment problem. Here is the third solution. The flow-chart shown in Figure 4.7 shows the flow of the Case structure, as used in this program segment.

```
1   Declare Score As Integer
2   Declare Rating As Character
3   Write "Enter score: "
4   Input Score
5   Select Case Of Score
6     Case 10:
7       Set Rating = "A"
8       Break
9     Case 9:
10    Case 8:
11      Set Rating = "B"
12      Break
13    Case 7:
14    Case 6:
15      Set Rating = "C"
16      Break
17    Case 5:
18    Case 4:
19    Case 3:
20    Case 2:
21    Case 1:
22      Set Rating = "D"
23      Break
24  End Case
25  Write Rating
```

What Happened?

When this Case statement is executed, Score is evaluated and the Cases are examined. If a constant equal to Score is found in one of the Cases, the corresponding statement is executed. To see what happens in the Case structure more clearly, let's walk a test value through the program. As a Mystery Shopper, you have been asked to rate a new style of backpack. The quality of the material and the size of the backpack are wonderful, but the straps hurt your shoulders so you give it a Score of 7. The following happens:

- Line 5 says that the value of the variable (Score) will be compared to the values listed in the cases.
- Line 6 compares Score to the value of 10; because Score is not 10, the program jumps over lines 7 and 8 to line 9.
- Line 9 checks to see if Score has the value of 9; because Score is not 9, the program proceeds to line 10. Since Score is not 8, the program jumps to line 13.
- Line 13 checks to see if Score has the value of 7; because Score is 7, the program continues to execute every statement until a Break is encountered.
- Nothing happens on line 14 but line 15 sets the value of (Rating) to "C".

- Line 16 is a command to break out of the Cases. If a Break statement is not included at the end of each Case, all the subsequent Cases will be executed—often with unfortunate results.
- Because a match has been found in one of the Cases and a Break statement has been executed, the program skips lines 17–23 and jumps to line 24, the end of the Case structure; execution proceeds to line 25 and the value of Rating is displayed—i.e., a C displays.

Figure 4.7 Flowchart for the Case structure

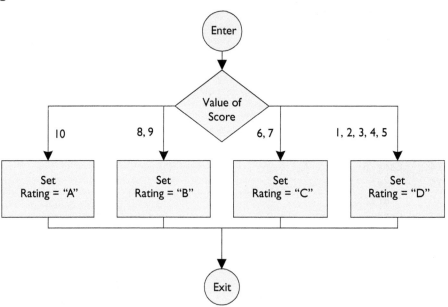

What would happen in Example 4.14 if the value of Score was 12? Or 0? In both instances, the Case structure would never find a match for Score. But the program would still get to line 25, which says to display the value of Rating. So whatever value had been previously stored in the variable Rating would be displayed. This could be an A from a previous product that you rated, a D, or gibberish from the computer's storage area. It is a good idea to have a default message coded in your program for this possibility. For example, you might put in a Default statement before the End Case statement that would store a nonexistent rating value such as "Z" in the variable Rating in case a value outside the range of 1–10 was entered or you could have a default display message that might say "No rating available".   ●

Example 4.15 **A Fortunate Use of the Case Statement**

Now that you are starting to write programs, you need to use your skill to create something that can be enjoyed by others. You decide to write a fortune-telling program for children at a local after-school care center. The child can enter a number (perhaps his or her age or a favorite number) and the program will deliver the child's fortune. In order for this game to be interesting, there must be a lot of possible fortunes. But using If-Then-Else clauses would make coding extremely long and tedious. This situation is ideal for the Case statement.

For the purposes of this example, we will only display five fortunes but, once you study the pseudocode, you will see that it is a simple matter to add another five fortunes, or 10, or 100, or as many as you like. Also, when the game becomes stale (i.e., the children have seen each fortune several times), it is easy to change the fortunes. The pseudocode for the fortune teller program is as follows:

```
1   Declare Fortune As Integer
2   Write "Enter your favorite whole number between 1 and 5:"
3   Input Fortune
4   Select Case of Fortune
5       Case 1:
6           Write "You will get a lot of money soon."
7           Break
8       Case 2:
9           Write "You will marry your one true love."
10          Break
11      Case 3:
12          Write "Study hard! There might be a quiz tomorrow."
13          Break
14      Case 4:
15          Write "Be kind to your teacher."
16          Break
17      Case 5:
18          Write "Someday you will become a game master."
19          Break
20      Default:
21          Write "You entered an invalid number."
22  End Case
```

What Happened?

In this example, the user enters a number that is stored in the integer variable, Fortune. That value is then compared with the number in each Case until a match is found. When a match is found, the corresponding Write statement is executed and the fortune is displayed. If the user enters a number that is not in the requested range, no match is found and the Default value—the message that the entry is invalid—is displayed.

The value of the Case statement is clear from this example. The fortunes can be changed easily, and more fortunes can be added with only one change in the code: the range of values requested needs to be updated.

Self Check for Section 4.4

4.14 Using each method indicated, construct a multiple-alternative structure that displays "Low" if X is equal to 0, "Medium" if X is equal to 1 or 2, or "High" if X is greater than 2 but less than or equal to 10. Assume that X is an integer. Be careful to distinguish between comparisons, using the comparison operator (==), and assignments, using the assignment operator (=).

a. Use a sequence of If-Then statements.

b. Use nested If-Then-Else statements.

c. Use a Case statement.

4.15 Suppose Choice is a variable of Character type. Write pseudocode for a multiple-alternative structure that tells the program to do one of three things, specified as follows:

- Do YesAction if Choice is "y" or "Y"
- Do NoAction if Choice is "n" or "N"
- If Choice is any other character, display the message "Signing off! Byebye."

4.5 Applications of Selection Structures

In this section, we discuss two important applications of selection structures: defensive programming and menu-driven programming.

Defensive Programming

Defensive programming involves the inclusion of statements within a program to check for improper data during execution. The program segment that catches and reports an error of this sort is called an **error trap.** In this section, we will show how to prevent two common "illegal operations"—division by 0 and taking the square root of a negative number. (Chapter 5 presents another aspect of defensive programming—data validation—checking that input data are in the proper range.)

Avoiding Division by Zero

If a division operation is performed during execution of a program and the number being divided by (the divisor) is 0, execution will halt and an error message will be displayed. In such a situation, we say that the program has *crashed.* Example 4.16 illustrates how to program defensively against this type of error with the aid of an If-Then-Else selection structure.

Example 4.16 **Displaying the Reciprocal of a Number**

The reciprocal of a number is just 1 divided by that number. Thus, the reciprocal of 8 is 1/8, and the reciprocal of 2/3 is 1/(2/3) = 3/2. Notice that to get the reciprocal of a fraction, we just flip it—interchange its numerator and denominator. Every number, except 0, has a reciprocal. We say that the reciprocal of 0 *is not defined* because there is no real number equal to 1/0. The following program segment displays the reciprocal of the number entered by the user unless that number is 0, in which case it displays an appropriate message.

```
1   Write "Enter a number."
2   Write "This program will display its reciprocal."
3   Input Number
4   If Number != 0 Then
5      Set Reciprocal = 1/Number
6      Write "The reciprocal of " + Number + " is " + Reciprocal
```

```
7  Else
8     Write "The reciprocal of 0 is not defined."
9  End If
```

In this program segment, the Else clause is the error trap. An error trap anticipates and checks for a value that would cause a problem in the running of the program. This error trap handles the possibility of a request for division by zero. By anticipating this illegal operation, we prevent the program from crashing.

Computers Don't Know Everything: Be Sure Your Display Is What *You* Want

Making It Work

If you enter the number 5 in Example 4.16, the reciprocal is 1/5. However, the line

```
Set Reciprocal = 1/Number
```

will set the value of the reciprocal to the mathematical value of $1 \div 5$, which is 0.2. The display will say

```
The reciprocal of 5 is 0.2
```

And if you input 2.5 when prompted for Number, the computer will store the value of $1 \div 2.5$ in Reciprocal. This value is 0.4. While these values are mathematically correct, the display might not be what you want. You might want the user to see that the reciprocal of a number is simply 1 divided by that number. In other words, you might want your display to look like

```
The reciprocal of 5 is 1/5
```

or

```
The reciprocal of 2.5 is 1/2.5
```

Can you rewrite the pseudocode to display the reciprocal of a number as a fraction, rather than as a decimal number? One way would be to change the Write statement, which outputs the reciprocal to these two lines:

```
Write "The reciprocal of " + Number + " is " + 1 + "/" + Number
Write "The value of the reciprocal of " + Number + " is " + Reciprocal
```

For an input of 5, the display would then be

```
The reciprocal of 5 is 1/5
The value of the reciprocal of 5 is 0.2
```

For an input of 6.534, the display would be

```
The reciprocal of 6.534 is 1/6.534
The value of the reciprocal of 6.534 is 0.15305
```

Dealing with Square Roots

In some applications, it's necessary to find the square root of a number. Most programming languages contain a built-in function that computes square roots. A function is a procedure that computes a specified value and can be called by a programmer at any time in a program. A typical square root function has the form Sqrt(X) where X represents a number, a numeric variable, or an arithmetic expression.

The square root of a positive number is a number which, when multiplied by itself, gives back the original number. For example, the square root of 16 ($\sqrt{16}$) is 4 since 4 * 4 = 16. However, another square root of 16 is -4. For every positive number, there are two possible square roots—a positive root and a negative root. Another example is the square root of 64, which is either +8 or -8 since +8 * +8 = 64 and -8 * -8 = 64. Given a positive number X, the square root function, Sqrt(X), gives the positive square root of X. So, Sqrt(4) = 2 and Sqrt(64) = 8. Moreover, since 0 * 0 = 0, we have Sqrt(0) = 0.

Here's how this function works. When Sqrt(X) is encountered in a statement, the program finds the value of X and then calculates its positive square root. For example, the statements

```
Set Number1 = 7
Set Number2 = Sqrt(Number1 + 2)
Write Number2
```

will display the number 3. First the number 7 is stored in the variable Number1. In the next line, the expression inside the parentheses is evaluated as follows:

```
Number1 + 2 = 7 + 2 = 9
```

Then the Sqrt() function computes the square root of 9, which is 3. Next, that value is stored in the variable, Number2 and the value of Number2 is displayed.

In the above program segment, the square root function appears on the right side of an assignment statement. In general, the square root function may be used anywhere in a program that a numeric constant is valid, as shown in the following:

- Write Sqrt(16) is valid because 16 is a positive number and the Write statement says to output the result of taking the square root of 16.
- Input Sqrt(Number) is not valid because an Input statement must take in a value—it cannot take in a function.

Since the square root of a negative number (for example, Sqrt(-4)) is not a real number, taking such a square root is an *illegal operation* and normally causes the program to crash. Example 4.17 illustrates how to guard against a program crash when using the Sqrt() function.

Example 4.17 **Avoid Illegal Operations with the Sqrt() Function**

This program segment inputs a number, Number. If Number is not negative, it computes and displays its square root. If Number is negative, it displays a message indicating that the square root is not defined. Note that in this situation, it is perfectly fine to have Number = 0, because the square root of 0 is 0.

```
1  Write "Enter a number."
2  Write "This program will display its square root."
3  Input Number
4  If Number >= 0 Then
```

```
5      Write "The square root of " + Number + " is " ↵
                + Sqrt(Number) + "."
6   Else
7      Write "The square root of "+ Number +" is not defined."
8   End If
```

What Happened?

In the If-Then-Else structure, the Then clause displays the square root of the input Number if this operation is valid (if Number is greater than or equal to 0). For example, if the user inputs 25, the program segment outputs the following:

```
The square root of 25 is 5.
```

On the other hand, if Number is less than 0, the Else clause reports the fact that taking the square root in this case is an illegal operation. If, for example, the user inputs the number −16, the output would be as follows:

```
The square root of -16 is not defined.
```

Fill in the blank lines of the following code segment which is slightly different from Example 4.17 but will give the same result:

```
Write "Enter a number."
Write "This program will display its square root."
Input Number
If Number < 0 Then
  Write Fill in the code
Else
  Write Fill in the code
End If
```

Program Defensively

Include error-trapping structures in your programs to catch and report the following kinds of errors:

1. Division by 0
2. A negative number input to the square root function
3. Input data that is out of the allowable range

Any one of these errors may cause your program to crash.

Make Sure Your Programs Pass a Lot of Tests

When your program contains selection structures, it's important to make enough test runs so that all blocks, or branches, of the structures are executed. For example, to test the code corresponding to Example 4.17, we must run the program at least twice. We must try at least once with a positive value for Number and at least once with a negative value for Number to make sure both the Then clause and the Else clause work correctly.

Menu-Driven Programs

One of the major goals of a programmer is to create programs that are user-friendly. For complex programs in which the user is presented with many options, listing these options in menus, instead of requiring the user to memorize commands, enhances user-friendliness. Such programs are sometimes referred to as **menu-driven**.

Menus are usually arranged in a row near the top of the screen. To display the options available on a particular menu, the user clicks the mouse on that menu's name. In this section, we will describe a more traditional approach to creating a menu-driven program by demonstrating how you can display a menu of options on the screen and have the program perform the task that the user has selected from that menu.

In a menu-driven program of this kind, the first screen that a user sees displays the main menu, which is a list of the program's major functions. For example, in a program that manages the inventory of a business, the main menu might include options to add to, delete from, or change items in the inventory.

In program design terms, the items displayed on the main menu usually correspond to separate modules. Each module is a part of the whole program and solves a particular problem or completes a specific task. Selecting one of the main menu choices may lead the user to another more detailed submenu (corresponding to additional submodules) or may lead directly into the specified task.

Example 4.18 describes the pseudocode for a part of a business's website. As shown in Example 4.18, a multiple-alternative structure is used to branch to the appropriate module once the user has selected an option. The main menu for an imaginary company, the Legendary Lawn Mower Company, might be as follows:

```
            The Legendary Lawn Mower Company
                    Inventory Control
Leave the program . . . . . . . . . . . .Enter 0
Add an item to the list . . . . . . . . .Enter 1
Delete an item from the list . . . . . . Enter 2
Change an item on the list . . . . . . . Enter 3
```

Example 4.18 **The Legendary Lawn Mower Company Keeps Its Inventory**

The inventory control menu given above can be implemented by the following pseudocode:

```
1  Write "          The Legendary Lawn Mower Company"
2  Write "                  Inventory Control"
3  Write "    Leave the program  . . . . . . . . . . .    Enter 0"
4  Write "    Add an item to the list . . . . . . . .    Enter 1"
5  Write "    Delete an item from the list . . . . . .   Enter 2"
6  Write "    Change an item on the list . . . . . . .   Enter 3"
7  Write "          Selection --> "
8  Input Choice
9  Select Case Of Choice
```

```
10    Case 0:
11       Write "Goodbye"
12       Break
13    Case 1:
14       Call AddItem module
15       Break
16    Case 2:
17       Call DeleteItem module
18       Break
19    Case 3:
20       Call ChangeItem module
21       Break
22  End Case
```

What Happened?

- Lines 1–7 display the heading and menu options.
- Line 8 takes the user's input and stores it in the variable named Choice.
- Lines 9–21 use the multiple-alternative Case structure to send the user to the appropriate module or program segment.

Section 4.6 presents another example of how menus can help structure a program and make it easier to use.

Self Check for Section 4.5

4.16 If A = 4 find the value of the following:

a. Sqrt(A)

b. Sqrt(2 * A + 1)

4.17 Rewrite the following code using defensive programming techniques. Be sure to incorporate checks against both program crashes discussed in this section!

```
Set C = Sqrt(A)/B
Write C
```

4.18. You are given the following formula for calculating the average scores for students in a certain class. Notice that all students begin with a handicap of 20 points.

```
Average = (20 + TotalExamScore)/NumberExamsTaken
```

a. Can you spot where there may be a program crash?

b. Write a program to allow the teacher to input a student's total exam score and the number of exams that the student has taken. Then compute and display the student's average. The variables are Average, TotalExamScore, and NumberExamsTaken.

4.19. Indicate whether each of the following statements is true or false.

a. A menu displays various program options for the user.

b. Menu-driven programs are considered more user friendly than programs that require the memorization of commands.

4.20. Write a program segment that displays a menu with options to OrderHamburger, OrderHotdog, and OrderTunaSalad, and then inputs the user selection.

4.6 Focus on Problem Solving: A New Car Price Calculator

In each Focus on Problem Solving section throughout this textbook we will develop a longer program that makes use of much of the material in the current chapter. In this chapter, this same problem will be implemented using RAPTOR in Section 4.7. The program developed here contains selection structures and menus to help compute the cost of a new car purchased with various options.

Problem Statement

Universal Motors makes cars. They compute the purchase price of their autos by taking the base price of the vehicle, adding in various costs for different options, and then adding shipping and dealer charges. The shipping and dealer charges are fixed for each vehicle at $500 and $175, respectively, but regardless of the particular model, the buyer can select the following options: type of engine, type of interior trim, and type of radio. The various choices for each option and the associated prices are listed in Table 4.5.

Universal Motors would like to have a program that inputs the base price of a vehicle and the desired options from the user, and then displays the selling price of that vehicle.

Table 4.5 Options available for Universal Motors' vehicles

Engine	Purchase Code	Price
6 cylinder	S	$150
8 cylinder	E	$475
Diesel	D	$750
Interior Trim	**Purchase Code**	**Price**
Vinyl	V	$50
Cloth	C	$225
Leather	L	$800
Radio	**Purchase Code**	**Price**
AM/FM/CD/DVD	R	$100
with GPS	G	$400

Problem Analysis

This problem has very clearly defined input and output. The input consists of the base price (BasePrice), the engine choice (EngineChoice), the interior trim choice (TrimChoice), and the radio choice (RadioChoice). After the user has entered a choice for an option, the program must determine the corresponding cost of that option: EngineCost, TrimCost, and RadioCost.

The only item output is the selling price (SellingPrice) of the vehicle. To determine SellingPrice, the program must also know the (fixed) value of the shipping and dealer charges (ShippingCharge and DealerCharge). Then the following computation is simple: SellingPrice = BasePrice + EngineCost + TrimCost + RadioCost + ShippingCharge + DealerCharge

Program Design

Roughly speaking, the following are the things our program must do:

1. Input the base price
2. Process the various option choices to compute additional costs
3. Total all the costs
4. Display the final selling price

We will input the base price in the main module and then transfer control to several submodules, one for each available option. Within each submodule, a menu will be displayed allowing the user to enter a choice for that option (see Table 4.5). Then the submodule will use this selection to determine the corresponding option cost. After all option selections are made, another module will compute the total cost and display the results. Thus, the Main module will contain the following submodules:

- Compute_Engine_Cost
- Compute_Interior_Trim_Cost
- Compute_Radio_Cost
- Display_Selling_Price

The hierarchy chart shown in Figure 4.8 shows the program modules and their relationship to one another.

Figure 4.8 Hierarchy chart for a new car price calculator

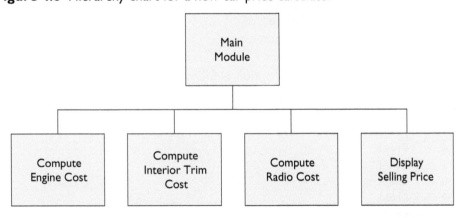

We now describe each of the modules in more detail.

Main Module

This module displays a welcome message, inputs the base price, and calls the other modules. In the Main module, we also declare all the variables that will be used by more than one module. The pseudocode for the Main module follows.

```
1   Start Program
2   Declare BasePrice, EngineCost As Float
3   Declare TrimCost, RadioCost As Float
4   Display a welcome message
5   // Prompt for and input the vehicle's base price:
6   Write "Enter the base price: "
7   Input BasePrice
8   Call Compute_Engine_Cost module
9   Call Compute_Interior_Trim_Cost module
10  Call Compute_Radio_Cost module
11  Call Display_Selling_Price module
12  End Program
```

A note about line 5: recall that the symbol (//) indicates a comment. Everything that follows this symbol on that line is text that a computer ignores when a program is executed but which contains information that may be helpful to other programmers at a future date.

Compute_Engine_Cost Module

This module displays a menu to allow the user to specify the type of engine desired and then determines the cost of this engine option as follows:

```
Display the menu and input user selection
Determine the cost of the selected option
```

This module needs a variable, EngineChoice, to hold the user's preference. The refined pseudocode follows:

```
1   Declare EngineChoice As Character
2   // Display the menu and input user selection:
3   Write "S - 6 cylinder engine"
4   Write "E - 8 cylinder engine"
5   Write "D - Diesel engine"
6   Write "Selection? "
7   Input EngineChoice
```

Determine the cost of the selected option as follows:

```
1   Select Case Of EngineChoice
2     Case 'S':
3       Set EngineCost = 150
4       Break
5     Case 'E':
6       Set EngineCost = 475
7       Break
8     Case 'D':
9       Set EngineCost = 750
```

```
10     Break
11   Default:
12     Write "Invalid selection"
13 End Case
```

Compute_Interior_Trim_Cost Module

This module has the same structure as the Compute_Engine_Cost module. It displays a menu to allow the user to specify the type of interior trim desired and then determines the cost of this trim option as follows:

```
Display the menu and input user selection
Determine the cost of the selected option
```

Its refinement is as follows:

```
1   Declare TrimChoice As Character
2   Display the menu and input user selection:
3   Write "V - Vinyl interior trim"
4   Write "C - Cloth interior trim"
5   Write "L - Leather interior trim"
6   Write "Selection? "
7   Input TrimChoice
```

In this case we will use several If-Then-Else clauses to demonstrate how either selection structure produces the required result. Determine the cost of the selected option as follows:

```
1   If TrimChoice == 'V' Then
2     Set TrimCost = 50
3   Else
4     If TrimChoice == 'C' Then
5       Set TrimCost = 225
6     Else
7       If TrimChoice == 'L' Then
8         Set TrimCost = 800
9       Else
10        Write "Invalid selection"
11      End If
12    End If
13  End If
```

Compute_Radio_Cost Module

The Compute_Radio_Cost module is similar to the Compute_Engine_Cost and Compute_Interior_Trim_Cost modules, but it provides only two options for the user, so we use a single If-Then-Else statement as follows:

```
1   Declare RadioChoice As Character
2   //Display the menu and input user selection:
3   Write "R - AM/FM/CD/DVD Radio"
4   Write "D - add GPS"
5   Write "Selection?"
6   Input RadioChoice
```

Determine the cost of the selected option as follows:

```
1  If RadioChoice == 'R' Then
2    Set RadioCost = 100
3  Else
4    If RadioChoice == 'G' Then
5      Set RadioCost = 400
6    Else
7      Write "Invalid selection"
8    End If
9  End If
```

Display_Selling_Price Module

This module computes and displays the selling price of the vehicle with the selected options. To determine the selling price, it uses variables determined in the previous modules, plus two new ones—ShippingCharge and DealerCharge.

```
1  Declare ShippingCharge, DealerCharge, SellingPrice As Float
2  Set ShippingCharge = 500
3  Set DealerCharge = 175
4  Set SellingPrice = BasePrice + EngineCost + TrimCost ↵
               + RadioCost + ShippingCharge + DealerCharge
5  Write "The total selling price for your vehicle ↵
               is $ " + SellingPrice
```

Program Code

In writing the program code, we make a few additional enhancements to the program.

- We include header and step comments for each module.
- When output is displayed on the screen, new lines are generated one after the other as specified by the code. When the screen is full, the next Write statement will cause the screen to scroll up. This means that all the text will move up one line with the top line of text disappearing from the screen and the new text will be displayed at the bottom of the screen. It is often desirable, however, to clear the screen of all text, so that the data that follows is displayed all by itself at the top of the screen. Most programming languages contain a statement that clears the screen. It is advisable to use this statement at the beginning of every program. In this program, a **clear screen statement** would also be appropriate prior to displaying each of the vehicle options menus.

Program Test

Test runs of the program should use various base prices and option combinations to ensure that the calculations and purchase codes in all branches of the Case and If-Then-Else statements work properly. For example, in the Compute_Radio_Cost module, to test the If-Then-Else structure, the characters 'R', 'G', and another character should be input on different test runs. As your programs become more professional and more complex, you will include code to deal with as many possibilities as you can imagine. For example, you would include code in the `Compute_Radio_Cost` module to take into account what would happen if a user typed in a number or a special character, such as the @ sign, rather than a letter. Then, during the testing phase, you would run the program with various inputs that test the system.

Self Check for Section 4.6

These Self Check questions refer to the new car price calculator problem in this section.

4.21 Replace the `Case` statement in the `Compute_Engine_Cost` module with `If` statements.

4.22 Replace the `BasePrice` prompt and input statements in the `Main` module by a module that allows the user to choose among three car models, each with a different base price. The user will input the model designation `'X'`, `'Y'`, or `'Z'`, and the program will determine the corresponding base price— $20,000, $25,000, or $28,000, respectively.

4.7 Running With RAPTOR (Optional)

In this section, we will learn how to use RAPTOR to create executable programs that include decisions, using the RAPTOR `Selection` symbol. We will use an example from this chapter to demonstrate how to create running programs using decisions, and we will also complete and run the New Car Price Calculator from the previous section. In order to create these programs, we need to learn how to use RAPTOR's `Selection` symbol and, for our programs to correspond to the modular programming techniques described in this text, we will also learn to use RAPTOR's `Call` symbol.

The `Selection` Symbol

The **Selection symbol** (shown in Figure 4.9) allows you to code `If-Then` and `If-Then-Else` statements. When you drag the `Selection` symbol to the screen and double-click the diamond, the `Enter Selection Condition` dialog box opens, as shown in Figure 4.10. Here is where you enter the condition that will determine which branch the code will take.

The `Selection` symbol includes `Yes` and `No` branches. Consider them carefully when you write your condition and when you enter the results. For example, if you want your program to end when the `Count` is greater than 5, you have two options for your test condition, as shown in Figure 4.11.

Figure 4.9 The `Selection` symbol

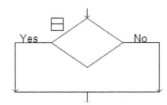

Figure 4.10 The Enter Selection Condition dialog box

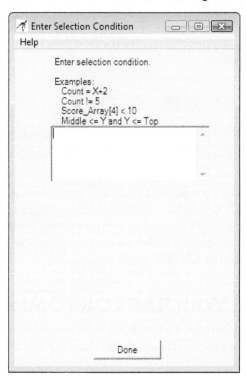

Figure 4.11 Coding options for the Selection symbol

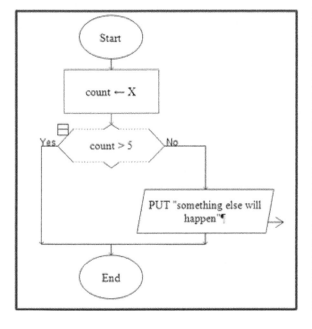
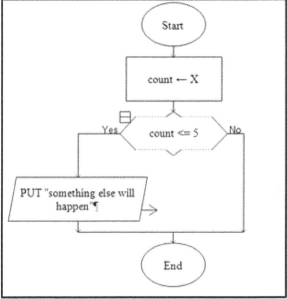

The Assignment Operator and the Comparison Operator in RAPTOR

Making It Work

You can enter any of the types of selection conditions that have been discussed in the book, including compound conditions that use logical operators with a RAPTOR Selection symbol. There is just one difference.

Throughout this text we have discussed the distinction between the single equals sign (=) which is an assignment operator and the double equals sign (==) which is a comparison operator. However, RAPTOR allows you to use either a single or a double equals sign to indicate a comparison within a test condition. RAPTOR "understands" that a single equals sign indicates comparison by its placement in the diamond shape. RAPTOR also accepts the double equals sign as a comparison operator. For example, if the condition you wish to check is "Is the value of Count equal to 5?" you could enter either of the following into the Enter Selection Condition

        Count = 5 or Count == 5

In this text we will use the double equals sign to indicate a comparison because it is an important distinction which, in a typical programming language, can wreak havoc on a program if used incorrectly. Therefore, you should become accustomed to using it and we encourage you to make sure you use the proper symbols in your RAPTOR programs.

You can use the Selection symbol to create nested decisions and you can nest a Selection statement inside a loop (to be covered in Chapter 6). Figure 4.12 illustrates how to create an If-Then-Else structure. In Figure 4.12, the program ends if Count is greater than 5, it displays a happy message if Count is between 1 and 5 and then ends, and it displays a sad message if Count is 0 or less.

Figure 4.12 A nested If-Then-Else structure

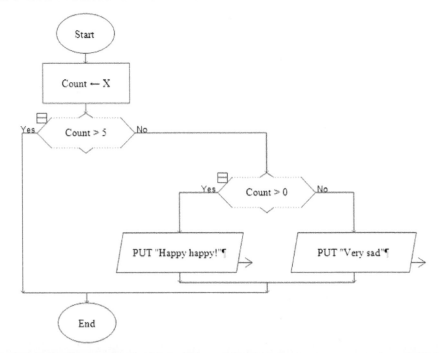

The Call Symbol and Subcharts

The Call **symbol,** as shown in Figure 4.13, is used to call submodules from the main program, as these submodules, named **subcharts** in RAPTOR, are needed.

Figure 4.13 The Call symbol

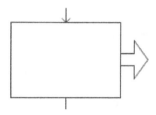

Subcharts help break a RAPTOR program into logical parts, called as needed by the main program, to simplify design, ensure that flowcharts are manageable, and reduce the chance for errors.

When you start a RAPTOR program, you'll see a main tab in the upper-left corner of the work area. To create a subchart, simply right-click the main tab and select Add subchart from the menu, as shown in Figure 4.14. Enter the name of your subchart and a new editing window will appear. The name you give your subchart is automatically created in this new window after you click yes when prompted.

Figure 4.14 Creating a subchart

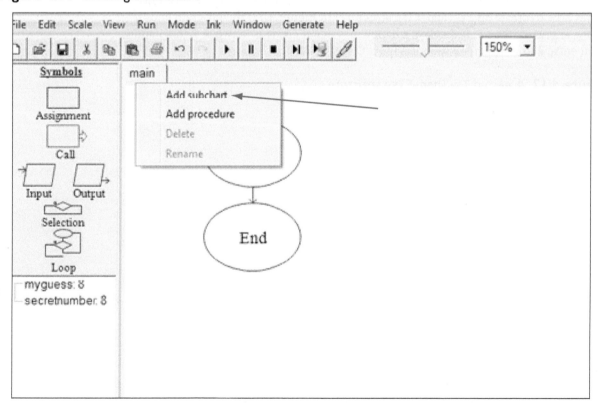

Figure 4.15 shows a new subchart named Calculations.

Figure 4.15 A new subchart named Calculations

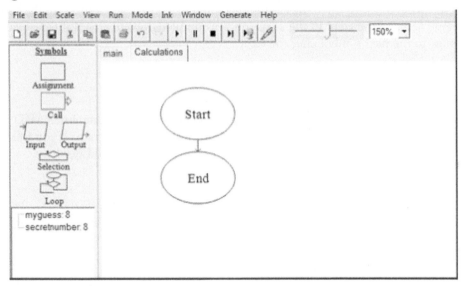

Now you can begin to build your subchart. After you have created your program, to call a subchart, simply insert the Call symbol where you want it in your program, and enter the name of the subchart that you want it to be called. Figure 4.16 shows a sample program that uses a Call statement to access a subchart, which will do calculations.

Figure 4.16 Using a Call symbol within a program

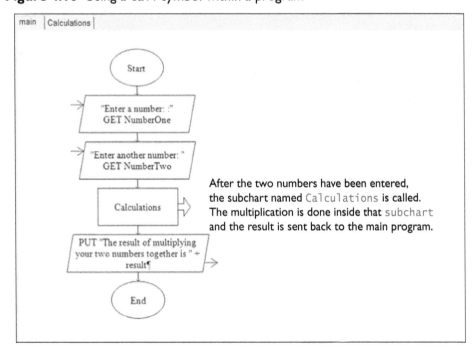

A subchart may be called from the main flowchart or from other subcharts or even from within itself but be careful if you decide to try this! It can easily result in an infinite loop (a loop that runs forever).

As the program runs, when the Call is encountered, control will transfer to the subchart. After all the steps in the subchart are completed, control will automatically return to the next symbol after the Call.

An Example

At this point, we will take an example from the chapter and re-create it in RAPTOR using a Selection symbol to create the decision part of the program. If you follow along and create the program, you can run it yourself and get valid results.

Example 4.19 Calculating a Paycheck

The problem statement is the same as that shown in Examples 4.7 and 4.8. It is repeated here for your convenience.

The weekly pay for workers at a given company is calculated as follows:

- Workers who earn less than $10 per hour are paid at 1.5 times their regular pay rate for overtime hours.
- Workers who earn $10 or more per hour are paid their regular hourly rate, regardless of how many hours they work in a week.
- In this company, working more than 40 hours in a week is considered overtime.

We will use the pseudocode developed in Example 4.7 for our program, but the pseudocode from Example 4.8 would work just as well. You can save your program, if you follow along with these instructions, with the filename paycheck.rap.

In order for the program to run and produce results that we can see, we need to add code to get input and to display output. The input will include a value for a worker's pay rate and the number of hours worked in a given week. Each step will be shown so that you can create the program yourself.

Numeric variables needed:

    PayRate, Hours, OvertimeHours, OvertimePay, TotalPay

The variables are created as follows:

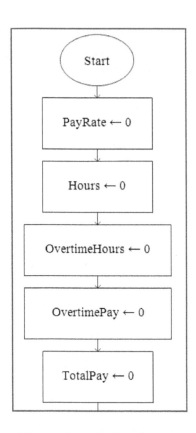

We will first create a welcome message—an output message that briefly describes what the program will do:

```
PUT "This program will calculate the
weekly paycheck for an employee,
including overtime if applicable."¶
```

Next we will prompt the user for the required information:

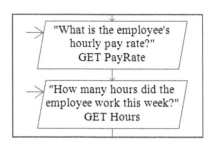

The processing part comes next. Here is where we use the Selection symbol. This program requires an If-Then-Else structure because, regardless of whether the test condition is true or false, something will happen; that is, TotalPay will be calculated. We could test to see if the PayRate is less than 10 AND the Hours are greater than 40 or we could use the alternate test (see Example 4.8). We will choose the method that uses the AND logical operator.

To do this, drag the Selection symbol to the work area under the second Input symbol and enter the condition as shown:

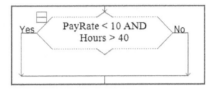

Because of the way we wrote our test condition, we must code for no extra money for overtime hours if the answer to the test condition is no (or false). If the answer is yes (true), then the employee is eligible for extra pay for overtime hours and we will code the program correspondingly. We will do the false option first. Drag an Assignment symbol to the No branch of the Selection symbol and calculate TotalPay as shown:

```
TotalPay = Hours * PayRate
```

If the result of the test condition is Yes, this means the employee will receive a pay that includes 40 hours at the regular pay rate and all hours over 40 at time and a half. The formula for this is given in Example 4.7 and is done in three steps. First, the OvertimeHours are calculated and then OvertimePay is calculated. Finally, TotalPay is calculated. In RAPTOR, we will use three Assignment boxes, all dragged to the Yes branch of the Selection symbol. The entire Selection symbol now looks like this:

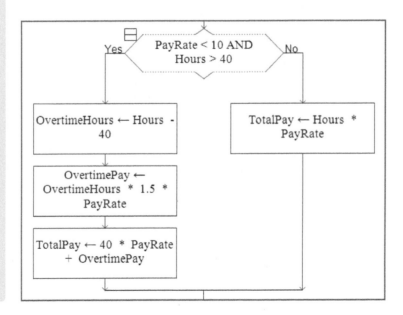

Finally, we display the results. After the selection structure is exited, regardless of whether the employee gets extra money for overtime hours, a total pay amount has been calculated. Therefore, we only need one Output symbol, as shown here:

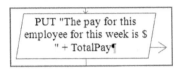

We should now test our program. The testing should include running the program to make sure there are no errors and should also include using enough test data to ensure that all possibilities provide accurate results. First, run the program with the following data: Assume that a worker earns $5 an hour and worked 10 hours. This data is chosen because we can easily do the math in our heads. A person who worked 10 hours at the rate of $5 an hour should have a paycheck of $50. If you run the program as created here, the Master Console display should look like this:

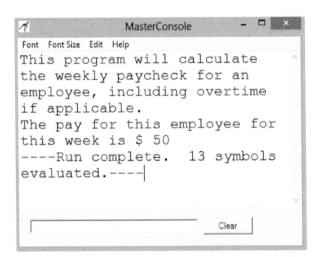

Next, check all the options for an employee and create test data to check each option. A list of the options and possible test data are given below, followed by the results that should be achieved if you create and run this program with this data:

- An employee who works more than 40 hours and earns less than $10 an hour
  - test data: 45 hours, $5/hr
  - result: The pay for this employee for this week is $ 237.50
- An employee who works more than 40 hours and earns exactly $10 an hour
  - test data: 45 hours, $10/hr
  - result: The pay for this employee for this week is $ 450
- An employee who works more than 40 hours and earns more than $10 an hour
  - test data: 45 hours, $15/hr
  - result: The pay for this employee for this week is $ 675

- An employee who works exactly 40 hours and earns less than $10 an hour
  - test data: 40 hours, $5/hr
  - result: `The pay for this employee for this week is $ 200`
- An employee who works exactly 40 hours and earns exactly $10 an hour
  - test data: 40 hours, $10/hr
  - result: `The pay for this employee for this week is $ 400`
- An employee who works exactly 40 hours and earns more than $10 an hour
  - test data: 40 hours, $15/hr
  - result: `The pay for this employee for this week is $ 600`
- An employee who works less than 40 hours and earns less than $10 an hour
  - test data: 30 hours, $5/hr
  - result: `The pay for this employee for this week is $ 150`
- An employee who works less than 40 hours and earns exactly $10 an hour
  - test data: 30 hours, $10/hr
  - result: `The pay for this employee for this week is $ 300`
- An employee who works less than 40 hours and earns more than $10 an hour
  - test data: 30 hours, $15/hr
  - result: `The pay for this employee for this week is $ 450`

You may have noticed that, when the result is not a whole number, RAPTOR includes more than two decimal places. For example, when the test data is 57.7 hours worked at an hourly pay rate of $ 5.36, the result will be:

`The pay for this employee for this week is $ 356.7080`

In most programming languages, there are several ways to change this output to the two-digit form you probably want for currency. However, in RAPTOR, at this point, we will simply ignore the extra decimal places or, by using one of the methods shown in the following Making It Work section, we can ensure that all decimals after the first two are zero.

Making It Work

Formatting Numeric Output

Most programming languages have a function that allows you to set the number of decimal places you want. For example, in JavaScript, the `toFixed()` method will take any number and display it with a specified number of decimal places:

If a variable named `myNum` =5.56739, then:

- `myNum.toFixed(1)` = 5.6
- `myNum.toFixed(2)` = 5.57
- `myNum.toFixed(3)` = 5.567

In RAPTOR, we can use a method which is included with the program that will be discussed in Chapter 9 or, for now, we can force our numbers to remove decimal values after two places so, for example, 5.56739 will display as either 5.5600 or 5.5700. As you learn more programming logic, you will be able to find a way to write RAPTOR code to make the display more accurate. For now, we will use either the RAPTOR floor() or ceiling() method to eliminate extra decimal numbers.

- **ceiling()** returns the lowest integer value greater than or equal to the provided argument. For example, ceiling(15.9) is 16, ceiling(3.1) is 4, and ceiling(23) is 23.
- **floor()** returns the highest integer value less than or equal to the provided argument. For example, floor(15.9) is 15, floor(3.1) is 3, and floor(23) is 23.

Therefore, to force all decimal places after the first two to be zero in RAPTOR, we can do the following: First multiply the number we have (5.56739, in this case) by 100 to get 556.739. Then use the floor() function: floor(556.739) = 556. Similarly, if we use the ceiling() function, ceiling(556.739) = 557. Next we can divide that number by 100 to get a number with only two decimal places. In this case, 556/100 = 5.56 and 557/100 = 5.57.

We can add the following Assignment boxes to our program, before the ending Output display to format the output so that only two decimal places are shown, even though RAPTOR will add two zeros because all numbers with a decimal part default to a display of four places.

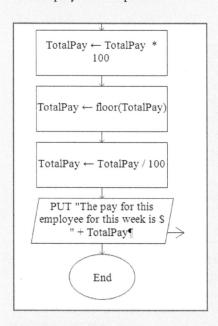

Now, if you try the program with the test data: hourly rate = $6.67 and hours worked = 53.5, your output will be:

```
The pay for this employee for this week is $ 401.8600
```

even though the actual value of the employee's pay is 401.8675.

Run It: The New Car Price Calculator

Now, we will use RAPTOR to implement the New Car Price Calculator program that was developed, using pseudocode, in the Focus on Problem Solving section. In some subsequent chapters we will use RAPTOR to re-create the Focus on Problem Solving program of that chapter and in other chapters we will develop a new, more complex program. If you follow along and create these programs yourself, you should be able to see how a longer program works.

The problem statement is repeated here for your convenience:

Universal Motors makes cars. They compute the purchase price of their autos by taking the base price of the vehicle, adding in various costs for different options, and then adding shipping and dealer charges. The shipping and dealer charges are fixed for each vehicle at $500 and $175, respectively, but regardless of the particular model, the buyer can select the following options: type of engine, type of interior trim, and type of radio. Universal Motors would like to have a program that inputs the base price of a vehicle and the desired options from the user, and then displays the selling price of that vehicle. The exact specifications match those given earlier in the text in Table 4.5.

Developing the Program

The design of this program will mirror the program developed in Section 4.6. We will have a main program that will call five subcharts (i.e., submodules).

The main module will display an introduction to describe the purpose of the program and will get initial input from the user. Then, we will call a subchart to declare variables (described below) as well as subcharts to do the tasks described in Section 4.6: computing the engine cost, the interior trim cost, the radio cost, and, finally, to display the selling price. You may wonder why the program in Section 4.6 called four submodules but here we will use five. The explanation of this fifth subchart is as follows:

Initializing Variables

This particular program requires many variables. In RAPTOR, each variable declaration uses a separate Assignment symbol. Initializing more than a few variables results in a long list of Assignment boxes that do not have much to do with the logic of the program. Therefore, for convenience, we can call a RAPTOR subchart as soon as the program begins, which will contain all our initial variable declarations. It keeps this long list of Assignment boxes out of the way and allows us to focus on the rest of the program. However, it is not necessary and, if you wish, you can initialize your variables in the main program.

Let's get started. Open a new RAPTOR program. We will save our program with the filename car_calculator.rap. To create the first subchart, drag a Call symbol to the left side of the work area directly beneath the Start symbol. Double-click inside the Call symbol to open the Enter Call dialog box. Here is where you enter a call. At this point, we simply need to call a new module that we will create. Since this module will consist of variable declarations, we will call it Variables. Enter Variables in the procedure call box and click Done. RAPTOR will ask if you want to create a new tab and you should click Yes.

Figure 4.17 Creating the Call to the Variables subchart

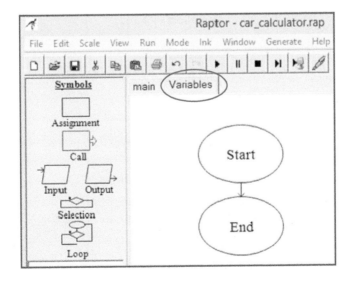

You will now see your main work area and a new tab at the top, named Variables.
You can click on the Variables tab and begin creating variables.

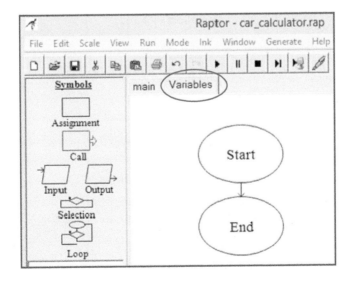

For this program, we need eight numeric variables, two named constants, and we will add a little personalization to the program by incorporating the user's name and the type of car desired, so we will add two string variables.

Since a variable's data type in RAPTOR is created when the variable is given a value, we will create most of our `number` variables by giving them an initial value of 0 and most `string` variables by giving them an initial value of an empty space (" "). Some variables, our named constants, have predetermined values that will not change as the program runs. We can set these values now.

Create the following `number` variables with the initial value of 0:

    BasePrice, EngineCost, TrimCost, RadioCost, SellingPrice

Create the following `string` variables with the initial value of " ":

    EngineChoice, TrimChoice, RadioChoice

Create the following named constants:

    ShippingCharge = 500
    DealerCharge = 175

We will personalize our output by asking the user for his or her name and the make of car to purchase. Then, we can use this information in the output display. Create the following `string` variables with an initial value of " ":

    Name and CarMake

A partial list of what your `Variables` subchart will look like is shown in Figure 4.18.

Figure 4.18 The `Variables` subchart in progress

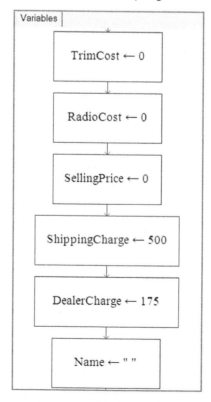

Creating the Introduction and Getting User Information

Now, return to the main tab to begin creating the program. We will start with a brief message that will appear in the MasterConsole when a user starts the program.

This is a simple Output message so drag an Output symbol under the Variables Call and enter text such as: "This program will help you calculate the cost of a new car."

For this message and for all text that is output to the MasterConsole, the exact wording is up to you, as the programmer. You might consider using two Output symbols so your MasterConsole will initially look like this:

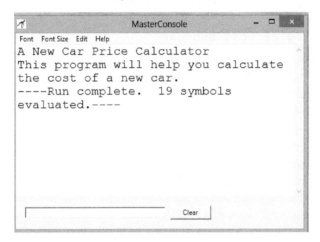

Next, use three Input symbols to get the user's name, the make of car the user wants to buy, and the car's base price. Recall that we already created two string variables, Name and CarMake, and a number variable to store the BasePrice. The input should be stored in these variables. At this point your program will look like this:

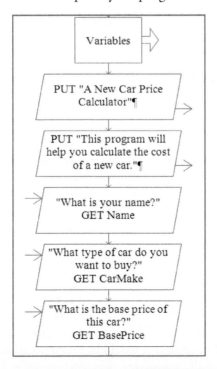

Creating the **Subcharts** to Compute the Cost

The next three subcharts will find the costs of the engine, interior trim, and radio features. The costs are determined by what the user chooses as an option for each of these features. We will put each feature into a separate subchart and use Calls to access each one. All of these subcharts require the use of the Selection symbols in RAPTOR.

In Section 4.6 we used a Case structure for one feature and If-Then-Else structures for the other features. However, a Case structure is simply a shorthand form of an If-Then-Else structure and is not available in RAPTOR. Therefore, all of our decisions will use one or more Selection symbols. This is exactly how you would create a Case structure if you were to do it with a flowchart.

The **Compute_Engine_Cost** subchart

First create a new tab called Compute_Engine_Cost by dragging a new Call symbol under the last Input symbol, double-clicking in the Call symbol, and entering Compute_Engine_Cost in the Enter Call box. This will create our second subchart. Click on this tab to begin creating this part of the program.

We will create a menu that will show the user what the choices are. The problem statement allows the user to choose between a 6-cylinder, 8-cylinder, or a diesel engine. If we ask the user to enter the full choice, such as "6-cylinder", for example, there is a lot of room for user error. Users often misspell words, enter things in uppercase when the computer is looking for lowercase, or, in this example, may use a space or an underscore instead of a hyphen. For the program to work, the user must enter exactly what the computer looks for. Therefore, to ensure fewer user errors, we will identify a single character for the user to enter to pick his or her selection. In this example, as in Section 4.6, an 'S' will represent the 6-cylinder option, an 'E' will represent the 8-cylinder option, and a 'D' will represent the choice of a diesel engine.

Making It Work

Sometimes Case Is Very Important

While RAPTOR is not case sensitive when it comes to variable names and RAPTOR keywords, the contents of a variable must match exactly. If the variable EngineChoice holds the character "e", it will not be identified as the 8-cylinder option because 'e' is not the same as 'E'.

We need to explain to the user what to enter. Most programming languages will display a prompt on the same screen as the rest of the program. In RAPTOR, as is often the case in programming on a web page, we know that the prompt comes in the form of a pop-up window. We need to explain the user's options and how to enter his or her choice in our Enter Input box. Your explanation should look something like this: "Enter 'S' for 6-cylinder, 'E' for 8-cylinder, or 'D' for a diesel engine" and the user's entry should be stored in the EngineChoice variable. Notice that single quotes are used inside the double quotes—the entire output is the text within the double quotes and that output will include the single quotes.

In RAPTOR, the prompt pop-up box has two functions. It serves as the Write statement we have used in our pseudocode to explain what the user is to enter, and it functions as an Input statement. The value typed in by the user in response to the prompt is stored in the specified variable as it would be in our pseudocode's Input statement.

Finally, we will use multiple Selection symbols to actually find the cost of the user's chosen engine type. There are three possible engine types, but we will need a fourth choice as well. The last option will take care of the possibility that the user did not enter an S, an E, or a D. Later, as you learn more programming, you will learn better ways to deal with this type of user error but, for now, we will simply end the program if the user does not enter a valid option in any of the features.

Begin by dragging the Selection symbol directly under the Input symbol. The Selection symbol contains a diamond-shaped box with two branch points. The test condition goes inside the diamond. If the answer to the test is "yes", one thing will happen. If the answer is "no", something else will happen. Notice that we cannot simultaneously check for an S or an E or a D. We must check these options one at a time. Therefore, this first Selection symbol will check if the user entered an "S" as shown:

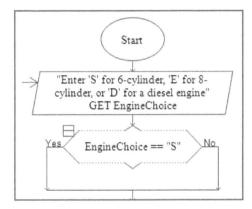

If the user did enter an "S", the answer will be "yes" and the result is simply to set the value of EngineCost to 150, as described in the initial problem. This is done by dragging an Assignment symbol to the Yes branch of the Selection symbol and setting EngineCost to its new value. However, if the answer is "no", we need to check the next option, that is, is EngineChoice == "E"? This is another If-Then-Else structure so drag a second Selection symbol to the No branch of the first Selection symbol. Here, we will create our second test condition (is EngineChoice == "E"?), as shown:

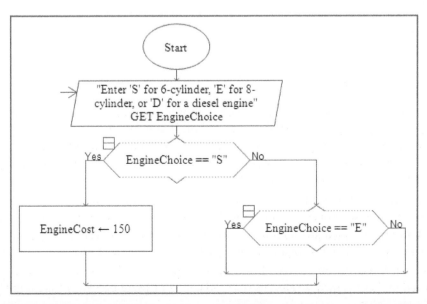

If the answer is "yes" we can set EngineCost to 475 by using an Assignment symbol on the Yes branch of the second Selection symbol. But if the answer is "no" we must use a third Selection symbol to check for the possibility that EngineChoice == "D".

Again, if the answer to this test is "yes" it is a simple matter to set the value of EngineCost to 750, the cost of a diesel engine. But if the answer is "no" then we know the user did not pick any of the valid engine options. We will output a message to the user saying that this was not a valid entry. At this point, the value of EngineCost has not changed from its initial value–the value we gave it when we originally initialized this variable. It still contains the value of 0. We will use this fact, at the end of the program, to see if the user made valid choices for a car throughout the program.

Therefore, the final code for this subchart is as shown in Figure 4.19.

Figure 4.19 The Compute_Engine_Cost subchart

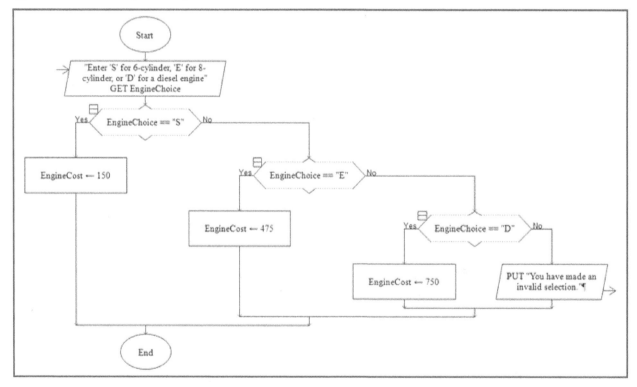

Notice that, regardless of which branch is chosen from any of the Selection symbols, the program proceeds to the End symbol. If you follow any one of the arrows, you will see that there is only one way to proceed: to the End. When the program reaches the End of a subchart, control is passed back to the main module, directly below the Call that initiated the code in this subchart.

At this point, you should run your program to make sure that there are no errors. The program will not do anything with the information you input; yet, you can check to make sure that there are no logical or syntax errors. For example, if you have misspelled the name of a variable, you can fix it now. You should run four tests, checking to see that there are no errors when you enter "S", "E", "D", or any other character at the prompt for EngineChoice. Testing the program at each phase makes debugging a great deal easier than waiting for the end when you have many more combinations of tests to run and where it may be difficult to pinpoint the source of a bug. In RAPTOR, as you run your tests, look at the watch window on the left side to be sure that your variables are being assigned the correct values. For example, if you run this program as it is so far with the following test data, your watch window should look like the one shown in Figure 4.20.

> Name = "Lorenzo", CarMake = "Rolls Royce", EngineChoice = "D"

Figure 4.20 The watch window and MasterConsole with a test run

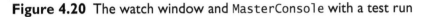
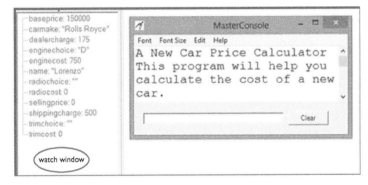

Now we are ready to continue creating this program. The next two subcharts are created in a manner similar to this one. We will only show the finished product because you can create the subcharts for the Compute_Interior_Trim_Cost subchart and the Compute_Radio_Cost_subchart as you did for this subchart.

The Compute_Interior_Trim_Cost subchart

First create a new tab called Compute_Interior_Trim_Cost by dragging a new Call symbol under the Call to the Compute_Engine_Cost subchart. The menu and nested If-Then-Else structures will look as shown in Figure 4.21.

Before continuing, be sure to test all the options in this subchart by running the program four times with test data to cover the three possible choices as well as the possibility that the user enters a character other than one of the specific options.

The Compute_Radio_Cost subchart

Create a new tab called Compute_Radio_Cost by dragging a new Call symbol under the Call to the Compute_Interior_Trim_Cost subchart. The menu and nested If-Then-Else structures will look like the structure shown in Figure 4.22.

Before continuing, be sure to test all the options in this subchart by running the program three times with test data to cover the two possible choices as well as the possibility that the user enters a character other than an "R" or a "G". We are now ready to find the final calculations and display the results.

Figure 4.21 The Compute_Interior_Trim_Cost subchart

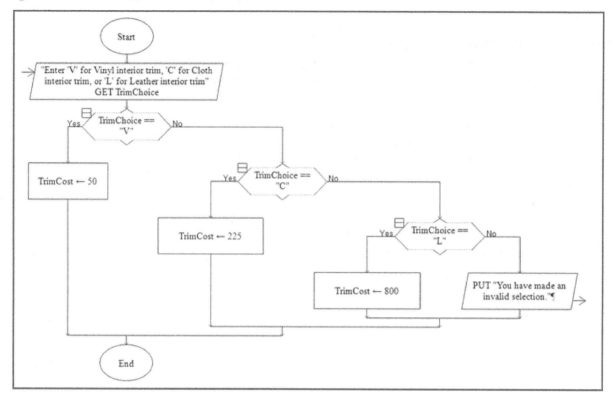

Figure 4.22 The Compute_Radio_Cost subchart

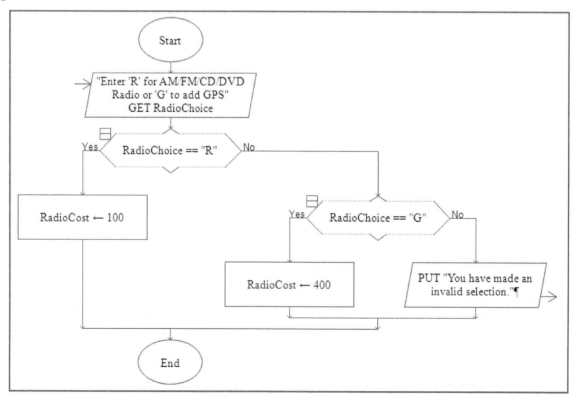

The `Display_Selling_Price` subchart

Now we can put all our information together and display the results. The program that was developed in Section 4.6 created a bare-bones output. We will add a little more to our output to personalize what the user sees.

Create a new tab called `Display_Selling_Price` by dragging a new `Call` symbol under the last `Call`. Click on this tab to enter this `subchart`. Before we calculate the final cost of a new car, we need to make sure that the user made valid selections for the three options. Recall that, for each feature (engine type, interior trim, and radio), if the user did not make a valid entry, we did not assign a new value to the corresponding variable (`EngineCost`, `TrimCost`, or `RadioCost`). In any case where an invalid selection was entered, the corresponding variable would still contain its original value which is 0. We will use this fact, combined with one more `Selection` symbol, to check if any user choice was invalid. The test condition for this `Selection` box will be a compound condition—we will check if either `EngineCost` or `TrimCost` or `RadioCost` is 0. If the answer is `Yes` to this condition, we will display a message stating that a car price cannot be calculated. But if none of these variables contain 0 as its value, a final cost can be calculated. In the `Display_Selling_Price` subchart create the following `Selection` structure:

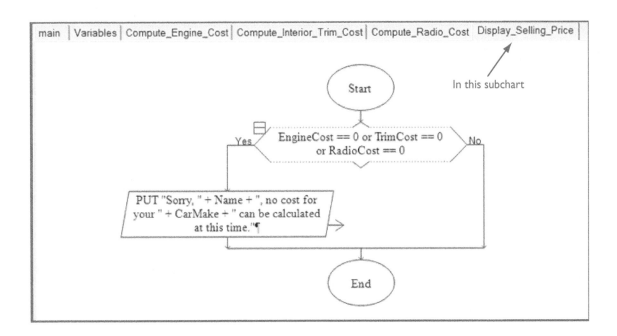

Note how the output is entered. Double quotes enclose all text, taking care to include spaces and punctuation where necessary. Text is concatenated with variables using the concatenation symbol (+). Also, note that the compound condition in this case uses two instances of the `OR` operator.

The last thing we must do is calculate the cost of the car if all user entries are valid and display that result. The following `Assignment` box calculates the car cost and is placed in the `No` branch of the `Selection` structure. The `Output` symbol is placed underneath with an appropriate message to the user:

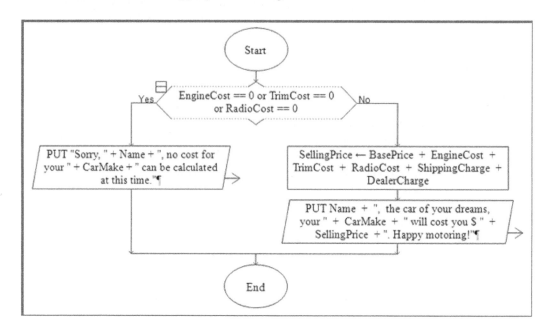

Check It Out

If you have tested the three `subcharts` that get user inputs about car features, you can now test this final module and run the entire program. You should perform at least four tests: making an invalid selection for each of the three feature options and one test where all entries are valid.

Assume your user is named Penelope. She wants to buy a Ford with a base price of $ 3,000. The output, with any invalid selection, should look similar to the one shown in Figure 4.23. However, if she wants a 6-cylinder engine, leather interior, and a GPS and she enters the correct selections for each choice, the output should be as shown in Figure 4.24.

Figure 4.23 The final output with an invalid selection

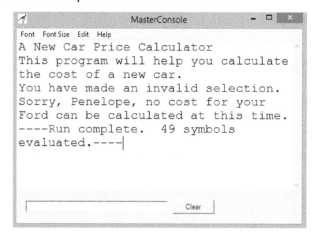

If you want, you can add more outputs to this program to list the options the user has selected. In the next chapter, after learning how to use the repetition structure, you can even allow the user the option to change a feature or compare costs.

Figure 4.24 The final output with a valid selection

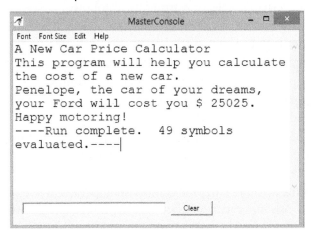

Chapter Review and Exercises

Key Terms

American Standard Code for
    Information Interchange
ASCII code
assignment operator
Call symbol
Case (Switch) statement
ceiling() function
character
clear screen statement
comparison operator
defensive programming
dual-alternative structure
Else clause
error trap
floor() function

If-Then structure
If-Then-Else structure
logical operator
menu-driven (program)
multiple-alternative structure
nested
relational operator
selection (decision) structure
selection symbol
single-alternative structure
subcharts
test condition
Then clause
truth tables

Chapter Summary

In this chapter, we have discussed the following topics:

1. The single-alternative selection structure as follows:
   - It contains a single block of statements to be either executed or skipped
   - It is implemented by an `If-Then` statement

2. The dual-alternative selection structure as follows:
   - It contains two blocks of statements, one of which is to be executed, while the other is to be skipped
   - It is implemented by an `If-Then-Else` statement

3. The multiple-alternative selection structure as follows:
   - It contains more than two blocks of statements, one of which is to be executed, while the others are to be skipped
   - It can be implemented by a sequence of `If-Then` statements, nested `If-Then-Else` statements, or a `Case` statement

4. Relational and logical operators as follows:
   - Relational operators are: the comparison operator that compares the value of one thing with another (==), the not equal operator (!=), the less than operator (<), the less than or equal to operator (<=), the greater than operator (>), and the greater than or equal to operator (>=)
   - Logical operators are `NOT`, `AND`, and `OR`
   - The order of operations in the absence of parentheses is that arithmetic operations are done first (in their usual order), then relational operations (all with equal precedence so that they can be done in any order), and finally, the logical operators, `NOT`, `AND`, and `OR`, executed in that order

5. The ASCII code is listed as follows:
   - In ASCII code, a number is associated with each character
   - ASCII code can be used to order arbitrary character strings

6. Defensive programming as follows:
   - Programmers must anticipate and prevent errors that might result from using improper data
   - A selection structure can be used to prevent instances of division by zero
   - The square root function, `Sqrt()`, is a commonly used function but attempting to take the square root of a negative number can cause a program crash—defensive programming ensures that a program will not be asked to take the square root of a negative number

7. The built-in square root function as follows:
   - It is of the form `Sqrt(X)`, where X is a number, numeric variable, or an arithmetic expression
   - It may be used anywhere in a program where a numeric constant is valid

8. Menu-driven programs as follows:
   - They present options for the user in the form of menus
   - They use a multiple-alternative structure to handle the user's option selection

Review Exercises

Fill in the Blank

1. A single-alternative structure is also known as a(n) _____ structure.

2. A dual-alternative structure is also known as a(n) _____ structure.

For Exercises 3 to 8: Replace the blank with one of the following words: arithmetic, relational, or logical

3. `<=` is a(n) _____ operator

4. `+` is a(n) _____ operator

5. `%` is a(n) _____ operator

6. `OR` is a(n) _____ operator

7. `NOT` is a(n) _____ operator

8. `!=` is a(n) _____ operator

Multiple Choice

9. Which expression is equivalent to the following expression but does not use the `NOT` operator: `NOT (A > B)`

   a. `A < B`

   b. `A <= B`

   c. `B < A`

   d. `B <= A`

10. Which expression is equivalent to the following expression:
    `A > 8 AND A < 18`

    a. `NOT (A < 8) AND NOT (A > 18)`

    b. `NOT (A <= 8) AND NOT (A >= 18)`

    c. `NOT (A > 8 OR A < 18)`

    d. `A < 8 OR A > 18`

11. A multiple-alternative structure cannot be implemented by using which of the following: (select all that apply)

    a. A single `If-Then` statement

    b. Several `If-Then` statements

    c. Several `If-Then-Else` statements

    d. A single `Case` statement

12. If `Char1 = "/"` and `Char2 = "?"`, which of the following expressions are `true`? (select all that apply)

    a. `Char1 < Char2`

    b. `Char1 <= Char2`

    c. `Char1 > Char2`

    d. `Char1 >= Char2`

13. The term defensive programming refers to which of the following (select all that apply):
    a. Ensuring that input data are in the proper range
    b. Ensuring that a division by 0 does not take place
    c. Ensuring that the square root operation is valid
    d. Techniques that include all the above points

True or False

14. If X = 0, determine whether each of the following expressions is `true` or `false`.
    a. T F   X >= 0
    b. T F   2 * X + 1 != 1

15. If First = "Ann", determine whether each of the following expressions is `true` or `false`.
    a. T F   First == "ann"
    b. T F   First != "Ann"
    c. T F   First < "Nan"
    d. T F   First >= "Anne"

16. If X = 1 and Y = 2 determine whether each of the following expressions is `true` or `false`.
    a. T F   X >= X OR Y >= X
    b. T F   X > X AND Y > X
    c. T F   X > Y OR X > 0 AND Y < 0
    d. T F   NOT(NOT(X == 0) AND NOT (Y == 0))

17. If X = 0 and Response = "Yes", determine whether each of the following expressions is `true` or `false`.
    a. T F   (X == 1) OR (Response == "Yes")
    b. T F   (X == 1) AND (Response == "Yes")
    c. T F   NOT (X == 0)

18. If Num1 = 1 and Num2 = 2, determine whether each of the following expressions is `true` or `false`.
    a. T F   (Num1 == 1) OR (Num2 == 2) AND (Num1 == Num2)
    b. T F   ((Num1 == 1) OR (Num2 == 2)) AND (Num1 == Num2)
    c. T F   NOT (Num1 == 1) AND NOT (Num2 == 2)
    d. T F   NOT (Num1 == 1) OR NOT (Num2 == 2)

19. T F   The ASCII coding scheme associates a number between 0 and 127 with every lowercase and uppercase letter as well as with other keyboard characters.

20. T F   If Char1 and Char2 are characters, then Char1 == Char2 if and only if their ASCII codes are the same.

21. T F   If Name = "John", then Name > " John".

22. T F   If Name = "John", then Name >= "JOHN".

23. T F   "**?" < "***".

24. T F   "** " < "***".

25. T F   A Case statement can be used to select an alternative based on the value of a variable of character type.

26. T F   A menu-driven program requires the user to memorize a list of commands in order to select options offered by the program.

27. T F   In a menu-driven program, the options on the main menu often correspond to separate program modules.

Short Answer

28. Suppose that X = "A". What is displayed when code corresponding to the following program segment is run?

```
If X == "B" Then
    Write "Hi"
End If
Write "Bye"
```

29. Suppose that X = 0. What is displayed when code corresponding to the following program segment is run?

```
If X == 1 Then
    Write "Hi"
Else
    Write "Why?"
End If
Write "Bye"
```

30. Give the ASCII code for each of the following characters:
   a. &
   b. 2
   c. @

31. What character corresponds to each of the following ASCII codes?
   a. 33
   b. 65
   c. 126

32. If the string "}123*" is less than the string MyText (according to the ASCII code), with which character must MyText begin?

33. Give the ASCII code for each of the following strings, character by character:
   a. why?
   b. Oh my!

34. Write a program segment that inputs Age and displays "You are too young to vote" if Age is less than 18 (and displays nothing else).

35. Draw a flowchart that corresponds to Exercise 34.

36. Write a program segment that inputs Age, displays "Yes, you can vote" if Age is 18 or older and displays "You are too young to vote" if Age is less than 18, and displays nothing else. Remember to use the comparison operator when checking the value of Age in your If-Then-Else statements.

37. Draw a flowchart that corresponds to Exercise 36.

38. Write a program segment that contains two If-Then statements and which inputs Num, then displays "Yes" if Num == 1 and displays "No" otherwise.

39. Write a program segment that contains a single If-Then-Else statement and which inputs Num, then displays "Yes" if Num == 1 and displays "No" otherwise.

40. List the programming symbols for the relational operators.

41. List three logical operators used in programming.

42. Write expressions equivalent to the following without using the NOT operator:

   a. NOT (N > 0)

   b. NOT ((N >= 0) AND (N <= 5))

43. Write expressions equivalent to the following using a single relational operator:

   a. (X > 1) AND (X > 5)

   b. (X == 1) OR (X > 1)

Exercises 44 to 48: Be sure to use the hierarchy of order of operations.

44. Evaluate the following expressions, using the values for A, B, and C as given. Note that T means true and F means false.

   | A = T | B = F | C = F | D = T |

   a. A OR B OR C OR D

   b. A AND B AND C AND D

   c. A AND B OR C AND D

   d. A OR B AND C OR D

45. Evaluate the following expressions, using the values for J, K, L, and M as given. Note that T means true and F means false.

   | J = F | K = F | L = T | M = T |

   a. NOT J OR K AND L OR M

   b. NOT J AND NOT K AND NOT L AND NOT M

   c. J AND K OR L AND M

   d. NOT J OR NOT K OR NOT L OR NOT M

46. Evaluate the following expressions, using the values for W, X, Y, and Z as given. Note that T means true and F means false.

   | W = T | X = T | Y = F | Z = T |

   a. W OR X OR X AND Z

b. W OR X OR X AND NOT Z

c. W AND Y AND Y OR X AND Z

d. W AND X AND NOT Y AND Z

47. Evaluate the following expressions, using the values for A, B, C, and D as given. Note that T means true and F means false.

A = T   B = T   C = T   D = F

a. A OR B OR C OR D

b. A OR (B OR (C OR D))

c. A AND B AND C AND D

d. A AND B AND (C OR D)

48. Evaluate the following expressions, using the values for R, S, P, U, and W as given. Note that T means true and F means false.

R = F   S = F   P = F   U = T   W = T

a. (S OR P AND U) OR (NOT R AND NOT S)

b. (R AND NOT S) OR (P AND W) AND NOT (U OR W) OR S

c. (U AND W) OR (R AND S AND NOT P) OR NOT (U AND W)

49. Evaluate the following expression, given that X = 3, Y = 5, and Z = 2. Your answer will either be true or false.

(NOT (X < Y) OR (Y > Z)) AND (X > Z)

50. Evaluate the following expression, given that A = 3 and B = 2. Your answer will either be true or false.

(A + 6)^2 - (B + 4 * A) <= A^3 + B * 5

51. Evaluate the following expression, given that A = 1 and B = 3. Your answer will either be true or false.

B^3 % A > B^3 * A

52. Write 3 short program segments that input Num, then display "Yes" if Num == 1, display "No" if Num == 2, and display "Maybe" if Num == 3. Implement this program segment by:

a. A sequence of If-Then statements

b. Nested If-Then-Else statements

c. A Case statement

53. Write a program segment that inputs a number X and does all of the following:

a. Displays the reciprocal of its square root, $1/_{Sqrt(X)}$, if X > 0

b. Displays "Error: Division by zero", if X = 0

c. Displays "Error: Square root of negative number", if X < 0

54. Which type of selection structure does the flowchart in Figure 4.25 represent?

Figure 4.25 Flowchart for Exercises 54 to 57

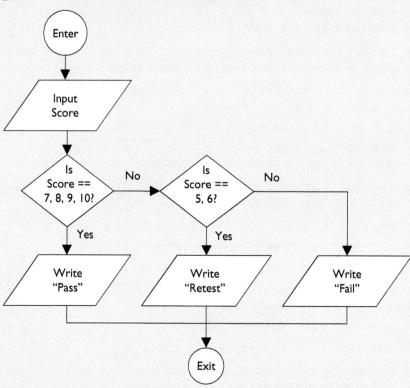

55. Write pseudocode that uses If-Then statements to achieve the same action as that indicated by the flowchart shown in Figure 4.25. Assume that Score is an integer between 1 and 10 inclusively.

56. Write pseudocode that uses nested If-Then-Else statements to implement the flowchart in Figure 4.25. Assume that Score is an integer between 1 and 10 inclusive.

57. Write pseudocode that uses a Case statement to achieve the same action as that indicated by the flowchart in Figure 4.25. Assume that Score is an integer between 1 and 10 inclusive.

58. What is displayed when the code corresponding to the following program segment is run?

```
Set X = 5
If X > 0 Then
   Write X
End If
If NOT ((X == 0) OR (X < 0)) Then
   Write "Not"
End If
If (X ∧ 2 >= 0) AND ((2 * X - 1) != 0) Then
   Write "And"
End If
```

59. Suppose that we replace the first statement in Exercise 58 by

    ```
    Set X = -5
    ```

    What would be displayed when the code is run using this value?

60. Using the code shown below, what will be displayed when the input is as follows:

    a. −1
    b. 0
    c. 1

    ```
    Input Number
    If Number < 0 Then
      Write "1"
    Else
      If Number == 0 Then
        Write "2"
      Else
        Write "3"
      End If
    End If
    Write "DONE"
    ```

61. What is displayed when the code corresponding to the following program segment is run and the input is as follows:

    a. −1
    b. 0
    c. 1

    ```
    Set Number1 = 1
    Input Number2
    Select Case Of Number2
      Case -1:
        Write "A"
        Break
      Case 0:
        Write "B"
        Break
      Case Number1:
        Write "C"
        Break
    End Case
    ```

62. This program segment is supposed to display HELLO if Grade == "A" and display GOODBYE, otherwise. Correct the logic error so that it works correctly.

    ```
    If Grade != "A" Then
      Write "HELLO"
    Else
      Write "GOODBYE"
    End If
    ```

63. This program segment is supposed to display NEGATIVE if Number is less than 0, SMALL if Number lies between 0 and 5 (inclusive), and LARGE if Number is greater than 5. Correct the logic error so that this pseudocode works correctly.

```
If Number < 0 Then
  Write "NEGATIVE"
Else
  If Number > 5 Then
    Write "SMALL"
  Else
    Write "LARGE"
  End If
End If
```

64. What is displayed when the code corresponding to the following program segment is run?

```
Set Y = 1
If Sqrt(Y - 1) == 0 Then
  Write "YES"
Else
  Write "NO"
End If
```

65. What is displayed when the code corresponding to the program segment below is run with the following:

a. X = 4

b. X = 0

```
Declare X As Integer
Input X
If X != 0 Then
  Write 1/X
Else
  Write "The reciprocal of 0 is not defined."
End If
```

66. Which block of statements, the Then clause or the Else clause, provides the error trap in Exercise 65?

67. Consider the following statement:

```
Set Number3 = Sqrt(Number1)/Number2
```

If Number1 and Number2 were input by the user and properly validated to ensure that Number1 is greater than or equal to 0 and Number2 is not zero, is any additional defensive programming necessary?

Programming Challenges

For each of the following Programming Challenges, use the modular approach and pseudocode to design a suitable program to solve it. Where appropriate, use defensive programming techniques.

1. Input a number entered by the user and display "Positive" if it is greater than zero, "Negative" if it is less than zero, and "Zero" if it is equal to zero.

2. Develop a menu-driven program that inputs two numbers and, at the user's option, finds their sum, difference, product, or quotient.

3. Input a number (X) and create a program that allows the user to select finding the area (Area) of one of the following:
   - The area of a square with side X, Area = X * X
   - The area of a circle with radius X, Area = 3.14 * X^2
   - The area of an equilateral triangle with side X, Area = Sqrt(3)/4 * X^2

   Note: Because X represents a dimension, we require that X > 0. Be sure to include this requirement in your program.

4. Consider the equation Ax² + B = 0.
   - If B/A < 0, this equation has two solutions. The solutions are:
     (1) X₁ = Sqrt(-B/A)
     (2) X₂ = -Sqrt(-B/A)
   - If B/A = 0, this equation has one solution which is X = 0
   - If B/A > 0, this equation has no real number solutions

   Write a program to have the user input any numbers for the coefficients, A and B, for this equation. If A = 0, terminate the program. Otherwise, solve the equation.

5. Compute the income tax due on taxable income entered by the user, given the data as shown in the following table. Be sure to include error checking to make sure the user does not enter a negative number. Assume all entries are integer values.

Taxable Income		Tax Due
From	To	
$0	$49,999	$0 + 5% of amount over $0
$50,000	$99,999	$2,500 + 7% of amount over $50,000
$100,000	...	$6,000 + 9% of amount over $100,000

6. Write a program that allows the user to input a total dollar amount for an online shopping order and computes and outputs the shipping cost based on the following schedule:

Order Total	Ship within USA	Ship to Canada
Less than $50.00	$6.00	$8.00
$50.01–$100.00	$9.00	$12.00
$100.01–$150.00	$12.00	$15.00
Over $150.00	Free	Free

7. Write a program that allows the user to enter his or her name. The program should output a username for entry into a website. The user should be prompted to enter a first name, middle initial, and last name. If the user doesn't have a middle initial, the entry should be "none." In this case, the output will be a username that concatenates the first and last names with a dot between them. If the user has a middle initial, the output username should be in the form `first.middle_initial.last`. For example, a user whose name is Harold Nguyen would have `Harold.Nguyen` for his username and a user whose name is Maria Anna Lopez would have `Maria.A.Lopez` for a username.

Repetition Structures: Looping

In this chapter, we will begin to explore the topic of repetition structures (also called loops). We will discuss different types of loops and more advanced loop applications. The discussion of loops continues in Chapter 6.

After reading this chapter, you will be able to do the following:

- Distinguish between pre-test and post-test loops
- Identify infinite loops and loops that never get executed
- Create a flowchart using the loop structure
- Use relational and logical operators in loop conditions
- Construct counter-controlled loops
- Use counter-controlled loops to increment or decrement the counter by any integer value
- Construct For loops
- Create test conditions to avoid infinite loops and loops that never get executed
- Construct sentinel-controlled loops
- Use the following functions: Int(), Floor(), and Ceiling()
- Apply loops to data input and validation problems
- Apply loops to compute sums and averages

Doing the Same Thing Over and Over and Knowing When to Stop

You may not remember, but you probably learned to walk about the time you were a year old. As you took your first step you had to figure out how to execute the following process:

- Put one foot in front of the other

At some point you did just that, and it was a major accomplishment. But this didn't get you very far. If you wanted to walk across the room, you needed to extend this process to the following:

- Put the left foot in front of the right foot
- Put the right foot in front of the left foot
- Put the left foot in front of the right foot
- Put the right foot in front of the left foot and so forth

This is not a very efficient way to describe what you did. A detailed list of your actions as you ambled all over the house would be very long. Because you did the same thing over and over, the following is a much better way to describe your actions:

- Repeat
  - Put the left foot in front of the right foot
  - Put the right foot in front of the left foot
- Until you get across the room

This way is short, convenient, and just as descriptive. Even if you want to take hundreds or thousands of steps, the process can still be described in four lines. This is the basic idea of a loop.

Walking is just one of many examples of loops in your daily life. For example, if you have a large family and need to prepare lunches in the morning for everyone, you can do the following:

- Repeat
  - Make a sandwich
  - Wrap the sandwich
  - Place the sandwich in a lunch bag
  - Place an apple in the lunch bag
  - Place a bag of chips in the lunch bag
- Continue until lunches have been made for everyone in the family

Where else do you encounter a looping process? How about reading your email (one message at a time) or brushing your teeth? If you have a programming class on Tuesdays at 11:00 a.m., you go to class every Tuesday at 11:00 a.m. until the end of the semester. You do the "go to programming class" loop until the end of the semester. After you read this chapter (one word at a time), you'll be ready to place loops in your programs as well.

5.1 An Introduction to Repetition Structures: Computers Never Get Bored!

You have already learned that all computer programs are created from three basic constructs: sequence, decision, and repetition. This chapter discusses repetition, which in many ways is the most important construct of all. We are lucky that computers don't find repetitious tasks boring.

Regardless of what task we ask a computer to perform, the computer is virtually useless if it can perform that task only once. The ability to repeat the same actions over and over is the most basic requirement in programming. When you use any software application, you expect it to open the application and do certain tasks. Imagine if your word processor was programmed to make your text bold only once or if your operating system allowed you to use the copy command only once. Each computer task you perform has been coded into the software by a programmer, and each task must have the ability to be used over and over. In this chapter, we will examine how to program a computer to repeat one or more actions many times.

Loop Basics

All programming languages provide statements to create a **loop**. The loop is the basic component of a **repetition structure**. These statements are a block of code, which under certain conditions, will be executed repeatedly. In this section, we will introduce some basic ideas about these structures. We will start with a simple illustration of a loop shown in Example 5.1. This example uses a type of loop called a **Repeat...Until loop**. Other types of loops are discussed throughout this chapter.

Example 5.1 **Simply Writing Numbers**

This program segment repeatedly inputs a number from the user and displays that number until the user enters 0. The program then displays the words List Ended.

```
1  Declare Number As Integer
2  Repeat
3    Write "Please enter a number: "
4    Input Number
5    Write Number
6  Until Number == 0
7  Write "List Ended"
```

In the pseudocode, the loop begins on line 2 with the word Repeat and ends on line 6 with Until Number == 0. The **loop body** is contained in lines 3, 4, and 5. These are the statements that will be executed repeatedly. The body of a loop is executed until the **test condition** following the word Until on line 6 becomes true. In this case, the test condition becomes true when the user types a 0. At that point, the loop is exited and the statement on line 7 is executed.

What Happened?

Let's trace the execution of this program, assuming that the user enters the numbers 1, 3, and 0, in that order:

- When the execution begins, the loop is entered, the number 1 is input, and this number is displayed. These actions make up the first pass through the loop. The test condition, "Number == 0?" is now "tested" on line 6 and found to be false because at this point, Number == 1. Therefore, the loop is entered again. The program execution returns to line 2, and the body of the loop is executed again. (Recall that the double equals sign, ==, is a comparison operator and asks the question, "Is the value of the variable Number the same as 0?")

- On the second pass through the loop, the number 3 is input (line 4) and displayed (line 5), and once again the condition (line 6), Number == 0 is false. So the program returns to line 2.

- On the third pass through the loop, the number 0 is input and displayed. This time the condition Number == 0 is true, so the loop is exited and execution transfers to line 7, the statement after the loop.

- The words List Ended are displayed and the program is complete.

The flowchart for Example 5.1 is shown in Figure 5.1.

Iterations

We have said that the loop is the basic component of a repetition structure. One of the main reasons a computer can perform many tasks efficiently is because it can quickly repeat tasks over and over. The number of times a task is repeated is always a significant part of any repetition structure, but a programmer must be aware of how many times a loop will be repeated to ensure that the loop performs the task correctly. In computer lingo, a single pass through a loop is called a loop **iteration**. A loop that executes three times goes through three iterations. Example 5.2 presents the iteration process.

Example 5.2 **How Many Iterations?**

This program segment repeatedly asks the user to input a name until the user enters "Done."

```
1  Declare Name As String
2  Repeat
3    Write "Enter the name of your brother or sister: "
4    Input Name
5    Write Name
6  Until Name == "Done"
```

What Happened?

This pseudocode is almost the same as shown in Example 5.1 except that the input in this example is string data instead of integer data. The loop begins on line 2 with the word Repeat and ends on line 6 with Until Name == "Done". The loop body is

Figure 5.1 A simple repetition structure flowchart

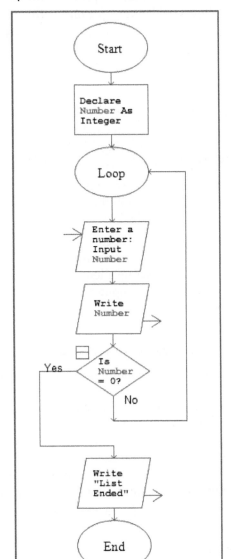

contained in lines 3, 4, and 5. How are the iterations counted? Each time these statements are executed, the loop is said to have gone through one iteration.

- Let's assume that this program segment is used to enter a list of a user's brothers and sisters. If Hector has two brothers named Joe and Jim and one sister named Ellen, the loop would complete four iterations. Joe would be entered on the first iteration; Jim on the second iteration; Ellen on the third iteration, and the word Done would be entered on the fourth iteration.
- If Marie, on the other hand, has only one sister named Anne, the program would go through two iterations—one to enter the name Anne and the second to enter the word Done.

- And if Bobby were an only child, the program would only complete one iteration since Bobby would enter Done on the first iteration.

Later in this chapter, we will see how to create a loop that does not require the test condition count as one of the iterations.

Beware the Infinite Loop!

In Example 5.1, we saw that the user was prompted to enter any number and that number would be displayed on the screen. If the user started with the number 234,789 and worked his way down, entering 234,788, then 234,787, and so forth, the computer would display 234,790 numbers (including the 0 that terminates the loop).

However, after the user entered the last number, 0, the loop would end. It would be a lot of numbers, but it would end. On the other hand, what would happen if the loop was written as shown in Example 5.3?

If, as shown in Example 5.3, a loop's test condition is never satisfied, then the loop will never be exited, and it will become an **infinite loop**. Infinite loops can wreak havoc on a program, so when you set up a loop and put in a test condition, be sure that the test condition can be met. Computers don't mind doing a task many times but forever is simply too many!

Example 5.3 **The Dangerous Infinite Loop**

In this example, we change the test condition of Example 5.1 to a condition that is impossible to achieve. The user is asked to enter a number on line 3, and line 4 takes in the user's input, which is stored in the variable Number. Line 5 sets a new variable, ComputerNumber equal to that number plus one. The loop will continue to ask for and display numbers until the value of Number is greater than ComputerNumber. That condition will never be met because on each pass through the loop, regardless of what number the user enters, ComputerNumber will always be one greater. Thus, the loop will repeat and repeat, continually asking for and displaying numbers.

```
1  Declare Number, ComputerNumber As Integer
2  Repeat
3    Write "Please enter a number: "
4    Input Number
5    Set ComputerNumber = Number + 1
6    Write Number
7  Until Number > ComputerNumber
8  Write "The End"
```

When will it end? Never. The words "The End" will never be displayed.

Don't Let the User Get Trapped in a Loop

There is one more important point to mention about Examples 5.1 and 5.2. In both of these examples, we have test conditions that can easily be met. As soon as a user enters 0 for the number in Example 5.1, the loop ends. As soon as the user enters the word Done in Example 5.2, the loop ends. But how would the user know that 0 or Done is the cue for the program segment to end? It is important for the programmer to make it clear, by means of a suitable prompt, how the user will terminate the action of the loop. In Example 5.1, the following would be a suitable prompt:

```
Write "Enter a number; enter 0 to quit."
```

In Example 5.2, the following would be a suitable prompt:

```
Write "Enter the name of your brother or sister:"
Write "Enter the word 'Done' to quit."
```

In the type of loops we used in these two examples, the loop continues until the user ends it. Other loops end without a user input. Regardless of what type of loop you write, you always wish to avoid the possibility that the loop will continue without an end. Therefore, you must ensure that the test condition can be met and, if the user must enter something special to end the loop, be sure it's clear.

Relational and Logical Operators

The condition that determines whether a loop is re-entered or exited is usually constructed with the help of relational and logical operators. We will briefly review these operators.

The following are the six standard **relational operators** and the programming symbols that we will use in this book to represent them:

- equal to (or "is the same as"): ==
- not equal to: !=
- less than: <
- less than or equal to: <=
- greater than: >
- greater than or equal to: >=

All six operators can be applied to either numeric or character string data. Recall that the double equals sign, the comparison operator (==) is different from the assignment operator (=). While the assignment operator assigns the value on the right side of the equals sign to the variable on the left side, the comparison operator compares the values of the variable or expression on the left side of the operator with the value of the variable, expression, number, or text on the right side. It returns only a value of false (if the two values are different) or true (if the two values are the same). When a comparison operator is used, neither the value on the left side nor the statement on right side changes from its initial value. The result of any relational operator is always a value of true or false.

The basic logical operators, OR, AND, and NOT, are used to create more complicated conditions (**compound conditions**) from given simple conditions. If S1 and S2 are conditions (such as Number <= 0 or Response == "Y") then we have the following:

- S1 OR S2 is true if *either* S1 is true or S2 is true or both are true; it is false if both S1 and S2 are false.
- S1 AND S2 are true if *both* S1 and S2 are true; it is false if either S1 or S2 or both are false.

- NOT S1 is true if S1 is false; the condition is false if S1 is true.

If Number = 3 and Name = "Joe", then we have the following compound conditions:

- (Number == 1) OR (Name == "Joe") is true but (Number == 1) AND (Name == "Joe") is false because one of the simple conditions (Number == 1) is false.
- NOT ((Number == 1) OR (Name == "Joe")) is false because (Number == 1) OR (Name == "Joe") is true.

Constructing Flowcharts with a Loop Structure

The use of flowcharts in program design is a topic often debated. Some programmers cannot imagine designing a program without flowcharts, while other programmers rarely use them. Most programmers, however, follow the same approach that is used in this textbook; we combine pseudocode and flowcharts in our designs. There are certain programs that lend themselves more easily to design with pseudocode and others that work better with flowcharts. Repetition structures are often more easily visualized with flowcharts than with pseudocode because the loop can be seen pictorially.

Self Check for Section 5.1

5.1 What numbers will be displayed if code corresponding to the following pseudocode is run?

a.
```
Declare Number As Integer
   Set Number = 1
   Repeat
     Write 2 * Number
     Set Number = Number + 1
   Until Number == 3
```

b.
```
Declare Number As Integer
   Set Number = 1
   Repeat
     Write 2 * Number
     Set Number = Number + 1
   Until Number > 3
```

5.2 What will be displayed if code corresponding to the following pseudocode is run? Assume the user is 17 years old.
```
   Declare Age As Integer
   Declare NewAge As Integer
   Declare Number As Integer
   Set Number = 2
   Write "Enter your age: "
   Input Age
   Repeat
     Set NewAge = Age + Number
```

```
      Write "In " + Number + " years you will be " + NewAge
      Set Number = Number + 1
   Until Number == 4
```

5.3 Indicate whether each of the following conditions is `true` or `false`.

   a. `5 == 5`

   b. `5 != 5`

   c. `5 < 5`

   d. `5 <= 5`

   e. `5 > 5`

   f. `5 >= 5`

5.4 If `C1 = "Jo"` and `C2 = "jo"`, indicate whether each of the following is `true` or `false`.

   a. `C1 >= "Ann"`

   b. `(C1 == "Jo") AND (C2 == "Mo")`

   c. `C1 == "Jo "`

   d. `(C1 == "Jo") OR (C2 == "Mo")`

   e. `C1 <= "Joe"`

   f. `NOT(C1 == C2)`

5.2 Types of Loops

As you learn to write more complicated programs, you will find that loops are one of your most indispensable tools. You'll use loops to load data, manipulate data, interact with the user, and much more. In fact, it would be difficult to imagine any program that does significant processing that does not contain loops. Just as one size does not fit all when it comes to choosing a screwdriver and nails for a carpentry project, loops come in various types as well. One type of loop may work well for one specific program's need, while another type fits a different program's design. In this section, you will learn about several types of loops and how and why one may be chosen over another in a specific situation.

Pre-Test and Post-Test Loops

Basically, all repetition structures can be divided into two fundamental types: **pre-test loops** and **post-test loops.** The following loop (from Example 5.1) is an example of a post-test loop because the test condition occurs *after* the body of the loop is executed:

```
Declare Number As Integer
Repeat
  Write "Enter a number: "
  Input Number
  Write Number
Until Number == 0
Write "List Ended"
```

The Do . . . While Loop

In the previous section, we used the pseudocode `Repeat . . . Until` for a post-test loop. Many languages include a slightly different syntax for post-test loops. These loops begin with a `Do` statement and close with a `While` statement. The following example shows this syntax in pseudocode and does the same thing as the `Repeat . . . Until` example:

```
Declare Number As Integer
Do
  Write "Enter a number: "
  Input Number
  Write Number
While Number != 0
Write "List Ended"
```

Notice, though, that the test condition is altered to fit the requirements of the `Do . . . While` loop. In a `Repeat . . . Until` loop, the loop is executed *until* a specified condition *becomes* true. In a **Do . . . While loop**, the loop is executed *while* a specified condition *remains* true.

In a pre-test loop, the test condition occurs *before* the body of the loop is executed. The **While loop** is one type of a pre-test loop. This significant difference warrants some careful examination and is illustrated in Examples 5.4 through 5.6.

Creating Loop Examples With RAPTOR

While most of the examples in this chapter can be implemented with RAPTOR, it is recommended that you read the first part of Section 5.6 before attempting to implement loops in RAPTOR. You may have to alter the way test conditions are written in the textbook examples for your programs to work in RAPTOR.

Example 5.4 **Writing Numbers with a Pre-Test Loop**

The following program segment does almost the same thing as shown in Example 5.1. However, in Example 5.1, we tested to see if the `Number == 0` after a number had been displayed. In the following, we test to see if `Number == 0` on line 4, before the first number has been displayed:

```
1  Declare Number As Integer
2  Write "Enter a number; enter 0 to quit."
3  Input Number
4  While Number != 0
5    Write Number
6    Input Number
7  End While
8  Write "List Ended"
```

What Happened?

In this pseudocode, the statement on line 4 begins with the word `While` and is followed by the test condition `Number != 0`, which as you remember, means "is `Number` not equal to 0?" The last statement in the loop is `End While` on line 7. All the statements between the `While` and the `End While` (lines 5 and 6) comprise the body of the `While` loop. When the loop is entered, the test condition is evaluated. If it is found to be `true`, the body of the loop is executed and control then returns to line 4, the top of the loop. If the test condition is found to be `false`, then the loop is exited and the statement following `End While` on line 8 is executed next.

Let's walk through the execution of this program segment using the same values that we tried in Example 5.1 to see what happens now. We'll take the first value the user enters for `Number` to be 1, and then on the next two passes through the loop the user will enter the numbers 3 and 0. In this case, execution flows as follows:

- When execution begins, the number 1 is input (line 3).
- On line 4, the `While` statement is executed. It checks the test condition `Number != 0`, which is found to be `true` since `Number = 1` at this point. Thus, the body of the loop is executed.
- Lines 5 and 6 are the body of the loop. Line 5 causes a 1 to be displayed, and line 6 asks for another number. The user inputs a 3. Then control returns to the top of the loop, on line 4. Lines 1, 2, and 3 are never executed again in this program segment.
- Line 4 tests the condition again and because `Number` now equals 3, the test is `true` and a second pass is made through the loop.
- This time 3 is displayed (line 5) and 0 is input (line 6) and control returns to the top of the loop.
- Once again, the test condition is evaluated on line 4. Because `Number` is now equal to 0, the test condition is found to be `false`. Therefore, the loop is exited *before* the 0 is displayed and control jumps to line 8.
- Line 8 causes the words `List Ended` to be displayed and the program is complete.

In Example 5.1, if the numbers 1, 3, and 0 are input, then the numbers 1, 3, and 0 are all displayed (and then the words `List Ended`). In Example 5.4, with the same input, only the numbers 1 and 3 are displayed (and then the words `List Ended`). What makes the display for this example different from Example 5.1? That's the key to understanding pre-test and post-test loops. In Example 5.1, because the condition was tested after the loop body statements were executed, the last number input (0) was also displayed. In Example 5.4, because the condition was tested before the loop body statements were executed, the last number input (0) caused the condition to fail before a 0 could be displayed.

What would happen, if in Example 5.4, the user inputs a 0 on line 3? In this case, the test on line 4 would ask "Is `Number` not equal to 0?" and the answer would be "no" because `Number` *is* equal to 0. Therefore, the test condition would be `false`, the loop body statements would never be executed, and control would immediately jump to line 8.

What would happen if, in Example 5.4, we left out line 3? In Example 5.1, the post-test loop, the first value of Number, was input by the user within the loop body and then the condition was tested. In Example 5.4, we asked the user to input a value for Number before the test condition. If we left off this line, the first line of this loop would be a test of the value of a variable named Number. Unless that variable had been given a value somewhere else in the program, the programmer would have no control at all over what would happen in the first pass of this loop. If the variable Number had a value of 0 from a previous assignment, the loop would never execute. If it had a value of 23 from a previous assignment, the loop would work fine, although a 23 would be displayed, even if the user did not want to see 23. And, if the memory location assigned to Number had never been assigned any value, the program might crash completely or execute in an undetermined manner, depending on the computer's operating system, the language used, and so on. So the initial value of a variable used is a very important consideration!

Example 5.5 **Using the Pre-Test Loop Wisely**

In Example 5.2 we saw that, no matter how many names a user entered, the last name on the displayed list would be Done. This is surely not desirable. We can eliminate this unwanted display by changing the pseudocode of Example 5.2 to a pre-test loop, shown as follows:

```
1  Declare Name As String
2  Write "Enter the name of your brother or sister:"
3  Write "Enter the word Done to quit."
4  Input Name
5  While Name != "Done"
6     Write Name
7     Input Name
8  End While
```

What Happened?

Now, if Hector from Example 5.2 enters Joe, Jim, Ellen, and Done the display would be:

```
Joe
Jim
Ellen
```

The word Done would not be displayed because after the third iteration of the loop, the value of Name would be Done, the test condition on line 5 would confirm that the condition no longer is true, and the loop body would not be executed a fourth time.

With this pseudocode, our only-child, Bobby, would not see the word Done on his list of no brothers and sisters. He would simply enter the word Done at the first prompt, the condition would be tested on line 5, found to be false, and control would jump to whatever instructions came after line 8. The loop would never be entered.

There are several basic differences between pre-test and post-test loops. They are:

- By definition, a pre-test loop has its test condition (the statement that determines whether the body of the loop is executed) at the top. A post-test loop has its test condition at the bottom.
- The body of a post-test loop is always executed at least once, but the body of a pre-test loop won't be executed at all if its test condition is initially false.
- Before a pre-test loop is entered, the variables that appear in its test condition must be initialized; that is, they must be assigned some value. This isn't necessary in the post-test loop because the test condition variables may be initialized within the body of the loop.

Figure 5.2 illustrates the logical differences between pre- and post-test loops through flowcharts. Example 5.6 demonstrates how to use a pre-test loop to display squares of numbers.

Either a pre-test loop or a post-test loop can be used to accomplish a given task; although as you will discover, some tasks are easier to accomplish with pre-test loops and others with post-test loops.

Figure 5.2 Pre- and post-test loop flowcharts

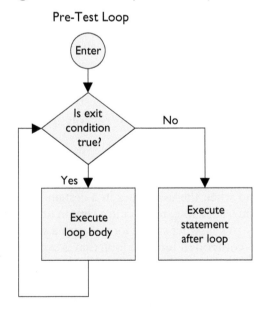

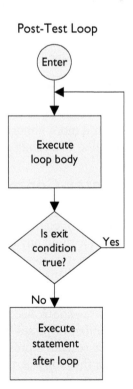

Example 5.6 **Numbers Squared**

The following program segment uses a pre-test loop to display the squares of numbers input by the user until he or she enters zero or a negative number. The zero or negative number is not displayed.

```
Declare Number As Integer
Write "Enter a number:"
Input Number
While Number > 0
  Write Number^2
  Input Number
End While
```

Notice that we initialize the variable Number by using an Input statement just prior to entering the loop. Trace this pseudocode with the test data 4, 3, 2, 1, and -1 to see for yourself how it works. Check that the numbers you would expect to see written to the screen are 16, 9, 4, and 1.

Indent the Body of a Loop

To make it easier to read your pseudocode and the corresponding program code, you should indent the body of a loop relative to its first and last statements. For example, compare the loop on the right, which is indented, with that on the left, which is not, as follows:

Not indented	Indented
Repeat	Repeat
Input Number	Input Number
Write Number	Write Number
Until Number == 0	Until Number == 0

As you begin to write longer and more complicated programs, this style becomes more and more important. It will enable you to quickly identify where loops begin and end as you debug a program.   ●

Counter-Controlled Loops

All the loops that we have seen so far end when the user types in a certain value. There are, of course, many times when you want a loop to execute a certain number of times without any user input. One way to construct such a loop is with a special type of pre-test loop known as a **counter-controlled loop**—a loop that is executed a fixed number of times, where that number is known prior to entering the loop for the first time.

A counter-controlled loop contains a variable (the **counter**) that keeps track of the number of passes through the loop (the number of loop iterations). When the counter reaches a preset number, the loop is exited. In order for the computer to execute the loop a certain number of times, it must keep track of how many times it goes through the loop. It stores this number in the counter.

Using a Counter

To keep track of how many times a loop has been executed using a counter, you must define, initialize, and either **increment** (to count up) or **decrement** (to count down) the counter. Self-Check Exercises 5.1 and 5.2 use a counter without actually defining it as such. The code to keep a count like this may seem a bit strange at first, but it will quickly make sense. Although there are small syntax differences in different programming languages, the code for a counter in any language is always similar. It is illustrated in Example 5.7 and described in the following list:

1. **Define a counter:** the counter is a variable. It is always an integer because it counts the number of times the loop body is executed and you cannot tell a computer to do something 5 3/4 times. Common variable names for counters are `counter`, `Count`, `I`, or `j`. For now, we will call our counter `Count`.

2. **Initialize the counter:** set the counter at a beginning value. Although a counter can begin at any integer value—often determined by other factors in the program—for now, we will usually set our counter equal to 0 or 1 (`Set Count = 0` or `Set Count = 1`, depending on the program's requirements).

3. **Increment the counter:** the computer counts the way you did when you were young. To count by ones, the computer takes what it had before and adds one. So the code for a computer to count by ones looks like `Count + 1`. Then, to store the new value where the old value was, you use the statement `Set Count = Count + 1`. This takes the old value, adds one to it, and stores the new value where the old value was.

Example 5.7 **Using a Counter to Display the Squares of Numbers**

A common use of counter-controlled loops is to print tables of data. For example, suppose we want to display the squares of a certain number of positive integers, where that number is to be entered by the user and stored in a variable named `PositiveInteger`. The pseudocode for this process is shown as follows:

```
1  Declare PositiveInteger As Integer
2  Declare Count As Integer
3  Write "Please enter a positive integer: "
4  Input PositiveInteger
5  Set Count = 1
6  While Count <= PositiveInteger
7    Write Count + "  " + Count^2
8    Set Count = Count + 1
9  End While
```

What Happened?

Let's walk through this pseudocode, one line at a time.

- Lines 1 and 2 declare the two integer variables.
- Line 3 asks the user to input a positive integer.

- Line 4 stores the value entered by the user in a variable named `PositiveInteger`.
- Line 5 sets `Count` equal to its first value—we initialize it to 1—before entering the loop.
- Line 6 is the beginning of the loop. It tests to see if `Count` is less than or equal to `PositiveInteger`. We want the loop body statements to execute so that the number and its square are displayed, for all numbers from 1 up to and including the value of `PositiveInteger`. In other words, if you entered 3 for `PositiveInteger`, you would want to see the following:

    1   1
    2   4
    3   9

- Line 7 writes the value of `Count` and the square of `Count` to the screen, separated by a space.
- Line 8 increments `Count` by 1 within the loop. Then the program goes back to the beginning of the loop on line 6.
- Line 9 is only reached when the value of `Count` becomes greater than the value of `PositiveInteger`.

A flowchart corresponding to this pseudocode is shown in Figure 5.3.

What would happen if, in Example 5.7, the user inputs a value of 1 for `PositiveInteger`? Line 6 would test to see if `PositiveInteger` was less than or equal to `Count`. This would be `true` and the loop body would execute once. Then `Count` would be incremented to 2, which is greater than `PositiveNumber` so the loop would be exited. The display would be as follows:

    1   1

What would happen if, in this example, the user inputs a value of 0 for `PositiveInteger`? The test condition would immediately be `false`, the loop body would never execute, and there would be nothing displayed.

Try this: Go through Example 5.7 by hand, using 6 as the value entered for `PositiveInteger`. Check to make sure your results are as follows:

    1   1
    2   4
    3   9
    4   16
    5   25
    6   36

Counting Up, Down, and Every Way

Counters don't just have to count by ones and counters don't just have to count up. You can start a counter with any number you want and count up to a certain number, as we did in Example 5.7, or you can count down to a certain number, as illustrated in Example 5.8. We can start a counter at any number and count up (or down) by twos, fives, or by any whole number.

Figure 5.3 A flowchart that uses a counter in a loop

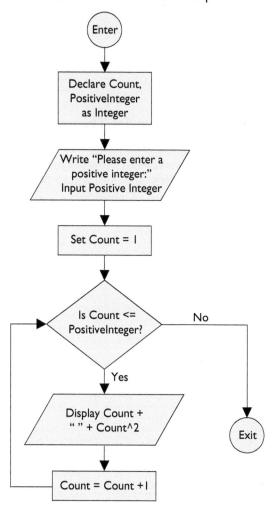

Example 5.8 **Countdown to Blastoff Using a Decremental Counter**

Let's display a countdown for a rocket to blast off to the moon. The countdown begins at 100 and counts down to 1 at one-second intervals as follows:

```
1  Declare Count As Integer
2  Set Count = 100
3  Write "Countdown in . . . ";
4  While Count > 0
5    Write Count + " seconds"
6    Set Count = Count - 1
7  End While
8  Write "Blastoff!"
```

Notice that in this example, as in our previous example, the counter has two purposes. Not only does it count how many times the loop has been repeated but also

it is used in the output. This may not always be true. Sometimes a counter simply counts the number of iterations in a loop and sometimes, as here, it serves a dual purpose.

Example 5.9 illustrates a loop with a counter that is used only to count the number of iterations but is not used in the output.

Example 5.9 A Few of Your Favorite Things

Let's assume you are writing a program to allow users to create a profile on a website. In this program segment, a counter is used to allow the user to enter his or her three favorite leisure time activities. The three activities will be displayed, but the counter is used only to keep track of the number of iterations.

```
1   Declare Count As Integer
2   Declare Activity As String
3   Set Count = 1
4   Set Activity = " "
5   Write "Enter 3 things you like to do in your free time:"
6   While Count < 4
7      Input Activity
8      Write "You enjoy " + Activity
9      Set Count = Count + 1
10  End While
```

If the user enters biking, football, and computer programming for the three activities, the display would look like this:

```
You enjoy biking
You enjoy football
You enjoy computer programming
```

The flowchart for this program segment is shown in Figure 5.4 .

What &Why

It is possible to use the counter to keep track of the number of iterations, to use it as part of the display, and to combine this with displaying other variables. Here, we will spruce up the output of Example 5.9 and use the counter to help us do that.

```
1   Declare Count As Integer
2   Declare Activity As String
3   Set Count = 1
4   Set Activity = " "
5   Write "Enter 3 things you like to do in your free time:"
6   While Count < 4
7      Input Activity
8      Write Count + ". You enjoy " + Activity
9      Set Count = Count + 1
10  End While
```

Now, if the user enters biking, football, and computer programming for the three activities, the display would look like this:

1. You enjoy biking
2. You enjoy football
3. You enjoy computer programming

Figure 5.4 A flowchart that uses the counter to keep track of the number of iterations

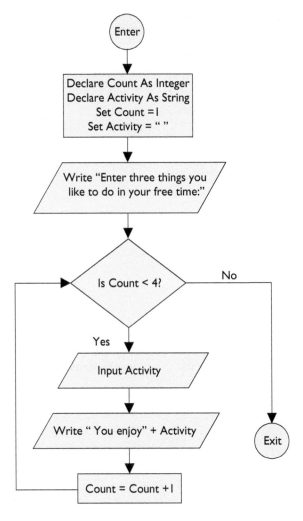

Self Check for Section 5.2

5.5 Create flowcharts for the program segments of Examples 5.5 and 5.6.

5.6 The following program is supposed to input numbers from the user and display them as long as 0 is not entered, but a statement is missing. What is the missing statement? Insert it in its proper place.

```
Declare Number As Integer
Input Number
While Number != 0
   Write Number
End While
```

5.7 The variable that stores the number of times a loop has completed is called a _____.

5.8 True or false? It is possible to increment a counter by 14 on each loop iteration.

5.9 True or false? It is possible to decrement a counter by any multiple of 4.

5.10 True or false? The counter can be any real number.

5.11 What numbers will be displayed when a code corresponding to the following pseudocode is run?

a.
```
Declare N, K As Integer
Set N = 6
Set K = 3
While K <= N
   Write N + " " + K
   Set N = N - 1
End While
```

b.
```
Declare K As Integer
Set K = 10
While K >= 7
   Write K
   Set K = K - 2
End While
```

5.12 Create a pseudocode that does the same thing as the following program segment but uses a post-test loop instead of a pre-test loop. You can use either a Repeat . . . Until or a Do . . . While structure.
```
Declare W As Integer
Declare Count As Integer
Set Count = 1
Set W = 2
While Count < 4
   Write Count * W
   Set Count = Count + 1
End While
```

5.3 The For Loop

Most programming languages contain a statement that makes it easy to construct a counter-controlled loop. To create a built-in counter-controlled loop, we introduce the For loop. The **For loop** provides a shortened method to initialize the counter, to tell the computer how much to increase or decrease the counter for each pass through the loop, and to tell the computer when to stop.

The For Statement

We will use the following pseudocode to represent the statement that creates a built-in counter-controlled loop that increases the value of the counter by 1 on each iteration:

```
For (Counter = InitialValue; Test Condition; Counter++)
   body of the loop
End For
```

This kind of statement will repeatedly execute the body of the loop starting with Counter equal to the specified InitialValue and incrementing Counter by 1 on each pass through the loop. Counter++ acts just like the statement Set Counter = Counter + 1. This continues until the Test Condition is met. While we will discuss each part of the For loop in detail in this section, Example 5.10 demonstrates how the simplest For loop works.

Example 5.10 **The Action of a For Loop**

```
For (Count = 1; Count <= 4; Count++)
   Write Count
End For
```

In this example, the loop is executed with Count equal to 1 on the first pass, then 2, then 3, and finally 4. The output of this program segment consists of the numbers 1, 2, 3, and 4.

There are three statements within the parentheses after the word For, separated by semicolons. The first statement sets the counter to an initial value. The second statement describes the test condition. The last statement tells the computer how much to increase or decrease the counter on each subsequent pass through the loop. In Example 5.10, the counter was incremented by 1 on each pass. However, a general form of a For loop is as follows:

```
For(Counter = InitialValue; Test Condition; Increment/Decrement)
   body of the loop
End For
```

Let's discuss each of the three statements in a bit more detail. In a typical For statement, Counter must be a variable, Increment or Decrement is normally a number, and InitialValue and Test Condition may be constants, variables, or expressions.

The Initial Value

The first statement sets the counter to its initial value. The initial value can be any integer constant, such as 1, 0, 23, or -4. The initial value can also be another numeric variable. For example, if a variable named LowNumber was set equal to an integer prior to entering the For loop, the counter could be initialized to the value of LowNumber. The first statement in the For loop would then look like this: Count = LowNumber. Similarly, the counter could be set equal to an expression containing a numeric variable and a number, such as `Count = (LowNumber + 3)`. However, the counter itself must be a variable and the initial value must be an integer.

- `Count = 5` is a valid initialization of a counter.
- `Count = NewNumber` is a valid initialization of a counter, if `NewNumber` is an integer variable.
- `Count = (NewNumber * 2)` is a valid initialization of a counter if `NewNumber` is an integer variable.
- `Count = (5/2)` is not a valid initialization of a counter because 5/2 is not an integer.
- `23 = Count` is not a valid initialization of a counter.

The Test Condition

The test condition is, perhaps, the most important statement of the three. It is important to understand what the test condition represents, where the test is made, and what happens after the condition is tested. The test condition asks the question, "Is the counter within the range specified by this condition?" If the test condition is, for example, `Count < 10`, then the question asked is, "Is the value of `Count` less than 10?" If the answer to that question is "yes" then the loop executes again. If the answer is "no" then the loop is exited. This means that when `Count` is equal to 10, the loop will be exited. However, if the test condition were `Count <= 10`, the question asked is, "Is the value of `Count` less than or equal to 10?" In this case, the loop will not be exited until `Count` is at least 11.

Another important consideration about test conditions in any loop, including `Repeat...Until`, `Do...While`, and `While` loops as well as `For` loops, is when the check of the test condition occurs. As we have seen, the test condition is checked at the end of a loop in a post-test loop and at the beginning in a pre-test loop. This is clear from the language of those loops, but it is not so clear with a `For` loop. In a `For` loop, the test condition is checked at the beginning. If the initial value of the counter passes the test condition, the loop is entered once. After the loop body executes once, the counter is then either incremented or decremented, and the test condition is checked again.

The test condition can also be a number, another variable with a numeric value, or an expression containing variables and numbers. For example, if `NewNumber` is an integer variable:

- `Count < 5` is a valid test condition and a loop with this condition will execute until `Count` has the value of 5 or more.
- `Count >= 6` is a valid test condition and a loop with this condition will execute until `Count` becomes 5 or less.
- `Count >= NewNumber` is a valid test condition and will execute until `Count` becomes less than the value of `NewNumber`.
- `Count < (NewNumber + 5)` is a valid test condition. A loop with this condition will execute until `Count` becomes greater than or equal to the value of `NewNumber + 5`.

The Increment/Decrement Statement

The increment or decrement statement does the same thing that the Set Count = Count + 1 or Set Count = Count - 1 statements used in Examples 5.7–5.9 did. However, many programming languages use a shorthand method to increment or decrement the counter. In our pseudocode, we will use a similar shorthand as follows:

- Count++ increments the variable named Count by 1 (i.e., it counts up).
- Count-- decrements the variable named Count by 1 (i.e., it counts down).
- To increase or decrease a counter by any integer other than 1, we will use the following shorthand:
  - Count+2 increments Count by 2. For example, if Count = 0 initially, it will equal 2 on the next pass through the loop, 4 on the next pass, and so on. This shorthand is comparable to the following pseudocode: Count = Count + 2.
  - Count-3 decrements Count by 3. For example, if Count = 12 initially, it will equal 9 on the next pass through the loop, then 6, then 3 and so on. This shorthand is comparable to the following pseudocode: Count = Count - 3.
  - Therefore, Count+X will increase Count by the value of X and Count-X will decrease Count by the value of X after each pass through the loop.

Examples 5.11 and 5.12 demonstrate incremental and decremental For loops.

Example 5.11 **An Incremental For Loop**

A For loop that increments a counter by 5 and displays how to count by fives from 0 to 15 would, thus be written as follows:

```
For (Count = 0; Count <= 15; Count+5)
   Write Count
End For
```

In this program segment, the counter is the variable named Count and it is initialized to the constant 0. The increment is 5; Count+5 tells the computer to add 5 to the value of Count for each pass through the loop. The test condition is the expression Count <= 15.

What Happened?

On the first pass through this loop, Count = 0, a 0 is written to the screen, and 5 is added to Count. Then the test condition is checked. The check determines that Count is not greater than 15, so another pass is made through the loop. On the second pass, Count = 5, a 5 is written to the screen, and 5 is added to Count. The test condition is checked again. Since 10 (the new value of Count) is not greater than 15, the loop is executed again. On the third pass, Count = 10 so a 10 is written to the screen, and 5 is added to Count. The test condition then determines that Count is still not greater than the limit (15 is equal to 15 but not greater than 15) and the loop is executed one more time.

On this last pass through the loop, Count = 15 so a 15 is written to the screen, Count is again incremented by 5 so its value is now 20. This time, when the test condition is checked, `Count` fails the test and the loop ends. The output of this program segment would be as follows:

```
0
5
10
15
```

? What &Why

The pseudocode that corresponds to the For loop of Example 5.11 is as follows:

```
Set Count = 0
While Count <= 15
    Write Count
    Set Count = Count + 5
End While
```

Notice that the variable `Count` is initialized before entering the `While` loop and the increment/decrement statement occurs inside the loop body in this pseudocode that corresponds to a For loop. To implement a For loop in RAPTOR, a flowchart similar to this comparable pseudocode must be used.   ●

Example 5.12 A Decremental For Loop

A For loop that decrements a counter by 5 and displays how to count down by fives from 15 to 0 would thus be written as follows:

```
For (Count = 15; Count >= 0; Count-5)
    Write Count
End For
```

In this program segment, `Count` is initialized to the constant 15. The decrement is 5; `Count-5` tells the computer to subtract 5 from the value of `Count` for each pass through the loop. The test condition is the expression `Count >= 0` and it means that, when `Count` becomes less than 0, the loop will end. The output of this program segment would be as follows:

```
15
10
 5
 0
```

The For Loop in Action

To summarize our discussion to this point, a For loop works as follows: when the loop is entered, the `Counter` is set equal to an `InitialValue`. If the `InitialValue` immediately passes the test of the `Test Condition`, then the body of the loop is executed. If the `Counter` doesn't pass the test, the loop is skipped and the statement following `End For` is executed next.

On each pass through the loop, the `Counter` is increased or decreased by the value of `Increment/Decrement`. Then, if the new value of the `Counter` passes the `Test Condition`, the body of the loop is executed again. When the value of the `Counter` no longer is within the range of the `Test Condition`, the loop is exited and the statement following `End For` is executed next. Example 5.13 demonstrates the use of an expression as a test condition.

Example 5.13 **Using an Expression for a Test Condition**

In the following For loop, the test condition is not a constant but an expression. In this loop, the counter is increased by 3 with each iteration until it reaches the value of two more than the variable named myNumber:

```
Set MyNumber = 7
For (Count = 1; Count <= (MyNumber + 1); Count+3)
   Write Count
End For
```

The display after this segment is executed will look like this:

```
1
4
7
```

What Happened?

On the first pass, Count = 1. The test condition states that the loop should be executed again so long as Count is less than or equal to MyNumber + 1, which is 8. On the second pass, Count = 1 + 3 = 4. On the third pass, Count = 4 + 3 = 7. On the fourth pass, Count = 7 + 3 = 10. At this point, Count fails the Test Condition so the loop ends.

Example 5.14 allows the user to control the test condition.

Example 5.14 **Using a For Loop to Display the Squares of Numbers**

The following For loop has the same effect as the While loop that we constructed in Example 5.7. It displays a table of numbers and their squares from 1 to PositiveInteger. The test condition in this example depends on the user's input of a value for PositiveInteger.

```
1  Declare Count As Integer
2  Declare PositiveInteger As Integer
3  Write "Please enter a positive integer: "
4  Input PositiveInteger
5  For (Count = 1; Count <= PositiveInteger; Count++)
6     Write Count + " " + Count^2
7  End For
```

The flowchart showing the action of the incremental For loop of Example 5.14 is shown in Figure 5.4 . This flowchart also illustrates the While loop of Example 5.7. The logic is the same; the differences are particular to the programming language used and the preferences of the programmer.

Examples 5.15–5.17 provide a few more examples and illustrate additional features of For loops.

Example 5.15 **Using a For Loop to Count by Twos**

This program provides an example of a For loop with an increment value that is not equal to 1. It displays the odd numbers between 1 and 20.

```
1  Declare Count As Integer
2  For (Count = 1; Count <= 20; Count+2)
3    Write Count
4  End For
```

The numbers that would be displayed on the screen would be all the odd numbers from 1, going up to and including 19.

What Happened?

On the first pass through this loop, Count is initialized to 1 (line 2), displayed (line 3), and incremented by 2 (due to the Count+2 statement on line 2). Now Count = 3, so on the second pass, the test condition (Count <= 20 on line 2) is also checked. Since 3 is not greater than 20, execution proceeds to line 3 again. A 3 is displayed and Count is incremented by 2 again. This continues until the 10th pass. On this loop iteration, the value of Count (19) is displayed and Count is incremented to 21. Since Count now exceeds the limit of the test condition (20), the loop is exited.

Example 5.16 **Stepping Down**

By using a negative value for the loop increment/decrement, we can step backward through a loop. In this case, we are decrementing the counter. That is, we have the counter variable decrease in value from iteration to iteration. For a negative increment, the loop is exited when the value of the counter becomes less than the loop's limit value.

```
1  Declare Count As Integer
2  For (Count = 9; Count >=5; Count-2)
3    Write Count
4  End For
```

The numbers that will be written to the screen if this program segment was coded and run would be 9, 7, and 5.

What Happened?

- Line 2: the counter, Count, is initialized to 9 and the code also says that on each pass through the loop Count will be decreased by 2 until it no longer is greater than or equal to 5.
- Line 3: the initial value of Count, 9, is displayed.
- Next, -2 (the decrement) is added to Count. The value of Count is now 7. Since the limiting value is 5 and Count is still not less than 5, a second pass is done.
- On the second pass, 7 is displayed and Count is decreased to 5. It is still not less than 5, so another pass can be executed.
- Finally, on the third pass 5 is displayed and Count is set equal to 3. Because 3 is less than the limiting value (5), the loop is exited.

Example 5.17 **The Prisoner in the Loop**

If the loop increment is positive and the initial value is greater than the limiting value, then the body of the loop is skipped as follows:

```
1  Declare Count As Integer
2  Write "Hello"
3  For (Count = 5; Count < 4; Count++)
4    Write "Help, I'm a prisoner in a For loop!"
5  End For
6  Write "Goodbye"
```

What Happened?

In this example, the initial value of Count is set to 5 and Count will be incremented by 1 for each iteration of the loop. Unfortunately, the test condition says to execute the loop only while Count is less than 4. Since Count starts out greater than 4, it can never be less than 4 so the body of the loop is skipped. Line 4 will never be executed and whoever is in the loop body is trapped there forever. Thus, the output produced by the code corresponding to this pseudocode is shown as follows:

```
Hello
Goodbye
```

The Careful Bean Counter

We round out this section of the chapter with several examples that illustrate some of the pitfalls that can be encountered in both For and While loops. One of the most common errors in a program is using a counter incorrectly. It is the programmer's decision to pick an initial value, an increment or decrement amount, and a test condition. These choices determine how many times the loop executes. It is very important to check your initial value and test condition value carefully to make sure your loop repeats exactly as many times as you need. With that in mind, we'll do some bean counting in Examples 5.18 through 5.24.

Example 5.18 **Count Four Beans**

```
1  Declare Count As Integer
2  Declare Beans as Integer
3  Set Beans = 4
4  For (Count = 1; Count <= Beans; Count++)
5    Write "bean"
6  End For
```

What Happened?

Let's see what happens with this program. On the first pass, Count = 1, which is less than Beans (4) and one "bean" is displayed. Then the counter is incremented to 2, which is still less than 4 so a second "bean" is displayed and Count is incremented to 3. This is still less than 4, so the loop repeats, a third "bean" is displayed, and Count is incremented to 4. A fourth "bean" is displayed and Count is incremented to 5. Now Count is greater than Beans (4) so the loop stops. We have displayed four "bean"s, as instructed.

Example 5.19 shows another way to do the same thing.

Example 5.19 **Count Four Beans Another Way**

```
1   Declare Count As Integer
2   Declare Beans As Integer
3   Set Beans = 4
4   For (Count = Beans; Count >= 1; Count--)
5     Write "bean"
6   End For
```

What Happened?

We begin this program with Count = 4 (the value of Beans). On the first pass, one "bean" is displayed and Count is decremented to 3. Since 3 is greater than 1, the loop continues again, a second "bean" is displayed, and Count is decremented to 2. This is still greater than 1, so a third "bean" is displayed and Count is decremented to 1. This passes the test condition because the value of Count is equal to the test condition. A fourth "bean" is displayed and Count is decremented to 0. Now Count fails the test condition and the program ends. We have displayed four "bean"s.

We see how the bean counting is done with a counter-controlled loop using a While loop structure in Example 5.20. This program does exactly the same thing as Example 5.18.

Example 5.20 **Count Four Beans with a While Loop**

```
1   Declare Count As Integer
2   Declare Beans As Integer
3   Set Beans = 4
4   Set Count = 1
5   While Count <= Beans
6     Write "bean"
7     Set Count = Count + 1
8   End While
```

What Happened?

In this case, after the third loop, when Count = 4, it's still less than or equal to Beans, so the loop repeats once more and a fourth "bean" is displayed. Then Count is incremented to 5, and the test condition is no longer true so the program ends, with four "bean"s correctly displayed.

If you aren't careful, the loop might not execute for the correct number of iterations. It's important to consider the initial value of the counter as well as the way you write the test condition, as you will see in Examples 5.21 through 5.24.

Example 5.21 **Use the Test Condition Carefully: Not Enough Beans**

This program snippet attempts to display four "bean"s but fails to do so.

```
1  Declare Count As Integer
2  Declare Beans As Integer
3  Set Beans = 4
4  Set Count = 1
5  While Count < Beans
6     Write "bean"
7     Set Count = Count + 1
8  End While
```

In this example, a "bean" is displayed and Count, which initially has a value of 1, is incremented to 2. A second "bean" is displayed and Count is incremented to 3. A third "bean" is displayed and Count is incremented to 4. Now Count is not less than Beans so the program ends, but we have only displayed three "bean"s.

For the loop in Example 5.21 to correctly display four "bean"s, we should have set Count = 0 instead of 1. In Example 5.22, we see what happens with a different incorrect limit condition.

Example 5.22 **Use the Test Condition Carefully: Too Many Beans**

```
1  Declare Count As Integer
2  Declare Beans As Integer
3  Set Beans = 4
4  Set Count = 0
5  While Count <= Beans
6     Write "bean"
7     Set Count = Count + 1
8  End While
```

What Happened?

In this case, Count starts at 0, a "bean" is displayed, Count is incremented to 1, and the test condition is true so another pass is executed. The second time around, a second "bean" is displayed and Count is incremented to 2. The test condition is still true. A third "bean" is displayed, Count takes the value of 3, and the test condition is still true. Then the fourth "bean" is displayed and Count gets incremented to 4. But now, when Count = 4, after the fourth "bean" has been displayed, the test condition is still true because Count is still less than or equal to Beans. Therefore, the loop continues for another pass. Now a fifth "bean" is displayed, Count is incremented to 5, and it finally fails the test so the program ends. But we have displayed five "bean"s instead of four.

Example 5.23 **Try It Yourself**

The following pseudocode would display five "bean"s. Can you see why?

```
1  Declare Count As Integer
2  Declare Beans As Integer
3  Set Beans = 4
4  Set Count = Beans
5  While Count >= 0
6     Write "bean"
7     Set Count = Count - 1
8  End While
```

Example 5.24 **Try Again**

How many "bean"s would the following pseudocode display? Can you figure out what needs to be changed in order to correctly display four "bean"s? You can check your answer; it's the same as the answer to Self Check Question 5.18.

```
1  Declare Count As Integer
2  Declare Beans As Integer
3  Set Beans = 4
4  Set Count = Beans
5  While Count >= 0
6     Write "bean"
7     Set Count = Count + 1
8  End While
```

Before we end this section, we will take a look at the specific syntax of For loops in several programming languages—C++, JavaScript, and Visual Basic. The logic and sequence of execution in all the languages is the same, but the syntax for Visual Basic is quite different from C++ and JavaScript.

Making It Work

The For Loop

The code in these three languages corresponds to Example 5.18.

C++ code:

```
void main()
{
   int Beans = 4;
   int Count;
   for (Count = 1; Count <= Beans; Count++)
   {
      cout << "bean";
   }
   return;
}
```

JavaScript Code

```javascript
function main()
{
  var Beans = 4;
  var Count;
  for (Count = 1; Count <= Beans; Count++)
  {
    document.write("bean");
  }
}
```

Note the similarities between JavaScript and C++!

Visual Basic code:

```
Private Sub btnBeanCount_Click
  Dim Beans as Integer
  Dim Count as Integer
  Beans = 4
  For Count = 1 To Beans Step 1
    Write "bean"
    Next Count
End Sub
```

Self Check for Section 5.3

5.13 What numbers will display when code corresponding to the following pseudocode is run?

a. Declare N As Integer
   Declare K As Integer
   Set N = 3
   For (K = N; K <= N+2; K++)
     Write N + " " + K
   End For

b. Declare K As Integer
   For (K = 10; K <= 7; K-2)
     Write K
   End For

5.14 What output will display when code corresponding to the following pseudocode is run?

a. Declare N As Integer
   Declare K As Integer
   Set N = 3
   For (K = 5; K >= N; K--)
     Write N
     Write K
   End For

```
b. Declare K As Integer
   For (K = 1; K <= 3; K++)
     Write "Hooray!"
   End For
```

5.15 Write a program (using pseudocode) that contains the statement

```
For (Count = 1; Count <= 3; Count++)
```

and that would produce the following output if it were coded and run:
10
20
30

5.16 Rewrite the following pseudocode using a For loop instead of the While loop shown:

```
Declare Number As Integer
Declare Name As String
Set Number = 1
While Number <= 10
   Input Name
   Write Name
   Set Number = Number + 1
End While
```

5.17 Rewrite the pseudocode of Self Check Question 5.16 using a post-test loop instead of a pre-test loop.

5.18 Find and explain the error(s) in the following pseudocode and then fix the pseudocode to produce an output of four "bean"s if it were run.

```
Declare Beans As Integer
Declare Count As Integer
Set Beans = 4
Set Count = Beans
While Count >= 0
   Write "bean"
   Set Count = Count + 1
End While
```

5.4 Applications of Repetition Structures

Throughout the rest of the book, you will see many examples of how the repetition (or loop) structure is used to construct programs. In this section, we will present a few basic applications of this control structure.

Using Sentinel-Controlled Loops to Input Data

Loops are often used to input large amounts of data. On each pass through the loop, one item or set of data is entered into the program. A professor teaching a large biology lecture class might use a loop to enter all the grades for an exam. The test condition for such a loop must cause it to be exited after all data has been input. Often the best way to force a loop to end is to have the user enter a special item (a **sentinel value**) to act as a signal that input is complete. The sentinel item (or **end-of-data marker**) should be chosen so that it cannot possibly be mistaken for actual input data. For example, using the biology professor's class as an illustration, since all student grades are between 0 and 100, the sentinel value could be the number -1. No student would get -1 for a grade, so when the value of -1 was encountered, the loop would end. Example 5.25 is a simple example of a **sentinel-controlled loop** that uses a sentinel value to determine whether the loop is to be exited.

Example 5.25 A Sentinel-Controlled Loop for Paychecks

Suppose that the input data for a program that computes employee salaries consists of the number of hours worked by each employee and his or her rate of pay. The following pseudocode could be used to input and process this data:

```
1   Declare Hours As Float
2   Declare Rate As Float
3   Declare Salary As Float
4   Write "Enter the number of hours this employee worked:"
5   Write "Enter -1 when you are done."
6   Input Hours
7   While Hours != -1
8     Write "Enter this employee's rate of pay: "
9     Input Rate
10    Set Salary = Hours * Rate
11    Write "An employee who worked " + Hours
12    Write "at the rate of " + Rate + " per hour"
13    Write "receives a salary of $ " + Salary
14    Write "Enter the number of hours the next employee worked:"
15    Write "Enter -1 when you are done."
16    Input Hours
17  End While
```

What Happened?

In this program segment, lines 4, 5, and 6 prompt for an initial value of Hours and receive the input to start the loop off. It is crucial that the input prompt makes it clear to the user that the number -1 will signify when all employees have been processed.

If the value input for Hours is the sentinel value -1, then the test condition in the While statement is false, the loop is exited, and input is terminated. Otherwise the loop body is executed, inputting Rate, computing and displaying the salary, and again inputting Hours. Then, the process is repeated. The flowchart shown in Figure 5.5 illustrates the pseudocode of this example.

Another way to allow the user to signal that all data have been input is to have the program ask, after each input operation, whether this is the case. Example 5.26 and the corresponding flowchart shown in Figure 5.6 show a program segment that illustrates this technique.

Figure 5.5 A sentinel-controlled loop for paychecks

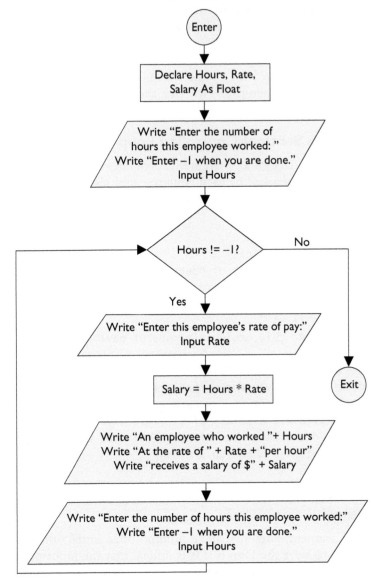

Example 5.26 **To Know When to Stop, Just Ask**

```
1   Declare Hours As Float
2   Declare Rate As Float
3   Declare Salary As Float
4   Declare Response As String
5   Repeat
6     Write "Enter the number of hours worked."
7     Input Hours
8     Write "Enter the rate of pay: "
9     Input Rate
10    Set Salary = Hours * Rate
11    Write "An employee who worked " + Hours
```

```
12     Write "at the rate of " + Rate + " per hour"
13     Write "receives a salary of $ " + Salary
14     Write "Process another employee? (Y or N)"
15     Input Response
16  Until Response == "N"
```

Figure 5.6 Using a prompt inside a loop instead of a sentinel

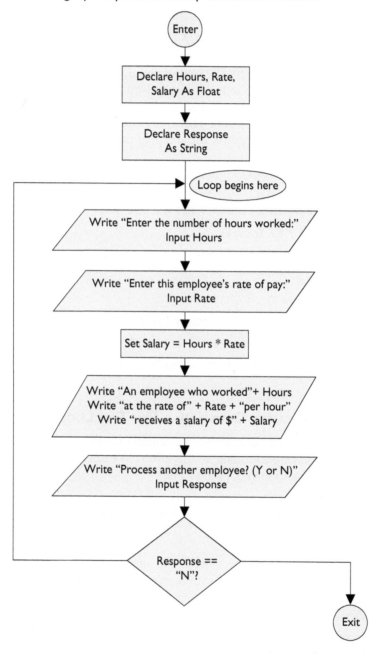

Here, the user enters the letter "Y" if there is more data to input or "N" otherwise. Of course, this means the variable Response must be of character or string type. The test condition, Response == "N", then determines whether the loop is reentered.

Data Validation

In Chapter 4 we discussed defensive programming and how to avoid mathematical pitfalls like dividing by zero or taking the square root of a negative number—two examples of times when data must be validated. You might write a program to accept orders for a small toy business. The customer will enter the number of wind-up mice ordered—one, two, a hundred, or even zero. To ensure that the user does not enter a negative number when entering a quantity of items to order, we use pseudocode similar to the following:

```
Write "How many wind-up mice do you want to order? --> "
Input Number
```

However, despite the input prompt, the user might enter a negative number. Since it's impossible to sell a negative number of wind-up mice, you must ensure that the user will enter a positive whole number or zero. Therefore, you should include statements in the program that **validate** (check) the number input and request a new number if the first number is outside of the accepted range. Examples 5.27 and 5.28 use loops to accomplish this.

Example 5.27 **Validating Data with a Post-Test Loop**

```
Declare MiceOrdered As Integer
Repeat
  Write "How many wind-up mice do you want to order? "
  Input MiceOrdered
Until MiceOrdered >= 0
```

This pseudocode validates the number entered using a post-test loop. The prompt

```
"How many wind-up mice do you want to order?"
```

is repeated until the number entered (MiceOrdered) is positive.

Example 5.28 **Validating Data with a Pre-Test Loop**

Sometimes when we validate data, we want to emphasize the fact that the user has made an error by displaying a message to this effect. We can do this with a pre-test loop, as illustrated in the following pseudocode:

```
1  Declare MiceOrdered As Integer
2  Write "How many wind-up mice do you want to order?"
3  Input MiceOrdered
4  While MiceOrdered < 0
5    Write "You can't order a negative number of mice."
6    Write "Please enter a positive number or zero. "
7    Input MiceOrdered
8  End While
```

Notice that in validating input data with a pre-test loop, we use two Input statements (and accompanying prompts). The first is positioned before the loop and is always executed; the second is contained within the loop and is executed only if the data entered is not in the proper range. Although this method to validate input data is a little more complicated than that used in Example 5.27, it's also more flexible and user-friendly. Within the body of the data validation loop, you can provide whatever message best suits the situation.

The Int() Function

Sometimes it's important that the number entered by the user is an integer—a whole number that can be negative, positive, or zero. For example, a shopping cart program written for a website cannot accept orders for noninteger values of the number of items to be ordered. A guessing game program, for example, where the user is asked to guess a number (we will create a game like this in Chapter 6) requires that the guess is an integer. Inputs with fractional parts are not allowed, but such a program could allow positive or negative numbers as well as zero. How such input is validated depends on the programming language.

In this text, we will introduce the Int() function to do the job. A **function** is a procedure that computes a specified value. We have already used the square root function Sqrt() earlier in the book. That function takes in a number and computes its square root. The **Int() function** takes any number and turns it into an integer. Other functions that do almost the same thing are the Floor() and Ceiling() functions, both of which are discussed in this section. Most programming languages include such functions.

The Int() function is written in the form Int(X), where X represents a number, a numeric variable, or an arithmetic expression. The function turns whatever numeric value X has into an integer by discarding the fractional part (if there is any) of the value of X.

If there is a computation to be done inside the parentheses of the Int(X) function, it's done first. Then the resulting value is turned into an integer. This is what makes Int(X) a function. It has been internally programmed within the programming language, to do whatever steps are necessary to turn a number, a numeric value, or any expression that results in a number into an integer. Example 5.29 demonstrates how we will use the Int() function.

Example 5.29 **The Int() Function**

This example demonstrates how the Int() function works on integers, floating point numbers (i.e., numbers with a decimal part), variables, and arithmetic expressions consisting of any combination of these values.

The left side of each of the following expressions takes the numeric values inside the parentheses and makes them into integers, as shown on the right side of each expression:

- Int(53) = 53 → the integer value of an integer is just that integer.
- Int(53.195) = Int(53.987) = 53 → the integer value of a floating point number is just the integer part, with the fractional part discarded.

If we have two variables, `Number1 = 15.25` and `Number2 = -4.5`, then we have the following:

- `Int(Number1) = 15` → `Number1` represents the value `15.25` and the `Int()` function turns the value of `Number1` into its integer part.
- `Int(Number2) = -4` → `Number2` represents `-4.5` and the integer part of this is `-4`.
- `Int(6 * 2) = 12` → first the `Int()` function does the math inside the parentheses and then returns the value as an integer.
- `Int(13/4) = 3` → `13/4 = 3.25` and the integer part of `3.25` is `3` so `Int(13/4) = 3`.
- `Int(Number1 + 3.75)` → `= 19` since `Number1 = 15.25`, the value of `15.25 + 3.75 = 19.00`, but the `Int()` function turns `19.00` (a floating point number) into `19` (an integer).

The `Int()` function may appear anywhere in a program that an integer constant is valid. For example, if `Number` is a numeric variable, then each of the following statements is valid:

- `Write Int(Number)`
- `Set Y = 2 * Int(Number - 1) + 5`

However, the statement `Input Int(Number)` is not valid.

Example 5.30 demonstrates how we use the `Int()` function to validate integer input.

Example 5.30 **Using the `Int()` Function for Data Validation**

This program segment uses two loops. First, it checks that the variable we named `MySquare` entered by the user is actually an integer, and then it uses another loop to display a table of the squares of all integers from 1 to the value of `MySquare`.

```
1  Declare MySquare As Integer
2  Declare Count As Integer
3  Repeat
4     Write "Enter an integer: "
5     Input MySquare
6  Until Int(MySquare) == MySquare
7  For (Count = 1; Count <= MySquare; Count++)
8     Write Count + " " + Count^2
9  End For
```

What Happened?

Let's walk through this program segment, line by line.

- Lines 1 and 2 declare the variables.
- Line 3 begins the first loop.
- Line 4 prompts the user for an integer.

- Line 5 takes in the number the user enters and stores it in a variable named MySquare. Of course, the user can type any number, but for now, let's pretend the user types 17.5.

- Line 6 checks to see that what the user typed is actually an integer. How does it do this? In our sample situation, the user typed 17.5, so line 6 asks "Is the integer value of MySquare the same as the value of MySquare?" In this case, the answer is no. We know that MySquare = 17.5. We also know that Int(MySquare) = the integer value of 17.5, which is 17 and is not the same as 17.5. So now the answer to the question asked on line 6 forces the program to go back up to line 3. The user would be prompted again for an integer on line 4. He or she would enter something else and that value would replace the value of 17.5 in MySquare. So let's pretend that this time the user enters 6. Now we're back to line 6 again and the test is run again: "Is the value of Int(MySquare) = MySquare?" This time the answer is yes because Int(MySquare) = 6 and MySquare also = 6.

- This first loop will be repeated over and over until the user finally enters an integer and the program moves on.

- Line 7 begins the second loop. It starts with a counter named Count equal to an initial value of 1. Count will be incremented by 1 each pass through this second loop, until it reaches the test value, which is the value of MySquare. In our pretend example, MySquare has the value of 6.

- Line 8 writes the display we want. The first time through this loop, it will display a 1 (the value of Count on the first iteration) and a 1 (the value of Count^2). Then control returns to line 7. Count is now equal to 2, line 8 writes 2 (the value of Count) and 4 (Count^2). This process continues until Count = 6, the value of MySquare.

Notice that the For loop will be executed only if MySquare is greater than or equal to 1. In that case, the table of squares will be displayed; otherwise, the For loop will be skipped. The result, at the end, assuming that the user entered the integer value of 6 on line 5 is as follows:

```
1   1
2   4
3   9
4   16
5   25
6   36
```

The flowchart shown in Figure 5.7 shows the flow of execution of this program segment and illustrates a flowchart for a program that includes two different types of loops.

What would happen if the user entered -3, a valid integer, on line 5? Nothing would be displayed since the test on line 7 would fail. This program segment will only display the squares of numbers that are greater than zero, even though zero and negative numbers are valid integers with valid squares.

Figure 5.7 Using two types of loops in a program

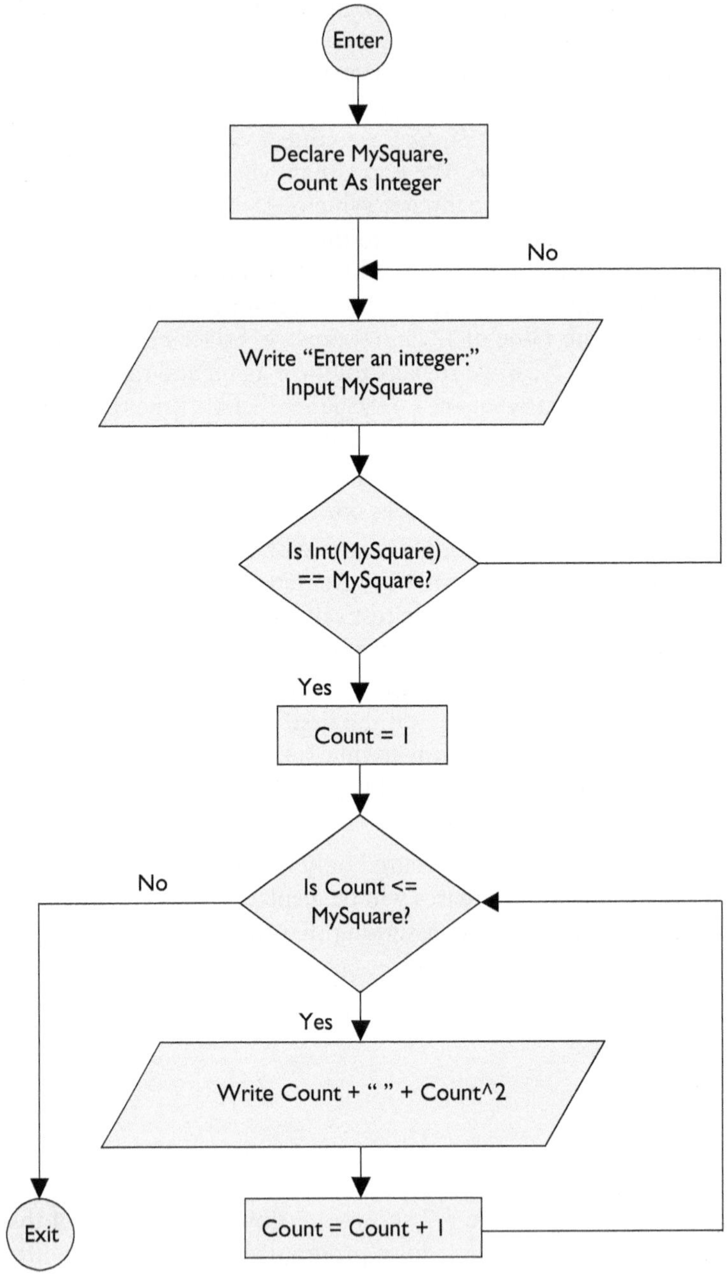

The Floor() and Ceiling() Functions

Many programming languages have functions which, when used appropriately, can do the same thing as the Int() function. We took a brief look at these functions in the Running With RAPTOR section of the previous chapter and will discuss them in further detail now. The **Floor() function** takes any number and turns it into an integer by discarding the decimal part, just as the Int() function has been described in this text. The **Ceiling()** function takes any number and rounds it up to the next integer value. While the Ceiling() function would not normally be used to validate integer input, the Floor() function can be used interchangeably with the Int() function for this purpose.

Example 5.31 **How the Floor() and Ceiling() Functions Work**

This example compares the result of using the Floor() and Ceiling() functions on various values:

```
Floor(62) = 62              Ceiling(62) = 62
Floor(62.34) = 62           Ceiling(62.34) = 63
Floor(79.89) = 79           Ceiling(79.89) = 80
```

As with the Int() function, both Floor() and Ceiling() work on numbers, numeric variables, and valid expressions. If we have two variables, NumberOne = 12.2 and NumberTwo = 3.8, then we have the following:

```
Floor(NumberOne) = 12       Ceiling(NumberOne) = 13
Floor(NumberTwo) = 3        Ceiling(NumberTwo) = 4
Floor(NumberOne * 4) = 48   Ceiling(NumberOne * 4) = 49
```

The Floor() and Ceiling() functions may appear in a program anywhere an integer constant is valid, just as with the Int() function. If Number is a variable with the value 7.83, the following statements are valid:

- Write Floor(Number) will display 7
- Write Ceiling(Number) will display 8
- Set Y = Floor(Number) assigns the value of 7 to Y
- Set Y = Ceiling(Number) assigns the value of 8 to Y
- Set X = Floor(Number/2) assigns the value of 3 to X
- Set X = Ceiling(Number/2) assigns the value of 4 to X

Example 5.32 demonstrates how we can use the Floor() function to validate integer input.

Example 5.32 **Using the Floor() Function for Data Validation**

This program segment is based on the pseudocode of Example 5.28. In that example a While loop was used to ensure that a customer did not try to order a negative number of wind-up mouse toys. However, the program also needs to ensure that the customer enters an integer value for the number of toys ordered. In this example, we will use the Floor() function to validate integer data. Later, we will see how to validate both positive input and integer input at the same time.

```
1  Declare MiceOrdered As Integer
2  Write "How many wind-up mice do you want to order? "
3  Input MiceOrdered
4  While Floor(MiceOrdered) != MiceOrdered
5     Write "You must enter a whole number."
6     Input MiceOrdered
7  End While
```

What Happened?

Line 4 is the point of interest in this example. By comparing `Floor(MiceOrdered)` with the value of `MiceOrdered`, we can see if the amount entered was an integer. The only time the `Floor()` of a number will be the same as that number is when the number is an integer.

Making It Work

Validating More than One Condition

Example 5.32 only checks to see if the value entered is an integer. However, negative values like -3 or -12 are integers and are not valid entries for a customer's order. The program must check two things: is the value entered an integer? And is that integer not negative? Can you think of a way to combine these two conditions in one loop?

This can be done with a compound condition, using logical operators. While there is always more than one way to solve this type of problem, see if you can rewrite the program segment using the following single compound condition:

```
While (Floor(MiceOrdered) != MiceOrdered) OR (MiceOrdered <= 0)
```

Example 5.33 Using the `Ceiling()` Function for a Pay Raise

Kim Smart works for a small business doing the payroll. She noticed that the payroll program her boss used was set up to pay hourly employees only in full-hour increments. Thus, a person who worked 25.2 hours as well as a person who worked 25.9 hours would both get paid for only 25 hours. The previous programmer had used the `Int()` function to convert floating point numbers to integer values. Kim decided that the previous programmer was probably unaware of the fact that this method would always underpay a worker unless the worker put in an exact integer value for the number of hours worked. Kim fixed the situation by using the `Ceiling()` function and hoped that her boss would not notice that now most employees were getting a better deal. In the following program segment, we see how this is done. Notice also that Kim used a compound condition to validate the input of both the number of hours worked and the pay rate.

```
1  Declare Hours As Float
2  Declare Rate As Float
3  Declare Pay As Float
4  Write "Enter number of hours worked: "
5  Input Hours
6  Write "Enter hourly pay rate: "
7  Input Rate
8  While (Hours < 0) OR (Rate < 0)
9    Write "Negative values are not allowed."
10   Write "Re-enter number of hours worked: "
11   Input Hours
12   Write "Re-enter hourly pay rate: "
13   Input Rate
14 End While
```

```
15  Set Pay = Ceiling(Hours) * Rate
16  Write "The pay for this employee is $ " + Pay
```

What Happened?

There are two lines of particular interest in this program segment. Line 8 is the compound condition. Because OR is used, the While loop will be entered if either Hours or Rate have been input as negative numbers. In this program segment, the user is required to re-enter both values (Hours and Rate) even if only one value was originally entered incorrectly. Later in the text, we will discuss methods to make this duplication unnecessary.

Line 15 uses the Ceiling() function within a calculation. This is a valid use of a function; it can be used anywhere that an integer value is acceptable. For example, if Hours was entered as 36.83 and Rate was entered as 9.50, the statement on line 15 would do the following:

First, Ceiling(Hours) would be evaluated: Ceiling(36.83) = 37. Then, this value would be multiplied by Rate (9.50) and the result, 351.50, would be stored in Pay.

Computing Sums and Averages

You may wonder why it is so important to discuss how sums and averages are computed in a program. It is not immediately obvious to someone new to programming how often programs use summing, but sums are used for many purposes other than simply adding numbers.

Computing Sums

Computers compute sums by using an **accumulator**, which is a variable that holds the accumulated result. The process of accumulating a value is used over and over in many computer programs. To use a calculator to sum a list of numbers, you add each successive number to the running total. In effect, you are looping because you are repeatedly applying the addition operation until all the numbers have been added. To write a program to sum a list of numbers, you do essentially the same thing, as illustrated in Example 5.34.

Example 5.34 **Using a Loop to Compute a Sum**

The following pseudocode adds a list of positive integers entered by the user. It uses 0 as a sentinel value. This number is entered by the user to indicate that input is complete.

```
1  Declare Sum As Integer
2  Declare Number As Integer
3  Set Sum = 0
4  Write "Enter a positive number. Enter 0 when done: "
5  Input Number
6  While Number > 0
7     Set Sum = Sum + Number
8     Write "Enter a positive number. Enter 0 when done: "
9     Input Number
```

```
10   End While
11   Write "The sum of the numbers input is " + Sum
```

What Happened?

In this program segment, we have a variable named Sum. In this context, such a variable is called the accumulator, which makes sense since it *accumulates* all the numbers. When the loop is finished, the accumulator, Sum, contains the sum of all the numbers entered and the sum is displayed. A flowchart for this example is shown in Figure 5.8 . Notice that the test condition in the flowchart tests if Number is the same as 0, while the pseudocode in this example checks if Number is greater than 0. Both tests work but the test in our pseudocode (Number > 0) guards against negative input.

Figure 5.8 Using an accumulator to sum numbers

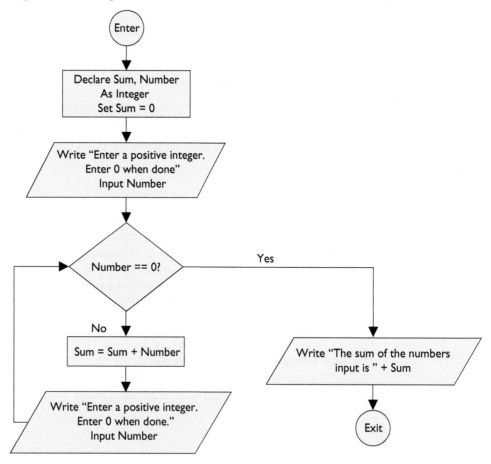

To understand how this algorithm works, let's trace execution of this pseudocode if input consists of the numbers 3, 4, 5, and 0:

- Lines 1 and 2 define the variables, Sum and Number. Prior to entering the loop, we initialize the variable Sum to 0 (line 3) so that it will not be an undefined variable when the right side of the statement on line 7 (Set Sum = Sum + Number) is evaluated. For the same reason, we input the initial value of Number from the user prior to entering the loop.

- Lines 4 and 5 ask for and obtain the first value of Number.
- Line 6: On the first pass through the loop Number equals 3, so the test condition is true and the loop body is executed.
- Line 7: The current values of Sum and Number are added. Before the addition is performed, the values are 0 and 3. After the addition is performed Sum = 3.
- Lines 8 and 9: The next number is requested and 4 is input and assigned to Number. The old value of Number (3) is lost.
- A second pass is now made through the loop in which Number = 4 and this value is added to the current running total (3) to increase the value of Sum to 7. In this pass, the number 5 is input and now Number = 5.
- Since Number is still not 0, the loop body is executed once more. The new value of Sum is the previous value (7) plus the new value of Number (5), or 12.
- Another number is requested and input. This time the user enters 0.
- Now Number is 0, so the test condition is false. The loop is exited and the current value of Sum, 12, is displayed.

Initialize Your Variables

Making It Work

When a variable is declared in a program, it's always a good idea to give it an initial value. When you declare a variable you are actually setting aside a space in the computer's memory as a storage space. That space may be empty, or it may have a value left over from some previous command or variable that is no longer being used. In Example 5.34 we have a variable named Sum. If we did not initialize it to equal 0 and, by a stroke of bad luck, the storage space the computer assigned to Sum had a value of 186 left in it by a previous program statement, then our sum would begin with Sum = 186. And our answer would be incorrect. To avoid this and other problems that may arise when variables are declared, it's best to make sure that they have the value you want them to start with by simply setting them to that value at the time you declare them.

Computing Averages

To calculate the average (or mean) of a list of numbers, we compute their sum and divide that sum by the number of data items in the list. Thus, the process of finding an average is similar to that of finding a sum, but here we also need a counter to keep track of how many numbers have been entered. Example 5.35 shows the pseudocode for finding the mean of a list of positive numbers.

Example 5.35 **Computing Your Exam Average**

Now that you understand a little about programming, you might want to write a program to calculate various averages in the courses you are taking this semester. The following program pseudocode shows how. Because we use variables and a sentinel-controlled loop, you can reuse this code to calculate your average in each of your courses. It doesn't matter if you have 3 exams or 33 exams. When this pseudocode is turned into real program code, it can be used again and again.

```
1   Declare CountGrades As Integer
2   Declare SumGrades As Float
3   Declare Grade As Float
4   Declare ExamAverage As Float
5   Set CountGrades = 0
6   Set SumGrades = 0
7   Write "Enter one exam grade. Enter 0 when done."
8   Input Grade
9   While Grade > 0
10    Set CountGrades = CountGrades + 1
11    Set SumGrades = SumGrades + Grade
12    Write "Enter an exam grade. Enter 0 when done."
13    Input Grade
14  End While
15  Set ExamAverage = SumGrades/CountGrades
16  Write "Your exam average is " + ExamAverage
```

What Happened?

- Lines 1–6 declare and initialize the variables.
- Line 7 asks for the first exam grade and also explains that when you are finished entering the exam grades for a particular set, you can end by entering 0.
- The first grade is input on line 8.
- Lines 9–14 are the loop. In this example, we used a While loop, which does two things—it sums the grades entered and it keeps count of how many grades were entered.
- On Line 10 we keep track of how many grades are entered. For each pass through the loop, CountGrades is incremented by 1. If you enter three grades before you end the program by entering 0, the loop will execute three times and CountGrades will be equal to 3. If you enter 68 grades, the loop will execute 68 times and CountGrades will be equal to 68.
- Line 11 keeps a sum of all the exam scores. To compute your exam average, you must divide the sum of all your exam grades by the number of exams, so lines 10 and 11 keep track of the information we need to compute the average at the end.
- Lines 12 and 13 ask the user for the next exam grade and gets the next input. Here, if you're done, you can enter a 0.
- Line 14 ends the loop when the user enters a zero.
- Line 15 computes the average and line 16 displays that average.

In Example 5.35, what would happen if your four exam grades for your basket weaving class were 0, 98, 96, and 92? The first grade you would enter would be 0. Line 9 says to do the loop only while Grade > 0. So the loop would never be executed, even though you would actually have an exam average in this class. Furthermore, if any student grade was 0, the loop would exit and this would exclude the student's other grades. How could you change the test condition on line 9 to take this situation into account?

And what would happen on line 15? If the first exam grade was 0, the loop would not execute and the program would jump to line 15. The value of SumGrades is 0 and the value of CountGrades is also 0. Then the statement:

    ExamAverage = SumGrades/CountGrades

would try to execute but a "division by zero" error would occur.

We showed how to avoid this situation using defensive programming techniques in Chapter 4. To rewrite this program so that it allows for an initial grade of 0 and also checks to be sure that the "division by zero" error does not occur, you may want to include an If-Then statement inside a loop. This process is covered in detail in Chapter 6.

? What &Why

Self Check for Section 5.4

5.19 Write pseudocode using a post-test loop that inputs a list of characters from the user until the character * (an asterisk) is input.

5.20 Suppose you want to input a number that should be greater than 100. Write pseudocode that validates input data to accomplish this task in the following two ways:
a. Using a pre-test (While) loop.
b. Using a post-test (Repeat . . . Until or Do . . . While) loop.

5.21 Give the number displayed by each of the following statements:
a. Write Int(5)
b. Write Int(4.9)

5.22 Give the number displayed by each of the following statements:
a. Write Floor(3.9)
b. Write Floor(786942)
c. Write Ceiling(3.9)
d. Write Ceiling(2 * 3.9)

5.23 Given the following values of the variables, what is stored in NewNum?
X = 4.6   Y = 7   Z = 0
a. Set NewNum = Int(X) + Ceiling(Y)
b. Set NewNum = Floor(X * Z)
c. Set NewNum = Int(Z) - Y

5.24 Use a For loop to sum the integers from 1 to 100.

5.25 Modify the program of Self Check Question 5.24 so that it finds both the sum and the average of integers from 1 to 100.

5.5 Focus on Problem Solving: A Cost, Revenue, and Profit Problem

Now let's put it all together. The program developed in this section uses a counter-controlled loop to display a table of data. It also features data validation (using post-test loops) and finds the mean (average) of a set of numbers.

Problem Statement

The CEO of KingPin Manufacturing Company wants to compute the costs, revenue, and profit of various production levels of its only product—kingpins. From past experience, the company knows that when a certain number of kingpins, X, are produced and sold, then the following is true:

- The total cost to the firm (in dollars), C, of producing them is: C = 100,000 + (12 * X).
- This is how much it costs KingPin Manufacturing to make X number of kingpins.
- The total revenue received by the firm (in dollars), R, is: R = X * (1000 - X) This is how much money the company takes in for selling X number of kingpins.

For example, if 200 kingpins are produced and sold, then the following is true:

- X = 200.
- Total cost is C = 100,000 + 12(200) = $102,400.
- Total revenue is = 200(1000 - 200) = $160,000.
- The difference, R - C, is the firm's profit (in this case, $57,600).

Of course, the company is most interested in its profit. The CEO wants to see the effects of various production levels (the number of kingpins produced, X) on the profit. So she asks you to write a program to create a table listing the costs, revenue, and profit corresponding to a wide range of production levels. She also wants the table to display the average profit of all these production levels.

Problem Analysis

As is often the case, the best way to attack a problem is to start with the desired output and then determine the input and formulas needed to produce this output. In this example, the output we want to see is a table of different production levels showing the cost, revenue, and profit associated with each production level. We will have the program display a table with four columns. The first (left) column will list a range of different production levels (different numbers of kingpins produced) and the other three columns will display the cost, revenue, and profit corresponding to each production level. Thus, the column headings and a few of the rows in the table would look something like that shown in Table 5.1.

The problem description does not specify the number of rows that the table is to contain, nor does it specify the range of production levels. So upon further consultation with the KingPin CEO, we decide to do the following:

- Let the user input the number of production levels to be listed—that is, the number of rows in the table. We will use the variable NumRows for this input.

Table 5.1 Display for KingPin Manufacturing Company program

Number	Cost	Revenue	Profit
100	101200	90000	−11200
200	102400	160000	57600
300	103600	210000	106400

(*Note:* The negative number in the first row of the profit column represents a *loss* of $11,200.)

- Specify that the largest production level (in the left column) will be 1000.
- Use evenly distributed production levels to make a comparison of the other items (cost, revenue, and profit) clear.

Thus, in the left column we will display production levels starting from a number, X, and incrementing by some fixed number up to $X = 1000$. For example, suppose that the user input for NumRows is 5. Then the left column of the five table rows would contain the following entries (values of X): 200, 400, 600, 800, 1000. Notice that the spacing between the values of X is $1000/5 = 200$. However, if the user inputs 4 for NumRows, there would be four rows with the values of X being 250, 500, 750, and 1000. In general, to determine the correct spacing between the values of X in the left table column, we divide 1000 by the number of rows in the table. That is, we declare a variable named Spacing and set Spacing = 1000/NumRows.

This seems to be a straightforward step, but there is a potential problem. The production levels must be whole numbers since KingPin never produces just a part of a pin, but the result of the division may have a fractional part. For example, if NumRows = 3, then 1000/NumRows is 333.33....

To ensure that Spacing has an integer value, we use the Int() function introduced earlier in this chapter to truncate the result of the division: Spacing = Int(1000/NumRows). Now if NumRows = 3, Spacing = Int(1000/3) = 333, and the production levels that appear in the table are 333, 666, and 999.

To obtain the entries in any row of the Cost and Revenue columns, we substitute the row's value of X (from the left column) into the supplied formulas. This is shown as follows:

- Cost = 100000 + 12 * X
- Revenue = X * (1000 - X)

To find the profit entry in any row, we just subtract the cost of production (Cost) from the amount of money the company takes in (Revenue), as follows:

- Profit = Revenue - Cost

The average (or mean) profit is obtained by adding all the individual profits (all the amounts in the Profit column of the table), obtaining a figure we will call Sum, and then applying the following formula:

- Average = Sum/NumRows

Program Design

To design this program using a modular approach, first we determine its major tasks. The program must perform the following operations:

- Input the necessary data
- Compute the table entries
- Display the table
- Display the average profit

We should also provide a welcome message, which is a general description of the program to be displayed at the beginning of a program run. Moreover, since the values of Cost, Revenue, and Profit will be calculated and displayed (through a loop) one row at a time, the second and third tasks are done almost simultaneously. Taking these points into consideration, a better approach might be to create the following major tasks:

(1) Display a welcome message
(2) Input data from the user
(3) Display the table
(4) Display the average profit

The third of these tasks makes up the bulk of this program, and should be further subdivided. In displaying the table, first we must do some housekeeping tasks such as setting up the table, displaying titles, initializing variables, and so forth. Then we can perform the necessary calculations to create the table entries. Thus, we break task 3 into two subtasks:

(3a) Do table housekeeping
(3b) Do table calculations

Task (3b) actually does several small jobs. It computes the table entries, displays them, and accumulates the profits so it can be further subdivided. However, as you will see, all these operations are performed within a single loop, so we will let this task stand as is. The hierarchy chart shown in Figure 5.9 shows the relationships among the program task modules.

We now design, using pseudocode, each program module. First, we give a rough outline of the program; then we refine it as necessary.

Figure 5.9 Hierarchy chart for the cost, revenue, and profit problem

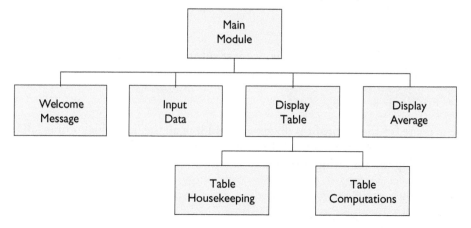

Main Module

The Main module only needs to call its immediate submodules; they will perform all the necessary program tasks. In the Main module, we also declare all the variables that will be used by more than one submodule. However, in most real programs, variables are declared "locally" (i.e., within their specific modules) and their values are passed from one module to another as necessary. The topic of where to declare variables and how to pass their values from one submodule to another is a very important topic and is covered in depth in Chapter 8. We are declaring our variables in the Main module for simplicity at this point. The resulting pseudocode is as follows:

```
Start Main module
  Declare NumRows As Integer
  Declare Sum As Float
  Call Welcome_Message module
  Call Input_Data module
  Call Display_Table module
  Call Display_Average module
End Program
```

Welcome_Message Module

This module displays general information and briefly describes the program. It must do the following:

- Display a title for the program, which will be "A Cost/Revenue/Profit Table".
- Display a brief overall description of the program.
- Describe, in general, how the user input affects the table.

Input_Data Module

This module is straightforward. It does the following:

- Prompt for, input, and validate the number of rows desired in the table, NumRows

To validate the input, notice that we want NumRows to be a positive integer. We can check both conditions (that NumRows is greater than zero and that NumRows is an integer) with the aid of a logical operator. The pseudocode is as follows:

```
Repeat
  Write "Enter the number of desired production levels."
  Write "It must be an integer greater than or equal to 1."
  Input NumRows
Until (Int(NumRows) == NumRows) AND (NumRows >= 1)
```

Display_Table Module

This module calls its two submodules and declares the only variable that is used solely in the two of them as follows:

```
Declare Spacing As Integer
Call Table_Housekeeping module
Call Table_Computations module
```

Table_Housekeeping Module

This module does a few minor things in preparation for the computation and display of the table entries that take place in the next module. It must do the following:

- Display the following table title:

  ```
  Write "KingPin Manufacturing Company"
  ```

- Display the following table headings:

  ```
  Write "Number     Cost      Revenue      Profit"
  ```

- Calculate the spacing for the production levels (X) in the left column, remembering that this variable must be an integer as follows:

  ```
  Declare Spacing As Integer
  Declare NumRows As Integer
  Set Spacing = Int(1000/NumRows)
  ```

- Initialize the sum of the profits to 0 as follows:

  ```
  Set Sum = 0
  ```

Table_Computations Module

This module is the heart of the program and contains the bulk of the computation. It consists of a single counter-controlled loop, which for each production value (X) does the following:

- Calculates the corresponding values of Cost, Revenue, and Profit
- Displays these values (on a single line)
- Adds the value of the Profit to a running total, Sum, for use in computing the average profit

Here is where we declare the variables X, Cost, Revenue, and Profit because they are used only in this module. Thus, the pseudocode is as follows:

```
Declare X As Integer
Declare Cost As Float
Declare Revenue As Float
Declare Profit As Float
Declare Sum As Float
For (X = Spacing; X <= 1000; X+Spacing)
   Set Cost = 100000 + (12 * X)
   Set Revenue = X * (1000 - X)
   Set Profit = Revenue - Cost
   Set Sum = Sum + Profit
   Write X + "    " + Cost + "    " + Revenue + "    " + Profit
End For
```

Display_Average Module

This module computes and displays the average profit as follows:

```
Declare Average As Float
Set Average = Sum/NumRows
Write "The average profit is " + Average
```

Program Code

The program code is now written using the design as a guide. At this stage, header comments and step comments are inserted into each module, providing internal documentation for the program. There are a few more points concerning coding that are specific to this program and often apply to many other programs.

To improve the look of the output, we should begin the program by using the programming language's clear screen statement to remove any text that is currently displayed on the screen. A clear screen statement would also be appropriate prior to printing the table of cost, revenue, and profit.

Most programming languages contain statements that help the programmer to format output. For example, in this program, we would like our table to look as professional as possible. The data in the table should line up in columns, and the dollar amounts should be preceded by dollar signs and contain commas in the appropriate places. If we just use our Write statements to create the output, part of it might look like that shown in Table 5.2.

Table 5.2 Unformatted table of KingPin Manufacturing Company results

Number	Cost	Revenue	Profit
800	109600	160000	54000
900	110800	90000	−20800
1000	112000	0	−112000

However, using the special formatting statements that most languages supply, these same table rows could look like that shown in Table 5.3.

Table 5.3 Formatted table of KingPin Manufacturing Company results

Number	Cost	Revenue	Profit
800	$ 109,600	$ 160,000	$ 54,000
900	110,800	90,000	−20,800
1000	112,000	0	−112,000

Program Test

To test this program adequately, we must run it with several sets of input data.

- To test the data validation Repeat loop, we input (in separate runs) values of NumRows that are not positive or not integer.
- To verify that the computations are being done correctly, we make a few program runs using simple input data so that the results can be checked easily with a calculator. For example, we might input (in separate runs) the

values 10 and 3 for NumRows. By using a value like 3, we also check that non-integer values for 1000/NumRows are handled correctly.

- We should also verify that the math we have programmed in the Table_ Computations module is functioning correctly. Remember that the computer will do exactly what we tell it to do. We might have erroneously programmed a plus sign for a multiplication sign or made some other incorrect entry into a formula. To check, we should run through a few calculations by hand or with a calculator to verify that our calculations match those of the computer's results.

Self Check for Section 5.5

All of these Self Check questions refer to the Cost, Revenue, and Profit Problem described in this section.

5.26 For each of the following production levels, calculate the corresponding Cost, Revenue, and Profit.
- X = 0
- X = 600

5.27 For each of the following input values, give the resulting value for Spacing and list the values of X displayed in the Number (left) column of the resulting table.
- NumRows = 8
- NumRows = 7

5.28 Write the pseudocode to validate the input value of NumRows (in the Input_ Data module) using a While loop.

5.29 Replace the For loop in the Table_Computations module with a While loop.

5.6 Running With RAPTOR (Optional)

In this section, we will learn how to use the RAPTOR Loop symbol to create executable programs that include both repetition and selection structures. We will use an example from this chapter to demonstrate how to use loops in RAPTOR, and we will develop a longer and a more interesting program that will allow the user to create secret encrypted messages.

Repetition: The Loop Symbol

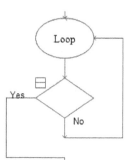

The Loop symbol allows you to code loops. When you drag the Loop symbol to the screen and double-click the diamond, the Enter Loop Condition dialog box opens, as shown in Figure 5.10 . Here is where you enter the condition that will determine whether to exit the loop.

Figure 5.10 The Enter Loop Condition dialog box

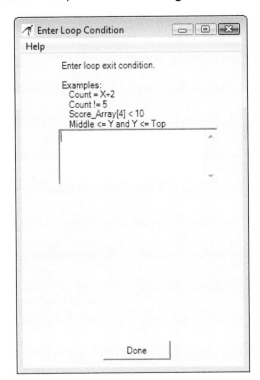

You can enter any of the types of conditions that have been discussed in the book, including compound conditions that use logical operators, noting that, in RAPTOR, the single equals sign (=) may be used in place of the comparison operator, the double equals sign (==).

There are several other important considerations about the way the Loop symbol has been designed. First, you cannot change the Yes and No branches. In RAPTOR Novice or Intermediate modes, a loop will be exited if the answer to the test condition is "yes". Therefore, you must remember to write your condition so that you want the loop to end when the answer is "yes".

The second consideration is whether you want a pre-test loop or a post-test loop. In the pre-test loop, a value to be tested is input before the loop is entered. Therefore, it is possible that, depending on the value input, the loop may never be executed. In the post-test loop, the value to be entered is input for the first time after the loop has been entered so any other statements in the post-test loop will execute at least once. Figure 5.11 demonstrates the difference between these structures.

You can combine loops with other structures, such as selection structures and you can also nest one loop inside another.

Figure 5.11 Using pre-test and post-test loop structures

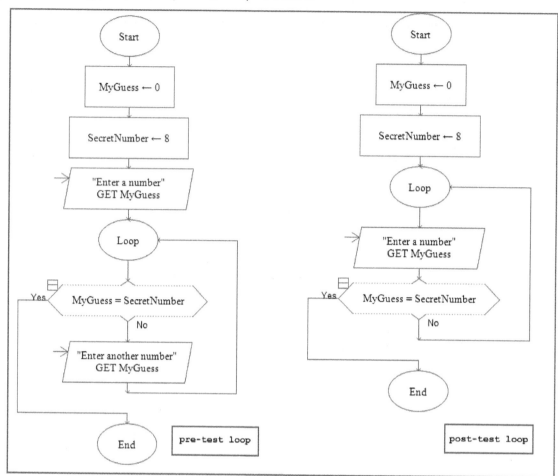

One last consideration concerns the For loop in RAPTOR. A For loop is merely a shorthand method of coding a loop. It allows you to enter three lines of code on a single line. You cannot use this shorthand when you design a program with a flow-chart nor can you implement For loops, as such, with RAPTOR. You must use a counter-controlled loop, as described in Section 5.3.

Take care that you include all the steps when creating loops with RAPTOR. In particular, don't forget to include an Assignment statement to increment or decrement your test condition; otherwise you'll find yourself running an endless loop!

A Short Example

Before we create a longer working program, we will redo an example provided earlier in this chapter to demonstrate how to use the RAPTOR Loop symbol. If you follow along and create the program, you can run it yourself and get valid results. Example 5.9 is repeated here.

Example 5.36 **From Example 5.9: A Few of Your Favorite Things**

Let's assume you are writing a program to allow users to create a profile on a website. In this program, a counter is used to allow the user to enter his or her three favorite leisure time activities. The three activities will be displayed, but the counter is used only to keep track of the number of iterations.

For this program, we need only two variables—a number variable, Count, and a string variable, Activity. We can initialize these variables in the RAPTOR main area instead of creating a separate subchart for variables as we have done in the past. To begin, open a new RAPTOR program and save the program with the filename activities.rap. Create the two variables and an output message that explains what the program does, as shown.

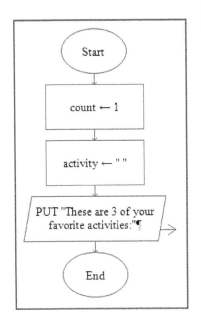

Next, we will prompt the user for the required information. Drag a Loop symbol under the prompt. In the pseudocode developed earlier in this chapter, the test condition for the loop was Count < 4. Since Count was given an initial value of 1, the condition would remain true for three iterations—while Count = 1, 2, and 3. When Count became equal to 4, the condition failed (would become false) and the loop exited. However, in RAP-TOR, the loop will be exited when the test condition becomes true so we need to rethink how we create our test condition. Here, we have given Count an initial value of 1. Instead of instructing the loop to continue while Count is less than 4, we need to instruct the loop to exit when Count becomes equal to 4. The test condition for our RAPTOR program will be Count = 4 or, if we wished to, we could also write Count > 3. The program with the test condition entered into the Loop structure is shown.

Next, we will create the statements in the loop body.

- The first statement is an Input that prompts the user for a favorite activity and stores the user's entry in Activity.

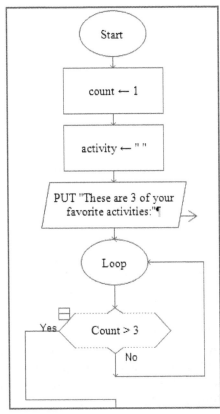

- The second statement is an Output that concatenates the result of the input with text and with the value of Count at this point.
- The third statement is an Assignment that increments the value of Count.

The loop should look like the one shown:

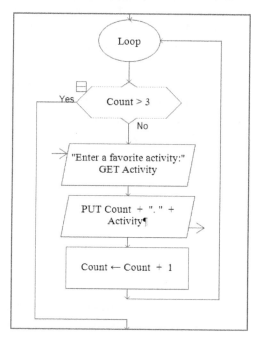

If you run this program and enter swimming, studying, and sewing at the prompts, your MasterConsole should give the display shown.

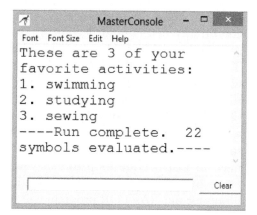

Run It: Encryption: The Secret Message Encoder

In this chapter, rather than recreating the Cost, Revenue, and Profit Problem from Focus on Problem Solving section, we will develop a different program. This new program will use an encryption algorithm to encode a message entered by the user. Nowadays, security is a serious consideration for software developers. This text cannot address the complex encryption algorithms that are incorporated into real-life software, but this section will give you a little taste of this profound subject.

What is Encryption?

Encryption is the process of transforming information using an algorithm to make it unreadable to anyone who does not have the "key" (i.e., the algorithm used). The possessor of this key can then decrypt the information; that is, transform it back to a readable state. In this section we will only encrypt a message but if you understand the process used, you can easily create a decryption algorithm of your own.

Problem Statement

The program will allow a user to enter a word, a sentence, or even a short paragraph. It will transform the text to make it unreadable by using the ASCII values for keyboard characters. The display will show the original message and the encrypted version. Later you can remove the display of the original message if you wish.

Developing the Program

In general terms, the plan for this program is extremely simple.

- Input: The user will input a message and select whether to have this original message displayed.
- Processing: Each character in the message will be changed, using the encryption algorithm, to a different character.
- Output: The original message will be displayed. The encrypted message will be displayed underneath the original.

However, the processing part of the program is complicated. We must convert each character in the message to its ASCII value, then change the ASCII value of that character to a new ASCII value, and then display the character that corresponds to the new ASCII value. To do this, we will use several functions that are available in RAPTOR. Most programming languages have similar functions to do these tasks. A brief discussion of each of these functions is now given.

The `Length_Of()` function

The **`Length_Of()` function** will return the number of characters in any string of text. The value returned is an integer and must be stored in a numeric variable. For example, if `sentenceLength` is a numeric variable and `mySentence` is a string variable, the following RAPTOR snippet will result in `sentenceLength` having the value 13.

This is because the phrase `"RAPTOR rules!"` contains thirteen characters, including the space between the two words.

Using Indexing

We can access the individual characters in a string using a "square bracket notation." This is known as **indexing**. For example, to write just the first character in the string variable `MyString`, we use `Write "MyString[1]"`, or to set `MyCharacter` equal to the

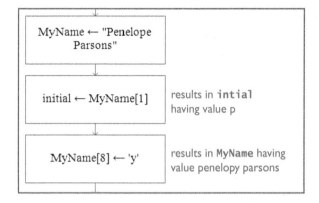

results in **intial** having value p

results in **MyName** having value penelopy parsons

third character in MyString, we use Set MyCharacter = MyString[3]. For example, if the string variable MyName has the value "Penelope Parsons", then the RAPTOR snippet shown here will result in initial having the value 'P'. The second assignment statement shown changes the value of MyName from "Penelope Parsons" to "Penelopy Parsons".

The To_ASCII() function

To_ASCII() is a function that returns the numeric ASCII value that is associated with the given ASCII character. To_ASCII('P') will return a value of 80, since 80 is the numeric ASCII value for the 'P' character. Or for example, if the character variable MyInitial has the value 'P', then an assignment like the following:

newInitial = To_ASCII(MyInitial)

gives the variable newInitial the value '80'.

The To_Character() function

To_Character() is a function that returns the ASCII character that is associated with the given numeric ASCII value. To_Character(80) will return a value of 'P', since 80 is the numeric ASCII value for the P character. Or, for example, if the variable MyAscii has the ASCII value '80' then an assignment like the following:

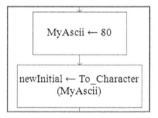

newInitial = To_Character(MyAscii)

gives the variable newInitial the value 'P'.

Developing the Encrypting Algorithms

We need to create a program that will allow the user to enter a message to be encoded. The program will then encrypt the message and display the encrypted message. While computers have developed extremely sophisticated encryption algorithms, we will use a very simple one. We will merely replace each letter of the alphabet with a different letter. One way to do this is to reverse the order of the alphabet. In other words, an A will become a Z, a B will become a Y, an F (the sixth letter) will become a U (the sixth letter from the end) and so on. In our encrypted code, the word ANNA will become ZMMZ and ZACK will become AZXP. We'll develop a simple encoding scheme for numbers and other characters.

The table of ASCII values is available in Appendix B. You can use this table to check that your program encodes messages correctly and, if you wish, to create more complex encoding algorithms. The user will enter a short message, and we need to change each letter in the message to a new character. To do this, we will develop several algorithms. The ASCII table shows that the values for the uppercase letters in the alphabet are 65 through 90. Lowercase letters are ASCII values 97 through 122.

The 10 digits (0–9) are ASCII values 48 through 57 and all other keys, including punctuation and special characters, are ASCII values 32 through 47, 58 through 64, and 123 through 126.

First, we will develop the algorithm to change A to Z, B to Y, C to X, and so on. In other words, we want to write an expression that will change 65 to 90, 66 to 89, 67 to 88, and so on. We can see that 65 + 90 = 155, 66 + 89 = 155, 67 + 88 = 155, etc. Thus, 155 - 65 = 90, which is what we want. In fact, for all ASCII values between 65 and 90, subtracting the original ASCII value from 155 will give us the ASCII value for the new character. The first algorithm, to encrypt uppercase letters, thus, is as follows:

```
newCode = 155 - oldCode
```

We can use similar reasoning to develop an algorithm to encrypt lowercase letters. For these letters, we want to convert ASCII 97 to 122, 96 to 121, 95 to 120, and so on. Since 97 + 122 = 219, 96 + 121 = 219, etc., the second algorithm will be

```
newCode = 219 - oldCode
```

Finally, we want to change numbers and other characters to something else. We'll use a very simple algorithm for this part. We'll just add 3 to whatever the ASCII value is. This will result in 2 (ASCII value 50) becoming 5 (ASCII value 53), the ampersand, & (ASCII value 38) becoming a closing parentheses, (ASCII value 41) and the question mark, ? (ASCII value 63) becoming an uppercase A (ASCII value 65). For this page, we will ignore the last four ASCII values (123, 124, 126, and 126). The final algorithm for numbers, punctuation, and special characters is as follows:

```
newCode = oldCode + 3
```

Now we need to develop the logic that will implement these algorithms. We'll sketch it out with informal pseudocode before creating it in RAPTOR.

- First, prompt for and display the message. We will display the message simply to ensure that our program is working with the correct information but, at the end, you can delete this output to make the Secret Message more realistic.

- Next declare variables. We need a string variable for the message and character variables to hold a single character of the message as well as one to hold the new (encrypted) character. We need numeric variables to hold our constants (155, 219, and 3) and the ASCII value of each character in the message, a variable to hold the length of the message, and a counter.

- The encryption of each character will be done in a loop. The loop will go around as many times as there are characters in the message. For each character, we will check if it is uppercase, lowercase, or another character. Depending on what type of character it is, we will convert its ASCII value to the new value, as determined by one of the three algorithms. At the end of each pass through the loop, the new character will be displayed.

- At the end of the loop, the entire encrypted message will be displayed on the MasterConsole.

Starting off: Creating the Introduction and Getting The Message

Open a new RAPTOR program and save it with the filename `secret_message.rap`.
Create a new `subchart` named `Variables` and create the following variables with
these initial values in that subchart:

```
asciiChar = 0
count = 1
msg = " "
newChar = 0
upCase = 155
lowCase = 219
specialCase = 3
oneChar = ' '
msgLgth = 0
```

Now return to the `main` tab and use an `Input` box to get the user's message. Then,
find out the number of characters in the message. We need this value to determine
how many iterations will be there in the loop. To do this, we use the `Length_Of()`
function and store the result in the `msgLgth` variable. Add an `Output` box to display
the original message and a second `Output` box to display the text `"Encoded message
is: "`. As the loop works, each encrypted character will be displayed so the end result
will be a single display of this text with the encrypted message underneath. At this
point, your RAPTOR program will look as shown in Figure 5.12.

Figure 5.12 Beginning the Secret Message Program

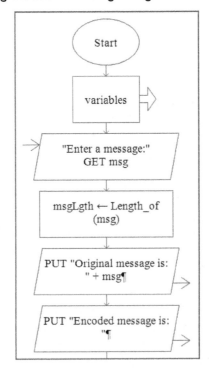

Encoding the Message

The "meat" of the program is the loop that encrypts the message, one character at a time. Therefore, we want the loop to execute for as many characters as are in the message. That number is stored in msgLgth. The counter, Count, begins at 1 and will be used in the test condition. The loop will end when Count is one more than msgLgth. Drag a Loop symbol to your program under the last Output box and enter the test condition.

Each time the loop is entered, the first thing it must do is get a character from the message to encrypt. We can store a character in a new variable by using indexing. The first character in any string in RAPTOR has the index value of 1. The second character has the index value of 2. This, conveniently, corresponds to the value of Count at any time the program is running. So we can get a single character by storing that character in a variable, oneChar if we use an Assignment box to set oneChar to the value of msg[Count]. For each iteration, this statement takes the value of the character in msg that corresponds to the place indicated by Count and stores it in oneChar.

The plan is to take the character we identified and change it to a different character. We will do that by finding out the character's ASCII value and then, depending on whether it is an uppercase, lowercase, or other type of character, change it to a different character, using the algorithms we have developed. The first thing we must do is find the ASCII value of the character. This is easily accomplished with the To_ascii() function. We store the ASCII value of this character in the variable, asciiChar. The loop part of RAPTOR program will look as shown.

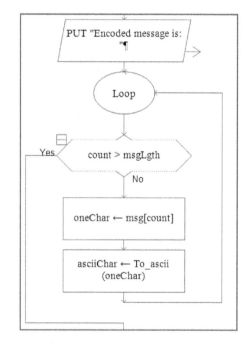

Now that we know the ASCII value of the character in question, we can transform it. We know, from the table of ASCII values, that the character is an uppercase letter if its ASCII value is between 65 and 90, it is a lowercase letter if its ASCII value is between 97 and 122, and it is some other character if it is less than 65, between 91 and 96 (inclusive) or greater than 122. However, to make our encrypting a little less confusing to the reader, we will also identify where the message contains spaces between words. The ASCII value for a space is 32 so, if the character stored in asciiChar is 32, we will leave it as is.

To transform the character, we will use nested Selection boxes. The first Selection box will check if asciiChar is an uppercase character. If this is not true, we will use a second Selection box to check if asciiChar is a lowercase character. If this is not true, we will use a third Selection box to check if asciiChar is the empty space. If this is not true, then we know asciiChar is a special character. Create nested `Selection` boxes with test conditions as follows:

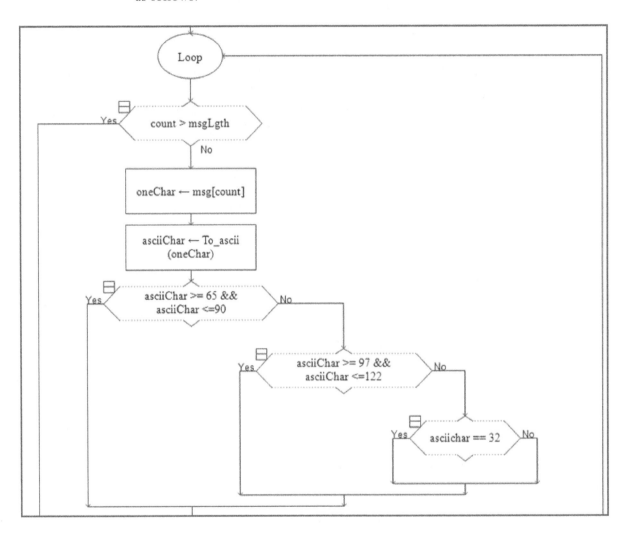

Creating the algorithms

We have already shown how to convert each character, from A to Z or a to z into another character, with A converting to Z, B to Y, C to X, and so on. We simply take the ASCII value of the character and subtract that value from the predetermined values (155 for uppercase and 219 for lowercase). We have also decided that we would transform a special character by simply turning it into the character that comes three characters before it. This is done by subtracting 3 from the ASCII value of the character. If the character is a space, nothing needs to be done because we want to leave empty spaces as spaces in the encrypted message.

Therefore, in each appropriate branch of the `Selection` boxes, store the ASCII value of the encrypted character in a variable, `newChar` as follows:

- `newChar = upCase - asciiChar` → for uppercase
- `newChar = lowCase - asciiChar` → for lowercase

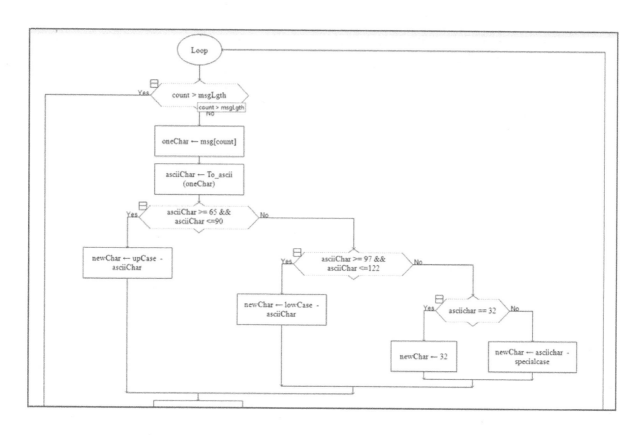

- newChar = 32 → if asciiChar is an empty space
- newChar = asiiChar - specialCase → for all special characters

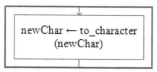

After a single iteration, regardless of what branch of the nested Selection statements is executed, the variable newChar will hold the ASCII value of the new (encrypted) character. Now, we must transform that ASCII value to a readable character. This is done using the RAPTOR To_Character() function (shown on left).

We need to display this character on the screen. The second time around, we want to display the next character but we want to have the characters display all on one line. Up to now, in RAPTOR, each time an Output box executes, the display begins on the line under the previous output. However, if we uncheck the End Current Line box at the bottom of the Enter Output Here dialog box, all the characters to be displayed in this loop will be on the same line. Create an Output box that simply displays the new value of newChar, being sure to uncheck the End Current Line box.

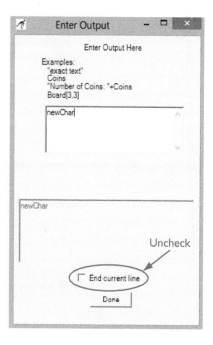

The final thing is to increment the counter, so create an `Assignment` box to set `Count` to `Count + 1.`

Your complete program will look like that shown in Figure 5.13.

Figure 5.13 The `Secret Message Encoder` program

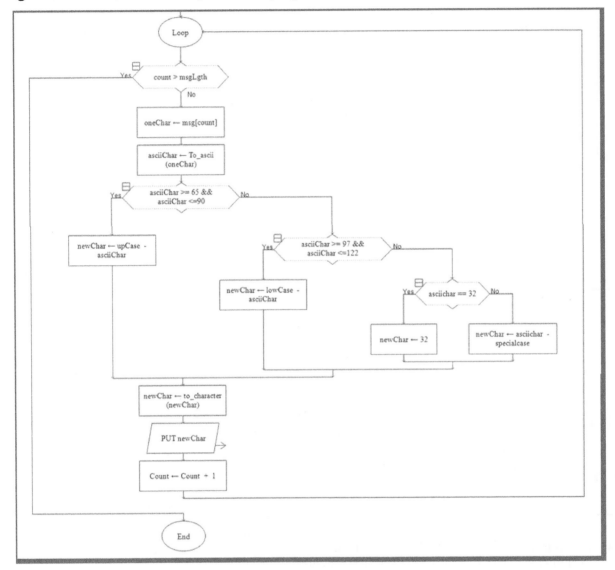

Check It Out

Test your program by entering the following secret message:

```
#RAPTOR - The secret will be revealed! Meet me at 9 pm.
```

Notice that the sample secret message tests all possible conditions; it includes upper and lowercase characters as well as special characters, numbers, and spaces. Be sure your output looks as shown:

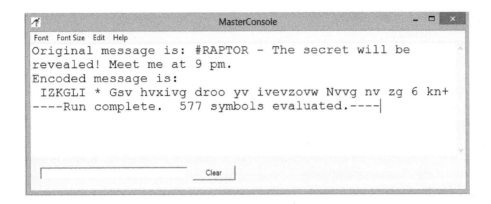

In the next chapter we will learn to nest loops and you can easily edit this program to allow the user to enter as many messages as desired. Also, with a little thought, you can add code to decrypt a secret message. Have fun with this!

Chapter Review and Exercises

Key Terms

accumulator
Ceiling() function
compound conditions
counter
counter-controlled loop
Do...While loop
decrement
encryption
end-of-data marker
Floor() function
For loop
function
increment
indexing [ ]
infinite loop
Int() function

iteration
Length_Of() function
loop
loop body
post-test loops
pre-test loops
relational operators
Repeat...Until loop
repetition structure
sentinel value
sentinel-controlled loop
test condition
To_ASCII() function
To_Character() function
validate
While loop

Chapter Summary

In this chapter, we have discussed the following topics:

1. Pre-test and post-test loops are as follows:
   - Structure of a pre-test loop
     ```
     While test condition
        body of the loop
     End While
     ```

- Structure of a post-test loop
  ```
  Repeat
      body of the loop
  Until test condition
  ```

2. Differences between pre-test `While` and post-test `Repeat...Until` and `Do... While` loops are as follows:
   - For pre-test loops, the test condition is at the top of the loop; for post-test loops the test condition is at the bottom
   - The body of a post-test loop must be executed at least once; this is not true for a pre-test loop
   - Variables appearing in the test condition for a pre-test loop must be initialized prior to entering the loop structure

3. Using flowcharts to visualize the flow of execution of loops

4. Counter-controlled loops are as follows:
   - The shorthand statement of a `For` loop has the following form:
     ```
     For(Counter = InitialValue; Test Condition; Increment)
         body of the loop
     End For
     ```
   - The importance of choosing the initial value of the counter and the test condition carefully to ensure that the loop is executed for the number of times required

5. The use of three built-in functions: `Ceiling()`, `Floor()`, and `Int()` is as follows:
   - `Ceiling(X)` rounds any valid number or expression up to the next integer value
   - `Floor(X)` turns a floating point number into an integer by discarding the fractional part
   - `Int(X)` normally turns a floating point number into an integer by discarding the fractional part

6. The use of sentinel-controlled loops for data input

7. Some applications of loops are as follows:
   - Validating data to ensure that data are in the proper range
   - Computing sums and averages

Review Exercises

Fill in the Blank

1. The counter variable in a `For` loop will decrease in value on each pass through the loop if the value of the loop's increment is _____.

2. If a `For` loop's increment is positive, then the body of the loop will not be executed if the initial value is _____ the limiting value.

3. To _____ data means to ensure that they are in the proper range.

4. Using the `Floor()` function has the same effect as using the _____ function.

True or False

5. If `Number = 3`, indicate whether each of the following statements is `true` or `false`:

    a. T F `(Number * Number) >= (2 * Number)`

    b. T F `(3 * Number - 2) >= 7`

6. Indicate whether each of the following statements is `true` or `false`:

    a. T F `"A" != "A "`

    b. T F `"E" == "e"`

7. If `N1 = "Ann"` and `N2 = "Anne"`, indicate whether each of the following statements is `true` or `false`:

    a. T F `(N1 == N2) AND (N1 >= "Ann")`

    b. T F `(N1 == N2) OR (N1 >= "Ann")`

    c. T F `NOT (N1 > N2)`

8. T F The body of a pre-test loop must be executed at least once.

9. T F The body of a post-test loop must be executed at least once.

10. T F A counter-controlled loop cannot be constructed using a `While` statement.

11. T F A counter-controlled loop cannot be constructed using a `Repeat...Until` loop.

12. T F The following statement is valid: `Input Int(X)`

Short Answer

13. Consider the following loop:

```
Declare Number As Integer
Set Number = 2
Repeat
   Write Number
   Set Number = Number - 1
Until Number = 0
```

    a. Is this loop a pre-test loop or a post-test loop?

    b. List the statements in the body of the loop.

    c. What is the test condition for this loop?

14. Give the output of the loop in Exercise 13.

15. Consider the following loop:

```
Declare Number As Integer
Set Number = 2
While Number != 0
   Write Number
   Set Number = Number - 1
End While
```

a. Is this loop a pre-test loop or a post-test loop?

b. List the statements in the body of the loop.

c. What is the test condition for this loop?

16. Give the output of the loop in Exercise 15.

17. Draw a flowchart for the pseudocode in Exercise 13.

18. Draw a flowchart for the pseudocode in Exercise 15.

19. Consider the following counter-controlled loop:

```
Declare K As Integer
For (K = 3; K <= 8; K+2)
    Write K
End For
```

• What is the name of the counter variable?

• Give the values of the initial value, the increment, and the limiting value.

20. Give the output of the loop in Exercise 19.

21. Add statements to the following pseudocode to create a post-test loop which validates the input data:

```
Declare Number As Integer
Write "Enter a negative number: "
Input Number
```

22. Redo Exercise 21 using a pre-test loop.

23. Give the value of each of the following expressions:

a. Int(5)

b. Int(4.7)

24. Let Num1 = 2 and Num2 = 3.2. Give the value of each of the following expressions:

a. Int (Num2 – Num1)

b. Int (Num1 – Num2)

25. Let Num1 = 6.8 and Num2 = 3.1. Give the value of each of the following expressions:

a. Floor(Num1 + Num2)

b. Ceiling(Num2 + Num1)

c. Floor(Num2 - 2)

d. Ceiling(Num1 - 2)

26. What is the output of code corresponding to the following pseudocode?

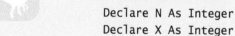

```
Declare N As Integer
Declare X As Integer
Set N = 4
Set X = 10/N
Write X
Set X = Int(X)
Write X
```

27. Use a `While` loop in a program segment that inputs numbers from the user until the number entered is an integer.

28. Given the following loop, fill in the compound condition necessary to ensure that the input is both an integer and positive.

```
Declare Number As Integer
Write "Enter your favorite positive whole number"
Input Number
While _____
   Write "The number must be a positive whole number."
   Write "Try again:"
   Input Number
End While
```

29. Complete each statement regarding the following pseudocode, which sums a set of numbers. (*Note:* N is any integer greater than or equal to 1.)

```
Declare A As Integer
Declare B As Integer
Declare N As Integer
Set A = 0
For (B = 1; B <= N; B++)
   Set A = A + (2 * B - 1)
   Set B = B + 1
End For
Write A
```

a. The accumulator for this program is the variable _____.

b. The counter variable for this program is _____.

30. If N = 4 in the pseudocode in Exercise 29, then what number is displayed when the corresponding code is run?

31. Rewrite the code in Exercise 29 using a `While` loop instead of the `For` loop.

32. Draw a flowchart corresponding to the pseudocode in Exercise 29.

33. Is the loop in Exercise 29 a pre-test loop or a post-test loop?

34. Add statements to the pseudocode in Exercise 29 that find the average of N numbers, (2 * B - 1), generated within the loop.

35. Write pseudocode that will average a list of numbers input by the user. Use the following variables:

- `Number As Integer`
- `Sum As Integer`
- `Average As Float`
- `Count As Integer`

Also:

- Use a `While` loop to enter the numbers.
- Use a sentinel to test when the user wants to stop entering numbers.
- Assume the user enters valid data.

36. Draw a flowchart corresponding to the pseudocode in Exercise 35.

37. Add data validation to the program segment of Exercise 35 to check that the user enters only positive integer values.

38. Draw a flowchart that corresponds to the program segment of Exercise 37.

39. Change the pseudocode of Exercise 35 to allow the user to include all floating point numbers (negative numbers as well).

40. What would be the output if the following pseudocode was run, assuming that the user enters 3 at the prompt?

```
Declare Number As Integer
Declare Product As Integer
Write "Enter a number: "
Input Number
Do
    Set Product = Number * 5
    Write "The product of " + Number + " and 5 is " + Product
    Set Number = Number - 1
While Number > 0
```

Programming Challenges

For each of the following Programming Challenges, use a modular approach and pseudocode to design a suitable program to solve it. Whenever appropriate, validate the input data.

1. Find the sum of the squares of the integers from 1 to MySquare, where MySquare is input by the user. Be sure to check that the user enters a positive integer.

2. Input a list of people's ages from the user (terminated by 0) and find the average age. Be sure to check that the user enters only positive numbers.

3. The number N factorial, denoted by N!, is defined to be the product of the first N positive integers:

    $$N! = 1 \times 2 \times \ . \ . \ . \ \times N$$

    For example:

    $$5! = 1 \times 2 \times 3 \times 4 \times 5 = 120$$
    $$7! = 1 \times 2 \times 3 \times 4 \times 5 \times 6 \times 7 = 5{,}040$$

    Find N!, where N is a positive integer input by the user. (*Hint:* initialize a Product to 1 and use a loop to multiply that Product by successive integers.) Be sure to check that the user enters a positive integer.

4. Allow the user to enter a series of temperatures in degrees Celsius (C) terminated by the input of -999. For each one, find the corresponding temperature in degrees Fahrenheit (F). The conversion formula is:

    $$F = 9 * C/5 + 32.$$

5. A biologist determines that the approximate number, Number, of bacteria present in a culture after a certain number of days, Time, is given by the following formula:

Number = BacteriaPresent * 2^(Time/10)

where BacteriaPresent is the number present at the beginning of the observation period. Let the user input BacteriaPresent, the number of bacteria present at the beginning. Then compute the number of bacteria in the culture after each day for the first 10 days. Do this in a loop so that the user can see the results in a table. The output table should have headings for Day and Number of Bacteria Present (on that day).

6. Help users calculate their car's miles per gallon. Write a program to allow a user to enter the number of miles driven and the number of gallons of gas used. The output should be the miles per gallon. Use a Do...While (post-test) loop to allow users to enter as many sets of data as desired.

More about Loops and Decisions

6

In this chapter, we continue to explore the topic of repetition structures. We will discuss how loops are used in conjunction with the other control structures—sequence and selection—to create more complex programs. We continue the discussion of different types of loops, including using loops for data validation, using nested loops, and using loops for data input.

After reading this chapter, you will be able to do the following:

- Create and use loops with selection structures
- Apply loops to data input problems
- Combine loops with `Select Case` statements
- Understand how to create output on separate lines with a newline indicator
- Include random numbers in loops by using the `Random()` function
- Create and use nested loops

Loops Within Loops

In Chapter 5 you learned how to create various types of simple loops. A loop was compared to the process of learning to walk—putting one foot in front of the other over and over and over. When you walk across a room, you are completing the "put one foot in front of the other" loop many times. But you may be walking across the room to pick up a book you need to complete a homework problem. So you do the "put one foot in front of the other loop" until you get to your bookcase. Then you search for your book and, after you find it, you turn around and do the "put one foot in front of the other" loop again until you get back to your desk. In this chapter, you will learn various ways to use loops within longer programs or to solve more complex problems. This is done by combining loops with the other control structures that we have learned.

Loops are often combined with other loops by putting one loop inside the other. Imagine, for now, that you work as a bagger in a grocery store. It is your job to fill bags with groceries while the cashier rings up a purchase. So you put one grocery item after another into one bag until that bag is full, then you fill another bag, and another until a customer's order is done. This is an example of a loop inside a loop. For a single customer, this situation can be expressed as follows:

```
Repeat
  Open a grocery bag
  While there is room in the bag
    Place an item in the bag
  End While
  Place filled bag in the customer's grocery cart
Until all the customer's groceries have been bagged
```

In fact, you could put these two loops inside a larger outer loop to continue the whole process for many customers until your shift ends. Or you could include a decision statement within the outer loop, which would allow you to stop the process if it is time for a lunch break.

6.1 Combining Loops with If-Then Statements

Early in this textbook you learned that virtually all computer programs are composed of code written using the three control structures: sequence, selection, and repetition. Now that we have learned about each of these structures separately, we can put them together to form programs that do everything from displaying a greeting on the screen to creating a word processor to performing calculations for a space ship to travel to Mars.

We have already combined selection structures and repetition structures with the sequence structure. In this section, we will combine repetition structures and selection structures. We'll begin by showing you how to use an If-Then structure within a loop. This will allow the loop to end, if necessary, before it completes all the iterations specified in the test condition.

Exiting a Loop

It's possible to break out of a loop if the user has entered an incorrect value that would cause an error or a problem within the loop, or if the user has entered a required response and the program can continue without further iterations. Examples 6.1 and 6.2 demonstrate these situations.

Example 6.1 **Exiting the Loop When There's No More Money**[1]

In this program segment pseudocode, you will imagine that you have a specific amount of money to spend. You're shopping online, and this program segment will keep track of the cost of your purchases and let you know when you have either reached your spending limit or bought 10 items. At the end, the program will display your exact purchase amount. The pseudocode uses a new statement, Exit For, to kick us out of the "purchasing loop" if the spending limit is exceeded. When an Exit For statement is encountered, the statement following the end of the For loop (the one after End For) is executed next. The flowchart that corresponds to this pseudocode is shown in Figure 6.1.

```
1  Declare Cost As Float
2  Declare Total As Float
3  Declare Max As Float
4  Declare Count As Integer
5  Set Total = 0
6  Write "Enter the maximum amount you want to spend: $ "
7  Input Max
8  For (Count = 1; Count < 11; Count++)
9    Write "Enter the cost of an item: "
10   Input Cost
11   Set Total = Total + Cost
12     If Total > Max Then
13       Write "You have reached your spending limit."
14       Write "You cannot buy this item or anything else."
15       Set Total = Total - Cost
16       Exit For
17     End If
18   Write "You have bought " + Count + " items."
19 End For
20 Write "Your total cost is $ " + Total
```

[1]To create programs in RAPTOR that are shown in this text with For loops, refer to the flowcharts that correspond with the examples. RAPTOR uses the same logic for a For loop as a While loop.

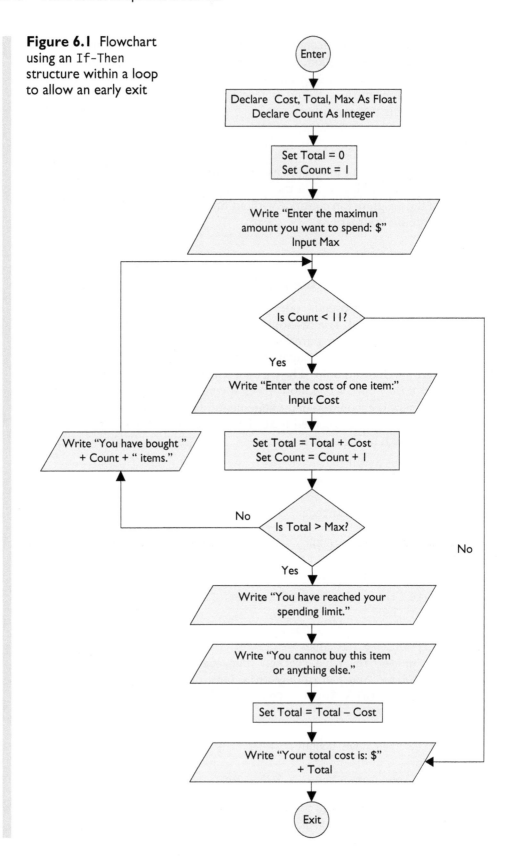

Figure 6.1 Flowchart using an `If-Then` structure within a loop to allow an early exit

What Happened?

- Lines 1–7 declare the necessary variables (Cost, Total, Max, and Count) and allow the user to input the maximum amount to spend.
- The For loop begins on line 8 and allows the user to input up to ten items.
- Lines 9 and 10 prompt for and input the cost of one item.
- Line 11 keeps a total of the cost of all the items.
- Line 12 uses an If-Then structure to check if the user has spent over the limit. If the last item entered puts the user over the limit, lines 13–16 are executed. The user receives a message that this last item costs too much to buy and that the spending limit has been reached (lines 13 and 14).
- Line 15 subtracts off the cost of the last item from the total since this item cannot be bought.
- Line 16 exits the loop and control proceeds to line 18, which tells the user how many items he has purchased and then, on line 20, displays the total up to, but not including, the cost of the last item entered. In general, if an Exit For statement is encountered in a For loop, control is immediately transferred to the program statement that follows End For. The exact syntax to accomplish this will differ, of course, from one programming language to the next, but the result will be the same; the loop is exited early.
- However, if an item entered does not put the total cost over the spending limit—that is, if the answer to the question on line 12 is "no" (Total is not greater than Max)—then the Then-clause is never executed and the next step is line 18. This displays the number of items purchased so far. Control returns to line 8 where Count is incremented and then checked to see if the user has entered 10 items.
- The program ends when the user enters 10 items or when the user enters fewer than 10 items and the total cost is greater than Max, whichever comes first.

Next, we'll look at how to use an If-Then-Else structure within a loop for **data validation**. The loop continues only while the user enters appropriate data. In this example, the appropriate data is an integer, and the loop is exited if the entry is not an integer.

Example 6.2 **Summing Integers and Only Integers**

This program segment pseudocode asks the user to enter 10 integers and computes their sum. The loop ends when the user has entered all 10 integers or exits early if the user enters a noninteger value. To accomplish this, we make use of the If-Then-Else structure and the Int() function. A flowchart corresponding to this example is shown in Figure 6.2.

```
1   Declare Count As Integer
2   Declare Sum As Integer
3   Declare Number As Float
4   Set Sum = 0
5   For (Count = 1; Count <=10; Count++)
6       Write "Enter an integer: "
7       Input Number
8       If Number != Int(Number) Then
```

```
9        Write "Your entry is not an integer."
10       Write "The summation has ended."
11       Exit For
12     Else
13        Set Sum = Sum + Number
14     End If
15   End For
16   Write "The sum of your numbers is: " + Sum
```

What Happened?

- Lines 1–7 declare the three variables (Count, Number, and Sum), initialize Sum, begin the For loop, and accept a number from the user. By declaring Number as a Float, we have allowed the user to enter any number. However, the prompt asks for an integer so we must test (on line 8) to make sure the user has followed the directions.

- In line 8, the number the user entered is tested. Recall that the Int() function turns any number, Float or Integer, into the integer value of that number. Therefore, if the user enters 5.38 for Number, the value of Int(Number) will be 5. In this case, the result of the test on line 8 will be true. The value of Number (which is 5.38) will not be the same as the value of Int(Number) (which is 5). Thus, the next lines to be executed will be lines 9 and 10.

- The user will see the following display:

  Your entry is not an integer.

  The summation has ended.

- Line 11 will force the loop to end. As mentioned in the previous example, the exact syntax to accomplish this will differ from language to language, but the result will be the same. When the user has entered a noninteger value, the loop will not complete all 10 iterations.

- However, if the user entered the number 4 on line 7, then the value of Int(Number) on line 8 would be exactly the same as the value of Number. Since the test on line 8 would return a value of false, the Then clause of the If-Then-Else statement would not be executed. Control would jump to line 12, the Else clause.

- The summation would continue on line 13. Then control would return to the top of the For loop and another number would be entered.

- This will continue until one of two things happens—either the user enters a noninteger number or the user enters 10 integers. Line 16 will be executed regardless of which of the two events occurs.

Since the Floor() function also converts a floating point number to an integer by dropping the fractional part of the number, it can be substituted for Int() in this program and anywhere else that Int() appears in program segments in the text.

There is one more thing to mention about this pseudocode. If a user entered any nonnumeric character on line 7, in most programming languages the program would stop or display an error message. However, the purpose of this example is to demonstrate how to validate numeric input so, for now, we will not address the possibility of a nonnumeric entry.

Figure 6.2 Flowchart using an If-Then-Else structure inside a loop to validate data input

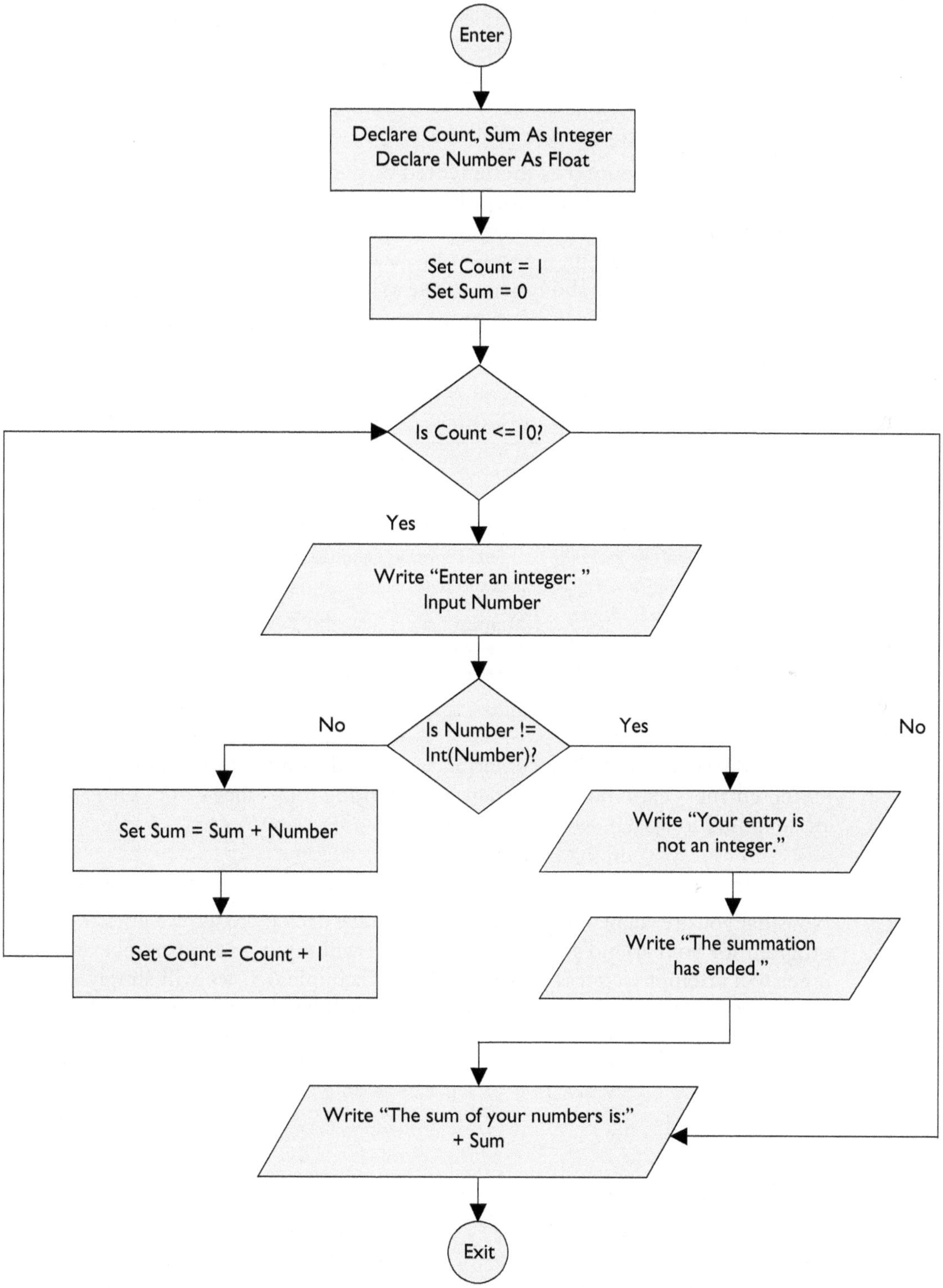

 **Making It Work**

Notice that, in Example 6.2, the test condition states that the loop should continue while Count <= 10. In Example 6.1, the test condition stated that the loop should continue while Count < 11. Since, in both examples, Count is incremented by 1 during each pass, both of these conditions will require the loop to complete 10 iterations. The decision about how to write the test condition, in these cases, is simply a matter of programmer preference.

In a For loop, the counter is incremented or decremented, by default, after the loop body is executed but before the test condition is tried again (i.e., at the bottom of the loop body). In a Repeat . . . Until, Do . . . While, or While loop, the placement of the increment or decrement of the loop is up to the programmer. The decision about what to use as a test condition is then based on the desired outcome. The following four little program segments create different displays because of the placement of the counter increment and the value of the test condition:

Set Count = 1	Set Count = 1	Set Count = 1	Set Count = 1
While Count <= 3	While Count <= 3	While Count < 3	While Count <= 2
Write Count + "Hello"	Set Count = Count + 1	Write Count + "Hello"	Set Count = Count + 1
Set Count = Count + 1	Write Count + "Hello"	Set Count = Count + 1	Write Count + "Hello"
End While	End While	End While	End While
Display	**Display**	**Display**	**Display**
1 Hello	2 Hello	1 Hello	2 Hello
2 Hello	3 Hello	2 Hello	3 Hello
3 Hello	4 Hello		

Clearly, the choice of the test condition, combined with the placement of the counter increment is extremely important when writing loops that work exactly as they are supposed to work!

Now that you are adept at programming, you have decided to write a guessing game program for your friend's children. One child will input a secret number and the other will attempt to guess that number. In Example 6.3, we will simply use the words Clear Screen to signify that the screen will be cleared as soon as the secret number is entered.

Example 6.3 **A Simple Guessing Game**

The pseudocode in this example shows how to develop a simple guessing game. One person inputs a secret number and the second person must guess that number. As soon as the first person enters a secret number, the `Clear Screen` statement will clear the screen so the second person cannot see the number. While the syntax for this command differs from language to language, every programming language has a way to hide user entries immediately, as you may have seen when entering a password into a website.

The problem you face when creating this game is that there are a great many numbers in the world. If you allow the user who is guessing the secret number to keep guessing until he or she is correct, the game could go on for a very, very long time. So you decide to allow the user five chances to guess the secret number. Therefore, your loop must allow five guesses, or if the person guesses correctly before the fifth try, the loop must be exited. A flowchart corresponding to this example is shown in Figure 6.3. The pseudocode for this little game is as follows:

```
1  Declare SecretNumber As Integer
2  Declare Count As Integer
3  Declare Guess As Integer
4  Write "Enter a secret number: "
5  Input SecretNumber
6  Clear Screen
7  For (Count = 1; Count <= 5; Count++)
8    Write "Guess the secret number: "
9    Input Guess
10   If Guess == SecretNumber Then
11     Write "You guessed it!"
12     Exit For
13   Else
14     Write "Try again"
15   End If
16 End For
```

Figure 6.3 Flowchart using an If-Then-Else structure inside a loop for a guessing game

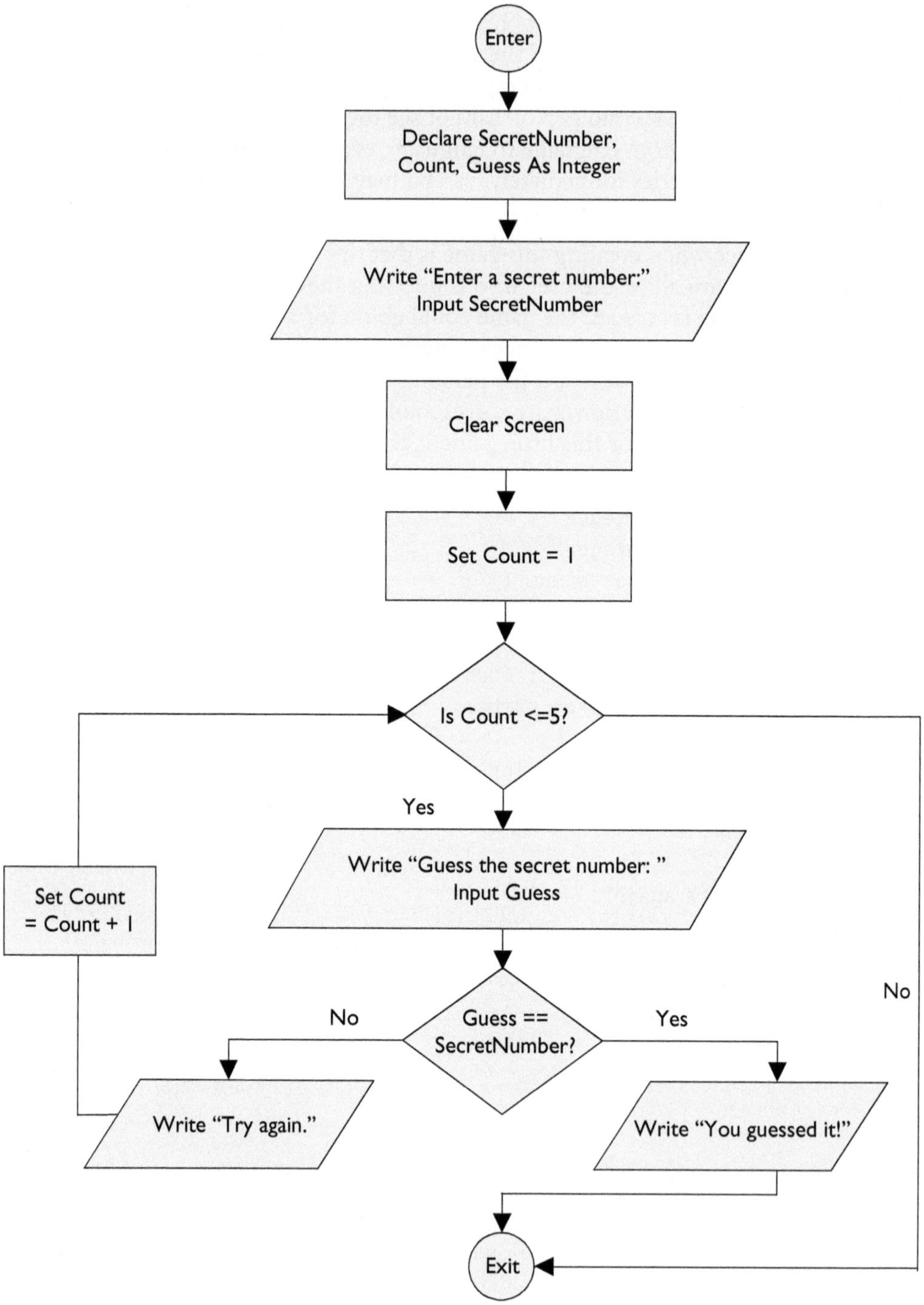

The first three examples in this chapter used For loops in combination with If-Then or If-Then-Else statements. However, any type of loop can be combined with selection statements, as we will see in Examples 6.4 and 6.5.

Example 6.4 **The Guessing Game Repeats**

In this example, we will rewrite the pseudocode of Example 6.3 using a Do . . . While post-test loop. The Exit statement on line 13 functions as the Exit For statement did in previous examples. It allows the program control to pass immediately to whatever comes immediately after the end of the loop.

```
1   Declare SecretNumber As Integer
2   Declare Count As Integer
3   Declare Guess As Integer
4   Write "Enter a secret number: "
5   Input SecretNumber
6   Clear Screen
7   Set Count = 1
8   Do
9     Write "Guess the secret number: "
10    Input Guess
11    If Guess == SecretNumber Then
12      Write "You guessed it!"
13      Exit
14    Else
15      Write "Try again"
16    End If
17    Set Count = Count + 1
18  While Count <= 5
```

Before we end this section, we will write one more program using a While loop combined with an If-Then-Else statement for data validation. In Example 6.5, we write pseudocode for a program that will compute the square root of a number and display that result. Recall from Chapter 4 that most programming languages contain a function that computes square roots and, in this text, we have defined that function to be Sqrt(). Also, as you know, Sqrt() can only compute the positive square root of a positive number. Therefore, the program will have to test the input to ensure that only positive numbers are entered.

Example 6.5 **Computing Valid Square Roots with a While Loop**

This program segment uses a While loop to allow the user to find the square roots of as many positive numbers as desired and an If-Then-Else statement to validate data input.

```
1   Declare Number As Float
2   Declare Root As Float
3   Declare Response As Character
4   Write "Do you want to find the square root of a number?"
5   Write "Enter 'y' for yes, 'n' for no: "
```

```
 6  While Response == "y"
 7    Write "Enter a positive number: "
 8    Input Number
 9    If (Number >= 0) Then
10      Set Root = Sqrt(Number)
11      Write "The square root of " + Number + " is: " + Root
12    Else
13      Write "Your number is invalid."
14    End If
15    Write "Do you want to do this again?"
16    Write "Enter 'y' for yes, 'n' for no: "
17    Input Response
18  End While
```

Self Check for Section 6.1

6.1 Redo the pseudocode for Example 6.4 to ensure that the input (the user's Guess) is a valid integer.

6.2 True or False? If-Then-Else statements can only be combined with For loops.

6.3 True or False? It is not possible to put a loop inside an If-Then statement.

6.4 If NumberX= 3 and NumberY = 4.7 determine whether each of the following statements is true or false:

a. NumberX = Int(NumberX)

b. NumberY = Int(NumberY)

6.5 If NumberX = 6.2, NumberY = 2.8, and NumberZ = 9, determine whether each of the following is true or false:

a. NumberZ = Floor(NumberX + NumberY)

b. NumberZ = Floor(NumberZ)

6.6 The following pseudocode allows the user to enter up to 10 numbers and see those numbers displayed on the screen. It contains one error. Identify the error and fix it.

```
Declare Count As Integer
Declare Number As Integer
Declare Response As String
For (Count = 1; Count < 10; Count++)
  Write "Enter a number: "
  Input Number
  Write "The number you entered is: " + Number
  Write "Do you want to continue?"
  Write "Enter 'y' for yes, 'n' for no:"
  Input Response
  If Response == "n" Then
    Write "Goodbye"
    Exit For
  End If
End For
```

6.2 Combining Loops and Decisions in Longer Programs

In this section, we will use loop structures combined with If-Then structures to create several longer and more complex program segments.

Example 6.6 shows how we can keep track of how many positive numbers and how many negative numbers are input by a user. A program segment such as this could be embedded in a larger program, with modifications, to keep track of various types of entries. For example, a college might enter demographic information on students and want to keep track of how many students are older than a certain age. A business might want to track how many items a user purchased that are above or below a certain cost.

Example 6.6 **Keeping Track of User Inputs**

This program segment inputs numbers from the user (terminated by 0) and counts how many positive and negative numbers have been entered. A flowchart for this program segment is shown in Figure 6.4.

```
1   Declare PositiveCount As Integer
2   Declare NegativeCount As Integer
3   Declare Number As Integer
4   Set PositiveCount = 0
5   Set NegativeCount = 0
6   Write "Enter a number. Enter 0 when done: "
7   Input Number
8   While Number != 0
9     If Number > 0 Then
10      Set PositiveCount = PositiveCount + 1
11    Else
12      Set NegativeCount = NegativeCount + 1
13    End If
14    Write "Enter a number. Enter 0 when done: "
15    Input Number
16  End While
17  Write "The number of positive numbers entered is " ↵
           + PositiveCount
18  Write "The number of negative numbers entered is " ↵
           + NegativeCount
```

What Happened?

- Lines 1–5 declare and initialize the counters, PositiveCount and NegativeCount.
- Lines 6 and 7 ask for and accept input of the first number, Number, from the user.
- The loop begins on line 8 and continues iterations as long as Number is not 0.
- Then within the loop, each number that has been entered is examined by the If-Then-Else structure.
- Line 9 checks to see if the number is positive.
- If this is true, the Then clause on line 10 is executed. PositiveCount is incremented by one so this keeps track of how many positive numbers have been entered.

Figure 6.4 Using selection structures with loops to keep track of counts

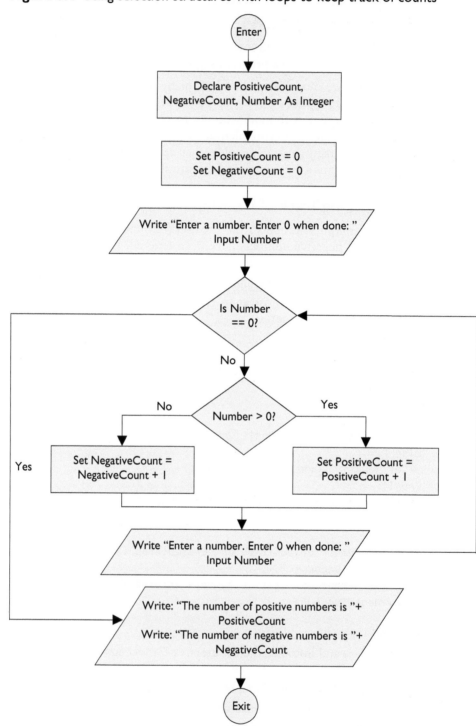

- If the number is negative, the Else clause on lines 11 and 12 are executed
  and NegativeCount is incremented by one, keeping track of how many negative numbers have been entered. Remember, in an If-Then-Else structure,
  when the If statement is true, the Else clause is skipped.

- Line 13 ends the `If-Then-Else` clause.
- Since any number entered must be positive, negative, or zero, all possibilities have been accounted for. The program continues to line 14 where the user is prompted for another number.
- The next number is input (line 15) and control returns to line 8 where the number is checked to see if it is zero. If it is not zero, the loop goes through another pass.
- If the number is zero, the loop is exited and `PositiveCount` and `NegativeCount` contain, respectively, the total number of positive and negative numbers entered. Control goes to lines 17 and 18 where the results of the positive and negative counts are displayed.

Example 6.7 combines `Select Case` statements with a loop in a longer program segment that might be used by a business.

Example 6.7 Keeping Track of Shipping Costs

Today, everyone who opens a small business must have an online presence. Customers expect to order from websites so online businesses need a program to calculate costs. In this example, we will use a loop and two `Select Case` statements to allow a customer to order as many items as desired. The business owner can offer various discounts to the customer, based on the cost of items. Shipping costs and sales tax will also be calculated, based on the total cost of the purchase. The shipping cost is dependent on the total amount purchased, while tax is calculated at a single rate. In our example, the discounts will be as shown but it would take very little work to alter the program for different discounts, shipping costs, and tax rates.

- The tax rate for our program is 6%.
- Discounts are offered as follows:
  - Items that cost $20.00 or less receive a 10% discount.
  - Items that cost between $20.01 and $50.00 receive a 15% discount.
  - Items that cost between $50.01 and $100.00 receive a 20% discount.
  - Items that cost over $100.00 receive a 25% discount.
- Shipping costs are calculated on the total purchase price and are as follows:
  - If the total purchase is $20.00 or less, shipping is $5.00.
  - If the total purchase is between $20.01 and $50.00, shipping is $8.00.
  - If the total purchase is between $50.01 and $100.00, shipping is $10.00.
  - Purchases over $100.00 receive free shipping.

The pseudocode for this program is as follows:

```
1  Declare ItemCost As Float
2  Declare ItemTotal As Float
3  Declare Tax As Float
4  Declare Ship As Float
5  Declare Count As Integer
6  Declare NumItems As Integer
7  Declare TotalCost As Float
8  Set ItemTotal = 0
```

```
 9  Set TotalCost = 0
10  Write "How many items are you buying? "
11  Input NumItems
12  For (Count = 1; Count <= NumItems; Count++)
13    Write "Enter the cost of item " + Count
14    Input ItemCost
15    Select Case Of ItemCost
16      Case: <= 20.00
17        Set ItemCost = ItemCost * .90
18        Break
19      Case: <= 50.00
20        Set ItemCost = ItemCost * .85
21        Break
22      Case: <= 100.00
23        Set ItemCost = ItemCost * .80
24        Break
25      Case: > 100.00
26        Set ItemCost = ItemCost * .75
27        Break
28    End Case
29    Set ItemTotal = ItemTotal + ItemCost
30  End For
31  Select Case Of ItemTotal
32    Case: <= 20.00
33      Set Ship = 5.00
34      Break
35    Case: <= 50.00
36      Set Ship = 8.00
37      Break
38    Case: <= 100.00
39      Set Ship = 10.00
40      Break
41    Case: > 100.00
42      Set Ship = 0.0
43      Break
44  End Case
45  Set Tax = ItemTotal * 0.06
46  Set TotalCost = ItemTotal + Tax + Ship
47  Write "Your item total is $ " + ItemTotal
48  Write "Shipping costs will be $ " + Ship
49  Write "The total amount due, including sales tax,"
50  Write " is $ " + TotalCost
```

What Happened?

- Lines 1 through 9 declare and initialize the variables needed for the program. The variables that refer to costs (ItemCost, ItemTotal, Tax, Ship, TotalCost) are floating point variables since prices usually include both dollars and cents. The variables `Count` and `NumItems` are integer variables.

- Lines 10 and 11 prompt for and input the number of items the customer wishes to buy. This variable, `NumItems`, will be used as the test condition in the loop.

- The loop begins on line 12 and continues iterations as long as the counter is not greater than the number of items the customer is buying.

- Lines 13 and 14 allow the customer to input the cost of an item.

- Lines 15 through 28 constitute the first `Select Case` statement. Here is where the discount is applied. For example, a 10% discount is achieved by finding 10% of the amount and subtracting it from the amount, as shown:

```
ItemCost - 0.10 * ItemCost = 0.90 * ItemCost
```

So, for a 10% discount, what is really needed is 90% of `ItemCost`. This pseudocode avoids the extra step and simply calculates 90% of the `ItemCost`. Similarly, for a 15% discount, 85% of `ItemCost` is the same as subtracting 15% from the amount.

- You will recall how a `Select Case` statement works: if `ItemCost` matches the first `Case` (i.e., `ItemCost` is less than or equal to 20.00), line 17 will be executed and, due to the `Break` statement on line 18, the remaining lines of code in this `Select Case` statement (lines 19–27) are skipped. If, however, an item costs, for example, $98.52, its value is checked on line 16 and, since it does not match this `Case`, lines 17 and 18 are skipped. Then the value is checked on 19 and, once again, it does not match this `Case` so lines 20 and 21 are skipped. However, this `ItemCost` does fall in the range of the `Case` specified on line 22 so line 23 is executed. The `Break` statement on line 24 forces lines 25–27 to be skipped as soon as a `Break` statement is encountered. In other words, with a `Select Case` statement, only the instructions following the matching `Case` are executed and all the other instructions are skipped. Therefore, the cost of each item is checked and, depending on that cost, the appropriate discount is applied. The discounted price of the item is now stored in `ItemCost` until the loop repeats and a new item's cost is entered.

- Line 29 keeps a sum of the total cost to the consumer. After calculating this total, control is returned to the top of the `For` loop. If `Count` is still not greater than `NumItems`, another `ItemCost` is entered on line 14 and the discount is applied to that item.

- When all the items have been entered, discounted, and added to the total cost, the `For` loop is exited (line 30).

- Lines 31 through 44 calculate the shipping cost, based on the total price of the purchase. In this program, we use another `Select Case` statement for this task.

- Line 45 computes the tax based on the total cost of the items, not including shipping costs, at a rate of 6%.

- Line 46 computes the total cost to the customer, including tax and shipping.

- Lines 47–50 display the results to the customer.

Making It Work

Can you think of ways to improve this program? There are several things that could be added or changed, which would increase the usability of the program. Computers calculate floating point numbers to many decimal places. If this program was coded in a real programming language, the output would be formatted so that costs are displayed with only two decimal places.

Data validation code should also be added to ensure that the customer enters a positive integer value for the number of items to purchase. A suitable message should be displayed if the customer enters 0 for the number of items to purchase. A prompt should be added if the customer enters a noninteger value or a negative number to check if the customer made an error in typing or if the customer truly wants to exit the program.

The program would also be more useful if the tax rate was assigned to a variable. That way, if the tax rate changed at a future date, the business owner could simply change the value of that variable instead of searching through the code for all the places where the tax rate was used.

In fact, it is always better to write code that can be used in the most general case. In the pseudocode of this example, the discount rates are set specifically to be 10%, 15%, 20%, and 25%. Shipping costs are also set specifically to be $5.00, $8.00, $10.00, or free. Can you think of how to write this program to make these items less specific and, therefore, easier for a user to change if necessary?

You will explore these possibilities in the Self Check questions.

The Length_Of() Function

We have already used the Length_Of() function in a RAPTOR program earlier in the text. Here, we will review how that function works for those who are not using RAPTOR with this book. Most programming languages contain a built-in function that is similar to the **Length_Of() function**. This function accepts a value inside the parentheses and returns a different value to the variable assigned to the result. The Length_Of() function takes a string or a string variable inside the parentheses and returns the number of characters in that string, as demonstrated in Example 6.8.

Example 6.8 **The Length_Of() Function**

This example demonstrates how the Length_Of() function works on strings. Since the Length_Of() function returns an integer, the variable on the left side of each expression must be an integer variable. In the following examples, it is to be assumed that MyLength has been declared as an integer.

- MyLength = Length_Of("Hello") assigns the value of 5 to MyLength because Hello has five characters.
- MyLength = Length_Of("Good-bye!") assigns the value of 9 to MyLength because the string has nine characters, including the hyphen and exclamation point.

- If Name = "Hermione Hatfield" then:

    MyLength = Length_Of(Name) assigns the value of 17 to MyLength
- If TheSpace = " ", then:

    MyLength = Length_Of(TheSpace) assigns the value of 1 to MyLength
    because a space is counted as one character

The Print Statement and the New Line Indicator

At this point we will introduce a new pseudocode statement: the **Print statement**. In the pseudocode that we have used so far, the Write statement indicates output to the screen with the assumption that each new Write statement would begin on a new line. In most programming languages, output will be displayed in one continuous line on the screen unless the programmer specifically instructs the program to go to the next line. The code to indicate a new line varies from language to language, but the result is the same: to get output on separate lines; the programmer must indicate this to the computer in one form or another. For some problems discussed in this chapter and later in the text, the Write statement is not a realistic portrayal of what may actually happen in some languages.

The Print statement will also be used in our pseudocode to indicate output to the screen, just as the Write statement does, including the ability to concatenate variables and text. However, until a **newline indicator** is used, it is to be assumed that output from any subsequent Print statements will be on the same line. The newline indicator that we will use is **<NL>**.[2]

For example, notice how the output displayed by the following two program segments differs:

Code	Code
Write "Hi"	Print "Hi"
Write "Ho"	Print "Ho" <NL>
Write "Done"	Print "Done"
Display	**Display**
Hi	HiHo
Ho	Done
Done	

Example 6.9 utilizes the Print statement and the <NL> indicator.

---

[2]To create output in RAPTOR that does not automatically begin on a new line with each Output symbol, refer to the Running With RAPTOR section in Chapter 5. Recall that you must uncheck the End Current Line box at the bottom of the Enter Output Here dialog box.

Example 6.9 **Using the `Length_Of()` Function for Formatting**

In this example, we will practice using an `If-Then` statement nested in a loop to format screen display. Later in this chapter we will add to this program to create more interesting formatting. The pseudocode shown below allows the user to enter his or her name, and the name will be displayed with a line of symbols (chosen by the user) under the name. The number of symbols will match the number of characters in the name. To do this, we will use the `Length_Of()` function. The `Print` statement allows output within a loop to be displayed on a single line. The pseudocode for this program is as follows:

```
1   Declare Name As String
2   Declare Symbol As Character
3   Declare Number As Integer
4   Declare Choice As Character
5   Declare Count As Integer
6   Set Count = 0
7   Write "Enter your name: "
8   Input Name
9   Write "Choose one of the following symbols: "
10  Write " * or # "
11  Input Symbol
12  Write "Do you want a space between each symbol?"
13  Write "Enter 'Y' for yes, 'N' for no"
14  Input Choice
15  Set Number = Length_Of(Name)
16  Print Name <NL>
17  While Count <= Number
18    If Choice == "y" OR Choice == "Y"
19      Print Symbol + " "
20      Set Count = Count + 2
21    Else
22      Print Symbol
23      Set Count = Count + 1
24    End If
25  End While
26  Print <NL>
27  Write "How does that look?"
```

What Happened?

- Lines 1 through 6 declare and initialize the variables needed for the program.
- Lines 7–14 prompt for and accept initial values from the user.
- Line 15 extracts the number of characters in the user's name through the `Length_Of()` function.
- Line 16 displays the user's name on the screen. It uses the `Print` statement but ends with the `<NL>` indicator. This means that the next output statement will begin on the next line.
- Line 17 begins the `While` loop.

- The If statement on line 18 does two things. It checks the value of Choice to see if the user wants to put a space between each symbol, and it adds a little programming to make this program segment more "user-friendly." By using a compound condition, with an OR operator, the program allows for a user to type in either an uppercase or a lowercase response. You may have noticed that sometimes, when you use any computer program, either upper or lower case responses are accepted but sometimes the case is significant. Good programmers try to think ahead of the users and account for many possible user responses when writing code.

- If the user has entered a "y" (or a "Y"), the program continues to line 19 where the chosen symbol is displayed with a space, and the counter is incremented on line 20.

- By using the Print statement on line 19 without the <NL> indicator at the end, the next time this line is executed the second output will be displayed on the same line.

- Let's think about line 20 for a moment. We want our display to be the person's name with a line of symbols underneath. If the user does not select a space between symbols, then the number of symbols will match the number of characters in the name. The loop has been written to execute until the value of Count matches the value of Number (the number of characters in the name). However, if the user wants a space between symbols and we simply increment Count by 1 on each pass, the line of symbols would extend twice as long as the name. If we increment Count by 2 in this case, instead of 1, the loop will now end when the number of characters in the symbol line (a symbol and a space for each iteration) matches the number of characters in the name.

- If the user has entered any character except y or Y, the Else option will be executed. In this case, a symbol with no space will be displayed (line 22) before the counter is incremented on line 23. The Print statement on line 22 without the <NL> indicator allows the next symbol (when this line is executed on the next iteration) to be displayed on the same line.

- Control returns to line 17 after either of the If-Then-Else options have been completed. The loop executes again and again until the counter is greater than Number and then it ends. In this way, the number of symbols displayed will match the number of characters in Name.

- Line 26 forces the next output to be on the following line. If we leave this line off, the statement "How does that look?" would be on the same line as the line of symbols.

Following is the code for this program in C++ along with the display, assuming the user has entered Joe for Name, # for Symbol, and has not chosen to put spaces between symbols. Notice that the new line indicator in C++ is endl.

Making It Work

```
int count = 0; int number = 0;
string name = " ";
char symbol = '#'; char choice;
cout << "Enter your name: ";
```

```
cin >> name;
number = name.length();
cout << "Choose a symbol: * or # ";
cin >> symbol;
cout << "Do you want a space between each symbol?";
cout << "Enter Y for yes, N for no.";
cin >> choice;
cout << name << endl;
while (count <= number)
{
    if ((choice == 'Y') || (choice == 'y'))
    {
        cout << symbol << "  ";
        count = count + 2;
    }
    else
    {
        cout << symbol;
        count = count + 1;
    }
}
return 0;
```

Display:

```
Joe
###
```

Self Check for Section 6.2

For Self Check for Section 6.7 and 6.8 refer to Example 6.7.

6.7 Which of the following variables should be checked for validity? For each variable you select, identify what needs to be validated.
ItemCost, ItemTotal, Tax, Ship, Count, NumItems

6.8 Walk through the pseudocode provided in Example 6.7 and find out what would be displayed at the end if the customer purchased the following three items:
A widget for $55.98
A wonka for $23.89
A womble for $103.50

6.9 Write a program segment that asks a user to enter the username he or she wants and checks the length of the entry. The username can be between 1-15 characters, inclusive. Since the space you have allowed for the username can only hold 15 characters, check to make sure the user's entry is no longer than this.

6.10 Create a program segment using Print statements, the <NL> indicator, and loops to display the following:

```
& & & & & & & & & &
# # # # # # # # # #
& & & & & & & & & &
```

6.11 The following pseudocode allows the user to enter five numbers and displays the absolute value of the inverse of each number. It is missing something. Find the missing condition and fix the pseudocode.

```
Declare Count As Integer
Declare Number As Float
Declare Inverse As Float
Set Count = 1
Do
  Write "Enter a number: "
  Input Number
  If Number > 0
    Set Inverse = 1/Number
  Else
    Set Inverse = (-1)/Number
  End If
  Write Inverse
  Set Count = Count + 1
While Count <= 5
```

6.3 Random Numbers

Random numbers are numbers whose values form an unpredictable sequence. They have many interesting applications in programming. Although one of their major uses is to provide an element of chance in computer games, they also have other important functions, as in simulating situations or processes in business, mathematics, engineering, and other disciplines. In this section, we will discuss how to use random numbers in your programs.

The Random() Function

Most programming languages contain a function that is used to generate a sequence of random numbers, although the name of this function and the way it works varies from language to language. To illustrate the use of random numbers, we will define a function of the following form: **Random()**. When the program encounters the expression Random(), which may appear anywhere that an integer constant is valid, it generates a random number from 0.0 to 1.0, including 0.0 but not 1.0. This may, initially, not seem very helpful. After all, how many situations can you think of that can use a random number like 0.2506 or 0.0925? While randomly generated numbers like these may have some esoteric uses, it is far more common to require integer random numbers in a specific range. For example, in simulating the roll of a single die (one of a pair of dice), the possible outcomes are 1, 2, 3, 4, 5, and 6. Therefore, we normally manipulate the generated number to turn it into an integer in the range we require. This may take several steps.

For the purposes of illustration, the random numbers generated here as examples will have four decimal places (the actual number of decimal places generated depends on the computer system and the specific language's compiler or interpreter). For example, `Random()` might generate `0.3792` or `0.0578`. If we multiply the random number by 10, we will generate numbers between 0 and `9.9999`, as shown in the following:

- If `Random()` = `0.3792`, then `Random()` * `10` = `3.7920`
- If `Random()` = `0.0578`, then `Random()` * `10` = `0.5780`
- If `Random()` = `0.1212`, then `Random()` * `10` = `1.2120`
- If `Random()` = `0.9999`, then `Random()` * `10` = `9.9990`

We have increased the range from `0.000` up to, but not including, 10. And we still do not have integer values. But we do have the `Floor()` function! If we take the `Floor()` of any random number, we will simply drop the decimal part, as you can see from the following:

- If `Random()` = `0.3792`, then `Floor(Random()` * `10)` = `3`
- If `Random()` = `0.0578`, then `Floor(Random()` * `10)` = `0`
- If `Random()` = `0.1212`, then `Floor(Random()` * `10)` = `1`
- If `Random()` = `0.9999`, then `Floor(Random()` * `10)` = `9`

We now have random numbers between 0 and 9. Finally, if we wish to generate a random number between 1 and 10, we can simply add 1 to the expression to get:

- If `Random()` = `0.3792`, then `(Floor(Random()` * `10)` + `1)` = `4`
- If `Random()` = `0.0578`, then `(Floor(Random()` * `10)` + `1)` = `1`
- If `Random()` = `0.1212`, then `(Floor(Random()` * `10)` + `1)` = `2`
- If `Random()` = `0.9999`, then `(Floor(Random()` * `10)` + `1)` = `10`

To use the random number generator in a program, you assign its value to an integer variable. To generate random numbers in any range desired, change the multiplier and/or the number added, as needed. Example 6.10 demonstrates this.

Example 6.12 provides a more advanced illustration of how random numbers can be used to make a probability prediction.

Earlier in this chapter, we created a simple guessing game in Example 6.3. Now, with the help of the `Random()` function, we can create a more interesting guessing game. Example 6.13 illustrates how to do this.

Example 6.10 Generating Random Numbers with the `Random()` Function

If `NewNumber` is an integer variable, then:

- `NewNumber = Floor(Random()` * `10)` + `1` will result in a random number between 1 and 10 (inclusive)
- `NewNumber = Floor(Random()` * `100)` + `1` will result in a random number between 1 and 100 (inclusive)
- `NewNumber = Floor(Random()` * `10)` + `4` will result in a random number between 4 and 13 (inclusive)
- `NewNumber = Floor(Random()` * `2)` will result in either 0 or 1
- `NewNumber = Floor(Random()` * `2)` + `1` will result in either 1 or 2

- NewNumber = Floor(Random() * 6) + 7 will result in a random number between 7 and 12 (inclusive)

After examining these examples, we can conclude that, to generate a sequence of N random integers beginning with the integer M, use:

$$Floor(Random() * N) + M$$

Example 6.11 **Flipping a Coin**[3]

This simple program segment uses the Random() function to simulate a coin toss. If a 1 is generated, the program displays Heads and, if a 0 is generated, the program displays Tails. We put the coin toss in a While loop, which can be run as often as the user wants.

```
1   Declare Number As Integer
2   Declare Response As Character
3   Write "Do you want to flip a coin?"
4   Write "Enter 'y' for yes, 'n' for no: "
5   Input Response
6   While Response == "y"
7     Set Number = Floor(Random() * 2)
8     If Number = 1 Then
9       Write "Heads"
10    Else
11      Write "Tails"
12    End If
13    Write "Flip again? Enter 'y' for yes, 'n' for no: "
14    Input Response
15  End While
```

Line 7 uses the Random() function to generate either a 0 or 1. That value is then stored in the variable Number and is used to determine the result of the coin toss.

Example 6.12 **Winning at Dice**

Suppose a pair of dice is rolled and its sum is recorded. For example, if the first die comes up 3 and the second comes up 6, we record the value 9. Your friend suggests that now that you are such an expert with computers, you might be able to use a computer to predict a good strategy for playing a game that uses dice. She asks you to write a program to generate what outcomes are most likely. She wants to know if it is more likely that the sum of a roll of a pair of dice will be 5 or 8.

We can answer this question by simulating an experiment with a program that uses random numbers. For each roll of the dice, we need to generate two random numbers— one for each die—in the range from 1 to 6. Then we add these numbers and keep track of the number of times the sum is 5 or 8. If we roll the dice (generate a pair of random numbers) thousands of times, the sum (5 or 8) with the larger count is presumably the one that is more likely to occur. Here's a program that carries out this plan.

[3]To generate a random number in RAPTOR, use the RAPTOR's random function. The function returns a random number in the same range as discussed here. To generate a random integer from A to B, assuming A and B are positive integers and A is less than B, use floor((random * B) + A). For example, you can simulate the roll of a die (a random number from 1 to 6) with floor((random * 6) + 1).

```
 1  Declare FiveCount As Integer
 2  Declare EightCount As Integer
 3  Declare K As Integer
 4  Declare Die1 As Integer
 5  Declare Die2 As Integer
 6  Declare Sum As Integer
 7  Set FiveCount = 0
 8  Set EightCount = 0
 9  For (K = 1; K <= 1000; K++)
10    Set Die1 = Floor(Random() * 6) + 1
11    Set Die2 = Floor(Random() * 6) + 1
12    Set Sum = Die1 + Die2
13    If Sum == 5 Then
14      Set FiveCount = FiveCount + 1
15    End If
16    If Sum == 8 Then
17      Set EightCount = EightCount + 1
18    End If
19  End For
20  Write "Number of times sum was 5: " + FiveCount
21  Write "Number of times sum was 8: " + EightCount
```

The best thing about this program, if it were actually coded and run, is that the computer would give us results in few seconds! It would take a person many hours to do this by hand. And, of course, if you think that 1,000 rolls of the dice is not enough to make an adequate prediction, just change the value of 1,000 to 10,000 or 2 million and you'll still get results in seconds. You can try this yourself using RAPTOR.

What & Why

What do you think? If we code and run this program segment, which sum do you think is more likely to occur? Can you justify your reasoning?

Consider the number of ways the sum of 5 can be obtained by rolling the dice and compare that with the number of ways the sum of 8 can be obtained by rolling the dice.

When two dice are rolled, the possible sums are 2, 3, 4, 5, 6, 7, 8, 9, 10, 11, and 12. However, the possible combinations of two dice are as follows:

Possible ways to roll the 11 possible sums						Possible ways to roll a 5	Possible ways to roll an 8
1 + 1 = 2	2 + 1 = 3	3 + 1 = 4	4 + 1 = 5	5 + 1 = 6	6 + 1 = 7	(1,4)	(2,6)
1 + 2 = 3	2 + 2 = 4	3 + 2 = 5	4 + 2 = 6	5 + 2 = 7	6 + 2 = 8	(4,1)	(6,2)
1 + 3 = 4	2 + 3 = 5	3 + 3 = 6	4 + 3 = 7	5 + 3 = 8	6 + 3 = 9	(2,3)	(3,5)
1 + 4 = 5	2 + 4 = 6	3 + 4 = 7	4 + 4 = 8	5 + 4 = 9	6 + 4 = 10	(3,2)	(5,3)
1 + 5 = 6	2 + 5 = 7	3 + 5 = 8	4 + 5 = 9	5 + 5 = 10	6 + 5 = 11		(4,4)
1 + 6 = 7	2 + 6 = 8	3 + 6 = 9	4 + 6 = 10	5 + 6 = 11	6 + 6 = 12		

There are 36 possible combinations and 11 possible sums. Since there are 4 ways to get a sum of 5 from 36 possible results, the probability of rolling a 5 is 4/36 (approximately 11.1%). Similarly, since there are five ways to get a sum of 8 from the 36 possible results, the probability of rolling an 8 is 5/36 (approximately 13.9%).

This means that, were you to roll two dice many, many times, over the long run, for every 100 times the dice are rolled and summed, there will be approximately 11 times that the sum will be 5 and approximately 14 times when the sum will be 8.   ●

Example 6.13 **Another Guessing Game**

This program allows the user (presumably a young child) to play a guessing game with the computer. The program generates a random integer (stored in a variable named Given) from 1 to 100, and the child has to guess this number.

```
1   Declare Given As Integer
2   Declare Guess As Integer
3   Set Given = (Floor(Random() * 100)) + 1
4   Write "I'm thinking of a whole number from 1 to 100."
5   Write "Can you guess what it is?"
6   Do
7     Write "Enter your guess: "
8     Input Guess
9     If Guess < Given Then
10      Write "You're too low."
11    End If
12    If Guess > Given Then
13      Write "You're too high."
14    End If
15  While Guess != Given
16  Write "Congratulations! You win!"
```

What Happened?

In this pseudocode, once the random integer is generated, the loop allows the user to repeatedly guess the value of the unknown number. To hasten the guessing process, the If-Then statements tell the user whether the guess is below or above the number sought. When the number guessed matches the number given, the loop is exited and the game is over.

Can you see a problem with the pseudocode provided in Example 6.13? If, for example, the random number generated was 64 and the child playing the game guessed 87, the display would say that this guess is too high. A clever child might quickly figure out that his or her next guess should be less than 87. The next guess might be 18 and the computer would tell the child that this guess was too low. Our clever child would realize that the number then had to be between 19 and 86 and

What &Why

would continue to make guesses that zoom in on the correct number, using the messages "You're too high" and "You're too low" as hints. But what if the child continued to make guesses without regard to the messages? This program could go on indefinitely. This pseudocode should have some limitations. For example, the whole program might be contained in a loop that restricts the number of guesses or asks the player if he or she wants to end the guessing process and see the correct number displayed. We will return to this program in the Focus on Problem Solving section.   ●

Not Really Random: The Pseudorandom Number

What does it actually mean to generate a random number? For a number (in a given set of numbers) to be selected truly at random, there must be an equal chance for any number to be selected.

However, no one can just tell a computer, "Pick any number between 0 and 1." A computer must receive instructions from a program. A programmer must write a program to instruct the computer about how to select a number in a given range. Random numbers are often produced by means of a **mathematical algorithm**—a formula (in a program) that instructs the computer how to pick some number in the range we specify. The algorithm might include instructions to multiply a number by something, divide by something else, raise the result to a power, and so forth. But the algorithm requires some beginning value to manipulate. This starting number is called the **seed value**.

The number generated by the algorithm is used as the seed to generate the next random number. If the same seed is used each time the program calls for a random number, the numbers generated are not really random. So the numbers generated like this are not unpredictable, even though they are all equally likely to occur. Such numbers are called **pseudorandom** but are generally just as useful as those that are truly random.

When a function that generates random numbers in this way is encountered in a program, some programming languages always use the same seed to generate the pseudorandom numbers unless specified otherwise. Therefore, if the starting value of the algorithm does not change, the same sequence of numbers will be produced each time the program is executed. This is useful for debugging purposes, but after a program is functioning correctly, you must force the computer to use a different seed on each run so that the random numbers produced will indeed be unpredictable. This is usually accomplished by placing a statement at the beginning of the program or program module that changes the seed from run to run. One way to make a pseudorandom number less predictable is to use a seed that is not predetermined. For example, you could use the number of milliseconds since the beginning of the current year as a seed. While this is not truly a random number, it will only occur once a year and therefore, is not likely to be repeated. This type of seed forces a random number generator to start with a different seed each time it is run because the time will be different in each run.

6.12 Give the range of the random numbers generated by the following statements:

    a. `Set Num1 = Floor(Random() * 4)`

    b. `Set Num2 = Floor(Random() * 2) + 3`

    c. `Set Num3 = Floor(Random() * X) - 2`, where X = 5

6.13 Write a program that displays 100 random integers between 10 and 20 (inclusive).

6.14 Write a program that uses random numbers to simulate rolling a single die and displays the results. Allow the user to input the number of rolls of the die.

6.15 Rewrite the pseudocode provided in Example 6.13 to use:

    a. one `If-Then-Else` structure instead of two `If-Then` statements

    b. one `Select Case` statement instead of two `If-Then` statements

6.16 What is a pseudorandom number and how does it differ from a truly random number?

6.4 Nested Loops

Often, programs employ one loop that is contained entirely within another. In such a case, we say that they are **nested loops**. The larger loop is called the **outer loop** and the one lying within it is called the **inner loop**. Students sometimes find it difficult to follow the logical sequence of steps that occurs when nested loops are implemented. Therefore, we will spend quite a bit of time developing short program segments with nested loops and will step through each line of each program carefully. Now, more than ever, it is important to walk through (**desk check**) the pseudocode with paper and pencil, carefully writing down the values of each variable at each step.

Nested For Loops

In a nested loop program, the outer loop works as a regular loop. The inner loop is simply part of the loop body of the outer loop. The flowchart shown in Figure 6.5 demonstrates the flow of a program with a nested loop where the inner loop completes three iterations and the outer loop completes two iterations. We will walk through the logic of this flowchart.

In Figure 6.5, the outer loop begins by testing the value of the integer variable, OutCount. The test condition says to repeat this loop, while OutCount is less than or equal to 2. When the loop begins, OutCount = 1 so the body of this loop is entered. The first thing that happens is that an integer variable, InCount, is initialized to 1.

Figure 6.5 Flowchart of nested For loops

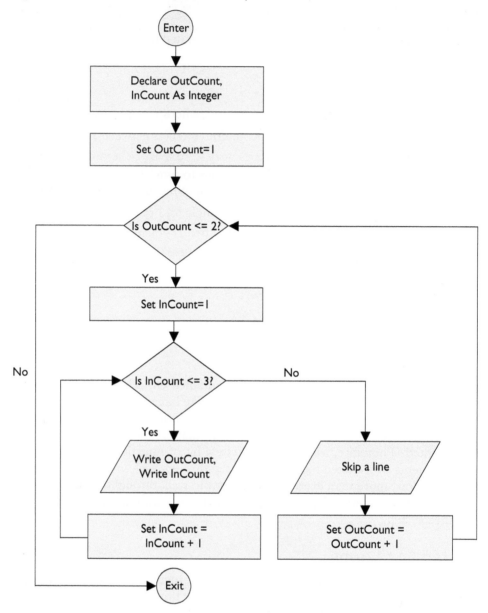

Next, the inner loop is entered. The entire inner loop must be contained in the outer loop. In this case, the test condition specifies that the inner loop will continue until InCount is greater than 3. Therefore, the inner loop body is executed for three iterations. The body of this loop displays the value of OutCount on one line and the value of InCount on the next line.

On the first pass through the inner loop, OutCount = 1 and InCount = 1. That is what is displayed. On the second pass, OutCount is still 1 but InCount has been incremented to 2. So a 1 is again displayed and, under it, a 2 is displayed. On the third pass, OutCount is still 1 and now InCount is 3. The fifth and sixth lines of the display are 1 and 3. Then, since InCount is incremented to 4, it fails the test condition and the inner loop is exited.

Next, a line is skipped and then OutCount is incremented to 2. Now we begin the outer loop a second time. Notice that the counter for inner loop, InCount, must be set equal to 1 again at this point. If this did not happen, the inner loop would never execute a second time because the value of InCount was 4 when the inner loop ended the first time.

The inner loop now goes through three more iterations, as before. This time it displays the new value of OutCount (2) each time around as well as the new values of InCount (1, 2, and 3). When InCount reaches 4, the inner loop is exited, a line is skipped, and OutCount is incremented to 3.

The program now ends since OutCount fails the test condition. The display, after the program is coded and run, will look as follows:

```
1
1
1
2
1
3

2
1
2
2
2
3
```

Examples 6.14 and 6.15 use For loops to further illustrate the order in which the loop iterations (the passes through the loops) take place when we nest one loop inside another. The flowchart for Example 6.14 is shown in Figure 6.6.

Example 6.14 **Using Nested For Loops to Display a Lot of Beans**

Let's say we want to write a program that will count twenty "bean"s and put them in four groups with five "bean"s in each group.

The inner loop counts five "bean"s. We know how to create this simple loop. We could repeat the loop four times to get the result we want, but that would be a long and boring process. Instead, we can put the little loop to display five "bean"s per group inside an outer loop, which simply says to repeat the inner loop four times.

The pseudocode for this program segment is as follows with a corresponding flowchart:

```
1  Declare OutCount As Integer
2  Declare InCount As Integer
```

```
3   For (OutCount = 1; OutCount <=4; OutCount++)
4     For (InCount = 1; InCount <=5; InCount++)
5       Write "bean"
6     End For(InCount)
7     Write " "
8   End For(OutCount)
```

Figure 6.6 Flowchart for Nested For Loops

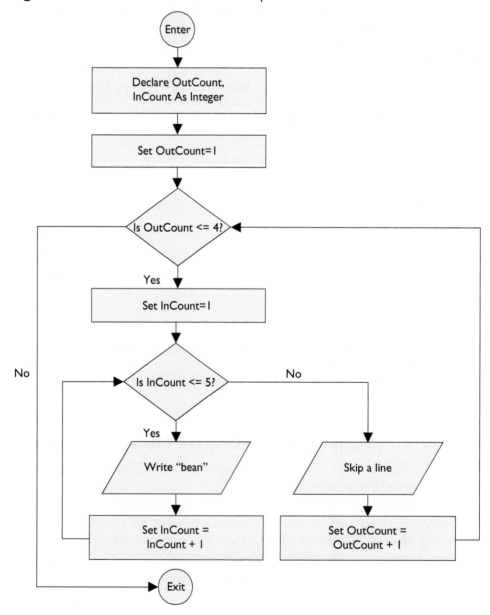

What Happened?

- Line 3 begins the outer loop. We want this loop to go through four iterations because each iteration displays one group of five "bean"s. So line 3 checks to make sure that the counter for the outer loop (OutCount) is not greater than 4. If OutCount is greater than 4, the program jumps to line 8. Otherwise, it proceeds to line 4.

- Line 4 begins the inner loop. This loop displays one "bean" and increments InCount by 1 each time it runs through a pass. We want it to complete five iterations which will display five "bean"s. When InCount reaches past 5, the limit condition is not true, the inner loop ends for the first time, and the program proceeds to line 7.

- Line 5 simply displays the word "bean". The next "bean" will be displayed right under this "bean", and this will continue until the loop is exited.

- The Write " " statement on line 7 simply displays a blank line. If we leave this line out, all 20 "bean"s would be displayed without a break. After this, OutCount is incremented by 1, the value is checked to see if it is still less than or equal to 4, and, if it is, the inner loop begins again.

- Note that when the inner loop begins each time, a new outer loop iteration happens; InCount is reset to 1 so it can go through five passes again.

- Each time the inner loop runs, a list of five "bean"s is displayed. Each time the outer loop runs, the inner loop displays the list of five "bean"s and the display skips a line. So we get four groups of five "bean"s.

Two Ways to Nest For Loops

Making It Work

If For loops have any statements in common, then one of them must be nested entirely within the other. They may not partially overlap! The inner loop must end before control passes again to the outer loop and their counter variables normally must be different. To illustrate, the following sets of pseudocode show two different valid ways in which three For loops may be nested.

Example A	Example B

```
For (I = . . .)
  For (J = . . .)
    Loop body
  End For(J)
  For (K = . . .)
    Loop body
  End For(K)
End For(I)
```

```
For (I =  . . . )
  For (J =  . . . )
    For (K =  . . . )
      Loop body
    End For(K)
  End For(J)
End For(I)
```

In Example A, two completely separate loops (J and K) are nested inside the outer loop (I). In Example B, the K loop is nested completely inside the J loop, and the J loop is nested completely inside the I loop. Both ways are perfectly acceptable, but the results will often differ. The type of nesting that is chosen for any specific program will depend on the program's requirements.

Nesting Other Kinds of Loops

Example 6.14 illustrates the nesting process with For loops. However, it is possible to nest one type of loop inside a different type of loop. The following examples demonstrate how to nest While, Repeat...Until, Do...While, and For loops.

In Chapter 5, we used a loop to calculate an exam average for one student in one class by inputting each exam grade. This works for one student, but you could use an outer loop to have the program accept information for all the students in a class. Example 6.15 demonstrates how to use nested loops to allow the user to find exam averages for many students. The example nests a For loop inside a While loop. The flowchart tracing the flow of execution for this example is shown in Figure 6.7.

Example 6.15 **Everyone's Exam Averages**

This program segment pseudocode allows a user to enter exam scores for as many students as the user wants using a While loop. In this example, it is assumed that each student has only three exams in the class, but the program can easily be altered to enter more or less exam scores by simply changing the limit condition in the nested For loop and the divisor on line 16. The pseudocode for this program segment is as follows:

```
1  Declare Count As Integer
2  Declare Name As String
3  Declare Score As Float
4  Declare ExamTotal As Float
5  Declare ExamAverage As Float
6  Set ExamTotal = 0.0
7  Set ExamAverage = 0.0
8  Write "Enter a student's name or enter * to quit: "
9  Input Name
10 While Name != "*"
```

```
11    For (Count = 1; Count < 4; Count++)
12      Write "Enter exam score number " + Count
13      Input Score
14      Set ExamTotal = ExamTotal + Score
15    End For
16    Set ExamAverage = ExamTotal/3
17    Write "Student: " + Name
18    Write "Exam average: " + ExamAverage
19    Write "Enter another student's name or '*' to quit:"
20    Input Name
21    Set ExamTotal = 0.0
22  End While
```

What Happened?

- The outer loop is a While loop and it begins on line 10, after the first name has been input. If the user has initially entered an asterisk (*), this loop will never be entered and nothing is displayed. Otherwise, control immediately goes to the inner loop, which begins on line 11.

- The inner loop is a For loop. Since for this example, we have assumed that each student has taken three exams, the counter is set to begin at 1 and to go through three iterations. For each iteration, one exam score (Score) is entered and a total is kept (ExamTotal).

- Line 12 uses the value of Count in the display. On the first pass through this loop, the value of Count is 1 so the prompt says "Enter exam score number 1". On the second pass, Count is 2 so the prompt says "Enter exam score number 2", and so on.

- Line 14 keeps a sum of these scores.

- When three scores have been entered, Count is incremented to 4, the test condition is no longer valid so the inner loop is exited. Control goes to the next line in the outer loop.

- Line 16 computes that student's exam average, and lines 17 and 18 display the result.

- Lines 19 and 20 give the user the opportunity to enter another student's scores or to end the program. Line 21 resets the ExamTotal to zero so the next student's sum will begin with 0. Control then returns to the top of the outer While loop. If the name entered is not an asterisk, the inner loop runs again.

- This process continues until the exam scores have been entered, averages calculated, and results displayed for all the students.

Figure 6.7 Flowchart of nested `While` and `For` loops

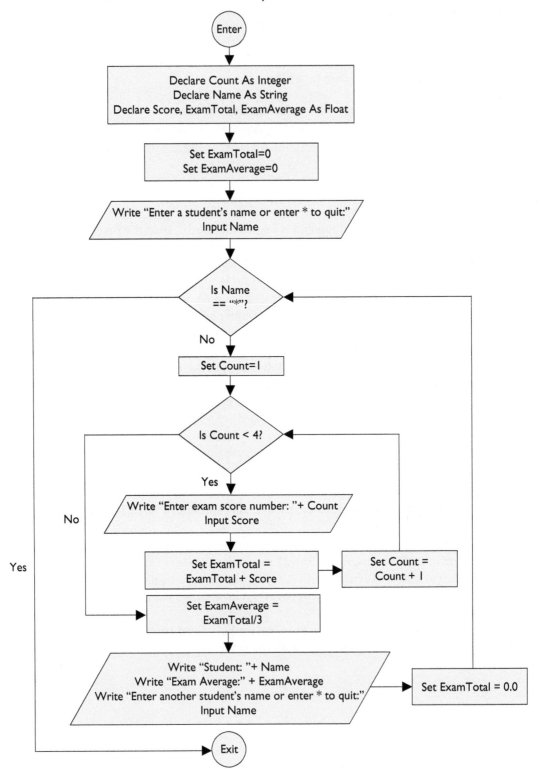

Example 6.16 contains nested `Repeat...Until` and `While` loops. A flowchart tracing the flow of execution in this example is shown in Figure 6.8.

Example 6.16 **Using `Repeat...Until` and `While` Nested Loops**

This pseudocode makes use of a post-test `Repeat...Until` loop to allow the user to sum several sets of numbers in a single run. The outer loop allows the entire program to be executed again if the user desires. It also contains statements that initialize the sum to 0, input the first number, explain that 0 is the sentinel value, and then display the sum computed by the inner `While` loop.

```
1   Declare Sum As Float
2   Declare Number As Float
3   Declare Response As Character
4   Repeat
5     Set Sum = 0
6     Write "I can do addition for you!"
7     Write "Enter the first number you want to add: "
8     Write "Enter 0 when you're done."
9     Input Number
10    While Number != 0
11      Set Sum = Sum + Number
12      Write "Enter your next number or 0 if you are done: "
13      Input Number
14    End While
15    Write "The sum of your numbers is " + Sum
16    Write "Sum another list of numbers? (Y or N)"
17    Input Response
18  Until Response == "N"
```

Notice that with the exception of its last three statements, the body of the outer `Repeat...Until` loop contains the usual pseudocode for summing a set of numbers input by the user. The last statements in this loop ask the user if he or she would like to do another sum, input this response, and then use it in the test condition for the outer `Repeat...Until` loop.

Figure 6.8 Flowchart of nested `Do...While` (or `Repeat...Until`) and `While` loops

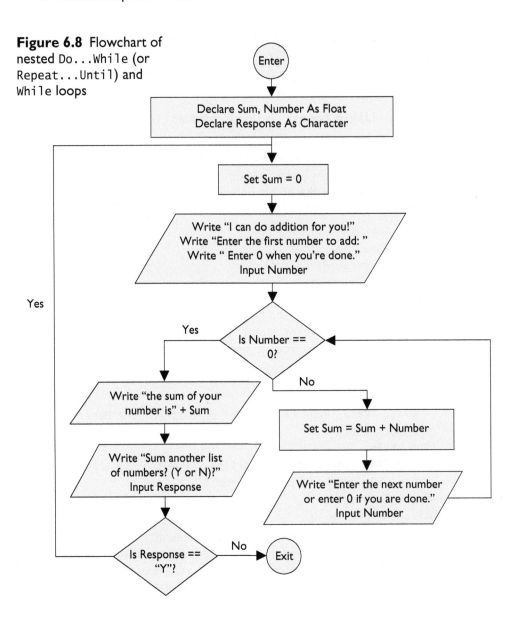

Example 6.17 **Drawing Squares with Nested Loops**

Example 6.9 demonstrates how to draw a line of symbols under a user's name using a combination of a loop and an `If-Then-Else` structure. In this example, we will build on this concept and use nested `While` loops to draw a square on the screen. You can add other options to this program; some of these will be part of the Self Check questions and the Programming Challenges at the end of this chapter. The pseudocode for this program is as follows:

```
1   Declare Count1 As Integer
2   Declare Count2 As Integer
3   Declare Symbol As Character
4   Declare Side As Integer
```

```
 5   Write "Choose a symbol (any character from the keyboard): "
 6   Input Symbol
 7   Write "Enter the length of a side of the square: "
 8   Input Side
 9   Set Count1 = 1
10   Set Count2 = 1
11   While Count1 <= Side
12     While Count2 <= Side
13       Print Symbol
14       Set Count2 = Count2 + 1
15     End While
16     Print <NL>
17     Set Count2 = 1
18     Set Count1 = Count1 + 1
19   End While
```

What Happened?

In this program segment, the user can choose any symbol from the keyboard, which is stored in the variable Symbol. The user also chooses the length of the sides of the square, which is stored in the integer variable, Side.

Since a square has the same length as width, the program needs to draw X number of symbols horizontally for X rows (if X represents the value of Side). The inner loop draws one row of symbols. The outer loop repeats the inner loop for the correct number of rows.

Notice that the Print statement on line 13, inside the inner loop, will allow symbols to be displayed all on one line. Line 16, however, simply says Print <NL>. This statement just instructs the output to begin on a new line. In a statement like this, there is no output to the screen.

A Mental Workout: Mind Games

By now you probably have realized that computers don't process information like humans. People can understand concepts like "pick up some bread when you're at the store" or "put that book down" or "make my coffee with a little cream and sugar." Computers can't process statements like that. Computers need exact, precise directions. In some ways, this makes it easier to write instructions because there can be no errors. A computer would never give you a cup of coffee that is too sweet or with too little cream. Unless you specify the exact amount of cream and sugar, you would get nothing. On the other hand, if you write a coffee preparation program correctly, you would always get a perfect cup of coffee. As you can see, there are pros and cons to this way of "thinking." The downside is that it is often much more difficult for humans to create and follow such a program. The upside is that, when it works, it always works and always works correctly.

Examples 6.18–6.20 use nested loops. A computer finds these instructions easy to process, but they can be challenging for a beginning programmer. The following examples will help you practice and understand loops, nested loops, and the pure logical thinking needed to write programs that do what you want them to do.

Example 6.18 **Workout Number 1: Beginner**

This pseudocode makes use of nested While loops.

```
1   Declare X As Integer
2   Declare Y As Integer
3   Declare Z As Integer
4   Set X = 1
5   While X < 4
6     Write "Pass Number " + X
7     Set Y = 1
8     While Y < 10
9       Set Z = X + Y
10      Write X + " + " + Y + " = " + Z
11      Set Y = Y + 3
12    End While(Y)
13    Set X = X + 1
14  End While(X)
```

What Happened?

The display, after this pseudocode is coded and run will look like this:

```
Pass Number 1
1 + 1 = 2
1 + 4 = 5
1 + 7 = 8
Pass Number 2
2 + 1 = 3
2 + 4 = 6
2 + 7 = 9
Pass Number 3
3 + 1 = 4
3 + 4 = 7
3 + 7 = 10
```

Now we'll walk through the pseudocode and see exactly how this program works. As you begin to write programs in a programming language, you will need to walk through your code with a pencil and paper to see exactly what is happening. The best way to do this is to keep track of the value of each variable at every step of the program. This program has three variables so we will identify the value of each variable as the code is executed, line by line.

```
Outer Loop, Pass 1: X = 1 at start
Display: Pass Number 1
  Inner Loop, Pass 1: Y = 1 at start
  X = 1 , Y = 1, Z = 2
  Display: 1 + 1 = 2
  Y = Y + 3 so Y = 4
  Inner Loop, Pass 2: Y = 4 at start
  X = 1, Y = 4, Z = 5
  Display: 1 + 4 = 5
```

```
    Y = Y + 3 so Y = 7
    Inner Loop, Pass 3: Y = 7 at start
    X = 1, Y = 7, Z = 8
```
Display: 1 + 7 = 8
```
    Y = Y + 3 so Y = 10
    Inner Loop ends and X is incremented to 2
Outer Loop, Pass 2: X = 2 at start
```
Display: Pass Number 2
```
    Inner Loop, Pass 1: Y = 1 at start
    X = 2 , Y = 1, Z = 3
```
Display: 2 + 1 = 3
```
    Y = Y + 3 so Y = 4
    Inner Loop, Pass 2: Y = 4 at start
    X = 2, Y = 4, Z = 6
```
Display: 2 + 4 = 6
```
    Y = Y + 3 so Y = 7
    Inner Loop, Pass 3: Y = 7 at start
    X = 2, Y = 7, Z = 9
```
Display: 2 + 7 = 9
```
    Y = Y + 3 so Y = 10
    Inner Loop ends and X is incremented to 3
Outer Loop, Pass 3: X = 3 at start
```
Display: Pass Number 3
```
    Inner Loop, Pass 1: Y = 1 at start
    X = 3 , Y = 1, Z = 4
```
Display: 3 + 1 = 4
```
    Y = Y + 3 so Y = 4
    Inner Loop, Pass 2: Y = 4 at start
    X = 3, Y = 4, Z = 7
```
Display: 3 + 4 = 7
```
    Y = Y + 3 so Y = 7
    Inner Loop, Pass 3: Y = 7 at start
    X = 3, Y = 7, Z = 10
```
Display: 3 + 7 = 10
```
    Y = Y + 3 so Y = 10
    Inner Loop ends and X is incremented to 4
Now X fails the Outer Loop test condition so the program segment
ends.
```

Example 6.19 demonstrates a harder example of the use of nested loops.

Example 6.19 **Workout Number 2: Intermediate**

In this pseudocode, a pre-test `While` loop is nested within a post-test `Do...While` loop.

To save space, we will assume that the following five variables have been declared as `Integer` type: `X`, `Y`, `Z`, `Count1`, and `Count2`. The pseudocode begins immediately following those declarations.

```
 1   Set Y = 3
 2   Set Count1 = 1
 3   Do
 4     Set X = Count1 + 1
 5     Set Count2 = 1
 6     Write "Pass Number " + Count1
 7     While Count2 <= Y
 8       Set Z = Y * X
 9       Write "X = " + X + ", Y = " + Y + ", Z = " + Z
10       Set X = X + 1
11       Set Count2 = Count2 + 1
12     End While
13     Set Count1 = Count1 + 1
14   While Count1 < Y
```

What Happened?

The display, after this pseudocode is coded and run will look like this:

```
Pass Number 1
X = 2, Y = 3, Z = 6
X = 3, Y = 3, Z = 9
X = 4, Y = 3, Z = 12
Pass Number 2
X = 3, Y = 3, Z = 9
X = 4, Y = 3, Z = 12
X = 5, Y = 3, Z = 15
```

Now we'll walk through the pseudocode and see exactly how this program works. Try doing it yourself with a paper and pencil and see if you get the same results as those shown. If not, check the explanation, shown below.

- Line 1 sets the variable Y equal to 3. Throughout the program, Y remains at this constant value.
- Line 2 initializes the counter for the outer loop, Count1, to 1. Note that the counter for the outer loop does not need to be reset during the program because once the outer loop ends, the program segment is complete. This is not the case for an inner loop, as we shall see.
- The outer Do...While loop begins on line 3. The loop will happen at least once because the test condition is not reached until the first iteration is complete. However, if we look down at line 14 we see that the test condition for this loop is While Count1 < Y. Y starts at 3 and its value does not change throughout the program so we see that the outer loop will complete only two iterations—when Count1 = 1 and when Count1 = 2.
- Line 4 sets a value of X. On the first pass, X will begin at 2 (Count1 + 1), on the second pass, X will begin at 3, and on the third pass, X will begin at 4.
- Line 5 initializes the counter for the inner While loop. This step is important. The inner loop ends when the counter has reached a certain value. If the counter were not reinitialized in the outer loop, the inner loop would never execute more than once.
- Line 6 displays the heading of the first or second pass, depending on the value of Count1.

- Line 7 begins the inner loop. The test condition for this loop is `Count2 <= Y`. Since Y remains at 3 throughout the program, we see that the inner loop will run for three iterations: while `Count2` is 1, 2, and 3.
- The inner loop body (lines 8–11) assigns a value to Z, outputs the values of X, Y, and Z, increments the inner counter, `Count2`, and increments X. Here is what happens:
  - On the first pass through the inner loop, while we are still in the first pass of the outer loop, Z is set to the value of Y * X which is 3 * 2.
  - Line 9 displays "X = 2, Y = 3, Z = 6".
  - Line 10 increments X, so X now equals 3.
  - `Count2` is then incremented to 2, the test condition is still valid, and the inner loop is executed again. This time Z = 3 * 3 so the values displayed are "X = 3, Y = 3, Z = 9". X is incremented again on line 10 to 4.
  - `Count2` is incremented to 3. Another pass through the inner loop is made. This time Z = 3 * 4 and the values displayed are "X = 4, Y = 3, Z = 12".
  - `Count2` is incremented to 4 and fails the test condition. The inner loop is exited and control goes to the outer loop on line 13.
- `Count1` now is incremented to 2 so it is still less than Y and the outer loop makes another pass.
- Line 4 resets the value of X. This time X will have the value of 3 when we begin the inner loop.
- Line 5 resets the value of `Count2` to 1 so the inner loop will run again.
- Line 6 displays the new header: "Pass Number 2".
- On this second pass, X begins with the value of 3. Therefore, the display (line 9) on the first pass will be "X = 3, Y = 3, Z = 9". Then X is incremented to 4 on line 10.
- A second pass is made through the inner loop when `Count2` is incremented to 2. The display now will be "X = 4, Y = 3, Z = 12". X is incremented to 5.
- A third pass is made through the inner loop when `Count2` is incremented to 3. The display is "X = 5, Y = 3, Z = 15".
- When `Count2` is incremented to 4, the inner loop is exited.
- `Count1` is then incremented to 3 and also fails the outer loop test so the outer loop is exited and the program ends.

Let's try one more. Example 6.20 will include two `While` loops and an `If-Then-Else` statement. The math is simple; the logic is a lot harder. Before you look at the line-by-line explanation, walk through the pseudocode with a pencil and paper. Keep track of the value of each variable at each step. Also, write down the display as you walk through the code to see if your display matches the one shown.

Example 6.20 **Workout Number 3: Expert**

This pseudocode makes use of nested `While` loops and `If-Then` statements. Three `Integer` variables have been declared: A, B, and C.

```
1  Set A = 1
2  Write "Cheers!"
3  While A < 3
4     Set C = A
```

```
 5     Write A
 6     Set B = 1
 7     While B < 4
 8       Set C = C + A
 9       Write C
10       If (A == 1 AND C >= 4) Then
11          Write "Let's do this some more!"
12       Else
13          If (A == 2 AND C >= 8) Then
14             Write "Who do we appreciate?"
15          End If
16       End If
17       Set B = B + 1
18     End While(B)
19     Set A = A + 1
20   End While(A)
```

What Happened?

The display, after this pseudocode is coded and run will look like this:

```
Cheers!
1
2
3
4
Let's do this some more!
2
4
6
8
Who do we appreciate?
```

Now we'll walk through the pseudocode and see exactly what happens.

- Line 1 initializes the variable A.
- Line 2 simply displays the heading: "Cheers!".
- The outer loop begins on line 3. The variable A is tested to see if it is less than 3. Since it starts at 1 and is incremented by 1 at the end of each loop, there will be two passes through this outer loop—while A = 1 and A = 2.
- Line 4 sets the variable C equal to the value of A, and line 5 displays the value of A. At this point A = 1 and C = 1. The screen so far displays "Cheers!" on one line and "1" on the next line.
- Line 6 sets the initial value of B to 1. Notice that it is set before entering the inner loop so it is set to 1 for each iteration of the outer loop.
- Line 7 begins the inner While loop. Since the test condition says the loop will continue while B is less than 4, we know the inner loop will continue for three iterations.
- Line 8 sets C equal to its previous value plus the value of A. Now C equals 2. A "2" is displayed on the screen (line 9) under the "1".

- Line 10 is the first part of the If-Then-Else statement. It tests to see if A = 1 AND if C has reached 4. On the first pass, while the first condition is true, the second is not. As we know, the logical operator AND only returns a value of true if both conditions are true so line 11 is skipped.

- Line 12 begins the Else clause. Line 13 tests to see if A = 2 AND if C has reached the value of 8. Since neither condition is true, line 14 is skipped.

- B is incremented to 2 on line 17 and control passes back to line 8 where C is set to a new value: C now equals 2 + 1 or 3. The "3" is displayed under the "2".

- The If-Then-Else statements are tested again on lines 10 and 13 but, since the conditions fail these tests, lines 11 and 14 are skipped again.

- B is incremented to 3 and control passes back to line 8. C is now set equal to 4. A "4" is displayed under the "3".

- Line 10 once again tests the values of A and C. At this point A does equal 1 AND C equals 4 so line 11 is executed. "Let's do this some more!" is now displayed under the "4".

- The Else clause on lines 12–14 is skipped since the If clause was true.

- B is incremented to 4 so the inner loop ends.

- Control returns to line 3 and the outer loop begins again. Take note of the values of all the variables at this point: A = 2, B = 5, and C = 4.

- However, on line 4, C is reset to 2.

- Line 5 displays a "2" under the statement "Let's do this some more!"

- Now the inner loop begins again, on line 7 but first B is reset to 1 on line 6.

- The inner loop repeats, as before, except this time the first value of C (line 8) is 4 since C = C + A means C = 2 + 2. A "4" is displayed under the "2" (line 9).

- On this and the next two passes through the inner loop, the If clause on line 10 will never be true since now A = 2.

- On the second pass through the inner loop (B = 2), C will become 6 (line 8) and a "6" will be displayed.

- On the third pass through this loop (B = 3), C will be 8 and an "8" will be displayed.

- At this point, A = 2, B = 3, and C = 8. When control reaches line 13, both conditions in the Else clause are true since A does equal 2 and C is equal to 8. Therefore, the statement on line 14 is executed and "Who do we appreciate?" is displayed under the "8".

- Now B is incremented to 4 (line 17) and the inner loop ends.

- Finally, A is incremented to 3 on line 19 and the outer loop ends.

- Note that, when this program ends, the final values of the variables are A = 3, B = 4, and C = 8.

Once you have walked through this program segment with a paper and pencil and you are sure you understand what happens, you are ready to tackle the Self Check questions for this section.

6.17 What is the output of the code corresponding to the pseudocode shown?

```
Declare I, J As Integer
For (I = 2; I <= 4; I++)
  For (J = 2; J <= 3; J++)
    Write I + " " + J
  End For(J)
End For(I)
```

6.18 What is the output of the code corresponding to the pseudocode shown?

```
Declare I, J, K As Integer
For (I = 1; I <= 5; I+3)
  Set K = (2 * I) - 1
  Write K
  For (J = I; J <= (I+1); J++)
    Write K
  End For(J)
End For(I)
```

6.19 Draw a flowchart corresponding to the pseudocode of Self Check for Question 6.18.

6.20 Refer to Example 6.17 in this section and add pseudocode to validate the following input: Side

6.21 Refer to Example 6.17 in this section and change the pseudocode to allow the user to draw either a square or a rectangle.

6.22 Write pseudocode containing two nested Repeat...Until loops that input and validate a number, MyNumber, to be greater than 0 and less than 10.

6.23 How would you change the pseudocode provided in Example 6.19 so that the outer loop would complete four iterations?

6.24 How would the display provided in Example 6.19 change if line 8 said Set Z = Y + X?

6.5 Focus on Problem Solving: A Guessing Game

In this chapter (Example 6.13), we created a very simple guessing game using a loop, two selection structures, and random numbers. The Project Manager at a small educational software company has seen this program and decided it would make a good game for young children. The game can help young children learn numbers, understand the concepts of "higher" and "lower," and help them begin to take a logical approach to problem solving. Since we have already written the skeleton of the game in Example 6.13, we are happy to tackle this project.

The program as written so far is a good start. We repeat the pseudocode here, for convenience.

```
1  Declare Given As Integer
2  Declare Guess As Integer
```

```
 3   Set Given = Floor(Random() * 100) + 1
 4   Write "I'm thinking of a whole number from 1 to 100."
 5   Write "Can you guess what it is?"
 6   Do
 7     Write "Enter your guess: "
 8     Input Guess
 9     If Guess < Given Then
10       Write "You're too low."
11     End If
12     If Guess > Given Then
13       Write "You're too high."
14     End If
15   While Guess != Given
16   Write "Congratulations! You win!"
```

Problem Statement

But a real game programmer could not use the program as is. In this section, we will elaborate on this program to add features that make the game more realistic. While we will still have a long way to go before this simple program could be marketed, you will get a feel for the process involved in developing a marketable program. We will add the following features:

- The program only runs once so we must add code to allow the game to be played as often as desired.
- The program requires input, which must be validated.
- The program needs to end after a specific number of guesses.
- We will add features to allow the user to control how the game works as follows:
  - The program uses a random number between 1 and 100. We will change this to allow the player to control the range of numbers.
  - We will allow the player to decide how many guesses can be made before the program ends.

Problem Analysis

For this problem, we do not have to work backward from a desired output to figure out the input needed. We are revising a skeleton program by adding modules and code to give us the features we want. This is not unusual for a programmer in the real world. Programmers rarely write code from scratch. Much programming work consists of debugging, re-using, or enhancing other people's code.

First, we need to add a Welcome module to explain the game. Then, we need to add a Setup module to define the options available. These options are as follows:

- Should the range of numbers be the default value of 1–100 or selected by a player?
- Should the number of guesses be a default value of 20 or selected by a player?

We need to add validation wherever necessary and, finally, we need to put the actual game inside a Game module and add a loop to allow the player to decide whether to play again or not.

The core of this program is the code that allows a player to guess a secret number by zeroing in on it from clues that indicate if the guess is too high or too low. Using a modular approach, we will develop the complete program with the following modules:

1. `Main` module, which calls the submodules into action
2. `Welcome_Message` module, which displays a welcome message
3. `Setup` module, which allows the user to personalize the game by selecting the range of numbers to be used and the number of guesses to be allowed
4. `Game` module, which is the actual game and will give the player an option to play again

The hierarchy chart shown in Figure 6.9 shows the division of programming tasks for this program.

Figure 6.9 Hierarchy chart for the guessing game problem

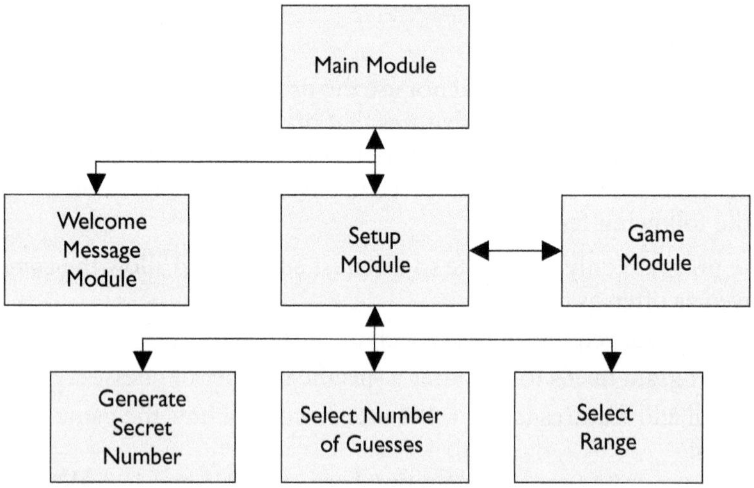

Program Design

To design this program using a modular approach, we will describe the major tasks of each module. First, we give a rough outline of the program, then we refine it as necessary.

Main Module

The `Main` module only needs to call its immediate submodules; they will perform all the necessary program tasks. In the `Main` module, we also declare all the variables that will be used by more than one submodule. Later in this book, when we discuss functions and subprograms (Chapter 9), we will learn how to declare variables within subprograms and pass their values from one subprogram to another. This is a more appropriate and realistic way to write code, but, for now, we will simply declare our variables once, in the `Main` module and assume that they are, therefore, available to all the subprograms. The resulting pseudocode is as follows:

```
Begin Program
   Declare Given As Integer
   Declare HighRange As Integer
```

```
      Declare LowRange As Integer
      Declare NumGuess As Integer
      Declare Guess As Integer
      Declare Response As Character
      Call Welcome_Message module
      Call Setup module
End Program
```

Welcome_Message Module

This module displays general information and briefly describes the program. It will consist only of Write statements, as follows:

```
Begin Welcome Message
  Write "Guess My Secret Number!"
  Write "This game allows you to guess a secret number by"
  Write "using information provided for you with each guess."
  Write "You only get a limited number of guesses,"
  Write "so think carefully about each guess."
End Welcome Message
```

Setup Module

This module will ask the user to personalize the program parameters. It will receive information from the user about how to set up one game and then will call the Game module to begin playing. The tasks are as follows:

- Set the default values for the Integer variables to be used: the secret number (Given), the range of numbers (LowRange and HighRange), and the number of guesses (NumGuess), as well as a Character variable (Response) for the player's responses to questions.

- Ask the user if the range of numbers to be used when generating the secret number should be between 1 and 100 (the default) or changed to something else. If the user opts to select a different range, the user's input must be validated to ensure that the range consists only of whole numbers and that the high end of the range is greater than the low end. This requires three validation code segments. First, the value of LowRange (the lower limit of the range) must be checked to see if it is an integer. Then, the value of HighRange (the upper value of the range) must also be checked to see if it is an integer. Finally, the HighRange value must be validated to ensure that it is greater than the lower limit value. We will use two If-Then statements to accomplish this inside a loop, which checks both items.

- Ask the user if the number of guesses allowed (NumGuess) should be left at 20 (the default) or set to another value. Once again, if the user opts to change the number of guesses allowed, we must validate the input to ensure that a valid integer value has been entered since the number of guesses must be a whole number greater than 0.

- Pick a value for the secret number from a computer-generated random number in the range specified.

- Call the Game module to begin play.

The second-to-last item in this list requires a little extra attention. In Example 6.13, the secret number was simply set equal to a random number from 1 to 100. This was done using the Random() function. However, in the expanded program, we do not know what the range for selecting the secret number will be. If a player picks a range, the lower limit and upper limit are the values that are assigned to the variables LowRange and HighRange.

Now, we must find a way to use the Random() function to select a number in any given range. We know that the Random() function produces a number from 0 up to but not including 1. Let's take one example and work through it to help us arrive at a general formula to get a random number in the desired range. Let's assume that the player chooses a range from 4 to 12 for the secret number. Therefore, LowRange = 4 and HighRange = 12. We want a random number generated from the following choices: 4, 5, 6, 7, 8, 9, 10, 11, and 12. This is a total of nine numbers.

HighRange − LowRange in this case equals 8 but (HighRange - LowRange + 1) = 9. We know that Floor(Random() * 9) will result in a number between 0 and 8, a total of nine integers. This formula works for any values of HighRange and LowRange; the difference between the two values, plus 1, gives us the number of choices we want.

While Random() * (HighRange - LowRange + 1) will generate a random number from 0 through 8, we need to shift the starting value so that it is 4. If we shift the number generated by 4 we get:

$$\text{Floor(Random() * (HighRange - LowRange + 1)) + 4}$$

This will generate the numbers 4, 5, 6, 7, 8, 9, 10, 11, or 12.

Of course, this will not work in the general case. We need to find a way to write the shift in general terms. If we add the value of LowRange to the generated random number, we can shift the numbers up to the value of LowRange.

The final formula for generating a random number between any two integer values and assigning that value to a variable named Given is, therefore:

```
Given = Floor(Random() * (HighRange - LowRange + 1) + LowRange
```

If you are not convinced, check the values that will be generated for several other values of HighRange and LowRange. For example, if HighRange = 35 and LowRange = 22, the secret number will be as follows:

```
Given   = Floor(Random() * (HighRange - LowRange + 1)) + LowRange
        = Floor(Random() * (35 - 22 + 1)) + 22
        = Floor(Random() * 14) + 22
        = 22, 23, 24, 25, 26, 27, 28, 29, 30, 31, 32, 33, 34, or 35
```

Try some other values to convince yourself that this works.

Now we can write the pseudocode for this module. Since this module is rather long and accomplishes several distinct tasks, comments have been added to the pseudocode to help distinguish what is happening at various stages of this module. The pseudocode is as follows:

```
Begin Setup
    Set HighRange = 100   // default value for upper limit
    Set LowRange = 1      // default value for lower limit
    Set NumGuess = 20     // default value for number of guesses
    Set Response = ' '
```

```
Set Given = 0
/* Comment: The following pseudocode allows the user to select a
range of numbers to be used for the secret number. The default
values (HighRange = 100 and LowRange = 1) will not be changed if
the user does not type 'y' when asked for a Response. */
Write "A secret number will be generated between 1 and 100."
Write "You can change these values to any values "
Write "that you want (whole numbers only)."
Write "Do you want to select your own range?"
Write "Type 'y' for yes or 'n' for no: "
Input Response
If Response == 'y' Then
  Write "Enter the low value of your desired range: "
  Input LowRange
  While Int(LowRange) != LowRange
    Write "You must enter a whole number. Try again: "
    Input LowRange
  End While
  Write "Enter the high value of your desired range: "
  Input HighRange
  While (Int(HighRange) != HighRange) OR (HighRange <= LowRange)
    If Int(HighRange) != HighRange Then
      Write "You must enter a whole number. Try again: "
      Input HighRange
    End If
    If HighRange <= LowRange Then
      Write "The upper value must be greater than "
      Write "the lower value. Try again: "
      Input HighRange
    End If
  End While
End If
/* Comment: The following pseudocode allows the user to select how
many guesses will be allowed for each run of the game. The default
value (NumGuess = 20) will not be changed if the user does not type
'y' when asked for a Response. */
  Write "The game normally allows a player 20 guesses."
  Write "Do you want to change the number of guesses allowed?"
  Write "Type 'y' for yes or 'n' for no."
  Input Response
  If Response == 'y' Then
    Write "Enter the number of guesses you want to allow: "
    Input NumGuess
    While (Int(NumGuess) != NumGuess) OR (NumGuess < 1)
      Write "You must enter a whole number greater than 0."
      Write "Try again: "
      Input NumGuess
    End While
  End If
```

```
/* Comment: The following pseudocode generates a random number in
the range specified. */
  Set Given = Floor(Random() * (HighRange - LowRange + 1)) + LowRange
  Call Game Module
End Setup
```

Game Module

This module is the heart of the program. It uses the values of variables sent over from the Setup module. Later in this text we will learn how programming languages pass variables from one module to another and back again, but for now we will just accept that the values of Given, HighRange, LowRange, and NumGuess are passed from the Setup module into the Game module. Therefore, whatever values these variables have when the Setup module is finished will be the values they have when the Game module begins. The pseudocode for the Game module is as follows:

```
Begin Game
  Declare Count As Integer
  Set Count = 1
  Write "I'm thinking of a whole number "
  Write "between " + LowRange + " and " + HighRange
  Write "Can you guess the number?"
  Write "You have " + NumGuess + " chances to guess."
  Input Guess
  If Guess == Given Then
    Write "Wow! You won on the first try!"
  Else
    While (Count <= NumGuess OR Guess != Given)
      While (Int(Guess) != Guess)
        Write "You must guess a whole number."
        Write "Guess again: "
        Input Guess
      End While
      If Guess < Given Then
        Write "Your guess is too low. Guess again:"
        Input Guess
      Else
        If Guess > Given Then
          Write "Your guess is too high. Guess again:"
          Input Guess
        Else
          Write "Congratulations! You win!"
        End If
      End If
      Set Count = Count + 1
    End While
  End If
```

```
/* Comment: Next, a suitable message is displayed if the player has
used up all the allowed guesses and has not correctly guessed the
secret number. Then, in either case (the player won or lost), an
option to play again is given.*/
    If (Count > NumGuess AND Guess != Given) Then
      Write "Sorry. You have used up all your guesses."
    End If
    Write "Do you want to play again?"
    Write "Type 'y' for yes, 'n' for no: "
    Input Response
    If Response != 'y' Then
      Write "Goodbye"
    Else
      Call Setup
    End If
End Game
```

Program Code

The program code is now written using the design as a guide. At this stage, header comments and, where needed, more step comments are inserted into each module, providing internal documentation for the program.

This type of program—a computer game—would probably be used in a graphical environment so artists and graphic designers would be brought in to develop a graphical interface.

Program Test

The program test phase of developing this program is extremely important. As always, we need to test the program with many different sets of data. We need to be sure that we test each set of data with each possible option. For example, we need to test what happens when a player guesses correctly on a first guess when the range is set to the default, when the range is set by the player, using several possible ranges, where the range is set by the player and the number of guesses allowed is the default, as well as in each of these cases when the number of guesses is set by the player. In a program such as this, with many options that are set by the user, a bug may exist in one combination of events that may not show up in most or all other combinations. The testing should be done in a systematic, planned manner. You, as the programmer at this level, should use desk-checking to walk through the program pseudocode with all the possible data sets, as follows:

- In this testing phase, a programmer would add temporary code so that, when the secret number is assigned to Given, that value will be displayed. This is so that the programmer can test the results of the game using both correct and incorrect data. This code would, of course, be deleted from the final product.

- Tests should be made using the default values as follows:
  - Check to see what happens in the Setup module when the user inputs 'n' or any character other than 'y' for responses to questions about the range and the number of guesses.
  - Check the Game module, inputting values above and below the secret number as well as the actual correct secret number.
  - Check what happens when the first guess is correct.
  - Check what happens when all twenty guesses are incorrect.
- Tests should be made using values other than the defaults.
  - Check what happens when appropriate and inappropriate values are entered for high and low values of the range. These tests should include both positive and negative integers, 0, and noninteger values.
  - Check what happens when appropriate and inappropriate values are entered for the number of guesses, as for the range.
  - Check the Game module as listed above but in each of the following cases:
    - The user changes the range but does not change the default value for the number of guesses.
    - The user changes the number of guesses but does not change the default values for the range.
    - The user changes all default values.

Self Check for Section 6.5

For all of these Self Check questions refer to the Guessing Game problem described in this section.

6.25 If HighRange = 13 and LowRange = 10, what possible numbers will be generated by the following formula?
Given = Floor(Random() * (HighRange - LowRange + 1)) + LowRange

6.26 If HighRange = 7 and LowRange = 0, what possible numbers will be generated by the following formula?
Given = Floor(Random() * (HighRange - LowRange + 1)) + LowRange

6.27 What should the values of HighRange and LowRange be, in the formula in the Self Check Question 6.25, to produce the following possible numbers: 40, 41, 42, 43, 44, 45

6.28 How could you change the formula in the Self Check Question 6.26 so that the range of numbers starts at 5?

6.29 Write the pseudocode in the Game module to output the results of testing a single guess (too high, too low, or correct) using a Select Case statement instead of an If-Then-Else structure.

6.30 Add pseudocode to the segment in the Setup module that asks the player to input a Response to the question "Do you want to change the number of guesses allowed?" that outputs a suitable message if the player does not type 'y'. Your pseudocode should check to make sure that the player did not type an incorrect character by mistake. In other words, validate the input to make sure that the player really meant to answer "no."

6.6 Running With RAPTOR (Optional)

In this section, since we do not need to introduce any special features of RAPTOR, we can create a rather complex program using nested loops and selection structures. However, to get accustomed to nesting structures with RAPTOR, we will first implement two examples from this chapter. Then we will create a program to validate a password entered by a user which must conform to specified criteria.

Two Short Examples

Before we create the longer working program, we will redo Examples 6.18 and 6.20. Since the logic of both these examples was discussed at length already, we will simply show what the RAPTOR programs would look like. If you follow these programs and run them in RAPTOR, your results should be as shown.

Example 6.21 Making Example 6.18 Run: the Beginner Workout

We will repeat the pseudocode of this example followed by its implementation in RAPTOR and the output in the MasterConsole.

Pseudocode:

```
1   Declare X As Integer
2   Declare Y As Integer
3   Declare Z As Integer
4   Set X = 1
5   While X < 4
6     Write "Pass Number " + X
7     Set Y = 1
8     While Y < 10
9       Set Z = X + Y
10      Write X + " + " + Y + " = " + Z
11      Set Y = Y + 3
12    End While(Y)
13    Set X = X + 1
14  End While(X)
```

RAPTOR implementation and `MasterConsole` output

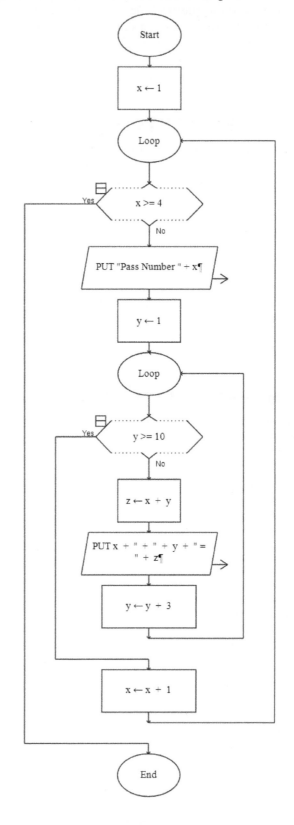

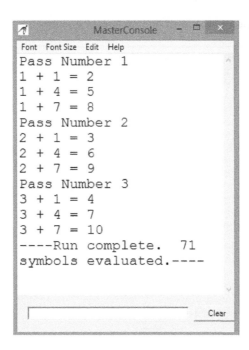

Example 6.22 **Making Example 6.20 Run: the Expert Workout**

We will repeat the pseudocode of this example followed by its implementation in
RAPTOR and the output in the MasterConsole.

Pseudocode:

```
 1  Set A = 1
 2  Write "Cheers!"
 3  While A < 3
 4    Set C = A
 5    Write A
 6    Set B = 1
 7    While B < 4
 8      Set C = C + A
 9      Write C
10      If (A == 1 AND C >= 4) Then
11        Write "Let's do this some more!"
12      Else
13        If (A == 2 AND C >= 8) Then
14          Write "Who do we appreciate?"
15        End If
16      End If
17      Set B = B + 1
18    End While(B)
19    Set A = A + 1
20  End While(A)
```

RAPTOR implementation and `MasterConsole` output

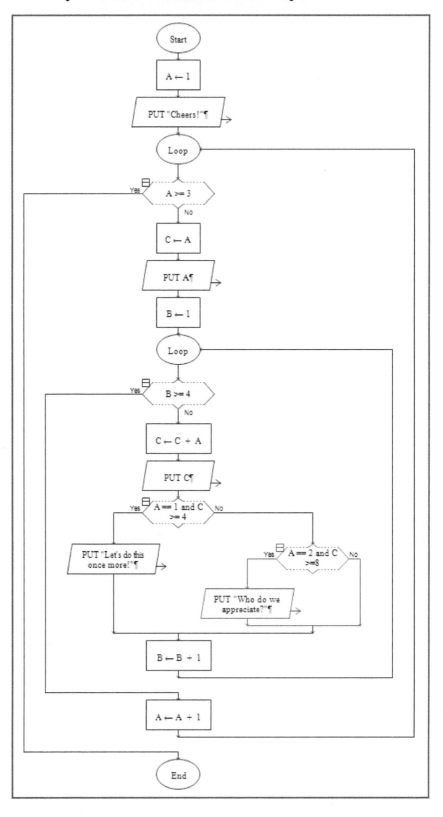

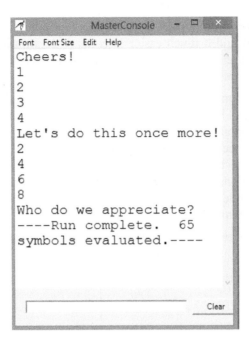

Run It: Validating a Password

A common programming task is to validate input. We have discussed how to validate input to ensure that the input is an integer or is only positive or nonzero. In this section, we will take validation further. We will assume that a user has been asked to create a password that adheres to specific conditions. Then we will create a RAPTOR program to validate the user's entry.

Problem Statement

The program will allow a user to enter a password, the password will be validated but if it does not pass validation, the user will be prompted to enter a new password. The loop to re-enter a new password will continue until the user enters a valid password or chooses to quit the program. The conditions for a valid password will be as follows:

- The password must be between 4 and 8 characters
- It must include one of the following special characters: '#', '*', or '$'
- It may consist of numbers, letters, or special characters, but it may not begin with a number

Developing the Program

We have often said that the best way to approach a programming problem is to identify the required output. In this case, the output is not a display on the screen. Rather, we must ensure that the input complies with the three given conditions.

If we break this program down into modules—or, in RAPTOR terms, into subcharts—we will find it much easier to code. After an initial welcome message that explains to the user what to do and gets the first entry input, we will use a subchart to check the password's validity.

To create this program, start a new RAPTOR program and save it with the filename password.rap. This program will require quite a few variables. It is unlikely that, in a "real" program all the variables would be created in a separate module. However, to save space in the RAPTOR work area and to make it easier to focus on the significant aspects of this program—the loops and decisions—we will put all our variable declarations and initializations into a single subchart called Variables. As we develop the code to validate each password condition, we can add necessary variables to this subchart.

Begin by creating instructions to the user, creating a Variables subchart, and getting the initial user input, as shown.

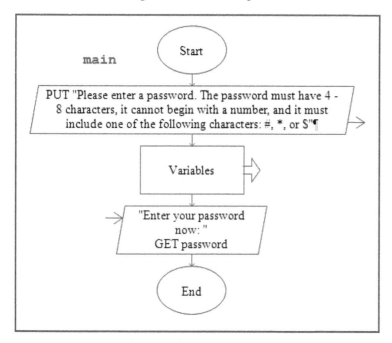

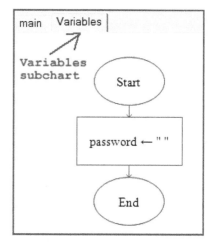

After the initial password is entered, we need to check that it passes the three requirements. We will use a subchart to do this so create a Call to a new subchart named Validate and place it directly under the Input box in main.

Validation of these three criteria could be handled in several different ways. In our program, we will check each criteria and, for simplicity, if the password fails any of the three, we will ask the user to re-enter a new password once, at the end of the validation process.

The Validate subchart

This module will validate the user's password by checking each of the three criteria in sequence. We will put the entire validation process in a loop because, if a password fails any of the criteria tests, a new password will be entered and checked. Since the first password entered in main must be checked, the loop must execute at least once. Therefore, a post-test loop is most appropriate for this program.

We will define a Boolean variable that is named pwOK and set its initial value to false. This will be the test condition. At the end of the loop, if all criteria are passed, we can set pwOK to true. Define this variable in the Variables subchart now. Then drag a Loop symbol to the work area in Validate. The test condition is: pwOK == true. Now we are ready to check the three criteria.

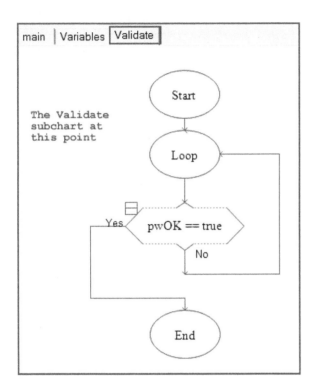
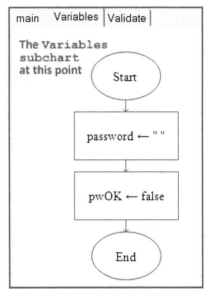

Check the length of the password (4–8 characters)

To ensure that the password entered is at least 4 and no more than 8 characters, we need a numeric variable to hold the value of the length of the password that is being checked. We will call this password pwLength. We will also use a Boolean variable called numChar that will be either true or false, depending on whether the password passes the test of its length. Initialize these two variables in the Variables subchart, assigning the value of 0 to pwLength and true to numChar.

Next, we return to the Validate subchart and begin to code the test of the first criteria. We will use the Length_Of() function to determine the number of characters in the password and will store that value in pwLength. If pwLength is between 4 and 8 (inclusive), we will set numChar to true. If not, we will set numChar to false. You may wonder why it is necessary to set numChar to true when it was initialized to be true. Recall, however, that this program is in a loop. The user may be asked to re-enter a failing password several times for any of the reasons set out by the required conditions. We only truly know the value of numChar at the first pass through the loop. After that, we cannot be sure what its value was from a previous test. We use a Selection statement with a compound condition. At this point, the loop will look like this:

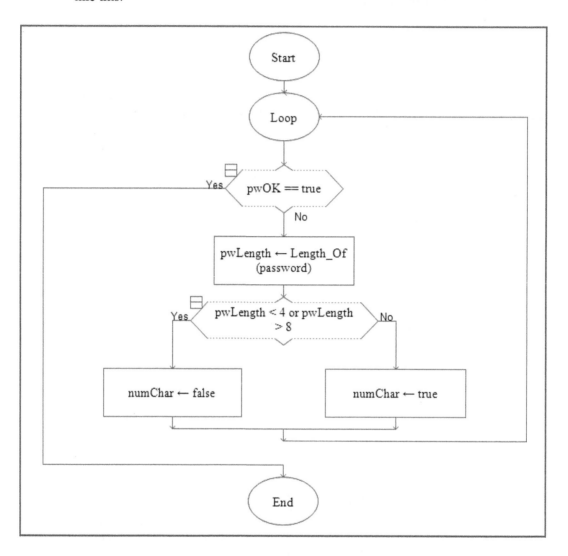

You probably should not try to run your program as it is right now. Can you think of why this is so? At this point your program prompts the user for a password. Then it goes to the Variables subchart where pwOK is set to false. From there it goes to the Validate subchart which is entered if pwOk is not true. The program then retrieves the length of your password and sets numChar to either true or false. And then the loop checks again to see if pwOk is true. Since pwOK has never been changed, it remains false, the loop is re-entered and does the same thing again. And again and again . . . At this point you have an infinite loop.

If you wanted to check to make sure that you have coded everything properly at this point you would need to add some things. At the very least, you should code to change pwOK to true after the length of the password is checked. To save space, we will assume you have completed all steps correctly and will continue without checking the code at this point.   ●

Check the first character of the password (cannot be a number)

Now, we will check to see if the first character is a number. For this we need another Boolean variable, which we will call charOne. Add this variable, initially set to true to your Variables subchart. We will use a Selection box to check the first character in the user's password; if it is a number, we will set charOne to false but if it is not a number, we will set charOne to true.

To do this, we will call upon the To_ascii() function that was discussed in Chapter 5 and we will use the table of ASCII values to see that the digits 0 through 9 have ASCII values 48–57. We also use indexing (also described in Chapter 5) to identify the first character of a String variable. Add the following Selection box to the Validate subchart directly under the end of the previous Selection box:

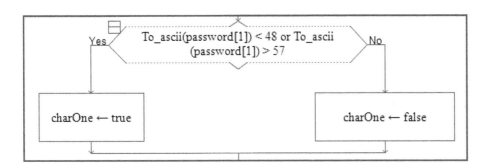

Notice that we combined the To_ascii() function with indexing to retrieve the first character of the password. We could have accomplished this in three steps:

- Set a new character variable, perhaps named FirstChar, to the value of the first character in password:
  - Set FirstChar = password[1]
- Set a new numeric variable, perhaps named FirstAscii, to the ASCII value of FirstChar:
  - Set FirstAscii = To_ascii(FirstChar)
- Use the value of FirstAscii in the Selection statement:
  - If (FirstAscii < 48 or FirstAscii > 57) Then . . . and so on

However, by combining all these steps into one, we make our code cleaner and more efficient.

Check that the password contains one of the special characters (#, *, or $)

This final check is more complicated than the previous two. We need to compare each character in the password with each of the three possible special characters. We'll use another `Boolean` variable named `specChar` to indicate whether a special character is located. We will use a `Selection` box with a compound condition to compare one character in the password with each of the three special characters. If a character in the password is either a "#", a "$", or a "*", we can set `specChar` to `true`. If that character is not one of the special characters, it will be set to `false`.

However, since we need to do this for each character in the password, we can use a `Loop` with a counter, combined with the indexing property, to check all the characters. Therefore, add the following variables with their initial values to your `Variables` subchart: `specChar = false` and `count = 1`.

Before you begin the loop, you need to set `count` to 1. Even though it has already been initialized to 1 in `Variables`, when the program executes, the value of `count` will be its value at the end of one iteration. It must be set back to 1 again or the program will not work.

The loop will continue until one of two outcomes is `true`; either a special character has been identified or all the characters in the password have been checked. Thus, the test condition for the `loop` is:

```
specChar == "true" OR count > pwLength
```

Next, drag a `Selection` box into the `Loop` body. The test condition should check if a single character which is identified as `password[count]` is one of the three special characters. Use a compound condition with two `OR` statements to check all three of these characters. By using `count` as the index value for the targeted character in `password`, the loop can check each character in the password. If a special character is found (the "yes" branch of the `Selection` statement), `specChar` can be set to `true`. For each character checked, if that character is not a special character (the "no" branch of the `Selection` box), `specChar` should be set to `false`. This way the loop will end as soon as the first special character is found. It does not matter if all the characters are not checked because the criteria only specify that at least one character must be a special character.

The final thing that must be done is to increment the value of count. This is done outside the Selection statement, within this inner loop. Your loop should look as follows:

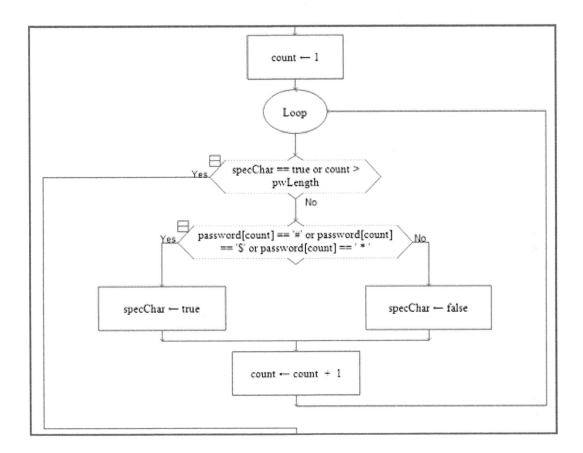

Intermediate testing

It is now possible for you to test your program before you put the finishing touches on it. You can enter various combinations of valid and invalid passwords and keep track of what is happening by looking at the Watch Window on the far left, under the Symbols.

There are some interesting things to note about the results in the Watch Window. For one, RAPTOR is not case sensitive. This means that, regardless of whether you enter charOne for a variable name or CHARONE or Charone, in the Watch Window, this variable will always show up as charone. Another important thing to note concerns the Boolean variables that we have used. We know that a Boolean variable has only two possible values: true or false. A computer doesn't read English. To the computer, a true value translates to a high voltage or, in machine language, to a 1. A false value is, in computer-ese, either low voltage or 0. This is what will show up in RAPTOR's Watch Window. All your Boolean variables will either have a 0 (for false) or 1 (for true) in the Watch Window.

With this in mind, run your program a few times with some test values. If you use the following values for password, you should see the results shown here in your Watch Window.

Password entered		Watch Window results
Liz	charone: 1	true, 1st character is not a number
	count: 3	3 characters in the password
	numchar: 0	false, password has too few characters
	password: "Liz"	Password identified
	pwlength: 3	Password length identified
	pwok: 0	false, password is not OK
	specchar: 0	false, no special character
4Lizrd	charone: 0	false, 1st character is a number
	count: 7	7 characters in the password
	numchar: 1	true, password has 4–8 characters
	password: "4Lizrd"	Password identified
	pwlength: 7	Password length identified
	pwok: 0	false, password is not OK
	specchar: 0	false, no special character
4Liz*rd	charone: 0	false, 1st character is a number
	count: 6	Special character identified at index 5
	numchar: 1	true, password has 4–8 characters
	password: "4Liz*rd"	Password identified
	pwlength: 7	Password length identified
	pwok: 0	false, password is not OK
	specchar: 1	true, special character found

Password entered		Watch Window **results**
Lizzy*!	charone: 1	true, Ist character is not a number
	count: 1	Password passed, count re-initialized
	numchar: 1	true, password has **4–8** characters
	password:"Lizzy*!"	Password identified
	pwlength: 7	Password length identified
	pwok: 1	true, password passed all tests
	specchar: I	true, special character found

Validating the whole password

We have now checked all the password requirements and must decide whether to ask the user to re-enter a new password, if any of the criteria did not pass or decide if we are done. For each condition, we have identified a Boolean variable which will be true if the password passes that condition or false if the password fails that condition. Therefore, if all three of these Boolean variables are true, we have a valid password. But if any are still false the user has to try again. We will use another Selection statement to check this and will use and statements in our compound condition. If the password has failed, then we will ask the user to enter a new password. Before the new password is added, we must set specChar back to false. The initial Boolean variable that is used in the test condition of the outer loop, pwOK, was set to false at the start and has not changed. Therefore, if this branch of the last Selection statement is taken, the user will enter a new password and the outer Loop will begin again.

But if all three tests have passed, we will set pwOK to true in the "yes" branch of this Selection statement, the Loop will end, and control will return to main. At this time we can output a message to the user to indicate that the password has been accepted. This Selection statement should look like the following:

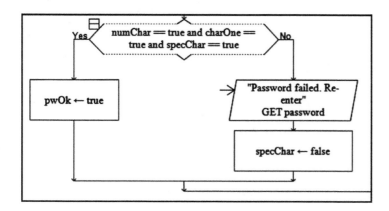

Your complete program with the subcharts will look like those shown in Figures 6.10–6.12.

Figure 6.10 The `main` module: Password Validator program

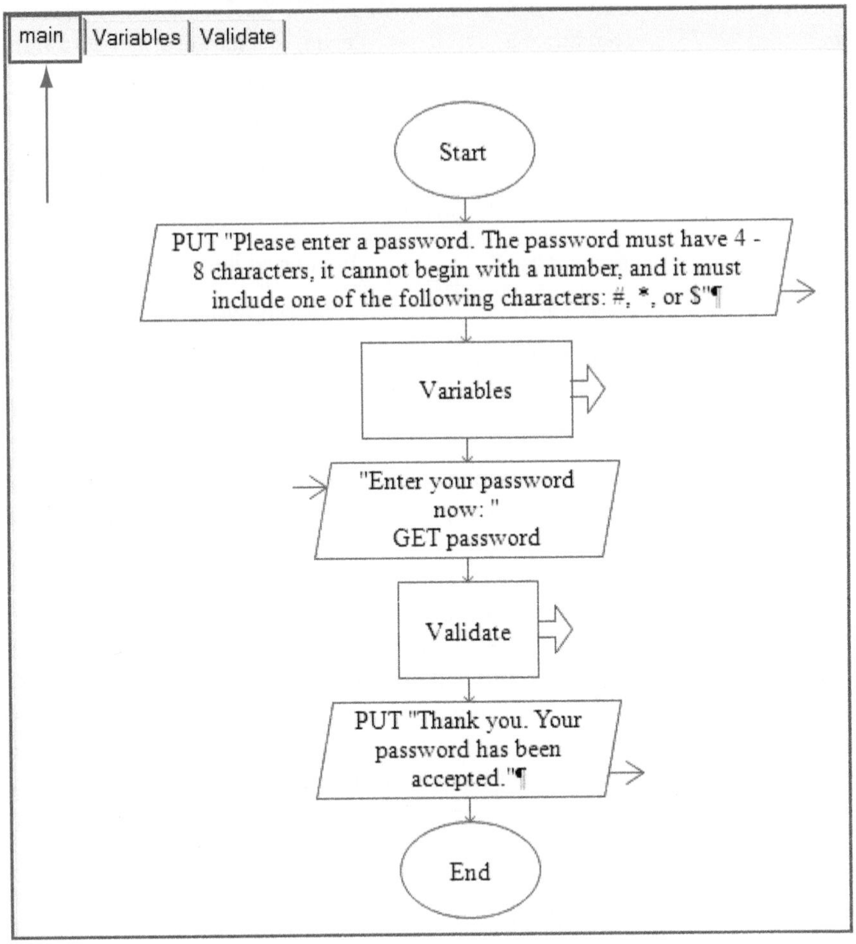

Figure 6.11   The Variables module: Password Validator program

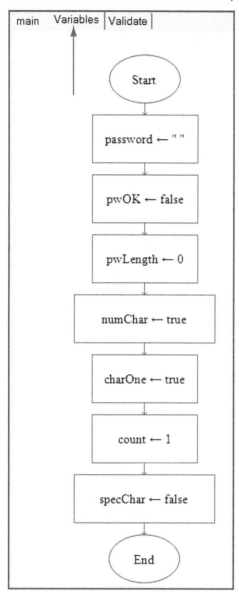

Figure 6.12 The Validate module: Password Validator program

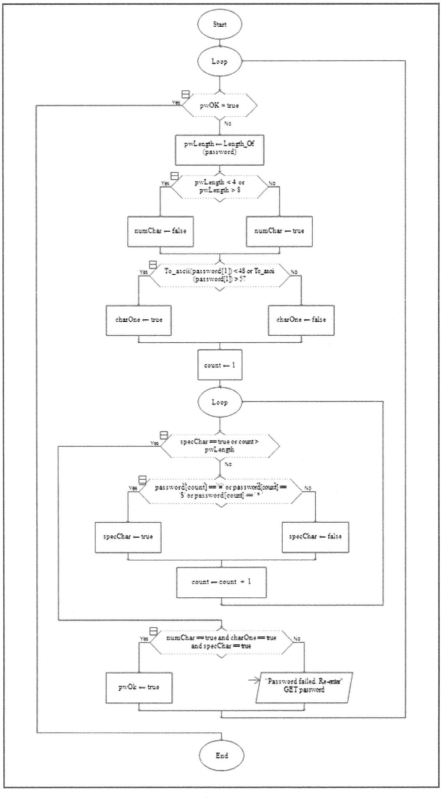

Key Terms

data validation
desk check
inner loop
Length_Of() function
mathematical algorithm
nested loops
newline indicator <NL>

outer loop
Print statement
pseudorandom numbers
Random() function
random numbers
seed value

Chapter Summary

In this chapter, we have discussed the following topics:

1. How to combine loops with selection structures
   - If-Then and If-Then-Else structures can be combined with all types of loops: For, While, Do...While, and Repeat...Until loops
2. Some applications of loops:
   - Inputting data until the user enters a sentinel value
   - Validating data—ensuring that data are in the proper range
   - Computing sums and averages
3. How to combine loops with Select Case statements
4. Random numbers as follows:
   - Random numbers can be generated within a specified range using the Random() function and, if necessary, a shift factor
   - In a computer program, random number generators do not generate true random numbers, but with correct programming, pseudorandom numbers can be generated and used with comparable results
5. How to correctly nest loops; that is, use one loop inside another
6. How to combine nested loops with selection structures to create complex programs
7. The Print statement and <NL> indicator are used to control when output should be displayed on a new line.

Review Exercises

Fill in the Blank

1. _____ are numbers that form an unpredictable sequence in which each number is equally likely to occur.

2. _____ are numbers that belong to a sequence, generated by a mathematical algorithm, in which each number is equally likely to occur.

3. The starting value of an algorithm used to generate a range of random numbers is called the _____.

True or False

4. Indicate whether each of the following statements is true or false:

   a. T F You cannot have both a `Select Case` statement and an `If-Then` structure within a single loop.

   b. T F You cannot put a loop inside an `If-Then` structure.

   c. T F You cannot nest more than one inner loop inside an outer loop.

5. If `Number = 3`, indicate whether each of the following statements is `true` or `false`:

   a. T F `Int(Number * Number) = Number * Number`

   b. T F `Int(Number/2) = Number/2`

6. If `Number = 3.5`, indicate whether each of the following statements is `true` or `false`:

   a. T F `Floor(Number * Number) = Number * Number`

   b. T F `Floor(Number/2) = Number/2`

7. If `Number = 16`, indicate whether each of the following statements is `true` or `false`:

   a. T F `Sqrt(Number) = Floor(Sqrt(Number))`

   b. T F `Floor(Sqrt(Number/2)) = Sqrt(Floor(Number/2))`

8. T F If `Number` is an integer variable, then `Number = 8` after the following statement is executed:

   `Number = Length_Of("Wow!")`

9. T F If `Number` is an integer variable and `MyString = "One potato"` then the following statement is valid:

   `Number = Length_Of(MyString)`

10. If `Number = 7`, indicate whether each of the following statements is `true` or `false`:

    a. T F `Sqrt(Number) = Int(Sqrt(Number))`

    b. T F `Sqrt(Number * Number) = Int(Sqrt(Number * Number))`

11. If `Number = 5`, indicate whether each of the following statements is `true` or `false`:

    a. T F `Random() * Number = 1, 2, 3, 4, or 5`

    b. T F `Floor(Random() * (Number - 2)) = 3, 4, or 5`

    c. T F `Floor(Random() * (Number + 2)) + Number = 7, 8, 9, 10, 11, 12, or 13`

12. T F If one `For` loop is nested within another, then the counter variables for the two loops should be different.

13. T F If one `For` loop is nested within another, then the limit values for the two loops must be different.

14. T F A `While` loop may not be nested within a `For` loop.

15. T F Two nonoverlapping loops may not be nested within a third loop.

Short Answer

16. If `Number = 6`, give the range of possible integers produced by the following expressions:

    a. `Floor(Random() * Number)`

    b. `Floor(Random() * Number) + 3`

    c. `Floor(Random() * (Number + 3))`

17. Write an expression that produces random integers in each of the following ranges:

    a. 1 through 6

    b. 0 through 1

18. Write an expression that produces random integers in each of the following ranges using the variable `Range`.

    a. 1 through 4

    b. 0 through 3

    c. 2 through 7

19. Write a program segment that simulates flipping a coin 25 times by generating and displaying 25 random integers, each of which is either 1 or 2.

20. Write a program segment that simulates rolling a die 50 times by generating and displaying 50 random integers in the range 1 to 6.

21. Add statements to the following pseudocode that creates a post-test loop which validates the input data:

    ```
    Write "Enter a negative number: "
    Input Number
    ```

22. Redo Exercise 21 using a pre-test loop.

23. Let `Num1 = 2` and `Num2 = 3.2`. Give the value of each of the following expressions:

    a. `Int(Num2 - Num1)`

    b. `Floor(Num1 - Num2)`

24. Let `Num1 = 5.6` and `Num2 = 3`. Give the value of each of the following expressions:

    a. `Floor(Num1 * Num2)`

    b. `Int(Num1 * Num2)`

25. What is the output of code corresponding to the following pseudocode, assuming N and X are integer variables?

```
Set N = 4
Set X = 0
While N < 12
  Set X = 12 / N
  Write X
  Set X = Floor(X)
  Write X
  Set N = N + 4
End While
```

26. What is the output of code corresponding to the following pseudocode, assuming N and X are integer variables?

```
For (N = 4; N <= 9; N+4)
  Set X = 10/N
  Write X
  Set X = Int(X)
  Write X
End For
```

27. Use a While loop in a program segment that inputs numbers from the user until the number entered is an integer.

28. What is the output of the code corresponding to the following pseudocode?

```
Declare I, J As Integer
For (I = 1; I <=3; I++)
  For (J = 4; J <= 5; J++)
    Write I * J
  End For(J)
End For(I)
```

29. Suppose that the variables I and J in Exercise 28 are interchanged (each I is changed to J and vice versa). What is the output now?

30. What is the output of the code corresponding to the following pseudocode?

```
Declare HelloCount As Integer
Set HelloCount = 1
Repeat
  Repeat
    Write "Hello"
  Until HelloCount >= 1
  Set HelloCount = HelloCount + 1
Until HelloCount == 3
```

31. Suppose that the first statement in Exercise 30 is changed as follows:

```
Set HelloCount = 2
```

What is the output now?

32. What is the output of the code corresponding to the following pseudocode?

```
Declare Dash As Character
Declare A, B, C As Integer
Set Dash = '-'
For (A = 1; A <=3; A++)
  Write A
  For (B = 1; B <= A; B++)
    Write B
  End For(B)
  For (C = 1; C <= A; C++)
    Write Dash + Dash + Dash
  End For(C)
End For(A)
```

33. What is the output of code corresponding to the following pseudocode?

```
Declare Dash As Character
Declare A As Integer
Declare B As Integer
Declare C As Integer
Set Dash = '-'
Set A = 1
While A <= 3
  Write A
  Set B = 1
  While B <= A
    Write B
    Set B = B + 1
  End While(B)
  Set C = 1
  While C <= A
    Write Dash + Dash + Dash
    Set C = C + 1
  End While(C)
  Set A = A + 1
End While(A)
```

34. Create flowcharts for Exercises 32 and 33 and compare them. Are they the same or different?

35. What is the output of code corresponding to the following pseudocode if the user's name is Sammy?

```
Declare Dash As Character
Declare Count As Integer
Declare Number As Integer
Declare Name As String
Set Dash = "-"
Set Count = 1
```

```
Write "What's your name?"
Input Name
Set Number = Length_Of(Name)
While Count <= Number
  Write Dash
  Set Count = Count + 1
End While
Write Name
Set Count = 1
While Count <= Number
  Write Dash
  Set Count = Count + 1
End While
```

Programming Challenges

For each of the following Programming Challenges, use the top-down modular approach and pseudocode to design a suitable program to solve it. Whenever appropriate, validate the input data.

1. Alberta Einstein teaches a business class at Podunk University. To evaluate the students in this class, she has given three tests. It is now the end of the semester and Alberta asks you to create a program that inputs each student's test scores and outputs the average score for each student and the overall class average. (*Hint*: The outer loop should allow for Ms. Einstein to input all the students, one by one, and the inner loop should accept the three exam scores and compute the average for each student.)

2. Create a program that will find and display the largest of a list of positive numbers entered by the user. The user should indicate that he/she has finished entering numbers by entering a 0.

3. For a list of numbers entered by the user and terminated by 0. Write a program to find the sum of the positive numbers and the sum of the negative numbers. (*Hint*: This is similar to an example in this chapter. Be sure to notice that the example given in this chapter counts the number of positive and negative numbers entered, but this problem asks you to find the sums of the positive and negative numbers entered.)

4. Create a program that will simulate the process of dealing cards from a 52-card deck by generating 1,000 random integers in the range 1–52. Assume that numbers 1–13 represent clubs, 14–26 represent diamonds, 27–39 represent hearts, and 40–52 represent spades. Display the number of times each suit occurred in the 1,000 "deals."

5. Create a program that formats the output of a user's name using the Length_Of() function. You will need to use the Print statement and the <NL> indicator to create this pseudocode. The user should be able to select the symbol used to form the borders of the name. If the user's name is

Howard Heisenberg and he chooses a * as the symbol, the output should look like this:

```
*************************
** Howard Heisenberg **
*************************
```

6. The child's card game, War, consists of two players each having a deck of cards. For each play each person turns over the top card in his or her deck. The higher card wins that round of play and the winner takes both cards. The game continues until one person has all the cards and the other has none. Create a program that simulates a modified game of War. The computer will play both hands, as PlayerOne and PlayerTwo, and, for each round will generate two random numbers and compare them. If the first number is higher, PlayerOne's score is increased by 1 and if the second number is higher, PlayerTwo's score is increased by 1. If there is a tie, no score is incremented. When one "player" reaches a score of 10, that player should be deemed the winner and the game ends. The range of numbers should be 1–13 to simulate the values of cards in a deck.

Arrays:
Lists and Tables

7

Although the value of a variable may change during execution of a program, in all our programs so far, a single value has been associated with each variable name at any given time. In this chapter, we will discuss the concept of an array—a collection of variables of the same type and referenced by the same name. We will discuss one-dimensional arrays (lists) and two-dimensional arrays (tables). You will learn how to set up and use arrays to accomplish various tasks.

After reading this chapter, you will be able to do the following:

- Declare and use one-dimensional arrays
- Manipulate parallel arrays
- Understand the relationship in programming between databases and parallel arrays
- Represent character strings as arrays
- Use the Length_Of() function to validate data in character arrays
- Declare and use two-dimensional arrays
- Combine one- and two-dimensional parallel arrays in a program

Organize It with Lists and Tables

Chances are that you frequently use lists in your daily life. The following is a common example:

Shopping List

1. Milk
2. Bread
3. Eggs
4. Butter

Or if you've ever done a home improvement project, you might have developed a list such as the following:

Tools Required List

1. Hammer
2. Saw
3. Screwdriver

If you write individual items on separate random pieces of paper, you might get them confused and end up going to the grocery store for a saw. By presenting a convenient method of organizing and separating your data, a list prevents this from happening.

Sometimes a single list isn't powerful enough for a given purpose. In this case, we use a table—a collection of related lists—such as the following:

Phone Book

A. Name List	B. Address List	C. Phone List
1. Ellen Cole	1. 341 Totem Dr.	1. 212-555-2368
2. Kim Lee	2. 96 Elm Dr.	2. 212-555-0982
3. Jose Rios	3. 1412 Main St.	3. 212-555-1212

Notice that this table contains three separate (vertical) lists that are all related horizontally. For example, to call someone you would scan down the Name List for the appropriate name, then look across that line to the Phone List to find the corresponding phone number. Could anything be more convenient? Thanks to a little organization and structure; you can easily find what you're looking for, even if the individual lists are hundreds of items long.

Everyone from farmers (weather tables) to accountants (ledgers) to sports fans (player statistics) uses lists and tables. If you use a spreadsheet program, you're using an electronic table and if you write a computer program with a lot of data that "goes together," you might organize it as a list or a table called an **array**. Often, programs that use data from databases store that data in arrays in order to manipulate and process it.

7.1 One-Dimensional Arrays

A **one-dimensional array** is a list of related data of the same type (for example, integers or strings) referred to by a single variable name with an index number to identify each item. In this section, we will discuss how to set up and manipulate these arrays, and we will present several advantages of their use.

Array Basics

Since an array stores many data values under the same variable name, we must have some way to refer to the individual elements contained within it. Each **element** is an item in the array and has its own value. To indicate a particular element, programming languages follow the array name by an **index number** enclosed in parentheses or brackets. For example, if the name of an array is `Month` and the index number is 3, the corresponding array element might be indicated by `Month[3]`.

The name of the array is similar to the name of a variable. For example, we might have an array called `Scores` that contains the final exam scores for a certain class of 25 students. Therefore, the array would have 25 scores. Each score is an element, and the array must indicate which particular element the program refers to at any time. This is done by using the index number. The first element of an array in most programming languages is referred to with the index number 0, although some may use 1 as the first index value. An array with 25 elements will have index numbers that range from 0 to 24. The first index value is a significant fact to keep in mind, especially when you manipulate arrays with loops. In our pseudocode, we follow the more common practice of starting array indexes with 0.

An individual element of an array is referred to by writing the array name followed by its index number surrounded by brackets. For example, since the first element of an array has index number 0, the first element of the array `Scores` would be referred to as `Scores[0]`, and in that same array the second element is `Scores[1]` and the third is `Scores[2]`. We read these as "Scores sub 0", "Scores sub 1", and "Scores sub 2". Here, 0, 1, and 2 are called the **subscripts**—or index numbers—of the array elements.

An array element such as `Scores[2]` is treated by the program as a single (or simple) variable and may be used in input, assignment, and output statements in the usual way. Thus, to display the value of the third student's final exam score, we use the following statement:

```
Write Scores[2]
```

Example 7.1 shows how to enter elements in an array.

Example 7.1 Entering Elements in an Array

If we wanted to input the final exam scores of a class of 25 students using an array named `Scores`, which has 25 elements, we could use a loop as follows:

```
For (K = 0; K < 25; K++)
  Write "Enter score: "
  Input Scores[K]
End For
```

What Happened?

- On the first pass through the loop, the input prompt is displayed ("Enter score: ") and the Input statement pauses execution, allowing the user to enter the first test score. Because K = 0, this value is then assigned to the first element of the array Scores, which is Scores[0].
- On the second pass through the loop, K = 1 and the next value input is assigned to Scores[1], the second element of Scores.
- On the third pass through the loop, the value input is assigned to Scores[2].
- Because this loop began with K = 0, we only need to go to K = 24 to complete all 25 passes through the loop and load all 25 values.

After 25 passes through this little loop, all the scores have been entered. This is certainly a more efficient way to write code than to type 25 Write and Input statements for 25 different variables! We will see that using arrays not only makes it much easier to load large amounts of data but also makes manipulating that data easier and more efficient.

Declaring Arrays

Arrays are stored in a computer's memory in a sequence of consecutive storage locations. As you know, when you declare a variable the computer sets aside a small amount of memory to store the value of that variable. The data type of the variable, the name of the variable, and the value of the variable are one little package and that package is stored in a small amount of memory. When you create an array, you tell the computer what the data type is and how many elements the array will contain. Then a space in the computer's memory is set aside for that array. If an array has five elements, the computer will set aside space with five equal parts, one part for each element of the array. Therefore, each element of the array has the same sized space in computer memory, the same array name, and the same data type. And all the elements are stored in consecutive locations in memory. The index (or subscript) number of the element sets it apart from the other members in the array.

Making It Work

Declaring Arrays in C++, Visual Basic, and JavaScript

While not always necessary, it is a good idea to inform the program, prior to the first use of an array, how many storage locations to set aside (or allocate) for that array. The array declaration statement can include the array name and the size of the memory space needed for that array. In program code, this is done by declaring the array in a statement at the beginning of the program or program module in which it is used. It is also possible to declare arrays without specifying the size, and this is used in some cases where the programmer may want the size of the array to be open ended. The declaration statement varies from language to language. The following shows how an array named Age, consisting of a maximum of six integer values, would be declared in three popular languages:

- In C++, the following statement:

```
int Age[6];
```

allocates six locations referred to as Age[0], Age[1], . . . , Age[5].

- In Visual Basic, the following statement:

      Dim Age(6) As Integer

  allocates six locations referred to as Age(0), Age(1), . . . , Age(5).
- In JavaScript, the following statement:

      var Age = new Array(6);

  allocates six locations referred to as Age[0], Age[1], . . . , Age[5].

In JavaScript the data type of the array will be determined when its elements are assigned values. However, all the elements of a JavaScript array must still be of the same data type.

Notice that the arrays begin with the subscript 0, and therefore, end with a subscript that is one less than the number of elements in the array.

In this book, for an array of integers, we will use the following pseudocode:

    Declare Age[6] As Integer

to allocate six locations referred to as Age[0], Age[1], . . . , Age[5]. In memory, this array would occupy six consecutive storage locations, and assuming that the elements have been assigned the values 5, 10, 15, 20, 25, and 30, the array can be pictured as follows:

Address	Age[0]	Age[1]	Age[2]	Age[3]	Age[4]	Age[5]
Contents	5	10	15	20	25	30

It would have been possible to create six integer variables with the values 5, 10, 15, 20, 25, and 30. We could have named them Age5, Age10, Age15, and so forth. But there are many advantages associated with using arrays. Arrays make it easy to manipulate many variables at a time, using only a few lines of code. Example 7.2 shows the declaration and use of an array.

Example 7.2 **When It Rains, It Pours, So Use an Array**[1]

This program uses arrays to find the average monthly rainfall in Sunshine City for the year 2014, after the user has entered the rainfall for each month. First the program computes the average of the monthly rainfall for a year and then displays a list of the months, identified by number (January is month 1, February is month 2, and so forth), each month's rainfall, and the year's average monthly rainfall. In the program, we will show all the variable declarations needed, not just those for the arrays.

```
1  Declare Rain[12] As Float
2  Declare Sum As Float
3  Declare Average As Float
4  Declare K As Integer
5  Set Sum = 0
```

[1]Before attempting to implement the examples in this chapter with RAPTOR, be sure to read the information in the Running With RAPTOR section (Section 7.6) on how RAPTOR creates and initializes arrays.

```
 6  For (K = 0; K < 12; K++)
 7    Write "Enter rainfall for month " + (K + 1)
 8    Input Rain[K]
 9    Set Sum = Sum + Rain[K]
10  End For
11  Set Average = Sum/12
12  For (K = 0; K < 12; K++)
13    Write "Rainfall for month " + (K + 1) + " is " + Rain[K]
14  End For
15  Write "The average monthly rainfall is " + Average
```

What Happened?

- Line 1 declares an array named Rain, which will consist of 12 elements of type Float.
- Lines 2 and 3 declare two floating point variables, Sum and Average. The initial value of Sum is set to 0 on line 5.
- Line 4 declares one integer variable, K. This variable will serve as a counter and will also identify each month when we write the display later.
- Lines 6–10 include the first For loop, where the user inputs the 12 rainfall figures (one for each month) into the array Rain. The loop also totals the value of the rainfall amounts for 12 months. At this point, note the following:
  - The variable K has been initialized to 0 and is set to count to 11. This will result in 12 passes through the loop, which is what we need to load values for 12 months in a year. Since we want to associate each element of the Rain array with its corresponding value of K, we begin the loop with K = 0.
  - However, the first month of the year is month 1, which is why the Write statement on line 7 asks the user to "Enter rainfall for month " + (K + 1). On the first pass, the Write statement asks for month 1 and on the 12th pass, the Write statement asks for month 12.
- Line 8 gets the input and stores the value. On the first pass, the user inputs a value for Month 1 since K + 1 = 1 and the value is stored in Rain[0] since K = 0. On the next pass, the user inputs a value for month 2 since K + 1 is now 2, but the value is stored in the second element of the Rain array, which is Rain[K] or Rain[1]. On the last pass, the user enters a value for month 12, which is stored in Rain[11].
- Line 11 computes the average value of monthly rainfall amounts for the whole year.
- At this point, the computer has stored rainfall amounts as 12 variables, but all the variables are elements of the array named Rain. The computer also knows the average of the yearly rainfall. All that is left is to tell us the results.
- The second For loop on lines 12–14 displays the month (K + 1) and the amount of rainfall for that month, which was stored in Rain[K] on line 8. This line is pretty important; when we say Write Rain[K], it's the same as saying Write the value stored in element K of the Rain array.
- Line 15 writes the average of the rainfall for all the months.

The subscript or index value of an array element can be defined as a number, a variable, or any expression that evaluates to an integer. For example, if an array is named Food and a variable named Num has the value of 5, all of the following will assign "cake" to the 6th element of Food:

- Food[5] = "cake"
- Food[Num] = "cake"
- Food[10 - Num] = "cake"

If you need to be further convinced about the advantages of using arrays to manipulate a large amount of related data, try to rewrite the pseudocode shown in Example 7.2 without an array. Instead of an array named Rain, declare 12 variables (January, February, March, April, May, June, July, August, September, October, November, and December) for the values of each month's rainfall amounts. Then rewrite the pseudocode to display each month, its rainfall amount, and the average for the year. ●

What & Why

In Example 7.2, the variable we used as a counter to load the array and to identify the number of the month we were referring to at any time was K. Initially, we set the value of K to 0, which meant that there were certain conditions that had to be met. We could not refer to the month as simply K. Instead we had to use K + 1 since there is no month 0. We also were required to set the test condition so that the loop ends when K = 11 to ensure 12 passes. However, we could also have written this program segment with the initial value of K = 1. If you rewrite this pseudocode with K = 1, what changes will you need to make so that the program does the exact same thing as shown in Example 7.2? This is the first Self Check question of this section.

What & Why

The following program segments show how C++, Java, and JavaScript code is implemented to load the Rain array, display its contents, and calculate and display the average of all entries. For clarity, in all code samples the variable names have been kept exactly the same as the pseudocode. ●

Before we move on we will use Example 7.2 to illustrate how the monthly rainfall pseudocode would look in three programming languages.

When It Rains . . . with C++

The C++ code for Example 7.2 is as follows:

Making It Work

```
1   int main()
2   {
3     float Sum; float Average;
4     float Rain[12];
5     int K;
6     Sum = 0; Average = 0;
7     for (K = 0; K < 12; K++)
8     {
9       cout << "Enter rainfall for month " << (K + 1) << endl;
10      cin >> Rain[K];
11      Sum = Sum + Rain[K];
12    }
13    Average = Sum/12;
```

```
14     for (K = 0; K < 12; K++)
15     {
16       cout << "Rainfall for month " << (K + 1) << " is " ↵
                << Rain[K] << end1;
17     }
18     cout << "The average monthly rainfall is " << Average << end1;
19     return 0;
20   }
```

When It Rains ... with Java

The Java code for Example 7.2 is as follows:

```
1   public static void main(String args[])
2   {
3     float Sum; float Average;
4     Rain[] = new float[12];
5     int K;
6     Scanner scanner = new Scanner(System.in);
7     Sum = 0; Average = 0;
8     for (K = 0; K < 12; K++)
9     {
10      System.out.println("Enter rainfall for month" + (K + 1);
11      Rain[K] = scanner.nextFloat();
12      Sum = (Sum + Rain[K]);
13    }
14    Average = Sum/12;
15    for (K = 0; K < 12; K++)
16    {
17      System.out.println("Rainfall for month" + (K + 1) + ↵
                            " is " + Rain[K]);
18    }
19    System.out.println("The average monthly rainfall is " ↵
                            + Average);
20  }
```

When It Rains ... with JavaScript

The JavaScript code for Example 7.2 is as follows:

```
1   <html> <head>
2   <title>Rainfall</title>
3   <script type="text/javascript">
4   function raining()
5   {
6     var Sum = 0; var Average = 0; var K;
7     var Rain = new Array(12);
8     for (K = 0; K < 12; K++)
9     {
10      Rain[K] = parseFloat(prompt("Enter rainfall for month "));
```

```
11      Sum = Sum + Rain[K];
12    }
13    Average = Sum/12;
14    for (K = 0; K < 12; K++)
15    {
16      document.write("Rainfall for month " + (K + 1) + ↵
                        " is " + Rain[K] + "<br />");
17    }
18    document.write("The average monthly rainfall is " + Average);
19  }
20  </script> </head>
21  <body>
22    <input type = "button" value = "click to begin" ↵
              onclick = "raining()" />
23  </body></html>
```

There are a few noteworthy points:

- Most of the syntax for the actual logic of the program is identical for all the languages. The main differences are in how the languages handle starting a program and how they retrieve and display data. In C++, the statement `int main()` begins the program, while in Java, the program begins with `public static void main(String args[])`, and in JavaScript the main function, called `raining()` in this example, is accessed from a button on the web page (see line 22).

- In C++, the `cout` and `cin` statements allow for input and output. In Java, an object, called a `scanner object` is created. It allows input to be placed into a buffer. The item in parentheses (in this case, `System.in`) tells the computer where the input is coming from (the keyboard in this case). For example:

  ```
  System.out.println("Enter rainfall for month" + (K + 1));
  ```

  tells the computer to output what is inside the parentheses. The use of `println` does the same thing as `endl` in C++—it tells the computer to move to the next line after executing this line of code. Then the line:

  ```
  Rain[K] = scanner.nextFloat();
  ```

  tells the computer to look at the `scanner object`, get the next floating point data that is in the buffer and store it in `Rain[K]`.

In JavaScript, the prompt statements get input from the user and store what the user enters in the variable or array element on the left side of the statement. In JavaScript, everything entered by a user is initially stored as text so the prompt is enclosed within the `parseFloat()` method. This changes the user's input from text to floating point data. The prompt appears as a small window on a web page screen with a box for user input. Thus, the line:

```
Rain[K] = parseFloat(prompt("Enter rainfall for month "));
```

prompts the user for a value, converts the value to a number, and stores it in `Rain[K]`. Output is created with the `document.write()` statements. Whatever is inside the parentheses will be displayed on the web page. The `<br />` tag is an indicator to move to the next line on the display.

Self Check for Section 7.1

For Self Check Questions 7.1 and 7.2 refer to Example 7.2.

7.1 Rewrite the pseudocode to load the array, Rain, with 12 rainfall amounts using K = 1 as the initial value of K.

7.2 Rewrite the pseudocode of Example 7.2 using While loops instead of For loops.

In Self Check Questions 7.3 and 7.4, what is displayed when code corresponding to the given pseudocode is executed?

7.3
```
Declare A[12] As Integer
Declare K As Integer
Set A[2] = 10
Set K = 1
While K <= 3
   Set A[2 * K + 2] = K
   Write A[2 * K]
   Set K = K + 1
End While
```

7.4 In this exercise, Letter is an array of characters and the characters that have been input are F, R, O, D, O.
```
Declare Letter[5] As Character
Declare J As Integer
For (J = 0; J <= 4; J++)
   Input Letter[J]
End For
For (J = 0; J <= 4; J+2)
   Write Letter[J]
End For
```

7.5 The following program segment is supposed to find the average of the numbers input. It contains one error. Find and correct it.
```
Declare Avg[10] As Integer
Declare Sum, K As Integer
Set Sum = 0
For (K = 0; K <= 9; K++)
   Input X[K]
   Set Sum = Sum + X[K]
End For
Set Average = Sum/10
```

7.6 State two advantages of using arrays instead of a collection of simple (unsubscripted) variables.

7.2 Parallel Arrays

In programming, we often use **parallel arrays**. These are arrays of the same size in which elements with the same subscript are related. For example, suppose we wanted to modify the program of Example 7.2 to find the average monthly rainfall and snowfall. If we store the snowfall figures for each month in an array named Snow, then Rain and Snow would be parallel arrays. For each K, Rain[K] and Snow[K] would refer to the same month so they are related data items. Example 7.3 illustrates this idea further.

Example 7.3 **You'll Be Sold on Parallel Arrays**

This program segment inputs the names of salespersons and their total sales for a given month into two parallel arrays (Names and Sales) and determines which salesperson has the greatest sales (Max). Figure 7.1 shows the flowchart for this pseudocode. It's helpful to walk through the flowchart to visualize the logic used to solve this problem. The pseudocode assumes that Max, K, and Index have been previously declared as Integer variables.

Pseudocode

```
 1  Declare Names[100] As String
 2  Declare Sales[100] As Float
 3  Set Max = 0
 4  Set K = 0
 5  Write "Enter a salesperson's name and monthly sales."
 6  Write "Enter *, 0 when done."
 7  Input Names[K]
 8  Input Sales[K]
 9  While Names[K] != "*"
10    If Sales[K] > Max Then
11      Set Index = K
12      Set Max = Sales[Index]
13    End If
14    Set K = K + 1
15    Write "Enter name and sales (enter *, 0 when done)."
16    Input Names[K]
17    Input Sales[K]
18  End While
19  Write "Maximum sales for the month: " + Max
20  Write "Salesperson: " + Names[Index]
```

What Happened?

- In this program segment, we do not use a For loop to input the data because the number of salespersons may vary from run to run. Instead, we use a sentinel-controlled loop with an asterisk (*) and a 0 as the sentinels. The user indicates that there are no more salespeople to enter by entering the asterisk (*) for the name and 0 for the amount.

- Lines 1 and 2 declare two arrays. Names is an array of String elements and Sales is an array of Floats. You may wonder why these arrays have been declared to have 100 elements each, when the program is going to allow the user to enter as many salespeople as necessary. In some programming languages, you may have to specify the size of the array. It's better to declare an array for a larger number of elements than you plan to use. In this

Figure 7.1 Flowchart for Example 7.3

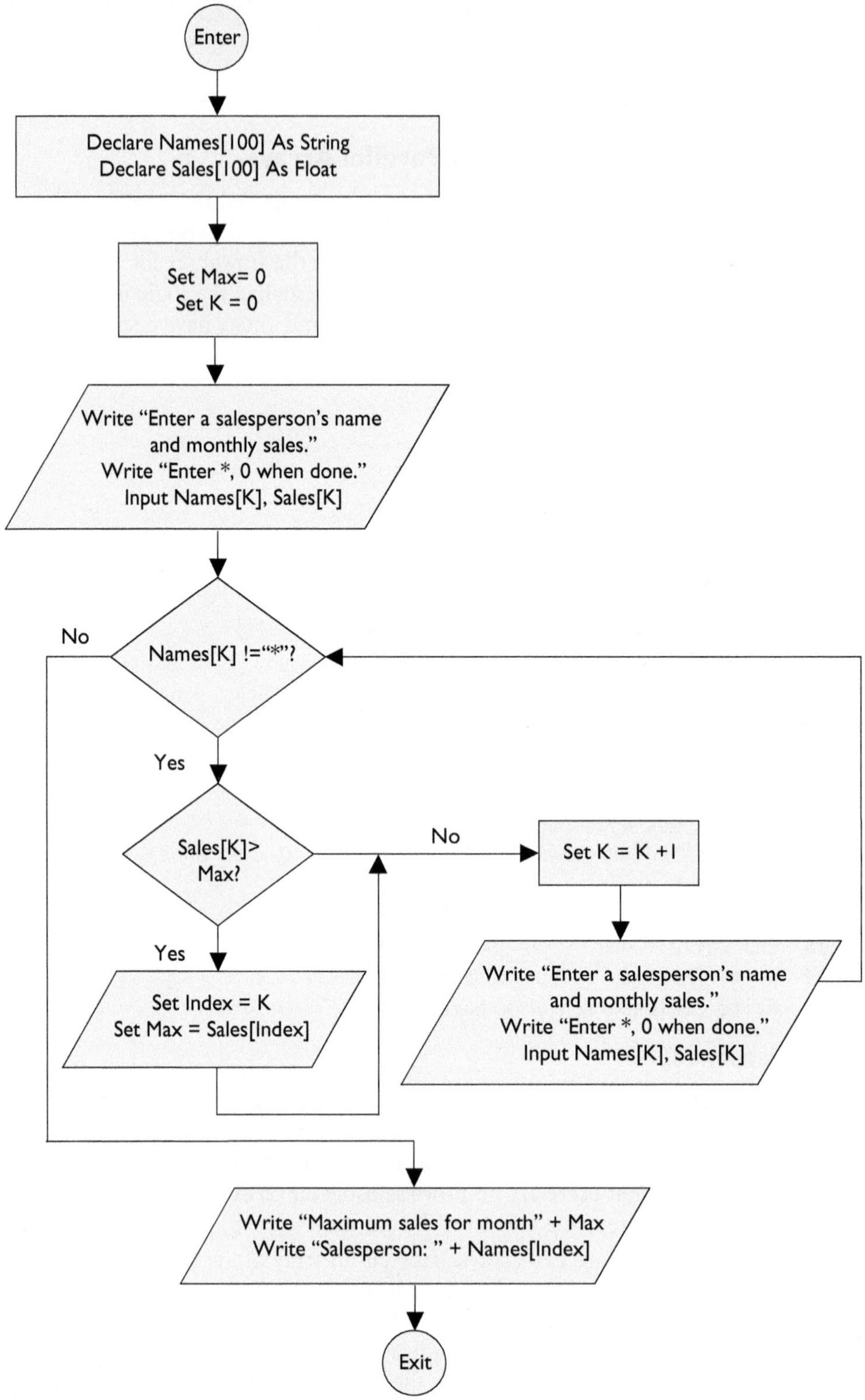

program segment, the maximum number of salespeople that can be entered is 100, but we assume that is plenty. If there are only 38 salespeople, the rest of the elements of the array are simply unused.

- Let's look at what happens on lines 5–8 in more detail. Line 5 requests the input (a salesperson's name and his/her monthly sales amount). Line 6 explains to the user how to finish entering data. Lines 7 and 8 are of some special interest. When a user enters a name and an amount, the first value entered is stored in the Names array and the second value entered is stored in the Sales array. This is very important! The information must be entered in the correct order. Imagine that the fifth entry was for a saleswoman named Josephine Jones whose sales totaled $4,283.51. If the information was entered in the wrong order, Names[4] would store 4283.51. This would not be the correct name, but a computer doesn't care what text is entered into a string so a string of numbers would be a legitimate entry. However, when the user entered "Jones" into the Float array, Sales, at best the program would simply halt or give an error message or, worse, it would crash.

- Line 9 begins the loop to do the work of this program. It continues until the asterisk is entered.

- Line 10 checks to see if the value of the current salesperson's monthly sales is greater than the maximum value to that point (Max). The variable Max holds the maximum value, so that as the entries are made, Max will continually change every time an entry has a larger sales amount.

- Line 11 sets the variable named Index equal to the value of K. K is just an integer. If the value in Sales[K] is greater than the Max value, we want the new Max value to be the value of whatever Sales[K] is at this point in the program. Let's say for example, that Sales[3] is the high value at one point in the program. We need a way to associate that value with the salesperson who sold that amount. The variable Index keeps track of that. Regardless of what the value of K becomes as the program proceeds, until there is a higher value for Sales[K], the person associated with Names[Index] (in this case, Names[3]) remains the high seller.

- In line 12, if the current salesperson has sold more than whatever value was in Max, the new Max is set equal to sales amount of the current salesperson. If the current salesperson has not sold more than the value of Max, nothing changes.

- Lines 14–17 increment the counter and get another set of data. The loop continues until the user ends it by entering the two sentinel values.

- Line 18 simply ends the While loop and lines 19 and 20 display the results.

In Example 7.3, what would happen if a salesperson had sold nothing for that month? The values entered would be the salesperson's name for the Name array and 0 for the Sales array. Would this create a problem? No, because the test condition tests only for the salesperson's name. As long as the salesperson who sold nothing was not named "*", the program would continue.

And what would happen if the user decided to end the input by entering "*" for the Name array but 23 instead of 0 for the Sales array? Would the program end? Yes, it would because the test condition on line 9 (`Names[K] != "*"`) would no longer be true, the `While` loop would not execute, and the value 23 would not be compared with other values.

You may be wondering why we ask the user to enter a 0 for the sales amount if the program segment is only interested in the salesperson's name. When this program is coded and run, there are two inputs required for each entry. The user must enter something for the sales amount. We could just easily have specified "`Enter *, -8,983 when done`" on lines 6 and 15, but we picked 0 since it makes sense that a normal monthly sales figure wouldn't be nothing. However, we have to specify some number since `Sales` is an array of numbers.   ●

Avoiding Errors

There is a small problem with the program in Example 7.3. If the user enters "`*`" at the first `Input` statement (line 7), the `While` loop is never entered. Then the variable `Index` on line 20 is undefined. Can you think of a way to rectify this problem?

One possible solution would be to initialize `Index` to an impossible value, like -1, before the loop begins. If the loop is entered, the value of `Index` is changed to `K`. But if the loop is never entered, `Index` retains its initial value. Then before the final display, a selection statement could check the value of `Index`. If it is still -1, the output might say something like "`No names were entered.`" and a program crash would be avoided.

Some Advantages of Using Arrays

There are many advantages to using arrays and even more advantages to using parallel arrays. As you have already seen, arrays can reduce the number of variable names needed in a program because we can use a single array instead of a collection of simple variables to store related data. Also arrays can help create more efficient programs. Once data are entered into an array, that data can be processed many times without having to be input again.

Example 7.4 illustrates this point.

Example 7.4 **Arrays Save You Time and Effort**

Professor Merlin has asked you to help him. He has 100 students in his four classes but he is not sure that all of them took his last exam. He wants to average the grades for his last exam in four sections of his medieval literature course and then determine how many students scored above the average. Without arrays you would have to enter all the test scores, find their average, and then enter them again to determine how many exceed the average. But you know how to use arrays, so you won't need to enter the input a second time. The following pseudocode does the job. We assume that the variables have been declared as given:

- Integer variables: `Sum`, `Count1`, `Count2`, and `K`
- Float variables: `Score` and `Average`

```
1   Declare Medieval[100] As Float
2   Set Sum = 0
3   Set Count1 = 0
4   Write "Enter a test score (or 999 to quit): "
5   Input Score
6   While Score != 999
7     Set Medieval[Count1] = Score
8     Set Count1 = Count1 + 1
9     Set Sum = Sum + Score
10    Write "Enter another score or 999 to quit: "
11    Input Score
12  End While
13  Set Average = Sum/Count1
14  Set Count2 = 0
15  Set K = 0
16  While K < Count1
17    If Medieval[K] > Average Then
18      Set Count2 = Count2 + 1
19    End If
20    Set K = K + 1
21  End While
22  Write "The average is:" + Average
23  Write "The number of scores above the average is: " + Count2
```

What Happened?

In the first While loop, which inputs the scores, the Count1 variable serves as a subscript for the array Medieval and also counts the number of scores input. Since we don't know exactly how many students took the exam, we must use a sentinel-controlled loop here. However, when it's time to determine the number of items above the average (Count2), we know the number of items that have been input. A second While loop is used (lines 16–21) with a limit value of one less than Count1 to determine the number of scores above the average.

Let's think about this limit value for a moment. The value of Count1 on line 12, at the end of the While loop, is equal to the number of scores entered. For example, since Count1 is initialized to 0 on line 3, each time Professor Merlin enters a score for a student, Count1 has the value of 1 less than the number of students up to that time. This is done so that the value of the first score will be stored in Medieval[0]. However, Count1 is incremented on the line following the score input (line 8). Therefore, when all the scores have been entered and the While loop is exited, Count1 will have the same value as the number of scores that have been entered. For example, if the Professor has 23 students in a class, he will store those students' scores in Medieval[0] through Medieval[22] but, on exiting the While loop, Count1 will equal 23.

The While loop that begins on line 16 needs to compare each score (each element of the Medieval array) with the value of Average. Therefore, if there are 23 scores entered in Medieval[0] through Medieval[22], the loop must make 23 passes. The counter for this loop, K, begins at 0 and, since it increments by 1 for each pass, by the time K has reached 22, it will have completed 23 passes. This is why we set the limit condition of this loop on line 16 to K < Count1.

Another benefit of using arrays is that they help create programs that can be used with greater generality. If we use 30 simple variables to hold the values for 30 test scores, we can only have 30 test scores. If five students register late for a class and we need variables for 35 students, we have to declare five more variables. However, because we do not have to use all the elements that were allocated to an array when it was declared, arrays give us more flexibility, as shown in Example 7.5. We could initialize an array for scores with space for 50 elements, even if we only use 30, or later in the semester, use 35. The unused spaces in the computer's memory are set aside for a value, if one is entered.

Example 7.5 **Arrays Make Programming Easy and Concise**

Professor Merlin received a list of all his students from the head of his department. The names are listed in alphabetical order from A to Z. But Professor Merlin is not a forward-thinking professor. He likes his student class list to appear in reverse alphabetical order from Z to A. He asks you to write a program to allow him to input a list of names and display them in reverse alphabetical order. This is easy to do using arrays, even if the number of names to be input is unknown at the time the program is written.

```
 1  Declare Names[100] As String
 2  Set Count = 0
 3  Write "Enter a name. (Enter * to quit.)"
 4  Input TempName
 5  While TempName != "*"
 6    Set Names[Count] = TempName
 7    Set Count = Count + 1
 8    Write "Enter a name. (Enter * to quit.)"
 9    Input TempName
10  End While
11  Set K = Count - 1
12  While K >= 0
13    Write Names[K]
14    Set K - K - 1
15  End While
```

What Happened?

This program segment inputs the list of names into the array Names and then displays the elements of that array in reverse order by "stepping backward" through a While loop whose control variable (K) is also the array subscript. The purpose of the variable TempName is to hold the string entered by the user temporarily. If that string is really a name and not the sentinel value "*", the first While loop is entered and the string is assigned to the next array element.

Note that when the first While loop ends, the value of Count is one greater than the highest subscript of the Names array. This is why we begin the second While loop with the new counter, K, set equal to the value of Count - 1.

A Word About Databases

Nowadays, virtually all companies and organizations store enormous amounts of data in **databases**. Databases consist of many tables that are linked in many ways. As we have seen, a table can contain lists of related data; in other words, a table is a group of parallel lists. The information in the tables can be retrieved and processed for a large variety of purposes.

How Databases May Be Used

Imagine a database used by a company that provides and sells online computer games. The company might have one or more tables that store information about people who play each game. If this imaginary company offers fifteen games—say, five word games, five adventure games, and five brain teaser games—the owners might want to do some market research. While each table relating to one game might include players' information, such as the player's name, username, age, contact information, dates played, scores, and so on, the market research might only be interested in some of this data. The owners might want to identify which age groups gravitate to which types of games or if scores are a factor in deciding which players keep returning to a certain game. By performing what is called a **query**, the owner can get this information quickly from the database.

Using the same tables in the database, the company's market research team can compile many types of information. Queries can discover which games are played most often on weekends, during daytime hours, how many players of what ages, gender, or even location are most likely to play which types of games and much more.

The company can also, using the information in the database, offer users of the site options to view statistics of other players or even find ways to get players to work together.

How Do Arrays Fit In?

The data retrieved from databases is processed and displayed through computer programs. When these programs are written, often the required information from the tables is temporarily stored in parallel arrays. It is manipulated, processed, and the results are output not directly from the database but from the arrays in the programs that are written by programmers. Therefore, while it is important to understand how to get and use information to load arrays directly from a user, understanding how to use arrays has a much more far-reaching purpose. Working with arrays is central to virtually all computer applications in today's world.

Self Check for Section 7.2

7.7 Write a program segment that inputs 20 numbers in increasing order and displays them in reverse order.

7.8 Redo Example 7.2 so that a user will enter values for both snowfall and rainfall for each month using parallel arrays, `Rain` and `Snow`.

7.9 Add to the program you created in Self Check Question 7.8 so that the display shows corresponding values for snowfall and rainfall for each month. Before displaying the averages for snowfall and rainfall, each output line should look like this:

```
month X:   Snowfall: Snow[X -1], Rainfall: Rain[X - 1]
```

7.10 Give two examples of situations where parallel arrays would be useful.

7.11 True or False: An array of names and an array of numbers cannot be parallel because they are of different data types.

7.12 Imagine you are starting your own small business selling widgets that you create in your home workshop. You want to keep track of your customers in a database. List the information you might store in a table about customers.

7.13 Add to the imaginary database you created in Self Check Question 7.12 by listing information you might want to store in a table about your inventory.

7.3 **Strings as Arrays of Characters**

In the first section of this chapter, we described one-dimensional arrays and some ways to use them. In this section, we will discuss how arrays are related to the topic of character strings.

In Chapter 1, we introduced character strings (or more simply, strings) as one of the basic data types. Some programming languages do not contain a string data type. In those languages, strings are implemented as arrays whose elements are characters. Even in programming languages that contain this data type, strings can be formed as arrays of characters. In this section, we will consider strings from this point of view. If you have been using the RAPTOR sections of this text you will recall how we used the RAPTOR indexing property to access specified characters in a string of text. When indexing is used, a string is processed as an array of characters in the manner that will be described in this section.

When defining a string as an array of characters in our pseudocode, we will always indicate the data type in the `Declare` statement. This practice is normally required when writing actual code. For example, the following statements

```
Declare FirstName[15] As Character
Declare LastName[20] As Character
```

define the variables `FirstName` and `LastName` to be strings of at most 15 and 20 characters, respectively.

Concatenation Revisited

Whether we consider strings as a built-in data type or as arrays of characters, we can perform certain basic operations on them, as shown in Example 7.6.

Example 7.6 **Stringing Arrays Together**

This program segment inputs two strings from the user, concatenates them, and displays the result. You will recall that concatenation means to join two items, and the + symbol is used to perform the **concatenation operation**.

```
Declare String1[25] As Character
Declare String2[25] As Character
Declare String3[50] As Character
Write "Enter two character strings. "
Input String1
Input String2
Set String3 = String1 + String2
Write String3
```

In this pseudocode, notice that String1, String2, and String3 are defined as arrays of characters, but when they are used in the program, the array brackets do not appear. For example, we write

```
Input String1
Input String2
```

rather than

```
Input String1[25]
Input String2[25]
```

This usage is typical of actual programming languages and also conforms to our previous way of referencing strings when they were considered as a built-in data type.

After the two strings have been input, the statement

```
Set String3 = String1 + String2
```

concatenates them and the Write statement displays the result. If code corresponding to this pseudocode is run and the user enters the strings "Part" and "Time" for String1 and String2, the program's output would be as follows:

```
PartTime
```

Concatenation versus Addition

Making It Work

The use of the concatenation operator in the following line of Example 7.6

```
Set String3 = String1 + String2
```

merits a short comment at this point.

If, for example, a person had three Integer variables as follows:

```
Var1 = 10, Var2 = 15, Var3 = 0
```

the statement:

```
Set Var3 = Var1 + Var2
```

would result in Var3 = 25.

However, if Var1, Var2, and Var3 were String variables with values as follows:

```
Var1 = "10", Var2 = "15", Var3 = "0"
```

the statement

```
Set Var3 = Var1 + Var2
```

would result in Var3 = "1015"

In our pseudocode, as well as in most programming languages that use the same symbol for concatenation as for addition, it is the data type declaration that tells the computer which operation (addition or concatenation) to perform.

In a language like JavaScript (or RAPTOR), you must use parentheses to ensure that the computer knows when the + sign indicates addition. The following JavaScript code snippet will demonstrate this:

```
function concatenation()
{
    var Var1 = 24;
    var Var2 = 12;
    document.write("Var1 concatenated with Var2 is: " + Var1 + ⏎
             Var2 + "<br />");
    document.write("Var1 added to Var2 is: " + (Var1 + Var2));
}
```

The output from this program would be:

```
Var1 concatenated with Var2 is: 2412
Var1 added to Var2 is: 36
```

String Length versus Array Size

The length of a string is the number of characters it contains. For example, the array String3 of Example 7.6 is declared as an array of 50 elements, but when "PartTime" is assigned to String3, only the first eight array elements are used. Thus, the length of the string "PartTime" is 8.

In some algorithms (see Example 7.7), it is useful to know the length of a string that has been assigned to a given array of characters. For this purpose, programming languages contain a Length_Of() function, which we will write as follows:

```
Length_Of(String)
```

We have discussed this function earlier in the text and used it in several RAPTOR programs. We will now review its characteristics and applications in the context of character arrays.

The value of the Length_Of() function is the length of the given string or string variable and may be used in a program wherever a numeric constant is valid. For example, when code corresponding to the following pseudocode is run:

```
Declare Str[10] As Character
Set Str = "HELLO"
Write Length_Of(Str)
```

the output will be the number 5 because the string "HELLO" is made up of five characters.

Recall that when an array is declared, the number specified in the declaration statement determines the number of storage locations in the computer's memory allocated to that array. If the array represents a string (an array of characters), then each storage location consists of one byte of memory. When a string is assigned to this array, the beginning elements of the array are filled with the characters that make up the string, a special symbol is placed in the next storage location, and the rest of the array elements remain unassigned. For example, a string named Str declared as an array of 8 characters and assigned the value "HELLO" can be pictured to look in memory as follows:

Address	Str[0]	Str[1]	Str[2]	Str[3]	Str[4]	Str[5]	Str[6]	Str[7]
Contents	"H"	"E"	"L"	"L"	"O"	#		

Here, the symbol # represents the character that is automatically placed at the end of the assigned string. Thus, to determine the length of the string contained in Str, the computer simply counts the storage locations (bytes) associated with the variable Str until the terminator symbol, #, is reached.

Example 7.7 illustrates how the Length_Of() function can be used to validate input when that input must be within a certain range of characters.

Example 7.7 Using the Length_Of() Function To Validate Input

It is sometimes necessary to ensure that a string of text does not exceed a certain limit or is within a given range of allowable characters. The following program segment demonstrates the use of the Length_Of() function to validate that a user's input for a username on a website is between 1 and 12 characters.

```
1   Declare Username[12] As Character
2   Declare Valid As Integer
3   Write "Enter your username. It must be at least 1 but ⏎
            no more than 12 characters:"
4   Input Username
5   Set Valid = Length_Of(Username)
6   While Valid < 1 OR Valid > 12
7     If Valid < 1 Then
8       Write "Username must contain at least one ⏎
              character. Please try again:"
9     Else
10      If Valid > 12 Then
11        Write "Username cannot be more than 12 ⏎
                characters. Please try again:"
12      End If
13      Input Username
14      Set Valid = Length_Of(Username)
15    End If
16  End While
```

What Happened?

The Length_Of() function finds out how many characters are in the character array, Username, and this integer is stored in Valid. Let's discuss the logic in the While loop from line 6 through line 16. This loop will not be entered if Valid is a number between 1 and 12 so nothing will occur. But if Valid is either less than 1 or greater than 12, the loop will begin. If there is nothing stored in Username (i.e., Valid < 1), the If-Then statement on line 8 will execute. If this condition is not true, then Valid must be greater than 12 (or the loop would have been skipped) so line 11 will execute. Either way, a new Username is input (line 13) and its length is checked again on line 14.

Example 7.8 illustrates how strings can be manipulated by manipulating the arrays in which they are contained.

Example 7.8 Using the Length_Of() Function with Character Arrays

This program segment inputs a person's full name with first name first, then a space, and then the last name. It stores the initials of that person as characters and displays the name in the following form: LastName, FirstName.

This pseudocode uses three strings. One stores the input name as FullName. The user is directed to enter his or her first name, then a space, and then the last name. The other two variables will store the first and last names as FirstName and LastName. It also makes use of two character variables to store the initials, FirstInitial and LastInitial. The trick to identifying which part of the input string is the first name and which part is the last name is to locate the blank space in the user's entry.

We will assume that the following arrays and variables have been declared:

- Character arrays: FullName[30], FirstName[15], LastName[15]
- Character variables: FirstInitial, LastInitial
- Integer variables: J, K, Count

```
1   Write "Enter a name in the following form: firstname lastname:"
2   Input FullName
3   Set Count = 0
4   While FullName[Count] != " "
5     Set FirstName[Count] = FullName[Count]
6     Set Count = Count + 1
7   End While
8   Set FirstInitial = FullName[0]
9   Set LastInitial = FullName[Count+1]
10  Set J = 0
11  For (K = Count + 1; K <= Length_Of(FullName) - 1; K++)
12    Set LastName[J] = FullName[K]
13    Set J = J + 1
14  End For
15  Write LastName + ", " + FirstName
16  Write "Your initials are " + FirstInitial + LastInitial
```

What Happened?

After the person's full name is input, the counter-controlled While loop on lines 4–7 assigns the characters in FullName to FirstName until the blank between the first and the last names is encountered. At this point, the value of Count is the length of

FirstName, and because the blank corresponds to the index Count, the first character in LastName corresponds to the index Count + 1. Thus, the two assignment statements that follow the While loop on lines 8 and 9 correctly store the person's initials. The new variable, J, (line 10) ensures that the letters of the last name are stored in the correct locations in the LastName array. The For loop on lines 11–14 copies the correct part of FullName to LastName. Finally, the Write statement on line 15 displays the person's name, last name first with a comma between the two parts of the name. We also display the person's initials, which have been stored in FirstInitial and LastInitial.

Array Indexes

Making It Work

In this chapter, we have emphasized the fact that the first element of an array is 0 and, therefore, an array with five elements will have index values from 0 to 4. However, this may not always be the case. Some programming languages use 1 as the beginning value for an array index. While this is rare nowadays, the program used in this book, RAPTOR, still uses an index of 1 as the first index of an array. All the other logic of dealing with arrays is the same but, when writing programs, this is a feature that must be considered. The Running With RAPTOR section of this chapter will give you practice dealing with this type of array.

Self Check for Section 7.3

7.14 True or false? If a string variable Str has been declared to be an array of 25 characters, then the length of Str must be 25.

7.15 Write a program segment to ensure that a user enters the year of his or her birth with exactly 4 digits.

7.16 Suppose that a string variable, Name, has been declared as an array of characters and has been assigned a value. Write a program segment that displays the first and last characters of Name.

7.17 Write a program segment that declares string variables String1 and String2 to be arrays of 25 characters, inputs a value for String1 from the user, and copies this value into String2.

7.4 Two-Dimensional Arrays

In the arrays you have seen so far, the value of an element has depended upon a single factor. For example, if one element in an array holds a student's ID number, the value of this number depends on which student is being processed. Sometimes it's convenient to use arrays whose elements are determined by two factors. For example, we might have several test scores associated with each student, in which case the value we look for would depend on two factors—the particular student *and* the particular test in which we are interested. Another example might be the records of the monthly sales for salespeople for a year. Each salesperson has 12 numbers (one for each month's sales) associated with him or her, so the value we look for would depend on which salesperson *and* which month is of interest. In these cases, we use two-dimensional arrays.

An Introduction to Two-Dimensional Arrays

A **two-dimensional array** is a collection of elements of the same types stored in consecutive memory locations, all of which are referenced by the same variable name using two subscripts. For example, `MyArray[2,3]` is one element of a two-dimensional array named `MyArray`. Example 7.9 illustrates one use of two-dimensional arrays.

Example 7.9 Introducing Two-Dimensional Arrays

Suppose we want to input the scores of 30 students in five tests into a program. We can set up a single two-dimensional array named `Scores` to hold all these test results. The first subscript of `Scores` references a particular student; the second subscript references a particular test. For example, the array element `Scores[0,0]` contains the score of the first student on the first test and the array element `Scores[8,1]` contains the score of the ninth student on the second test.

This situation may be easier to understand if you picture the array elements in a rectangular pattern of horizontal rows and vertical columns. The first row gives the scores of the first student, the second row gives the scores of the second student, and so forth. Similarly, the first column gives the scores of all students on the first test, the second column gives all scores on the second test, and so forth (see Figure 7.2). The entry in the box at the intersection of a given row and column represents the value of the corresponding array element. The following is shown in Figure 7.2.

- `Scores[1,3]`, the score of Student 2, Boynton, on Test 4, is 73
- `Scores[29,1]`, the score of Student 30, Ziegler, on Test 2, is 76

Figure 7.2 The two-dimensional array named Scores

	Test 1	Test 2	Test 3	Test 4	Test 5
Student 1: Arroyo	92	94	87	83	90
Student 2: Boynton	78	86	64	73	84
Student 3: Chang	72	68	77	91	79
.	.	.	.	.	.
.	.	.	.	.	.
.	.	.	.	.	.
Student 30: Ziegler	88	76	93	69	52

Declaring Two-Dimensional Arrays

Like their one-dimensional counterparts, two-dimensional arrays must be declared before they are used. We will use a declaration statement for two-dimensional arrays that is similar to the one we've been using for one-dimensional arrays. For example, we will declare the array of Example 7.9 using the following statement:

```
Declare Scores[30,5] As Integer
```

The numbers 30 and 5 inside the brackets indicate the number of elements in this array. This statement allocates 150(30 × 5) consecutive storage locations in the computer's internal memory to hold the 150 elements of the array Scores. The Scores array has 30 rows and each row has 5 columns. Example 7.10 illustrates some basic points about using two-dimensional arrays.

Example 7.10 **The Basics of Two-Dimensional Arrays**

Consider the following pseudocode:

```
1  Declare ArrayA[10,20] As Integer
2  Declare ArrayB[20] As Integer
3  Declare FirstPlace As Integer
4  Set FirstPlace = 5
5  Set ArrayA[FirstPlace,10] = 6
6  Set ArrayB[7] = ArrayA[5,10]
7  Write ArrayA[5,2 * FirstPlace]
8  Write ArrayB[7]
```

What Happened?

Here, the Declare statements on lines 1 and 2 declare two arrays—the first, ArrayA, is two dimensional with 10 rows and 20 columns (200 elements) and the second, ArrayB, is one dimensional with 20 elements. Because FirstPlace is 5, the following is true:

- The assignment statement on line 5 sets ArrayA[5,10] equal to 6. In other words, the value of the 6th row, 11th column of ArrayA is equal to 6.
- The assignment statement on line 6 sets ArrayB[7] equal to the value of ArrayA[5,10], which is a 6. So now the value of the 8th element in ArrayB = 6.
- The Write statements on lines 7 and 8 display the value of the element in the 6th row, 11th column of ArrayA and the value of the 8th element of ArrayB so the number 6 will be displayed twice.

Using Two-Dimensional Arrays

As you have seen, counter-controlled loops, especially the For variety, provide a valuable tool for manipulating one-dimensional arrays. In the two-dimensional case, as shown in Example 7.11, nested For loops are especially useful.

Example 7.11 Nested Loops for Loading a Two-Dimensional Array

This program segment inputs data into a two-dimensional array, Scores, whose elements are test scores. The first subscript of Scores refers to the student being processed; the second subscript refers to the test being processed. For each of the 30 students, the user is to input five test scores. The pseudocode is as follows:

```
1  Declare Scores[30,5] As Integer
2  Declare Student As Integer
3  Declare Test As Integer
4  For (Student = 0; Student < 30; Student++)
5    Write "Enter 5 test scores for student " + (Student + 1)
6    For (Test = 0; Test < 5; Test++)
7      Input Scores[Student,Test]
8    End For(Test)
9  End For(Student)
```

What Happened?

This pseudocode results in one input prompt for each student. The prompt instructs the user to enter the five scores for that student. For example, if the code corresponding to this pseudocode is run, the following text will be displayed:

```
Enter 5 test scores for student 1
```

and then execution will pause for input. After the user enters the five scores, he or she will see the following:

```
Enter 5 test scores for student 2
```

and so forth.

Example 7.12 demonstrates the use of nested loops to display the contents of the array.

Example 7.12 Using Nested Loops to Display the Contents of a Two-Dimensional Array

Suppose that a two-dimensional array Scores has been declared and assigned data as described in Example 7.11. Student is an integer variable that is used to identify the element of Scores for a particular student's record. Notice that, if the user enters a value of 4 for Student, this actually corresponds to the elements in the 4th row (subscript 3) of Scores. The following pseudocode displays the test scores of a student specified by the user:

```
1  Write "Enter the number of a student, and his or her test scores
      will be displayed."
2  Input Student
3  For (Test = 0; Test < 5; Test++)
4    Write Scores[Student - 1,Test]
5  End For
```

The pseudocode shown in Examples 6.11 and 7.12 is somewhat not user-friendly because it requires the user to refer to students by number (student 1, student 2, and so forth) rather than by name. Example 7.13 presents a more comprehensive example that corrects this defect by using a second (parallel) one-dimensional array of names.

Example 7.13 **The Friendly Version Puts It All Together**

This program inputs the names and test scores for a class of students and then displays each name and that student's average test score. It uses a one-dimensional array, Names, whose elements are strings. This array holds the student names; a two-dimensional array, Scores, of numbers holds a numeric identification number for the student (the first value in the two-dimensional array) and that student's 5 test scores.

We assume that there is a maximum of 30 students in the class, but that the exact number is unknown prior to running the program. Thus, we need a sentinel-controlled While loop to input the data. However, during the input process, we discover how many students are in the class, and we can use that number to process and display the array elements. For the sake of clarity, we declare all the variables used in this program.

```
 1  Declare Names[30] As String
 2  Declare Scores[30,5] As Integer
 3  Declare Count As Integer
 4  Declare Test As Integer
 5  Declare K As Integer
 6  Declare J As Integer
 7  Declare StudentName As String
 8  Declare Sum As Float
 9  Declare Average As Float
10  Set Count = 0
11  Write "Enter a student's name; enter * when done."
12  Input StudentName
13  While StudentName != "*"
14    Set Names[Count] = StudentName
15    Write "Enter 5 test scores for " + Names[Count]
16    Set Test = 0
17    While Test < 5
18      Input Scores[Count,Test]
19      Set Test = Test + 1
20    End While(Test)
21    Set Count = Count + 1
22    Write "Enter a student's name; enter * when done."
23    Input StudentName
24  End While(StudentName)
25  Set K = 0
26  While K <= Count - 1
27    Set Sum = 0
28    Set J = 0
```

```
29    While J < 5
30      Set Sum = Sum + Scores[K,J]
31      Set J = J + 1
32    End While(J)
33    Set Average = Sum/5
34    Write Names[K] + ": " +      Average
35      Set K + K + 1
36  End While(K)
```

What Happened?

By now you can easily recognize what many parts of the pseudocode do; therefore, rather than go through this program line by line, we will concentrate on the more advanced logic.

- Lines 1–12 declare all the variables, set the initial counter to 0, and get the "seed" value for the next loop (the first student's name). To avoid inputting the sentinel value, "*", into the array Names, we temporarily assign each input string to the variable StudentName. If the value of StudentName is not "*", the While loop is entered and that string is assigned to the next element of Names. As soon as "*" is entered, the While loop is exited so it is never input into the Names array.

- The While loop on lines 13–24 is the most complicated part. It inputs the student names into the one-dimensional array, Names, and the five test scores into the two-dimensional array, Scores. How does it do this?

  - The statement on line 14, Set Names[Count] = StudentName, loads the first student into the first element of the array, Names[0]. On the next time around this loop, the next name entered will be loaded into the second element of Names[1], and so forth.

  - Line 15 asks the user to enter the five test scores for whichever student was entered on the previous line. The inner loop, on lines 17–20, loads each of the test scores into the two-dimensional array. The first dimension of this array, Scores[30, 5] is the *number* (Count) that identifies the student and the second dimension is a score. If Martin has been entered as the third student and his test scores are 98, 76, 54, 92, and 89, then the following values are stored in Scores:

    ```
    Scores[2,0] = 98
    Scores[2,1] = 76
    Scores[2,2] = 54
    Scores[2,3] = 92
    Scores[2,4] = 89
    ```

- Line 21 increments the value of Count to prepare for the next student.

- After the five test scores for one student have been loaded into the two-dimensional array, lines 22 and 23 prompt for and input another student's name. If there are no more students, Count has the value of the number of entries in the array, Names, and each student is identified in Scores by the number corresponding to his/her array subscript in Names. Note that Count has the value of the number of entries, which is one more than the highest subscript.

- When all the students and their test scores have been loaded into the two arrays, the program control goes to the outer `While` loop on lines 26–36. In effect, the outer loop says, "Using the student identified by number `K`, add up his/her test scores and divide that sum by 5 to get the average."
- The inner loop on lines 29–32 gets each test score and does the sum.
- Line 33 computes the average and line 34 displays the name of the student and his/her average.
- The outer loop makes another pass, as long as `K` (the variable that identifies the student) is less than or equal to `Count - 1`.

Higher Dimensional Arrays

Making It Work

Although they are not used very often, arrays with three or even more subscripts are allowed in some programming languages. These higher dimensional arrays can be used to store data that depends upon more than two factors (subscripts).

Self Check for Section 7.4

7.18 How many storage locations are allocated by each statement?
- `Declare A[4,9] As Integer`
- `Declare Left[10], Right[10,10] As Float`

7.19 A two-dimensional array named `Fog` has two rows and four columns with the following data:

```
5    10   15   20
25   30   35   40
```

a. What are the values of `Fog[0,1]` and `Fog[1,2]`?

b. Which elements of `Fog` contain the numbers 15 and 25?

7.20 What is displayed when code corresponding to the following pseudocode is executed?

```
Declare A[2,3] As Integer
Declare K As Integer
Declare J As Integer
Set K = 0
While K <= 1
  Set J = 0
  While J <= 2
    Set A[K, J] = K + J
    Set J = J + 1
  End While(J)
  Set K = K + 1
End While(K)
Write A[0,1] + " " + A[1,0] + " " + A[1,2]
```

7.21 How many times are the prompts on lines 3 and 4 of the following pseudo-code displayed?

```
1  For (I = 0; I < 5; I++)
2    For (J = 0; J < 12; J++)
3      Write "Enter rainfall in state " + I
4      Write " in month " + J
5      Input Rain[I, J]
6    End For(J)
7  End For(I)
```

7.22 Imagine you own a small business that sells jewelry (rings, bracelets, and pendants) that you make. You create each piece in silver, gold, and stainless steel. Create a program that allows you to store the following data:
- each item's name is stored in a one-dimensional array
- a two-dimensional array holds an identification number for each item plus the number of that item you have in stock in gold, silver, and stainless steel

7.5 Focus on Problem Solving:
The Magic Square

A magic square is a two-dimensional array of positive integers, which has the following characteristics:

- The number of rows equals the number of columns
- All entries must be positive integers
- The sum of all the entries in each row, each column, and the two diagonals are identical

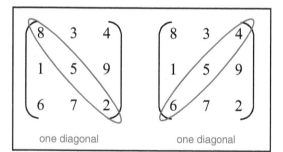

one diagonal   one diagonal

In a two-dimensional array, one diagonal goes from the upper left corner to the lower right corner and the other goes from the lower left corner to the upper right corner. The diagonals of a 3 × 3 square are shown here.

In this section, we will use the concepts in this chapter to create the pseudocode for a program that will allow a user to enter numbers into a two-dimensional array. The program will then test to see if the numbers entered form a magic square.

Problem Statement

The user should be prompted to enter values into a two-dimensional array. The values will be checked to ensure that the entries are positive integers. The values in the rows will be summed, the values in the columns will be summed, and the values in the diagonal elements will be summed. The sums will be compared. When one sum differs from another, a message will be displayed stating that these values do not form a magic square. If all the sums are the same, a message will be displayed stating that the values entered do form a magic square.

Problem Analysis

A magic square must be a two-dimensional array with the same number of rows and columns. We can think of a two-dimensional array as a matrix. A **matrix** is a rectangular grid of numbers. If there are M rows and N columns in the grid, we call it an M × N matrix (read this as "M by N matrix"). Therefore, our two-dimensional array should be a square or an N × N matrix, where N represents the number of rows and columns. While a magic square can consist of as many rows and columns as desired, for our purposes, we will use a 4 X 4 matrix—that is, an array with four rows and four columns. After the program is coded and tested, the number of rows and columns can be increased or decreased with one fell swoop of the keyboard—simply by changing the value assigned to the number of rows and columns.

Step 1: Populate the array. The array we use will be named Magic and each entry will be of the form Magic[A, B] where A represents the row and B represents the column. Getting the values for Magic requires input from the user. After each entry is input, we should validate it to ensure that it is a positive integer. We can do this with nested loops. The logic for this part, in general terms, is as follows:

```
Begin at the first column (column counter = 0)
While column counter < N (where N is the number of columns)
   Set row counter to 0
   While row counter < N
     Get a value for this location: Magic[row, column]
     Check if the value is a positive integer
     Increase row counter
   End While (row counter)
   Increase column counter
End While (column counter)
```

Step 2: Do the sums. We need, at most, ten sums. There will be four sums of the values in the four rows, four sums of the values in the columns, and two sums of the values in the diagonals. However, we might not need to do all these sums. As soon as one sum does not match another sum, we know we do not have a magic square. So the logic for this part of the program, while a bit complex, is virtually all that is needed to complete this problem.

We can take one sum and compare it with all the subsequent sums. As soon as the sum differs from the first sum, we can jump out of the loop that does the sums and display the message that the data does not form a magic square.

In general terms, the logic for this part of the program will consist of a loop to sum the values of the rows, a loop to sum the values of the columns, and two sums for the diagonals. Before we begin to do all the sums, we can get an initial sum, store this value in an integer variable which we will call SumOne, and use it to compare each sum. As soon as one sum does not match SumOne, we can leave this part of the program and move on to Step 3.

Step 3: Display the results. The results are simple. Either the numbers entered by the user form a magic square or they do not.

The variables and the array needed for this program, therefore, are:

- Magic is a two-dimensional array with four rows and four colums
- RowCount is an Integer variable
- ColCount is an Integer variable
- rows and cols are two Integer variables
- SumOne and SumCount are two Integer variables
- Flag is a Boolean variable
- Diag1 and Diag2 are two Integer variables
- newSum is an Integer variable

Program Design

As with virtually all programs, we will begin this program with a welcome message. In this case, the welcome message will explain briefly what the program does and what is to be entered.

Thus, our program will consist of the following modules.

1. The Main module calls its submodules into action and displays the welcome message. It will explain what the user is to enter. Then it will, in sequence, call the other submodules that perform all the required processes.

2. The Enter_info module declares the array and accepts entries for each array element. When complete, control returns to the main module.

3. The Check_sums module gets an initial sum, then calls submodules to find the sums of the rows, the columns, and the diagonals:

    a. Check_row_sums – sums each row in the array and compares each sum with the first sum.

    b. Check_column_sums – sums each column in the array and compares each sum with the first sum.

    c. Check_diag_sums – sums the two diagonals in the array and compares these sums with the first sum.

    Each submodule will, at its end, either have Flag set to 1 or 0. When the Check_row_sums submodule returns control to the Check_sums module, if Flag is still 0, the Check_column_sums module will be called. If Flag is 1, the Check_sums submodule will end because the array has been identified as not a magic array. If Flag is still 0, the next submodule, Check_column_sums will be called. At the end of Check_column_sums, a similar situation exists. When control returns to Check_sums, either the Check_diag_sums will be called (if Flag is still 0) or the Check_sums module will end and return control to the main module. Finally, if the Check_diag_sums module is called, when it is finished, it will return control to Check_sums which will then return control to main.

4. The Display_results module displays the results.

Passing Values to Submodules

In this section, as we have in the past, submodules are called and values are sent from one submodule to another with the assumption that they retain their values when passed from one place to another. It should be noted that we are doing this for simplicity at this point. In real programming languages a great deal of attention must be paid to how the values of variables are passed from one part of a program to another. Chapter 9 discusses this important concept in depth.

Keeping in mind that it is not always possible to use variables interchangeably from one submodule to another without special treatment that will be discussed later in the text, the pseudocode for each module follows:

Main Module

```
Start
    Identify the program, explain to the user what to enter, and what
    will be determined (i.e., user entries will either form a magic
    square or not)
    Call Enter_info submodule
    Call Check_sums submodule
    Call Display_results
End Program
```

Enter_info Module

This module will define some variables and will get input from the user to populate the two-dimensional array which we will call Magic. Since we have chosen to use a 4 X 4 matrix for our program, we will define the number of rows and columns to be 4. It is in this single place where, by changing this value, we can change the matrix size at one time and the program will still work.

The pseudocode for this module is as follows:

```
1   Declare cols, rows, ColCount, RowCount As Integer
2   Declare Magic[4, 4] As Integer
3   Set cols = 4
4   Set rows = 4
5   Set ColCount = 0
6   Set RowCount = 0
7   While RowCount < rows
8       While ColCount < cols
9           Write "Enter the value of the cell in row " + (RowCount + 1) ↵
                + ", column " + (ColCount + 1)
10          Input Magic[RowCount, ColCount]
```

```
11        While ((Magic[RowCount, ColCount] != floor(Magic[RowCount, ⌐
                  ColCount])) OR (Magic[RowCount, ColCount] < 0))
12          Write "Please enter a positive integer: "
13          Input Magic[RowCount, ColCount]
14        End While(Magic[RowCount, ColCount])
15        Set ColCount = ColCount + 1
16      End While(ColCount)
17      Set RowCount = RowCount + 1
18      Set ColCount = 0
19    End While(RowCount)
```

The logic used to input the values into this two-dimensional loop is similar to what we will use to determine all the sums so it is a good idea to spend a bit of extra time on the nested loops in this pseudocode. Each row of the array has four elements:

```
Magic[row0,col0], Magic[row0,col1], Magic[row0,col2], Magic[row0,col3]
Magic[row1,col0], Magic[row1,col1], Magic[row1,col2], Magic[row1,col3]
Magic[row2,col0], Magic[row2,col1], Magic[row2,col2], Magic[row2,col3]
Magic[row3,col0], Magic[row3,col1], Magic[row3,col2], Magic[row3,col3]
```

Lines 11–14 validate the user's input, ensuring that only positive integers are stored in the array.

For each row, we need to get four inputs—one for each column. And we need to do this for four rows. The outer loop that begins on line 7 starts with RowCount = 0. The inner loop that begins on line 8 starts with ColCount = 0 and accepts input for four iterations. Each time the inner loop goes around a value of Magic is input. During this time, the value of the row (RowCount) does not change, but the value of the column (ColCount) is increased at the end of each iteration. Once the four columns on the first row have been filled, the inner loop is exited and RowCount is increased (line 17). The outer loop begins again, this time targeting the second row. The value of ColCount is set back to 0 (line 18) so the four columns of the second row are filled when the inner loop executes. This happens again and again until all the rows are filled. We will revisit this logic—using an outer loop to focus on one row and an inner loop to access each column in that row—when we create the modules to sum the rows, columns, and diagonals.

Check_sums Module

Once the array is populated, this module is called. It will first find a "test" sum (the sum of the first row of the array) which will be used to see if the other sums match and then it will call submodules to get the sums of the rest of the rows, the columns, and the diagonals. Recall that a magic square only exists if every sum matches every other sum. This is why we can initially pick any row or column as our test sum; if any other sum doesn't match this one, there is no magic square. Here, we select the first row.

For the sake of efficiency, we will create this program so that it will stop finding sums when one sum doesn't match the test sum. Therefore, we will use a Boolean variable as a flag to indicate when a sum is found that does not match the test sum. A **flag** is a variable that can be set to false (or 0) initially and, when the data we are searching for is found, its value is changed to true (or 1). We will introduce three new variables here:

- SumCount is an Integer variable used to indicate a single row in the test sum
- SumOne is an two Integer variable that will hold the value of the test sum
- Flag is a Boolean variable

The pseudocode for this module is as follows:

```
1   Declare SumCount, SumOne As Integer
2   Declare Flag As Boolean
3   Set SumCount = 0
4   Set SumOne = 0
5   Set ColCount = 0
6   Set Flag = 0
7   While ColCount < cols
8       Set SumOne = SumOne + Magic[SumCount,ColCount]
9       Set ColCount = ColCount + 1
10  End While(ColCount)
11  Call Check_row_sums
12  If Flag == 0 Then
13      Call Check_column_sums
14  End If
15  If Flag == 0 Then
16      Call Check_diag_sums
17  End If
```

The loop that begins on line 7 calculates the sum of the four colums in the first row. This value is stored in SumOne and will now be used to compare every sum in the following three modules.

Line 11 calls the module to check the sums of the rows. If any of these does not match SumOne, the value of Flag will be set to 1, as we shall see in the next submodule. This will indicate that the array does not form a magic square. Once the rows have been summed, control from the Check_row_sums module will return to line 12 of this submodule. If Flag = 1, then no further sums need to be found. But if Flag still is 0, the columns and diagonals must be checked. Therefore, line 12 checks this condition and, if Flag is 0, the Check_column_sums module is called. Once all the columns have been summed, control returns to line 15 of this submodule. Again, the value of Flag is checked and, if it is still 0, the sums of the diagonal must be checked so the Check_diag_sums module is called.

Finally, when this submodule ends, control will return to the main module where the Display_results module will be called (line 16).

The **Check_row_sums** Module and the **Check_column_sums** Module

These two modules are almost identical so a detailed explanation is given only of the first; the pseudocode for the second will then be shown. The main difference between the two is that the variables identifying rows and columns will simply be switched.

In the `Check_row_sums` module, we begin by setting the row counter (`RowCount`) to 0. Nested loops are used. The outer loop identifies a single row. The inner loop adds up the values of all the column entries in that row. We will store that sum in a new integer variable, `NewSum`, which is set to 0 each time a new row sum begins. We also compare the value of `NewSum` whenever a row's sum is finished with the value of `OneSum` from the previous module. If the two sums are the same, nothing happens. But if they are different, `Flag` is set to 1. Therefore, when the row sums are finished, if one row sum differs from `OneSum`, the `Flag` indicates that this is not a magic square.

The pseudocode for this module is as follows:

```
1   Set RowCount = 0
2   While RowCount < rows AND Flag == 0
3     Set NewSum = 0
4     Set ColCount = 0
5     While ColCount < cols AND Flag == 0
6       Set NewSum = NewSum + Magic[RowCount,ColCount]
7       Set ColCount = ColCount + 1
8     End While(ColCount)
9     If NewSum != OneSum Then
10      Set Flag = 1
11    End If
12    Set RowCount = RowCount + 1
13  End While(RowCount)
```

The pseudocode for the `Check_column_sums` module is almost the same but the outer loop identifies a single column and the inner loop sums up the rows in that column:

```
1   Set ColCount = 0
2   While ColCount < cols AND Flag == 0
3     Set NewSum = 0
4     Set RowCount = 0
5     While RowCount < rows AND Flag == 0
6       Set NewSum = NewSum + Magic[RowCount,ColCount]
7       Set RowCount = RowCount + 1
8     End While(RowCount)
9     If NewSum != OneSum Then
10      Set Flag = 1
11    End If
12    Set ColCount = ColCount + 1
13  End While(ColCount)
```

Check_diag_sums Module

The diagonals of our 4 X 4 matrix are the values shown in the grid below. The first diagonal, which we will call `Diag1`, starts at the upper left corner and ends at the lower right corner. The second diagonal, which we will call `Diag2`, starts at the lower left corner and ends at the upper right corner.

It would be easy to simply create these sums by using the values of these array elements. For example, the sum of the diagonals are:

```
Diag1 = Magic[0,0] + Magic[1,1] + Magic[2,2] + Magic[3,3]
Diag2 = Magic[3,0] + Magic[2,1] + Magic[1,2] + Magic[0,3]
```

However, we need to find a way to sum the diagonals that can be used for an N X N matrix of any size. This takes a bit more thought.

If we look at the rows and columns in each diagonal we notice several things. In Diag1, we want to add elements with increasing row and column values. If we write a loop to add values that have increasing row and column values in general, we can get the sum for Diag1, as follows:

```
1   Set Diag1 = 0
2   Set ColCount = 0
3   Set RowCount = 0
4   While RowCount < rows
5      Set Diag1 = Diag1 + Magic[RowCount,ColCount]
5      Set RowCount = RowCount + 1
6      Set ColCount = ColCount + 1
7   End While
```

For Diag2, however, we want to add the element that starts at the highest numbered row (the last row), first column to the element in the next highest row, second column, and so on until we get to the element in the first row, last column. We can use pseudocode that is almost identical to that of Diag1 but begin at RowCount = (rows - 1) (the highest row) and decrement RowCount for each iteration. This will also require that we change the test condition of the loop so that it ends after Row-Count is 0. The pseudocode for this part is as follows:

```
1   Set Diag2 = 0
2   Set ColCount = 0
3   Set RowCount = rows - 1
```

```
4  While RowCount >= 0
5     Set Diag2 = Diag2 + Magic[RowCount,ColCount]
5     Set RowCount = RowCount - 1
6     Set ColCount = ColCount + 1
7  End While
```

We could check whether each of these sums is the same as SumOne within each loop but, since there are only two diagonals and, regardless of the size of the array, there will always be only two diagonals, we can do this check in one step after we find both Diag1 and Diag2, as follows:

```
1  If Diag2 != SumOne OR Diag2 != SumOne Then
2     Set Flag = 1
3  End If
```

Control now returns to the last line of the Check_sums module which then returns control to the main module. The Display_results module is then called from main.

The Display_results Module

This module is simple. If Flag is 1, a message is displayed to tell the user that the entries do not form a magic square. If Flag is still 0, a message is displayed, explaining that the entries do form a magic square. The pseudocode for this module is as follows:

```
1  If Flag == 1 Then
2     Write "Sorry, this is not a magic square."
3  Else
4     Write "Hooray! Your entries do form a magic square!"
5  End If
```

Program Code

The program code is now written using the design as a guide. At this stage, header comments and step comments are inserted, as necessary, into each module, providing internal documentation for the program.

Program Test

This program should be tested by using values that form a magic square and values that do not form a magic square. The simplest way to check if the program will identify a magic square is to enter all values that are the same such as all 1s or all 2s. However, you can search the Internet for more interesting values that will work. Two such solutions are provided below in Figure 7.3. Almost any other entries that you use, selecting arbitrary values, will result in an array that does not form a magic square.

A working copy of this program, created in RAPTOR, is included with the Student Data Files but it would be a good exercise to create this program in RAPTOR yourself, if you have been using RAPTOR throughout the book. If you do this, remember that the test conditions and some initial values in RAPTOR loops must be reworked to ensure that the loop is exited when the test question is true and

Figure 7.3 Two ways to form a magic square

Magic Square Option 1				Magic Square Option 2			
1	14	14	4	16	3	2	13
11	7	6	9	5	10	11	8
8	10	10	5	9	6	7	12
13	2	3	15	4	15	14	1

the loop is re-entered when the test condition is `false` as well as to account for the fact that RAPTOR arrays begin with the index value of 1. You can check the values given in Figure 7.3 to make sure your program correctly identifies a magic square.

Self Check for Section 7.5

For Self Check Questions 7.23–7.27 refer to this section.

7.23 Add code to the `Enter_info` module to display the values in `Magic` after the user enters his or her numbers.

7.24 Add code to the `Check_sums` module to display the value of the initial sum, `SumOne`.

7.25 Add code to the three submodules (`Check_row_sums`, `Check_column_sums`, and `Check_diag_sums`) to display the first sum (`NewSum`) that does not match `SumOne`.

7.26 Change the 4 X 4 array to a 6 X 6 array.

7.27 Add code to give the user the option to select the size of the array.

7.6 Running With RAPTOR (Optional)

In RAPTOR, an array is created a bit differently from the way it has been done so far in this text. In the text, 0 is the first index of an array. This is the way most programming languages (such as C++ and Java) create arrays. However, in RAPTOR, the first element of an array has an index of 1. So, the first element of an array named `RaptorItems` is `RaptorItems[1]`, the second element is `RaptorItems[2]`, and so forth. Thus, a RAPTOR program to fill the `RaptorItems` array with the numbers 2, 4, 8, 16, and 32 would look as follows in the text's pseudocode:

```
Set K = 1
While K <= 5
  Set RaptorItems[K] = 2^K
  Set K = K + 1
End While
```

You can see how this short program would look in RAPTOR in Figure 7.5.

Although this is a minor difference between the text and RAPTOR versions of arrays, it has an important consequence. You must amend the pseudocode you create for text exercises involving arrays if you want these programs to work in RAPTOR. Specifically, when converting your pseudocode to a RAPTOR program, make sure that your arrays start with an index of 1, and you must make sure that any test conditions in loops that depend on array indexes are coded properly.

To declare an array in RAPTOR, you use an Assignment symbol, as you do for a variable but put square brackets ([ ]) after the array name. When you declare an array, you can set its size by putting a number inside the brackets. If you do not know initially how many elements you need, put in any number. RAPTOR will automatically add array elements, if needed, to your programs. You must, however, fill the array with an initial value. If your array is to be an array of numbers, the initial value for all the elements is normally set to 0; if it is to be an array of strings, the normal initial value will be the empty string (""); and if you want an array of characters, the normal initial value will be the blank space (' '). Figure 7.4 shows how various types of arrays, each named RaptorArray, are declared in RAPTOR.

Figure 7.5 shows the RAPTOR program that fills the array named RaptorItems with the values 2, 4, 8, 16, and 32 and the output in the MasterConsole.

In this section, we will use our programming skills with parallel arrays to create an application that can be used in a classroom. Our program will create a math test with questions created at random so that they are new each time a student

Figure 7.4 Declaring and initializing arrays in RAPTOR

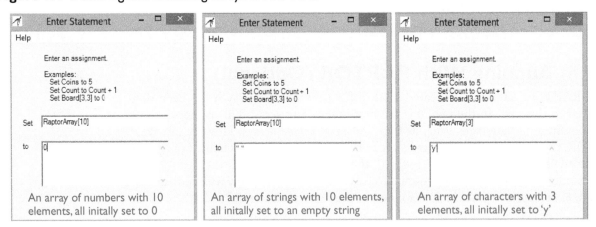

Figure 7.5 Filling an array in RAPTOR

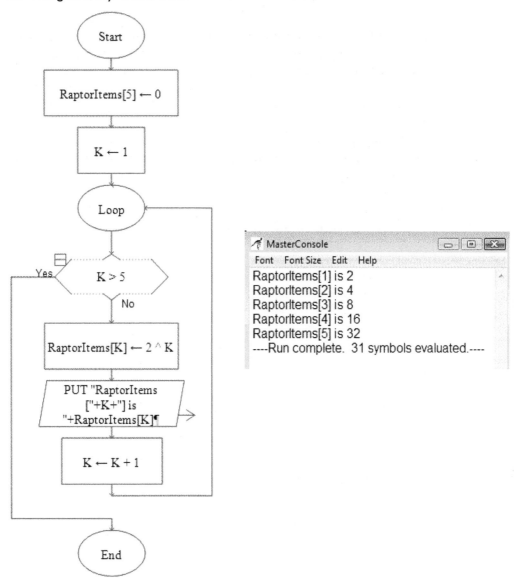

takes the test. It will also grade the student's test and output the results. However, before we begin this ambitious project, we will redo Example 7.3 from earlier in this chapter to practice how to use parallel arrays with RAPTOR.

A Short Example

Example 7.14 **You'll Be Sold on Parallel Arrays**

We will repeat the pseudocode of Example 7.3 here and then create the program in RAPTOR. This program inputs the names of salespersons and their total sales for the month into two parallel arrays (Names and Sales) and determines which salesperson has the greatest sales (Max).

Pseudocode:

```
 1  Declare Names[100] As String
 2  Declare Sales[100] As Float
 3  Set Max = 0
 4  Set K = 0
 5  Write "Enter a salesperson's name and monthly sales."
 6  Write "Enter *, 0 when done."
 7  Input Names[K]
 8  Input Sales[K]
 9  While Names[K] != "*"
10    If Sales[K] > Max Then
11      Set Index = K
12      Set Max = Sales[Index]
13    End If
14    Set K = K + 1
15    Write "Enter name and sales ↵
             (enter *, 0 when done)."
16    Input Names[K]
17    Input Sales[K]
18  End While
19  Write "Maximum sales for the ↵
             month: " + Max
20  Write "Salesperson: " + ↵
             Names[Index]
```

RAPTOR implementation

In RAPTOR, Max is a reserved word so we have changed the name of the variable, Max, to Best. It is declared in our list of variables. Note that, because of the way RAPTOR handles the loop's test condition, we changed the condition so that the loop will exit when the test condition is true. We also used K = 1 for the starting value since RAPTOR arrays begin with index = 1. The declaration of variables is shown followed by the RAPTOR implementation of the program.

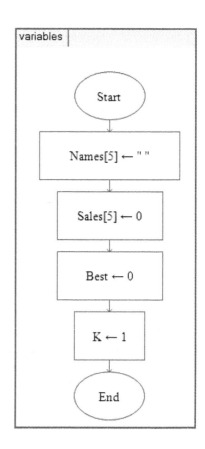

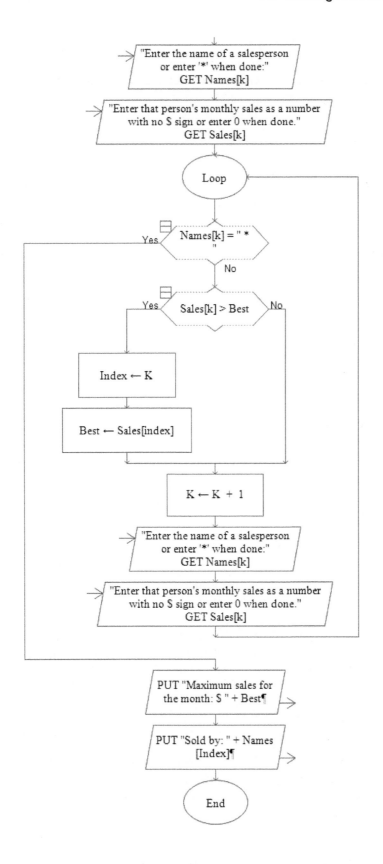

Run It: Self-Grading Math Test

The program that we will create here will generate a simple math test with ten questions. The questions will be created by selecting two random numbers between 1 and 100 and asking the student to give their sum. Student responses will be evaluated and, at the end, the student will get a grade and a list of questions that were missed. We use only ten simple addition problems in order to make the program easy to follow. However, once created, this program can be edited to make the math problems much more complex or to test different mathematical operations. The number of questions in the test can also be changed with ease.

If you want to create this program as you read this section, open a new RAPTOR program and save it with the filename grader.rap.

Problem Statement

This program will generate addition problems at random, get student inputs with the answers to each problem, compare student answers with the correct answers, and display the student's grade and a list of questions that were answered incorrectly.

Developing and Creating the Program

There are several clearly defined aspects of this program which will make it easy to develop the program with submodules (i.e., subcharts). We need to create questions, get the student to take the test, grade the test, and display the results. Therefore, we will have the following subcharts:

- Variables: The subchart we normally create in RAPTOR as a matter of convenience to declare the variables used in the program.
- Load_questions: This subchart will load two parallel arrays. One will store the questions and the other will store the answers. These arrays will contain, in our program, ten elements each because our test will have ten questions. Each question will comprise two randomly generated numbers between 1 and 100.
- Take_test: This subchart will display the questions to the students and store his or her responses in another array. This new array will also be parallel to the two previously created arrays.
- Grade_test: In this subchart, each response is compared with the correct response by using a loop and parallel arrays. If a response is incorrect, a total of incorrect responses is incremented, and the question that corresponds to each incorrect response is stored in a new array. This list of incorrect responses will be displayed at the end.
- Display_results: This subchart will calculate the student's score, using the number marked wrong and the total number of questions. It will display that score and the list of questions that were answered incorrectly.

For this program, the welcome message will be short and sweet. Besides the single line of output, the main module will only call the other submodules. Your main module should look as shown. You can create the Calls and subcharts now and follow along as we develop the code for each subchart.

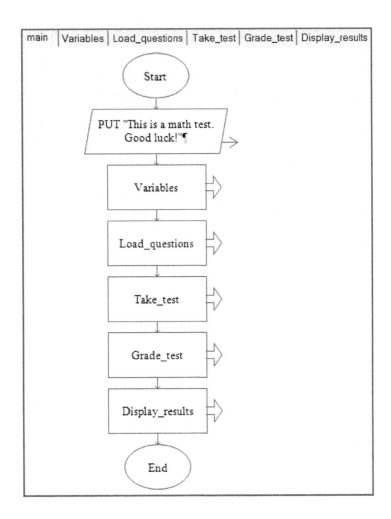

As we develop each module, we will add the variable declarations and their initial values to the Variables subchart.

The Load_questions subchart

We want to generate addition problems using two random numbers for each problem. We also need to keep track of the numbers generated because we will need them later on. Therefore, we will declare four arrays. The first and second, Num1 and Num2, are number arrays and will hold the ten pairs of numbers that we generate. Each pair—that is, Num1[1] and Num2[1], Num1[2] and Num2[2], and so on—will be used in a single addition problem. These arrays are parallel. The sum of any pair of numbers should be stored in a third parallel array, Answers, which is also of the number data type. The fourth parallel array, Questions, will be an array of strings and will hold the addition questions to be given to the student.

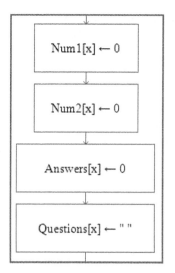

First declare and initialize these four arrays in the Variables subchart and declare a number variable, x.

Let's take a moment to explain the variable x, which is the index value of these four arrays. We have said that this math test will have ten questions. But we may not want to go through ten questions each time we run a test to see if our program works. Similarly, we may decide in the future to double the number of questions in the test. By declaring a single number variable, here called x, and setting its value to a number, we can change the number of questions in the test (and everything else about the test, as you will see) by changing the value of x in one place. For this program, x = 10. This variable should be the first thing declared in the Variables subchart.

Why must x be declared before the arrays are declared? If you can't think of the reason immediately, try to run your program (which will do nothing so far but should work without errors) both ways.

If x does not exist when it is used in the array declaration, you will get an error. ●

Now we are ready to create our addition problems.

The random function in RAPTOR: The random function in RAPTOR returns a number in the range of 0.0 up to but not including 1.0, as we have discussed earlier in the text (see Chapter 6). The code to create a random integer between 1 and 100 is familiar. It uses the floor() function and is:

```
floor(random * 100) + 1
```

We will use a loop to load the ten elements of our two number arrays, Num1 and Num2 with random numbers. Our loop will begin at 1 and will continue for ten iterations or until our counter is larger than x.

However, we can complete two more tasks in this same loop. Once we have generated two random numbers, we can store their sum in the parallel array, Answers. We can also create the questions that the student will see and store those questions in the string array, Questions.

For each iteration through the loop, the counter, which we will call count, will increase by 1. We can also use count as the index value for each of the parallel arrays. The limit value of this loop will be the number of elements in the array (i.e., the number of questions in our test) so the test condition in the loop is count > x.

The Num1 and Num2 arrays will each hold a single random number. The addition question will ask the student what is the sum of these two numbers. The displayed question should be of the form:

```
"What is the sum of A + B?"
```

assuming A and B are numbers stored in Num1 and Num2, respectively.

We will create the statement that will store the question in the Questions array and will change for each new value of Num1 and Num2. We do this by concatenating text and the array values of Num1 and Num2, using count as the index value of all three arrays, as follows:

```
Questions[count] ← "What is the sum of " + Num1[count] + " + " + ↵
                    Num2[count] + "?"
```

The answers to each question should be stored in another parallel array, Answers. The answer to each addition question is the sum of the numbers in Num1 and Num2. When we use the + operator without concatenating any text, the computer performs the mathematical addition operation. We can load Answers with the sum of the two numbers generated at each iteration by using the following:

```
Answers[count] ← Num1[count] + Num2[count]
```

Therefore, the Load_questions subchart should look like this:

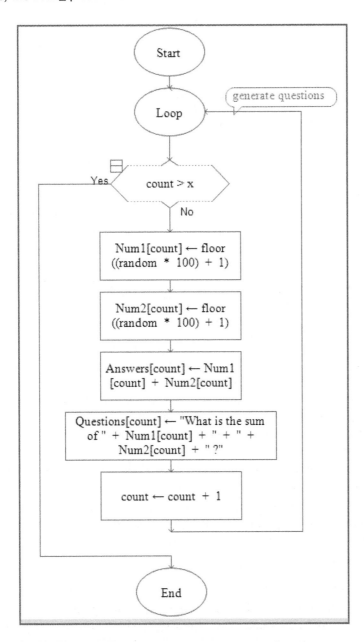

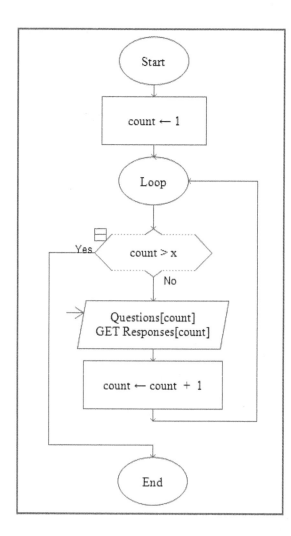

The `Take_test` subchart

For this submodule, we want the questions to be displayed, one at a time, and want to give the student a chance to enter an answer. We need one more array which we will call `Responses`. Create this array in the `Variables` subchart. As with all the other arrays, it will have x number of elements.

We need a loop to do one thing: display a question and store the response. We need to set a counter to 1. The loop should continue for as many questions as we have which, in this program is x. The loop, therefore, should end when the counter is greater than x. The `Take_test` subchart looks as shown.

The `Grade_test` subchart

This submodule is a little complicated. We want to compare the responses of the student (`Responses`) with the correct answers (`Answers`). Since our arrays are parallel, the comparison is easy. But we also want to keep track of how many answers are incorrect and, if an answer is incorrect, we want to hold that problem somewhere to display later so that the student knows where he or she made mistakes. We need to create one more array, called `Incorrect`, which should be created in the `Variables` subchart. `Incorrect` should also contain x elements. We need a variable to hold the number of incorrect responses. We will call that numeric variable `wrong` and, when it is declared in the `Variables` subchart, will have an initial value of 0.

Thus, the loop will have as many iterations as there are questions. For each iteration, it will compare a value of an element in `Responses` with the corresponding element in `Answers`. A `Selection` statement will be used at this point, and the branch taken will depend on the result of the comparison. If the value of `Answers` is the same as the value of `Responses`, we can store a message in the new array, `Incorrect`, that indicates that this answer was correct (`"OK"`). If the student's response was incorrect (i.e., the value of `Responses` is not the same as the value of `Answers`), we need to increment the value of `wrong`, which keeps track of the number of incorrect responses and we also want to hold the incorrect question. We do this by storing the value of `Questions` for that element into the parallel element of `Incorrect`.

At the end of the loop, each element of the `Incorrect` array will either hold the value `"OK"` (when a student response was correct) or hold the value of a question that has been missed. The RAPTOR program that does these tasks is shown:

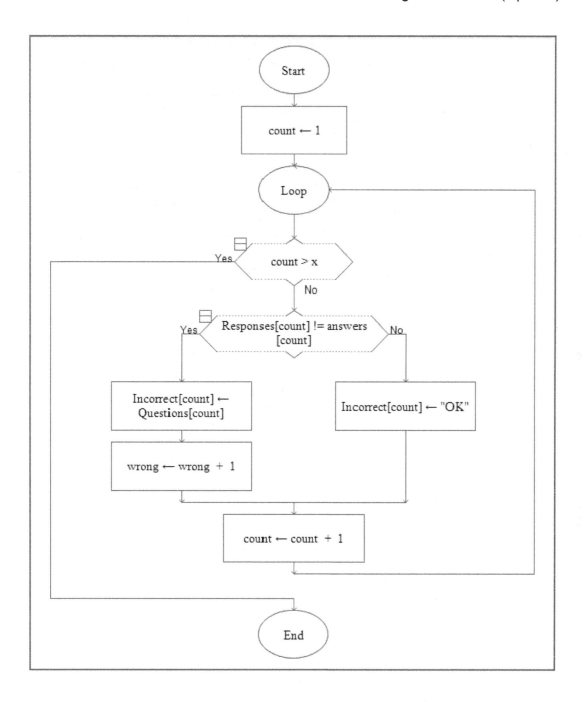

The `Display_results subchart`

This subchart will find the student's grade on this math test and display that information as well as the number of questions missed. One new variable is needed which we will call `score`. Create this variable in the `Variables` subchart with an initial value of 0. The student's score is simply the percent of correctly answered questions. We don't know how many were answered correctly but we do know how many were answered incorrectly (wrong) and how many questions are there (x). So the number answered correctly is what's left when the number wrong is subtracted from the total number. Multiplying this fraction by 100 turns the value into a percent:

```
score ← ((x - wrong)/x) * 100
```

We can then output messages telling the student his or her score (score) and the number incorrect (wrong). We also want to output a list of the missed questions. To do this, we need another loop with a nested decision structure. The loop will have x iterations. For each iteration, if the value of the corresponding element in Incorrect is "OK", nothing will happen. But if the value in an element of Incorrect is not "OK" then we know this was a missed question and we can display that value. In this way the output will consist of a list of all the questions missed by that student.

The flowchart for this subchart in RAPTOR is as shown in the next page:

Check It Out

It is now time for you to run your program. If you have created the program as shown in this section, your initial display would look similar to the one shown. Note, of course, that, since the questions are generated from random numbers, your questions will (and should) be different from those shown here. In fact, each time the program runs, the questions should be different. If they are not, you should recheck your program and make sure your random numbers are being generated correctly.

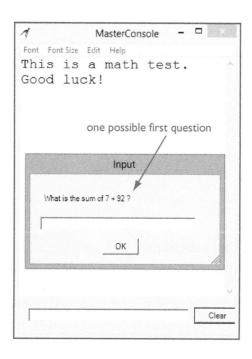

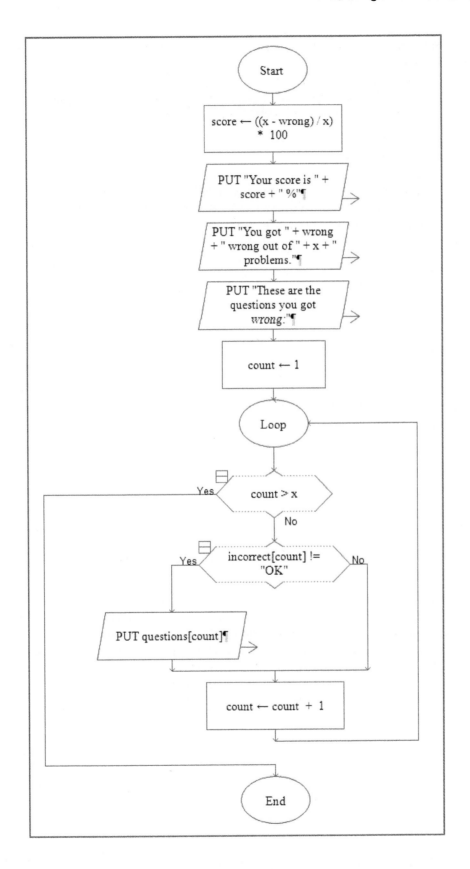

If, for example, you enter 3 incorrect responses, your final display should look similar to the one shown:

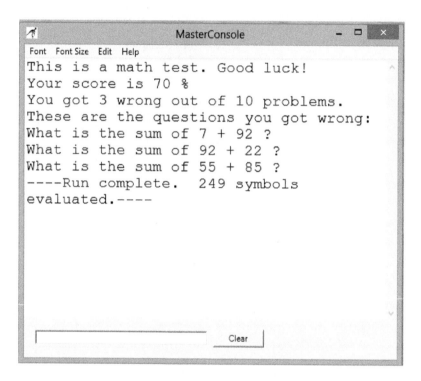

Generating More and More Math Tests

The beauty of this program is in its versatility. By changing the value of x in one place, you can have a test with 5, 50, 500 or as many questions as you want. By changing a few plus signs to minus, multiplication, or division signs you can have many different types of tests, although you might need to also change the syntax of the Questions array. You can increase or decrease the difficulty level of the test by changing the range of generated random numbers.

In fact, you could add a menu to the main program and offer various types of tests to the user. Then, depending on the user's selection, Calls could be made to different subcharts which contain code almost identical to what we have created but altered slightly to generate very different math tests. This is how real-life programs are created. Whenever possible, a variable or an array is used in lieu of a hard-coded value to increase versatility. Altering this program to create different math tests will be part of the Programming Challenges in this chapter.

Key Terms

array	matrix
concatenation operation	one-dimensional array
database	parallel arrays
driver	query
element (of an array)	subscript
flag	table
index number	two-dimensional array
list	

Chapter Summary

In this chapter, we discussed the following topics:

1. One-dimensional arrays as follows:
   - The `Declare` statement is used to define a one-dimensional array with its data type
   - Arrays and parallel arrays are used in input, processing, and output operations
   - There are many advantages to using arrays, including reducing the number of program variables and creating more efficient and more general programs
2. The relationship between parallel arrays and databases
3. Viewing strings as arrays of characters as follows:
   - A `String` variable can be declared as an array with elements that are of `Character` type
   - The `Length_Of()` function is used to find the length of a `String`
   - Strings can be manipulated by examining the array in which the string is located
4. Two-dimensional arrays as follows:
   - Two-dimensional arrays are declared as `Array[X,Y]` where `X` represents the number of rows and `Y` represents the number of columns
   - Two-dimensional arrays are used in input, processing, and output operations

Review Exercises

Fill in the Blank

1. A variable that is used to indicate whether a certain action has taken place is called a(n) _____.
2. Each element in an array is identified by its _____.

3. The Declare statement allocates _____ storage locations to the array Name[25].

4. The length of the string called MyName which contains the name "Arnold" is _____.

5. If the arrays Score1, Score2, and Score3 have the same size and the corresponding elements contain related data, they are said to be _____ arrays.

True or False

6. T F The elements of an array are stored in consecutive storage locations in the computer's internal memory.

7. T F One advantage of using subscripted variables (an array) is that they take up fewer storage locations than the same number of unsubscripted variables.

8. T F An array may have some elements that are numbers and other elements that are strings.

9. T F If a declaration statement allocates 100 storage locations to an array, the program must assign values to all 100 elements.

10. T F The following statement:
    Declare Array1[10], Array2[20] As Integer
    allocates storage space for 200 variables.

11. T F In two parallel arrays, all corresponding elements must be of the same data type.

12. T F Array elements are normally stored in a computer's memory in a sequence of consecutive storage locations.

13. T F Parallel arrays must be of the same size.

14. T F Parallel arrays must be of the same data type.

15. T F A database consists of many tables.

16. T F The length of a string in a Character array that has been declared as:
    Declare Chr[10] As Character
    is always 10.

17. T F One- and two-dimensional arrays must be declared in the same statement.

18. T F If we know that 100 elements have been allocated to the two-dimensional array A, then both subscripts of A must run from 0 to 9; that is, A must have 10 rows and 10 columns.

Short Answer

19. Write a program segment that inputs up to 25 whole numbers (integers) from the user, terminated by 0, into an array called Numbers.

20. Write a program segment that displays the contents of a previously declared array of strings called Names. Assume that the last entry in Names is "ZZZ", which should not be displayed.

21. What is the output of code corresponding to the following pseudocode?

```
Declare N As Integer
Declare K As Integer
Declare X[100] As Integer
Set N = 4
Set K = 1
While K <= N
  Set X[K] = K^2
  Set K = K + 1
End While
Write X[N/2]
Write X[1] + " " + X[N - 1]
```

22. What is the output of code corresponding to the following pseudocode if the user inputs 2, 3, 4, 5?

```
Declare Number As Integer
Declare Count As Integer
Declare Sums[5] As Integer
Set Count = 0
Set Sums[0] = 0
While Count < 4
  Write "Enter a number: "
  Input Number
  Set Sums[Count + 1] = Sums[Count] + Number
  Set Count = Count + 1
End While
While Count >= 0
  Write Sums[Count]
  Set Count = Count - 1
End While
```

23. What is the output of code corresponding to the following pseudocode?

```
Declare A[20] As Integer
Declare B[20] As Integer
Declare K As Integer
For (K = 1; K <= 3; K++)
  Set B[K] = K
End For
For (K = 1; K <= 3; K++)
  Set A[K] = B[4-K]
  Write A[K] + " " + B[K]
End For
```

24. Explain why a variable that is used as a flag to indicate when a condition becomes true or false is normally a Boolean variable.

For Short Answer Questions 25 and 26 refer to the following pseudocode:

```
Declare Name[20] As Character
Declare K As Integer
Set K = 0
While K < 8
  Set Name[K] = "A"
  Set K = K + 1
End While
Set Name[8] = " "
Set Name[9] = "B"
```

25. Write a single statement that displays the first and last characters in Name.

26. Write a program segment that displays the characters in Name except the blank.

    In Short Answer Questions 27–30, an array has been declared by the following:

    ```
    Declare FullName[25] As Character
    ```

    and contains a person's first and last names, separated by a blank.

27. Write a statement that displays the length of the string in the array FullName.

28. Write a program segment that displays the number of letters in the person's first name.

29. Write a program segment that displays the person's initials, with a period after each initial.

30. Write a program segment that displays the person's last name.

31. Assume you are writing a program for a man who sells picture frames that he makes in his garage. List at least three types of information that he might require to be stored in parallel arrays if he wanted to keep track of his customer database.

32. Write a program segment that declares a two-dimensional array X of integers with five rows and five columns and inputs 25 integers into this array from the user.

33. Write a program segment that sums the elements in each row of the array X of Exercise 32 and displays these five numbers.

34. What is the output of code corresponding to the following pseudocode?

```
Declare Q[10,10] As Integer
Declare R, C, As Integer
For (R = 1; R <= 3; R++)
  For (C = 1; C <= 3; C++)
    If R == C Then
      Set Q[R,C] = 1
    Else
      Set Q[R,C] = 0
    End If
  End For(C)
End For(R)
For (R = 1; R <= 3; R++)
```

```
      For (C = 1; C <= 3; C++)
         Write Q[R,C]
      End For(C)
   End For(R)
```

Programming Challenges

For each of the following Programming Challenges, use the modular approach and pseudocode to design a suitable program to solve it.

1. Input a list of positive numbers, terminated by 0, into an array Numbers[]. Then display the array and the largest and smallest number in it.

2. Create a program that allows the user to input a list of first names into one array and last names into a parallel array. Input should be terminated when the user enters a sentinel character. The output should be a list of email addresses where the address is of the following form: first.last@mycollege.edu

3. Input a list of employee names and salaries stored in parallel arrays. The salaries should be floating point numbers in increments of 100. For example, a salary of $36,000 should be input as 36.0 and a salary of $85,900 should be input as 85.9. Find the mean (average) salary and display the names and salaries of employees who earn within a range of $5,000 from the mean. In other words, if the mean salary is $45,000, all employees who earn between $40,000 and $50,000 should be displayed.

4. Write a program that allows a small business owner to input, in parallel arrays, the type of item, its cost, and the number in stock. The program should output this information in the form of a table. You can assume that columns will be correctly formatted at a later time. The output will look something like this:

```
Item Name        Cost         Number in Stock

Widget           25.00        4

    .              .                .

    .              .                .

    .              .                .

Wombet           47.50        9
```

Question 5 is designed specifically to accompany the Running With RAPTOR Math Test that was created in this chapter.

5. Revise the Math Test created in the Running With RAPTOR section in this chapter to create a math exam that tests the following:
   - There should be 20 division questions
   - The questions should be of the form Num1 / Num2
   - Num1 can be any number between 0 and 10, inclusive
   - Num2 can be any number between 1 and 100, inclusive
   - The output should include the student's score, number wrong, and a list of the questions missed

Searching and Sorting Arrays

8

We have learned that arrays hold lists of related data and that parallel arrays can increase the number of relationships we can have between data. When we write programs we often find that we need to **search** a one-dimensional array (or list) to locate a given item or to **sort** it in a specified order. Consequently, there are many algorithms available to perform each of these tasks. In this chapter, we will present several techniques for searching and sorting an array. Sorting and searching techniques form the backbone of relational database management systems that are used in every aspect of commerce and government throughout the world today.

After reading this chapter, you will be able to do the following:

- Use the serial search technique to search an array for a specified element
- Use the bubble sort technique to sort an array into a specified order
- Use the binary search procedure to search an array for a specified element
- Use the selection sort procedure to sort an array into a specified order
- Combine sorting and searching algorithms with parallel arrays to locate data in related arrays

Searching and Sorting

One characteristic of human beings that may distinguish us from other animals is our need to classify. Humans like to bring order out of chaos. And, in many cases, bringing order out of chaos is more than a desire; it is a requirement.

Imagine if, as you fold your big pile of laundry, you put each item into a dresser drawer, regardless of what type of item it was. When one drawer was filled to the top, you started on the next drawer and then the next, and so on, until all the laundry was folded and put away. How would you go about finding your green tee-shirt with the picture of a raptor on it when you wanted to wear it the next day? Or the match to your white gym sock with the red trim? You know these items are in your dresser but you might find them on top of the first drawer or you might have to search through every item in every drawer before finding what you want.

This could prove annoying. But multiply that annoyance by a factor of 1,000 or a million and imagine what it would be like for a large clothing chain store if it kept a database of all inventory by simply appending each new item to a list. Each time a customer wanted to buy an item online, a computer program would have to try to match the desired item to thousands of items in the list.

Without the ability to keep data in some order (sorted) or the ability to quickly and efficiently locate a needed item (searching), you might be kept waiting for a very long time when you try to complete a shopping order online, find the song you want to hear in an online music site, or register for your classes at school next semester.

This is why this chapter focuses on various methods used to sort and search through data that is stored in arrays.

8.1 Introduction to Searching and Sorting

When we write programs we often find that we need to search through a one-dimensional array to locate a given item or to sort that array in some particular order. Consequently, there are many algorithms that have been designed by programmers to perform each of these tasks. In this chapter we present only two sorting algorithms and two searching algorithms but there are many others. The important thing for you to learn is, while you could probably think of ways to write your own original programs to search or sort, you can apply these algorithms and save yourself a lot of time and effort. You should also know how to evaluate algorithms that are available for a task and be able to select which best serves your purpose in a given situation.

The Serial Search Technique

Suppose you have arrived at the airport to meet your best friend who is flying in from her overseas vacation. You know her flight number but not the arrival time or gate, so you consult the posted flight information, which is given in the following tabular form:

Flight	Origin	Time	Gate
43	Kansas City	4:15 p.m.	5
21	St. Louis	5:05 p.m.	4
96	London	5:23 p.m.	2
35	Dubuque	5:30 p.m.	7
...	...	...	...
...	...	...	...
...	...	...	...

To find the arrival time and gate of your friend's flight, you scan the leftmost column until you locate her flight number and then you move across that row to read the corresponding time and gate in the last two columns.

In computer lingo, you have performed a *table lookup*. In data processing terminology, the item you were seeking (your friend's flight number) is called the **search key**. The search key is a particular item in the list of all such items (all the flight numbers); we call this list the **table keys**. In general, the data in the table are called the *table values*. The way in which you looked for a desired flight number, checking the numbers in the order listed, makes this a **serial search**.

Basic Steps in a Serial Search

1. **Load the table:** this is where we input the data in the table, often from a file (see Chapter 10), into parallel arrays, one for each column of the table.
2. **Search the array of table keys:** here, we compare the search key with the elements of this array, one by one, until a match occurs or the end of the array is reached.
3. **Display the search key and corresponding table values:** or if the search key is not found in the array, display a message to this effect.

Use a Flag to Indicate a Successful Search

Pointer

In Step 2 of the search procedure described above, we loop through the array of table keys to see if any element is identical to the given search key. There can be two results: the search will be successful—the item we are seeking (the search key) will match one of the table keys—or the search will fail—no match will occur.

When we exit the loop and carry out Step 3 of the procedure, we must know which of these two possibilities has occurred so that the appropriate message can be displayed. An elegant way to indicate whether the search was successful is to use a variable known as a flag. We have used flags earlier in the text in other types of programs.

Recall that a **flag** is a `Boolean` variable used to indicate whether a certain action has taken place. Usually a value of 0 indicates that the action has not occurred; a value of 1 indicates that it has occurred. In a serial search, we set the flag equal to 0 before we begin the search. If a match occurs within the search loop, we change the flag's value to 1. This means that if the search loop never finds the item we are looking for, the flag's value will never change and it will be 0 at the end. But if the search loop finds what we are looking for, the flag is changed to 1. Thus, when we exit the loop the value of the flag can be used to verify the success or failure of the search and to display the proper message.

Pseudocode for a Serial Search

Consider a list of table keys contained in an array named `KeyData`. The array has `N` elements. We want to find an item called `Key`, which, we hope, is one of the elements in the array. The flowchart shown in Figure 8.1 pictures the logic used in this serial search. In this flowchart, the variable `Found` is the flag for the search and `Index` is the array subscript.

The pseudocode for performing this serial search follows:

```
//Set the subscript (Index) of the current table key to 0
Set Index = 0
//Set a flag (Found) to 0
Set Found = 0
While (Found == 0) AND (Index < N)
  If KeyData[Index] == Key Then
    Set Found = 1
  End If
  Set Index = Index + 1
End While
If Found == 1 Then
  Write KeyData[Index - 1]
Else
  Write "The item you are searching for was not found."
End If
```

In this pseudocode, the variable `Index` is used within the loop to hold the current array subscript. The variable `Found` is a flag that indicates whether the search has been successful. Note that we could, alternatively, have used a `For` loop with the counter, `Index`, running from 0 to `N - 1` but a `While` loop is more efficient because it is exited as soon as `Key` is found; the `For` loop would unnecessarily continue to check the remaining elements of the array for `Key`. When we exit from the `While` loop, we check the value of `Found`. A value of 1 indicates that the search was successful and that the item, `Key`, has been found among the table keys. The value of `Index - 1` tells us the location of `Key` in `KeyData` because `Index - 1` is the subscript that identifies the element in the array where the item is located. If the value of `Found` is 0 when we exit the loop, we know that the search item, `Key`, was not found and we display this fact. Example 8.1 provides a particular instance of the serial search technique.

Figure 8.1 Flowchart for a serial search

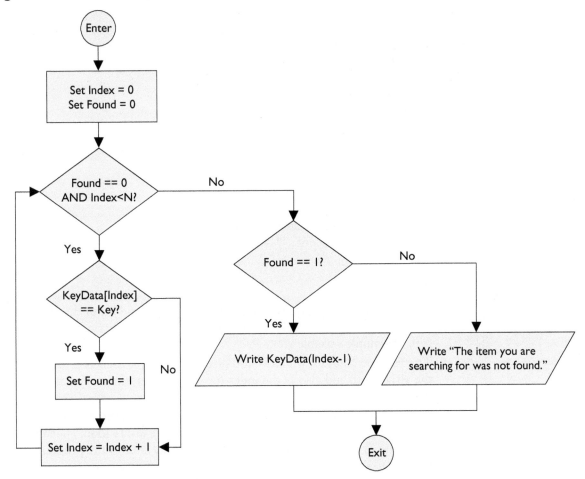

Example 8.1 **A Serial Search with Parallel Arrays**

This program segment displays the test score for a particular student when the student's identification number is input by the user. It searches an array called IDNumbers, which consists of identification numbers for the ID number that is entered by the user (IDKey). Then it does the following:

- Displays the corresponding student name and test score contained in two parallel arrays named Names and Scores, if the number IDKey is found in the IDNumbers array or
- Displays an appropriate message if the IDKey is not found in the IDNumbers array

We assume that the arrays IDNumbers, Names, and Scores have already been declared and loaded with the necessary data. We also assume that the number of elements in each of these parallel arrays is N and that the variables IDKey, Index, and Found have been declared as Integer variables.

```
 1  Write "Enter a student ID number: "
 2  Input IDKey
 3  Set Index = 0
 4  Set Found = 0
 5  While (Found == 0) AND (Index < N)
 6    If IDNumbers[Index] == IDKey Then
 7      Set Found = 1
 8    End If
 9    Set Index = Index + 1
10  End While
11  If Found == 0 Then
12    Write "Student ID not found"
13  Else
14    Write "ID Number: " + IDKey
15    Write "Student name: " + Names[Index - 1]
16    Write "Test score: " + Scores[Index - 1]
17  End If
```

What Happened?

- Lines 1 and 2 of this program segment prompt for and input the ID number for the student we are seeking. Notice that the ID number of the student we seek is a simple variable (IDKey).

- The variable (Index), which is initialized on line 3, is used as a counter in the While loop and also as the index (or subscript) of the arrays, as we search through the arrays.

- The variable (Found), which is initialized on line 4, is used as our flag. If we find the ID number of the student we want in the While loop, Found is set to 1 (on line 7) so we know what message to display later in the program.

- Notice that line 4 sets the value of Found to 0 while the statement on line 5 compares the value of Found with 0. This is an example of how both the assignment and the comparison operators are used in a program.

- Lines 5–10 contain the While loop that does the following things:
  - The conditions under which the loop will continue are set up here. Line 5 contains a compound condition with an AND operator. You will remember that this means both parts of the condition must be true for the loop to continue. This line says that as long as the IDKey has not been found (Found will still contain the value of 0) AND Index is less than the number of elements in the ID numbers array (Index < N), continue doing the loop. As soon as one of those conditions is not true, the loop ends. This allows the loop to end as soon as a match is found.
  - The If-Then clause on lines 6–8 checks to see if the ID number of the student in the array whose subscript is Index matches the IDKey. If that is the case, the flag (Found) is set to 1. There is no Else clause here because if there is no match, nothing needs to be done.
  - Line 9 increments the counter (Index), which counts the number of times through the loop to ensure that we only loop through as many times as

there are students in the array and sets the correct subscript for the comparison, which begins at the next pass through the loop.

- Line 10 ends the `While` loop.

- At this point there are two possibilities. In one case, the loop has gone around `N` times so all ID numbers in the `IDNumbers` array have been checked and no match has been found. In this case, `Found` still is 0. The only other possibility is that a match has been discovered and `Found` has the value of 1. The value of `Index` is one higher than it was when the match was found.

- Lines 11–17 display the appropriate message depending on whether a match has been found.

Self Check for Section 8.1

8.1 Why would you choose to use an algorithm for searching an array such as the serial search algorithm presented in this section instead of developing your own program code to search an array?

8.2 True or false? The serial search algorithm requires that the array to be searched is in order, either alphabetical or numerical.

8.3 Write a program segment that searches an array of 100 names, `Client`, for the name `"Grokofiev"`. If the name is found, the program should display `"This client is found"`; if not, it should display `"This client is not in this list"`.

8.4 Add to the program created in Self Check Question 8.3. In the new program, assume there are parallel arrays, `Client` and `DateSeen`. Search for the name `"Grokofiev"` and, if found, the program should display `"Grokofiev was last seen on XXX"` where XXX represents the date that corresponds to the entry for `"Grokofiev"` in the `DateSeen` array. If `"Grokofiev"` is not found, the display should be `"Client Grokofiev is not in the list"`.

8.2 The Bubble Sort Technique

When we sort data we arrange it in some prescribed order. For numbers, the "prescribed order" would normally be ascending (from smallest to largest) or descending (from largest to smallest). For names, the prescribed order is usually alphabetical.

As long as the number of items to be sorted is relatively small (say, fewer than 100), the **bubble sort** algorithm provides a reasonably quick and simple way to sort. To apply this technique, we make several sweeps (or passes) through the data, and on each pass we compare all adjacent pairs of data items and interchange the data in an adjacent pair if they are not already in the proper order. We continue making passes until no interchanges are necessary in an entire pass, which indicates that the data is sorted.

Swapping Values

If you brought a peanut butter sandwich for lunch and your friend brought a cheese sandwich, the two of you could swap lunches in one motion. You hold out your sandwich, your friend holds out his; he takes your sandwich and you take his. For even a fraction of a second, one of you holds two sandwiches and the other holds none. A computer cannot make this kind of exchange. In a computer each value is stored in its own location in memory. If you put a cheese sandwich in the location that previously held a peanut butter sandwich, the peanut butter sandwich will be replaced by the cheese sandwich and disappear into cyberspace. So before we discuss the bubble sort algorithm, first we must understand how the computer swaps the values of two items.

How would you change the contents of two boxes if each box can only contain one item at a time? We start with `Blue` in Box1 and `White` in Box2 and want to end up with `White` in Box1 and `Blue` in Box2. But if we put `Blue` into Box2, we have lost the value of `White`. That's the problem a computer programmer faces. So we create an empty temporary storage space to save the contents of Box1 while we change its value to `White`, as shown in Figure 8.2.

Figure 8.2 Trading places: the swap routine

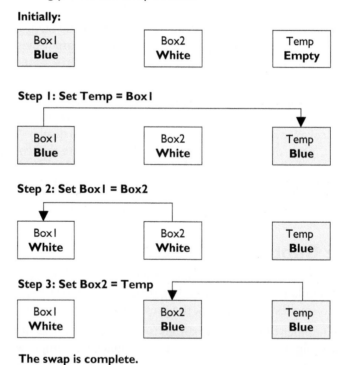

Example 8.2 shows the pseudocode for the box shuffle. We'll name our variables `Box1` and `Box2` and assume that `Box1` initially contains the string `"Blue"` and `Box2` initially contains `"White"`. We will also use a variable named `Temp` which initially contains a blank space.

Example 8.2 **Swapping Boxes**

```
Set Temp = " "      /* The Temp variable is initialized to contain just
                       a blank space */

Set Temp = Box1     /* Now the value "Blue" is in two places—it's still
                       in Box1 and also in Temp */

Set Box1 = Box2     /* Now the value of Box1 is "White" and "White" is
                       still in Box2 but we have held the value of "Blue"
                       in Temp */

Set Box2 = Temp     /* The value of Box2 has been replaced by "Blue"
                       and the swap is complete—Box1 and Box2 have
                       exchanged values. The variable Temp still has
                       "Blue" but we don't care since Temp is not used for
                       anything else. */
```

The method used to interchange the values of two variables that was demonstrated in Figure 8.2 and in Example 8.2 is called a **swap routine**. It will be used many times from now on in this book and will become one of your most important tools as you continue to write programs. If you spend a few extra minutes now to ensure that you understand how the swap routine works, you will be glad you did! We'll do one more example using the swap routine now.

Example 8.3 **Colorful Tee-shirts**

This example will demonstrate once again how to use the swap routine. In this program segment the user is asked to enter two colors for a club tee-shirt. The shirt can be either yellow or green and the logo can be either black or red. The display will be of the form "You have selected a XXX shirt with a YYY logo" where XXX represents the shirt color and YYY represents the logo color. If the user enters colors in the wrong order, they must be swapped. We assume that three String variables have been previously declared: Temp, Shirt, and Logo.

```
 1  Write "Pick two colors: either yellow or green and ↵
              either red or black."
 2  Write "Enter your first color: "
 3  Input Shirt
 4  Write "Enter your second color: "
 5  Input Logo
 6  If (Shirt != "yellow") OR (Shirt != "green") Then
 7    Set Temp = Shirt
 8    Set Shirt = Logo
 9    Set Logo = Temp
10  End If
11  Write "You have selected a " + Shirt + " shirt with a " ↵
              + Logo + " logo."
```

What Happened?

In this program, if the user enters either "yellow" or "green" on line 3, the If-Then clause on lines 6 through 10 is skipped. We also assume, for our purposes here, that the user follows directions and, if "yellow" or "green" has been selected for the first input, only either "red" or "black" will be selected for the second input on line 5.

But if the user enters either "red" or "black" on line 3, then we know one of the shirt colors ("green" or "yellow") has been entered on line 5. In this case, we want to switch the values in Shirt and Logo so a correct tee-shirt color can be ordered with one of the two available logo colors. The swap routine, on lines 7–9, makes this switch.

First, the incorrect color (either "red" or "black" is stored in Temp on line 7. Then Shirt is given a correct shirt color (the value presently in Logo) on line 8. Finally, the incorrect logo color is replaced with a valid logo color by retrieving that value from Temp on line 9.

Using the Bubble Sort Algorithm

To illustrate the bubble sort, first we will do a simple example by hand. Figure 8.3 demonstrates how to sort five numbers in a data set so they are arranged from smallest to largest. The numbers are initially stored as follows:

    9   13   5   8   6

A computer can only do one thing at a time, so first it must compare two numbers and decide if they need to switch places. After it makes this decision, it can move on to the next pair. This is why, in this example, there are three passes and each pass has four steps. Figure 8.3 shows, for each pass, the data at the start of the pass on the left and the results of the four comparisons in the next four columns. If an interchange takes place, the arrows cross, indicating which items have been swapped.

In the first pass (the top row of Figure 8.3), the first number (9) is compared with the next number (13) to see if the first is larger than the second. Since 9 is less than 13, no swap is made. Then the second number (13) is compared with the third number (5). In this case, because 5 is less than 13, the numbers are switched. Remember that the computer can only do one thing at a time. Each time you see an exchange in Figure 8.3, a swap routine, using a temporary variable as a holding place, has been used. Further, a computer can't think, as you might, "Well, 5 is also smaller than 9 so I should switch the 5 and 9." It will do that on the next pass, but it can't do it yet. After the 5 and 13 are swapped, the number in the third place (which is now 13) is compared with the number in the fourth place (8). Once again, since 8 is less than 13, they are swapped. Now 13 is in fourth place and 13 is compared with the number in the last place (6). Because 13 is larger than 6, they are swapped. One pass is complete.

On the second pass, we return to the first number. It is still a 9. But now the second number is a 5, so when these two are compared, the 5 moves to first place. Now the pass continues as before. By the end of the second pass you will see that the second-largest number has moved down to the fourth place.

The bubble sort gets its name from the fact that, when sorting in ascending order, the larger numbers "sink" to the bottom (the end) of the list and the smaller ones "bubble" to the top. After the first pass the largest number will be at the bottom of the list; after

Figure 8.3 The bubble sort

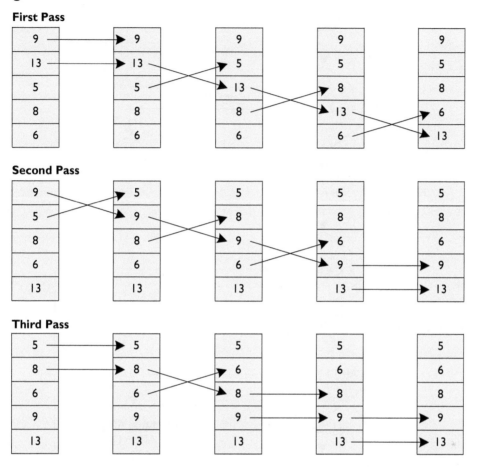

First Pass

Second Pass

Third Pass

Fourth Pass
No interchanges take place; the numbers are sorted.

the second pass the second largest will be next to last; and so forth. In this example, only three passes are needed to sort the numbers. This is simply a result of the way the original list was given. If the list had been written differently, we might have needed up to four passes to sort. In general, to sort N items, it will take at most N - 1 passes through the list to sort them (and one additional pass to determine that they are sorted).

The bubble sort of an array named A of N numbers in ascending order is described in the following general pseudocode. Figure 8.4 shows a flowchart of the bubble sort logic.

General pseudocode for the bubble sort:

```
While (array A is not sorted)
   For (K = 0; K < N - 1; K++)
      If A[K] > A[K + 1] Then
         Interchange A[K] and A[K + 1]
      End If
   End For
End While
```

Figure 8.4 Flowchart for the bubble sort

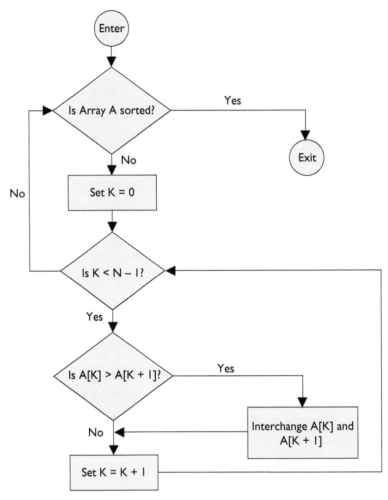

This pseudocode is somewhat vague. We can neither just say "interchange two values" because as we have seen, we need to use the swap routine nor can we simply say "while the array is not sorted". In Figure 8.3, we saw that while the maximum number of passes needed to sort N numbers is N - 1, some data can be sorted in fewer passes. If we had a list of 100 numbers to sort and only 2 numbers were out of order, it would be inefficient to allow the loop to continue for 99 passes. Therefore, we should include some way to indicate that the data is sorted and that the loop can end. We should refine the previous pseudocode as follows:

1. We use the swap routine to interchange array elements A[K] and A[K + 1] by temporarily copying one of them to a temporary location and then swapping their values:

```
Set Temp = A[K]
Set A[K] = A[K + 1]
Set A[K + 1] = Temp
```

Try it by executing these statements with A[K] = 3 and A[K + 1] = 5.

2. To determine when the list is sorted, we borrow a technique from the serial search algorithm given in Section 8.1 and use a flag. In the bubble sort algorithm, a flag value of 0 indicates that during the latest pass, an interchange took place. Therefore, we initialize the flag to 0 and continue to re-enter the While loop as long as its value remains 0. Once inside the loop, we immediately set the flag equal to 1 and change it back to 0 if an interchange takes place. If no interchange takes place (meaning the data is sorted), the flag remains 1 and the loop is exited.

Example 8.4 gives detailed pseudocode for a typical bubble sort.

Example 8.4 **Input Numbers in Any Order, See Them Sorted!**

This program implements the bubble sort procedure described above. It inputs numbers from the user, sorts them in descending order (from largest to smallest), and then displays the results. Imagine how convenient this would be for Professor Merlin. He could enter his students' test scores in any order and in a few seconds, all the scores could be sorted. This might help him decide how much the grades should be curved.

In this program segment, the numbers are input into an array named TestScores. Each test score entered is stored in a variable named OneScore. The variable, Flag, will indicate when enough passes have been made to sort the whole array, regardless of whether the array is full (with 100 elements) or partially full.

After you read the pseudocode and the explanation, pick some values for test scores of your own and walk through the pseudocode to verify that it works and that you understand what each line does.

```
1   Declare TestScores[100] As Float
2   Declare Count As Integer
3   Declare Flag As Boolean
4   Declare K As Integer
5   Declare OneScore As Float
6   Declare Temp As Float
7   Write "Enter a test score; enter -9999 when done: "
8   Input OneScore
9   Set Count = 0
10  While OneScore != -9999
11    Set TestScores[Count] = OneScore
12    Set Count = Count + 1
13    Write "Enter a test score; enter -9999 when done: "
14    Input OneScore
15  End While(OneScore)
16  Set Flag = 0
17  While Flag == 0
18    Set Flag = 1
19    Set K = 0
20    While K <= (Count - 2)
21      If TestScores[K] < TestScores[K + 1] Then
```

```
22          Set Temp = TestScores[K]
23          Set TestScores[K] = TestScores[K + 1]
24          Set TestScores[K + 1] = Temp
25          Set Flag = 0
26        End If
27       Set K = K + 1
28     End While(K)
29   End While(Flag)
30   Write "Sorted list . . . "
31   Set K = 0
32   While K <= (Count - 1)
33     Write TestScores[K]
34       Set K = K + 1
35   End While(K)
```

What Happened?

- Lines 1–15 declare and load the array, TestScores, with up to 100 scores. The counter, Count, is initialized to 0. The first While loop (lines 10–15) accomplishes the input of all the scores and counts how many scores are entered by the user. The array, TestScores, was originally declared to have 100 elements, so this program segment can only sort up to 100 numbers. However, it will stop asking for numbers when the user enters the sentinel value of -9999, so Professor Merlin could use this program for a class of 20 or 50 or any number up to 100.

- At the end of this loop, the value of Count is the same as the number of scores entered into the array. In other words, if Professor Merlin has entered 45 test scores, Count also equals 45. Can you see why? On line 8 the first score is entered and on line 9 Count is set equal to 0. Then, within the loop (lines 10–15), Count is incremented *after* the value of OneScore is stored in TestScores[0]. Now, there is one element in the array and Count equals 1. In effect, Count "catches up" with the number of elements in the TestScores array. However, later in the program we want Count to keep track of the subscripts of the elements in the array. For example, if there are 45 elements in the array, the subscripts on these elements are, as you know, 0 through 44. We must remember this as we continue with the program.

- Line 16 begins the interesting part. The Flag is set equal to 0. The next While loop (lines 17–28) implements the general bubble sort procedure given prior to this example.

Let's walk through lines 17–28 with a few test values. Assume you have input the following four test scores: 82, 77, 98, and 85.

Line 17 sets up the condition for the outer loop (the While loop) of the sorting process. When Flag no longer is 0, this loop will end. Line 18 changes the value of Flag to 1. Line 20 begins the inner loop. It begins with the variable, K, which line 19 sets to 0. This variable is used to identify the indexes of array elements. K will be incremented by 1 for each pass through this loop. The test condition says to continue the loop until K = (Count - 2). Remember that Count is equal to the number of elements in the array, but the indices of the array begin at 0 and go up through the value of Count - 1. The bubble sort compares one element in the array with the next element so the last comparison is between the next-to-last element and the last element. This is why we only need K to go up to the next-to-last element, Count - 2. In our example, we have four elements in the array so the loop will end after three passes when K = 2.

On the first pass, line 21 tests to see if TestScores[0] is less than TestScores[1]. In this example TestScores[0] = 82 and TestScores[1] = 77 so the first element is not less than the second and no swap is made. Now (line 27) K = 1.

On the second pass through this loop, we compare TestScores[1] (77) with TestScores[2] (98). Since 77 is less than 98, the swap is made (lines 22–24) and Flag is set to 0. At this point, the value of Flag does not come into play; it will be significant later on. Now TestScores[1] contains the value 98 and TestScores[2] contains the value 77.

Now K = 2 and the loop compares TestScores[2] (77) with TestScores[3] (85). Since 77 is less than 85, these values are swapped. Flag is still equal to 0. However, K is now 3, which is greater than the test condition so the loop ends. At this point the array contains the following values:

```
TestScores[0] = 82
TestScores[1] = 98
TestScores[2] = 85
TestScores[3] = 77
```

Notice that the lowest value has "bubbled" down to the last place after all the comparisons have been made.

Control now goes back to line 17. The value of Flag is checked, and since it's still 0, the inner loop begins again. Line 18 sets Flag to 1, K is set back to 0, and lines 20–28 compare all the values again. In this iteration of the outer loop, the inner loop swaps TestScores[0] with TestScores[1] and then TestScores[1] with TestScores[2]. Flag is set back to 0. When K becomes greater than 2, the inner loop ends again and the array now looks as follows:

```
TestScores[0] = 98
TestScores[1] = 85
TestScores[2] = 82
TestScores[3] = 77
```

Once again control goes back to line 17. Since Flag is 0, the outer loop begins again. Flag is now set to 1. This time no swaps will be made in the inner loop. This means that the Flag will never be set back to 0 because the If-Then statements on lines 21–26 are never executed.

Now, when control goes back to line 17, the test condition is false. Flag is not equal to 0, so the outer loop ends and all the values have been sorted. Control passes to line 30 and then to the little While loop at the end, which displays all the sorted values.

Other Sorts of Sorting

We can use the pseudocode presented in Example 8.4, with little or no modification, to perform several related sorting tasks, as follows:

- Virtually the same pseudocode can also be used to sort numbers in ascending order. The only modification needed here is to change the first line of the If statement to read as follows:

  If TestScores[K] > TestScores[K + 1] Then . . .

- Almost identical pseudocode can be used to sort names alphabetically. Of course in this case, the array TestScores must be declared to be an array of Strings, which we would probably rename something like Names, and OneScore must be a String variable, which would probably be renamed OneName. And, since alphabetical order is actually sorted from smallest to largest, the line that tests if one value is less than the next value would have to be reversed, as described above.

Self Check for Section 8.2

8.5 What is the output if the following program segment is coded and run?
```
Declare Bird As String
Declare Cat As String
Declare Temp As String
Set Bird = "black"
Set Cat = "green"
Set Temp = Bird
Set Bird = Cat
Set Cat = Temp
Write "My bird has " + Bird + "feathers."
Write "My cat is " + Cat + "."
```

8.6 What will be stored in each variable after the swap routine in the pseudocode shown below has been coded and run given that:
```
X = "X"     Y = "Y"     Z = "Z"
Set Z = X
Set X = Y
Set Y = Z
```

8.7 True or false? The bubble sort can only be used to sort a list of numbers.

8.8 How many interchanges take place in sorting the numbers 3, 2, 1 in ascending order using a bubble sort?

8.9 Write a program that sorts an array of 100 names, Client, in alphabetical order using the bubble sort method.

8.3 The Binary Search

In the previous sections, we described simple methods for searching and sorting arrays. However, for arrays that contain huge amounts of data, these methods are not very efficient. In this section, we will introduce a more efficient searching technique.

Use the Binary Search for Large Arrays

The **binary search** method is a good way to search a large amount of data for a particular item, which is called the *search key*. It is considerably more efficient than the serial search technique, discussed in Section 8.1. However, a binary search requires that the table keys, the array of data to be searched, is in numerical or alphabetical order.

To illustrate how the binary search method works, let's suppose that you want to look up a certain word (the target word) in a dictionary. If you used a serial search to find it, starting with the first page and going through the dictionary word by word, it might take hours or even days. A more reasonable approach would be as follows:

1. Open the dictionary to the target word's approximate location.
2. Check the target word against an entry on that page to determine if you have gone too far or not far enough.
3. Repeat Steps 1 and 2 until you have located the target word.

This example demonstrates the basic idea underlying the binary search procedure. To carry out a binary search, first we compare the search key (the **target**) with the table key midway through the given array. Because the array data is ordered, we can then determine in which *half* of the array the search key lies. We now compare the search key with the table key in the middle of this half, and in doing so it is possible to determine in which *quarter* of the array the search key is located. Then, we look at the middle entry in this quarter, and so forth, continuing this process until we find the search key.

The following general pseudocode performs a binary search, assuming that the array named `Array` is sorted in ascending order. The variable `Key` represents the item sought and the array `Array` is a given array of a certain number of table keys. Recall the following:

- The function `Int(X)` produces the integer obtained by discarding the fractional part of `X`, if any.
- A program flag is a variable that indicates whether a specified action has taken place. Typically, a flag value of `1` indicates that the action has occurred; a value of `0` indicates that it has not occurred.

Example 8.5 demonstrates the general pseudocode for the binary search.

Example 8.5 General Pseudocode for the Binary Search[1]

In the following pseudocode, the variables `Low` and `High` represent the smallest and the largest array indexes in the part of the array currently under consideration. Recall that an array begins with `0` as the first index, and the highest index number is actually one less than the number of elements in the array. If the highest index in this array is `N`, then the number of elements in the array is `N + 1`. The variable `Key` represents the value we are looking for.

[1]To implement this pseudocode and other examples in this section with RAPTOR, you should use the `floor()` function where `Int()` is indicated. You also, as always, should revise where necessary to account for the fact that the first element of a RAPTOR array has index = `1`. To create these examples as working programs you must first load arrays with sample data and sort the arrays.

Initially, we are searching the entire array, so Low = 0 and High = N. However, after the first attempt at locating Key, we are either searching the first half or the last half of the array, so either Low = 0 and High = Int(N/2) or Low = Int(N/2) and High = N.

The variable Index represents the middle element of the part of the array under consideration. Thus, Index is initially Int(N/2), and in general, it is the average of Low and High: Index = Int((Low + High)/2). Note how this works mathematically. If N is an even number, N/2 is an integer, but if N is an odd number, then N/2 is not an integer. Since the values of Low, High, and Index must be integer values, we use the Int() function to ensure that Index is an integer, regardless of whether N is even or odd. When N is odd, then Index will not be the exact middle, of course, but will be 0.5 below the mathematical middle. However, the search is not affected by this. In this general pseudocode, Array can be an array of any data type and Key is a variable of the same data type as Array.

```
1   Declare Low As Integer
2   Declare High As Integer
3   Declare N As Integer
4   Declare Index As Integer
5   Declare Found As Boolean
6   Set Low = 0
7   Set High = N
8   Set Index = Int(N/2)
9   Set Found = 0
10  While (Found == 0) AND (Low <= High)
11     If Key == Array[Index] Then
12        Set Found = 1
13     End If
14     If Key > Array[Index] Then
15        Set Low = Index + 1
16        Set Index = Int((High + Low)/2)
17     End If
18     If Key < Array[Index] Then
19        Set High = Index - 1
20        Set Index = Int((High + Low)/2)
21     End If
22  End While
```

What Happened?

In this pseudocode, after initializing the values of Low, High, Index, and Found, we enter the While loop. This loop will be re-entered if the search key has still not been located, in which case Found = 0, *and* if there are still array elements to check, in which case Low <= High.

Within the loop, we deal with the following three possible cases:

1. If Key == Array[Index], then we've located the search key, and Found is set equal to 1.
2. If Key > Array[Index], then we've got to check the upper half of the remaining array elements, and Low is adjusted accordingly.

3. If `Key < Array[Index]`, then we've got to check the lower half of the remaining array elements, and `High` is adjusted accordingly.

In the first case, the loop is exited. In the last two cases, `Index` is reset to the middle of the remaining part of the array and the loop is re-entered unless we've exhausted the array elements to be searched. Example 8.6 demonstrates a binary search.

Example 8.6 **Finding the Right House**

Table 8.1 shows how a binary search for the word `House` proceeds in the given list of eleven words.

Table 8.1 A Binary search for the word `House`

Subscript	Word	First Pass	Second Pass	Third Pass
0	Aardvark	Low	Low	
1	Book			
2	Dog		Index	
3	House			Low, Index
4	Job		High	High
5	Month	Index		
6	Start			
7	Top			
8	Total			
9	Work			
10	Zebra	High		

The words are stored in an array of strings named `Words`. The pseudocode for this example is as follows, assuming `Words` has been loaded, sorted alphabetically, and integer variables named `Low`, `High`, `Index`, `N`, and `Found` have been declared. A string variable, `Key`, has also been declared.

```
1   Set N = 10
2   Set Key = "House"
3   Set Low = 0
4   Set High = N
5   Set Found = 0
6   Set Index = Int(N/2)
7   While (Found == 0) AND (Low <= High)
8     If Key < Words[Index] Then
9       Set High = Index - 1
10      Set Index = Int((High + Low)/2)
11    Else
12      If Key > Words[Index] Then
13        Set Low = Index + 1
14        Set Index = Int((High + Low)/2)
```

```
15        Else
16          Set Found = 1      // Key must = Words[Index]
17        End If
18      End If
19   End While
```

What Happened?

On the first pass through the `While` loop:

- `N = 10` so `Index` is `Int(N/2)` which is 5
- `"House"` < `Words[5]` since the element of `Words` that has the index 5 is `"Month"`.
- `High` is set equal to 4 because `High = Index - 1`.
- `Index` becomes `Int((0 + 4)/2) = 2`

Now the range of items to be searched has been reduced to `Words[0]` through `Words[4]` and the middle of this range is `Words[2]`. On the second pass through the loop:

- `"House"` is greater than `Words[Index]` because `Words[2] = "Dog"`
- `Low` now becomes `Index + 1 = 3`
- `Index` is now `Int((4 + 3)/2) = 3`

The range of items to be searched is now between `Words[3]` (`Low`) and `Words[4]` (`High`). The middle of this range is 3.5 but `Int(3.5) = 3`. On the third pass the search ends.

- `"House"` which is the 4th element of the array has the subscript 3. So `Words[3] = "House"` and a match is found.

Example 8.7 **Combining Parallel Arrays and a Binary Search**

Professor Crabtree saves all her student records in parallel arrays. The array `Names` holds the students' names, listed alphabetically by last name. Each time she gives an exam or grades a homework assignment, she adds a new parallel array: `Exam1`, `HW1`, `HW2`, and so on. Now, Dr. Crabtree needs to locate the record of one student, Julio Vargas. She writes a program, which allows her to search for and retrieve Julio's whole record very quickly.

The pseudocode that corresponds to this program, shown here, assumes the following parallel arrays have been declared, filled with data, and that the following variables have been declared:

- `Names[100]` is an array of `Strings` with each element holding a student's last name
- `First[100]` is an array of `Strings` with each element holding a student's first name
- `Exam1[100]`, `HW1[100]`, and `HW2[100]` are parallel arrays of `Floats`.
- `Low`, `High`, `Found`, `N`, and `Index` are `Integer` variables.
- `Student` is a `String` variable.

```
1  Set N = 99
2  Set Low = 0
```

```
 3  Set High = N
 4  Set Found = 0
 5  Set Index = Floor(N/2)
 6  Write "Enter a student's name: "
 7  Input Student
 8  While (Found == 0) AND (Low <= High)
 9    If Student < Names[Index] Then
10      Set High = Index - 1
11      Set Index = Floor((High + Low)/2)
12    Else
13      If Student > Names[Index] Then
14        Set Low = Index + 1
15        Set Index = Floor((High + Low)/2)
16      Else
17        Set Found = 1
18      End If
19    End If
20  End While
21  If Found == 0 Then
22    Write "Student record not found."
23  Else
24    Write "Student record for: "
25    Write First[Index] + " " + Names[Index]
26    Write "Exam 1: " + Exam1[Index]
27    Write "Homework 1: " + HW1[Index]
28    Write "Homework 2: " + HW2[Index]
29  End If
```

What Happened?

This program searches through the Names array for the search key which is the value of the variable Student. This program differs from the previous example because, in this case, the user can enter the item to be found so the program can be reused to search for any student's record.

Once the search record has located the desired student's last name, we know the index number of that element in the Names array. However, since all the arrays are parallel, we now also know the index number of that student's information in all the arrays. In fact, with very little modification, this program could be used to display all homework grades, all exam scores, or any combination of items. This is the value of using parallel arrays.

We also note that this program substitutes the Floor() function where the Int() function had been previously used. For the purpose of this program, the two functions are interchangeable. If you try this program in RAPTOR which does not include the Int() function, you can always use the Floor() function to replace Int().

You can add more functionality to this program, such as finding a student's exam or homework average, computing a final course grade, and so on. The Self Check questions for this section will ask you to do some of these things.

Self Check for Section 8.3

8.10 True or false? The binary search requires that the list of table keys be ordered.

8.11 True or false? The binary search cannot be used to locate a numeric search key.

8.12 Rewrite the binary search pseudocode given in this section to perform a search for an element, Key, in an array named Array with N elements that has been sorted in descending order.

For Self Check Question 8.13 refer to Example 8.7

8.13 Assume that Professor Crabtree gave three exams and a final exam during one semester. The scores have been loaded into parallel arrays of Floats named Exam1, Exam2, Exam3, and Final. Arrays for students' names are also loaded, as described in Example 8.7. Write pseudocode to do the following:
  - Find the record for a student named "Mary Reilly". Calculate Mary's exam average for the course using the criteria that Professor Crabtree counts the final exam twice in her exam average:

    ```
    ExamAvg = (Exam1 + Exam2 + Exam3 + 2 * Final) / 5
    ```

  - Output Mary Reilly's full name and her exam average.

8.4 The Selection Sort

The **selection sort** procedure is a more efficient way to sort data stored in an array than the bubble sort technique presented in Section 8.2.

General Selection Sort Technique

The basic idea behind the selection sort is fairly simple. Here is how we would use it to sort an array in ascending order—from smallest to largest. We make several passes through the array as follows:

  - On the first pass, we locate the smallest array element and swap it with the first array element
  - On the second pass, we locate the second smallest element and swap it with the second element of the array
  - On the third pass through the array, we locate the next smallest element and swap it with the third element of the array

And so forth. . . . If the array contains N elements, it will be completely sorted after at most N - 1 passes.

To illustrate the selection sort, first we will do an example by hand. Figure 8.5 demonstrates the process for a data set consisting of the numbers 9, 13, 5, 8, 6. It displays the given data in the first (leftmost) column and the results of the four passes through this data in the next four columns, using arrows to indicate which data values have been swapped. Example 8.8 presents the general pseudocode for the selection sort.

Figure 8.5 Selection sort of the numbers 9, 13, 5, 8, 6

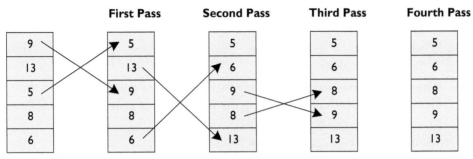

(On the fourth pass, no interchanges take place; the numbers are sorted.)

Example 8.8 **General Pseudocode for the Selection Sort[2]**

Now we will construct the pseudocode to sort an array named `Array` in ascending order. The array, `Array`, can be an array of `Integers`, `Floats`, `Strings`, or `Characters`, and `Littlest` must be of the same data type. For simplicity, we will declare `Array` as an array of `Floats` in this example. The array contains `N + 1` elements so the highest index value is `N`. Therefore, we need to make `N` passes through the loop to complete the selection sort.

The general skeleton of this program segment is as follows:

```
For (K = 0; K < N; K++)
  Find the smallest, Littlest, of Array[K], Array[K+1], ↵
      . . . , Array[N]
  If Littlest != Array[K] Then
    Swap array elements Littlest and Array[K]
  End If
End For
```

Of course, each of the two statements in the `For` loop requires further refinement, described as follows:

- To find the smallest element, `Littlest`, in a set of numbers, we set `Littlest` equal to the first number and then compare `Littlest`, successively, with the remaining numbers. Whenever we find a number smaller than `Littlest`, we set that number equal to `Littlest` and record the current subscript, `Index`. Thus, this step in the pseudocode above becomes:

```
Set Littlest = Array[K]
Set Index = K
For (J = K + 1; J <= N; J++)
  If Array[J] < Littlest Then
    Set Littlest = Array[J]
    Set Index = J
  End If
End For
```

[2]These examples can be implemented with RAPTOR, keeping in mind the caveats described in the previous section. To test the RAPTOR programs you create with the selection sort you must first load arrays with sample data. Be sure that you use unsorted data to see that your sort routine works properly.

- To swap array elements with subscripts `K` and `Index`, we use the swap routine technique as follows:

```
Set Temp = Array[K]
Set Array[K] = Array[Index]
Set Array[Index] = Temp
```

The refined pseudocode for sorting the array `Array`, consisting of `N + 1` elements, in ascending order using the selection sort procedure is as follows:

```
 1  Declare Array[K] As Float
 2  Declare Littlest As Float
 3  Declare K, N, Index, Temp As Integer
 4  For (K = 0; K < N; K++)
 5    Set Littlest = Array[K]
 6    Set Index = K
 7    For (J = K + 1; J <= N; J++)
 8      If Array[J] < Littlest Then
 9        Set Littlest = Array[J]
10        Set Index = J
11      End If
12    End For(J)
13    If K != Index Then
14      Set Temp = Array[K]
15      Set Array[K] = Array[Index]
16      Set Array[Index] = Temp
17    End If
18  End For(K)
```

Applying the Selection Sort Technique

The following example demonstrates how the selection sort might be implemented in a real program.

Example 8.9 **Sorting Large Arrays**

There are many ways the selection sort is used. In this example, we assume that an array of student ages is part of each student's record in Professor Crabtree's classes. The professor wants to see the range of ages of her students and, at a future date, plans to use the sorted data to compile other statistics. She asks you to write a program to sort the array named `Ages` in ascending order. To save space we will assume:

- `Ages[200]` is an array of `Integers` with each element holding the age of a student (in years).
- `Youngest`, `J`, `K`, `M`, `N`, `Temp` and, `Index` are `Integer` variables.

The pseudocode for this program is as follows:

```
1  Set N = 199
2  Set M = 0
3  Set Temp = 0
4  Set K = 0
```

```
 5    While K < N
 6      Set Youngest = Ages[K]
 7      Set Index = K
 8      Set J = K + 1
 9      While J <= N
10        If Ages[J] < Youngest Then
11          Set Youngest = Ages[J]
12          Set Index = J
13        End If
14        Set J = J + 1
15      End While(J)
16      If K != Index Then
17        Set Temp = Ages[K]
18        Set Ages[K] = Ages[Index]
19        Set Ages[Index] = Temp
20      End If
21      Set K = K + 1
22    End While(K)
23    Write "Ages sorted: "
24    While M < N + 1
25      Write Ages[M]
26      Set M = M + 1
27    End While(M)
```

What Happened?

The outer While loop of this program segment performs 199 iterations. Why do we only need 199 iterations to sort 200 items? On the first pass through the outer loop, the initial value of the variable Youngest is set equal to the value of the first element of the array, Ages[0]. This is then compared with the second element of the array, Ages[J] which, since J is one larger than K, is the next element in the array. On the second pass, the value of Youngest is compared with the third element of Ages. Continuing on with this reasoning, on the 199th pass, the value of Youngest is compared with the 200th element of Ages. This is why, for N elements in an unsorted array, we need N - 1 iterations of the outer loop to sort the elements.

Once inside the outer loop, the inner loop begins. The first If-Then statement checks to see if the value of the element in question is smaller than Youngest. If it is, Youngest is now set to that value. Also, Index is now set to the present value of J (the subscript of the element being checked). If this element is not smaller than Youngest, nothing changes. Then J is incremented and the loop continues, checking all elements of the array against Youngest and continually replacing the value of Youngest as a smaller and smaller value is discovered. After this loop has completed all its iterations one time, Youngest now holds the smallest value in the whole array.

Whenever the value of Youngest is replaced, Index takes on the value of J which identifies the subscript of the element that holds the new small value. At the end of this inner loop, the value of Index identifies the element of the array that has the smallest value in the whole array. A check is now made, in the second If-Then statement, to see if the element that the outer loop started with (K) is the same as Index.

If it is, then Ages[K] already holds the smallest value in the array. If it is not, we need to swap the value of Ages[K] with Ages[Index] to put the smallest value in this spot. The swap routine does this. If this is unclear consider this scenario:

Assume that the values of a 3-element array, Ages are:

    Ages[0] = 5,   Ages[1] = 8,   Ages[2] = 3

On the first pass, K = 0 so Youngest now equals the value of Ages[0] which is 5. At the end of the first pass through inner While loop, Youngest has been compared with Ages[1] and no switch is made since Ages[1] has a value greater than Youngest. At this point J = 1. Then it is incremented to 2. When Ages[2] is checked, since its value (3) is less than Youngest, the value of Youngest is replaced by 3. Now Index is set equal to J so Index now equals 2. The inner loop ends with Youngest = 3 and Index = 2 (J, by the way, equals 3, but this is irrelevant since its value will be set back appropriately before entering the inner loop again.)

Now the program proceeds to the second If-Then statement. It checks to see if K (which is still 0) is the same as Index (which is 2). Since this results in a Boolean true (i.e., it is true that K != Index), the swap occurs and the new value of Ages[0] is the value of Ages[Index] which is Ages[2] which is our smallest value. Now the smallest value is in the first element of the array.

The fact that now Ages[2] has the value of 5 and 5 is smaller than the value of Ages[1] (which is 8) is irrelevant. All this will be sorted out (literally and figuratively!) in subsequent iterations.

After all this has happened, the outer loop begins again, now starting with the second value in the array. At the end of the second pass, the second-smallest value is stored in the second element of the array. At the end of 2 passes through the outer loop the array has been sorted from smallest to largest. In this pseudocode, we include a small loop at the end to display the sorted array.

But perhaps the most interesting thing about this example is that a computer can complete this sort for an array containing many thousands of elements in a lot less time than it takes a person to read through this explanation.

Self Check for Section 8.4

8.14 True or false? The selection sort method requires that the given array is already ordered.

8.15 True or false? The selection sort method requires that the programming language contains a swap statement.

8.16 List two differences between the bubble sort algorithm and the selection sort algorithm.

8.17 Add pseudocode to Example 8.9 to produce the output shown. Assume that the ages in Ages[200] run from 16 years to 70 years and are all integer values.

Output for Self Check 8.17:

```
Number of students younger than 17: XXX
Number of students between 17 - 22: XXX
Number of students between 23 - 30: XXX
Number of students between 31 - 45: XXX
Number of students older than 45: XXX
```

8.5 Focus on Problem Solving: A Grade Management Program

In this section, we will use a common programming problem to practice using the concepts learned so far, especially those presented in this chapter. We will create a program for a college professor to help view the grades for each student in a class and to allow the professor to evaluate a class's results by displaying some simple statistics. The program will make use of parallel arrays and search and sort routines.

Problem Statement

Professor Hirsch has asked you to write a program to help manage the grades for his Technical Writing class. He wants the program to do several things. After entering the final numerical grade for each student, he wants the number to be translated into a letter grade. He also wants to be able to enter any student's name and see the data relating to that student (the student's ID number, numerical final grade, and letter grade). Finally, he wants to see a report that includes all the students and their information and a statistical summary that includes the class average, the highest and lowest scores in the class, and the number of people who scored above, below, and exactly at the class average.

Problem Analysis

We begin our analysis of the problem by examining the required output. In this problem, there are several types of required output.

Professor Hirsch wants to see all the students with their information (names, ID's, numerical scores, and letter grades) as well as a statistical summary at the bottom of the report. The statistical summary will look as follows:

```
Summary
The average score for this class is: Class Average
High score for the class: High Score
Low score for the class: Low Score
Number of scores above the average: Number Above
Number of scores below the average: Number Below
Number of scores equal to the average: Number At Mean
```

A typical report for a sample class is shown in Figure 8.6.

Figure 8.6 Sample report for Grade Management program

Grade Management Program			
Student Name	ID Number	Numerical Score	Letter Grade
Venit, Stewart	1231	98.2	A
Kim, John	1245	97.3	A
Vargas, Orlando	1268	94.6	A
Lee, Nancy	1288	88.7	B
Voglio, Nicholas	1271	86.9	B
Stein, Mandy	1213	84.2	B
Ettcity, Kate	1222	83.3	B
Lopez, Maria	1263	80.0	B
Moser, Hans	1244	78.9	C
Smith, Jane	1208	78.5	C
Goshdigian, Anne	1212	78.2	C
Alerov, Mark	1216	76.3	C
Iijima, Kazuko	1225	75.4	C
Fitch, James	1275	72.8	C
Chen, Karen	1236	71.5	C
Baptiste, Etienne	1279	70.1	C
Cooper, Martha	1260	68.2	D
McDonell, Chris	1251	64.5	D
Montas, Eric	1246	62.3	D
Drake, Elizabeth	1218	59.4	F
Summary			

```
The average score for this class is: 78.5
High score for the class: 98.2
Low score for the class: 59.4
Number of scores above the average: 9
Number of scores below the average: 10
Number of scores equal to the average: 1
```

Professor Hirsch also wants to be able to pull up the record for any single student. In this case, Professor Hirsch should be able to input a student's name and see that student's record displayed in a form similar to the following:

```
Student Name:
Student ID Number:
Student's final score:
Student's letter grade:
```

For this program, we will store the data for each student in four parallel arrays as follows:

- Names[50] is a String array that will hold the name of each student in the form: lastname, firstname
- IDNum[50] is an Integer array that will hold an identification number for each student. This is a number usually assigned by the college or, if Professor Hirsch desires, he can create his own student ID numbers.
- Final[50] is a Float array that will hold each student's numerical grade at the end of the semester.
- Grade[50] is a Character array that will hold each student's letter grade (A, B, C, D, or F).

The arrays in this program will be declared at this time to have 50 elements but, of course, that number can be changed to hold as many elements as Professor Hirsch desires. Later, if the Professor is happy with this program, we can add modules to hold homework grades, exam grades, attendance records, and so on. These values could be used by a module that will calculate the final numeric grade and send the results to the Final array for the reports. (See Chapter 9 for information on how to send data from one submodule to another.)

We need to load the students' data into the first three arrays (the Grade array will be populated within our program). To do this, we will use a loop and we need several input variables as follows:

- StudentName is a String variable
- StudentScore is a Float variable

The following output variables are also necessary:

- ClassAvg is a Float variable and will contain the average of all the scores
- HighScore is a Float variable and will contain the highest score in the class
- LowScore is a Float variable and will contain the lowest score in the class
- NumAbove is an Integer variable that will contain the number of scores above the mean
- NumBelow is an Integer variable that will contain the number of scores below the mean
- NumAvg is an Integer variable that will contain the number of scores that are equal to the mean

Program Design

As with virtually all programs, we will begin this program with a Welcome_Message module. In this case, the Welcome_Message module will explain briefly what the program does and will offer Professor Hirsch several options.

We need a module for input so that Professor Hirsch can enter his students' names, ID numbers, and final scores. This will be the Enter_Info module. Once the data has been input, it will be processed. First, the numerical grade for each student will be converted to a letter grade and stored in the parallel array, Grades. We will use a Case Statement to accomplish this in a Letter_Grade module.

The Statistics module will process the data. First, it will compute the average score. Once we have this value, we will use the bubble sort routine to sort the scores in descending order so that the report will display the scores from highest to lowest. Later, when Professor Hirsch offers to pay us more to increase the functionality of this program, modules can be added to allow the report to display in sorted order by names or by ID numbers. Remember that, when we sort one array, we must be sure to sort all the parallel arrays so all the information for any particular student can be easily accessed through its index number. Once the numeric scores in the Final array have been sorted, it is possible to identify the highest and lowest scores. The Statistics module will also count the number of scores above, below, or exactly the same as the mean (average). This module will also generate a report, as shown in the sample report of Figure 8.6.

Finally, the Display_Student module will allow Professor Hirsch to input one student's name. Using the serial search technique, that student's complete record will be located and displayed.

Thus, our program will consist of the following modules.

1. The Main module calls its submodules into action.
2. The Welcome_Message module displays a welcome message and explains how to use the program.
3. The Enter_Info module accepts all the information for each student and stores that information in three parallel arrays.
4. The Letter_Grade module converts the numerical score of each student into a letter grade which is stored in another parallel array.
5. The Statistics module processes the data. It computes the average score of all the students and determines the highest and lowest scores. It also counts the number of scores at, above, and below the average and generates a report to display this information along with detailed information about every student in the class.
6. The Display_Student module allows the user to search for the record of any student and have that information displayed.

Modules 2 and 3 are called from the Main module. Module 3 calls modules 4, 5, and 6. This division of programming tasks is illustrated in the hierarchy chart shown in Figure 8.7.

Figure 8.7 Hierarchy chart for the Grade Management program

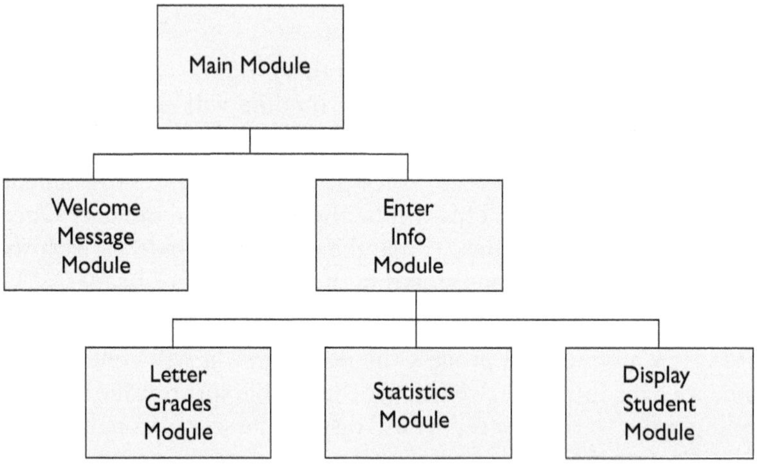

In our program, we will declare all variables and arrays that are used throughout the program in the Main module for simplicity. However, in most real programs, variables are declared "locally" (i.e., within their specific modules) and their values are passed from one module to another as necessary. The topic of where to declare variables and how to pass their values from one submodule to another is a very important topic and will be covered in depth in Chapter 9. With that in mind, the pseudocode for each module is given next.

Main Module

```
1   Begin
2     Declare Names[50] As String
3     Declare IDNum[50] As Integer
4     Declare Final[50] As Float
5     Declare Grade[50] As Character
6     Declare StudentName As String
7     Declare NumAbove, NumBelow, NumAvg, StudentCount As Integer
8     Declare StudentScore, ClassAvg, HighScore, LowScore,Sum As Float
9     Call Welcome_Message module
10    Call Enter_Info module
11  End Program
```

Welcome_Message Module

This module will present the program title, identify the programmer and other program data, and provide a brief explanation of what the program does. It will explain that the user must enter the data and then he or she will see a statistical summary for the course and be given the option to locate and view the record of a single student. This model consists solely of Write statements.

Enter_Info Module

This module will allow Professor Hirsch to input data for all the students in a class using a While loop. While the program is written to allow up to 50 students, a sentinel value is employed so the program can be used for fewer than 50 students. Recall that we have already declared all the necessary arrays and variables needed for this module so the pseudocode shown begins with entering the data. The variable StudentCount is initialized here and, at the end of this module, it holds the number of students in the class. For the purposes of this program, it is assumed that StudentCount retains its value when used in subsequent submodules. The pseudocode for this module is as follows:

```
1   Set StudentCount = 0
2   Write "Enter a student's full name; enter '*' when done."
3   Write "Use the form 'LastName, FirstName' for each entry."
4   Input StudentName
5   While StudentName != "*"
6     Set Names[StudentCount] = StudentName
7     Write "Enter this student's ID number: "
8     Input IDNum[StudentCount]
9     Write "Enter the final score for this student: "
10    Input Final[StudentCount]
11    Set StudentCount = StudentCount + 1
12    Write "Enter another name or enter '*' when done. "
13    Input StudentName
14  End While
15  Call Letter_Grade module
16  Call Display_Student module
17  Call Statistics module
```

At this point, three parallel arrays have been filled. StudentCount has the value corresponding to the number of elements in each array and also is one higher than the highest subscript of each array.

Letter_Grade Module

The numerical grade is stored in the Final array. Now we will convert that number to a letter grade according to the grade scale shown in Figure 8.8, provided by Professor Hirsch. The letter grades will be stored in a fourth parallel array, Grade. Since StudentCount has the value of the number of students in the class, we use StudentCount as the limit value of the For loop, comparing that value to a new counter.

Figure 8.8 Grade scale for the Grade Management program

Grade Scale	
Numerical Score	**Letter Grade**
90.0 – 100.0	A
80.0 – 89.9	B
70.0 – 79.9	C
60.0 – 69.9	D
under 60.0	F

The pseudocode for this module is as follows:

```
1   Declare I As Integer
2   For (I = 0; I < StudentCount; I++)
3     Set StudentScore = Final[I]
4     Select Case of StudentScore
5       Case >= 90.0:
6         Set Grade[I] = "A"
7       Case >= 80.0:
8         Set Grade[I] = "B"
9       Case >= 70.0:
10        Set Grade[I] = "C"
11      Case >= 60.0:
12        Set Grade[I] = "D"
13      Default:
14        Set Grade[I] = "F"
15    End Case
16  End For
```

Display_Student Module

This module will use the serial search technique to search for a specific student and, because of the characteristics of parallel arrays, will display all the information for the requested student. This pseudocode is written to search for a student by his or her ID number. However, it could easily be changed to allow the search to be based on the student's name. The pseudocode for this module is as follows:

```
1   Declare J As Integer
2   Declare IDKey As Integer
3   Declare Found As Integer
4   Set Found = 0
5   Set J = 0
6   Write "Enter the ID number for one student to view all the ↵
            information about that student: "
8   Input IDKey
9   While (Found == 0) AND (J < StudentCount)
10    If IDNum[J] == IDKey Then
11       Set Found = 1
12    End If
13    Set J = J + 1
14  End While
15  If Found == 0 Then
16    Write "Student ID was not found."
17  Else
18    Write "Student name: " + Names[J - 1]
19    Write "Student ID number: " + IDNum[J - 1]
20    Write "Student's final score: " + Final[J - 1]
21    Write "Student's letter grade: " + Grade[J - 1]
22  End If
```

Note that J is incremented at the end of the While loop. Therefore, when the correct student ID number is located and the loop ends, the value of J is one higher than the subscript of the desired array element. Therefore, the subscript of the array element to be displayed is J - 1.

Statistics Module

This module is the longest and most complicated of the program. The bubble sort technique is used to sort the elements of the numerical scores array, Final, in descending order. To keep all the information about each student together, the subscripts of all the parallel arrays must also match the sorted elements of the Final array.

After the Final array is sorted, all the scores are summed in order to compute the average. The program also counts the number of scores at, above, and below the average, and the high score and low score are identified. This last part is very simple since, after the scores are sorted, the first element of the Final array is the highest score and the last element of this array is the lowest score.

The last thing this module does is to create a report which includes all the information about all the students in descending order, by their final grade scores, and the summary of the statistics.

The pseudocode for this module is as follows. Comments have been included to explain what each part of the module accomplishes.

```
1   /*This section sorts the scores in descending order. It also
    puts the parallel arrays into the same order and identifies the
    highest and lowest scores. */
2   Declare HighScore, LowScore, Sum, TempFinal As Float
3   Declare NumAbove, NumBelow, NumAvg As Integer
4   Declare Flag, K, TempID As Integer
5   Declare TempName As String
6   Declare TempGrade As Character
7   Set Flag = 0
8   While Flag == 0
9     Set Flag = 1
10    For (K = 0; K <= StudentCount - 2; K++)
11      If Final[K] < Final[K+1] Then
12      //swap for Final array
13        Set TempFinal = Final[K]
14        Set Final[K] = Final[K + 1]
15        Set Final[K + 1] = TempFinal
16      //swap for IDNum array
17        Set TempID = IDNum[K]
18        Set IDNum[K] = IDNum[K + 1]
19        Set IDNum[K + 1] = TempID
20      //swap for Names[] array
21        Set TempName = Names[K]
22        Set Names[K] = Names[K + 1]
23        Set Names[K + 1] = TempName
24      //swap for Grade array
25        Set TempGrade = Grade[K]
26        Set Grade[K] = Grade[K + 1]
27        Set Grade[K + 1] = TempGrade
28        Set Flag = 0
29      End If
30    End For
31  End While
32  Set HighScore = Final[0]
33  Set LowScore = Final[StudentCount - 1]
34  /*This section computes the average score and determines how
    many scores fall at, above, and below that average. */
35  Set Sum = 0
36  Set NumAbove = 0
37  Set NumBelow = 0
38  Set NumAvg = 0
39  Set K = 0
40  //loop to get sum of all grades
41  While K < StudentCount
42    Set Sum = Sum + Final[K]
43    Set K = K + 1
44  End While
```

```
45   //compute the average
46   Set ClassAvg = Sum/StudentCount
47   // loop to count number greater than or less than the mean
48   For (K = 0; K < StudentCount; K++)
49     If Final[K] > ClassAvg Then
50       Set NumAbove = NumAbove + 1
51     Else
52       If Final[K] < ClassAvg Then
53         Set NumBelow = NumBelow + 1
54       Else
55         Set NumAvg = NumAvg + 1
56       End If
57     End If
58   End For
59   /* This section displays the report. The "/t" indicates a tab. */
60   Write "Student Name /t ID Number /t Final Score /t Letter Grade"
61   For (K = 0; K < StudentCount; K++)
62     Write Names[K] + "/t" + IDNum[K] + "/t" + Final[K] ↵
              + "/t" + Grade[K]
63   End For
64   Write "The average score for this class is: " + ClassAvg
65   Write "High score for the class: " + HighScore
66   Write "Low score for the class: " + LowScore
67   Write "Number of scores above the average: " + NumAbove
68   Write "Number of scores below the average: " + NumBelow
69   Write "Number of scores equal to the average: " + NumAvg
```

Program Code

The program code is now written using the design as a guide. At this stage, header comments and step comments are inserted into each module, providing internal documentation for the program. The following are several important points concerning the coding:

- The welcome message should be displayed on a blank screen using the programming language's clear screen statement.
- To produce a professional report similar to the one shown in Figure 8.6, we must format the output to ensure that the data in the report lines up in columns and that the numbers displayed have a consistent decimal representation. For a report such as this, unless Professor Hirsch specifies otherwise, the final scores for each student should be rounded to the nearest tenth or hundredth. This can be accomplished using the programming language's special print formatting statements.
- This program, as written, does not contain any error checking. Before the program is submitted to Professor Hirsch, error traps and error checking code should be added. The Self Check questions for this section will ask you to add some error checking.

Program Test

This program can be tested as written by entering data for a small class—perhaps just three or four students. The statistics should be calculated by hand and checked against the program's results. A more extensive test can be done by entering exactly the same data as shown in Figure 8.6 and comparing the results.

However, in a real programming environment, the code would include error traps in many places. Typical errors that the program should catch would include:

- Data entered as an incorrect data type, such as a name entered for an ID number
- Negative numbers entered for numerical grades

The program should also be tested to see what would happen if the user attempted to enter more than the 50 allowed entries.

Self Check for Section 8.5

For Self Check Questions 8.18–8.21 refer to the Grade Management program of this section.

8.18 Add code to the Enter_Info module to ensure that the user enters no more than 50 students.

8.19 Add code to the Enter_Info module to ensure that the user enters an appropriate ID number (an integer) and that the score is between 0 and 100 (inclusive).

8.20 Since ClassAvg has been declared as a Float, it is unlikely that there will be many student averages which match the ClassAvg exactly. Add code to the Statistics Module to calculate how many grades fall within a range of ClassAvg. The range should be between the Floor() of the ClassAvg and the Ceiling() of ClassAvg.

8.6 Running With RAPTOR (Optional)

We can create RAPTOR programs that use the search and sort algorithms discussed in this chapter. First, we will do several short examples to demonstrate how these techniques are implemented and then we will create a new and longer program.

The Serial Search

Example 8.10 A Serial Search Using Parallel Arrays

This example is similar to Example 8.1. We will assume that three parallel arrays have been loaded with the names of all students (Names) in a particular class, their identification numbers (IDNumbers), and their scores on the final exam (Scores).

The instructor can enter a student's ID number, and the output will either be that student's name, ID, and exam score or a message that no such student exists in that class. The program uses a serial search and the RAPTOR program looks as shown. The display does not show the variable or array declarations and initializations.

You can try this program yourself with your own data or load the three arrays with the following sample data.

Names	IDNumbers	Scores
Jenny Jacobs	2498	86
Ronny Weasley	0106	91
Luisa Vargas	3012	78
Ivan Gretsky	3215	74
Sonia Umani	1011	61
Stewie Stavros	2463	86
Ginger Robbins	1982	93
Tom Sawyer	2861	77
Haseen Patel	1442	95
Pam Princeton	2263	82

RAPTOR implementation and sample MasterConsole output given ID entered is 2463:

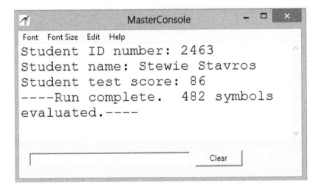

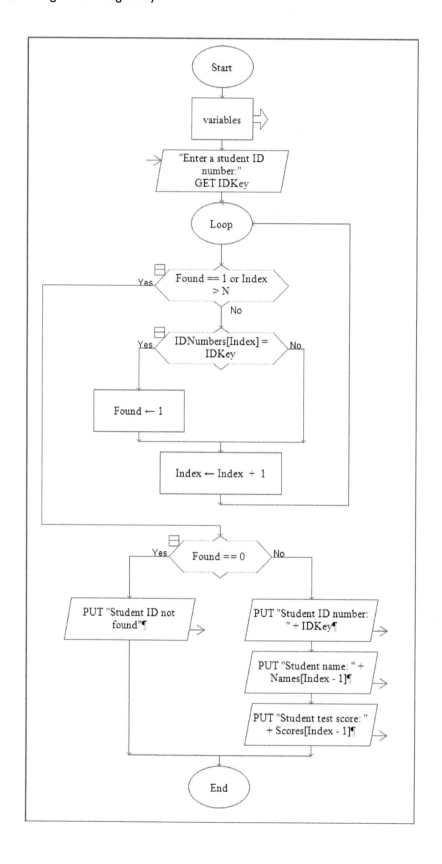

The Bubble Sort

Example 8.11 **Sorting Numbers with the Bubble Sort**

This example is similar to Example 8.4. We will assume that Professor Crabapple has entered all the scores on a test from all her students in her four Programming classes. But the students are listed alphabetically so the scores are in no particular order. If Professor Crabapple wants to see the range of scores or wants to assign a curve, based on various criteria, the scores need to be sorted into either ascending or descending order. Here, we will use RAPTOR to complete a bubble sort on the scores, sorting in descending order, assuming the array has already been loaded. The RAPTOR program is shown, following the `MasterConsole` output.

If the array is loaded with 20 sample scores which are displayed first, then sorted, the output will be as shown. Note that the RAPTOR implementation of loading and displaying the original array is not given in this program.

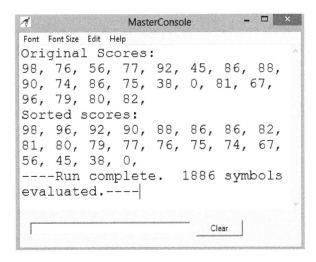

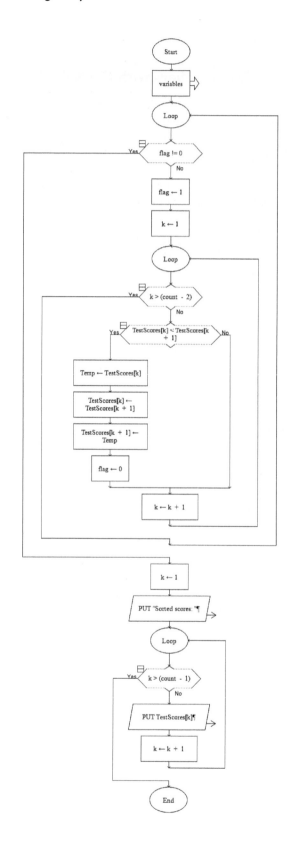

The Binary Search

Example 8.12 **Finding Your Pet with the Binary Search**

This example is similar to the binary search described in Example 8.6. We will assume that a pet store has kept the names of all pets it offers in an array, Pets. You want to buy a gecko to keep as a pet so you call the store to see if they sell geckos. The following program uses a binary search for the Key, "gecko", assuming the Pets array contains the following animal names:

"aardvark"	"ant"	"canary"	"cat",
"dog"	"duck"	"ferret"	"gecko"
"goldfish"	"goose"	"guinea pig"	"hamster"
"iguana"	"kangaroo"	"monkey"	"mouse"
"ostrich"	"parrot"	"pony"	"rabbit"
"rat"	"sheep"	"snake"	"tarantula"
"wombat"			

If the array is loaded with the data given and the user wants to buy a gecko, the output will be as shown below on the left, but if the user wants to buy an elephant, the output will be that shown on the right of the following MasterConsole displays.

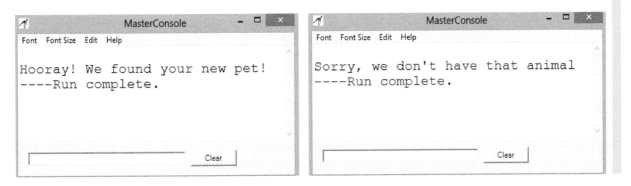

The RAPTOR program is shown next.

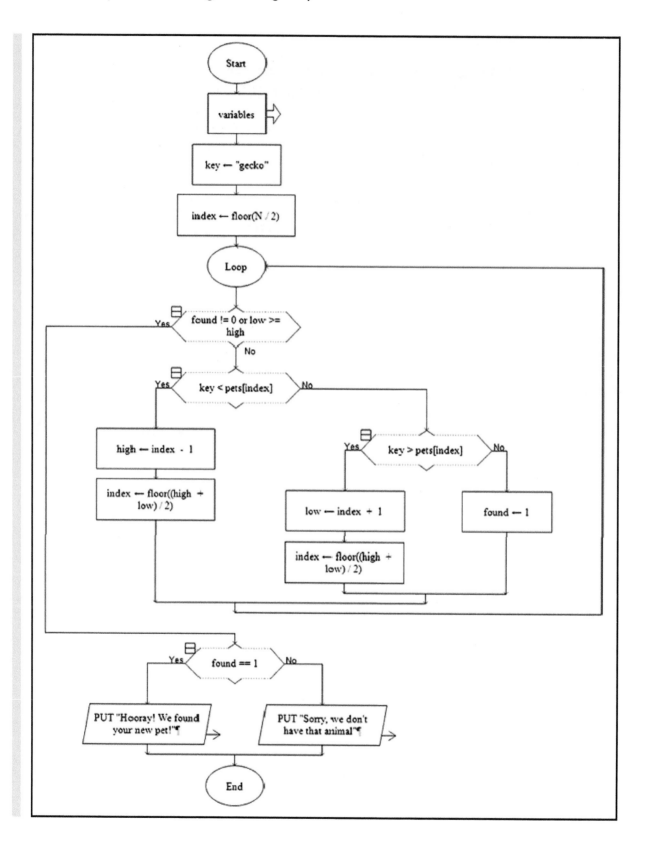

The Selection Sort

Example 8.13 **Sorting Large Arrays with the Selection Sort**

This example will parallel Example 8.9. In this program, an array, ages, has been loaded with the ages of 20 students. They are sorted in ascending order using the selection sort method. While this method is good for large amounts of data, in order for you to see the results of the sort, the array has been limited to only 20 values. However, with patience, you can enter hundreds of numbers to see more impressive results. The program is shown with the MasterConsole delivering both the original (unsorted) and sorted array values.

If the array is loaded with 20 ages, as shown, the output on the MasterConsole is:

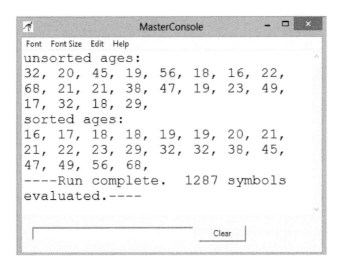

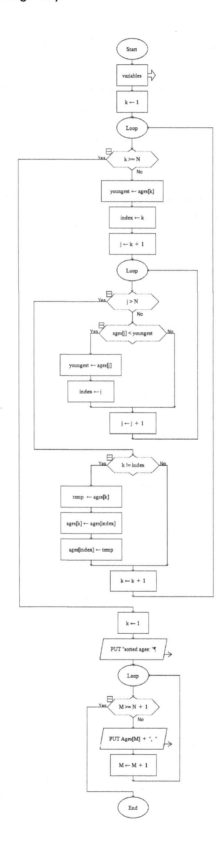

Run It: Soccer Camp

In this section, we will develop a program that requires a sorting algorithm but also requires some careful logical thought. The program will allow the owners of a soccer camp to divide campers into three groups based on the ages of the campers who sign up each year. If you wish to create this program, open a new RAPTOR program and save it with the filename `soccer.rap`.

Problem Statement

Nancy and Ned Norton run a children's soccer camp. Each year they divide the children into three leagues: `PeeWee`, `Junior`, and `Senior`. Sixty children have signed up and the Nortons need to find age ranges for the leagues. However, the age ranges for each league are dependent on the ages of the children who sign up. For example, if most children who sign up this year are between ages 5 and 12, a `Senior` would be a 12 year old. But if the children who sign up next year are between ages 7 and 17, a 12 year old would probably be in the `Junior` League. Therefore, we will create a program that will allow Nancy and Ned to load the children's ages in an array named `Ages` and will sort the ages in ascending order. Then, by identifying the youngest and oldest, we will find the range of ages represented. Finally, we will create age cutoffs for the three leagues. The output at the end will look like this where the ?s are replaced by the ages we calculate:

```
PeeWee League: ages ?? through ??
Junior League: ages ?? through ??
Senior League: ages ?? through ??
```

Developing and Creating the Program

There are several tasks that must be done which can be relegated to several subcharts. We can divide our tasks into subcharts as follows:

- `main`: The `main` module provides a welcome message and calls all the other subcharts.
- `Get_campers`: This subchart will allow Ned and Nancy to load the array with the ages of the children who signed up this year. Since they have room for 60 campers, the array should allow for 60 entries. However, because camp may not be full (and also because we might wish to test our program with fewer numbers), we will allow Ned and Nancy to input the number of values they wish to store in this array.
- `Sort_campers`: This subchart will sort the values entered in ascending order.
- `Create_leagues`: This subchart will divide the ages entered into three leagues with appropriate age ranges.
- `Display_leagues`: This subchart will display the results as defined in the Problem Statement.

Thus, the `main` module should look as shown.

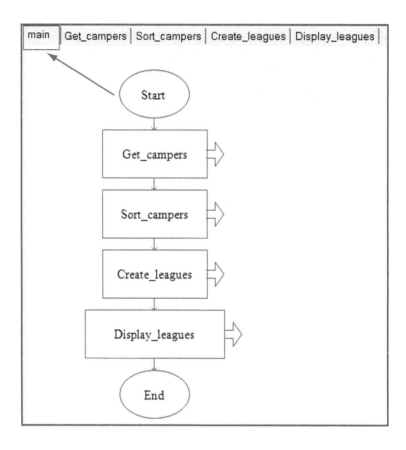

You can add a welcome message here, create a separate Welcome_message subchart, or put a message in the Get_campers subchart that might say:

> "This program will allow you to enter the ages of the campers who have signed up for Soccer Camp this year. It will then create three soccer leagues based on the ages of the campers."

The Get_campers subchart

This part of the program is not complicated. We will prompt for the number of ages to be entered and declare an array (Ages[60]) for a maximum of 60 campers, although all elements may not be used. We set Ages[60] to 0 because RAPTOR requires an initial value for an array, just as for a variable. However, when the array is filled, the user will enter floating point values to represent campers' ages. Then we will store the values entered using a loop. This subchart is shown:

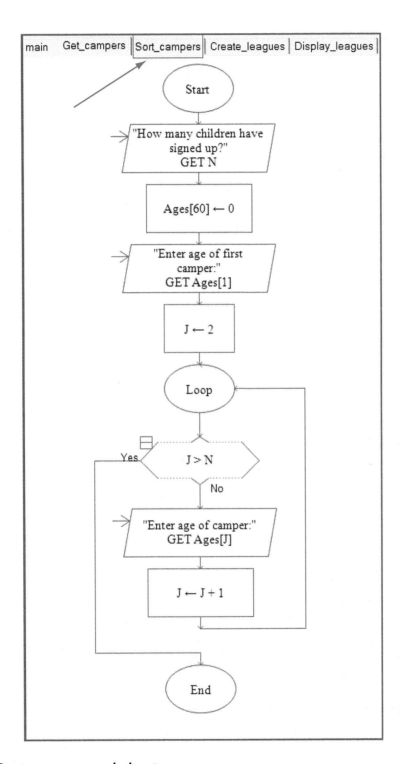

The `Sort_campers` subchart

We will use a bubble sort to sort the ages that have been stored in `Ages`. Since arrays
in RAPTOR begin with the subscript 1 and since the loop structure in RAPTOR

requires that the loop be exited when the answer to the test condition is "yes", the program to sort these values is as shown:

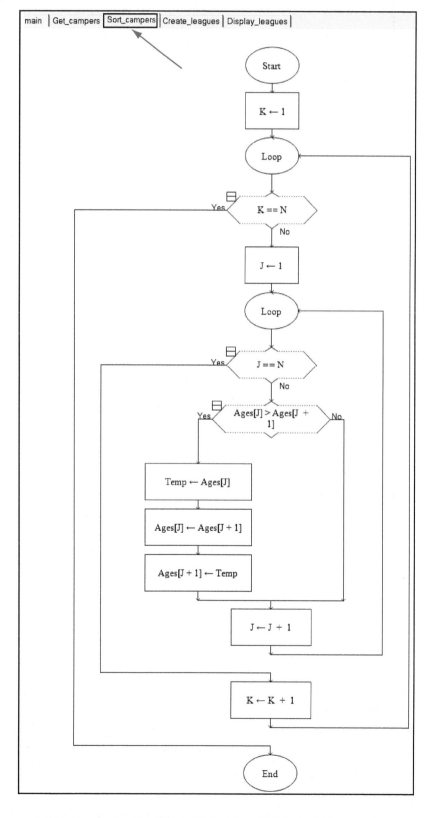

You can add a short loop to display the sorted values, if you wish to check your work. It would look, simply, like this:

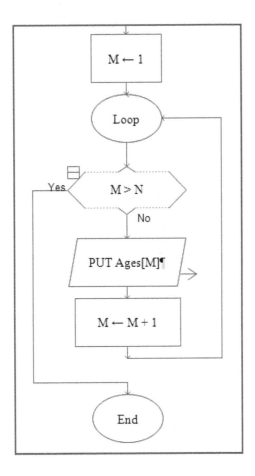

The `Create_leagues` subchart

This part of the program requires a little consideration. It is tempting to think, "Well, I have 60 ages. I can simply assign the first 20 to the `PeeWee` League, the next 20 to the `Junior` League, and the last 20 to the `Senior` League." This would not work.

Imagine that children whose ages are stored in elements `Ages[19]`, `Ages[20]`, and `Ages[21]` are all 9 years old. The first two of these children would be in the `PeeWee` League and the third child would be placed in the `Junior` League. Anyone who has ever known (or seen a movie about) a soccer mom would realize how such a division could cause serious trouble for Ned and Nancy!

A better way to determine the age limits on each league must be found to ensure that no children of the same age are put into different leagues. We can do this by finding the entire range of ages that exists for any particular year. Then we can divide those ages into three groups.

We already know the youngest child (the age stored in `Ages[1]` and the oldest child (the age stored in `Ages[N]` where `N` is the number of elements in the array). The range of ages, therefore, which we will store in a variable called `Range` is:

```
Range = Ages[N] - Ages[1]
```

Let's assume the youngest child is 5 and the oldest is 17. This makes the value of Range = 12. This is a nice number because it is divisible by 3 and we want three groups. This would mean that the PeeWee League would start at age 5 and end at age (5 + 4) since 12/3 = 4. So the PeeWee League would be from age 5 to age 9. The Junior League would then have to start with children who are older than 9. It would stop when the age reaches 13. And the Senior League would begin with children who are older than 13 and end with the oldest age, 17.

We need to polish this up a bit. First, if Range is not a number neatly divisible by 3, we must set a cutoff. For our purposes, we can simply use the floor() of Range/3. We will create a new variable called Step and set Step to:

    Step = floor(Range/3)

Now that we have thought about how to create league ranges, the Create_leagues subchart will be easy to implement. It is a sequence of Assignment statements. Once the range is identified, the value of Step tells us how many years to add to the starting age for each league. The variable PeeWee identifies the highest age allowed in the PeeWee League. The value of Junior identifies the highest value allowed in the Junior League. The highest value allowed in the Senior League is simply the last element in the sorted Ages array.

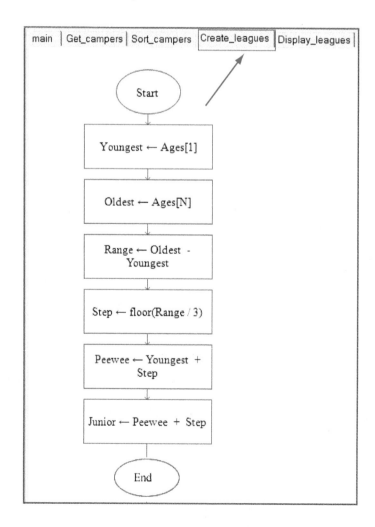

The `Display_leagues` subchart

This subchart displays the age ranges for the three leagues. We want to show that one league begins a bit after the other ends but, because of the limitations of the RAPTOR program, floating point numbers are displayed with four decimal places. While this may not be the prettiest output, it serves our purpose.

The `PeeWee` League's lowest age is the youngest child who signed up (`Ages[1]` which is presently stored in `Youngest`). The `PeeWee` League's upper age limit is the age identified in the previous subchart as `PeeWee`. The `Junior` League begins at the age just above the upper limit of `PeeWee`. We identify this as `PeeWee + 0.1`. Its upper limit was previously identified as `Junior`. The `Senior` League's lower limit is the value of `Junior` plus `0.1` and its upper limit is `Oldest`. Therefore, the `Display_leagues` subchart is:

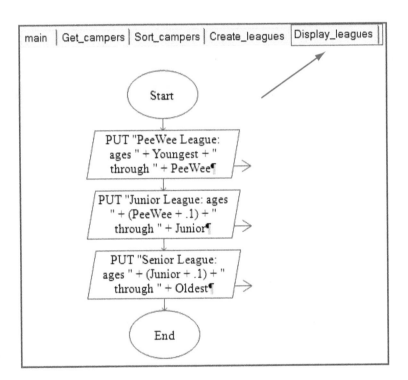

Check It Out

If you have created the program as shown in this section, try entering the following values and make sure your displays match the ones shown. In the next chapter we will learn how to limit the precision (i.e., the number of decimal places displayed) in RAPTOR but for now, the default of four decimal places is acceptable.

Test 1: enter 12 ages: 10, 8, 4, 9, 16, 8, 7, 14, 13, 5, 11, 14

```
MasterConsole                    _ □ ×
Font  Font Size  Edit  Help
PeeWee League: ages 4 through 8
Junior League: ages 8.1000 through 12
Senior League: ages 12.1000 through 16
----Run complete.  707 symbols
evaluated.----

[                    ]    Clear
```

Test 2: enter 19 ages: 10, 8, 6, 9, 16, 8, 7, 14, 13, 6, 11, 14, 7, 9, 12, 10, 17, 15, 10

```
MasterConsole                    _ □ ×
Font  Font Size  Edit  Help
PeeWee League: ages 6 through 9
Junior League: ages 9.1000 through 12
Senior League: ages 12.1000 through 17
----Run complete.  1694 symbols
evaluated.----|

[                    ]    Clear
```

Revise and Improve

You may have noticed that the League ranges, given the values of Test 2, are not exactly even. This is a consequence of using the floor() function to create the variable Step. In this case, the youngest child is 6 and the oldest is 17. Thus we have:

Range = (Oldest - Youngest)

so Range = (17 - 6) or Range = 11

Then Step = floor(Range/3)

Step = floor(11/3) or Step = floor(3.6667)

Step = 3

That is why the PeeWee League's range starts at 6 and goes through (6 + 3) or 9. The Junior League's range begins at (9 - 1) and ends at 12. What is left (12.1 through the oldest age, 17) must be the Senior League. In this case, that turns out to be almost six years. To ensure that this does not happen we need to reconsider how we identify the value of Step. One possible solution follows.

This revised method to identify a Step value for the range of ages in each League is not perfect but it allows for better accuracy in the League ranges. We will use the floor() function to identify Step if the fractional part of Range is less than 0.5 and use the ceiling() function if the fractional part is 0.5 or greater. The revised Create_leagues subchart looks as shown.

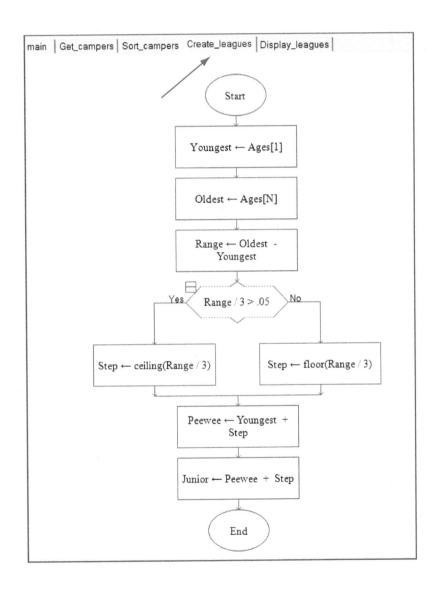

Check It Out Again

If we substitute the improved code in the Display_leagues subchart, the output for the two test cases is now as shown.

Test 1: enter 12 ages: 10, 8, 4, 9, 16, 8, 7, 14, 13, 5, 11, 14

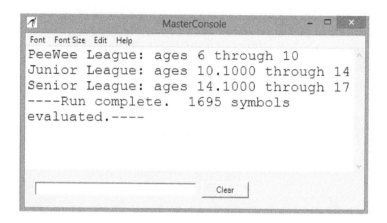

Test 2: enter 19 ages: 10, 8, 6, 9, 16, 8, 7, 14, 13, 6, 11, 14, 7, 9, 12, 10, 17, 15, 10

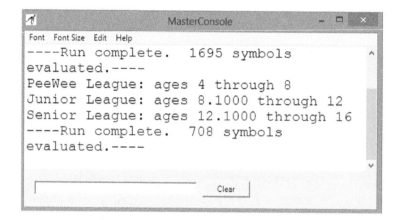

Key Terms

binary search
bubble sort
flag
search (an array)
search key
selection sort

serial search
sort (an array)
swap routine
table key
target

Chapter Summary

In this chapter, we discussed the following topics:

1. The serial search examines array elements in order, one-by-one, until the desired element is found

2. The bubble sort makes passes through the array, comparing consecutive pairs of elements on each pass and interchanging them if they are not in the correct order

3. The binary search is a more efficient search procedure used for large amounts of data
   - Pseudocode was discussed for a binary search for the element Key in an array called Array which has N + 1 elements and is sorted in either ascending or descending order, with the highest subscript in the array equal to N

4. The selection sort is a more efficient sort procedure used for large amounts of data
   - Pseudocode was discussed for a selection sort of an array called Array which has N + 1 elements and is sorted in ascending order, with the highest subscript in the array equal to N

5. When searching or sorting parallel arrays it is essential to keep parallel elements together.

Review Questions

Fill in the Blank

1. In a serial search, the item you are looking for is called the _____ _____.

2. In performing a bubble sort to arrange the numbers 5, 30, 25, 15 in ascending order, _____ interchanges will take place.

3. When performing a search of two parallel arrays, when the item is found in one array, its _____ value identifies the corresponding element in the other array.

4. At the end of the first pass through the outer loop of an array that is to be sorted in ascending order, using the selection sort method the _____ element will be the first element.

5. In a binary search of an array named MyArray, the first time the program runs, the value of Low will be _____.

True or False

6. T F Items must be sorted in descending order to perform a serial search.

7. T F On the first pass through a loop using a binary search, each element in the array is checked.

8. T F One problem with the selection sort routine is that it can only be used on arrays with numeric data types.

9. T F In a binary search, the values of Low (identified initially, the first element in the array) and High (identified initially, the last element in the array) will never change as the program executes.

10. T F In a serial search, the search key (the value being searched for) is compared with each element in an array until a match is found or there are no more elements in the array.

11. T F Both search algorithms presented in this chapter can be used with parallel arrays.

12. T F Before using the serial search method, you must sort the table keys in ascending order.

13. T F The bubble sort method cannot be used to arrange numeric data in descending order.

14. T F The binary search procedure can only be used with numeric data.

15. T F A binary search requires that the data be sorted before beginning the search.

Short Answer

16. How many interchanges take place when sorting the following numbers in descending order, using the bubble sort technique?

     6   9   5   8

17. What is the maximum number of passes that would be made to ensure that an array with 50 elements is sorted, using the bubble sort technique?

For Short Answer Questions 18–21 refer to the following array:

```
Pet[0] = "dog"      Pet[1] = "cat"      Pet[2] = "bird"
Pet[3] = "snake"    Pet[4] = "duck"     Pet[5] = "fish"
Pet[6] = "rabbit"   Pet[7] = "mouse"    Pet[8] = "pony"
Pet[9] = "frog"
```

18. Write a program segment to sort the given array in alphabetical order using the bubble sort method.

19. Write a program to perform a serial search on the given array for the key "duck".

20. Assuming you have sorted the given array, write a program to perform a binary search for the element "pony".

21. Write a program segment to sort the given array in alphabetical order using the selection sort method.

22. The following program segment is supposed to search an array A consisting of N elements for a value Key and set Found equal to 1 or 0, depending on whether Key is located. It contains two errors. Correct them. Assume that the array A and the other variables have already been properly declared.

```
Set Index = 0
Set Found = 0
While (Found == 1) AND (Index < N)
   If A[Index] == Key Then
      Set Found = 0
      Set Index = Index + 1
   End If
End While
```

23. In Exercise 22, which variable is the flag for this program segment?

24. What are the values of A[K] and A[K+1] after code corresponding to the following pseudocode is run?

```
Set A[K] = 10
Set A[K+1] = 20
Set Temp = A[K]
Set A[K] = A[K + 1]
Set A[K + 1] = Temp
Write A[K]
Write A[K + 1]
```

25. What are the values of A[K] and A[K+1] after code corresponding to the following pseudocode is run?

```
Set A[K] = 10
Set A[K + 1] = 20
Set A[K] = A[K + 1]
Set A[K + 1] = A[K]
Write A[K]
Write A[K + 1]
```

26. The following program segment is supposed to sort an array A consisting of N numbers in ascending order. It contains two errors. Correct them. Assume that the array A and the other variables have already been properly declared.

```
Set Flag = 0
While Flag == 0
   Set Flag = 1
   For (K = 0; K <= StudentCount - 1; K++)
```

```
            If A[K] <= A[K + 1] Then
                Set Temp = A[K]
                Set A[K] = A[K + 1]
                Set A[K + 1] = Temp
                Set Flag = 1
            End If
        End For
    End While
```

For Short Answer Questions 27–30 refer to the following pseudocode used to perform a binary search of the names "Arnold", "Draper", "Gomez", "Johnson", "Smith", "Wong" (stored in Array), for the name "Gomez". (Assume the array and all the variables have already been declared with their appropriate data types.)

```
Set N = 5
Set Key = "Gomez"
Set Low = 0
Set High = N
Set Index = Int(N/2)
Set Found = 0
While (Found == 0) AND (Low <= High)
    If Key == Array[Index] Then
        Set Found = 1
    End If
    If Key > Array[Index] Then
        Set Low = Index + 1
        Set Index = Int((High + Low)/2)
    End If
    If Key < Array[Index] Then
        Set High = Index - 1
        Set Index = Int((High + Low)/2)
    End If
End While
```

27. On entering the While loop for the first time, what is the value of Index?

28. After the first pass through the While loop, what are the values of Low and High?

29. How many passes are made through the While loop?

30. After the While loop is exited, what is the value of Found?

For Short Answer Questions 31–34 refer to the following pseudocode, which is used to perform a selection sort in ascending order on the names "Wong", "Smith", "Johnson", "Gomez", "Draper", and "Arnold" (which are stored in Array). (Assume that the array and all the variables have already been declared with their appropriate data types.)

```
Set N = 5
For (K = 0; K <= N; K++)
    Set Min = Array[K]
    Set Index = K
    For (J = K + 1; K < N; J++)
```

```
      If Array[J] < Min Then
         Set Min = Array[J]
         Set Index = J
      End If
   End For(J)
   If K != Index Then
      Set Temp = Array[K]
      Set Array[K] = Array[Index]
      Set Array[Index] = Temp
   End If
End For(K)
```

31. How many passes are made through the outer For loop?

32. After the first pass through the first inner For loop, what is the value of Index?

33. After the first pass through the outer For loop, which name is stored in Array[1]?

34. What changes must be made to this pseudocode to sort this array of six names in descending order?

Programming Challenges

For each of the following Programming Challenges, use the modular approach and pseudocode to design a suitable program to solve it.

1. Input a list of employee names and salaries, sort them ascending by salary, and determine the mean (average) salary as well as the number of salaries above, below, and, if any, exactly at the mean.

2. Determine the median selling price of all homes in a subdivision named Botany Bay sold during one year. Allow the user to enter the number of houses sold and store their selling prices in an array. The median of a list of N numbers is as follows:

   a. The middle number of the sorted list, if N is odd

   b. The average of the two middle numbers in the sorted list, if N is even

   (*Hint:* after inputting the prices into an array, sort that array.)

3. Given the following array, write a program to sort the array using a selection sort and display the number of scores that are less than 500 and those greater than 500.

Scores[0] = 198	Scores[1] = 486	Scores[2] = 651
Scores[3] = 85	Scores[4] = 216	Scores[5] = 912
Scores[6] = 73	Scores[7] = 319	Scores[8] = 846
Scores[9] = 989		

4. Assume the following array is parallel to the Scores array of Programming Challenge 3. Write a program to sort this Player array in alphabetical order, keeping the Scores array parallel. Use either of the sort routines

covered in this chapter. Include code to display each player's name and score. To get your column data to line up as shown, you can use the tab indicator, /t, in your Write statements, as shown in Section 8.5.

```
Player[0] = "Joe"        Player[1] = "Ann"
Player[2] = "Marty"      Player[3] = "Tim"
Player[4] = "Rosy"       Player[5] = "Jane"
Player[6] = "Bob"        Player[7] = "Lily"
Player[8] = "Granny"     Player[9] = "Liz"
```

Your display should look like this:

```
Ann       486
Bob       73
Granny    846
Jane      912
Joe       198
Lily      319
Liz       989
Marty     651
Rosy      216
Tim       85
```

5. Redo Programming Challenge 4 but sort by Scores. Sort the Scores in ascending order, keeping the Player array parallel. To get your column data to line up as shown, you can use the tab indicator, /t, in your Write statements, as shown in Section 8.5.

Your display should look like this:

```
Bob       73
Tim       85
Joe       198
Rosy      216
Lily      319
Ann       486
Marty     651
Granny    846
Jane      912
Liz       989
```

6. Write a program to load an array, Squares, with 100 numbers. Each element should contain the square of its index value. In other words, Squares[0] = 0, Squares[3] = 9, Squares[8] = 64, and so on. Then

prompt the user for a number from 0 through 1000 and write pseudocode to check if that number is a perfect square (i.e., if the user inputs X, check to see if X is a value in the array). Use a serial search for this program.

Bonus: Add pseudocode to check how many iterations must be made for each number entered by the user and, if you also complete Programming Challenge 7 in RAPTOR, you can compare the two values.

7. Redo Programming Challenge 6 but use a binary search.

Bonus: Add pseudocode to check how many iterations must be made for each number entered by the user, and, if you also complete Programming Challenge 6 in RAPTOR, you can compare the two values.

Bonus: Change the number of elements in the Squares array to 500. Run both kinds of searches (Programming Challenges 6 and 7) several times and keep track of how many iterations each program must make for each search. Does your data demonstrate that one algorithm is more efficient than the other? Justify your response.

Program Modules, Subprograms, and Functions

9

In Chapter 2, we introduced the idea of modular programming. We discussed how to design and code a program as a set of interrelated modules. In subsequent chapters, especially in the Focus on Problem Solving sections, we used this technique to help simplify the design of relatively complicated programs. In this chapter, we will discuss more advanced aspects of this topic, including the concepts of arguments and parameters, functions, and recursion.

After reading this chapter, you will be able to do the following:

- Use a data flow diagram to indicate the data being transmitted among the program's modules
- Use arguments and parameters to pass data between modules and functions
- Use value and reference parameters
- Define and specify the scope of a variable
- Use some functions commonly built into a programming language
- Create your own functions
- Create recursive functions to solve certain programming problems

Living and Programming in Manageable Pieces: Subprograms

As you know, a basic problem-solving strategy involves breaking a problem into modules and submodules and solving each subproblem separately. When we use this technique, we often use the data generated by one module in another module. For example, suppose you want to send your mother a bouquet of flowers and as luck would have it, you have just received an email from Ye Olde Flower Shop offering you a discount on a bouquet if you call in your order within the next few days. So the problem of how to send a gift of flowers to your mom has the following simple solution:

1. Locate a suitable bouquet and the store's phone number from the Ye Olde Flower Shop website: `Locate_Information` module.
2. Call Ye Olde Flower Shop: `Call_Shop` module.
3. Place your order: `Place_Order` module.

To solve this problem, the data collected in Step 1 (the phone number and bouquet name) are used in Steps 2 and 3, respectively. In the language of programming, we say that the phone number and bouquet name are exported from the `Locate_Information` module and imported by the `Call_Shop` and `Place_Order` modules, respectively.

Here's another example of passing data among modules. Consider the steps you take to file your federal income tax return. You must do the following:

1. Gather data about your income and (possibly) your expenses: `Gather_Data` module.
2. Fill out the forms: `Form_1040` module.
3. Send your return to the IRS.

As you fill out the main form (Form 1040), you may discover that you also have to complete two other documents. You might be required to submit Schedule A (deductions) and Schedule B (interest and dividends). So a refinement of Step 2 might look as follows:

2. Fill out Form 1040: `Form_1040` module.
   a. Fill out Schedule A: `Schedule_A` module.
   b. Fill out Schedule B: `Schedule_B` module.

The `Form_1040` module imports all data from the `Gather_Data` module and exports the following:

- The expense data (if necessary) to the `Schedule_A` module, which imports the data and exports the total deductions to `Form_1040`
- The interest and dividend income data (if necessary) to the `Schedule_B` module, which imports the data and exports the total interest and total dividend income to `Form_1040`

In the everyday world, you transfer data from one module to another in various ways. You may write information on a slip of paper, record it in a new form, or just remember it. In programming, this action is accomplished by using parameters and arguments.

9.1 Data Flow Diagrams, Arguments, and Parameters

In this section, we will describe how data is transmitted between program submodules, or **subprograms**.[1] We will discuss subprogram parameters, which allow the program to transmit information between modules, and **data flow diagrams**, which keep track of the data transmitted to and from each subprogram.

Most subprograms manipulate data. If a data item in the main program is needed in a certain subprogram, its value must be *passed to*, or *imported* by that subprogram. Conversely, if a data item processed by a subprogram is needed in the main program, it must be *returned*, or *exported* to that module. We say that we **pass a value** to a subprogram and that subprogram may or may not **return a value** to the calling program. To illustrate these concepts, let's consider the following programming problem.

A Big Sale: The Sale Price Computation Program

Katrina Katz owns a small pet store. She wants you to design a program that will compute and display the sale price of a discounted store item when she inputs the original price and its percentage discount.

We will briefly discuss the analysis and design for this problem and then use it to introduce the concepts of data flow diagrams, arguments, and parameters.

Problem Analysis

Our program must input the original price (OriginalPrice) of an item and its percentage discount (DiscountRate). Then it must compute the sale price (SalePrice) of the item and display this amount. To arrive at the sale price, first we compute the amount of the discount using the following formula:

    AmountSaved = OriginalPrice * DiscountRate/100

Note that dividing by 100 converts the discount rate, entered as a percentage, to a decimal. We need the decimal amount because AmountSaved represents currency. This also means that all variables will be declared as Float. Then we compute the sale price using the following formula:

    SalePrice = OriginalPrice - AmountSaved

Program Design

Our modular design for this program consists of a Main module and four submodules, constructed as follows:

Main Module

```
Call Welcome_Message module
Call Input_Data module
Call Compute_Results module
Call Output_Results module
```

---

[1]We will use the word *subprogram* to describe the code that implements a program *submodule;* later we will consider a specific type of subprogram—the *function*. Be aware that the words *subprogram* and *function* may have other meanings in some programming languages.

Welcome_Message Module

Display a brief description of the program

Input_Data Module

Prompt for and input the original price, OriginalPrice

Prompt for and input the percentage discounted, DiscountRate

Compute_Results Module

```
Set AmountSaved = OriginalPrice * DiscountRate/100
Set SalePrice = OriginalPrice - AmountSaved
```

Output_Results Module

```
Write "The original price of the item is $ " + OriginalPrice
Write "The discount is: " + DiscountRate + "%"
Write "The sale price of the item is $ " + SalePrice
```

Imported and Exported Data

The following occurs in the Sale Price Computation program:

- The Welcome_Message module does not import or export any data. This means that no data is passed to it, and it does not return any data to the Main module.

- The Input_Data module inputs data, OriginalPrice and DiscountRate, from the user and then exports (sends or returns) these values to the Main module so that they can be used by another module.

- The Compute_Results module imports the values of OriginalPrice and DiscountRate *from* the Main module and exports the value of SalePrice *to* the Main module. Alternatively, we can say that the values of OriginalPrice and DiscountRate are passed to the Compute_Results module, and the value of SalePrice is returned to the Main module. The value of AmountSaved is neither imported by nor exported from the Compute_Results module. It is only needed and used within the Compute_Results module.

- The Output_Results module displays the values of OriginalPrice, DiscountRate, and SalePrice, so it needs to import these values from the Main module. It does not export any data to another program module.

Data Flow Diagrams

In the process of designing a program like this, we can keep track of the data passed among the various modules by using a data flow diagram. This is a hierarchy chart that shows the data imported by and exported from each program module. For example, the data flow diagram for the Sale Price Computation program design is given in Figure 9.1. The arrows indicate the direction in which the data is passed.

Figure 9.1 Data flow diagram for the Sale Price Computation program

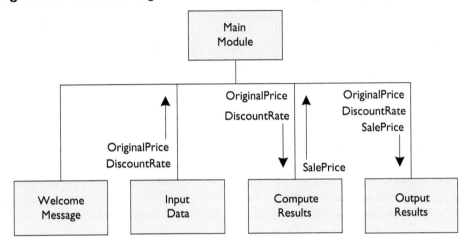

An Introduction to Arguments and Parameters

When data is passed between a calling module and a submodule, programming languages use **arguments** and **parameters** to transfer the data. In this discussion about parameters, we will use the Sale Price Computation program as an example. In our design of this program, the Output_Results module imports and displays the values of OriginalPrice, DiscountRate, and SalePrice. At the time that the Output_Results module is called, these variables will have values that were assigned within other subprograms and then transmitted to the main program. For example, Katrina Katz may have decided to put doghouses on sale. The original price of a doghouse might have been $150.00 and the discount may have been 30 percent; therefore, the sale price would end up being $105.00, and the values of these variables would be as follows:

```
OriginalPrice = 150.00
DiscountRate = 30.0
SalePrice = 105.00
```

These values must be sent from one module to another.

We will use the following pseudocode to call the Output_Results subprogram, and at the same time, pass the values of OriginalPrice, DiscountRate, and SalePrice to this subprogram as follows:

```
Call Output_Results(OriginalPrice,DiscountRate,SalePrice)
```

Notice that we place the relevant variable names in parentheses, separated by commas. This pseudocode transfers control to the Output_Results subprogram and simultaneously transmits the values of the indicated variables to this subprogram.

If we use this pseudocode for the Call statement, then the first line (the **header**) in the definition of the Output_Results subprogram must contain a corresponding list of three variables as follows:

```
Subprogram Output_Results(OldPrice,Rate,NewPrice)
```

Notice that the names of the variables listed in the `Call` statement and the subprogram header don't need to be the same. In fact, in most cases it is better if they are not the same for reasons that will be explained later in this chapter. However, the names of the variables listed in the `Call` statement and those in the subprogram header *must* agree in number, in type, and in the order in which they are given in the subprogram's list. In this case, we are sending (or passing) three values (stored in variables named `OriginalPrice`, `DiscountRate`, and `SalePrice`) so there must be three variables listed in the `Call` statement and in the subprogram header. Also, if a certain variable in the `Call` statement is of one type, then the corresponding variable in the subprogram header cannot be of a different type. For example, if the fourth variable in a `Call` statement is of type `Integer`, then the fourth variable in the subprogram header must be of type `Integer` as well. In this case, our three variables (`OriginalPrice`, `DiscountRate`, and `SalePrice`) are all `Floats` so the three variables in the `Call` statement (`OldPrice`, `Rate`, and `NewPrice`) must also be `Floats`.

The *order* in which the variables are sent to the calling submodule is extremely important. In this example, the calling submodule header is written as follows:

```
Subprogram Output_Results(OldPrice,Rate,NewPrice)
```

The value of the first variable that is sent over will be passed to the variable `OldPrice`, the value of the second variable will be passed to `Rate`, and the value of the third variable will be passed to `NewPrice`. We will take a closer look at what this means.

The items listed in parentheses in the `Call` statement are known as **arguments**, whereas those appearing in the subprogram header are known as **parameters**. Arguments (appearing in the `Call`) may be constants, variables, or more general expressions, but parameters (appearing in the subprogram header) *must* be variables. This means you can *send* data to a subprogram that is stored as a variable or is a constant or an expression. These values will be passed into the variables listed as parameters in the subprogram.

How Data Is Transferred between Modules

When a subprogram is called, the current values of the arguments are assigned to the corresponding parameters. This correspondence is made solely on the basis of the order of appearance in the two lists. For example, when the subprogram with the header

```
Subprogram Output_Results(OldPrice,Rate,NewPrice)
```

is called by the statement

```
Call Output_Results(OriginalPrice,DiscountRate,SalePrice)
```

the following occurs:

- The value of the first argument (`OriginalPrice`) is assigned to the first parameter (`OldPrice`).
- The value of the second argument (`DiscountRate`) is assigned to the second parameter (`Rate`).
- The value of the last argument (`SalePrice`) is assigned to the last parameter (`NewPrice`).

Examples 9.1 and 9.2 illustrate this concept.

Example 9.1 **Passing Data between Modules**

Suppose that the values of OriginalPrice, DiscountRate, and SalePrice are respectively, 200.00, 20.0, and 160.00. After the call to Output_Results, the variables within the Output_Results subprogram have the following values:

```
OldPrice = 200.00
Rate = 20.0
NewPrice = 160.00
```

Pictorially, we can represent the way the values of the arguments in the Call are transmitted to the parameters in the subprogram header as follows:

```
Call Output_Results( OriginalPrice, DiscountRate, SalePrice)
                          ↓              ↓            ↓

Subprogram Output_Results( OldPrice,     Rate,      NewPrice)
```

Argument and Parameter Names

Be aware that, while it is not required that you use different names for an argument and its corresponding parameter, it is normally better to do so. For example, the header for the Output_Results subprogram could be the following:

```
Subprogram Output_Results(OriginalPrice,DiscountRate,SalePrice)
```

Regardless of the names used for arguments and parameters, be sure that you use the name listed in the subprogram header to refer to a given parameter when you write the statements in that subprogram description.

Example 9.2 **More about Passing Data between Modules[2]**

This example continues to refer to the Sale Price Computation problem. The pseudocode for the Output_Results subprogram (with parameters OldPrice, Rate, and NewPrice) is as follows:

```
Subprogram Output_Results(OldPrice,Rate,NewPrice)
   Write "The original price of the item is $ " + OldPrice
   Write "The discount is: " + Rate + "%"
   Write "The sale price of the item is $ " + NewPrice
End Subprogram
```

On the other hand, the following pseudocode would work just as well:

```
Subprogram Output_Results(OriginalPrice,DiscountRate,SalePrice)
   Write "The original price of the item is $ " + OriginalPrice
   Write "The discount is: " + DiscountRate + "%"
   Write "The sale price of the item is $ " + SalePrice
End Subprogram
```

[2]While most of the examples in this chapter can be implemented in RAPTOR, you must read Section 9.6, Running With RAPTOR, before attempting to convert the pseudocode to a RAPTOR program. RAPTOR procedures allow you to pass data stored in variables from one subprogram to another, but this must be done in the manner described in Section 9.6.

Remember that the arguments that appear in a call to a subprogram may be constants, variables, or expressions. If variables appear in the call, in many programming languages they must be declared in the module that contains the `Call` statement. The parameters that appear in the subprogram itself, however, are declared in that subprogram's header.

Example 9.3 uses a `Call` statement that contains `String` values, which are sent to a subprogram with two parameters. It demonstrates the importance of sending values to subprograms in proper order.

Example 9.3 **A Horse of a Different Color**

Katrina Katz, our pet store owner, wants a subprogram that will display the type and color of a pet ordered by a customer. The following program segment has a `Call` statement that sends two arguments to the subprogram. The arguments are the color and type of the pet. In this `Call` statement, the arguments passed to the subprogram are actual values; they are not variables. However, the parameters in the subprogram header must be variables. In this example, they take on the values of "yellow" and "duck". The subprogram simply displays the information sent in the `Call` as follows:

```
Call Animal("yellow","duck")
Subprogram Animal(Color,Beast)
   Write "The pet you are buying is a " + Color + " " + Beast
End Subprogram
```

In this case, the display would be as follows:

```
The pet you are buying is a yellow duck
```

However, if the expressions in the calling statement were reversed, as shown below, the result would be significantly different.

```
Call Animal("duck","yellow")
Subprogram Animal(Color,Beast)
   Write "The pet you are buying is a " + Color + " " + Beast
End Subprogram
```

If this program segment were coded and run, the display would not be what the programmer intended; rather it would look as follows:

```
The pet you are buying is a duck yellow
```

Example 9.3 demonstrates how an improper `Call` statement, where the arguments are sent to the subprogram in the wrong order, can lead to a silly result. However, if your parameters were of different data types and you passed values in the wrong order, the consequences could be a lot worse. Attempting to store a `String` value in an `Integer` or `Float` variable will result in an error that may even cause the program to stop running.

The Benefits of Using Arguments and Parameters

Sometimes people who are new to programming wonder why we don't just name the arguments in the main program the same as the parameters in the subprograms. In the Sale Price Computation program, the variables in the `Call` statement are named `OriginalPrice`, `DiscountRate`, and `SalePrice`. But in the subprogram, `Output_Results`, these variables are named `OldPrice`, `Rate`, and `NewPrice`. We said that this is not necessary—the subprogram would work just as well if its parameters had the same names as the arguments passed to them. However, in real-life programs, it is natural and desirable that the parameters in a subprogram be assigned names that are different from those in the call to that subprogram (see the list of "benefits" given below).

Using arguments and corresponding parameters to pass data among program modules is an important feature of the programming process for the following reasons:

- It enhances the usefulness of subprograms. They can be designed and coded independently of the main program and even used in several different programs, if desired. Only the *structure* of the subprogram is important, not the naming of its variables.
- It makes it easier for different programmers to design and code different subprograms. The programmer of a particular subprogram only needs to know what kinds of variables are transmitted to or from that module. He or she doesn't need to be concerned about how these variables are named or used in the main program or in another subprogram.
- It makes it easier to test and debug a subprogram independently of the main program.

We will return to the Sale Price Computation program in Section 9.2.

Assigning Data Types to Parameters

Earlier in this section, we discussed the importance of passing arguments to the subprogram in the correct order and said that an error would occur if an argument of one type was passed to a parameter of a different data type. The values that are passed from the calling program or subprogram are declared in the program or subprogram where they originate. But we have not yet shown how to declare the data type of a parameter in pseudocode. In this book, we will use the following pseudocode to assign a type to a parameter:

```
Subprogram Subprogram_Name(String Var1, Integer Var2, Float Var3)
```

Therefore, if Katrina Katz wanted you to write a subprogram that would display the number, color, and type of pet that a customer is buying, the pseudocode for the first line of this subprogram would look as follows:

```
Subprogram Animal(Integer Number, String Color, String Beast)
```

Example 9.4 also demonstrates, in a simple, yet complete program, how to declare the data types of subprogram parameters.

Example 9.4 **Assigning Types to Parameters**

This program displays a sequence of asterisks (*****) before and after a message (which is stored as a String) entered by the user. It contains one subprogram (named Surround_And_Display), which imports the input string from the main program and displays that string enclosed within asterisks. In the following pseudocode, we will explicitly declare the necessary program variables:

```
Main
   Declare Message As String
   Write "Enter a short message: "
   Input Message
   Call Surround_And_Display(Message)
End Program
Subprogram Surround_And_Display(String Words)
   Write "***** " + Words + " *****"
End Subprogram
```

What Happened?

As usual, execution begins with the first statement in the main program. Thus, when code corresponding to this pseudocode is run, the user is prompted to enter a message, which is assigned to the variable Message. Then, the statement

```
   Call Surround_And_Display(Message)
```

calls the subprogram, transferring control to it and assigning the value of the argument Message to the parameter Words. Notice that, in the subprogram header, the data type of the parameter Words is indicated. In this program, the subprogram's Write statement

```
   Write "***** " + Words + " *****"
```

displays the value of Message preceded and followed by five asterisks. Then control returns to the next statement in the main program, which is End Program.

Self Check for Section 9.1

9.1 Draw a data flow diagram for the following problem: A salesperson's commission is 15 percent of total sales. Input the total sales and compute and display the commission.

For Self Check Questions 9.2–9.4 refer to the following pseudocode:

```
Main
    Declare Name As String
    Declare Age As Integer
    Write "Enter your name: "
    Input Name
    Write "Enter your age as a whole number: "
    Input Age
    Call Voting_Age(Name, Age)
End Program
```

```
Subprogram Voting_Age(String Voter, Integer VoterAge)
  If VoterAge >= 18 Then
    Write Voter + ", you are eligible to vote."
  Else
    Write "Sorry, " + Voter + ", you are too young."
End Subprogram
```

9.2 Identify the arguments in the program segment.

9.3 Identify the parameters in the program segment.

9.4 What, if anything, would change in the output if the variables in the Subprogram were changed from `Voter` and `VoterAge` to `Person` and `PersonAge`?

9.5 Write pseudocode for a program segment that inputs a name and uses the following subprogram to display the input name three times:

```
Subprogram Display_Name(String Name)
  Write Name
End Subprogram
```

9.6 What is the output when code corresponding to the following pseudocode is run?

```
Main
  Declare Num1, Num2, Num3 As Integer
  Set Num1 = 1
  Set Num2 = 2
  Set Num3 = 3
  Call Display(Num3, Num2, Num1)
End Program
Subprogram Display(Integer Num3, Integer Num2, Integer Num1)
  Write Num3 + " " + Num2 + " " + Num1
End Subprogram
```

9.7 Suppose the subprogram header in Self Check Question 9.6 was changed to the following:

```
Subprogram Display(Integer A, Integer B, Integer C)
```

a. What changes (if any) should be made to the subprogram body?

b. What changes (if any) should be made to the main program for the output to be the same as that of Self Check Question 9.6?

9.2 More about Subprograms

In Section 9.1, we introduced the concepts of subprogram arguments and parameters. In this section, we will delve more deeply into this subject.

Value and Reference Parameters

Previously, we used arguments and parameters for the sole purpose of passing data from the main program to a subprogram. Here, we will consider the reverse process—exporting data from a subprogram to the main program. This can occur automatically when control is transferred to the main program at the end of the subprogram, but there is an important difference in the way various programming languages implement this action. We illustrate this difference in Example 9.5.

Example 9.5 **Changing the Value . . . but Where?**

Consider the following pseudocode:

```
1  Main
2     Declare NumberOne As Integer
3     Set NumberOne = 1
4     Call Change_Value(NumberOne)
5     Write NumberOne
6  End Program
7  Subprogram Change_Value(Integer Number)
8     Set Number = 2
9  End Subprogram
```

What Happened?

The output of code corresponding to this pseudocode will differ, depending on the programming language used. In all languages, the variable NumberOne is set equal to 1 in the main program and this value is transmitted to the parameter Number of the subprogram when the latter is called. Then, the value of Number is changed to 2 in the subprogram and the subprogram ends. What happens next however, depends on the language as follows:

- In some programming languages when control is returned to the main program, the new value of Number is assigned to the corresponding variable, NumberOne, so the output in this case is 2.
- In other programming languages when control is returned to the main program, unless otherwise indicated, changes to the parameter Number do not affect the corresponding variable, NumberOne, in the main program. Hence, the output in this case is 1.

In this book, we will follow the lead of most programming languages and distinguish between the following types of subprogram parameters:

- **Value parameters** have this property: Changes to their values in the subprogram *do not* affect the value of the corresponding (argument) variables in the calling module. These parameters can only be used to **import data** into a subprogram.
- **Reference parameters** have this property: Changes in their values *do* affect the corresponding arguments in the calling module. They can be used to both **import data** into and **export data** from a subprogram.

The Inside Story: Pass by Value, Pass by Reference Revealed

The distinction between value parameters and reference parameters is extremely important because it can have a significant impact on how a program works. When you understand what is happening inside the computer, you will also understand how and when to use each type of parameter.

You already know that when a variable is declared, the computer sets aside a specific location in memory for the contents of that variable. When a variable is **passed by value** to a submodule, that submodule receives a copy of that variable. In other words, a separate storage location is created and the value of the variable is stored there also. So now the value of that variable exists in two places. It is in the location where it was stored originally and it is in a second location. The module that sends that variable to a submodule has access to the original location only; the submodule has access to the second location only—the copy. If the submodule does calculations that change the value of that variable, the changes are made only to the copy. When the submodule finishes its work, any changes that have been made to that variable remain in the copied location. The original variable in the main (or calling) module retains its original value.

On the other hand, when a variable is **passed by reference**, the submodule receives the actual storage location in the computer's memory where the value of that variable is stored. This means that if the submodule does anything that changes the value of that variable, the value is also changed in the main (or calling) module.

The Value of Value Parameters

Making It Work

You may wonder why, if a subprogram changes the value of a parameter, the corresponding argument shouldn't change in the calling module. It may seem as though value parameters don't serve any purpose, but there is a good reason why many programming languages support them. Value parameters enhance the independence of subprograms from the main program and each other, and this is a key ingredient in the modular programming method. In particular, the use of value parameters prevents the code in one subprogram from inadvertently affecting the action of the main program or another subprogram through unwanted changes to its variables.

How to Tell the Difference between Value and Reference Parameters

Every programming language that distinguishes between value and reference parameters has a way to indicate in the subprogram header whether a parameter is of value or reference type. In this book, we will place the symbols As Ref after the parameter name to indicate that it is of reference type, and therefore, changes to it will affect the corresponding argument in the calling module. If these words do not appear, then the parameter is of value type. For example, in the header

```
Subprogram Switch(Integer Number1, Integer Number2 As Ref)
```

Number1 is a value parameter and Number2 is a reference parameter. Examples 9.6 and 9.7 further illustrate and build on this usage.

Example 9.6 **Passing by Reference, Passing by Value**

Consider the following pseudocode:

```
1  Main
2    Declare MyNumber As Integer
```

```
 3    Declare YourNumber As Integer
 4    Set MyNumber = 156
 5    Set YourNumber = 293
 6    Call SwitchIt(MyNumber,YourNumber)
 7    Write MyNumber + " " + YourNumber
 8  End Program
 9  Subprogram SwitchIt(Integer Number1, Integer Number2 As Ref)
10    Set Number1 = 293
11    Set Number2 = 156
12  End Subprogram
```

What Happened?

- Line 1 tells us that we begin this segment in the Main module. On line 4, the integer variable MyNumber is set equal to the value of 156. On line 5, the integer variable YourNumber is set equal to the value of 293.
- Line 6 transfers control to the subprogram SwitchIt().
- Now we must jump to line 9 to see what is happening. The value of MyNumber is passed into Number1, the first parameter of SwitchIt(). The value of YourNumber is passed into Number2, the second parameter of SwitchIt(). At this point, the SwitchIt() parameters, Number1 and Number2, have been assigned values. Number1 = 156 and Number2 = 293. However, line 9 also adds that Number1 is a value parameter and Number2 is a reference parameter.
- Line 10 changes the value of Number1 to 293 and line 11 changes the value of Number2 to 156.
- Line 12 ends the subprogram, SwitchIt(), and control is transferred back to the main program on line 7. Note that control returns to the line directly after the Call statement, which in this case, is line 7.
- Line 7 simply writes the values of MyNumber and YourNumber to the screen, separated by a space. However, because Number1 is a *value parameter*, MyNumber retains the original value (156) it had when the subprogram was called. On the other hand, because Number2 is a *reference parameter*, YourNumber changes to the current value of Number2 (156). Thus, the output of code corresponding to this pseudocode is as follows:

```
156 156
```

We didn't actually switch the numbers, did we? To actually switch the values of MyNumber and YourNumber, both Number1 and Number2 must be specified as reference parameters.

Example 9.7 **The Sale Price Computation Program Revisited**

For another example of the use of value and reference parameters, let's return to the Sale Price Computation program described at the beginning of Section 9.1. For the sake of convenience, we repeat it here:

Katrina Katz owns a small pet store. She wants you to design a program that will compute and display the sale price of a discounted store item when she inputs the original price and its percentage discount.

Note the following:

- The `Input_Data` module inputs the presale price and the percentage discount (`OriginalPrice` and `DiscountRate`) from the user. These quantities must be exported to the main program; therefore, they must be reference parameters. In other words, we want the values of `OriginalPrice` and `DiscountRate` that are obtained in the `Input_Data` module to be retained when they are exported to the `Main` module to be used in the next step (computing the sale price).

- The `Compute_Results` module imports these quantities from the main program, computes the sale price (`SalePrice`) of the item, and exports the latter to the main program. Each time Katrina runs the program, new values for `OriginalPrice` and `DiscountRate` will be sent to this module. Since these values are not exported out of this module, they are value parameters. However, the `SalePrice` that is computed here must be exported to the `Main` module and then used in the `Output_Results` module. Therefore, this parameter must be a reference parameter.

- The `Output_Results` module imports `OriginalPrice`, `DiscountRate`, and `SalePrice` from the main program and displays their values. All parameters here are value parameters because `Output_Results` does not export any data to the main program.

The pseudocode for the entire program follows:

```
1   Main
2      Declare OriginalPrice As Float
3      Declare DiscountRate As Float
4      Declare SalePrice As Float
5      Call Welcome_Message()
6      Call Input_Data(OriginalPrice, DiscountRate)
7      Call Compute_Results(OriginalPrice, DiscountRate, SalePrice)
8      Call Output_Results(OriginalPrice, DiscountRate, SalePrice)
9   End Program
10  Subprogram Welcome_Message()
11     Write "This program is a sale price calculator."
12     Write "When you enter the original price of an item and ↵
                how much it has been discounted, the program ↵
                will display the original price, the discount rate, ↵
                and the new sale price."
13  End Subprogram
14  Subprogram Input_Data(Float Price As Ref,Float Rate As Ref)
15     Write "Enter the price of an item: "
16     Input Price
17     Write "Enter the percentage it is discounted: "
18     Input Rate
19  End Subprogram
20  Subprogram Compute_Results(Float OrigPrice, Float DiscRate, ↵
                               Float Sale As Ref)
21     Declare AmountSaved As Float
22     Set AmountSaved = OrigPrice * DiscRate/100
23     Set Sale = OrigPrice - AmountSaved
24  End Subprogram
```

```
25   Subprogram Output_Results(Float OldPrice, Float Rate, ↵
                               Float NewPrice)
26     Write "The original price of the item is $ " + OldPrice
27     Write "The discount is: " + Rate + "%"
28     Write "The sale price of the item is $ " + NewPrice
29   End Subprogram
```

What Happened?

- The program starts by declaring variables and then control transfers to the Welcome_Message() subprogram. Since the Welcome_Message() subprogram has no arguments, we simply include empty parentheses. This displays a welcome message and transfers control back to the main program.
- Control then transfers to the Input_Data subprogram. Because the Input_Data arguments are undefined (have not been assigned values), the parameters Price and Rate are initially undefined as well. However, they are assigned values by the Input statements in this subprogram, and since both are reference parameters, they are exported to the main program and assigned to OriginalPrice and DiscountRate, respectively.
- Control transfers to the Compute_Results subprogram, in which the value of Sale is computed and returned to the main program in the variable SalePrice. Because its value is used in the next subprogram, it must be a reference parameter.
- Control transfers to the Output_Results subprogram. The values of OriginalPrice, DiscountRate, and SalePrice are assigned to OldPrice, Rate, and NewPrice, respectively, and displayed.
- Control returns to the main program and execution terminates.

To summarize the preceding discussion, when a subprogram is called, the kind of parameter (value or reference) determines the way in which memory is allocated for the value of that parameter. If the parameter is of value type, then the following is true:

- A new (second) storage location is set up in memory to hold the value of that parameter while the subprogram executes.
- The value of the corresponding argument is copied into this location.
- Whenever the value of the parameter is modified by the subprogram, only the contents of this second storage location are changed, so the corresponding argument is unaffected.

If the parameter is of reference type, then the following is true:

- It is assigned the same storage location as the corresponding argument, which in this case must be a variable.
- Whenever the value of the parameter is modified by the subprogram, the contents of this common storage location are changed, so the value of the argument is modified as well.

Two Helpful Functions: ToUpper( ) and ToLower( )

Before we take another look at the important difference between passing by value and passing by reference, we introduce two functions that exist in most programming languages: ToUpper() and ToLower().

As you have gone through the exercises in this book, you may have noticed that often the prompt asking a user to enter information is case sensitive. This means that, for example, when the user is asked to indicate by entering "y" or "yes" that he or she wants to continue, the program will read an entry of "Y" or "YES" as a "no." In the early days of computer technology, people knew that they must always type in exactly what the computer requested. But today, computers are far more user-friendly. Browser search engines forgive misspellings and, unless specifically indicated, it is assumed that you can respond to computer-generated questions without regard to the case (upper or lower). This latter capability is due, in large part, to built-in functions that automatically change a user's response to either all upper-case or all lowercase.[3] Then the program can continue to evaluate the response and proceed as needed. These two functions are described briefly here and will be used to demonstrate the important distinction between passing parameters by value and by reference.

When a `String` value or variable is placed inside the parentheses of the **`ToUpper()` function**, all characters in that `String` are converted to uppercase. Similarly, when a `String` value or variable is placed inside the parentheses of the **`ToLower()` function**, all characters in the string are converted to lowercase. Example 9.8 demonstrates how this works.

Example 9.8 **Using the `ToUpper()` and `ToLower()` functions**

The following program segment shows two uses of the `ToUpper()` and `ToLower()` functions. The user is asked to enter a "Y" for "yes" but many users simply type "y". The `ToUpper()` function converts the response to uppercase. The body of the little game in this program will display a box formed of any word the user enters. The `Length_Of()` function is used to find how many characters are in a word entered by the user and this number is used in the loop that draws the box. The `ToLower()` function changes all characters in any word entered to all lowercase. The pseudocode for this example is as follows:

```
 1  Declare Response As Character
 2  Declare Word As String
 3  Declare Box As String
 4  Declare Count As Integer
 5  Declare X As Integer
 6  Write "Do you want to draw a word-box? Enter 'Y' or 'N'"
 7  Input Response
 8  While ToUpper(Response) == "Y"
 9    Write "Enter any word: "
10    Input Word
11    Set X = Length_Of(Word)
12    Set Box = ToLower(Word)
13    Set Count = 1
```

---

[3]There are also functions available in most languages to read only the first letter of a word so that an entry of **"yes"** would be interpreted as a **"y"** but we do not need to include those in this small example.

```
14          While Count <= X
15             Write Box
16             Set Count = Count + 1
17          End While(Count)
18          Write "Create a new box? Enter 'Y' or 'N'"
19          Input Response
20       End While(Response)
```

What Happened?

There are several lines of interest in this program. Line 8 uses the ToUpper() function to convert any Response to uppercase. Since ToUpper("Y") yields the same result as ToUpper("y"), the outer loop will be entered regardless of which case the user types. Any other entry is the equivalent to "no."

Line 12 uses the ToLower() function slightly differently. Here, the result of the function is assigned to a new variable, Box, which is used later in the program.

Here is what this program segment would display, assuming the user enters "Y" for the first input, "Help" for the second input, and "N" for the third:

```
help
help
help
help
```

Example 9.9 illustrates what can happen when one is not careful about passing parameters by value by reference.

Example 9.9 Pass Those Variables Carefully!

Natalie and Nicholas are co-presidents of the Gamers at College club (GAC). They have created a website and they want the site to be secure. Nick suggests that each member should have a secret login name and Natalie offers to write a program to achieve this. Unfortunately, Natalie did not study this chapter carefully and does not understand the difference between value parameters and reference parameters. She writes the following pseudocode:

```
1  Main
2    Declare Response As String
3    Declare First As String
4    Declare Last As String
5    Write "Do you want to start? Enter 'yes' or 'no' :"
6    Input Response
7    Set Response = ToLower(Response)
8    While Response == "yes"
9      Write "Enter this member's first name:"
10     Input First
11     Write "Enter this member's last name:"
12     Input Last
13     Call Secret_Login(First, Last)
14     Write "Member name: " + First + " " + Last
```

```
15        Write "Enter another member?"
16        Input Response
17        Set Response = ToLower(Response)
18     End While
19  End Program
20  Subprogram Secret_Login(String Part1 As Ref, String Part2 As Ref)
21     Declare Login As String
22     Declare Temp As String
23     Set Temp = Part1
24     Set Part1 = ToLower(Part2) + "**"
25     Set Part2 = ToLower(Temp)
26     Set Login = Part1 + Part2
27     Write "Your secret login is: " + Login
28  End Subprogram
```

What Happened?

Nick is not impressed with the results of the program and tells Natalie to determine what went wrong. Natalie runs the program twice, entering the names Mary Lamb and Jack Sprat. When she sees the following display she realizes what happened:

```
Your secret login is: lamb**mary
Member name: lamb** mary
Your secret login is: sprat**jack
Member name: sprat** jack
```

Luckily, it takes very little effort to fix the program. Do you know how to fix it? Natalie sent reference parameters to the subprogram Secret_Login. The value of the first name (First) was sent into Part1 but all changes to Part1 affected First. The same is true of Last; since it was sent into Secret_Login as a reference parameter, its value changed as changes were made to Part2 in the subprogram.

However, if line 20 were changed to

```
Subprogram Secret_Login(String Part1, String Part2)
```

then the display, given the entries of "Mary", "Lamb", "Jack", and "Sprat", would look as follows:

```
Your secret login is: lamb**mary
Member name: Mary Lamb
Your secret login is: sprat**jack
Member name: Jack Sprat
```

The Scope of a Variable

When a variable is input, processed, or output in a program module, we say that it has been *referenced* in that module. In certain situations, a variable that is declared in one program module cannot be referenced in another module. Trying to do so will result in an **undefined variable** error message when the program is compiled. The part of the program in which a given variable can be referenced is called the **scope** of that variable.

In many programming languages, the scope of a variable declared in a certain program module consists of that module together with all its submodules. We will follow this practice in this book. For example, in the Sale Price Computation program discussed earlier in this chapter:

- The variables `OriginalPrice`, `DiscountRate`, and `SalePrice` are declared in the main program. Because all other program modules are subprograms of the main program, we will consider the scope of these variables to be the entire program; they can be referenced in any module.
- The variable `AmountSaved` is declared in the `Compute_Results` subprogram, so its scope is limited to this subprogram; it cannot be used in any other program module.

Global and Local Variables

Notice that, in this book, variables declared in the main program have a scope that is the entire program. Such variables are called **global variables**. On the other hand, in some programming languages, a variable is only global if it is declared outside of, or prior to, all program modules including the main program.

In the Sale Price Computation program, the variables `OriginalPrice`, `DiscountRate`, and `SalePrice` are global variables. Variables that are declared in a particular subprogram, such as `AmountSaved` in the `Compute_Results` subprogram, are said to be local to that module. **Local variables** have the following properties:

- When the value of a local variable changes in a subprogram, the value of a variable with the same name outside that subprogram remains unchanged.
- When the value of a variable changes elsewhere in a program, a local variable with the same name remains unchanged in its subprogram.

Sometimes local and global variables come into conflict. For example, suppose a variable named `MyName` is declared in the main program, and another variable, also called `MyName`, is declared in a subprogram. We say that `MyName` has a multiple declaration in the program. The `MyName` declared in the main program is a global variable and thus may be assigned a value in any subprogram. But the `MyName` declared in the subprogram is local to that subprogram, so changes to its value do not affect a variable with the same name outside the subprogram. To resolve this conflict, the local declaration takes precedence. This means that the value of the main program variable, `MyName`, is not changed when the subprogram `MyName` is assigned a new value. Example 9.10 illustrates this situation.

Example 9.10 Keeping Track of the Value of `MyNumber`

Consider the following pseudocode:

```
1  Main
2     Declare MyNumber As Integer
3     Set MyNumber = 7654
4     Call Any_Sub()
```

```
 5    Write MyNumber
 6  End Program
 7  Subprogram Any_Sub()
 8    Declare MyNumber As Integer
 9    Declare YourNumber As Integer
10    Set MyNumber = 2
11    Set YourNumber = MyNumber * 3
12    Write YourNumber
13  End Subprogram
```

What Happened?

- What will be displayed after this program segment is coded and run? The main program begins by assigning MyNumber the value 7654. Then control is transferred to the subprogram. In the subprogram, MyNumber is a local variable and is set to 2, locally. The value assigned to it inside Any_Sub does not affect the value of the main program's variable, MyNumber.

- However, the value of the local variable, MyNumber, is valid within the subprogram. Therefore, YourNumber will be set equal to 2*3 since MyNumber, within the confines of the subprogram, Any_Sub, has the value of 2. The Write statement in Any_Sub will display the number 6.

- When control is returned to the main program, MyNumber still maintains its global value and the Write statement displays the number 7654.

Note that it is normally a bad idea to give the same name to two variables, except perhaps for counters. In fact, some languages don't support global variables at all.

The computer treats local variables in the same way as value parameters. Whenever a local variable is declared, even if it has the same name as a previously declared variable, it's allocated a new storage location in memory. Thus, in Example 9.10, from the computer's point of view, the main program MyNumber and the subprogram MyNumber are treated as two different variables. Changing one has no effect on the other.

Use Parameters, Not Global Variables, to Pass Data among Modules

In many programming languages, it's possible to pass data among modules by making use of global variables. By its nature, a global variable can be imported by or exported from every program module. Nevertheless, it is considered poor programming practice to use global variables for this purpose because doing so diminishes the independence of program modules. The proper way to pass data among program modules is through the use of arguments and parameters. We can use the property of local variables to our advantage, as demonstrated by the use of counters in Example 9.11.

Example 9.11 **Using Counters Locally**

Counters are often used in programs and subprograms. Luckily, the value of a counter in a subprogram does not affect the value of a counter in the main program or in another subprogram, as shown by the following pseudocode, which calculates the weekly gross pay (pretax) of employees in a small business:

```
1   Main
2     Declare Name As String
3     Declare NumEmployees As Integer
4     Declare Count As Integer
5     Write "How many employees do you have?"
6     Input NumEmployees
7     For(Count = 1; Count <= NumEmployees; Count++)
8       Write "Enter this employee's name: "
9       Input Name
10      Call Pay_Employee(Name)
11    End For
12  End Program
13  Subprogram Pay_Employee(String EmpName)
14    Declare Rate As Float
15    Declare Hours As Float
16    Declare Sum As Float
17    Declare Pay As Float
18    Declare Count As Integer
19    Set Sum = 0
20    Write "Enter the pay rate for " + EmpName
21    Input Rate
22    For(Count = 1; Count <= 7; Count++)
23      Write "Enter hours worked for day " + Count
24      Input Hours
25      Set Sum = Sum + Hours
26    End For
27    Set Pay = Sum * Rate
28    Write "Gross pay this week for " + EmpName
29    Write "is $ " + Pay
30  End Subprogram
```

What Happened?

This program finds the weekly gross pay for employees. Initially, the user enters the number of employees (NumEmployees) and the For loop on lines 7–11 gets an employee's name (Name) and sends that name to the subprogram (Pay_Employee(EmpName)) for each employee. The subprogram uses a For loop to get the number of hours worked by that employee for seven days (one week). At the end of each time this subprogram is called, the counter, Count, has the value of 8. However, the variable Count in the main program must maintain its original value. Because Count is declared in Main and also declared locally in Pay_Employees, the two values remain separate and changes to the value of Count in the subprogram have no effect on the value of Count in Main.

Self Check for Section 9.2

The following program is used in Self Check Questions 9.8 and 9.10

```
Main
  Declare X, Y, Z As Integer
  Set X = 1
  Set Y = 2
  Set Z = 3
  Call Display(Z, Y, X)
  Write X + " " + Y + " " + Z
End Program
Subprogram Display(Integer Num1,Integer Num2, Integer Num3 As Ref)
  Write Num1 + " " + Num2 + " " + Num3
  Set Num1 = 4
  Set Num2 = 5
  Set Num3 = 6
  Write Num1 + " " + Num2 + " " + Num3
End Subprogram
```

9.8 What is the output of code corresponding to this pseudocode?

9.9 Suppose that all occurrences of Num1, Num2, and Num3 in this program were changed to X, Y, and Z, respectively. What is the output of code for the modified program?

9.10 Determine the output of code for the given program if its subprogram header were changed as follows:

a. `Subprogram Display(Integer Num1,Integer Num2,Integer Num3)`
b. `Subprogram Display(Integer Num1 As Ref,Integer Num2 As ↵`
`                    Ref,Integer Num3 As Ref)`

9.11 What is displayed after the following program segment is coded and run? Assume all variables have been declared as String variables.

```
Set MyName = "Marty"
Set PetName = "JoJo"
Write ToUpper(MyName) + " and " + ToLower(PetName)
```

9.12 What is the output of code corresponding to the following pseudocode? Assume that variables declared in the main program are global variables.

a.
```
Main
    Declare X As Integer
    Set X = 0
    Call Simple()
    Write X
End Program
Subprogram Simple()
    Set X = 1
End Subprogram
```

```
b. Main
    Declare X As Integer
    Set X = 0
    Write X
    Call Simple()
End Program
Subprogram Simple()
    Set X = 1
End Subprogram
```

9.3 Functions

A **function**, as we have seen, is a special type of subprogram—one whose name can be assigned a value. In this section, we will discuss built-in functions, which are supplied by the programming language, and user-defined functions, which are program modules created by the programmer.

Built-in Functions

Programming languages typically provide a wide assortment of built-in functions. These are often referred to as a **library**. The code for these functions is supplied in separate modules, and doesn't need to be included within your program. In this book, you have already seen the following examples of built-in functions:

- Sqrt(X) computes the square root of the number X.
- Int(X) computes the integer obtained by discarding the fractional part of the number X.
- Ceiling(X) computes the integer obtained by rounding the number X up to the next integer.
- Floor(X) computes the integer obtained by discarding the fractional part of the number X.
- Random() generates a random integer (whole number) from 0.0 to 1.0, including 0.0 but not 1.0.
- Length_Of(S) computes the length of the string S.
- ToUpper(S) changes the value of all characters in a string, S, to uppercase.
- ToLower(S) changes the value of all characters in a string, S, to lowercase.

Built-in functions can be viewed as subprograms, which normally contain one or more parameters and return (export) at least one value. As with any subprogram, the arguments in the call to a built-in function may be constants, variables, or expressions of the appropriate type. However, built-in functions (including the ones listed above) differ from the subprograms discussed in Sections 9.1 and 9.2 in the following ways:

1. The header and definition of a built-in function do not appear in the program that calls that function.
2. When a built-in function is called, the function name is assigned a value (of the type specified for that function).
3. A built-in function is called by using the function name anywhere in the program that a constant of its type is allowed.

For example, the Sqrt() function is of type Float—it is assigned a Float value when it is called. Sqrt() may be used (called) anywhere in a program that a constant of type Float is allowed. Thus, all of the following are valid calls to the Sqrt() function (assuming that Num is a variable of numeric type and the value of the argument is not negative):

- Set X = Sqrt(10)
- Write Sqrt(2*(Num + 1))
- Call Display(Sqrt(Num))

Here are a few more functions that are commonly built into programming languages. While the exact name and form of any of the functions given here may differ from those used in a particular programming language, most common programming languages have built-in functions that perform the following tasks:

- Abs(X) computes and returns the absolute value of the real number X. The absolute value of a given number is the number obtained by ignoring the sign, if any, of the given number. This function is of type Float.
- Round(X) rounds the real number X to the nearest whole number and returns that number. It is of type Integer.
- Str(X) converts the number X into the corresponding string and returns that string. It is of type String.
- Val(S,N) converts the string S, if it represents a number, into a number of the appropriate type (Integer or Float) and sets N = 1. If S does not represent a number, this function sets both Val and N equal to 0. Val is of type Float and N is an Integer parameter of reference type.

Example 9.12 provides examples of using built-in functions.

Example 9.12 **Built-in Functions**

The following examples show the result of applying the indicated function to the specified argument:

- Abs(10) returns 10
- Abs(-10) returns 10
- Round(10.5) returns 11
- Round(100 * 10.443)/100 returns 10.44
- Str(31.5) returns "31.5"
- Str(-100) returns "-100"
- Val("31.5",N) returns the number 31.5 and N = 1
- Val("abc",N) returns the number 0 and N = 0

When a Number Is Not a Number

Although the string "31.5" and the number 31.5 may look similar, from a programming point of view they are quite different as follows:

- The number 31.5 is stored in memory as the binary equivalent of 31.5. Moreover, because it's of numeric type, it can be used in mathematical computations.

- The string "31.5" is stored in memory by placing the ASCII codes for "3", "1", ".", and "5" in consecutive storage locations. Because "31.5" is a string, we cannot perform arithmetic operations on it, but we can concatenate it with another string.

The Val() function is important in programming because it allows the programmer to convert a string to a numeric value, if appropriate, or signify to the program that the string cannot be converted to a numeric value. There are many programming situations that require this functionality.

Example 9.13 provides an application of the Val() function to the process of data validation. It demonstrates the technique of inputting numbers as strings, which prevents a program crash if the characters entered by the user do not form a valid number.

Example 9.13 **The Valuable Val() Function**

The following pseudocode prompts the user to enter an integer. It receives the input as a string, checks whether that string represents an integer, and repeats the prompt if it does not.

```
1  Declare InputString As String
2  Declare N As Integer
3  Declare Number As Integer
4  Repeat
5    Write "Enter an integer: "
6    Input InputString
7    Set Number = Val(InputString,N)
8  Until (N != 0) AND (Number == Int(Number))
```

What Happened?

The Repeat-Until loop on lines 4–8 validates the data input with the aid of the Val and Int() functions. If the string entered by the user is an integer, then both conditions in the Until statement on line 8 are true and the loop is exited. If the input string is not a number, then the first condition is false; if it is a number but not an integer, then the second condition is false. In either of these two cases, the loop is reentered and the user is again asked to input an integer.

Note that, if the number input is to be manipulated later by the program, it must be referred to as Number and not as InputString.

Making It Work

Accessing Built-in Functions

Although you don't need to include the code for a built-in function in the program you are writing, the file that contains that code may have to be linked to your program in order for the program to run. This is usually done by inserting a statement at the beginning of the program that tells the compiler, when it translates the program into machine language, where to locate the function's code and instructs the compiler to link that code to your program. These files are stored in libraries—collections of built-in functions, precompiled routines, and subprograms—which are linked normally in the beginning of the program.

Following is an example of the beginning of a C++ program. These are calls to C++ libraries that contain functions (and other information) needed for this specific program. These calls are identified, in C++, as **preprocessor directives**.

```
//** preprocessor directives
#include <iostream>    //** Header for input/output stream
#include <string>      //** Header for string type
#include <vector>      //** Header for vector class
#include <cstdlib>     //** Header for standard C library
#include <cctype>      //** Header for CType library functions
```

User-Defined Functions

Programming languages also allow you to create your own function subprograms, which are called **user-defined functions**.[4]

In some languages all subprograms are functions; in others functions are one special type of subprogram. In this book, we consider both subprograms and functions. The difference between a subprogram that is a function and one that is not (sometimes referred to as a **procedure**) is twofold:

1. A function's name may be assigned a value (of a specified type) in the code that defines it.
2. A function is called by placing its name (and desired arguments) anywhere in the program that a constant of the function's specified type is allowed.

In this book, we will begin a function's header with the word Function (instead of Subprogram). Example 9.14 illustrates these points.

Example 9.14 **A Cubic Function**

The following program defines and calls a function Cube() that imports a number, Side from the main program and returns its cube, Side^3, to the main program, where it is displayed:

```
1  Main
2     Declare LittleBox As Float
3     Set LittleBox = Cube(10)
4     Write LittleBox
5  End Program
6  Function Cube(Float Side) As Float
7     Set Cube = Side^3
8  End Function
```

---

[4]Here, the word *user* refers to the programmer (the user of the programming language) and not the person executing the program.

What Happened?

Line 1 begins the main program. Line 2 declares a `Float` variable named `LittleBox`, but no value is assigned to `LittleBox`. The value of `LittleBox` is set on the next line and needs a little more explanation.

The call to the function is made on line 3 where the variable, `LittleBox`, is given the value of what will happen to the number 10 after it has been acted upon by the `Cube()` function.

When this statement is executed, control transfers to line 6, to the function subprogram named `Cube()`. Notice that this function has one parameter, `Side`. Line 3 passes the value of 10 to the parameter, `Side`. Notice also that the function header declares the function type—the type for `Cube()`—as `Float`. Then, the statement

```
Set Cube = Side^3
```

assigns the value 1000 (i.e., 10^3) to the function. When the function ends, this value is returned to the main program, assigned to `LittleBox`, and displayed.

When to Use a Function

If the programming language you are using contains both functions and non-function subprograms, then either one may be used to implement a given program submodule. Which one you decide to use in a particular instance is a matter of style. Here is a guideline for deciding whether to use a function to implement a particular submodule: If the submodule in question computes and returns a single value to the calling module, then implement it with a function. Notice that the function in Example 9.14 satisfies this criterion.

To illustrate this point, and to provide another example of the use of a user-defined function, let's reexamine the Sale Price Computation program discussed in Sections 9.1 and 9.2. To facilitate our discussion, we will repeat the description for the problem.

> Katrina Katz owns a small pet store. She has asked you to design a program that will compute and display the sale price of any discounted item in her store when she inputs the original price and the percentage it is discounted.

The data flow diagram in Figure 9.2 makes it clear that the only submodule that returns a single value to the `Main` module is `Compute_Results`. Therefore, following the guidelines stated above, we would use subprograms to implement the `Welcome_Message`, `Input_Data`, and `Output_Results` modules, but use a function to implement the `Compute_Results` module. The pseudocode for the modified `Main` program and the `Compute_Results` subprogram (which now becomes the `NewPrice()` function) is given below. The pseudocode for the other three modules is identical to that given in Section 9.2.

```
1  Main
2     Declare OriginalPrice As Float
3     Declare DiscountRate As Float
4     Declare SalePrice As Float
5     Call Welcome_Message
6     Call Input_Data(OriginalPrice, DiscountRate)
```

Figure 9.2 Data flow diagram for the Sale Price Computation program

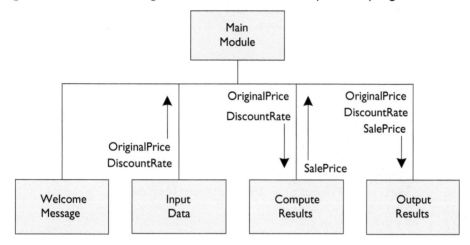

```
 7    Set SalePrice = NewPrice(OriginalPrice, DiscountRate)
 8    Call Output_Results(OriginalPrice, DiscountRate, SalePrice)
 9  End Program
10  Function NewPrice(Float OriginalPrice, Float DiscountRate) As Float
11    Declare AmountSaved As Float
12    Set AmountSaved = OriginalPrice * DiscountRate/100
13    Set NewPrice = OriginalPrice - AmountSaved
14  End Function
```

Before we end this section, we will look at Example 9.15 that shows a program that combines the use of parallel arrays and a user-defined function in a longer program.

Example 9.15 **Getting Good Mileage Out of a Function**

Penelope Pinchpenny is concerned about the amount of money she spends on gasoline. She asks you to write a program that will allow her to compare the miles per gallon she uses over ten different driving trips. She wants to compare highway miles with city miles, trips over flat distances and those on curvy hilly roads, and the like. After some careful thought, you come up with the following design:

The output required is a table that identifies the specific type of road trip, the total miles of each trip, and the miles per gallon used for each trip. Parallel arrays are ideal to use in this situation to store this information so you decide you will need the following:

A String array: `TripName[10]`

Two Float arrays: `TripMiles[10]` and `TripMPG[10]`

After Penelope enters information for each trip, you need to calculate the miles per gallon. You decide to create a function named `Answer()` to do this. You will need to send two pieces of information to the function—the number of miles traveled and the number of gallons of gas used. The result of the `Answer()` function must be stored in the appropriate element in the `TripMPG` array.

To save space, we assume that the following variables have been declared in the beginning of Main, as well as the three arrays previously mentioned: Count As Integer, K As Integer, Gallons As Float.

```
1   Main
2     Set Count = 0
3     While Count < 10
4       Write "Enter a description of this trip: "
5       Input TripName[Count]
6       Write "How many miles did you drive? "
7       Input TripMiles[Count]
8       Write "How many gallons of gas did you use on this trip?"
9       Input Gallons
10      Set TripMPG[Count] = Answer(TripMiles[Count], Gallons)
11      Set Count = Count + 1
12    End While(Count)
13    Set K = 0
14    Write "Trip Name \t Miles Traveled \t MPG"
15    While K < 10
16      Write TripName[K] + "\t" + TripMiles[K] + "\t" + TripMPG[K]
17      Set K = K + 1
18    End While(K)
19  End Program
20  Function Answer(Float Num1, Float Num2) As Float
21    Set Answer = Num1/Num2
22  End Function
```

What Happened?

Line 1 begins the main program. The first While loop on lines 3–12 does most of the work. Penelope enters a brief description of a given trip on line 5, and this value is stored in the first element of the TripName array. Next, she enters the miles traveled on line 7 and this value is stored in the first element of the TripMiles array. Then she enters the number of gallons used on line 9. Line 10 calls the function, Answer() and sends it the present values of TripMiles[Count] and Gallons. These values are sent to the arguments Num1 and Num2 in the function on line 20. The function simply divides the number of miles by the gallons used to find the miles per gallon result. That result is stored in the first element of the TripMPG array on line 10. The counter, Count, is then incremented and Penelope is prompted for the next set of data.

When all the data has been entered, the second While loop displays the table. Notice the \t symbol helps format the information.

Making It Work

Getting the Most Out of Functions

You may wonder why we gave the function a generic name like Answer() and why we called the arguments Num1 and Num2 instead of names that indicate their significance. You might be tempted to name the function something that shows its purpose more clearly, like mpg(numMiles,numGals). However, by giving the function a generic name, it can be reused in other programs. For example, this particular function could easily be used in a program to determine the cost of a pound of potatoes if you knew the price of a 10-pound bag or the exam average of a student if you knew the sum of the exam scores and the number of exams. In fact, you will be asked to do this in Self Check Question 9.18.

Where Should You Put the Functions and Subprograms?

Making It Work

You can see in Example 9.15 as well as in previous examples in this chapter that the functions and subprograms have been placed at the end of the code, after the Main program has ended. In general, we have followed this form:

```
Main
   Program statements
Function Any_Func()
   Function statements
End Function
Subprogram Any_Sub()
   Subprogram statements
End Subprogram
```

In most programming languages functions and subprograms can be placed anywhere in the code. Normally comments are inserted at the top of a function or subprogram to explain the code's purpose. The programming language's keyword that identifies what comes next as a function or subprogram (Function and Subprogram, in our pseudocode) alerts the computer about how to treat the code within that function or subprogram. Therefore, these statements will only be executed when they are called.

Normal conventions of programming dictate that all user-defined functions and subprograms are placed either at the beginning (before Main) or at the end (after EndProgram) of a program.

Self Check for Section 9.3

9.13 Determine the value of the following expressions:
   a. Sqrt(4)
   b. Int(3.9)

9.14 Determine the value of the following expressions:
   a. Abs(0)
   b. Round(3.9)
   c. Str(0.1)
   d. Val("-32",N)

9.15 What is the output of code corresponding to the following pseudocode?

```
Main
  Write F(1,2)
  Write G(-1)
End Program
Function F(X,Y) As Integer
  Set F = 5 * X + Y
End Function
Function G(X) As Integer
  Set G = X * X
End Function
```

9.16 a. Write a function named Area as follows:

```
Function Area(L,W) As Float
```

that computes the area of a rectangle of length L and width W.

b. Write an assignment statement that calls this function, using any values you want for the length and width.

For Self Check Questions 9.17 and 9.18 refer to Example 9.15

9.17 Add pseudocode to Example 9.15 to include another parallel array to store the number of gallons used on each trip and display this with the rest of the information.

9.18 Write a program that will allow the user to enter three exam scores, find their sum, and, using the Answer(Num1, Num2) function, computes and displays the exam average.

9.4 Recursion

When a subprogram calls itself, the process is called **recursion**, and the subprogram is said to be recursive. Some programming languages allow recursion; others do not. **Recursive algorithms** are algorithms that make use of recursive subprograms. Sometimes they can provide quick and simple solutions to complex problems.

The Recursive Process

To illustrate the concept of recursion, let's consider a simple programming problem: Given a positive integer, N, we will write a function, Sum(N), which computes the sum of the first N positive integers. To solve this problem we will set up a counter-controlled loop in which each successive integer is added to a running total. The pseudocode is as follows:

```
Function Sum(Integer N) As Integer
  Set Total = 0
  For (K = 1; K <= N; K++)
    Set Total = Total + K
  End For
  Set Sum = Total
End Function
```

This pseudocode provides a nonrecursive solution to the problem. To solve this problem recursively, we ask the question, "If we know the sum of the first N - 1 positive integers, how would we find the sum of the first N positive integers?" The answer is to add the integer N to the sum of the first N - 1 positive integers as follows:

    Sum(N) = (1 + 2 + . . . + (N - 1)) + N

or

    Sum(N) = Sum(N - 1) + N

For example, if N = 4, then

    Sum(4) = (1 + 2 + 3) + 4 or Sum(4) = Sum(3) + 4

This is the key to the recursive solution of the problem. We have effectively replaced the original problem with a lesser problem. Now we must find the sum of the first N - 1 positive integers; that is, we must find Sum(N - 1). But a similar argument gives us

    Sum(N - 1) = Sum(N - 2) + N - 1

and we can continue in this manner until we reach the following:

    Sum(2) = Sum(1) + 2.

Notice that we can't write Sum(1) = Sum(0) + 1, because Sum(0) makes no sense—we can't sum the first zero positive integers! However, since Sum(1) is the sum of the first positive integer, we have the following:

    Sum(1) = 1

Thus, we can define the function Sum(N) by the following pair of formulas:

    If N = 1, Sum(N) = 1.
    If N > 1, Sum(N) = Sum(N - 1) + N.

Then, we can use these formulas to compute Sum(N) for any value of N. To illustrate the technique, let N = 4; that is, we will find Sum(4), the sum of the first four positive integers. To do so, we apply the formulas above with, successively, N = 4, N = 3, N = 2, and N = 1. The computation goes as follows:

    N = 4: Sum(4) = Sum(3) + 4
    N = 3: Sum(3) = Sum(2) + 3

Now, substituting this expression for Sum(3) into the line above it gives us the following:

    N = 4: Sum(4) = [Sum(2) + 3] + 4 = Sum(2) + 7

What is Sum(2)?

    N = 2: Sum(2) = Sum(1) + 2

Substituting this expression for Sum(2) into the line above it gives us the following:

    N = 4: Sum(4) = [Sum(1) + 2] + 7 = Sum(1) + 9

and we already know:

    N = 1: Sum(1) = 1

Substituting this value for Sum(1) into the line above it gives us the following:

    N = 4: Sum(4) = 1 + 9 = 10

Compare this to the straightforward way of finding Sum(4) as follows:

    N = 4: Sum(4) = 1 + 2 + 3 + 4 = 10

The recursive solution shown here may seem awkward and even confusing but remember that you are looking at it from a human perspective. When a recursive solution is carried out in a program, it may require only a small amount of code that can be executed very quickly. Example 9.16 provides an illustration of this.

Example 9.16 **A Recursive Solution**

The following pseudocode provides a recursive solution to the problem of summing the first N positive integers, where N is a given positive integer:

```
1  Function Sum(Integer N) As Integer
2    If N == 1 Then
3      Set Sum = 1
4    Else
5      Set Sum = Sum(N - 1) + N
6    End If
7  End Function
```

What Happened?

To help explain how this pseudocode works, suppose that this function is called by the statement

```
Set Total = Sum(4)
```

where Total is an Integer variable that has previously been declared. When this statement is executed, control transfers to the function Sum(). N is set equal to 4 (line 1). Then execution proceeds as follows:

- **First call to the function:** Because N = 4, lines 2 and 3 are not executed and control goes to the Else clause on line 4. Then line 5 is executed. The right side of the assignment statement

  ```
  Set Sum = Sum(N - 1) + N
  ```

  is evaluated. At this point, since N = 4 and (N - 1) = 3, this gives us the following for the right side:

  ```
  Sum(3) + 4
  ```

  But, before this expression can be assigned to Sum, the function Sum(3) causes a call to the function Sum() with N = 3.

- **Second call to the function:** This is actually where the function calls itself. On this second call, lines 2 and 3 are still skipped because N does not equal 1. However, the Else clause is executed now with N = 3. At this point, (N - 1) = 2, so when the right side of the assignment statement is evaluated this time, we get

  ```
  Sum(2) + 3
  ```

  which causes the function to be called again, this time with N = 2.

- **Third call to the function:** Lines 2 and 3 are skipped again during this call and the Else clause is executed with N = 2. The right side of the assignment statement is evaluated, which gives us the following:

  ```
  Sum(1) + 2
  ```

  Now the function calls itself one more time, with N = 1.

- **Fourth (and last) call to the function:** Since N = 1, this time the Then clause on lines 2 and 3 is executed and Sum is set equal to 1. In this case, the function does not call itself and execution of this call to the function is completed.

- Control now returns to the assignment statement on line 5 as

    ```
    Set Sum = Sum(1) + 2
    ```

    in the third call to the function (where the last call to the function was made). Here, Sum(1) is replaced by 1 and Sum (on the left side) takes on the value 3. Execution of the third call is now complete.
- Control now returns to the assignment statement as

    ```
    Set Sum = Sum(2) + 3
    ```

    in the second call to the function. Here, Sum(2) is replaced by 3 and Sum (on the left side) takes on the value 6. Execution of the second call is now complete.
- Finally control returns to the assignment statement as

    ```
    Set Sum = Sum(3) + 4
    ```

    in the first call to the function. Here, Sum(3) is replaced by 6 and Sum (on the left side) takes on the value 10. Execution of the first call is now complete, and Total (in the initial calling statement) is set equal to 10.

Table 9.1 summarizes the action of the function Sum() if it is called from the main program with $N = 4$.

Table 9.1 Calling Sum(N) with $N = 4$

If Execution Is Here	Value of N	Value of Sum
Start of execution of first call to Sum()	4	Undefined
Start of execution of second call to Sum()	3	Undefined
Start of execution of third call to Sum()	2	Undefined
Start of execution of fourth call to Sum()	1	Undefined
End of execution of fourth call to Sum()	1	1
End of execution of third call to Sum()	2	3
End of execution of second call to Sum()	3	6
End of execution of first call to Sum()	4	10

Example 9.17 provides another example of recursion.

Example 9.17 **Using Recursion to Do Exponentiation**

We will write a recursive function that finds the Nth power, X^N, of the number X, where N is a given positive integer. We name this function Power(). To apply recursion, we have to express X^N in terms of X^{N-1}:

```
XN = X * XN-1
```

Thus, if we call our function Power(X,N), where X represents the base and N represents the exponent, we have the following:

```
If N > 1, Power(X,N) = X * Power(X,N - 1)
If N = 1, Power(X,N) = X (since X1 = X)
```

For example, when $X = 2$ and $N = 5$:

$$2^5 = 2 * 2 * 2 * 2 * 2 = 2 * (2 * 2 * 2 * 2) = 2 * 2^4$$

Therefore, we can replace the problem of finding the Nth power of X with that of finding the $(N - 1)^{st}$ power of X. This is the key to a recursive solution. Adapting the pseudocode of Example 9.16 to the current situation, we have the following:

```
1  Function Power(Float X, Integer N) As Float
2    If N == 1 Then
3      Set Power = X
4    Else
5      Set Power = Power(X,N - 1) * X
6    End If
7  End Function
```

What Happened?

Let's trace the execution of this function when it is called by the following statement:

```
Set Answer = Power(5, 3)
```

The statement above will assign the value $5^3 = 125$ to the variable Answer. The assignment statement transfers control to the function Power(), where X is set equal to 5 and N is set equal to 3. This is the first call to the recursive function, which calls itself a total of three times, as follows:

- The first call to the function begins on line 1: However, since $N = 3$, lines 2 and 3 are skipped and the Else clause on line 5 is executed. The right side of the assignment statement,

  ```
  Set Power = Power(X, N - 1) * X
  ```

  is evaluated. The right side yields the following:

  ```
  Power(5, 2) * 5
  ```

  and causes a second call to the function Power() with $X = 5$ and $N = 2$.
- The second call to the function is where the function calls itself the first time: The Else clause on line 5 is now executed again with $N = 2$ and the right side of the assignment statement is evaluated, which yields the following:

  ```
  Power(5, 1) * 5
  ```

  and causes Power() to be called again with $X = 5$ and $N = 1$.
- The function calls itself once more. On this third (and last) call to the function, since $N = 1$ in this function call, the Then clause on line 3 is executed and Power is set equal to 5. The function does not call itself here, and execution of the third call to the Power() function is complete.
- Control now returns to the right side of the assignment statement on line 5 as follows:

  ```
  Set Power = Power(5, 1) * 5
  ```

  in the second call to the function (where the third call was made). Here, Power(5, 1) is replaced by 5 and Power (on the left side) takes on the value 25. Execution of the second call is now complete.
- Control now returns to the right side of the assignment statement (still line 5) as follows:

  ```
  Set Power = Power(5, 2) * 5
  ```

in the first call to the function. Here, Power(5,2) is replaced by 25 and Power (on the left side) takes on the value 125. Execution of the first call is now complete and Answer is set equal to 125.

Self Check for Section 9.4

Use the following information for Self Check Questions 9.19–9.22:

The factorial of a positive integer N is denoted by N! and is read "N factorial". It is defined to be the product of the first N positive integers as follows:
N! = 1 × 2 ... × N

In particular, if N = 1, then N! = 1. Also, 2! = 1 × 2 = 2, 3! = 1 × 2 × 3 = 6, and so on. "Eight factorial" is written 8! and 8! = 8 × 7 × 6 × 5 × 4 × 3 × 2 × 1.

9.19 Express N! in terms of (N-1)!.

9.20 Write a recursive function, Factorial(N), which computes and returns N!.

9.21 Trace the action of the function Factorial(N), similarly to that of Example 9.16, if it is called by the following statement:

Set Answer = Factorial(3)

9.22 Use a For loop to write a nonrecursive function, Fac(N), which computes and returns N!.

9.5 Focus on Problem Solving: **A Fitness Plan**

In this section, we will develop a program that uses subprograms and one user-defined function. The function will be used for several purposes, demonstrating how a generic function can be used for varied tasks.

Problem Statement

Your friend, Pat Nerdoff, has realized that too many hours sitting in front of an array of computer screens has resulted in a very out-of-shape, albeit impressive computer programmer. Pat wants to get in shape and you offer to design a program that will track Pat's progress at the gym over a period of four weeks. The program will calculate Pat's initial Body Mass Index (BMI) and calculate Pat's progress toward a goal that includes a weight lifting, jogging, and a weight-loss regimen. Pat—or any user—should be able to input initial values and weekly updates. The program will display what percent the user has achieved toward a personal goal in each category and will provide new BMI values each week. A single function that we will create can be used to help accomplish these tasks.

Problem Analysis

This program needs the following initial information:

- The user's name
- The user's beginning BMI
- The user's fitness goals

The Body Mass Index (BMI)

A person's Body Mass Index is calculated with the following formula:

```
BMI = ((weight in pounds)/(height in inches)²) * 703
```

Therefore, we need the following input from the user:

- The user's height in feet (`feet`)
- The user's height in inches (`inches`)
- The user's weight in pounds (`pounds`)

We must be sure to explain to the user that we need input in feet separate from inches as in, for example, "5 feet, 6 inches" and then we can convert the height to inches as follows:

```
height = feet * 12 + inches
```

We can then calculate the user's beginning BMI:

```
BMI = (pounds / height^2) * 703
```

The User's Goals

For this program, in the interest of saving time and space, we will assume there are only four fitness goals: improving muscle tone for quadriceps and biceps, increasing jogging time, and lowering the BMI. The user will enter his or her goals as follows:

- Desired number of reps per session for quadriceps workout (`Quads`)
- Desired number of reps per session for biceps workout (`Biceps`)
- Desired number of minutes to jog per session (`Jog`)
- Target BMI level (`TargetBMI`)

Input, Calculations, and Output

Once we know what the user wants to accomplish, we will have him or her input the progress over the span of four weeks and calculate how close he or she has come to achieving these goals. We will do this by comparing each week's achievement with the user's goals using a function for each comparison. Then we will output, for each week, the results.

Program Design

In this program, the `Main` module is what has been referred to as the **driver program**. It will call a welcome message, which describes what the program does and then will call the rest of the submodules. We need a submodule to determine the user's BMI, one to find the user's fitness goals, another to input weekly updates, and one to display the results. The `Main` module will call three of these submodules but, since the display module must be called each time a weekly update is made, the display module will be called from within the update module. In general, the design of the program is as follows:

- `Main` module: This module will display a welcome message and call the other submodules.
- `Welcome` module: This module will display information about the program.

- `Initial_bmi` module: This module will get the user's beginning height and weight and will, by calling a function, calculate and display the beginning BMI value.
- `Fitness_goals` module: This module will prompt the user to enter goals for number of reps per session for a quad workout and a biceps workout and for the user's jogging goal. It will also allow the user to input the BMI goal. Since the user's height cannot change significantly in four weeks, a change in BMI must come from a change in weight, and this will identify how far the user has come toward the weight-loss goal.
- `Progress` module: In a loop, this module will prompt the user to enter values for the number of reps completed per session for one week in quads and biceps, for the number of minutes jogged per session that week, and for the user's weight. For each entry, a new percent of goal achieved will be calculated by calling a function we will create, `Quotient()`. This module will then call the `Display` module to output the results for each week.
- `Display` module: This module will display the results for each week.

The `Quotient()` Function

The formula to find the Body Mass Index (BMI) requires that the weight in pounds be divided by the height in inches. Then the result is multiplied by 703. We will ask the user to enter a target BMI and, for each week, determine how close the user is to achieving that target. To do this, we use a division operation. The way we find the percent of goal achieved for the quad workout is to divide the number of reps done in a given week by the amount entered in the initial goal and multiply the result by 100. The same method is used to find the percent of goal achieved for the biceps workout (reps done divided by reps desired, multiplied by 100). To find the percent of goal achieved for jogging, we must divide the number of minutes jogged by the end goal and multiply the result by 100. Each of these formulas requires a simple division operation. We can, therefore, create a single function which will divide one number by another. The function which we will call `Quotient()` will import two values from the program and return the result. If we design the function to be generic, this one function can be used for all division calculations required throughout the program.

This function will have two parameters and will return one value. The first parameter will be the dividend and the second is the divisor. We know that, whenever we have a division operation, we must ensure that the divisor is not zero. In this program, in the interests of saving time and space, we will simply set the result to 0 if the divisor is zero. This will avoid a program crash and will also return a result of 0 for any `Call` to this function with a value of 0. The code for this function is:

```
Function Quotient(Float x, Float y) As Float
  If y != 0 Then
    Set Quotient = x/y
  Else
    Set Quotient = 0
End Function
```

The general hierarchy chart for this program is shown in Figure 9.3.

Figure 9.3 General Hierarchy Chart for the Fitness Program

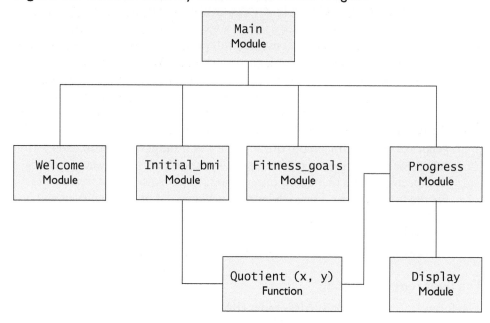

The subprograms are now designed as follows:

Main Module

The Main module will call the subprograms Welcome, Initial_bmi, Fitness_goals, and Progress. The pseudocode for this module is as follows:

```
Main
    Declare BMI, Height, BMIpoints As Float
    Declare Quads, Biceps, Jog As Integer
    Call Welcome() module
    Set initial values of all variables to 1
    Call Initial_bmi(BMI, Height)module
    Call Fitness_goals(Quads, Biceps, Jog, BMI, BMIpoints) module
    Call Progress(Quads, Biceps, Jog, Height, BMI, BMIpoints) module
End Program
```

Welcome Module

The Welcome module gets the user's name and displays a welcome message. It can be as short as the following or more elaborate:

```
Subprogram Welcome()
    Declare Name As String
    Write "What's your name?"
    Input Name
    Write "Welcome, " + Name + " to your Fitness Plan"
End Program
```

Initial_bmi() Module

In order to calculate the BMI we need to find out the user's height in inches and weight in pounds. But normally people do not think of their height in inches. So we will prompt the user to enter the height in two steps—number of feet and number of inches—and then convert this to inches. The BMI formula uses a person's height in inches squared and weight in pounds. Most people also do not think of their weight in terms of pounds and ounces (as they might do when buying luncheon meat) but they might think of their weight in parts of a pound (as in, "I weigh 125 and a half pounds") so we can simply prompt once for weight in pounds. After we get the height, we must square that value. Then, along with the weight, we can use these values to call the Quotient() function. The Quotient() function returns a value but the BMI formula requires that this number is multiplied by 703. Therefore, the pseudocode for this module is as follows:

```
1   Subprogram Initial_bmi(Float BMI As Ref, Float Height As Ref)
2     Declare Feet, Inches, Weight As Float
3     Set BMI = 0
4     Write "How tall are you? Enter number of feet first"
5     Input Feet
6     Write "How many inches (for example, if you are 5'6", ↵
             enter 6 for the number of inches)"
7     Input Inches
8     Set Height = Feet * 12 + Inches
9     Write "How much do you weigh (for example, if you ↵
             weigh 136.5 lbs, enter 136.5)?"
10    Input Weight
11    BMI = Quotient(Weight, Height^2) * 703
12    Write "Your BMI now is " + BMI
13  End Subprogram
```

You can see that we pass two arguments to the Quotient() function—Weight and Height—which are then assigned to the parameters x and y in the function. The value returned by the Quotient() function (i.e., Weight divided by Height^2) is not enough for a true BMI. We must multiply this result by 703, as we do on line 11. Since the Quotient() function will not alter the values of Weight or Height we do not need to worry about whether we pass these variables in as value or reference parameters. Control is now returned to the Main module and then passed to the Fitness_goals() module.

The values of Height and BMI are used in subsequent modules so these values must be returned (exported) to Main.

The Fitness_goals() module needs to receive (import) the value of BMI in order to find a new BMI goal so we send that value in when we call the module and include it as a parameter in the module name.

Fitness_goals() Module

This module prompts the user to enter goals. We will create the following variables and then write the pseudocode to input the goals and calculate a target BMI level.

Variables

- TargetBMI As Float (desired BMI)
- OK As Character (sentinel value for loop to check if entry is OK)

Pseudocode

```
1   Subprogram Fitness_goals(Integer Quads As Ref, Integer ↵
                             Biceps As Ref, Integer Jog As Ref, ↵
                             Float BMI, Float BMIpoints As Ref)
2     Declare variables
3     Write "Enter your goal for quads workout in number of ↵
            reps per session:"
4     Input Quads
5     Write "Enter your goal for biceps workout in number of ↵
            reps per session:"
6     Input Biceps
7     Write "Enter your goal for number of minutes you want to ↵
            jog or run per session:"
8     Input Jog
9     Write "Enter your target BMI number:"
10    Input TargetBMI
11    Set BMIpoints = BMI - TargetBMI
12    Write "It looks like you want to reduce your BMI by " ↵
            + BMIpoints + " points. Is that right? (y/n)"
13    Input ToLower(OK)
14    While (OK != "y")
15      Write "Let's try again. Enter your target BMI number:"
16      Input TargetBMI
17      Set BMIpoints = BMI - TargetBMI
18      Write "It looks like you want to reduce your BMI by " ↵
              + BMIpoints + " points. Correct? (y/n)"
19      Input OK
20    End While
21    Write "Your target BMI is " + (BMI - BMIpoints)
22  End Subprogram
```

The code to get the goals for biceps, quads, and jogging time (lines 3–8) is clear. At this point, however, for the BMI goal we want to find out how many points the user wants to shave off his or her Body Mass Index. We do not need to calculate a new BMI; we just ask the user to enter what is the desired BMI (lines 9 and 10). Then, by subtracting this value (TargetBMI) from the initial BMI we determine how many points the user wants to reduce (line 11). We give the user a chance to change this value using the loop on lines 14–20). The number of points to reduce the BMI by is stored in BMIpoints.

This module must import the value of BMI which will be used in subsequent modules so we will import it as a reference parameter. We need to export the values of Biceps, Quads, Jog, and BMIpoints to the Progress() module in order to calculate how much progress the user has made toward goal.

Control then reverts to the Main module where the Progress() module is called, sending it the values of BMIpoints, BMI, Height, Biceps, Quads, and Jog.

Progress() Module

This module will consist of a loop that begins on Week 1 and will continue for four iterations to get the progress toward goals in each of the four weeks. We need variables to hold the values of the number of reps completed each week for quads and biceps, the number of minutes jogged each week, and a new value for the user's weight to calculate a new BMI. For each goal, the new value will be divided by the old value to find the percent completed toward goal. Therefore, we must import the old values from Main. Each time a new value is entered, we can use the Quotient() function, sending in appropriate arguments.

The new variables needed are as follows:

Variables

- Week As Integer (counter for the loop)
- Brep As Integer (number of reps per session for biceps workout this week)
- Qrep As Integer (number of reps per session for quads workout this week)
- Jmin As Integer (number of minutes jogged this week)
- NewB As Float (percent of biceps workout goal achieved this week)
- NewQ As Float (percent of quads workout goal achieved this week)
- NewJ As Float (percent of jogging workout goal achieved this week)
- NewW As Float (new weight for this week)
- NewBMI As Float (new BMI calculated with new weight for this week)
- NewPoints As Float (number of BMI points lost or gained this week)
- BMIGoal As Float (percent of gain/loss of BMI points)

Pseudocode

```
1   Subprogram Progress(Integer Quads, Integer Biceps, Integer ↵
                        Jog, Float Height, Float BMI, Float BMIpoints)
2     Declare variables
3     Set Week = 1
4     While Week <= 4
5       Write "How many biceps reps did you do for week " + Week + "?"
6       Input Brep
7       Set NewB = Quotient(Brep, Biceps)
8       Write "How many quad reps did you do for week " + Week + "?"
9       Input Qrep
10      Set NewQ = Quotient(Qrep, Quads)
11      Write "How many minutes did you jog during week " + Week + "?"
12      Input Jmin
13      Set NewJ = Quotient(Jmin, Jog)
14      Write "What was your weight for week " + Week + "?"
15      Input NewW
16      Set NewBMI = Quotient(NewW, Height^2)
17      Set NewBMI = NewBMI * 703
18      Set NewPoints = BMI - NewBMI
19      Set BMIGoal = Quotient(NewPoints, BMIpoints)
20      Call Display(Week, NewQ, NewB, NewJ, BMIGoal, NewBMI)
21      Set Week = Week + 1
22    End While
23  End Subprogram
```

Notice how the Quotient() function is used on lines 7, 10, 13, 16, and 19 for four different purposes. To use one function for these varied reasons, we simply send different arguments to the same parameters.

This module must export the values of Week, NewQ, NewB, NewJ, BMIGoal, and NewBMI to the Display() module.

Display() Module

The Display() module is called four times—once for each iteration of the loop in the Progress() module. Each time it displays the week under consideration and reports the progress made by the user. The display will show how close, in percentage, the user is to goal in biceps workout, quadriceps workout, jogging time, and BMI. If the user surpasses the BMI goal, we will display a message to that effect. No new variables are needed for this module but the variables that are exported from the Progress() module are used. These variables are used in the display but are otherwise unaltered in the Display() module so they can be imported as value parameters. The pseudocode is as follows:

```
 1  Subprogram Display(Integer Week, Float NewQ, Float ⏎
                       NewB, Float NewJ, Float BMIGoal, Float NewBMI)
 2    Write "For Week " + Week
 3    Write "Percent of goal for biceps: " + NewB * 100 + "%"
 4    Write "Percent of goal for quads: " + NewQ * 100 + "%"
 5    Write "Percent of goal for jogging: " + NewJ * 100 + "%"
 6    Write "Your new BMI is now " + NewBMI
 7    If (BMIGoal > 1) Then
 8      Write "You have exceeded your goal for a BMI score!"
 9      Write "Congratulations!"
10    Else
11      Write "Percent of BMI goal: " + BMIGoal * 100 + "%"
12    End If
13  End Subprogram
```

We can now turn the hierarchy chart of Figure 9.3 into the data flow diagram shown in Figure 9.4.

Program Code

The program code is now written using the design as a guide. At this stage, header comments and step comments are inserted into each module to provide internal documentation for the program. There are many places where error checking should be added. Since we now understand how to create and use functions, it would simplify matters if we created a single function to check for inappropriate numeric entries such as a negative number entered where only positive values are acceptable or a noninteger value is entered for number of reps. Adding error checking functions will be part of the Self Check exercises in this section.

Program Test

The best way to test this program is to imagine that you want to use this program. See what happens when you use as many sets of test data as you can imagine. Several possible sets of test data are given in the Making It Work section below.

Figure 9.4 Data flow diagram for the Fitness program

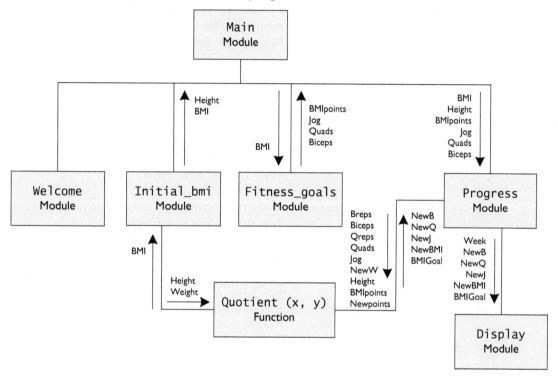

Test Data

While you are testing the data, you may change the test condition in the Progress() module to 1 or 2 so you don't need to enter four weeks of data.

Input Data Set 1	Output Set 1 (data rounded to 1 decimal place)
Name: Rocky	Welcome, Rocky, to your Monthly Fitness
Feet: 6	Progress Report
Inches: 2	Your beginning BMI is 30.9
Weight: 240.5 lbs	Your target BMI is 24
Quad goal: 30 reps	For Week 1
Biceps goal: 30 reps	Percent of goal for biceps: 60.0%
Jogging goal: 90 mins	Percent of goal for quads: 50.0%
Target BMI: 24	Percent of goal for jogging: 38.9%
Week 1:	Your new BMI is now: 30.2
Quads: 15 reps	Percent of BMI goal: 10.3%
Biceps: 18 reps	For week 2
Jogging: 35 mins	Percent of goal for biceps: 83.3%
Weight: 235.0 lbs	Percent of goal for quads: 73.3%

Week 2:	Percent of goal for jogging: 61.1%
Quads: 22 reps	Your new BMI is now: 28.6
Biceps: 25 reps	Percent of BMI goal: 33.6%
Jogging: 55 mins	
Weight: 222.5 lbs	

Input Data Set 2	**Output Set 2 (data rounded to 1 decimal place)**
Name: Barbie	Welcome, Barbie, to your Monthly Fitness
Feet: 5	Progress Report
Inches: 4	Your beginning BMI is 20.3
Weight: 118.25 lbs	Your target BMI is 16
Quad goal: 20 reps	For Week 1
Biceps goal: 20 reps	Percent of goal for biceps: 45.0%
Jogging goal: 45 mins	Percent of goal for quads: 45.0%
Target BMI: 16	Percent of goal for jogging: 33.3%
Week 1:	Your new BMI is now: 19.2
Quads: 9 reps	Percent of BMI goal: 25.0%
Biceps: 9 reps	For Week 2
Jogging: 15 mins	Percent of goal for biceps: 60.0%
Weight: 112.0 lbs	Percent of goal for quads: 75.0%
Week 2:	Percent of goal for jogging: 77.8%
Quads: 15 reps	Your new BMI is now: 18.8
Biceps: 12 reps	Percent of BMI goal: 35.0%
Jogging: 35 mins	
Weight: 109.5 lbs	

Be sure to check the loop in the `Fitness_goals()` module that asks you to reenter a new target BMI if the first entry is not satisfactory to make sure it works correctly.

Self Check for Section 9.5

For Self Check Questions 9.23 and 9.24 refer to the Fitness program of this section.

9.23 a. Create a function named `Positive()` that will check if a value entered is nonnegative (greater than or equal to 0). The function should take one value and return a value of either `true` (if the value imported is nonnegative) or `false` (if the value is negative).

b. List the places in this program where such a function should be called.

9.24 a. Create a function named `Zero()` that will check if a value entered is zero. The function should take one value and return a value of either `true` (if the value imported is not zero) or `false` (if the value is zero).

b. Write pseudocode to call this function from the `Quotient()` function to ensure that a division by zero error does not occur. Be sure to include the correct arguments and parameters in the two functions.

9.6 Running With RAPTOR (Optional)

So far we have used RAPTOR subcharts in our programs in the same manner as we use submodules or subprograms in our pseudocode. However, until now we have not concerned ourselves with the scope of our variables. We have assumed that, once a variable is declared and given a type and a value, it is available for use anywhere in the program. In this chapter, we learned that this is not normally true. In longer programs, variables must be declared specifically as global variables if we want them to be available to all parts of a program and that, in most programs, global variables are rarely used. A variable that is declared within a subprogram is not available to any other subprogram unless we send its value to that subprogram. We can simulate this situation with RAPTOR as well. We do this by using RAPTOR procedures.

RAPTOR also has some built-in procedures, similar to the built-in functions we discussed in this chapter. Some of them we have already used such as the Sqrt() function. We have learned that an Output statement such as

    PUT Sqrt(64)

will take the square root of 64 and display the result. But there are other functions that are actually Calls to procedures and must first be called before they can be used.

First we will learn to use RAPTOR procedure Calls, then we will create and use our own procedures, and finally we will create the Fitness Plan program from the Focus on Problem Solving Section in this chapter to demonstrate how to implement procedures.

RAPTOR Built-In Functions (Procedures)

In previous chapters we have seen that numeric output defaults to a floating point display with four decimal places. We learned a rather cumbersome method to ensure that a number will be displayed with two decimal places, but this often did not give the results we wanted. For example, if the result of a calculation was 4.5678, we could force the output to be 4.56, but if the result of a calculation was 4.5002, our method would result in an output of 4.5. RAPTOR has a procedure, **Set_Precision()** that will allow us to specify the exact number of decimal places to be displayed consistently. Unfortunately, there is no way to set the precision to 0; one decimal is the lowest number of places possible. Here is how to do it.

Create a new RAPTOR file named decimals.rap. Create variables named num1, num2, and result. Assign the values 73 to num1, 13 to num2, and num1/num2 to result. Your program will look like this so far (shown at right).

Now drag a Call symbol under the last Assignment symbol and enter Set_Precision(2) into the pop-up window. Then add an Output statement to output the value of result. To verify that this works, add two more Calls, using Set_Precision(3) and Set_Precision(7) underneath. Your program and its output, when run, will look as shown on the following page.

This function is very helpful when we need to output currency or make all numerical output consistent.

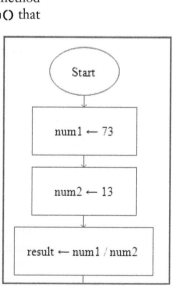

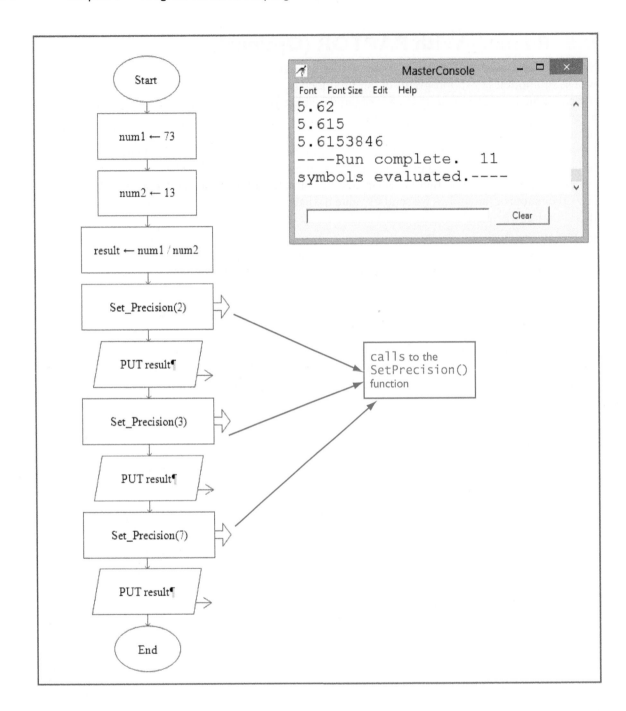

There are other functions available in RAPTOR that return values relating to the current date and time. We have not used these in any programs; however, you may want to incorporate them in your own programs. Most of them are listed in Table 9.2 and these functions are normally available in most programming languages.

Table 9.2 Date and Time functions in RAPTOR

RAPTOR function	Return value
Current_Year	Returns the current year
Current_Month	Returns the current month as a number (i.e., if it is July, the return is 7)
Current_Day	Returns the current day of the month (i.e., if it is May 28, the return is 28)
Current_Hour	Returns the hour in military time (i.e., 7:00 pm returns 19)
Current_Minute	Returns the number of minutes past the current hour (i.e., 7:10 pm returns 10)
Current_Time	Returns the number of milliseconds since midnight January 1, 1990

Example 9.18 Does RAPTOR Know What Time (and Day and Month and Year) It Is?

To use any of these date and time functions, set a variable equal to the function. A quick example of how these functions are used is shown with the variables minute, hour, day, month, and year getting their values from the Current_Minute, Current_Hour, Current_Day, Current_Month, and Current_Year functions. While clearly not perfect, these date and time functions can be used to create more complex programs with RAPTOR. Notice that, in RAPTOR, since these functions do not take any arguments, no parentheses are needed after the function name.

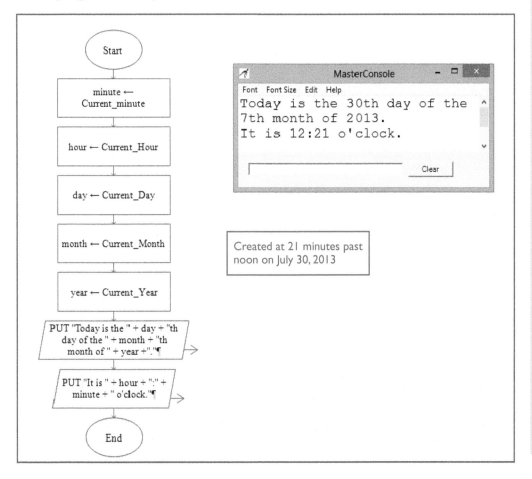

Creating a New Procedure

Procedures developed by the programmer are not available in RAPTOR Novice Mode. Therefore, the first thing you must do is to switch to Intermediate Mode:

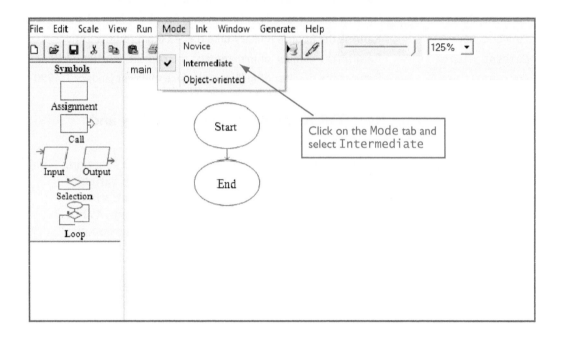

To create a procedure in RAPTOR, right-click on the tab in a subchart and select Add procedure:

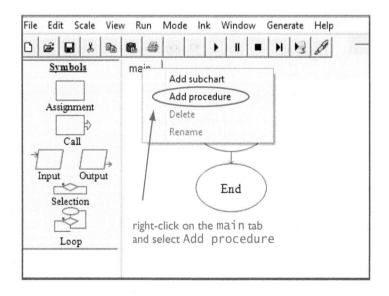

You will see the following window open. On the first line you enter the name of the procedure. The next six lines allow you to enter parameters. If the parameter is to be imported from a Call, check the Input box. If its value is to be output to the calling subchart, also check the Output box.

```
                    Create Procedure

        Names must begin with letter, and contain
        only letters, numbers and underscores.

        Examples:
          Draw_Boxes
          Find_Smallest


    Procedure Name
    |

    Parameter 1 (or blank)  ☑ Input   ☐ Output
    |

    Parameter 2 (or blank)  ☑ Input   ☐ Output
    |

    Parameter 3 (or blank)  ☑ Input   ☐ Output
    |

    Parameter 4 (or blank)  ☑ Input   ☐ Output
    |

    Parameter 5 (or blank)  ☑ Input   ☐ Output
    |

    Parameter 6 (or blank)  ☑ Input   ☐ Output
    |


        Ok                      Cancel
```

We'll use a very short example to demonstrate how to create and use a procedure,

Example 9.19 Finding The Distance Between Two Points

The Pythagorean Theorem is used to find the distance between two points. If the coordinates of the two points are $(x1, y1)$ and $(x2, y2)$, then the distance between them is given by

$$Distance = \sqrt{[(x1 - x2)^2 + (y1 - y2)^2]}$$

The pseudocode that corresponds to this formula requires five numeric variables, which we will call mydistance, myx1, myy1, myx2, and myy2 and a string variable, choice, to allow the user to repeat the process. We need to write a program that will allow the user to enter the coordinates of any two points and see the distance between those points. We'll use a loop in the main program to get values and, for each set entered, we will call a function (in RAPTOR, called a `procedure`) to do the calculation. We need to pass the values of the user's entries to the function and have the function return the calculated distance. The general pseudocode for this program is as follows:

```
main
   Declare and initialize variables
   Write "Calculate a distance? (y/n)"
   Input choice
   While choice == "y"
      Get values for myx1, myy1, myx2, and myy2
      Call the distance() function for the calculation
      Display the result: mydistance
      Prompt user to do another calculation or exit and input choice
   End While
End Program
```

To create this program in RAPTOR, open a new RAPTOR program and save it with the filename `distance.rap`. Create a `subchart` with the variables described and create the program shown on the next page. We will fill in the `procedure` and `procedure Call` (i.e., the function and function `Call`) next.

The `distance()` function will calculate the distance between two points in three steps. The formula requires that we find the difference between the two *x*-values and the two *y*-values and then takes the square root of the sum of the squares of these distances. Thus, the function needs to import four values: two *x*-values and two *y*-values. It needs to return one value—the calculated `mydistance`.

Therefore, the `distance()` function has five parameters, which we will call `point_x1`, `point_X2`, `point_y1`, and `point_y2`. These parameters will receive the values of the arguments, `myx1`, `myy1`, `myx2`, and `myy2`, which will be sent in when calling the function. Since these values do not need to be used again by the main program, they are only `Input` (value) parameters.

The fifth parameter will hold the value that is calculated. In RAPTOR the result of a `procedure` should not have the same name as the `procedure` name. Therefore, we will call the variable that holds the distance calculation `length`. This result is returned to the calling program so it is an `Output` (reference) variable. In RAPTOR you must send in, as an argument, the name of the variable you want the result assigned to. In our program, the result is assigned to `mydistance` so the value of `mydistance` will be received, when the `procedure` is called, from the `length` variable.

With this in mind, the `distance()` `procedure` window should be filled in as shown in the second image.

We are now ready to write our `distance()` procedure. We will use two local variables, `dx` and `dy` to hold the intermediate results of the differences between the two *x*-values and the two *y*-values. Then we will calculate the distance between the two points and store that value in the variable `length`. The third image shows the RAPTOR implementation of the `distance()` procedure.

We'll talk for a moment about the `Start` oval in the `procedure`. The information inside the parentheses is created automatically by RAPTOR. It reflects the

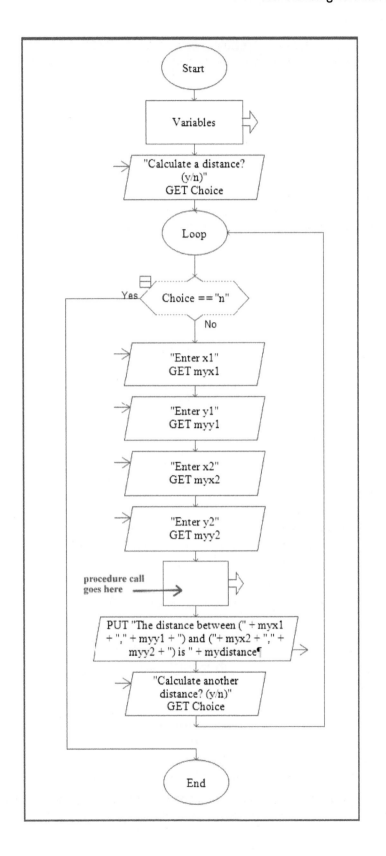

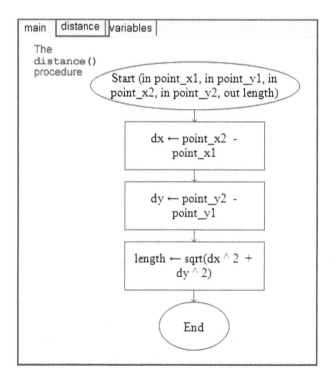

information we entered when we created the procedure. You can see that point_x1, point_y1, point_x2, and point_y2 are shown as Input variables by the keyword in. The variable length is an Output variable, as indicated by the keyword out.

When we call this procedure we must include four Input arguments to match these Input parameters and one Output argument to match the Output parameter.

We can now fill in the Call box in our main program as follows:

    distance(myx1, myy1, myx2, myy2, mydistance)

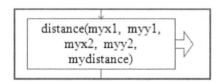

This Call will return a value to mydistance which we use in final output. If you run this program with the following values, your display should be as shown:

First run: choice = "y", myx1 = 3, myy1 = 4, myx2 = 0,

            myy2 = 0, choice = "y"

Second run: choice = "y", myx1 = 15, myy1 = 20, myx2 = 30,

            myy2 = 55, choice = "n"

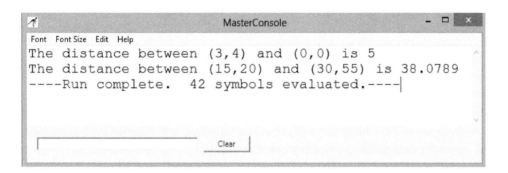

Run It: The Fitness Plan

In this section, we will develop a RAPTOR program that does the same thing as the Fitness Program in the Focus on Problem Solving section of this chapter. Because of some of the features and limitations of RAPTOR, the development of the program will differ slightly from that of the pseudocode in the Focus on Problem Solving section. However, the program will give the same results and you could, if you wish, by adding or altering the program slightly, use it to help with your own fitness goals.

Problem Statement

We will repeat the problem statement here for your convenience:

Your friend, Pat Nerdoff, has realized that too many hours sitting in front of an array of computer screens has resulted in a very out-of-shape, albeit impressive computer programmer. You offer to design a program that will track Pat's progress at the gym over a period of four weeks. The program will calculate Pat's initial Body Mass Index (BMI) and calculate Pat's progress toward a goal that includes a weight-lifting, jogging, and weight-loss regimen. Pat—or any user—should be able to input initial values and weekly updates. The program will display what percent the user has achieved toward a personal goal in each category and will provide new BMI values each week. A single function can be used to help accomplish each of these tasks.

Developing and Creating the Program

The program we developed earlier had a Main module and five submodules as well as a single function. We will re-create those here in RAPTOR. However, instead of a Welcome module, we will put a single "welcome" message in main and use a subchart for our global variables. Since RAPTOR procedures are limited to six parameters, we will develop this program as we have in the past, with subcharts that allow variables to be global and concentrate on using a single procedure to simulate the function, quotient(), used in the original program. This will help you understand the concepts of passing arguments to parameters more thoroughly.

We can divide our tasks as follows:

- main: The main module will get the user's name and welcome him or her to the program. Then it will call the other subcharts.
- Initial_bmi: This subchart will get the user's height and weight and calculate an initial BMI. It will do this by calling the procedure named quotient() which we will create.
- Fitness_goals: This subchart will input from the user the number of reps per session that are goals for the quadriceps workout and the biceps workout as well as the jogging goal in minutes and the number of BMI points the user wants to drop. The quotient() procedure is not called in this subchart.
- Progress: This subchart will contain a loop that will execute for four times, one for each week. For each week, the user will enter the number of quads and biceps reps done, the number of minutes jogged, and the user's weight. For the quads, biceps, and jogging workouts, the quotient() procedure must be called to find out the percent of goal achieved. For the BMI goal, the quotient() procedure is called twice. First, a new BMI is calculated using the user's new weight. Then the percent of progress toward goal is calculated by calling the quotient() procedure a second time. Each time quotient() is called, different arguments are exported.
- Display: This subchart is called from the Progress subchart at the end of each week's entries. It displays the results of the progress made toward the user's goals.
- quotient(): This procedure does one thing: it accepts two arguments plus the argument that holds the value of the result, divides the first by the second, and returns the result of that division.
- Variables: This subchart is normally included with our RAPTOR programs to keep variable declarations manageable. We will add variables as they are shown to be necessary throughout the program's development.

To create this program yourself, open a new RAPTOR program and save it with the filename fitness.rap. The main module should look as shown after you create the subcharts Initial_bmi, Fitness_goals, and Progress.

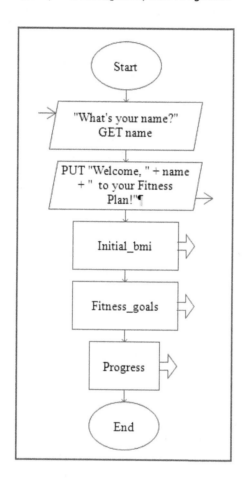

The quotient() procedure

We will create our quotient() procedure first because it is used throughout the rest of the program. The procedure will do one simple thing: it will divide one number by another. By now, you know that any division operation runs a risk of a program crash if the divisor is zero. Since this program will be relatively long, we will not include error checking for user input but we will take care of the situation that might be created if the divisor is 0. If this is the case, in our function, we will simply set the result to 0.

Since quotient() is a procedure, it must import and export variables. This procedure will have three parameters (the dividend, the divisor, and the quotient which is the result of the division). In all cases, the result must be returned to the calling subchart. Recall that in RAPTOR, rather than assigning a value to the function name, the result of a procedure's calculations must be assigned to an Output variable which, in this case, we call z. To create this procedure, right-click on the main tab and select Add procedure. Then fill in the window that opens up as shown.

Here, the procedure name is quotient, we use x to represent the dividend, y to represent the divisor, and z to represent the result. These three variables are all both Input and Output parameters. The flowchart for the quotient procedure is also shown.

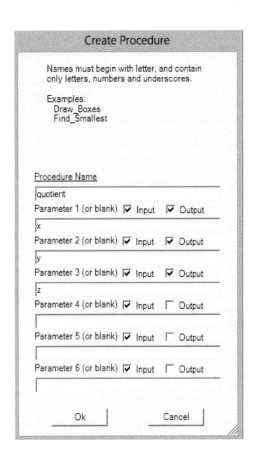

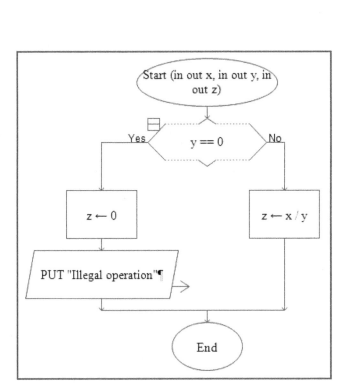

The Initial_bmi subchart

This subchart will mirror the Initial_bmi() subprogram created earlier in this chapter. First we get input from the user: height (in feet and inches) and weight (in pounds). We convert the number of feet to inches, add it to the value of inches, square this number, and store the result in height. Then we call the quotient() procedure, sending in values of weight and height.

One thing that must be noted is that the procedure's first parameter, x, becomes the numerator (or dividend) and the second parameter, y, becomes the denominator (or divisor). Therefore, each time this procedure is called we must make sure we send in our arguments in the correct order.

There is also something that is different in this step from the pseudocode previously developed. The pseudocode that calls the Quotient() function and creates the initial BMI, discussed earlier in this chapter, is:

```
BMI = Quotient(weight, height) * 703
```

But in RAPTOR, you cannot do all of this in one step. You must call the `procedure`, sending in three values. The first, `weight`, is the user's weight. The second, `height`, is the height we determined by converting to inches and squaring the result. The third argument is the name of the variable that we want the result to be stored in, in `main`. We call that variable `bmi`. The value of `z`, the third `quotient()` parameter, gets stored in `bmi`. In RAPTOR, the call to `quotient()` looks as shown to the right.

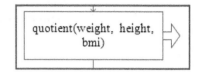

The `Initial_bmi()` subchart is:

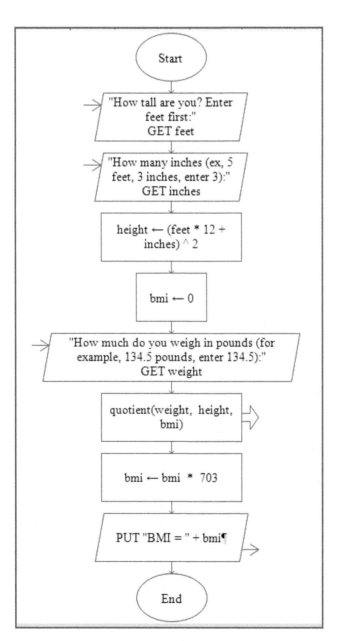

Initial_bmi subchart

After the procedure returns the result, the actual value of bmi must be calculated by multiplying this value by 703.

The Fitness_goals subchart

This subchart is pretty straightforward. We can mimic the pseudocode created in the Focus on Problem Solving section with one small change in how the test condition is written in the loop to reflect the way RAPTOR handles loops. For your convenience, the pseudocode is repeated here followed by the RAPTOR implementation.

```
1   Subprogram Fitness_goals(BMI As Ref)
2     Declare variables
3     Write "Enter your goal for quads (in number of reps ↵
                                    per session):"
4     Input Quads
5     Write "Enter your goal for biceps (in number of reps ↵
                                    per session):"
6     Input Biceps
7     Write "Enter your goal for number of minutes you want to ↵
              jog or run per session:"
8     Input Jog
9     Write "Enter your target BMI number:"
10    Input TargetBMI
11    Set BMIpoints = BMI - TargetBMI
12    Write "It looks like you want to reduce your BMI by " ↵
              + BMIpoints + " points. Is that right? (y/n)"
13    Input OK
14    While (OK != 'y')
15      Write "Let's try again. Enter your target BMI number:"
16      Input TargetBMI
17      Set BMIpoints = BMI - TargetBMI
18      Write "It looks like you want to reduce your BMI by " ↵
                + BMIpoints + " points. Correct? (y/n)"
19      Input OK
20    End While
21    Write "Your target BMI is " + (BMI - BMIpoints)
22  End Subprogram
```

The Progress subchart

This part of the program must run four times since the user is expected to enter four weeks' worth of progress. Of course, if we were developing a real application, the user would enter information for the first week, then close the program, return the second week to enter more information, and so on. But we cannot do that, at this point. For now we'll assume the user will enter information for all four weeks at one time. However, by using techniques we have discussed earlier in the book we can add code to this program to give week-by-week printouts.

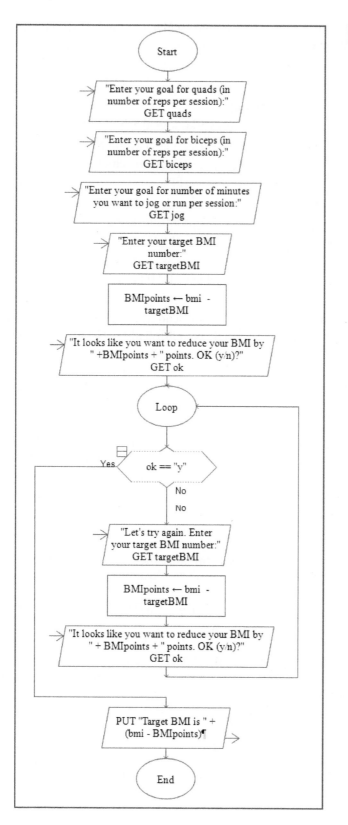

Fitness_goal subchart

This module requires some new variables, which we can declare and initialize in the `Variables` subchart. These are the same variables used in the Focus on Problem Solving section and are repeated here, with their initial values:

Variables

- `Wk` = 1 (counter for the loop)
- `NewB` ← 0 (percent of biceps workout goal achieved this week)
- `NewQ` ← 0 (percent of quads workout goal achieved this week)
- `NewJ` ← 0 (percent of jogging workout goal achieved this week)
- `NewW` ← 0 (new weight for this week)
- `NewBMI` ← 0 (new BMI calculated with new weight for this week)
- `newTarget` ← 0 (number of BMI points lost or gained this week)
- `BMIGoal` ← 0 (percent of gain/loss of BMI points)

Other variables (`brep`, `qrep`, `jmin`, `height`, `bmi`, and `BMIpoints`) are created "on the fly" within this `subchart` or are available to RAPTOR from a previous `subchart`.

For each week, we `Input` the user's values and calculate progress by finding the percentage of work done. To do this, we send in the weekly value and the goal to the `quotient()` function. The result is multiplied by 100 to give a percent. The `Progress` subchart is shown.

The `Display` subchart

This `subchart` displays the week number and the percent of goal reached for each type of workout. We can translate the pseudocode developed in the Focus on Problem Solving section directly to RAPTOR for this module. The pseudocode is repeated here, for your convenience, and the corresponding RAPTOR program follows.

```
1   Subprogram Display(NewBMI, NewJ, NewQ, NewB, Week,BMIGoal)
2     Write "For Week " + Week
3     Write "Percent of goal for biceps: " + NewB * 100 + "%"
4     Write "Percent of goal for quads: " + NewQ * 100 + "%"
5     Write "Percent of goal for jogging: " + NewJ * 100 + "%"
6     Write "Your new BMI is now " + NewBMI
7     If (BMIGoal > 1) Then
8        Write "You have exceeded your goal for a BMI score!"
9        Write "Congratulations!"
10    Else
11       Write "Percent of BMI goal: " + BMIGoal * 100 + "%"
12    End If
13  End Subprogram
```

Progress subchart

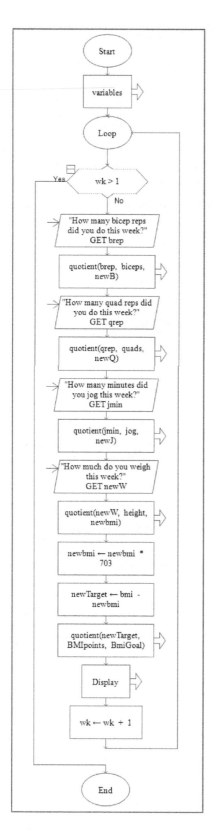

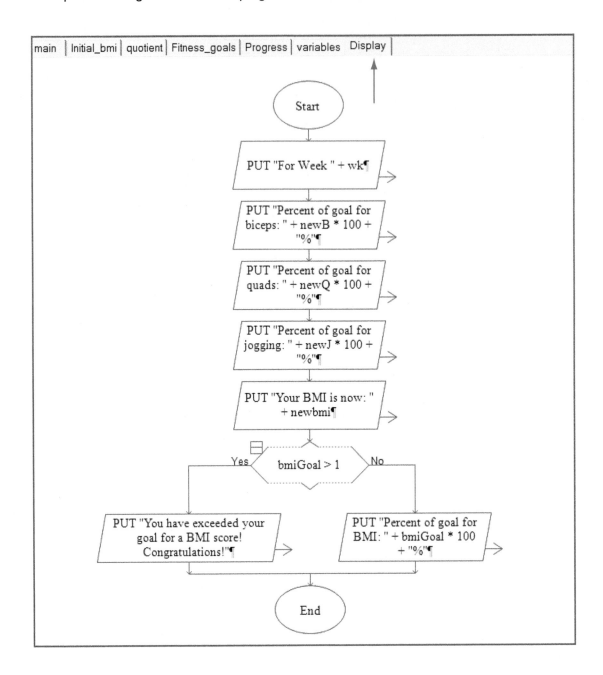

Check It Out

If you test this program, changing the test condition in the Progress subchart to 2 instead of 4 (simply for ease of testing) and use the same values as given earlier in the Focus on Problem Solving section, your MasterConsole display will be as shown.

Input Data Set 1

Name: Rocky
Feet: 6
Inches: 2
Weight: 240.5 lbs
Quad goal: 30 reps
Biceps goal: 30 reps
Jogging goal: 90 mins
Target BMI: 24
Week 1:
  Quads: 15 reps
  Biceps: 18 reps
  Jogging: 35 mins
  Weight: 235.0 lbs
Week 2:
  Quads: 22 reps
  Biceps: 25 reps
  Jogging: 55 mins
  Weight: 222.5 lbs

Output Set 1 (data given in 4 decimal places in RAPTOR)

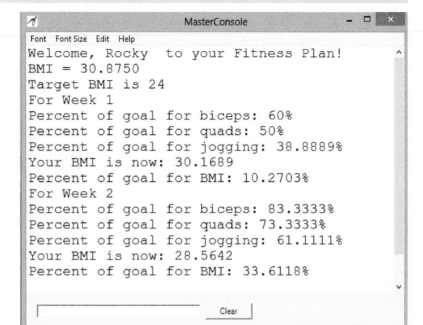

```
                        MasterConsole              — □  ✕
 Font  Font Size  Edit  Help
Welcome, Rocky   to your Fitness Plan!          ⌃
BMI = 30.8750
Target BMI is 24
For Week 1
Percent of goal for biceps: 60%
Percent of goal for quads: 50%
Percent of goal for jogging: 38.8889%
Your BMI is now: 30.1689
Percent of goal for BMI: 10.2703%
For Week 2
Percent of goal for biceps: 83.3333%
Percent of goal for quads: 73.3333%
Percent of goal for jogging: 61.1111%
Your BMI is now: 28.5642
Percent of goal for BMI: 33.6118%
                                                ⌄

 [                              ]    Clear
```

Input Data Set 2

Name: Barbie
Feet: 5
Inches: 4
Weight: 118.25 lbs
Quad goal: 20 reps
Biceps goal: 20 reps
Jogging goal: 45 mins
Target BMI: 16
Week 1:
  Quads: 9 reps
  Biceps: 9 reps
  Jogging: 15 mins
  Weight: 112.0 lbs
Week 2:
  Quads: 15 reps
  Biceps: 12 reps
  Jogging: 35 mins
  Weight: 109.5 lbs

Output Set 2 (data given in 4 decimal places in RAPTOR)

```
                        MasterConsole              — □  ✕
 Font  Font Size  Edit  Help
Welcome, Barbie   to your Fitness Plan!         ⌃
BMI = 20.2953
Target BMI is 16
For Week 1
Percent of goal for biceps: 45%
Percent of goal for quads: 45%
Percent of goal for jogging: 33.3333%
Your BMI is now: 19.2227
Percent of goal for BMI: 24.9734%
For Week 2
Percent of goal for biceps: 60%
Percent of goal for quads: 75%
Percent of goal for jogging: 77.7778%
Your BMI is now: 18.7936
Percent of goal for BMI: 34.9627%
                                                ⌄

 [                              ]    Clear
```

Key Terms

argument	pass by value
built-in functions	preprocessor directive
data flow diagram	procedure
driver program	recursion
export data	recursive algorithm
function	reference parameter
global variable	return a value
header (of subprogram)	scope (of a variable)
import data	subprogram
library (of functions)	`ToLower()` function
local variable	`ToUpper()` function
parameter	undefined variable
pass a value	user-defined function
pass by reference	value parameter

Chapter Summary

In this chapter, we have discussed the following topics:

1. Parameters and arguments
   - Data transmitted from one program module to another is exported from the former and imported by the latter.
   - A data flow diagram shows the relationships among the program modules and indicates the data imported and exported by each module.
   - To pass data from a module to a submodule, the `Call` statement (in the former) contains arguments and the subprogram header (in the latter) contains parameters.
   - The number and type of arguments in a `Call` statement must be the same as the number and type of parameters in the corresponding header; the data is passed from an argument to a parameter based solely on its position in the argument and parameter list.
2. Value and reference parameters
   - A change in the value of a value parameter in its subprogram does not affect the value of the corresponding argument, but a change in the value of a reference parameter in its subprogram does change the value of the corresponding argument.
3. The `ToUpper()` and `ToLower()` functions are used to change `Strings` to either all uppercase or all lowercase.

4. Scope of a variable
   - The scope of a variable is the part of the program in which that variable can be referenced (used).
   - The scope of a global variable is the entire program.
   - The scope of local variable is the subprogram in which it is declared and any subprograms within that subprogram.
   - If the same variable is declared locally and globally, it is treated as if it were two different variables, and the local declaration takes precedence.
5. Functions
   - A function is a subprogram whose name returns a value to the calling subprogram. The function name may appear anywhere in the program that a constant of that type is valid.
   - Built-in functions are supplied by the programming language software.
   - User-defined functions are functions created by the programmer. They are subprograms whose name may be assigned a value and are called in the same way as built-in functions.
6. Recursion
   - A recursive subprogram is a subprogram that calls itself.
   - To create a recursive function, F(N), which computes an expression that depends on a positive integer N, you must do the following:
     - Express F(N) in terms of F(N - 1).
     - Determine the value of F(1).
     - In the function definition, use an If-Then-Else statement that sets F equal to F(1) if N = 1, and which involves F(N - 1) if N > 1.

Review Exercises

Fill in the Blank

1. If a data item is transmitted from a subprogram to the main program, it is said to be returned to or _____ to the main program.

2. If a data item is transmitted from the main program to a subprogram, it is said to be passed to or _____ by the subprogram.

3. A diagram that shows the data transmitted between program modules is called a(n) _____.

4. A chart that shows the data that is imported to, processed by, and exported from each program module is called a(n) _____.

5. The part of the program in which a given variable can be referenced is called the _____ of that variable.

6. The scope of a(n) _____ variable is the entire program.

7. A(n) _____ is a type of subprogram whose name may be assigned a value.

8. A(n) _____ function is one that is supplied by the programming language; its code does not appear in the program that uses it.

9. When a subprogram calls itself, the process is called _____.

10. If N = 2 and Sum(N) is a function with Sum(1) = 5, then the statement

    ```
    Set Sum = Sum(N - 1) + N
    ```

    assigns the value _____ to Sum.

True or False

11. T F Changes to a value parameter in a subprogram affect the corresponding argument in the calling module.

12. T F Changes to a reference parameter in a subprogram affect the corresponding argument in the calling module.

13. T F The ToUpper() and ToLower() functions can take a variable of any data type.

14. T F The statement: Display ToUpper("Yes") is not allowed because "Y" is already uppercase.

Short Answer

Exercises 15–20 refer to the following program:

```
Main
   Declare X As Integer
   Set X = 1
   Call Display(2*X,X,5)
End Program
Subprogram Display(Integer Num1, Integer Num2,Integer Num3)
   Write Num1 +  " " + Num2 + " " + Num3
End Subprogram
```

15. What data is passed from the main program to the subprogram?

16. What data is imported by the subprogram Display?

17. Draw a data flow diagram for this program.

18. If code corresponding to this pseudocode is run but X is initially set to 4, what is the output of this program?

19. If code corresponding to this pseudocode is run, as given, with X = 1, what is the output of this program?

20. Suppose that in the subprogram, all occurrences of Num1, Num2, and Num3 were replaced by A, B, and C, respectively. If code corresponding to the resulting pseudocode were run as in Exercise 19, what would be the output now?

21. Write a subprogram called Input_Data() that inputs two numbers from the user and exports their values to the main program.

22. Write a subprogram called Flip() that imports two variables from the main program (into parameters X and Y), interchanges their values, and exports the results to the main program.

Exercises 23–28 refer to the following program. Assume that variables declared in the main program are global.

```
Main
   Declare X As Integer, Y As Integer
   Set X = 1
   Set Y = 2
   Call Sub(X,Y)
   Write X
   Write Y
End Program
Subprogram Sub(Integer Num1,Integer Num2 As Ref)
   Declare X As Integer
   Set Num1 = 3
   Set Num2 = 4
   Set X = 5
   Write X
End Subprogram
```

23. What is the scope of the following variables?
    a. X, declared in the main program?
    b. X, declared in the subprogram?

24. List the local and global variables in this program.

25. List the value and reference parameters in the subprogram Sub.

26. What is the output of this program if code corresponding to this pseudocode is run?

27. Suppose the subprogram header is changed to the following:

    ```
    Subprogram Sub(Integer Num1 As Ref,Integer Num2)
    ```

    If code corresponding to the new pseudocode is run, what is the output now?

28. Suppose the subprogram header is changed to the following:

    ```
    Subprogram Sub(Integer Num1,Integer Num2)
    ```

    If code corresponding to the new pseudocode is run, what is the output now?

In Exercises 29–35, give the value returned by the built-in function.

29. a. Abs(0)
    b. Abs(-1.5)

30. a. Round(3.8)
    b. Round(Abs(-1.4))

31. a. Str(10.5)
    b. Val("ten",N)

32. a. Str(Val("-1.5",N))
    b. Val(Str(87.6),N)

33. a. ToUpper("N")
    b. ToUpper("Nancy Newley")

34. a. ToLower("N")
    b. Length_Of(ToLower(Name)), where Name is a String variable and Name = "Nancy Newley"

35. Given the Float variables: Charge = -87.23 and Cost = 456.87
    a. Val(Str(Cost),N)
    b. Abs(Round(Charge))

36. Refer to Example 9.15. Add the following functionality to this program: Allow the user to enter the cost of a gallon of gas on each trip and use a function, Cost() to calculate the cost of purchasing gas for that trip. Display this information in the table with the rest of the information. You will need to add another parallel array, TripCost, to hold this information.

37. Suppose a program contains the following function:

    ```
    Function F(X) As Float
       Set F = X + 1
    End Function
    ```

    What is displayed when the statement

    ```
    Write F(3)
    ```

    in the main program is executed?

38. Given the function of Exercise 37, what is displayed when the statement:

    ```
    Write F(F(0))
    ```

    in the main program is executed?

39. Suppose a program contains the following function:

    ```
    Function G(X,Y) As Float
       Set G = X + Y
    End Function
    ```

    What is displayed when the statement

    ```
    Write G(4,5)
    ```

    in the main program is executed?

40. Given the functions of Exercises 37 and 39, what is displayed when the statement

    ```
    Write G(1,F(1))
    ```

    in the main program is executed?

41. Write a function

    ```
    Function Average(Num1,Num2) As Float
    ```

    that finds the mean, (Num1 + Num2)/2, of the numbers Num1 and Num2.

42. Write a Main module (main program) that inputs two numbers from the user, calls the Average() function of Exercise 41 to find the mean of these numbers, and displays the result.

Exercises 43–46 refer to the following program:

```
Main
   Declare K As Integer
   Input K
   Set Result = F(K)
   Write Result
End Program
Function F(N) As Integer
   If N == 1 Then
      Set F = 1
   Else
      Set F = N * F(N-1)
   Set N = N -1
   End If
End Function
```

43. What is the output of this program if K = 1?

44. If K = 3, how many times is the function F() called?

45. What is the output of this program if K = 3?

46. Write a nonrecursive function (using a loop) that has the same effect as F().

47. Write a recursive function Mult(M,N) that multiplies the positive integers M and N by using the fact that

    M × N = M + M + . . . + M (N times).

48. Write a nonrecursive function (using a loop) that has the same effect as the recursive function Mult(M,N) of Exercise 47.

Programming Challenges

For each of the following Programming Challenges, use pseudocode to design a suitable program to solve it. In your program, make use of subprograms or functions with parameters and arguments. Note: some of the Programming Challenges will require some reworking to be implemented in RAPTOR.

1. Input a list of positive numbers (terminated by 0) into an array, find the largest number in the array, and output the result. Use a subprogram to input the numbers, a function to find the largest number, and a subprogram to output the result.

2. Input a list of positive numbers (terminated by 0) into an array, find the mean (average) of the numbers in the array, and output the result. Use a subprogram to input the numbers, a function to find the mean, and a subprogram to output the result.

3. Develop a menu-driven program that inputs a number X, and at the user's choice, finds and displays the area (A) of one of the following:
   - A square with side X (use A = X^2)
   - A circle with radius X (use A = 3.14 * X^2)
   - An equilateral triangle with side X (use A = Sqrt(3)/4 * X^2)

   Use a function for the area of each shape.

4. The factorial of a positive integer N, denoted by N!, is defined by the following:

   ```
   N! = 1 × 2 × . . . × N     (Note:  0! = 1 )
   ```

   Using subprograms and functions, create a recursive program to compute N!. The user should input a positive integer and a subprogram should check that the input is correct (a positive integer). Then use recursion to compute the factorial. Create a subprogram that will call itself to do the multiplication until N = 1. Then display the result in the main program.

5. Create a program that will input a positive integer from the user. The program should check to make sure the entry is a positive integer and then check to see if the number is a prime number. A prime number is a number that is divisible only by itself and 1. The first five prime numbers are 2, 3, 5, 7, and 11; you can check this directly from the definition. If the number is prime, the program should display a message to this effect. If the number is not prime, the program should display the number and its factors. For example, if the user enters the number 3, the output should be:

   ```
   The number 3 is a prime number.
   ```

   However, if the user enters the number 6, the output should be:

   ```
   The number 6 is not a prime number.
   The factors of 6 are: 1, 2, 3, 6
   ```

6. Use functions and submodules as appropriate to allow a user to create an interesting display of text. The user should enter a string of text and a character or characters to use as a border. The main program should call the submodules as follows:

   - A submodule to get the user's text selection
   - A submodule to get the user's symbol selection
   - A submodule to allow the user to select a full border (to surround the text completely) or just a line of symbols either under or above the text.
   - A submodule to display the result

   Some sample inputs and output are as follows:

   ```
   Text:         Pat's Premium Pastry
   Symbol(s):    <>
   Border style: full border
   Display:      <><><><><><><><><><><><><><><>
                 <><> Pat's Premium Pastry <><>
                 <><><><><><><><><><><><><><><>

   Text:         Lizzy Lizard
   Symbol(s):    *
   Border style: underline
   Display:      Lizzy Lizard
                 ************
   ```

Sequential Data Files

10

In this chapter, we will introduce the important concept of a data file and discuss the use of sequential files for data input. We will also describe how to manipulate the records in these files in several ways.

After reading this chapter, you will be able to do the following:

- Identify the types of data files
- Identify records and fields within a data file
- Create, write data to, and read data from a sequential file
- Delete, modify, and insert records in a sequential file
- Use arrays for file maintenance
- Merge two data files so that their records stay in order
- Use the control break processing technique in certain programming situations

Keeping it On File

You really should save a copy of all the work you submit to your teachers throughout your college career. So let's assume you are diligent about doing this. But how do you save this work? When you finish an English class essay, do you just click the Save button? If you use a Windows-based computer, the operating system will probably save the file to a folder named MyDocuments. If this is what you do, at the end of approximately four years of college, assuming about ten courses a year, each with about ten assignments to be submitted, you will have at least 400 college-related files in your MyDocuments folder. Plus, of course, any other files you have saved throughout those years. And if you want to find one of those files—say, an essay written for a history class that you remember has the information you need to use in your senior sociology term paper, it will be pretty hard to find without opening a lot of files. It would be far better if you had organized your files from the beginning into folders. That is why businesses spend a great deal of time creating the best organizational system to use for storing data. While you may have to search through 400 files to find the one you want, unless a large business has a good organizational system, a worker might have to search through 40,000 or 400,000 files to find a record that is needed.

By keeping large amounts of data organized and stored uniformly, it's easy to locate and process the data. For example, in one folder in the computer network used by a small business there might be a subfolder named Payroll with folders inside this one for each month of the year. Inside each folder there might be files consisting of employees' time sheets and other payroll records. Another folder might contain subfolders for purchase orders, billing records, and so forth.

Regardless of the contents of a file, the information within it needs structure to make processing it predictable and easy. For example, a simple employee file might contain the following information:

Employee number

Employee name

Address

Department

Pay rate

The information about each employee would be stored in the same order. It would make no sense—and would be very confusing—if the employee number was stored after the employee name for some employees but after the address for other employees. If the collection of these records is filed alphabetically by employee name, then any person with access to the employee information folder can easily and quickly find the record for a particular worker. Once the appropriate record is located, that person can, for example, use it for a report, modify it, or delete it. On the other hand, sometimes the entire file needs to be processed. For example, when paychecks are disbursed, every employee gets one, so the person in charge of payroll simply accesses the entire file and processes all records sequentially, beginning with the first and stopping after the last.

There are many ways to organize a file system to save time and effort, but the important thing to remember is that just having a large quantity of related data is useless unless it's organized properly—so you can get to the information you need in short order.

10.1   An Introduction to Data Files

So far in this book we have assumed that all program input would be entered by the user from the keyboard and that all program output would be displayed on the screen. In the pseudocode, we have used the Input and Write statements to represent entering and displaying information. Data files provide another means of supplying input and producing output.

File Basics

A computer **file** is a collection of information that has been assigned a name and stored separately from the program that created it. Files may contain programs, in which case they are called **program files**, or they may contain data to be used by programs, in which case they are called **data files**. Of course, all files you create and save, such as homework assignments, a resume, and so on, are data files, but in this chapter we will focus on the type of file that is to be processed by a program that we will write ourselves—data files with records.

Input provided by the user (for example, by using a keyboard or a mouse) while the program is running is called **interactive input**. Input to a program from a data file is called **batch processing**. You have already seen in many examples that interactive input can be very useful; batch processing (using data files) has advantages too, as follows:

- Data files are usually better for input of large amounts of data.
- Data files can circumvent the need to reenter data in certain programming situations.
- Data files can be used by more than one program.
- Data files can store the output of a program for future review or for input to another program.

Text Files versus Binary Files

All files can be divided into two general types: **text files** and **binary files.** Text files consist solely of standard characters—roughly speaking, the symbols you can type on a keyboard. Examples of text files include certain operating system files, simple word processing or web page files, some program files, and specialized files produced by certain applications.

Files that don't fall into the text file category are often referred to as binary files. In addition to standard characters, they may contain other symbols and codes. Today, most operating system files, program files, and data files produced by applications are binary files.

Text files have one big advantage over binary files. They are much simpler for the following reasons:

- They are easier to create, whether from within the programming language software (as demonstrated later in this section) or by just typing their contents using a text editor. A text editor is a simple word processor whose output is stored as text files.
- They can be displayed on the screen or printed on a printer without using any special software.

- They are universal in nature. Virtually every computer system can correctly interpret the contents of a text file without any special software. For example, every word processor can create and display text files, so a text file created with one word processor can be accessed by any other. On the other hand, word processors normally store their data in a special (proprietary) file format, specific to that application. Consequently, a nontext document created with one word processor cannot always be viewed or modified by another one.

Records and Fields

Often, the information in a data file is broken into groups of related data called **records**. Think about a file that contains an airline's passenger reservations. Each reservation consists of the flight date, flight number, passenger name, and perhaps other information like the passenger's credit card number, telephone or email contact, and so on. All of the information relating to one passenger's flight reservation makes up a single record. One data item in a record is called a **field**. In this case, the fields would be the passenger's name, the flight date, the flight number, and so forth.

Here's another example of a file with records and fields. A teacher might have a data file that stores the names and test scores for the students in a certain class. A record in this file would consist of the student's name and test scores. If the teacher stored the students' first names separately from the last names, then first name and last name would be separate fields. However, if the teacher preferred, each student's full name could be stored in one field. Each exam score could be another field. To summarize: *files* are made up of *records* and records are made up of *fields*.

Figure 10.1 shows one way to depict the data stored in a data file. This file stores the names of the students in one class and each student's four exam scores. It has 30 records and each record consists of five fields. Here, the name is a single field that includes the student's first initial and last name. The other four fields are exam scores. The teacher would know that field 1 is the name, field 2 corresponds to Exam 1, field 3 corresponds to Exam 2, and so forth. For example, the first record contains the following fields:

```
"R. Abrams", 86, 64, 73, 84
```

Figure 10.1 Records and fields in a data file

	Field 1	Field 2	Field 3	Field 4	Field 5
Record 1	"R. Abrams"	86	64	73	84
Record 2	"J. Chavez"	94	87	83	90
Record 3	"H. Crater"	68	77	91	79
.	.	.	.	.	.
.	.	.	.	.	.
.	.	.	.	.	.
Record 30	"A. Zelkin"	76	93	69	52

Actually, the data of Figure 10.1 would be saved in a file as a sequence of consecutive characters. The fields are separated from one another by commas, and each record is terminated by a special symbol, which we will denote by <CR>. Thus, the first two records of this file would look as follows:

```
"R. Abrams",86,64,73,84<CR>"J. Chavez",94,87,83,90<CR>
```

Notice that fields that hold String values (the name, in this case) use quotes, while data in fields that store numerical data (the test scores in this example) are simply stored as numbers. If one field in our example was each student's telephone number, the number would be stored as a String (i.e, "123-555-1234") to show that this data cannot be manipulated as Integer or Float data can.

Sequential and Direct-Access Files

Data files can also be divided into two other categories:

- **Sequential files** contain records that must be processed in the order in which they were created. They are accessed in the same linear fashion as the scenes on an old VCR tape. For example, to print the 50th record in a sequential file, we must first read (or scan) the 49 records that precede it.
- **Direct-access files** are sometimes called **random-access files**. In this type of file, each record can be accessed independently of the rest. Locating a data item in a direct-access file is analogous to finding a certain track on a DVD.

Either type of file can be used to solve a given problem. A sequential file is generally the better choice if you have to frequently display and/or modify the entire file, as with a file that contains student grades. On the other hand, a direct-access file is more efficient if you have lots of data to store but expect to change or display small amounts at a time, as with an airline reservations management program. In the remainder of this chapter, we will limit the discussion to sequential data files.

Creating and Reading Sequential Files[1]

Now we will discuss two fundamental operations on sequential data files—creating a file and reading the contents of a file.

Creating a Sequential File

There are three basic steps involved in developing a program segment to create a sequential file.

1. You need to open the file, which may sound strange because you have to open something that doesn't exist yet. But **opening a file** actually means to create it and specify some information about it.
   - You must give the file an **external name**—the name under which the file will be saved. Operating systems have different rules about what is an acceptable filename. The safest way to name a file is to use a name that is no more than eight characters long, there should be no spaces in the name, and all the characters should be lowercase. Operating systems

[1]It is possible to work with data files using RAPTOR but not all the functionality described in this chapter is present in RAPTOR. Before attempting to use RAPTOR to implement the examples in the chapter you should read Section 10.6, Running with RAPTOR.

differ in the way they handle uppercase and lowercase characters, but regardless of what operating system is used, all lowercase characters are treated the same.

- You must give your file an **internal name**—the name by which the file will be known in the program code. This name must conform to the rules for variable names specified by the programming language.
- You must specify the **file mode,** which states the purpose for which you want to open the file. Typically, the purpose is either `Output mode` for writing (creating) data in the file or `Input mode` for reading (accessing) the contents of an existing file.

2. You need to create the contents of the file by writing data to the file.
3. The file must be closed, which terminates the process. The file is saved and the connection between the internal and external names is broken. **Closing a file** places a special symbol (an **end-of-file marker**) at the end of the file. When we begin to manipulate the data in the file you will understand the importance of the end-of-file marker.

The statements used to carry out these steps vary considerably depending on the programming language used to implement them. To show how the process works, we will use generic pseudocode statements.

- To open a file we will say the following:

  `Open "external_name" For Output As InternalName`

  For example, to create a file that we will save with the filename `grades` and refer to as `NewFile` within the program, use the following:

  `Open "grades" For Output As NewFile`

- To write a record (a line) of data to a file, we will use a `Write` statement, just as if we were displaying this information on the screen, but we will precede the data with the name of the file to which we are writing and use commas to separate the name of the file and the data items as follows:

  `Write InternalName, data`

  For example, if a file's internal name is `NewFile`, we would use the following to add the name `"John Doe"` and his test score, 85, to the file:

  `Write NewFile, "John Doe", 85`

  This statement creates a file record with two fields—the first containing a full name and the second containing that person's test score. It also places an **end-of-record marker**, the special symbol we denote by <CR>, after these data items to separate them from the next record.

- To close a file we use the following:

  `Close InternalName`

  For example, you `Close` the file `NewFile` as follows:

  `Close NewFile`

Example 10.1 illustrates how these statements are used to create a sequential file.

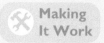

Programming Logic Transcends Syntax

It is important, when inputting data into a sequential file, to know what data type goes into each field. If you type a number when entering data for a text field (a String), the number will be entered as text and cannot be used in any computations.

Data is always stored with specific data types and, no matter what language or software you are using, the data type is always an integral part of the way that data is processed. This is true regardless of whether you are storing data as a variable, in an array, or in a data file. As you have seen, the most basic concepts of programming are applied over and over in all aspects of writing programs even when the syntax of each language differs.

Example 10.1 **Creating a Sequential File**

This program segment creates a file called "grades" containing records with two fields each. The first field is the student's name (a String variable named Student) and the second field is the student's test score (an Integer variable named Score).

```
1   Declare Student As String
2   Declare Score As Integer
3   Open "grades" For Output As NewFile
4   Write "Enter the student's name and test score."
5   Write "Enter 0 for both when done."
6   Input Student, Score
7   While Student != "0"
8     Write NewFile, Student, Score
9     Write "Enter the student's name and test score."
10    Write "Enter 0 for both when done."
11    Input Student, Score
12  End While
13  Close NewFile
```

What Happened?

- The statement on line 3

    ```
    Open "grades" For Output As NewFile
    ```

  assigns the internal name NewFile to a file that will be saved as "grades" and prepares it for Output (to be created).

- Lines 4 and 5 explain to the user what data is to be entered and how to stop entering data.

- Line 6 gets the initial student and score as input from the user. The input is separated by commas. This indicates to the program that the first data item goes into the first field and the second data item goes into the second field. Obviously, it is essential that the data be entered in correct order.

- Line 7 begins the While loop. Within this loop, the statement on line 8

```
    Write NewFile, Student, Score
```

transmits the input data to the file "grades" (whose internal name is NewFile).

- Lines 9–11 get data for another record and this Input-data/Write-record process continues until the user enters 0 for the student name and 0 for score, causing an exit from the loop.
- Finally, the statement on line 13

```
    Close NewFile
```

closes the file, ending the Output mode and the association of the names NewFile and "grades". This statement also ensures that the marker we call <EOF> is placed at the end of the file.

To see the effect of this program segment, suppose that the user input is as follows:

```
Jones, 86
Martin, 73
Smith, 84
0, 0
```

After execution, a file named "grades" would have been created, containing the following data:

```
"Jones",86<CR>,"Martin",73<CR>"Smith",84<CR><EOF>
```

Here, <CR> represents an end-of-record marker generated after each Write statement is executed and <EOF> is an end-of-file marker placed there when the file "grades" is closed.

Making It Work

Take Care Not to Lose Your Data!

If a file is opened for Output, and a file of that name already exists in the same folder, all data in the existing file will be lost! Although this is useful when modifying a file, it could be catastrophic if done accidentally.

Reading the Contents of a File

Once a file has been created, we can input (or Read) data contained within it into a program. To do so, we need to do the following:

1. Open the file. We use the same type of statement to perform this operation that we used to create a file, but we take the mode to be Input as follows:

```
Open "external_name" For Input As InternalName
```

For example, to open the file "grades", stored previously, and assign it the internal (program) name GradeFile so that we can access its contents, use the following:

```
Open "grades" for Input As GradeFile
```

Note that when a file is opened for Input, the **file pointer**, which indicates the current item in the file, is positioned at the beginning of the first record, or if the file does not contain any records, at the end-of-file marker. Recall that this marker, which we denote by <EOF>, was automatically placed at the end of the file when that file was created.

2. Assign the data in the file records to program variables. We do this by means of a Read statement of the following form:

```
Read InternalName, variable1, variable2, . . .
```

If you are given a file with internal name GradeFile and you want to Read the current record in this file so that you can assign the String data in its first field to the String variable called StudentName and assign the Integer data in its second field to the Integer variable called Score, use the following statement:

```
Read GradeFile, StudentName, Score
```

After a Read statement is executed, the file pointer moves to the beginning of the next record, or if the last file record has just been read, to the end-of-file marker.

The EOF() Function

To read all the records in a file into a program, we place a Read statement within a loop. On successive passes through this loop, the contents of successive records are input into program variables. To terminate the input process and force an exit from the loop, most programming languages contain an end-of-file (EOF) function. We will take this function to be of the following form:

```
EOF(InternalName)
```

The **EOF() function**, which may appear in the test condition of any loop or selection structure, has the value true if the end of the file InternalName has been reached; that is, if the file pointer is located at the end-of-file marker. Otherwise, the value of this function is false. We have discussed the Boolean data type, which assigns a value of either true or false to a variable. The EOF() function is also a Boolean. Since a function returns a value and, in the case of EOF(), that value is either true or false, it is a function of type Boolean. The use of the EOF() function is illustrated in Example 10.2.

Example 10.2 **Using the EOF() Function**

The following program segment displays the contents of the file "grades" created in Example 10.1, which has records of the following form: student_name, test_score:

```
1  Declare Student As String
2  Declare Score As Integer
3  Open "grades" For Input As GradeFile
4  While NOT EOF(GradeFile)
5    Read GradeFile, Student, Score
6    Write Student + " " + Score
7  End While
8  Close GradeFile
```

What Happened?

- In this program segment, the Open statement on line 3 prepares the file "grades" for Input. This allows the data from the file to be transferred to the program and assigns it the internal name GradeFile.

- Then, starting on line 4, the `While` loop is entered. The condition

  `NOT EOF(GradeFile)`

  is `true` if we have not reached the end-of-file marker for grades.
- On the first pass through the loop (lines 5 and 6), this condition will be `true` unless the file is empty.
- Within the loop, the statement on line 5

  `Read GradeFile, Student, Score`

  reads the next two data items (fields) from the file. This statement also assigns these data items to the variables `Student` and `Score`, respectively, and moves the file pointer to the next record or to the end-of-file marker, if the last record has just been read.
- The `Write` statement on line 6 displays the values of `Student` and `Score` on the screen, with two blank spaces between them.
- Then, on line 7, if more data remains in the file, the loop is reentered, or if the end of the file has been reached, the loop is exited.

Suppose that the file "grades" contains the following data:

`"Jones", 86<CR>"Martin", 73<CR>"Smith", 84<CR><EOF>`

Then, the screen output of this program segment would be as follows:

```
Jones 86
Martin 73
Smith 84
```

Self Check for Section 10.1

10.1. a. What is a text file?

   b. What advantage does a text file have over a nontext (binary) file?

10.2. What is the difference between a sequential file and a direct-access file?

10.3. Write a program that displays the contents of an existing file named "employee" containing a list of employee names in records with a single field of string type.

10.4. Write a program that creates the "employee" file of Self Check 10.3 by having the user enter a sequence of names from the keyboard.

10.2 Modifying a Sequential File

In this section, we continue the discussion of sequential files that was begun in Section 10.1. We will describe three basic file operations: deleting, changing, and inserting records within an existing sequential file. To carry out any of these operations, the entire file must be rewritten. Every record in it must be read, modi-fied if desired, temporarily stored somewhere else, and after all records have been processed, written back to the given file. A standard way of doing this makes use of a second file, called a **scratch file**, to store the contents of the given file temporarily. Arrays can also be used instead of a scratch file, as discussed later in this section. The process for file modification, using this technique is as follows:

1. Open the given file for Input and the scratch file for Output.
2. Input data concerning the change from the user.
3. Read records from the given file and write them to the scratch file until you reach the record to be modified.
4. Make the change: write a new or modified record to the scratch file, or in the case of a deletion, skip the specified record so that it does not get written to the scratch file.
5. Read the rest of the records from the given file and write them to the scratch file.
6. Close both files.
7. Replace the contents of the given file with that of the scratch file.

The flowchart shown in Figure 10.2 provides a visual representation of this process.

Examples 10.3–10.6 show how this general process can be applied to the specific operations of deleting, inserting, and changing records. In these examples, we assume that a file "grades" exists on disk whose records are made up of the following fields:

    student_name, test_score

(The file "grades" was created in Example 10.1.)

Deleting Records

To delete a record from a file, we create a file called "scratch" that is identical to the original file except for a record that has been deleted at the request of the user. The basic idea, using the file "grades" from the previous example, is as follows:

1. Successively, Read records from "grades".
2. If the current record is not the one to be deleted, write it to "scratch"; if it is the one to be deleted, do not write it to "scratch".

Example 10.3 shows the detailed pseudocode for this process.

The "grades" file does not change during the execution of the program segment in Example 10.3. To restore "grades" as the name of the updated (modified) file, we copy the records in the "scratch" file to "grades". Example 10.4 shows how to carry out this operation.

Figure 10.2 Flowchart for the general file modification process

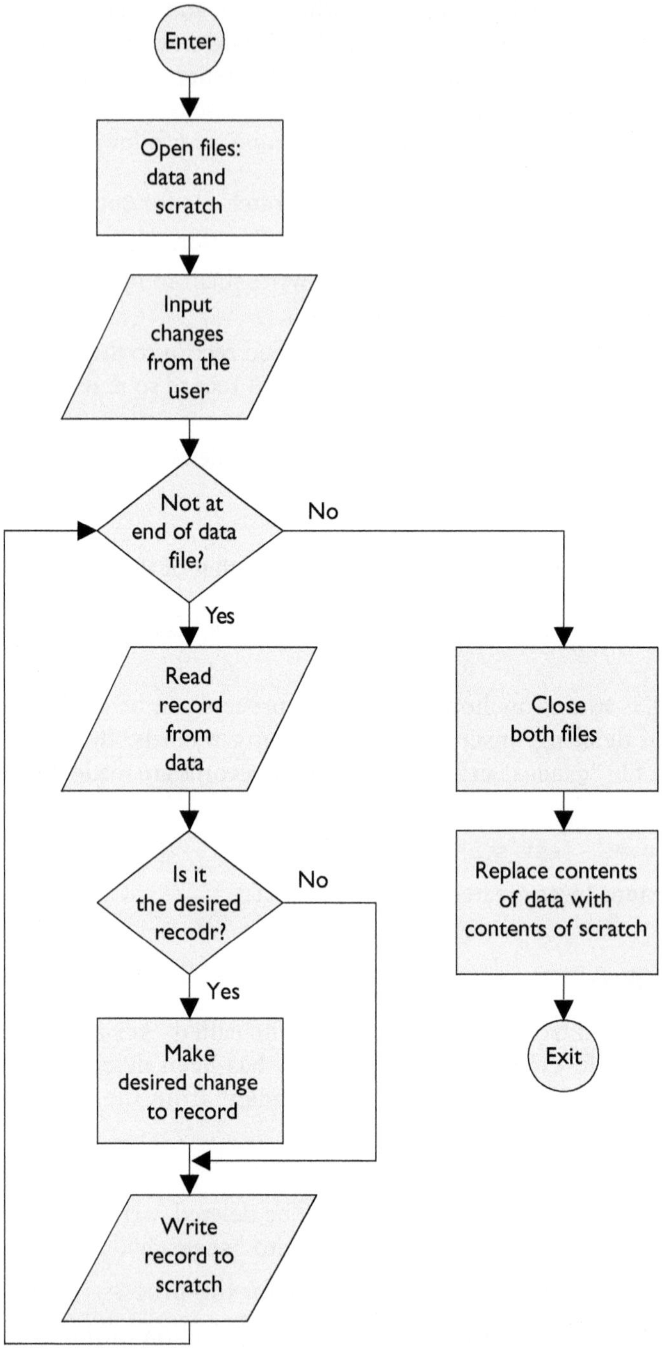

Example 10.3 **Deleting a Record from a Sequential File**

```
1   Declare Student As String
2   Declare DeleteName As String
3   Declare Score As Integer
4   Open "grades" For Input As GivenFile
5   Open "scratch" For Output As TempFile
6   Write "Enter name of student to be deleted:"
7   Input DeleteName
8   While NOT EOF(GivenFile)
9     Read GivenFile, Student, Score
10    If Student != DeleteName Then
11      Write TempFile, Student, Score
12    End If
13  End While
14  Close GivenFile, TempFile
```

What Happened?

In this program segment, the While loop (lines 8–13) reads all records, one at a time, from the file "grades", which has the internal name GivenFile. It then writes each record, except for the one specified for deletion, onto the file "scratch", which has the internal name TempFile. At the end of execution, "scratch" is identical to "grades", except for the deleted record. For example, suppose that prior to execution, "grades" contains

```
"Jones",86<CR>"Smith",94<CR>"Martin",73<CR><EOF>
```

and the user inputs the name "Martin". Then after execution, the record containing Martin's name and score would have been deleted and "scratch" would contain:

```
"Jones",86<CR>"Smith",94<CR><EOF>
```

Example 10.4 **Updating the File after Deleting Records**

This pseudocode makes a copy, called "grades", of the file "scratch".

```
1   Open "grades" For Output As TargetFile
2   Open "scratch" For Input As SourceFile
3   While NOT EOF(SourceFile)
4     Read SourceFile, Student, Score
5     Write TargetFile, Student, Score
6   End While
7   Close SourceFile, TargetFile
```

What Happened?

Recall that opening a file for Output erases all data in that file. Thus, after the Open statement on line 1, for all practical purposes, the file "grades" (known to the program as TargetFile) is empty. The While loop (lines 3–6) then reads each record from scratch (which has the internal name SourceFile) and writes it to "grades", effectively creating the latter as a copy of "scratch". It won't hurt anything if you leave the temporary "scratch" file as is. If you need to use a scratch file again in another program or later in the same program, when you open a file named "scratch" for Output again, all the contents of this old file will be erased anyway.

Modifying Records

To modify one or more records in a sequential file, basically you want to make a copy of the original file. The new file—the copy—will be the same as the original except that the records you want to modify are changed on the copy. Then you replace the original file with the copy that has the modifications. Example 10.5 shows how to change one of the data fields in a specified record of a sequential file.

Example 10.5 Modifying One Field in One Specific Record in a Sequential File

This program segment modifies a specified record in the "grades" file. The user will replace a given student's test score by a new one. Again, the basic idea is simple.

1. Read records from the "grades" file in succession.
2. If the current record is the one to be modified, write the new record to a "scratch" file. Otherwise write the current record to the "scratch" file.
3. Copy the "scratch" file to the "grades" file.

The following shows the detailed pseudocode:

```
 1   Declare Name As String
 2   Declare NewScore As Integer
 3   Open "grades" For Input As GivenFile
 4   Open "scratch" For Output As TempFile
 5   Write "Enter the name of the student: "
 6   Input Name
 7   Write "Enter new test score: "
 8   Input NewScore
 9   While NOT EOF(GivenFile)
10     Read GivenFile, Student, Score
11     If Student == Name Then
12       Write TempFile, Student, NewScore
13     Else
14       Write TempFile, Student, Score
15     End If
16   End While
17   Close GivenFile, TempFile
18   Copy the file "scratch" onto the file "grades"
```

What Happened?

In this program segment, the While loop copies all records from "grades" onto "scratch" except for the one to be modified. The latter is replaced (due to the If-Then-Else statement) by the one containing the input data. Thus, if prior to execution, "grades" contains

```
"Jones",86<CR>"Post",71<CR>"Smith",74<CR><EOF>
```

and the user enters the name "Smith" and the score 96, then after execution, the "grades" file will contain the following:

```
"Jones",86<CR>"Post",71<CR>"Smith",96<CR><EOF>
```

You should realize that line 18 is just rough pseudocode for the refinement shown in Example 10.4.

Inserting Records

Inserting a record into a specified location in a sequential file is the most complex of the three file modification operations. Example 10.6 shows how we achieve this.

Example 10.6 **Inserting Records into a Sequential File**

Let's assume that the contents of the "grades" file lists records alphabetically according to student name. Suppose a new student joins the class. Now we need to insert a new record. We must place data in each field of that record. In this example, "grades" has two fields—one for the student's name and one for the student's score. So we want to insert values that are stored in the variables called NewName and NewScore. These values will be entered by the user and will be inserted into this file at the appropriate place, retaining alphabetical order. Since this operation is somewhat difficult to accomplish in a sequential file, first we will give a general idea of how it's done using rough pseudocode as follows:

```
1  Open the "grades" file and a "scratch" file.
2  Input the NewName and NewScore from the user.
3  Read records (Student, Score) from "grades" and write them to
        "scratch" until desired location is reached.
4  Write the new record (NewName, NewScore) to "scratch".
5  Read the rest of the records in "grades" and write them to
        "scratch".
```

Although this plan is fairly straightforward, the following points need to be considered before refining the pseudocode:

- In Step 3, how do we know when we've reached the proper location in the "grades" file? Since the student names in "grades" are in alphabetical order, as we read records from this file, the position determined by the ASCII ordering of the String variable Student is increasing. So when we reach the first record for which NewName < Student we know that the new record must be inserted just before the current one. Thus, we rewrite Step 3 as follows:

```
3 Read records from "grades" and write them to "scratch"
        until NewName < Student.
```

- What if the condition NewName < Student never occurs? This means that NewName follows (alphabetically) every name in the file. Thus, in this case the new record must be added to the end of the file.

Taking these points into account, we arrive at the following refined pseudocode for the record insertion operation:

```
1  Declare NewName As String
2  Declare NewScore As Integer
3  Open "grades" For Input As GivenFile
4  Open "scratch" For Output As TempFile
5  Write "Enter name and score for the new student:"
6  Input NewName, NewScore
7  Set Inserted = 0
```

```
 8  While (NOT EOF(GivenFile)) AND (Inserted == 0)
 9    Read GivenFile, Student, Score
10    If NewName < Student Then
11      Write TempFile, NewName, NewScore
12      Set Inserted = 1
13    End If
14    Write TempFile, Student, Score
15  End While
16  If Inserted == 0 Then
17    Write TempFile, NewName, NewScore
18  End If
19  While NOT EOF(GivenFile)
20    Read GivenFile, Student, Score
21    Write TempFile, Student, Score
22  End While
23  Close GivenFile, TempFile
24  Copy "scratch" onto "grades"
```

What Happened?

The While loop that begins on line 8 reads records from the "grades" file and writes them onto the "scratch" file until the new record has been inserted (line 11), in which case the variable Inserted is set equal to 1 (line 12), or the end of the "grades" file is reached. Inserted, therefore, is a flag.

If the latter condition (end-of-file) occurs first, then the loop is exited without inserting the new record. In this case, Inserted still equals 0 so the If-Then structure (lines 16–18) that follows the While loop will insert the new record at the end of the "scratch" file. On the other hand, if the loop is exited due to the former condition (because the new record has been inserted), the variable Inserted has been set to 1. Therefore, the If-Then condition on line 16 will be false and the Then clause will be skipped. Then the While loop on lines 19–22 reads the rest of the records, if there are any, from "grades" and writes them to "scratch". Finally, line 23 closes GivenFile and TempFile and, in line 24, the updated "scratch" file is copied back to "grades". The rough pseudocode on line 24 should be refined by replacing it with the code given in Example 10.4.

This is what would happen if, before we ran this program segment, "grades" contains

"Jones",86<CR>"Smith",94<CR><EOF>

and the user inputs the name "Martin" and the score 71. Then, after the program segment is run, "grades" would contain the following data:

"Jones",86<CR>"Martin",71<CR>"Smith",94<CR><EOF>

This is a rather difficult program to follow so take a little time to walk through it, step by step, until you are sure you understand what each line does. It is helpful to write down some sample data and walk through the program with it. Here's some sample data to try (this is also a Self Check for Section 10.2). Assume that your "grades" file has the following data:

"Drake",98<CR>"Jones",86<CR>"Martin",71<CR>"Smith",94
<CR>"Venit",99<CR><EOF>

Try inserting these new records, one at a time, to see how each part of the program segment works. Be sure to notice which lines of pseudocode will be executed and which will be skipped for each of the following records:

```
"Cornswaller",77
"Throckmorton",67
"Zigler",88
```

Using Append Mode to Insert New Records

Making It Work

Some programming languages, such as C++, make it easy to insert new records at the end of an existing file. In this case, all that needs to be done is the following:

1 Open the desired file in append mode.
2 Input data from the user.
3 Write that data to the file.

The new record is automatically added (appended) to the end of the file.

Using Arrays in File Maintenance

Instead of using a scratch file in the modification process, sometimes it's preferable to load (i.e., input) the given file into arrays in the computer's internal memory. This is a desirable technique if there are a large number of changes to be made to the file. The relatively high speed of internal memory can often make such changes more efficiently than using a scratch file. The general procedure is as follows:

1. Open the given file for Input (to be read from).
2. Read the file records into parallel arrays, one array for each field.
3. Close the file (so that it can later be opened for Output).
4. Make the desired modifications to the arrays.
5. Open the file for Output (which erases all the original data in this file).
6. Write the contents of the arrays (the modified data) to the given file.
7. Close this file.

Example 10.7 illustrates this process.

Example 10.7 Using Arrays for File Maintenance

This program segment allows the user to add a second test score for each student in a file called "grades", which currently has records of the following form:

```
student_name (String), test_1_score (Integer)
```

We will load these records into two parallel arrays named Student (an array of strings) and Test1 (an array of integers). Then we will input the scores for the second test into a third parallel array of integers named Test2. Finally, we will write all this data back to the file "grades" so each record will now have three fields as follows:

```
student_name, test_1_score, test_2_score
```

The pseudocode is as follows:

```
1   Declare Student[100] As String
2   Declare Test1[100] As Integer
3   Declare Test2[100] As Integer
4   Declare Count As Integer
5   Open "grades" For Input As DataFile
6   Set Count = 0
7   While NOT EOF(DataFile)
8      Read DataFile, Student[Count], Test1[Count]
9      Set Count = Count + 1
10  End While
11  Close DataFile
12  Open "grades" For Output As DataFile
13  For (K = 0; K < Count; K++)
14     Write "Enter Test 2 score for " + Student[K]
15     Input Test2[K]
16     Write DataFile, Student[K], Test1[K], Test2[K]
17  End For
18  Close DataFile
```

What Happened?

Since our modified records will have three fields each, we declare three arrays to hold their values. The While loop loads the existing records with two fields in each record into the appropriate arrays and also counts the number (Count) of records. The For loop inputs the modifications (the new test scores) from the user and writes the modified records to the file "grades". As is usually required by the programming language, notice that the file is closed and reopened for Output after it has been loaded into memory and before it can be rewritten.

If prior to execution of this program segment, "grades" contains

```
"Jones",86<CR>"Post",71<CR>"Smith",96<CR><EOF>
```

and the user enters scores of 83, 79, and 88 for the three students in the file, then after execution, "grades" will contain the following:

```
"Jones",86,83<CR>"Post",71,79<CR>"Smith",96,88<CR><EOF>
```

Self Check for Section 10.2

For Self Check Questions 10.5–10.7, assume that a file named "payroll" exists with 500 records of the form:

```
employee_number (Integer), name (String), rate_of_pay (Float)
```

and that the records appear in order of increasing employee number. Use the following variable names: IDNum *for the employee number,* Name *for the employee name, and* Rate *for the rate of pay. Write a program segment that performs each of the following operations:*

10.5. It deletes a record with employee number 138.

10.6. It changes the rate of pay of employee 456 to 7.89.

10.7. It inserts the record
```
167,"C.Jones",8.50
```
into the appropriate place in the file to maintain its order.

10.8. Walk through Example 10.6 with the sample data given, inserting the three new records. Assume your "grades" file has the following data:
```
"Drake",98<CR>"Jones",86<CR>"Martin,"71<CR>"Smith",
94<CR>"Venit",99<CR><EOF>
```
Insert the following new records, one at a time, and write down which lines of pseudocode are executed and which are skipped for each record.
```
"Cornswaller",77
"Throckmorton",67
"Zigler",88
```

10.9. What is the difference between using a scratch file and using arrays in file maintenance? Why would you use arrays instead of a scratch file?

10.3 Merging Sequential Files

In Section 10.2, we described how to maintain a sequential file—how to delete, insert, and change its records. In this section, we discuss another operation on sequential files: **merging** (combining) the data from two files that have the same types of records into a single file in such a way that the proper ordering of the records is retained.

To carry out the merge process, we use a third file to hold the combined records of the two given files. The general procedure for creating this third **merged file** is as follows:

1. Open the two given files for Input. Open the file that will hold the merged records for Output. Assume File1, File2, and File3 are the internal file-names for these files.
2. Successively Read records from File1 and File2.
3. If the current record for File1 precedes that of File2, then Write the File1 record to File3; otherwise, Write the File2 record to File3.
4. Close the three files.

Steps 2 and 3 are the heart of the merge process. They are carried out with the aid of a loop which is exited when the end of one of the two given files is reached. Then the records remaining in the other file are read and written to the merged file. The following is a refinement of these two steps:
```
Read first record from each file
While (NOT EOF(File1)) AND (NOT EOF(File2))
  Compare current records for File1 and File2
  If File1 record precedes File2 record Then
    Write File1 record to File3
    Read another record from File1
  Else
    Write File2 record to File3
    Read another record from File2
  End If
```

```
End While
Read remaining records, if any, in File1 and write to File3
Read remaining records, if any, in File2 and write to File3
```

Example 10.8 provides detailed pseudocode for the file merge process that we've just described.

Example 10.8 **The Big Merger: Merging Two Files**

A company wants to merge two payroll files ("payroll1" and "payroll2") into a single file. Suppose that each record in these files has the following form:

employee_number (Integer), employee_name (String), rate_of_pay (Float)

We will assume that the records are ordered (in increasing order) by employee number and that the last record in each file is 0, "0", 0.0. We will merge these two files into a new file called "payroll". The following program performs the merge:

```
1   Declare Number1, Number2 As Integer
2   Declare Name1, Name2 As String
3   Declare Rate1, Rate2 As Float
4   Open "payroll1" For Input As File1
5   Open "payroll2" For Input As File2
6   Open "payroll" For Output As File3
7   Read File1, Number1, Name1, Rate1
8   Read File2, Number2, Name2, Rate2
9   While (Number1 != 0) AND (Number2 != 0)
10    If Number1 < Number2 Then
11       Write File3, Number1, Name1, Rate1
12       Read File1, Number1, Name1, Rate1
13    Else
14       Write File3, Number2, Name2, Rate2
15       Read File2, Number2, Name2, Rate2
16    End If
17  End While
18  While Number1 != 0
19    Write File3, Number1, Name1, Rate1
20    Read File1, Number1, Name1, Rate1
21  End While
22  While Number2 != 0
23    Write File3, Number2, Name2, Rate2
24    Read File2, Number2, Name2, Rate2
25  End While
26  Write File3, 0, "0", 0.0
27  Close File1, File2, File3
```

What Happened?

This program follows the outline that precedes Example 10.8. The first part of the pseudocode declares the field variables and opens the payroll files. The remainder of the pseudocode performs the merge as described earlier. Notice that the last two

While loops just read the records remaining in one of the files and write them to the merged file. Therefore, one of these loops is always skipped in any program run. Also notice that at the end of the merge process, the two original files are still intact; their contents have not been modified.

To understand this program better, walk through the pseudocode using files with the indicated records:

"payroll1":	"payroll2":
115, "Art", 11.50	120, "Dan", 14.00
130, "Ben", 12.25	125, "Eva", 15.50
135, "Cal", 13.75	0, "0", 0.0
0, "0", 0.0	

Then, after the merge, "payroll" should contain the following records:

```
115, "Art", 11.50
120, "Dan", 14.00
125, "Eva", 15.50
130, "Ben", 12.25
135, "Cal", 13.75
0, "0", 0.0
```

Here is something to think about: What happens to the last record in "payroll1" and "payroll2"? Both these records contain identical values (0, "0", 0.0). Are they ever read? Are they ever written to the merged file? (See Self Check Question 10.11.)

And speaking of identical records, what would happen if "payroll1" and "payroll2" contained some identical records? How does the pseudocode shown in Example 10.8 deal with this possibility? (See Self Check Question 10.12.)

Now, what would happen if both "payroll1" and "payroll2" contain the following record?

```
23, Hortense, 13.82
```

Walk through the pseudocode and see what happens in the merged file. Then try this: In "payroll1", Hortense's employee number is 23 but what if, in "payroll2", she is listed as number 68. In both files her pay rate remains the same. What would show up in the merged file? Can you think of a way to deal with this situation? ●

? What &Why

Self Check for Section 10.3

10.10. a. T F To merge two existing sequential files, we open three files—the existing ones for Input and a new file for Output.

b. T F To merge two sequential files, the fields in the records of both files must be arranged in the same order.

c. T F If we merge two sequential files using the <EOF> function, one with M records and the other with N records and no two records are the same, then the resulting file will contain M + N records.

For Self Check Questions 10.11–10.13 refer to Example 10.8.

10.11. What happens to the last record in "payroll1" and "payroll2"? Both records contain identical values (0, "0", 0.0). Are they ever read? Are they ever written to the merged file?

10.12. What would happen if "payroll1" and "payroll2" contained some identical records? How does the pseudocode shown in Example 10.8 deal with this possibility?

10.13. What changes must be made to the pseudocode of Example 10.8 to merge "payroll1" and "payroll2" if these files are sorted in descending order (largest to smallest) by employee number?

10.4 Focus on Problem Solving: Control Break Processing

In this section, we will present a programming problem, and in the course of solving it we will introduce a programming technique called **control break processing,** which can be used to deal with problems similar to the one presented here. This technique gets its name from the way the procedure is carried out. A data file is processed until a **control variable,** which represents a field in that file, changes value or reaches a preassigned level. This causes a **break** in the processing to take place and allows an action (usually a computation) to be carried out. Processing then resumes until another control break occurs, again initiating an action. This procedure typically continues until the end of the file is reached.

In order to learn how to use the control break processing technique, we will use a single example and follow the program development and design through.

Problem Statement

Harvey's Hardware Company has three locations in the town of Chippindale, and at each location there are several salespeople. Harvey wants to produce a combined monthly sales report for the three stores. The program that creates this report would read a data file called "salesdata", which contains records with the following fields:

    store (Integer), salesperson (String), sales (Float)

Here, store is identified by the number 1, 2, or 3; salesperson gives the name of a salesperson in that store; and sales is the monthly sales, in dollars, for that salesperson. In this file, all records for store 1 appear first, then those for store 2, and finally those for store 3. The last record has a 0 in the store column to indicate the end of the file.

The computer-generated sales report should include the following for each store:

- The store number
- A list of the salespeople at that store and the monthly sales for each of them
- The total monthly sales for that store

The total combined sales for the three stores should appear at the bottom of the report, on the "bottom line," of course.

Problem Analysis

As is most often the case, we begin our program development by examining the required output, as outlined in the problem specifications. The output for this problem is a sales report, most of which consists of a table with the following headings:

```
Store    Salesperson    Sales
```

In this table, we will list all salespeople who work in store 1, then those from store 2, and finally those from store 3. Thus, in the store column of this table, the beginning entries will all be 1, the middle entries will all be 2, and the remaining entries will all be 3. After listing all salespeople in a given store, the subtotal consisting of all sales for that store will be displayed. Finally, after the subtotal for store 3 is displayed, the grand total of all sales for the three stores will be displayed. A typical report of this kind is shown in Figure 10.3.

Figure 10.3 A typical sales report

```
               Harvey's Hardware Company
                 Monthly Sales Report

   Store        Salesperson                    Sales

   1            T. Arnold                       4444.44

   1            J. Baker                        5555.55

   1            C. Connerly                     6666.66

                Total sales for store 1:        16666.65

   2            T. Dashell                      7777.77

   2            E. Everly                       8888.88

                Total sales for store 2:        16666.65

   3            B. Franklin                     9999.99

   3            L. Gomez                        1111.11

   3            W. Houston                      2222.22

                Total sales for store 3:        13333.32

                Total sales for all stores:     46666.62
```

The input variables needed for this program correspond to the fields in each record of the file "salesdata". They are as follows:

- Store (Integer)
- Salesperson (String)
- Sales (Float)

The output variables are as follows:

- Subtotal—the total monthly sales for each store (Float)
- Total—the grand total of the three subtotals (Float)

To proceed from the given input (the data in the file) to the desired output (a report listing sales for each store and the total sales for all three stores), we use the technique of control break processing.

In this program, the control variable is the store number (Store) and the action is the display of a subtotal. The program will process records in a loop until the store number changes. At that point, control is transferred to a module that displays the sales subtotal for the store that was processed just prior to the change in store number. Then file processing continues; that is, control transfers back to the loop until a control break occurs again. The entire process terminates when the end of the file is reached.

Program Design

As indicated in the Problem Analysis section, the heart of this program is a module that reads file records, writes them to the report, and sums the sales for a particular store until a control break takes place. At this point, another module is called to display the store subtotal, and if the last store has been processed, to display the grand total of sales for all stores.

The remaining tasks are small ones: displaying a welcome message, opening the data file, initializing variables, and displaying the report headings. Thus, our program will consist of the following modules:

1. Main module, which calls its submodules into action
2. Welcome_Message module, which displays a welcome message
3. Setup module, which performs "housekeeping" tasks such as displaying the table title and headings, opening the data file, and initializing variables
4. Process_Records module, which reads and displays file records, and sums sales for each store
5. Display_Totals module, which displays the store subtotals and the grand total for all stores

Modules 2, 3, and 4 are called from the Main module and module 5 is called from the Process_Records module when a control break occurs. This division of the programming tasks leads to the hierarchy chart shown in Figure 10.4. The pseudocode for each module follows.

In this program, to allow you to concentrate on the new material (using data files for input and output and the control break processing technique), we will assume all variables are global.

Figure 10.4 Hierarchy chart for the Harvey's Hardware Company Sales Report program

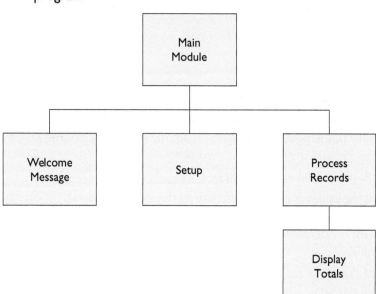

Main Module

```
1  Begin
2     Declare Sales, Subtotal, Total As Float
2     Declare Salesperson As String
3     Declare Store, PreviousStore As Integer
4     Call Welcome_Message module
5     Call Setup module
6     Call Process_Records module
7  End Program
```

Welcome_Message Module

This module displays a welcome message for the program. It will present the program title, identify the programmer and other program data, and provide a brief explanation of what the program does. It will consist, basically, of simple Write statements.

Setup Module

This module will do the following:

- Display a title and headings for the sales report.
- Open the "salesdata" file and Read its first record.
- Initialize certain program variables.

Here is more detailed pseudocode for the Setup module:

```
1  Write "Harvey's Hardware Company"
2  Write "    Monthly Sales"
```

```
3   Write " "
4   Write "Store number \t Salesperson \t Sales"
5   Open "salesdata" For Input As DataFile
6   Set Total = 0
7   Set Subtotal = 0
```

Process_Records Module

The variable PreviousStore, declared earlier in Main, enables us to determine when the control variable Store has changed. This initiates the action of computing totals.

This module loops through all the records in the salesdata file and does the following:

- Sends the data in each record to the report on the screen.
- Adds the sales for each salesperson to the store's subtotal.
- Reads a new record and checks if the store number has changed (i.e., if a control break has occurred). If so, it transfers control to the Display_Totals module.

The end of the file is reached when Store = 0. At this time, the loop is exited and the data file is closed. The pseudocode for this module is as follows:

```
1   Read DataFile, Store, Salesperson, Sales
2   Set PreviousStore = Store
3   While Store != 0
4     Write Store + "\t" + Salesperson + "\t" + Sales
5     Set Subtotal = Subtotal + Sales
6     Read DataFile, Store, Salesperson, Sales
7     If Store != PreviousStore Then
8       Call Display_Totals module
9     End If
10  End While
11  Close DataFile
```

Display_Totals Module

This module is called when a control break occurs. It displays the total sales for each store, and if the last store has been processed and the end of the file has been reached, it also displays the grand total of sales for all stores. If the last store has not yet been processed, this module resets Subtotal to 0 and sets the current store variable, PreviousStore, to the new store number. The pseudocode is as follows:

```
1   Write "Total sales for store " + PreviousStore + ": " + Subtotal
2   Write " "
3   Set Total = Total + Subtotal
4   If Store == 0 Then
5     Write "Total sales for all stores: " + Total
6   Else
7     Set PreviousStore = Store
8     Set Subtotal = 0
9   End If
```

Coding and Testing the Program

The program code is now written using the design as a guide. At this stage, header comments and step comments are inserted into each module, providing internal documentation for the program. Here are a few more points concerning the coding that are specific to this program:

- Both the welcome message and the sales report should be displayed on a blank screen. Recall that this is accomplished by using the programming language's clear screen statement.
- To produce a professional sales report, similar to the one shown in Figure 10.3, we will need to format the output. This means we must ensure that the data in the report lines up in columns and that the dollar amounts align on their decimal points. Our pseudocode has used the "\t" symbol to indicate a tab stop but each programming language has its own special print formatting statements.

This program can be adequately tested by creating a data file, "salesdata", which contains the input data given in Figure 10.3. The file can be created by using the technique described earlier in this chapter or by typing its contents in a text editor and saving the resulting document to disk using the name "salesdata".

Self Check for Section 10.4

For Self Check Questions 10.14–10.17 refer to the Harvey's Hardware Company Sales Report program developed in this section.

10.14. Add appropriate statements to the Setup module to accept input from the user for the month and year for which sales are being totaled.

10.15. Add an additional statement to the Setup module that includes columns to display the month and year that was input in Self Check Question 10.14. The headings should go alongside the other headings, under the report title.

10.16. What are the first and last values assigned to the variable PreviousStore during a run of this program with the data shown in Figure 10.3?

10.17. What changes, if any, would have to be made to the Process_Records module if Harvey opened more stores?

10.5 Focus on Problem Solving:
The Invoice Preparation Program

In this section, we will apply the material we have discussed in this chapter and the material on arrays to develop an Invoice Preparation program, which prepares a bill for items ordered from the Legendary Lawnmower Company. The program uses one-dimensional arrays and sequential data files and contains search and sort routines.

Problem Statement

The Legendary Lawnmower Company needs a program that will prepare invoices for parts ordered by its customers. The user will input the customer's name and the parts ordered (part numbers and quantities). Then the program will locate the part numbers in a data file to determine the part names and prices and print an invoice. This invoice should contain the customer's name and, for each part ordered, the quantity, part number, part name, part price, and total price. The parts ordered should be listed on the invoice in ascending part number order and the total amount due should be given at the bottom.

We will assume that the part numbers, names, and prices (the price list) are contained in a sequential file called "pricelist", with records of the form as follows:

```
part_number (Integer), part_name (String), part_price (Float)
```

Problem Analysis

The input for this program is of two types as follows:

1. The price list for the lawnmower parts is read from the "pricelist" file; its fields will be loaded into three parallel arrays named Numbers, Names, and Prices.

2. The following data are input from the user:
   - The customer name will be stored in a variable named Customer.
   - The part numbers and quantities of all parts ordered will be stored in arrays named OrderNums and OrderAmts.

We will use the variable ListCount to represent the number of records in the "pricelist" file. This is the number of elements in the arrays Numbers, Names, and Prices. The variable OrderCount will be used for the number of parts ordered by the user and is the number of elements in the arrays OrderNums and OrderAmts.

The output for this program is the invoice, most of which is in the form of a table with headings as follows:

```
Quantity   Part Number   Part Name   Unit Price   Item Cost
```

The entries in the Quantity, Part Number, Part Name, and Unit Price columns of the table are obtained from the data input into the OrderAmts, OrderNums, Names, and Prices arrays, respectively.

The entries in the Item Cost column are obtained by multiplying the unit price (the cost of the item) by the quantity ordered. For example, if the unit price of a part is $3.24 and the quantity ordered is 10, then the item cost for that part is $32.40.

The invoice also displays the total amount due for the parts ordered, AmountDue, which is the sum of all the ItemCost entries. A typical invoice is shown in Figure 10.5.

Figure 10.5 Sample invoice

```
INVOICE

THE LEGENDARY LAWNMOWER COMPANY

Customer: Hortense Cornswaller

Quantity Part Number   Part Name          Unit Price     Price
- - - - - - - - - - - - - - - - - - - - - - - - - - - - - - - - - - -

10       13254          Handle             $  15.65      $  156.50

         14000          *** Invalid part number ***

5        15251          Starter (recoil)   $  24.80      $  124.00

4        16577          Axle (small)       $   7.50      $   30.00
                                                         - - - - - -

                                           TOTAL DUE ... $  310.50
```

Program Design

This program needs to perform three major tasks:

1. Input data: We must load the price list from the "pricelist" file into parallel arrays and input the customer's order from the user.
2. Sort the parts ordered.
3. Output the invoice.

The first task contains two substantial subtasks—loading the price list data and inputting the parts order. Moreover, the third task requires that we search the price list for each of the ordered parts to determine its price. Thus, we arrive at the following modularization of this program. The Main module calls three submodules as follows:

1. The Input_Data module, which calls the submodules:
   Load_Price_List module
   Input_Parts_Order module
2. The Sort_Parts_Order module
3. The Print_Invoice module, which calls the submodule:
   Search_for_Part_Number module

   A hierarchy chart depicting this modularization is shown in Figure 10.6. Pseudocode describing each module is given below.

In this section we will assume all variables are global. This will allow you to focus on the complex logic required to understand this program that combines using data files, arrays, searching and sorting, and user input.

Figure 10.6 Hierarchy chart for the Invoice Preparation program

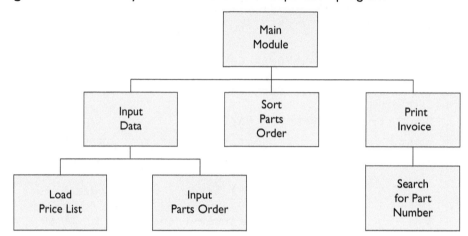

Main Module

The Main module declares the arrays and variables to be used in the program, displays a welcome message, and calls its submodules. Remember: The arrays Numbers, Names, and Prices store the data from the "pricelist" file. The arrays OrderNums and OrderAmts hold the part numbers and quantities input by the user. ListCount is the number of records in the "pricelist" file and OrderCount is the number of parts ordered by the user. The pseudocode for this module is as follows:

```
1  Main
2     Declare Numbers[100], OrderNums[50] As Integer
3     Declare OrderAmts[50] As Integer
4     Declare Names[100] As String
5     Declare Prices[100] As Float
6     Declare ListCount, OrderCount As Integer
7     Declare Customer As String
8     Display a welcome message
9     Call Input_Data module
10    Call Sort_Parts_Order module
11    Call Print_Invoice module
12  End Program
```

Input_Data Module

All this module does is to call its two submodules as follows:

```
Call Load_Price_List module
Call Input_Parts_Order module
```

Load_Price_List Module

This module reads the data in the sequential file "pricelist" and assigns it to three parallel arrays—Numbers, Names, and Prices. While reading the file, we use the counter named ListCount to count the number of records it contains. The counter not only serves as a subscript for the arrays, but also gives the number of elements in each array and can be used in the test condition of loops that process these arrays. The pseudocode for this module is as follows:

```
1  Open "pricelist" For Input As DataFile
2  Set ListCount = 0
3  While NOT EOF(DataFile)
4     Read DataFile, Numbers[ListCount], Names[ListCount], ↵
             Prices[ListCount]
5     Set ListCount = ListCount + 1
6  End While
7  Close DataFile
```

Input_Parts_Order Module

The customer places the order in this module. The module inputs the data for the parts order, which consists of the customer's name and the part numbers and quantities wanted. The part number for each part ordered is put into one array named OrderNums and the quantity the customer wants is input into a parallel array named OrderAmts. A counter (OrderCount) acts as a subscript for the two arrays and also determines the number of items in the order. At the end, the counter contains the number of elements in the arrays, but as you know, the highest subscript is actually OrderCount - 1.

```
1  Declare Num, Amt As Integer
2  Write "Enter the customer's name: "
3  Input Customer
4  Set OrderCount = 0
5  Write "Enter part number, quantity desired:"
6  Write "Enter 0, 0 when done."
7  Input Num, Amt
8  While Num != 0
9     Set OrderNums[OrderCount] = Num
10    Set OrderAmts[OrderCount] = Amt
11    Set OrderCount = OrderCount + 1
12    Write "Enter part number, quantity desired. Enter 0, 0 ↵
             when done."
13    Input Num, Amt
14 End While
```

Sort_Parts_Order Module

This module uses the bubble sort method (see Chapter 8) to sort the list of ordered part numbers (the array OrderNums) in ascending order. It also puts the parallel array, OrderAmts, into the same order as OrderNums so that the two arrays remain parallel. The pseudocode for this module is as follows:

```
1  Declare Flag, K, TempName, TempAmt As Integer
2  Set Flag = 0
3  While Flag == 0
4     Set Flag = 1
5        For (K = 0; K <= OrderCount - 2; K++)
```

```
 6        If OrderNums[K] > OrderNums[K+1] Then
 7          Set TempNum = OrderNums[K]
 8          Set OrderNums[K] = OrderNums[K+1]
 9          Set OrderNums[K+1] = TempNum
10          Set TempAmt = OrderAmts[K]
11          Set OrderAmts[K] = OrderAmts[K+1]
12          Set OrderAmts[K+1] = TempAmt
13          Set Flag = 0
14        End If
15     End For
16  End While
```

Print_Invoice Module

This module displays the invoice. (See Figure 10.5 for a sample.) This task entails displaying a title, the customer's name, the headings, the list of all parts ordered, and the total amount due. For each part ordered, we must search the price list for the corresponding name and price, and do one of the following:

- If the item is found, the quantity ordered, part number, part name, unit price, and total cost of that item are displayed on one line of the invoice.
- If the item is not found, the part number and an appropriate message is displayed on that line of the invoice.

The same loop that displays the above information also sums the total cost of the parts ordered by summing the ItemCost values so that the amount due can be displayed at the bottom of the invoice. The pseudocode for this module is as follows:

```
 1  Declare AmountDue, ItemCost As Float
 2  Declare K, Found, Index As Integer
 3  Set AmountDue = 0
 4  // Display a title for the invoice
 5  Write "Customer: " + Customer
 6  Write "Quantity \t Part Number \t Part Name \t Unit Price \t ↵
        Item Price"
 7  For (K = 0; K < OrderCount; K++)
 8     // Search the parts list for OrderNums[K]:
 9     Call Search_for_Part_Number module
10     /* Found = 1 indicates that search is successful, Index is the
        subscript of item found */
11     If Found == 1 Then
12        Set ItemCost = OrderAmts[K] * Prices[Index]
13        Write OrderAmts[K] + "\t" + OrderNums[K] + "\t" + ↵
              Names[Index] + "\t" + Prices[Index] + "\t" + ItemCost
14        Set AmountDue = AmountDue + ItemCost
15     Else
16        Write OrderNums[K] + " Invalid Part Number"
17     End If
18  End For
19  Write "TOTAL DUE  . . .  " + AmountDue
```

Recall that the \t symbol indicates a tab stop, and is used here to show that the output must be formatted to line up in columns.

Search_for_Part_Number Module

This submodule performs a serial search (see Chapter 8) of the array Numbers for the part number with subscript K, which is stored as OrderNums[K]. If this number is found, it sets the variable Index equal to the current subscript and sets the variable Found equal to 1; otherwise, there is no change to Found. The pseudocode for this module is as follows:

```
1  Set Index = 0
2  Set Found = 0
3  While (Found == 0) AND (Index <= ListCount - 1)
4    If Numbers[Index] == OrderNums[K] Then
5       Set Found = 1
6       Set Index = Index + 1
7    End If
8  End While
```

Program Code

The program code is now written using the design as a guide. At this stage, header comments and step comments are inserted into each module, providing internal documentation for the program. The following are several points concerning the coding that are specific to this program:

- The welcome message and the invoice should be displayed on a blank screen. Recall that this is accomplished by using the programming language's clear screen statement.
- To produce a professional invoice, similar to the one shown in Figure 10.5, we must format the output to ensure that the data in the invoice lines up in columns and that the dollar amounts align on their decimal points. This can be accomplished using the programming language's special print formatting statements.

Program Test

This program can be adequately tested by creating a data file, "pricelist", which contains the following records:

```
13254,"Handle",15.65
14153,"Wheel (6 in.)",5.95
14233,"Blade (20 in.)",12.95
14528,"Engine (260 cc)",97.50
14978,"Carburetor",43.00
15251,"Starter (recoil)",24.80
15560,"Adjusting knob",0.95
16195,"Rear skirt",14.95
16345,"Grass bag",12.95
16577,"Axle (small)",7.50
```

This file can be created by using the technique described in this chapter or by typing its content in a text editor and saving it under the name "pricelist". Then, if the programmer inputs the part numbers 13254, 14000, 15251, 16577 with corresponding quantities from the keyboard when the actual program code is run, the output should be similar to the sample invoice shown in Figure 10.5.

Self Check for Section 10.5

For Self Check Questions 10.18–10.20 refer to the Invoice Preparation program developed in this section.

10.18. Describe the contents of the invoice if the user enters 0,0 at the first input prompt in the Input_Parts_Order module.

10.19. Replace the outer pre-test loop in the Input_Parts_Order module by a post-test loop.

10.20. Write a Welcome_Message module and rewrite the Main module so that it consists solely of Declare and Call statements.

10.6 Running With RAPTOR: (Optional)

RAPTOR doesn't deal with data files as most "real" programming languages do. We can create data files and read from the files in RAPTOR, but sorting, inserting records, or merging two data files requires some fancy footwork and is really beyond the scope of this book. If you're very ambitious, after working through the examples in this section, try it! It will require some advanced consideration about how to extract only parts of data from an array of strings.

Creating Data Files with the Redirect_Output() Procedure

To create a data file in RAPTOR, you use a Call to the built-in Redirect_Output procedure. RAPTOR provides two options for this procedure.

1. In this Call to the procedure, any input until the procedure is turned off will be sent to a specified data file. A filename is used as an argument to Redirect_Output, as shown in the following examples:

   * Redirect_Output("sample.txt")
   * Redirect_Output("C:\MyDocuments\John.Doe\sample")

   Note that in the first example, only the filename is given. In this case, the data file will be created in the same directory as the current RAPTOR program. In the second example, the full path to the file is given. Also, in the second example, no file extension is specified. In this case, the data file will be created with no extension. However, the data file created will always be a simple text file.

2. In this Call to the procedure, the procedure is either turned on or off by including a yes/true or no/false argument, as follows:

- Redirect_Output(true)or Redirect_Output(yes)
- Redirect_Output(false) or Redirect_Output(no)

After Redirect_Output() is turned on, the data must be redirected to the data file by using a Call to the Redirect_Output() procedure. The name of the data file is used as the argument. This filename must be inside quotation marks as previously shown.

Once Redirect_Output() has been turned on and a destination for the data has been specified (the path to the data file), you need to create the code to input data. One variable is required for each field of the records in the data file. The Output box will PUT the value of those variables into each record. For example, to create a data file with records that have two fields, Name and Salary, two variables are required (probably called name and salary). As values for different employees are input, each name and salary will be stored in the data file on a single line as one record.

By calling the Redirect_Output() procedure and including a filename as the location for the data, the procedure is automatically turned on. However, the procedure must be turned off with a Call to the procedure at the end of the data entry process, this time by using either no or false as the argument.

Figure 10.7 shows a RAPTOR flowchart that will write four records, each with two fields, to a data file named "data.txt". The entries at the prompts were as shown and the contents of the file created are displayed (opened in a text editor).

Data entered:

name:	Amy	salary:	21,000
name:	Kim	salary:	23,500
name:	Pat	salary:	46,000
name:	Sandy	salary:	38,900

Displaying Data Files with the Redirect_Input() Procedure

To display the contents of a data file, the Redirect_Input() procedure is used. This works similarly to the Redirect_Output() procedure.

In a Call to Redirect_Input(), the filename (or the path to that filename) of the file to be read is used as the argument as follows:

```
Redirect_Input("sample.txt")
Redirect_Input("C:\MyDocuments\John.Doe\sample.txt")
```

RAPTOR uses the keyword **record** to identify a single record in a data file. The records are read, normally, within a loop. This is accomplished with GET statements. Input boxes are used to GET each record. In this example, the records consist of the names and salaries along with the extra text ("$ ") that we included. The prompt should be null (i.e., quotes with nothing inside: ""). Output boxes are used to display the output of each record. The output is displayed in the MasterConsole.

Figure 10.8 shows a RAPTOR flowchart that will write the four records stored in the "data.txt" file to the MasterConsole.

Figure 10.7 Program to write 4 records to a data file and the text file that is created

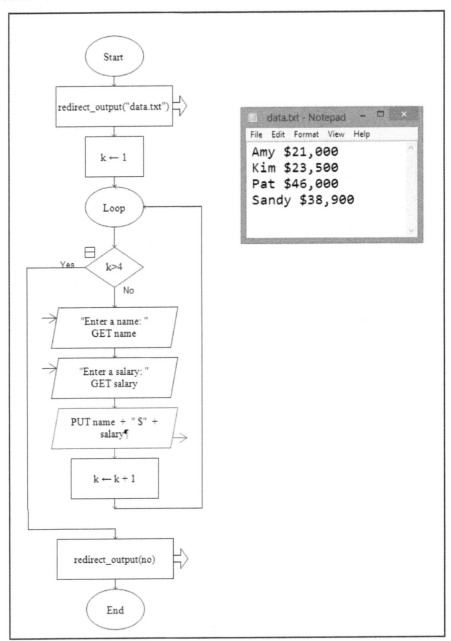

Input to an Array

You can also read the records of a data file and send them to an array. Instead of using the keyword record to get a record, use the array name as the destination for each record. The program shown in Figure 10.9 will read the records stored in "data.txt" into an array named employees. The Watch Window on the left of the screen shows the contents of the employees array after the program has run.

Figure 10.8 Program to display 4 records from a data file to the `MasterConsole`

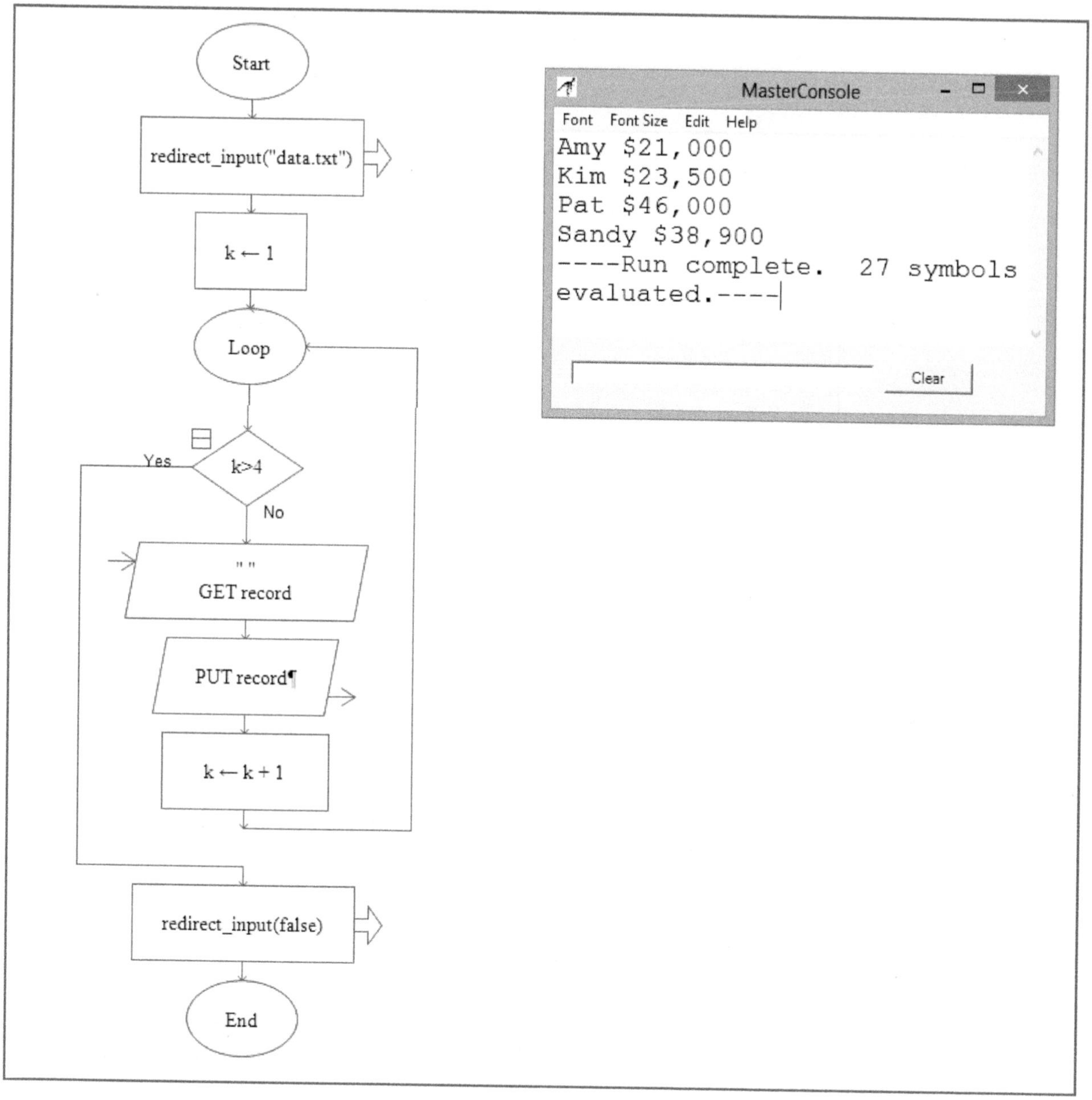

The `End_Of_Input` Function

RAPTOR's built-in function, `End_Of_Input`, can be used as the test condition of a loop. When reading records in a data file, if this function is used as the test condition, RAPTOR will end the loop when all the records have been read.

However, when all the records have been read and written to the `MasterConsole`, the `Redirect_Input` procedure must still be turned off with a `Call` to the procedure using `false` or `no` for the argument. Figure 10.10 shows the program that reads data from `"data.txt"` to an array but uses the `End_Of_Input` function as the test condition for the loop.

Figure 10.9 Program to store records from a data file to an array

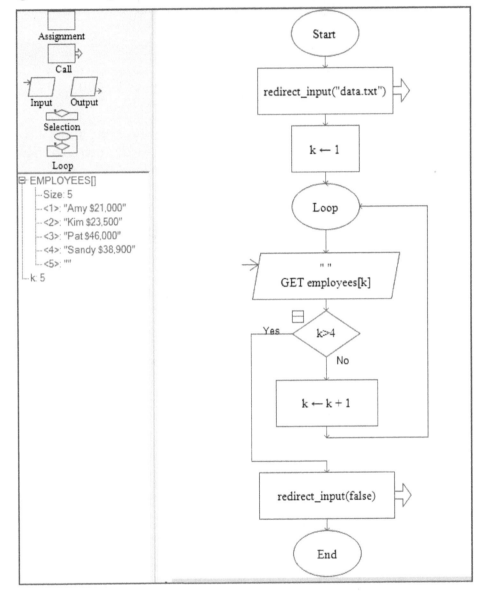

The Limitations

Unfortunately, the Redirect_Input() procedure does not separate each field in a record. Rather, each record is stored as one line of String data. Each Input line reads all the fields in one record (or everything that is on a single line in the data file). Therefore, the records can be output to the MasterConsole but the fields cannot be manipulated easily to sort, insert, or merge. This can be done, but it requires programming beyond what we need at this point. However, we will create a program that will demonstrate how to read data to and from a file, sort that data, and replace the original data file with a sorted version.

Figure 10.10 Using the `End_Of_Input` function to test for the end of data

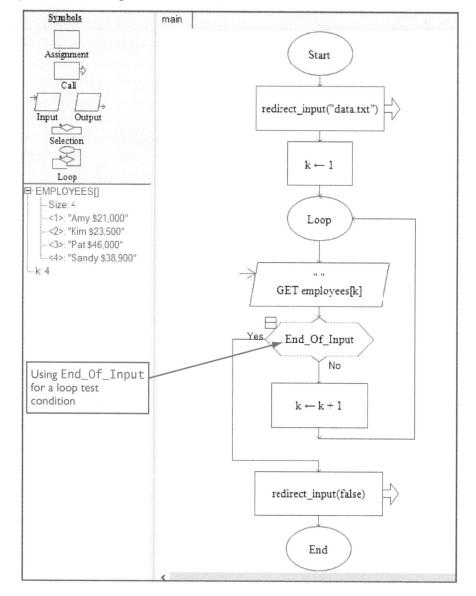

Run It: Professor Weisheit's Semester Grades

In this program we will combine all the features we have learned about using files with RAPTOR. Professor Weisheit (a wise professor) wants to enter his students' names and final grades into a text file. He wants us to write a program that will allow him to enter the data in any order and then produce a file sorted in alphabetical order. If you want to create the program as you continue to read, open a new RAPTOR file and save it with the filename "weisheit.rap".

We'll create our program with subcharts to break it into more manageable pieces. Our main module will call subcharts to allow Professor Weisheit to store the data in a file (Store_data), retrieve the data and store it in an array (Load_data), sort the array (Sort_data), and finally write the sorted data to a new text file (Store_sorted_data). The main program looks like this:

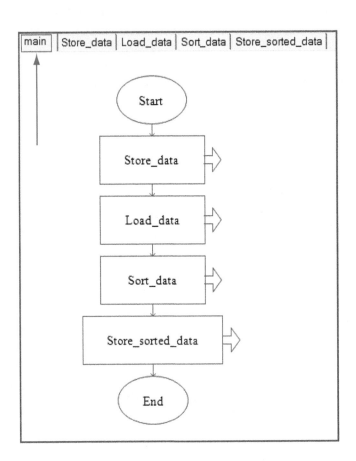

Store_data Subchart

This subchart will allow Professor Weisheit to enter data for as many students as he wants. Each record will be stored in a text file named "weisheit_grades.txt" which, for simplicity, we assume will be stored in the same place as the RAPTOR file. If Professor Weisheit wanted to store this file in his ProgramLogic course folder which is inside a folder named SpringSem on the professor's hard drive, the entire path to the file must be included (i.e., ("C:\SpringSem\ProgramLogic\weisheit_grades.txt").

First we must turn on the Redirect_Output() function which is done by simply calling the function and placing a filename in as a parameter. A loop allows the professor to enter all the data which is sent, one record at a time, to the file. We use "*" as a sentinel value to end the loop when all data has been entered. After the loop is exited, the Redirect_Output() function is turned off by entering either no or false as a parameter. The code for this subchart is shown:

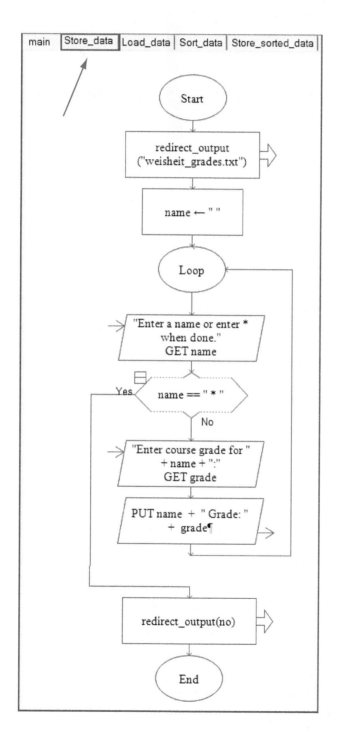

Before we continue, we will develop a data set so we can test this program as it grows. You can enter whatever data you want, but sample data is given:

Name	Grade		Name	Grade
Johnson, Jimmy	C		Harman, Harry	B
Andrews, Anna	B		Young, Zona	F
Lee, Lynn	C		Garcia, Jorge	D
Kendall, Keisha	A		Sazorin, Sally	B
Best, Bruce	C		Foraker, Frank	B
Montas, Maria	A		Rouen, Robert	A

Load_data Subchart

This subchart will retrieve the data in the "weisheit.txt" file and store that data in an array named students. There are a few things to notice.

- We use the Redirect_Input() function to tell the program where to get the data, putting the filename in as the parameter.
- We use the End_Of_Input function in the loop test so this subchart will work, regardless of whether you use the twelve names listed in the sample data or choose to enter only two or three names or decide to enter 125 names.
- The counter, count, has two functions. It keeps track of how many records we have and this is can be used later to identify how many elements are in the students array. It also serves as the index value for each array element as each record is stored in the array.
- The Redirect_Input() function does not have to be turned off because this task is done automatically by the End_Of_Input function.

The flowchart for this subchart is as follows:

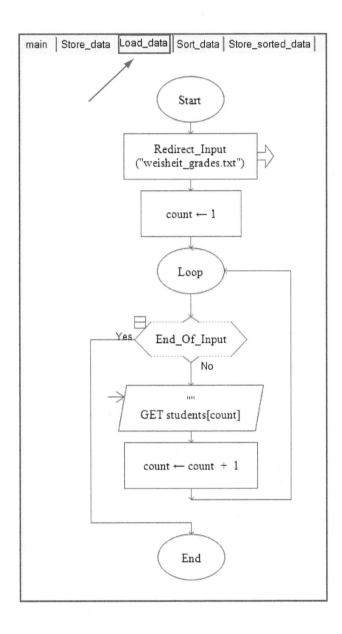

Notice that, at the end of this part of the program, the variable count will have a value that is one more than the number of elements in the newly created array, students. We need to keep this in mind when we sort the data.

At this point, if you run the program and use the sample data given, your students array should look as shown in the Watch Window of your RAPTOR screen:

```
count: 13
grade: "A"
name: "*"
STUDENTS[]
    Size: 12
    <1>: "Johnson, Jimmy Grade: C"
    <2>: "Andrews, Anna Grade: B"
    <3>: "Lee, Lynn Grade: C"
    <4>: "Kendall, Keisha Grade: A"
    <5>: "Best, Bruce Grade: C"
    <6>: "Montas, Maria Grade: A"
    <7>: "Harman, Harry Grade: B"
    <8>: "Young, Zona Grade: F"
    <9>: "Garcia, Jorge Grade: D"
    <10>: "Sazorin, Sally Grade: B"
    <11>: "Foraker, Frank Grade: B"
    <12>: "Rouen, Robert Grade: A"
```

Sort_data Subchart

This subchart will sort the data in our students array. We have said that RAPTOR does not divide the record into fields so each element of the students array is a string of text that includes the student's name and letter grade. We know that when we sort String data, the computer compares the first character of one element with the first character of the next element, using the elements' ASCII values. So, in our sample data, for example, the first entry is "Johnson, Jimmy Grade C" and it will be compared with the second entry, "Andrews, Anna Grade B". Since "J" is clearly larger (in ASCII values) than "A", these two elements will be exchanged. If the two entries have the same first character, the program will compare the second character and the next until two different characters are encountered. In general, considering the information we are using, this will not be a problem. If two students have the exact same name and different letter grades, the one with the better grade will be listed before the one with the lower grade.

Unfortunately, we cannot sort this program by grade as we could in a "real" language where the data would be stored in parallel arrays. For this program, we will only sort in alphabetical order by name. The Sort_data subchart uses the bubble sort technique that was discussed in Chapter 8. The subchart is as follows:

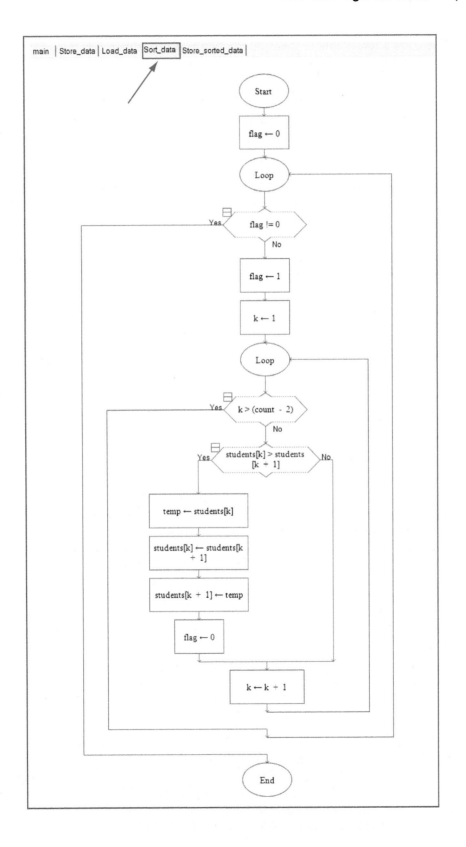

There are a few points to mention, though you probably recall these things from Chapter 8:

- The `flag` allows the loop to end when all the data has been sorted and may save time.
- The variable `count` has a value from the previous `subchart` that is one more than the number of elements in the `students` array. This is why the inner loop is set to end when the counter, `k`, is greater than (`count - 2`). For example, if we have 12 elements in `students`, `count` has the value of 13. But we only need to compare `students[11]` with `students[12]`. When k = 11, the element `students[k]` will compare its value with that of `students[k + 1]` so the loop must end when `k` becomes greater than 11. Thus the loop must end when `k` is greater than (`count - 2`).

You can add a quick loop at the end of this `subchart` to output the sorted data to the `MasterConsole` to make sure your sort routine works correctly. It will look like this:

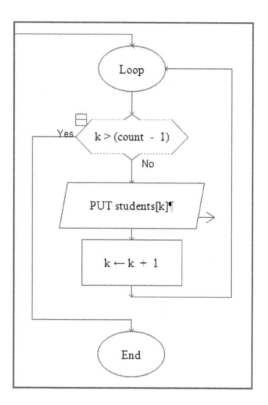

Store_sorted_data Subchart

This `subchart` will create a new file for Professor Weisheit which will contain all the original data but with the names in alphabetical order. We will name our new file `"weisheit_new.txt"`. First we Call the `Redirect_Output()` function, sending in the name of the new file. We need to retrieve each element of the sorted `students` array, one at a time, and write that data to a new `record` in the new file. To do this, we will use a loop. Recall that `count` holds the value that is one greater than the number of elements in `students`. We will use a new counter, `k`, which will begin at 1 (the index of the first element in `students`) and will, for each iteration, take an array element, and send it to `"weisheit_new.txt"` until `k = (count - 1)`. When the loop ends, we must turn off the `Redirect_Output()` function. The code is as shown:

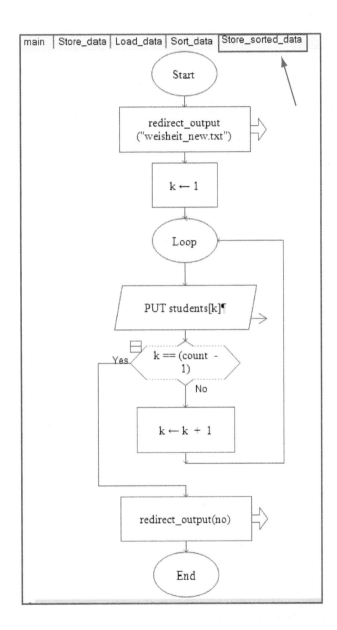

Check It Out

If you create this program and use the sample data as given, at the end of a run, your `Watch Window` will look as shown and your new file, `"weisheit_new.txt"`, will look as shown.

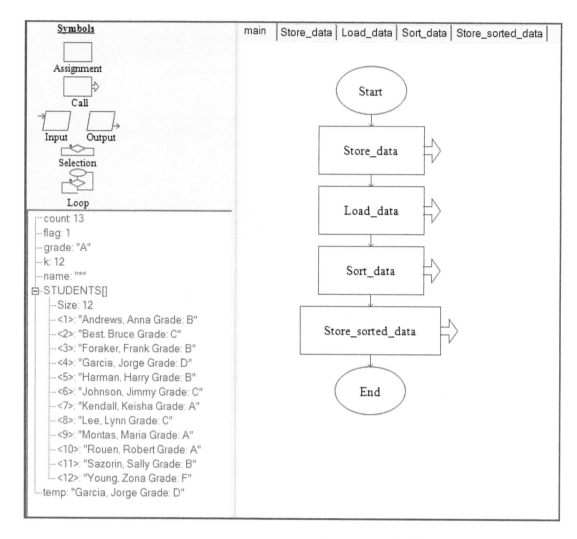

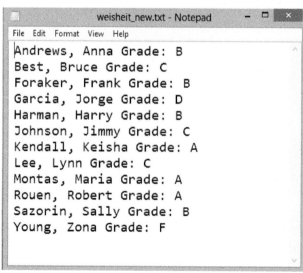

Key Terms

batch processing	file pointer
binary files	Input mode
break	interactive input
closing a file	internal name
control break processing	merged file
control variable	merging
data files	opening a file
direct access files	Output mode
end-of-file marker	program file
end-of-record marker	random-access files
EOF function	records (in a file)
external name	scratch file
field (in file record)	sequential files
file	text files
file mode	

Chapter Summary

In this chapter, we have discussed the following topics:

1. The difference between text files and binary files
2. The difference between sequential files and direct-access files
3. Steps to create a sequential file:
   - The Open statement opens the file for Output.
   - The Write statement writes the data to the file which creates the records.
   - The Close statement closes the file.
4. Steps to read the contents of a sequential file:
   - The Open statement opens the file for Input.
   - The Read statement assigns data in a record to program variables.
   - The EOF function is used to determine the end of the file.
   - The Close statement closes the file.
5. Steps to modify (delete, change, or insert) the contents of a sequential file:
   - Open the given file for Input and a scratch file for Output.
   - Input data concerning the change from the user.
   - Read records from the given file and Write them to the scratch file until you reach the one to be modified.
   - Make the change to this record.
   - Read the rest of the records from the given file and Write them to the scratch file.

- Close both files.
- Replace the original contents of the given file with that of the scratch file.

6. Steps to merge two sequential files into a third file:
  - Open the given files for Input and the merged file for Output.
  - Read the initial record in each file.
  - While records remain in both files, if the record in the first precedes the record in the second, Write the first record to the third file and Read another record from the first file. Otherwise, Write the record from the second file to the third file and Read another record from the second file.
  - Read the remaining records from either the first or second file and Write them to the third file.
  - Close all files.

7. Control-break processing uses a control variable to exit a loop or module periodically and perform an action.

Review Exercises

Fill in the Blank

1. A(n) _____ is a collection of data that has been given a name and stored in a file.

2. Data files are often made up of records, which consist of one or more items called _____.

3. A(n) _____ file consists solely of standard characters.

4. A(n) _____ file may contain nonstandard characters.

5. To access the fifth record in a(n) _____ file, we must read the first four records first.

6. To access the fifth record in a(n) _____ file, we don't need to read the first four records first.

7. In the technique of _____, the program exits a loop or module and performs an action whenever the value of a specified variable changes or reaches a predetermined level.

8. The "specified variable" of Exercise 7 is called the _____ variable for the process.

True or False

9. T F A program file contains data that is to be used by various programs.

10. T F A data file can be used by more than one program.

11. T F A data file can store a program's output for future use.

12. T F Word processors are designed to be able to read all binary files.

13. T F If a file is opened for Output, and a file of that name already exists in that folder, then all data on the latter file is erased.

14. T F The statement

    ```
    Write DataFile, Number
    ```

    transmits the value of `Number` to the file with internal name `DataFile`

15. T F When a file is opened for `Input`, data can be written from the program to that file.

16. T F When a file is closed, the connection between the internal and external names is terminated.

17. T F If a single record is to be changed in a sequential file, then the entire file must be rewritten to a temporary file.

18. T F Some programming languages contain statements that can be used to append records to data files.

19. T F After merging two sequential files that are sorted in ascending order, the resulting merged file will also be sorted in ascending order.

20. T F To merge two sequential files, they must first be opened for `Output`.

Short Answer

21. Write a program, by inputting names from the user, that will create a sequential file with the contents

    ```
    "Arthur"<CR>"Michael"<CR>"Sam"<CR><EOF>.
    ```

22. Write a program that will display the contents of the sequential file of Exercise 21 on the user's screen.

In Exercises 23–27, give the contents of the file named `"update"` *after each program segment is executed. Assume that the content of the file named* `"original"` *at the beginning of each program segment is*

```
"A",25<CR>"C",20<CR>"E",15<CR><EOF>
```

and that the following statements precede each program segment:

```
Open "original" For Input As GivenFile
Open "update" For Output As TempFile
```

23. ```
    Read GivenFile, Item, Number
    Write TempFile, Item, Number
    Close GivenFile, TempFile
    ```

24. ```
    While NOT EOF(GivenFile)
       Read GivenFile, Item, Number
       Write TempFile, Item, Number
    End While
    Close GivenFile, TempFile
    ```

25. ```
    While NOT EOF(GivenFile)
       Read GivenFile, Item, Number
       If Item != "C" Then
         Write TempFile, Item, Number
       End If
    End While
    Close GivenFile, TempFile
    ```
    ```

26.
```
Set InputItem = "D"
Set InputNumber = 90
While NOT EOF(GivenFile)
   Read GivenFile, Item, Number
   If InputItem < Item Then
      Write TempFile, InputItem, InputNumber
   End If
End While
Close GivenFile, TempFile
```

27.
```
Set InputItem = "C"
Set InputNumber = 75
While NOT EOF(GivenFile)
   Read GivenFile, Item, Number
   If InputItem == Item Then
      Write TempFile, InputItem, InputNumber
   Else
      Write TempFile, Item, Number
   End If
End While
Close GivenFile, TempFile
```

28. In the program segment of Exercise 23:

   a. Give two possible data types for the variable Item.

   b. Give two possible data types for the variable Number.

For Exercises 29–34 refer to the following pseudocode, which partially merges the files with internal names FileOne *and* FileTwo *into a third file named* Merged. *(Each record in* FileOne *and* FileTwo *contains a single field of string type.)*

```
Read FileOne, Name1
Read FileTwo, Name2
While (NOT EOF(FileOne)) AND (NOT EOF(FileTwo))
   If Name1 < Name2 Then
      Write Merged, Name1
      Read FileOne, Name1
   Else
      Write Merged, Name2
      Read FileTwo, Name2
   End If
End While
```

Suppose that the contents of FileOne *and* FileTwo *are*

```
FileOne: "Corinne"<CR>"Marjorie"<CR>"Shirley"<CR>"Tamara"<CR><EOF>
FileTwo: "Arthur"<CR>"Michael"<CR>"Sam"<CR><EOF>
```

29. After the first pass through the While loop, what are the contents of the file Merged?

30. How many passes are made through the While loop?

31. When the While loop is exited, what are the contents of the file Merged?

32. Which names are added to the end of the file Merged to complete the merging of the two files?

33. If FileOne and FileTwo had been given in reverse alphabetical order, what changes would have to be made to this pseudocode to merge these files into a file that is in reverse alphabetical order?

34. If FileOne and FileTwo had been given in reverse alphabetical order and the pseudocode were changed as in Short Answer 33, what would be the contents of Merged after the While loop is exited?

For Exercises 35–37 assume that a file named "test" has 25 records of the following form:

    score_1 (Integer), score_2 (Integer), score_3 (Integer)

Suppose we want to load the test file records into arrays Score1, Score2, and Score3.

35. Write a statement that declares these three arrays.

36. Write a program segment that loads the "test" file into the arrays.

37. Write a program segment that displays the contents of the arrays of Exercise 36 on 25 lines, each containing three test scores.

For Exercise 38, suppose that the file "data" consists of the following records:

    "Huey",1,2
    "Dewey",4,5
    "Louie",7,8

38. What is the output of code corresponding to the following pseudocode?

```
Declare Ducks[10] As String
Declare Numbers[10,20] As Integer
Open "data" For Input As DataFile
For (K = 0; K < 3; K++)
  Read DataFile, Ducks[K]
  For (J = 0; J < 2; J++)
    Read DataFile, Numbers[K,J]
  End For(J)
End For(K)
For (J = 0; J < 2; J++)
  For (K = 0; K < 3; K++)
    If K == 1 Then
      Write Ducks[K] + " " + Numbers[K,J]
    End If
  End For(K)
End For(J)
Close DataFile
```

Programming Challenges

For each of the following Programming Challenges, use the modular approach and pseudocode to design a suitable program to solve it. The Programming Challenges in this chapter can be implemented in RAPTOR but may need some modification. In RAPTOR, all data from a file must be loaded into an array to be manipulated. Be aware that RAPTOR processes each record in a data file as a complete entity; there is no way to distinguish one field from another. Any manipulation that must be done (sorting, searching, and so on) must be done to the array and the file must be rewritten from the resulting array.

1. a. Input names and three test scores of students from the user, terminated by "ZZZ",0,0,0, and create a data file "grades" with records of the following form:

   ```
   student_name (String), test_1 (Integer), test_2 (Integer),
   test_3 (Integer)
   ```

   b. Display the contents of the file "grades" created in Part a. Each student's record should appear on a separate line and include the total score (the sum of the three tests) for that student. For example, a line of output might be as follows:

   ```
   R. Abrams 76 84 82 242
   ```

   c. Modify the program of Part b so that at the option of the user, it displays either the entire contents of the file "grades" or just the record of a specified student. In either case, for each student displayed, also display his or her total test score.

2. Assume that a file named "inventory", which contains the inventory of parts for the Legendary Lawn Mower Company (from Section 10.5), already exists with records of the following form:

   ```
   part_Number (Integer), part_Name (String), quantity (Integer)
   ```

   Also assume that the records in this file are ordered by increasing part number. For each part of this problem, write a program that performs the indicated task.

   a. Input a part number from the user and delete the corresponding record from the "inventory" file.

   b. Input a part number and a quantity from the user and modify the record corresponding to that part number by changing the value of its last field to the quantity input.

   c. Input a new part number, part name, and quantity from the user and insert the corresponding record in the proper place in the "inventory" file.

3. a. The Last National Bank has two branches, each of which uses a sequential file containing a summary of customers' checking accounts in the following form:

   ```
   account_number(Integer), customer_name(String), balance(Float)
   ```

   The files, which are called "account1" and "account2", are ordered by account number in increasing order. (Assume that no two account numbers are the same.) Due to financial reverses, one of the branches must be closed, and the two files need to be merged into a single one called "account3". Write a program to perform this operation.

b. Suppose that some of the records in "account1" and "account2" are the same. Modify the appropriate module of the program so that only one of the duplicate account records is written to the file "account3".

4. The Eversoft Eraser Company has a list of its customers' names (not necessarily in alphabetical order) and telephone numbers in a file named "customer" with records of the following form:

last_name (String), first_name (String), phone_number (String)

a. Allow the user to input a last name, then search the file and display all names and phone numbers corresponding to that last name.

b. Load the file into parallel arrays and display the list of customers' names and phone numbers in alphabetical order.

5. The Department of Motor Vehicles in the state of Euphoria has finally decided to computerize its list of licensed drivers. The program you write should make use of an existing file named "licenses" with records of the following form:

driver_name (String), license_number (String),
number_of_tickets (Integer)

When a license number is input by the user, the corresponding driver's name and number of tickets should be output by the program. (Hint: load the "licenses" file into three parallel arrays and search one of these for the license number input.)

Object-Oriented and Event-Driven Programming

11

Throughout this book, we have used a single approach to develop our more complicated programs: top-down, modular design. In this chapter, we will discuss two other approaches to program design—object-oriented programming and event-driven programming. First we will discuss the basic concepts that underlie object-oriented programming (OOP), and then we will apply this material as we develop a more complex program. You will also learn how programmers use modeling to develop sophisticated and complicated programs. Finally, we will discuss events, the Graphical User Interface, and how event-driven programming combines the two.

After reading this chapter, you will be able to do the following:
- Use the basic terminology of object-oriented programming
- Define classes, create constructors, and create objects
- Understand the encapsulation, inheritance, and polymorphism features of OOP
- Understand how child (derived) classes extend parent (base) classes
- Understand how to develop an OOP program
- Use object-oriented program design with pseudocode
- Understand what UML is and how it is used to develop complicated programs and software
- Use objects to create a graphical user interface
- Handle events in programming for a GUI
- Create an event-driven program design

Objects are Everywhere

This chapter is about objects. Of course, this book is about programming and a program is basically a list of instructions. So in programming terms, what do objects have to do with writing programs? The answer is simple: Anything that has properties and a function (or functions) is an object. Properties are qualities, traits, or attributes common to a specific thing—or object. A function, in this context, is a process or operation executed by or to the object. Objects are all around us—your chair, this book, and a washing machine are objects. Even *you* are an object.

Consider the washing machine. It certainly has properties—it's made of metal; has a tub, motor, and gearbox; and has specific dimensions. After writing a long list of its properties, we may know what a washing machine looks like (which is fine), but we still don't have enough information to define it. We also have to talk about its functions—the processes it carries out: The machine turns on, fills with water, agitates, empties, fills again, rinses, spins, and turns off. Finally, we need to know what our object works on. In this case, our object normally works on items such as clothes, towels, and blankets. Combine all these pieces—properties, functions, and something to work on—and we can completely describe a useful object.

The following are important attributes of a washing machine, or for that matter, any useful object:

- You don't have to know how it works internally to use it.
- If someone has built a suitable one and it's available for purchase (or better yet, free), you don't have to build it yourself.

In programming, objects containing properties (data) and functions (processes) provide packaged solutions to help us solve problems. Defining and creating objects may initially seem unnecessarily complicated, but their use leads to elegant and efficient ways to handle complex problems. Moreover, by their very nature, objects ultimately simplify the programming process and ensure that we don't have to reinvent the wheel (or washing machine).

11.1 Classes and Objects

An **object** is a structure that comprises data (or attributes) and processes (or methods) that perform operations on that data. **Object-oriented programming (OOP)** refers to an approach to program design and coding that places an emphasis on the objects needed to solve a given problem and the relationships among them. In this section, we will discuss some of the basic concepts of object-oriented programming.

Classes

When learning a new subject, understanding its particular terminology is not always easy. In the case of object-oriented programming, we have the additional complication that often there are several terms that describe the same concept.

However, many of the new terms and concepts are analogous to the ones you are familiar with.

The fundamental entity in object-oriented programming is the class. A **class** is a data type that allows us to create objects. It provides the definition for a collection of objects by describing its **attributes** (data) and specifying the **methods** (operations) that may be applied to that data. For example, consider the following definition of the class `alarm_clock`:

- Its attributes include shape, color, display face, sound, and so forth.
- Its methods include changing volume, choosing sound, set snooze, how to turn it on and off, and so forth.

The `alarm_clock` *class* simply describes what an `alarm_clock` is and what can be done with it; an alarm clock *object*, on the other hand, is a particular example of an `alarm_clock`, such as an old-fashioned windup clock or an electric clock with digital display.

It is easy to see that, while both clocks can serve the same purpose—to wake you up—they are extremely different in appearance and in the way they work. Two objects of the same class type can share many attributes and methods, but how these are applied can create great differences.

As stated, a class is, in effect, a data type. We already know about some data types: `Integers`, `Floats`, `Strings`, and `Characters`. These are known as **primitive data types**. A primitive data type is predefined by the language and is named by a reserved keyword. A class is a data type created by the programmer. Another way to think of a class is to consider it a blueprint or prototype from which objects are created.

The purpose of defining a class is to allow us to create objects. An object is just a particular **instance** of its class. The relationship between a class and its objects is analogous to the relationship between a data type and variables of that type. For example, when we write the statement

```
Declare Number As Integer
```

the type `Integer` states what kind of data we are dealing with and what operations (+, −, and so forth) can be performed on it. The variable `Number` is a particular *instance* of the type `Integer`. It can be assigned a specific integer value to be used within the program. But there is a difference between a primitive data type, like `Integer`, and a class. The programmer creates the class and, by doing so, defines the attributes and methods associated with that class. This gives the programmer a great deal of power, as you will see when you begin object-oriented programming.

Objects

Let's take a closer look at the objects themselves. As you know, objects are made up of two components: data and operations on that data. We say that an object **encapsulates** data and operations. This means that an object is like a little package containing both the data and operations on that particular object. The operations are specified in the class definition; the data are specific to the particular object under consideration, although the type of data is also specified in the class definition.

If we continue the alarm clock analogy, the blueprint for an `alarm_clock` class includes its attributes (shape, color, display face, sound, and so forth) and its methods (changing volume, choosing sound, set snooze, how to turn it on and off, and so forth). We can create instances of the `alarm_clock` class by assigning values to its attributes and methods.

For example, we can say that the windup instance of the `alarm_clock` class (an object) encapsulates the following attributes (data) and methods (operations):

attributes: shape (round), color (blue), display (hours, minutes, with a second hand in a circular display), sound (loud clangs), and more

methods: volume settings (loud), sounds (one sound only), snooze (none), on/off (manual windup), and so forth

However, the electronic digital object, while possessing the same data and operations as the windup model, looks like a very different object. It looks like this:

attributes: shape (rectangular), color (black), display (digital hours and minutes), sound (rings or radio), and more

methods: volume settings (soft, medium, loud), sounds (beep, clang, radio), snooze (yes, set time from 5 to 15 minutes), on/off (electric or battery), and so forth

Note that there are several alternate names for the two components that make up an object:

- An object's data are called its *attributes*, *properties*, or *state*.
- An object's operations are called *methods*, *behaviors*, *services*, *procedures*, *subprograms*, or *functions*.

In this book, most often we will use the terms attributes (for data) and methods (for operations).

Defining Classes and Creating Objects

If you want to use objects in a program, the first step is to define a class for each kind of object. The class definition provides the structure (or blueprint) of the objects in it—the attributes they possess and the methods that may be applied to them. Example 11.1 illustrates the kind of pseudocode we will use to define a class.

Example 11.1 **The Cube Class**[1]

A cube is a box-shaped solid in which all sides are of equal length. The volume of a cube is obtained by taking the third power of the length of a side, Volume = (Side)^3. Suppose that we want to define a class called Cube that has the following:

- **Attributes**:
  - The length of a side (Side)
  - The volume (Volume) of the cube
- **Methods**:
  - Assign a value to the side: SetSide().
  - Compute the volume of the cube: ComputeVolume().
  - Return the value of the side to the program: GetSide().
  - Return the volume of the cube to the program: GetVolume().

We will discuss the specifics of these methods later in this section. The code in this example is a subprogram, which will be called by the main program. Later, in Example 11.2, we will see how this subprogram is used.

To define the class Cube, we use the following pseudocode:

```
1   Class Cube
2      //attributes of type Cube
3      Declare Side As Float
4      Declare Volume As Float
5      //methods of type Cube
6      Subprogram SetSide(Float NewSide)
7        Set Side = NewSide
8      End Subprogram
9      Subprogram ComputeVolume()
10       Set Volume = Side^3
11     End Subprogram
12     Function GetVolume() As Float
13       Set GetVolume = Volume
14     End Function
15     Function GetSide() As Float
16       Set GetSide = Side
17     End Function
18   End Class
```

---

[1]RAPTOR includes an OOP mode which allows you to try some of the examples in this chapter. However, before attempting to use RAPTOR in Object-oriented mode, you should read the information on UMLs in Section 11.3 and the Running With RAPTOR section, 11.6.

What Happened?

The Subprogram and Function notation that we have used in this pseudocode was introduced in Chapter 9. Recall that a function is a special type of subprogram; its name can be assigned a value. In this example, SetSide() and ComputeVolume() are subprograms but GetSide() and GetVolume() are functions. The values of these functions are called by and used in the main program, while the subprograms perform other operations within the class itself.

- Recall that the variables within parentheses in the subprogram header (for example, NewSide on line 6) are called parameters.
- If a particular subprogram has no parameters, notice that we still write the parentheses, ()—see for example, the subprogram ComputeVolume() on line 9.
- Recall that a function can be used whenever a variable, constant, or expression of its type is normally valid. For example, the function GetVolume() on lines 12–14 will set the value of GetVolume to the value of the variable Volume. A subprogram, on the other hand, will perform one or more operations on data. For example, the subprogram ComputeVolume() on lines 9–11 will compute the volume of the cube by cubing the value of the variable Side and assigning that value to the variable Volume.
- The methods SetSide() (line 6), GetVolume() (line 12), and GetSide() (line 15) are called **access methods**; they provide the rest of the program with access to the object's attributes.
- SetSide() imports a value of the attribute Side from the main program.
- GetSide() and GetVolume() allow the main program to make use of the values of Side and Volume.

This last point raises the question: Why not just pass the values of the variables Side and Volume back and forth to the program as parameters? The answer is one of the keys to understanding OOP. In object-oriented programming, normally we want to keep the class variables completely hidden from the rest of the program. This practice of **data hiding** has the following twofold purpose:

- It enhances the security of the object's data. The data cannot be altered except by the means intended, namely, by using one of the object's methods. Any object can be used throughout a program. For example, if you were writing an adventure game and had a Monster class that defined objects with one head and a tail, you would want to be sure that any time you created a new Monster object, the class had not been changed to a two-headed tailless creature because someone else had edited a Monster object elsewhere in the program.
- It helps to shield the inner workings of the object from the programmer. In OOP, objects work like black boxes. Although their interface with the outside programming world (their methods) is made public, the way in which a method gets its job done and the variables with which it works is kept private.

Public versus Private Attributes and Methods

It's possible to make some attributes and methods available to code outside an object of that class while keeping other methods and attributes hidden. We can explicitly state which members (attributes and/or methods) of a class are **public** (available to code outside an object of that class) and which are **private** (not available outside the class). Most programming languages use the keywords Public and Private. The relevant keyword, placed in front of the variable or method name, specifies the status of that class member. For instance, in Example 11.1, to declare all variables as Private and all methods as Public, we would rewrite the pseudocode as follows:

```
1   Class Cube
2      Declare Private Side As Float
3      Declare Private Volume As Float
4      Public Subprogram SetSide(Float NewSide)
5         Set Side = NewSide
6      End Subprogram
7      Public Subprogram ComputeVolume()
8         Set Volume = Side^3
9      End Subprogram
10     Public Function GetVolume() As Float
11        Set GetVolume = Volume
12     End Function
13     Public Function GetSide() As Float
14        Set GetSide = Side
15     End Function
16  End Class
```

Attributes are normally declared as Private to protect their integrity. Methods are declared as Public if they are part of the interface between the object and program, and declared as Private if they are only used internally, within the class itself. Object-oriented programming makes use of a third type of declaration as well. Attributes may be declared as **protected** (Protected) if they are meant to be available (Public) to derived classes (subclasses of the given class—see Section 11.2) but still hidden (Private) from the rest of the program. For the purposes of this book, we will assume all attributes are Private or Protected and all methods are Public.

Creating Objects

You will remember that defining a class is analogous to creating a data type and just as a data type (like Integer) cannot be referenced within the program, neither can the name of the class. So once we have defined a class, we need to create one or more objects of that class, which can be referenced within the program. In an OOP language, each time we create an object based on a class, we say we are creating an **instance** of the class. This means we must perform an **instantiation** operation. Instantiation is typically done by means of a declaration statement placed in the main program. For example, in this book, we use the statements

```
Declare Cube1 As New Cube
Declare Cube2 As New Cube
```

to create two objects, named Cube1 and Cube2, of the class Cube. The keyword New specifies that a new object of a certain class type is being created.

Once they are created, we can make use of the objects Cube1 and Cube2 in our program, but we need a notation for doing so. In this book, as in many object-oriented programming languages, we will use **dot notation** that allows us to use a single expression to refer to the object and method or attribute under consideration. For example, to assign a value of 10 to the Side attribute of Cube1 (see Example 11.1), we will use the following statement:

```
Call Cube1.SetSide(10)
```

This statement calls the method SetSide(), assigning the value 10 to its argument, NewSide, in the process. To ensure that this method is setting the Side of the object Cube1 (not that of Cube2) equal to 10, we place Cube1 in front of the subprogram name, separated from it by a dot (period). As another example, to display the Volume attribute of Cube2, we use the following statement:

```
Write Cube2.GetVolume()
```

Any method or property of a class is referred to as a **member** of that class. In general, to refer to a public member (attribute or method) called MemberName, of an object called ObjectName, we use the following notation:

```
ObjectName.MemberName
```

Example 11.2 further illustrates this notation.

Example 11.2 **Using an Object in a Class**

The following program makes use of the Cube1 object of the class Cube. The Cube class is defined in Example 11.1. This program inputs a number from the user that represents the length of the side of a cube and displays the volume of that cube.

```
1   Main
2      Declare Cube1 As New Cube
3      Declare Side1 As Float
4      Write "Enter the length of the side of a cube: "
5      Input Side1
6      Call Cube1.SetSide(Side1)
7      Call Cube1.ComputeVolume()
8      Write "The volume of a cube of side " + Cube1.GetSide() ⏎
                + " is " + Cube1.GetVolume()
10  End Program
```

What Happened?

Notice that there are four calls in this pseudocode to the methods of the object Cube1: to SetSide() (line 6), ComputeVolume() (line 7), GetSide() (line 8), and GetVolume() (line 8). In OOP language, each of these calls is referred to as a **message** to the appropriate instance. Refer to Example 11.1 and the following explanations to see what happens as objects in the Cube class are called:

- On line 5 a value is input for the side of a cube. Let's say, for example, that the input is 2 so the value of Side1 is 2.
- The first subprogram call on line 6: Call Cube1.SetSide(Side1) assigns the number input on line 5 to the subprogram variable Side. Side now has the value of 2.

- The next subprogram call on line 7: `Call Cube1.ComputeVolume()` sets `Volume = Side^3`. The value of `Volume` is 2^3 or 8.
- The statement on line 8: `Write "The volume of a cube of side " + Cube1.GetSide()+ " is " + Cube1.GetVolume()` will display the following:

    ```
    The volume of a cube of side 2 is 8
    ```

The Constructor

In Example 11.2, a program error will result if the main program calls the subprogram `ComputeVolume()` before its `Side` attribute is given a value. To prevent this, object-oriented programming languages supply an easy way, through the use of **constructors**, to initialize an object's attributes. You can think of a constructor as a model or a plan for constructing an object. In programming, a constructor is a special method included in the class definition that automatically performs specified setup tasks when an object is created. The constructor will initialize the object's attributes and establish the conditions that do not change in the class. A properly written constructor will leave the object in a valid state. In other words, a constructor in a class is a special method that can be used to create objects of the class.

Constructors are automatically called when an object (an instance of a class) is created. They are normally distinguished by having the same name as the class of the object they are associated with. The constructor is created when the class is created. In some cases, more than one constructor may be created.

As shown in Example 11.3, in our `Cube` class, for example, a constructor might be assigned values to the two attributes, `Side` and `Volume`, of 1 and 1, respectively. Then when the main program calls the subprogram `ComputeVolume()` before its `Side` attribute is given a value, the value of 1 is already there and ready to be replaced by whatever value is necessary.

Example 11.3 **Creating a Constructor for the Cube Class**

The following program shows how a constructor is created when we create the class `Cube`. The `Cube` class, as defined in Example 11.1, is revised as follows:

```
1   Class Cube
2     Declare Private Side, Volume As Float
3     // The Cube constructor:
4     Public Cube()
5       Set Side = 1.0
6       Set Volume = 1.0
7     End Constructor
8     Public Subprogram SetSide(NewSide)
9       Set Side = NewSide
10    End Subprogram
11    Public Subprogram ComputeVolume()
12      Set Volume = Side^3
```

```
13      End Subprogram
14      Public Function GetVolume() As Float
15        Set GetVolume = Volume
16      End Function
17      Public Function GetSide() As Float
18        Set GetSide = Side
19      End Function
20   End Class
```

Self Check for Section 11.1

11.1   What are the two major components of an object?

11.2   What is the relationship between a class and objects in that class?

11.3   What is the difference between public and private class members?

11.4   What is data hiding? Give an example of why it is important in an OOP program?

11.5   Define a class called InAndOut, including a constructor, that has one attribute named Value (of type Float) and two methods as follows:

   • SetValue() is a subprogram that imports a value of the attribute Value from the main program.
   • GetValue() is a function that returns the value of the attribute Value to the main program.

11.6   What is a constructor? Why are constructors used?

11.2   More Features of Object-Oriented Programming

In this section, we will continue our discussion of object-oriented programming (OOP) by describing additional features that provide OOP with versatility and power.

Benefits of Object-Oriented Languages

Object-oriented programming tools have been used for decades, but they gained great popularity in the late 1980s. There are two basic reasons for this development:

   1. During the 1980s, programs became more complex as demand grew for sophisticated applications such as word processors, graphics programs, and computer games. Software of this sort had so many options and possible outcomes that keeping track of the subprograms became a nightmare. Due to the self-contained nature of objects (encapsulation) and the properties of inheritance and polymorphism which we will discuss shortly, OOP is better equipped than top-down modular programming to deal with extremely complex software.

2. The graphical user interface (GUI), popularized by the Apple Macintosh in the mid-1980s, gradually became almost universal. Today, virtually all modern computers use a GUI interface. A GUI is made up of objects (windows, boxes, buttons, and so forth), so OOP became the natural way to program for these interfaces.

Inheritance and Polymorphism

In contrast with OOP, the approach that makes use of top-down modular design is known as **procedural programming**. Most early programming languages, such as FORTRAN and BASIC, did not support the use of classes and objects, and are known as procedural languages. On the other hand, most modern languages, such as C-based languages, Java, or JavaScript, allow the programmer to make use of objects, in addition to providing the tools found in a procedural language. In order to take full advantage of the power of OOP—to truly support object-oriented programming—a language must include the following features:

- **Encapsulation** is the incorporation of data and operations on that data into a single unit in such a way that the data can only be accessed through these operations. This is the fundamental idea behind classes and objects.
- **Inheritance** is the ability to create new classes that are based on existing ones. The methods (operations) and attributes (data) of the original class are incorporated into the new class, together with methods and attributes specific to the latter.
- **Polymorphism** is the ability to create methods that perform a general function, which automatically adapts itself to work with objects of different classes.

We discussed the concept of encapsulation in Section 11.1; we will discuss inheritance and polymorphism next.

Inheritance

We often classify things in everyday life. For example, trucks and cars are kinds of vehicles, and SUVs, convertibles, and sedans are kinds of cars. Mathematically, we can say that the set of cars is a subset of the set of vehicles, and the set of convertibles is a subset of the set of cars. To picture the relationships among these sets, we can use a kind of hierarchy chart, as shown in Figure 11.1.

Classifying objects can help to explain what they are and how they operate. For example, if we know what a car is, then, when a friend tells us he has just bought a convertible, he doesn't have to explain the attributes and functions that it has in common with a car. A convertible inherits these attributes and functions because it is part of the set of cars. Even if someone has never heard of a convertible, simply by stating that a convertible is a car, the common attributes and functions of cars are automatically understood. Our friend would then just present the special features of a convertible that distinguish it from any car.

This concept of classification and inheritance also works in object-oriented programming. Object-oriented languages allow us to create a subclass of an existing class. In this case, the existing class is called the **parent** or **base class**, and the subclass is

Figure 11.1 A hierarchy of vehicles

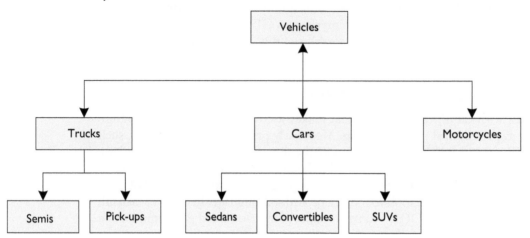

called the **child** or **derived class**. In creating a subclass, the attributes and methods of the base class automatically become members of the derived class, together with any additional attributes and methods defined specifically for the latter. In this way, we can say that the child class **extends** the parent class. A derived class is created to take advantage of the methods that have already been defined in an existing class. As an example, recall the Cube class of Section 11.1. Its members are as follows:

- Attributes: Side, Volume
- Methods: SetSide(), ComputeVolume(), GetSide(), GetVolume()

We may consider a cube to be a special type of box—one in which all sides are equal. If we want to define a class that models another kind of box, one with a square base but whose height is not the same as the sides of its base, we don't need to start from scratch; we can define this new class to be a subclass of Cube.

When we define a child class, we define it to be of the parent class type. Since it extends the parent class, we will use the following pseudocode to define a child class:

    Class ChildName Extends ParentName

Example 11.4 demonstrates how we would do this.

Example 11.4 **Using a Child Class for a Cube That Is Not Really a Cube**

The following pseudocode gives the definitions of the class Cube (from Section 11.1) and its child class, SquareBox. The SquareBox class makes use of all attributes and methods of the Cube class, although it changes the definition of the ComputeVolume() method and adds an attribute and two methods of its own. In this example, we have made the attributes of the Cube class available to the derived SquareBox class by declaring Side and Volume as Protected, rather than Private.

```
1  Class Cube
2    Declare Protected Side, Volume As Float
3    //create constructor
```

```
 4    Public Cube()
 5      Set Side = 1.0
 6      Set Volume = 1.0
 7    End Constructor
 8    Public Subprogram SetSide(Float NewSide)
 9      Set Side = NewSide
10    End Subprogram
11    Public Subprogram ComputeVolume()
12      Set Volume = Side^3
13    End Subprogram
14    Public Function GetVolume() As Float
15      Set GetVolume = Volume
16    End Function
17    Public Function GetSide() As Float
18      Set GetSide = Side
19    End Function
20  End Class
21  Class SquareBox Extends Cube
22    Declare Private Height As Float
23    //create constructor
24    Public SquareBox()
25      Set Height = 1.0
26      Set Side = 1.0
27      Set Volume = 1.0
28    End Constructor
29    Public Subprogram SetHeight(Float NewHeight)
30      Set Height = NewHeight
31    End Subprogram
32    Public Function GetHeight() As Float
33      Set GetHeight = Height
34    End Function
35    Public Subprogram ComputeVolume()
36      Set Volume = Side^2 * Height
37    End Subprogram
38  End Class
```

What Happened?

In this pseudocode, notice that we specify SquareBox to be a subclass of Cube with the following statement:

```
Class SquareBox Extends Cube
```

(Of course, each programming language has its own way of defining subclasses.) The derived class SquareBox has the following members:

- Its attributes are Side and Volume, both inherited from Cube, and its own attribute, Height.
- Its methods are SetSide() and GetSide(), inherited from Cube, and its own methods, SetHeight(), GetHeight(), and ComputeVolume().

A statement like

```
Declare Box As New SquareBox
```

creates an object called `Box` of the class `SquareBox` that can take advantage of all these attributes and methods. The `New` keyword specifies that a new object (`Box`) of a specific type (`SquareBox`) is to be created. For example, the following statements assign the values 10 and 20 to the `Side` and `Height` attributes, respectively:

```
Call Box.SetSide(10)
Call Box.SetHeight(20)
```

In Example 11.4, notice that a `ComputeVolume()` method appears in both the base class `Cube` and the derived class `SquareBox`. In such a case, for an object in the derived class, the definition in the derived class overrides the one in the base class. Example 11.5 clarifies this notion.

Example 11.5 Using the Child Class for the Volume of a Box

With the definition of the `SquareBox` class given in Example 11.4, the following pseudocode inputs values for the side and height of a box from the user and computes and displays its volume:

```
 1  Main
 2    Declare Box As New SquareBox
 3    Declare BoxSide, BoxHeight As Float
 4    Write "For a box with a square base and arbitrary height, ⏎
             enter the length of the sides of its base:"
 5    Input BoxSide
 6    Call Box.SetSide(BoxSide)
 7    Write "Enter the height of the box:"
 8    Input BoxHeight
 9    Call Box.SetHeight(BoxHeight)
10    Call Box.ComputeVolume()
11    Write "The volume of the box is " + Box.GetVolume
12  End Program
```

What Happened?

When the message

```
Call Box.SetSide(BoxSide)
```

is sent, the computer looks in the class definition `SquareBox` (the class of the object `Box`) for the method `SetSide()`. Because this method is not defined in `SquareBox`, the computer looks in the parent class, `Cube`, for this method and applies it to the object `Box`. This sets `BoxSide` equal to the value input. On the other hand, when the subprogram `SetHeight()` is called, this method is found in the definition of `SquareBox` and invoked. Similarly, when the message

```
Call Box.ComputeVolume()
```

is sent, it's received by the method `ComputeVolume()`, which is defined in `SquareBox`. Thus, the correct formula, `Volume = Side^2 * Height`, is applied at this point, and the `ComputeVolume()` method in `Cube` is never accessed.

Before we move on to discuss the next significant aspect of object-oriented programming, Example 11.6 demonstrates another example of inheritance.

Example 11.6 Using OOP to Solve the Parking Lot Problem

In this example, we will create one parent class and two child classes to demonstrate how inheritance works and how to create a constructor for a child class that uses some—but not all—of the members of the parent class. First we will create a class called Person and then add two subclasses, Faculty and Student, which will each inherit attributes and methods from the Person class and also will include some methods and attributes specific to each child class. The program is designed to solve a problem common to many colleges—the ever-present Parking Lot Problem.

The following pseudocode gives the definitions of the class Person and its child classes, Faculty and Student. Although both professors and students are people, at our imaginary college, OOPU, parking is at a premium so students must ride bikes to school while professors can drive cars. Cars may be parked in lots 1 through 5 and bikes must be parked in lots 6 through 10. In this example, the Faculty and Student child classes make use of some of the attributes and methods of the Person class, although each derived (child) class adds attributes and methods required to assign a parking lot.

The following pseudocode shows how the classes are defined, how two objects are created (ProfOne and StuOne), and what each object looks like at the end. Note that the constructors for the child classes must invoke the constructor for the parent class.

Create the parent class, Person

```
 1  Class Person
 2    Declare Protected Name, City, Vehicle As String
 3    Declare Protected Age As Float
 4    //Create a constructor for the Person class
 5    Public Person()
 6      Set Name = " "
 7      Set City = " "
 8      Set Age = 1.0
 9      Set Vehicle = " "
10    End Constructor
11    Public Subprogram SetName(String NewName)
12      Set Name = NewName
13    End Subprogram
14    Public Subprogram SetCity(String NewCity)
15      Set City = NewCity
16    End Subprogram
17    Public Subprogram SetAge(Float NewAge)
18      Set Age = NewAge
19    End Subprogram
20    Public Subprogram SetTravel(String NewVehicle)
21      Set Vehicle = NewVehicle
22    End Subprogram
23    Public Function GetName() As String
```

```
24    Set GetName = Name
25    End Function
26    Public Function GetCity() As String
27      Set GetCity = City
28    End Function
29    Public Function GetAge() As Float
30      Set GetAge = Age
31    End Function
32    Public Function GetTravel() As String
33      Set GetTravel = Vehicle
34    End Function
35  End Class
```

Create the first child class, Faculty

```
1   Class Faculty Extends Person
2     Declare Private Subject, Public ParkingLot As Integer
3     /*Create Faculty constructor: Note: since the Faculty class
        uses some attributes of the Person class, the constructor
        invokes the Person Constructor */
4     Public Faculty()
5       Call Person()
6       Set Subject = 1
7       Set ParkingLot = 1
8     End Constructor
9     Public Subprogram SetSubject(Integer NewSubject)
10      Set Subject = NewSubject
11    End Subprogram
12    Public Function GetSubject() As Integer
13      Set GetSubject = Subject
14    End Function
15    Public Subprogram ComputeParkingLot(Integer NewSubject)
16      Set ParkingLot = NewSubject
17    End Subprogram
18  End Class
```

Create the second child class, Student

```
1   Class Student Extends Person
2     Declare Private Subject, Public ParkingLot As Integer
3     /*Create Student constructor: Note: since the Student
        class uses some attributes of the Person class,
        the constructor invokes the Person constructor */
4     Public Student()
5       Call Person()
6       Set Subject = 1
7       Set ParkingLot = 1
8     End Constructor
9     Public Subprogram SetSubject(Integer NewSubject)
```

```
10        Set Subject = NewSubject
11     End Subprogram
12     Public Function GetSubject() As Integer
13        Set GetSubject = Subject
14     End Function
15     Public Subprogram ComputeParkingLot(Integer NewSubject)
16        Set ParkingLot = NewSubject + 5
17     End Subprogram
18  End Class
```

Begin the Main program to create two objects: ProfOne **and** StuOne

```
 1  Main
 2     Declare ProfLot, ProfSubject, StuLot, StuSubject As Integer
 3     Declare ProfName, ProfCar, StuBike, StuName As String
 4     Declare ProfOne As Faculty
 5     Write "What is this professor's name?"
 6     Input ProfName
 7     Call ProfOne.SetName(ProfName)
 8     Write "What type of car does this professor drive?"
 9     Input ProfCar
10     Call ProfOne.SetTravel(ProfCar)
11     Write "What is the professor's general subject area?"
12     Write "Enter 1: Liberal Arts, 2: Engineering, 3: Health ↵
              Science, 4: Business, 5: Education"
13     Input ProfSubject
14     Call ProfOne.SetSubject(ProfSubject)
15     Set ProfLot = ProfOne.ComputeParkingLot(ProfSubject)
16     Write "Professor " + ProfOne.GetName + ": You may park ↵
              your " + ProfOne.GetTravel() + " in Parking ↵
              Lot " + ProfLot
17     Declare StuOne As Student
18     Write "What is this student's name?
19     Input StuName
20     Call StuOne.SetName(StuName)
21     Write "What type of bike does this student have?"
22     Input StuBike
23     Call StuOne.SetTravel(StuBike)
24     Write "What is the student's major?"
25     Write "Enter 1: Liberal Arts, 2: Engineering, 3: Health ↵
              Science, 4: Business, 5: Education
26     Input StuSubject
27     Call StuOne.SetSubject(StuSubject)
28     Set StuLot = StuOne.ComputeParkingLot(StuSubject)
29     Write "Student " + StuOne.GetName + ": You may park ↵
              your " + StuOne.GetTravel() + " in Parking ↵
              Lot " + StuLot
30  End Program
```

What Happened?

If Professor Crabbe is an English teacher who drives a Porsche and Sammy is an Engineering student who rides a racing bike, after this program segment is run, the display will be as follows:

```
Professor Crabbe:
You may park your Porsche
in Parking Lot 1
Student Sammy:
You may park your racing bike
In Parking Lot 7
```

The Main program allows the user to create two objects. The Faculty object (ProfOne in this example) makes use of the Name attribute and the SetName(), SetTravel(), GetName(), and GetTravel() methods of the Person class but does not use the City or Age attributes or methods of Person. It also uses the attributes and methods specific to itself—the Subject and ParkingLot attributes and the SetSubject(), GetSubject(), and ComputeParkingLot() methods. The same is true for the Student object (StuOne in this example). The Faculty and Student constructors set initial (default) values for the attributes needed from Person as well as their own specific attributes.

Note that some members of the Person class were not used in the program of Example 11.6. However, these members may be important in other programs that use the Person class. This is one of the key aspects of OOP; the programmer creates classes that can be used in many and varied ways. A good programmer anticipates what may be needed in the future and allows for it in the present.

Polymorphism

In a hierarchy of classes, it's often the case that some methods are common to several classes, but their definitions may differ from class to class. For example, the ComputeVolume() method of Example 11.4 calculates the volume of a cube in the base class Cube and it uses a different formula to calculate the volume of a box with a square base in the derived class SquareBox. A module might contain definitions of many three-dimensional objects, like cubes, boxes, spheres, and cylinders, and each of these would need a different formula to compute its volume. It would be convenient if a programmer were able to use a single method, ComputeVolume(), to calculate the volume of any of these objects. Polymorphism allows for this kind of flexibility.

Polymorphism means "many shapes." In programming, polymorphism allows a method to take on many definitions when applied to objects in a hierarchy of classes. Although this OOP feature is implemented differently in various object-oriented languages, Example 11.7 shows the general way in which it works. It is merely a convenient coincidence that we are using an example of a class that computes the volumes of many shapes to illustrate the concept. Polymorphism works the same way, regardless of whether the program is about computing volumes of various shapes or providing payroll information for a large corporation with many types of employees (see the What & Why following Example 11.7).

Example 11.7 **Polymorphism in Action**

The following pseudocode shows how a method can take on different forms when applied to different objects. It makes use of the class definitions given in Example 11.4.

```
1   Main
2     Declare Box1 As New Cube
3     Declare Box2 As New SquareBox
4     Declare Side1, Side2, Height2 As Float
5     Write "Enter the length of the side of a cube: "
6     Input Side1
7     Call Box1.SetSide(Side1)
8     Call Box1.ComputeVolume()
9     Write "The volume of this cube is " + Box1.GetVolume()
10    Write "For a box with a square base and arbitrary ↵
              height, enter the length of the sides of its base:"
11    Input Side2
12    Call Box2.SetSide(Side2)
13    Write "Enter the height of the box:"
14    Input Height2
15    Call Box2.SetHeight(Height2)
16    Call Box2.ComputeVolume()
17    Write "The volume of this box is " + Box2.GetVolume()
18  End Program
```

What Happened?

The Declare statement on line 2 creates the object Box1 as an instance of the Cube class. Therefore, for all statements that refer to Box1, the Cube class definition is referenced. Like a child who inherits his parents' brown eyes, Box1 inherits the attributes and methods of the Cube class. In particular, on line 7, when the first message is sent to the method ComputeVolume(), the formula used is Volume = Side^3. This is the formula for Volume, which is defined in the Cube class.

The Declare statement on line 3 creates Box2 as an instance of the class SquareBox. So when a statement refers to Box2, the SquareBox class definition is referenced. However, SquareBox is a child of the Cube class. Thus, when an attribute or method is not defined in SquareBox, the definition of that attribute or method is used from the parent class, Cube.

On line 16, a second message is sent to ComputeVolume(), this time preceded by Box2. Since Box2 is of SquareBox type, the definition in SquareBox is used for the ComputeVolume() method. SquareBox defines Volume as Volume = Side^2 * Height.

SquareBox inherits some attributes and methods from its parent, Cube, but if a method (or attribute) that is already defined in the parent is redefined in the child, then the class closest to the calling instance takes precedence. In other words, even though Cube has a valid method to compute the volume, Box2 will never see that formula. Box2 will first go to SquareBox for a method to compute the volume and will use that one.

The two classes, `Cube` and `SquareBox`, both contain functions named `ComputeVolume()`. In procedural programming, it's normally not possible to have two functions with the same name be defined by different expressions. But in object-oriented programming, polymorphism allows this to happen since each class is self-contained. As we have seen from Example 11.7, even though `SquareBox` has access to the methods in `Cube`, if a method is defined differently in `Cube` and `SquareBox`, then the method in the child class (`SquareBox`) is used and the method in the parent class (`Cube`) is ignored.

Another example of polymorphism is present in Example 11.6 where both the `Faculty` and `Student` child classes have methods to assign a parking lot, but the computation in each `ComputeParkingLot()` method is different. This is another incidence of polymorphism, even though the parent class in this case, `Person`, does not have a `ComputeParkingLot()` method.

Example 11.7 demonstrates a simple example of polymorphism. However, polymorphism can handle much more complex programming issues. For example, imagine that we have created a program to provide the payroll department of a certain company with information about employee paychecks. The program contains a parent class called `Worker` with members that describe things common to all employees. It also has several child classes that contain members with information specific to different types of workers (such as truck drivers, clerical staff, etc.). The `Worker` parent class, among other things, computes the gross pay of an employee. This class contains a method called `ComputeGrossPay()`, which uses the results of two other methods in the class: `ComputeRegular()`, which calculates regular pay by multiplying the hourly rate by the number of hours worked up to 40 hours and `ComputeOvertime()`, which calculates the overtime pay by multiplying all hours worked over 40 by 1.5 times the hourly rate. Therefore, `ComputeGrossPay()` uses the formula

```
Gross = ComputeRegular(RegHours) + ComputeOvertime(OverHours)
```

where `RegHours` and `OverHours` are previously determined.

However, the company hires student workers who are paid overtime based on a different formula from the other workers. Student workers' overtime is calculated at 1.75 times the hourly rate for all hours over 40. There is a specific child class, `StudentWorker`, which can use the `ComputeGrossPay()` method but must use its own method for overtime pay in the calculation. This could be a problem since the `ComputeGrossPay()` method utilizes a `ComputeOvertime()` method, which is already in the parent class. We need a way to tell the parent class that, when dealing with an object of `StudentWorker` class, it must use the `ComputeOvertime()` method from the child class and not from its own class.

Polymorphism allows us to handle this problem. In some OOP languages this can be handled by declaring the `ComputeOvertime()` in the `Worker` class as a *virtual method* which is only accessed when instructed. This feature would allow `StudentWorker` to make use of the `ComputeGrossPay()` method in the parent class while substituting its own `ComputeOvertime()` method for the one defined in the parent class. Using virtual methods is one way to deal with this problem. Various OOP languages may use or handle this situation slightly differently but the end result is the same: polymorphism is the feature that allows this to happen.

Self Check for Section 11.2

11.7 In contrast to object-oriented programming, the top-down modular approach to programming is referred to as _____ programming.

11.8 Identify each of the following OOP features using one word:
   a. The incorporation of data and operations on that data into a single unit in such a way that the data can only be accessed by making use of these operations
   b. The ability to create new classes that are based on existing ones and to make use of their data and attributes
   c. The ability to create methods that perform a general function that automatically adapts to work with certain related classes

11.9 When we create a subclass of an existing class, the new class is called the _____ or _____ class; the original is called the _____ or _____ class.

11.10 Assume you have a parent class named Shape, which contains a method, ComputeArea() to compute the area of a shape based on a square (area = side × side). You have three child classes named Rectangle, Circle, and RightTriangle.
   a. How many methods, in total, would you need to use these classes to compute the areas of all rectangles (including squares), circles, and triangles?
   b. Write pseudocode for these four classes, including the attributes and methods needed to calculate these areas. Recall that the formulas for the areas of these shapes are as follows:
   - Area(square) = (side)^2
   - Area(circle) = 3.14 × (radius)^2
   - Area(rectangle) = length × height
   - Area(right triangle) = ½ × base × height

11.11 Define inheritance as it relates to base and derived classes.

11.3 Object-Oriented Program Design and Modeling

As you know, the top-down modular approach to program design (procedural programming) places an emphasis on determining the subprograms (procedures) that are needed in a program. On the other hand, object-oriented program design places an emphasis on determining the objects needed to solve the given problem. In fact, in most cases in which OOP is better suited to solve a given problem (such as in programming for a Graphical User Interface), there is no strong hierarchy of program modules.

Viewed in terms of the program development cycle—problem analysis, program design, program coding, and program testing—the analysis phase differs the most between the two approaches. In developing an OOP program, the analysis phase entails the following:

1. Identifying the classes to be used in the program
2. Determining the attributes needed for the classes

3. Determining the methods needed for the classes
4. Determining the relationships among the classes

The manner in which these steps are carried out is not so different from that of the top-down approach. The program designer works with the program specifications, imagining what kinds of situations the program will encounter—what types of specific cases it must handle—and determines the necessary objects, attributes, and methods from these scenarios.

There is a natural transition from the analysis phase of the program development cycle into the design phase. Here, as in the top-down technique, the methods (subprograms and functions) must be defined. Although this is easy to say, in real-life programs there may be hundreds or even thousands of methods. Encapsulating them in objects generally makes it easier to manage them. Finally, although the coding and testing phases proceed as in procedural programming, here too, a benefit of OOP emerges. It is likely that some preexisting objects can be recycled in this new program. Using reusable code speeds up both coding and testing. Example 11.8 illustrates the analysis phase of an object-oriented design.

Example 11.8 Designing with OOP: Managing Classes with Parent and Child Classes

Professor Crabbe has asked you to create a program to help her manage the grades in two of her courses. She teaches Programming Logic and Web Authoring classes and she has a different grading scheme for each course. Student grades in the Logic class depend heavily on exam scores while homework grades count minimally toward the final course grade. The Web Authoring class, however, is based mainly on homework projects, so homework grades contribute more toward the final course grade than exam grades. Also, Professor Crabbe uses two different scales to assign letter grades once she has computed the students' averages. She never changes her grading scale for her Web Authoring classes but she curves her grades in the Logic classes, depending on various factors, which she has included in a specific formula. Professor Crabbe wants a single program that will allow her to input students' names, exam averages, and homework averages for the semester, calculate the numeric average for the whole course, and produce a letter grade for each student.

1. As we begin to analyze the problem, we decide to use three classes of objects. We plan to have one base (parent) class and two derived (child) classes:
   - The base class (the parent class) is named `Crabby` and its members are the students, their semester exam averages, and their semester homework averages.
   - The first derived class (one child class) is named `Logic` and its members are the numeric averages for the semester and the letter grades.
   - The second derived class (the second child class) is named `Webauth` and its members are the numeric averages for the semester and the letter grades.
2. The attributes of these classes are as follows:
   - For the `Crabby` class: `Name` (`String`), `ExamAvg` (`Float`), `HomeworkAvg` (`Float`)
   - For the `Logic` class: `SemAvg` (`Float`), `LetterGrade` (`String`)
   - For the `Webauth` class: `SemAvg` (`Float`), `LetterGrade` (`String`)

3. The methods of these classes are as follows:
   - For the `Crabby` class: The methods are those that allow access to the attributes of this class, including `SetName()`, `GetName()`, `SetExamAvg()`, `GetExamAvg()`, `SetHomeworkAvg()`, and `GetHomeworkAvg()`.
   - For the `Logic` class: The methods are those that allow access to the attributes of the base class, `Crabby`, and two methods to do the computations, `ComputeSemAvg()` and `ComputeLetterGrade()`.
     - For example, `ComputeSemAvg()` for this class would be a subprogram that computes the semester average by weighting exams at 70 percent and homework at 30 percent:

       `SemAvg = ExamAvg × 0.7 + HomeworkAvg × 0.3`

     - The `ComputeLetterGrade()` might use the midpoint of all the students' averages as a C and then use another formula to assign the remaining grades based on the number assigned to the grade of C.
   - For the `Webauth` class: The methods are those that allow access to the attributes of the parent class, `Crabby`, and two methods to do the computations, `ComputeSemAvg()` and `ComputeLetterGrade()`.
     - For example, `ComputeSemAvg()` for this class would be a subprogram that computes the semester average weighting exams at 25 percent and homework at 75 percent:

       `SemAvg = ExamAvg × 0.25 + HomeworkAvg × 0.75`

     - The `ComputeLetterGrade()` might assign a grade using a common grading scale where 90-100 is an A, 80-89 is a B, and so forth.

The classes `Logic` and `Webauth` are related to `Crabby`. Each derived class has access to the attributes and methods of the base class. That is, the classes `Logic` and `Webauth` inherit the attributes and methods of `Crabby`. However, neither of the derived classes can access the methods and attributes of the other.

Now that we have determined the classes, attributes, and methods needed to solve this problem, we must design, code, and test the corresponding subprograms, as well as the program itself. In a real-life situation, we would have to add some other attributes and methods to these classes to consider more possibilities, such as what might happen if a student were enrolled in both of Professor Crabbe's classes simultaneously. However, this example demonstrates how a base class is used to hold general data that may be used in various ways by other, derived classes.

Making It Work

Could the programmer who wrote Professor Crabbe's grade management program make use of the `Person` class we created previously in Example 11.6? The `Crabby` class contains the `Name` member and this is also part of the `Person` class. In fact, it would be better to create `Crabby` as a child class of `Person` or even a child of the `Faculty` subclass. At this point, Professor Crabbe only needs to access the `Name` attribute of `Person`, but in the future she may want to correlate her students' grades with their ages or their majors. This information is available in the `Person` class or in the derived class, `Student`. Thinking ahead like this is essential in object-oriented programming.

Modeling Languages

In earlier chapters, we learned how to use flowcharts and hierarchy charts to help us design our programs. Programmers use these aids to construct a model of what a program will do and how it will accomplish its tasks before writing actual code. As programs get larger and encompass more capabilities, the models must also get larger and more complex. By using objects and OOP design, programmers can efficiently use and reuse code. But software developers also use modeling languages to design large programs. An **object modeling language** is a standardized set of symbols that includes ways to arrange these symbols to model parts of an object-oriented software design or system design.

A modeling language is any artificial language that can be used to express information, knowledge, or a system in a structure that is defined by a consistent set of rules. The rules are used to interpret the meaning of the components in the model. Modeling languages can be graphical or textual. Graphical modeling languages use diagrams that have symbols to represent concepts and lines to connect the symbols. The lines represent relationships between the symbols. A flowchart is a type of graphical model. Textual modeling languages typically use specific keywords to represent concepts or actions. In that way, textual modeling languages are similar to the pseudocode we have been using throughout this book.

In addition to computer programming, modeling languages are used in many different disciplines, such as information management, business processes, software engineering, and systems engineering. Modeling languages can be used to specify system requirements, structures, and behaviors. They are used to specify systems so that people (e.g., customers, designers, programmers, and analysts) can easily understand the system being modeled. The more mature modeling languages are extremely precise, consistent, and executable. Informal diagramming techniques applied with drawing tools can produce useful pictorial representations of system requirements, structures, and behaviors, but not much else.

Executable modeling languages applied with proper tool support (which make creating models easier), however, are even expected to simulate outcomes and generate code. In many ways, the RAPTOR flowchart-based environment used in this book is an executable modeling language. In fact, in OOP mode, RAPTOR requires the use of a UML (which is discussed in this section) to design a program as part of its implementation.

Executable modeling languages cannot take the place of programming code but they are a significant part of the design of object-oriented programs. By using them, programmers are able to address more challenging problems and team members can more easily visualize what other members of the programming team are doing.

Unified Modeling Language (UML)

Unified Modeling Language (UML) is a nonproprietary, general-purpose modeling language that is an industry standard for describing software-intensive systems. In 2000 UML was accepted by the International Organization for Standardization (ISO) as the industry standard for modeling software-intensive systems. UML 2.4.1

is the latest version. It was published in August 2011 by the Object Management Group (OMG). The OMG is a consortium focused on setting standards for object-oriented systems.

UML can be used to create an abstract model of a system, sometimes referred to as the **UML model**. It's beyond the scope of this book to demonstrate how to use UML or create a UML model, but you should be aware that when designing very large programs for intricate applications, you will need to use more sophisticated design tools such as a UML in addition to the ones described in this book.

Unified Modeling Language resulted from the combined efforts of three men (Ivar Jacobson, James Rumbaugh, and Grady Booch). In 1995, the Three Amigos (as they were nicknamed), collaborated to develop a nonproprietary Unified Modeling Language. Under their technical leadership, an international organization called the UML Partners was organized in 1996 to complete the UML specification. It was submitted to the OMG and was adopted by the OMG in November 1997. UML has changed considerably since then and the present version is now an international standard.

The UML Model

UML diagrams represent three different views of a system model:

- The **functional requirements view** emphasizes the requirements of the system from the user's point of view. It presents a graphical overview of what a system does, in terms of actions and goals, and any dependencies between them.

- The **static structural view** emphasizes the static structure of the system using objects, attributes, operations, and relationships. The static characteristics define what parts make up a system. This view includes diagrams that allow the designer to see the structure of a program by showing the classes, their attributes, and the relationships between the classes. It also includes diagrams that show the internal structure of a class and the relationships that this structure makes possible.

- The **dynamic behavior view** emphasizes the dynamic behavior of the system by showing collaborations among objects and changes to the internal states of objects. The dynamic characteristics of a system are the ways the system behaves in response to certain events or actions.

UML uses many different types of diagrams to represent the various aspects of a system. Three significant diagram categories are described as follows:

1. **Structure diagrams** emphasize what things must be in the system being modeled.

2. **Behavior diagrams** emphasize what must happen in the system being modeled.

3. **Interaction diagrams** are a subset of behavior diagrams; they emphasize the flow of control and data among the things in the system being modeled.

Each of the these categories contains several types of diagrams. This flexibility allows the designer to model just one part of the system. For example, if a designer only wants to see what methods and attributes are available to the classes in the system, a structure diagram will show just this aspect of the system. At another point, the designer might be interested in working on the interaction between several classes. A behavior diagram would allow the designer to focus on this aspect without worrying about the structure of all the other classes in the model.

Why Use UML?

Until now we have designed programs using a top-down procedural approach. In some ways, this approach is intuitive. You are given a problem to solve and, while you begin by thinking about the outcome, the way to achieve the outcome is to start at the beginning and work toward that goal. Object-oriented programming requires you to think differently about a problem. You want to write code that will not simply solve one problem or even many similar problems. You want to write code that can be used in many different situations. You want to write code that will allow a programmer to use a given class in many ways. This is why the concepts of encapsulation and polymorphism are so important; the way one part of a program uses a class to create certain objects is completely encapsulated. The class can be used in an entirely different manner in another part of the program without fear that one will interfere with the other.

In a well-designed OOP program, classes and subclasses have many uses. Creating software is a matter of writing enormous amounts of code. But the code uses and reuses many of the same classes, subclasses, and objects in different ways. UML is important because it helps designers monitor what they are doing and what they have done, and helps them devise ways to increase functionality and improve the program over time.

OOPU Can Benefit from a UML Model

Let's think about Professor Crabbe's request for a program to manage grades in classes with different grading systems. We have written the Grade Management program in a previous chapter. She might have used such a program. But Professor Crabbe's university, OOPU, also needed to solve the problem of assigning specific parking lots to faculty and students. Additionally, Professor Crabbe thought it would be interesting to correlate the majors of her students with their grades and with their courses. In fact, when the academic advisors heard Professor Crabbe's idea, they thought it would be great to see these results—not just for Professor Crabbe but for all students in all courses in all majors. This might help them when advising new students about course selections. And, at the same time, the administration decided to extend the program that is used to assign appropriate parking lots to students and faculty to include everyone who comes to OOPU—staff, administrators, and visitors.

Instead of writing new programs to accomplish each of these tasks—and the many other tasks that OOPU folks can think of as they see how valuable these programs are—the object-oriented programmer designs classes and objects that can be reused for each new task. As the programmer continues to add functionality to the program that originally simply assigned parking lots to faculty and students—and now has become much more than a parking lot assignment program—the object-oriented model allows the programmer to see what is happening between the objects, predict what can happen, and design ways to achieve future goals.

11.12 List the fundamental steps taken in analyzing a problem to be solved using object-oriented program design.

11.13 What is one advantage of OOP over procedural programming?

11.14 What is a modeling language?

11.15 What are the three views of a UML system model?

11.16 Why would a programmer use UML?

11.4 Graphical User Interfaces and Event-Driven Programming

One of the important applications of object-oriented programming (OOP) is to create programs that employ a **graphical user interface** (GUI). A **GUI** includes windows that contain components such as menus, buttons, boxes, and so forth, which allow users to make choices and issue commands simply and intuitively.

Window Components

Figure 11.2 displays a typical dialog box window. This particular dialog box is the Print dialog box for the Microsoft Windows GUI. Its buttons, boxes, and other elements are collectively known as **window components** or **controls**. From a programming point of view, **windows** and window components are objects. The names and functions of common window components are described below; their attributes and methods are discussed later.

Figure 11.2 A typical dialog box

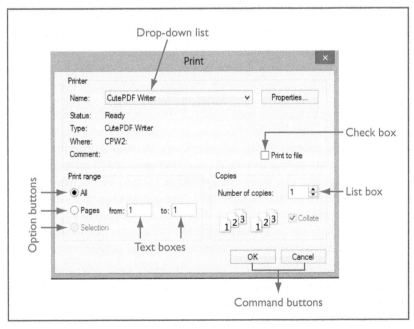

Refer to Figure 11.2 to see examples of the controls listed here.

Command buttons, like the "Properties", "OK", and "Cancel" buttons, are represented by labeled rectangles. When you click a command button, it initiates an action. The initial values assigned to all items before the user changes or selects anything are known as **default values**.

A **check box**, like the "Print to file check box", is represented by a small square, which may or may not contain a check mark. If a check mark is present, this indicates that the specified option is in effect (selected).

A **text box**, like the "from" or "to" text boxes, allows the user to input text into the dialog box.

Option buttons, which are represented by small circles, always appear in groups like the "Print range" group in Figure 11.2. These kinds of buttons are also called **radio buttons**. When the user clicks one of them, that button is selected and the others are automatically deselected. In a group of option buttons, only one of the corresponding options can be selected at any given time, but in a group of check boxes, several can be selected at any given time.

A **drop-down list box**, like the one labeled "Name", is used to display a list of items.

A **list box** is like a drop-down list box but displays either the entire list of items or a certain number of the items, allowing the user to scroll up and down through the entire list, with the first value at the top. In Figure 11.2 there is a list box next to "Number of copies".

A **label** is text in the dialog box that is not part of another window component. Often it's located near a component to help identify it. In Figure 11.2, "Printer", "Name", and "Status" are labels.

Creating GUI Objects in a Program

The major OOP languages have built-in classes, called class libraries, that supply the objects needed to write programs for a graphical user interface. Thus, there is no need to define windows, command buttons, and so forth. The way that these objects are created within a program depends on the language used.

- In some programming languages, GUI objects are created in the same way as any other objects, as instances of the class to which they belong
- In other programming languages, GUI objects are selected from a menu or toolbar and drawn on the screen

For example, in some programming languages, we can add a command button to a window by using a New statement to create the object and an Add statement to place it in the window. In languages that use a GUI interface such as Visual Basic or languages using the Dot-Net platform, we can click on a command button icon on a toolbar and then draw the button in the window. These actions create code that adds the button to the window. For simplicity's sake, in this chapter we will assume that windows and window components can be created in this second manner, without explicitly writing any code.

Each window and window component (command button, text box, and so forth) in a GUI has a set of attributes (or properties), such as name, position, and size. The following are some examples of GUI object properties:

Some properties of a window:

- name (by which it's known in the program)
- height and width (usually in pixels, the tiny dots that make up the screen image)
- title ("Area Calculator" shown in Figure 11.3)
- title font (the typeface and size of the window title)
- visible (true or false)—whether the window appears on the screen

Some command button properties:

- name (by which it's known in the program)
- caption ("Done" or "Calculate" shown in Figure 11.3)
- position (distance, in pixels, from the left and top edges of the window)
- enabled (true or false)—whether the button is active or inactive—the "Calculate" button is inactive, or grayed out, and will not respond to a mouse click; in Figure 11.3 the "Done" button is active and the "Calculate" button is inactive
- text boxes have properties similar to those of command buttons, but text boxes have a text property instead of a caption property. The text property holds the character string that currently appears inside the box.
- labels have properties that are very similar to those of text boxes.

Figure 11.3 A simple window

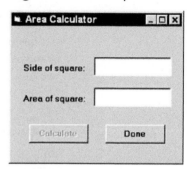

Option button properties include the following:

- name (by which it's known in the program)
- caption ("All", "Pages", or "Selection" shown in Figure 11.2)
- enabled (true or false)—whether the button is active or inactive
- value (true or false)—whether the option button has a bullet

Setting Properties

Since windows and window components are objects, their properties can be assigned values, just like the attributes of any object. Most GUI properties have default values, which are automatically used unless new ones are assigned. To change these default values, we can make use of assignment statements.

For example, in the Area Calculator window shown in Figure 11.3, if the name of the window is MainWindow, then the following statements:

```
Set MainWindow.title = "Area Calculator"
Set MainWindow.height = 100
```

specify that the title of the window is "Area Calculator" and that the height of the window is 100 pixels.

If the name of the right command button is QuitButton, then the following statements:

```
Set QuitButton.caption = "Done"
Set QuitButton.enabled = false
```

label the button as "Done" and cause it to be grayed out when the window is opened.

It isn't easy to remember the names of all the possible properties of all window components. To simplify matters, some languages allow you to specify properties by selecting items from menus or entering values into dialog boxes.

As objects, windows and their components also have methods (procedures) associated with them. We will discuss this aspect of GUI programming next.

Event-Driven Programming

So far in this chapter, we have discussed object-oriented programming (OOP) and some of the objects used in creating a graphical user interface (GUI). In this section, we will continue this discussion and introduce the concepts of events and event-driven program design.

Handling Events

In a procedural program, the flow of execution is determined by the code and the data it uses. Although the user can influence the flow through the input of data, it is the data that makes the difference and not the fact that the user entered it. However, in many programs the actions of the user (such as clicking the mouse) or system-related circumstances (such as the state of a timer) determine the flow of execution. These actions are called **events** and the resulting program is said to be **event-driven**. Although **event-driven programs** don't need to be written for a GUI or be object-based, the prime examples of event-driven programs employ a graphical user interface and are object-oriented.

To illustrate the concept of events and how they are handled by a program, let's return to the simple window displayed in Figure 11.3. For the sake of convenience, it's shown again in Figure 11.4. We will use this window and the components it contains as the interface for an event-driven program.

Figure 11.4 A GUI interface

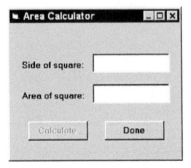

As you know, windows and the components contained within them are objects that have various attributes. Also associated with each object is a set of events and methods, called **event handlers** or **event procedures**. These event handlers enable the objects to carry out their functions. For example, the basic function of a command button is to allow the user to call for a specified action by clicking that button. Thus, the command button object needs a method to handle this event. In other words, there must be a way for the computer to recognize the click on a command button and then to call the appropriate subprogram. The programming language software ensures that this is done automatically. However, the programmer must design and write the code for this subprogram so that it performs the proper action when called.

The following is a list of some typical methods associated with the objects in a GUI. As usual, the names we use here may differ from those in an actual programming language.

Methods for a window include the following

- Open: opens (displays) the window
- StartUp: a programmer-written procedure that executes automatically when the window is opened
- Close: this closes the window (removes it from the screen)

Command button methods include the following

- Click: executes automatically when the button is clicked

Text box methods include the following

- Click: executes automatically when the box is clicked
- Change: executes automatically when the text within the box is changed

Option button methods include the following

- Click: executes automatically when the button is clicked

When a GUI program is run, the initial window appears on the screen and a StartUp procedure for this window (if there is one) is executed. From that point on, the flow of execution is determined by the events that occur. Example 11.9 shows a simple GUI program and how it works. We will present the pseudocode used to create a calculator that finds the area of a square.

Example 11.9 An Event-Driven GUI Calculator

To use the Area Calculator window shown in Figure 11.4 to find the area of a given square, the user types a number that represents the length of a side of the square into the upper text box. When this is done, the "Calculate" button becomes active so that it can respond to a mouse click. Then the user clicks this button to display the area of the square in the lower text box. To calculate the area of a different square, the user clicks inside the upper text box, which clears the numbers in both text boxes, grays out the "Calculate" button, and allows the process to be repeated. After calculating the areas of as many squares as desired, the user clicks the "Done" button to close the window and end the program. The following is the pseudocode that defines the methods and sets some of the attributes for the objects in this program.

```
1   Window
2      name = MainWindow
3      title = "Area Calculator"
4      Upper Label
5         text = "Side of square"
6      Lower Label
7         text = "Area of square"
8      Upper Text Box
9         name = InputBox
10        text = " "
11     Subprogram InputBox.Click()
12        Set InputBox.text = ""
13        Set OutputBox.text = ""
14        Set CalculateButton.enabled = false
15     End Subprogram
16     Subprogram InputBox.Change()
17        Set CalculateButton.enabled = true
18     End Subprogram
19     Lower Text Box
20        name = OutputBox
```

```
21      text = ""
22    Left Command Button
23      name = CalculateButton
24      caption = "Calculate"
25      enabled = false
26    Subprogram CalculateButton.Click()
27      Set OutputBox.text = Val(InputBox.text)^2
28    End Subprogram
29    Right Command Button
30      name = DoneButton
31      caption = "Done"
32    Subprogram DoneButton.Click()
33      Call MainWindow.Close
34    End Program
35  End Subprogram
```

All object properties, including those specified in the pseudocode above, are assigned when the program is compiled. When the program is started, the window shown in Figure 11.4 appears on the screen. Since there is no StartUp procedure defined for this window, execution pauses until an event occurs.

To see what is happening in this program, imagine that you are running the program, and when you perform an action, read the corresponding subprogram. Also, note the following:

- The Val() function (line 27) converts string data into numeric data
- The End Program statement in the last subprogram halts execution

Making It Work

Let's try it. Suppose your physics homework includes a problem that requires you to calculate the area of a square that is 3 inches by 3 inches. Rather than search in your backpack for your graphing calculator, you decide to test this program to find the answer by looking at the Area Calculator window, as shown in Figure 11.4.

First you click in the box next to the label "Side of square". This is the Upper Text Box in our pseudocode. When you click in the box (an event), control immediately goes to the subprogram, InputBox.Click() on line 11, which is triggered by the Click event. Line 12 would clear this text box if it had anything in it. Line 13 would clear the answer box (labeled "Area of square") if it had anything in it. Line 14 grays out the "Calculate" button since there is nothing, at this point, to calculate.

Next you enter a 3 in the "Side of square" text box. This is another event and the subprogram, InputBox.Change(), is activated (line 16). Line 17 enables the "Calculate" button so it's now ready for you to click it when you want to see the answer to your problem.

You trigger the third event when you click the "Calculate" button. Control goes to the subprogram that is activated by this event—the CalculateButton.Click()

subprogram on lines 26–28. Line 27 is the formula that calculates the area of a square. It does several things as follows:

- First, by using the Val function, the 3 that you entered is converted from a string value to a numeric value
- Then it takes that value and squares it to find the area. The statement on line 27:

```
Set OutputBox.text = Val(InputBox.text)^2
```

now sets the OutputBox to show the answer, 9.

At this point, you could go back to InputBox and enter another value, which would trigger the same events again. You could continue to do this as long as you wanted, and when you got tired of calculating areas of squares, you would finally click the "Done" button—the event that would send control to line 32, the subprogram that ends the program. Line 33 would close the window and line 34 would halt execution of the program.

Event-Driven Program Design

One of the striking differences between top-down programming and event-driven programming is that event-driven programming has no active main (or driver) program (i.e., no master controller). Execution begins by displaying the program's initial window and running its StartUp procedure, if any. But from then on, execution moves from subprogram to subprogram depending on the events that take place. Execution terminates when a statement that ends the program is encountered.

The analysis phase of an event-driven program design is similar to that of an object-oriented program. The following are the basic steps involved:

1. Identify the windows needed in the program.
2. Determine the relationships among the windows. For example, the programmer must figure out which window can open another so that the latter appears on the screen. Such relationships can be pictured in a flow diagram (see Figure 11.5). In a flow diagram, an arrow pointing from one window to another, as from Window 6 to Window 2 in Figure 11.5, means that the first can open or reactivate the second. A double arrow, pointing in both directions, as with Windows 2 and 3 in Figure 11.5, means that either window can open or reactivate the other.
3. For each window do the following:
   - Determine the components (command buttons, text boxes, and so forth) needed for that window
   - Draw a rough sketch of the resulting window
   - Determine the properties and methods needed for the window and each of its components; the methods don't need to be fleshed out in this phase

Figure 11.5 Flow diagram for a GUI program

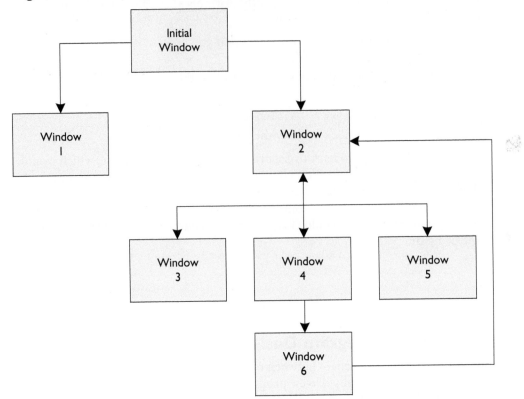

The third step of this process leads us into the design phase of the program development. Here, the methods for each object (and perhaps additional properties) are defined. We will illustrate the design process in detail in the next section.

Self Check for Section 11.4

11.17 Identify each of the following window components as a command button, an option button, a check box, or a text box:

  a. It can receive data input by the user

  b. When clicked, it initiates an action

  c. It allows the user to select one choice from a group of related choices

11.18 Give two properties of each of the following objects:

  a. A window

  b. A text box

  c. An option button

11.19 A command button has the name "OKbutton". Write assignment statements that set its caption property equal to "OK" and its enabled property equal to false.

11.20 Indicate whether each of the following statements is true or false:

  a. When the user clicks a command button during program execution, that action is considered to be an event.

  b. Event-driven programs must make use of a graphical user interface.

11.21 Which method would you use to respond to data after it is typed into a text box—its Click method or its Change method?

11.22 How would you modify the Area Calculator program of this section to do each of the following?

  a. Display the number 0 in both text boxes when the program starts

  b. Display the message "Invalid input" in the bottom text box if the user enters a negative number into the top text box and clicks the "Calculate" button. (*Hint:* use an If-Then-Else statement in the CalculateButton.Click() subprogram.)

11.23 Which of the following is the first step in developing an event-driven program?

  a. Write the Main program code

  b. Write the Click subprograms

  c. Determine which windows are needed

  d. Determine which buttons are needed

11.5 Focus on Problem Solving:
Another Grade Management Program

In this section, we will develop an event-driven program for a problem similar to the one discussed earlier in the book (Chapter 8) using a modular approach. Our new program uses the material covered in this chapter as well as the concepts developed throughout the book.

Problem Statement

One of your instructors, Professor Hirsch, would like to have a program that creates an electronic grade sheet so that he can monitor student scores in his classes. This program should allow the professor to enter the names of his students and their scores in three tests, compute the average test score for each student, and display this information whenever he wants.

Problem Analysis

First we want to determine the windows we will need to handle this problem. To do so, we imagine that we are teaching this class and think about the kinds of things that we will do with this program.

We need to create a file named "grades" to hold the grade sheet information. This file will hold the name, test scores, and test average for each student in the class. As we create the file, we will enter the names of students in the class at the same time.

Once the "grades" file has been created, we must be able to retrieve the file to display its information, enter test scores, or compute test averages.

Thus, the initial window should allow the user to select from two options: create the grade sheet or retrieve the grade sheet.

Now that we have determined the contents of the initial window, it's apparent that we need at least two additional windows as follows:

- CreateGradeSheet window
- RetrieveGradeSheet window

The CreateGradeSheet window should allow the user to enter the names of the students in the class. The RetrieveGradeSheet window would allow the user to specify the particular task to perform: display the grade sheet, enter test scores, or compute test averages. This leads to at least three more windows as follows:

- DisplayGradeSheet window
- EnterTestScores window
- ComputeTestAverages window

To see if additional windows are needed, we imagine that we are using the program to perform its stated functions. We pretend that we are Professor Hirsch and that we have just given the second exam. We pick the EnterTestScores window to enter these scores and realize that the program must know which score we are entering—test 1, test 2, or test 3. So we need to create one more window, a SelectTest window, to precede the actual entering of test scores.

Figure 11.6 displays a flow diagram that shows the windows described above and their relationship with one another.

Program Design

The program design consists of two stages. For each window indicated in Figure 11.6, we must:

1. Determine the objects (window components) needed to implement the user interface for that window
2. Write pseudocode that describes the attributes and methods for that window

Due to the space required to present these descriptions, we will not supply detailed pseudocode for every aspect of this program.

Initial window

We will use the following window components for the initial window:

- A label to describe the options that follow
- Two option buttons to allow selection of the display grade sheet or retrieve grade sheet option
- A command button ("OK") to put the selected option into effect
- A command button ("Quit") to allow the user to end the program

Figure 11.6 Flow diagram for the grade management program

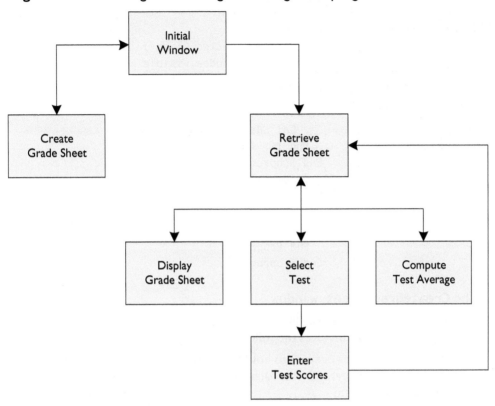

A sketch of this window (that the program designer might draw) and the actual window are shown in Figures 11.7 and 11.8, respectively. The pseudocode for this window's option buttons and command buttons follows.

Figure 11.7 A sketch of the initial window

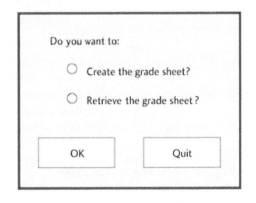

Pseudocode

```
1   Top option button:
2     name = Option1
3     caption = "Create the grade sheet?"
4     value = false [no bullet]
5     Subprogram Option1.Click()
6       Set Option1.value = true
7       Set Option2.value = false
8     End Subprogram
9   Bottom option button:
10    name = Option2
11    caption = "Retrieve the grade sheet?"
12    value = true [bullet]
13    Subprogram Option2.Click()
14      Set Option1.value = false
15      Set Option2.value = true
16    End Subprogram
```

Figure 11.8 The actual initial window

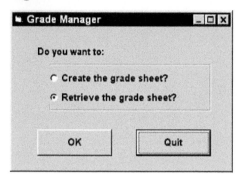

```
17  Left command button:
18    name = OKbutton
19    caption = "OK"
20    Subprogram OKbutton.Click()
21      Set InitialWindow.visible = false
22      If Option1.value == true Then
23        Call Create.Open
24      Else
25        Call Retrieve.Open
26      End If
27    End Subprogram
28  Right command button:
29    name = QuitButton
30    caption = "Quit"
31    Subprogram QuitButton.Click()
32      End Program
33    End Subprogram
```

The `CreateGradeSheet` window

The `window` components are shown in Figure 11.9. The pseudocode needed to implement this `window` involves the following:

1. Opening a file (for `Output`) to hold the required information—name, test scores, and test average—for each student in the class; this file has records of the following form:

   `student_name, test_1_score, test_2_score, test_3_score, average`

2. Inputting the student names from the user
3. Writing the names to the file and, at the same time, initializing all test scores and averages in the file to 0
4. Closing the file

The pseudocode for opening the file is housed in this `window`'s `StartUp` method. This method also initializes a counter, `StudentCount`, which will hold the number of students in the class for use by several other subprograms. If the current window has the `name` attribute `Create`, then the pseudocode for `StartUp` is as follows:

Figure 11.9 The create grade sheet window

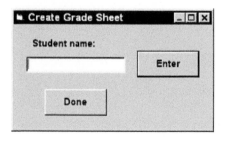

```
Subprogram Create.StartUp()
  Open "grades" For Output As GradeFile
  Set StudentCount = 0
End Subprogram
```

To input a student name, the user types it in the text box and clicks the "Enter" command button. Thus, all the code to input names and write the corresponding file records can be housed in the "Enter" command button's `Click()` method. In this pseudocode, we assume that the `name` attribute of the `text box` is InputBox. This method also increments the counter, `StudentCount`, that was initialized in the `window`'s `StartUp` method.

```
Subprogram Enter.Click()
  Write GradeFile, InputBox.text, 0, 0, 0, 0
  Set StudentCount = StudentCount + 1
  Set InputBox.text = ""
End Subprogram
```

Finally, the file is closed when the user clicks the "Done" button, which also closes the `CreateGradeSheet` window and reactivates (makes visible) the initial window.

```
Subprogram Done.Click()
  Close GradeFile
  Call Create.Close
  Set InitialWindow.visible = true
End Subprogram
```

The `RetrieveGradeSheet` window

This window and its methods have the following functions:

- When the window is opened, its `StartUp` method opens the file "grades" for Input and loads it into three parallel arrays—two one-dimensional arrays to hold the student names (`Names`) and test averages (`Averages`), and a two-dimensional array (`Scores`) to hold the scores in the three tests.
- The window allows the user to choose one of three options—display the grade sheet, enter test scores, or compute test averages.
- The window allows the user to exit the program and then copies the arrays back to the "grades" file, closes this file, and halts execution.

To implement these actions, we use the following:

- A `label` object at the top displaying the text "Select an option and click OK"
- Three option buttons with captions "Display the grade sheet", "Enter test scores", and "Compute test averages"
- Two command buttons at the bottom: one labeled "OK", which transfers execution to the proper window; the other labeled "Exit Program", which closes the grades file and halts execution

We leave the sketch of this window and the pseudocode for its components as a Self Check Exercise.

The `DisplayGradeSheet` window

When opened, this window displays the contents of the grade sheet (the `Names`, `Scores`, and `Averages` arrays) in the window itself. The code to do this is located in the window's `StartUp` method. This window also contains a single "OK" command button, which closes this window and reactivates the `RetrieveGradeSheet` window.

The `SelectTest` window

The `SelectTest` window (its `name` is `SelectTest`) contains three option buttons, stacked vertically. By clicking the appropriate option button, the user specifies whether he or she wants to enter scores for test 1, test 2, or test 3 into the

Scores array. This window also contains "OK" and "Cancel" command buttons. Clicking the "OK" button records the user's selection, closes the window, and opens the EnterTestScores window. Clicking the "Cancel" button closes the window and reactivates the RetrieveGradeSheet window. The pseudocode for this window is as follows:

```
 1   Top option button:
 2     name = Option1
 3     caption = "Enter scores for test 1"
 4     value = false
 5     Subprogram Option1.Click()
 6       Set Option1.value = true
 7       Set Option2.value = false
 8       Set Option3.value = false
 9     End Subprogram
10   Middle option button:
11     name = Option2
12     caption = "Enter scores for test 2"
13     value = false
14     Subprogram Option2.Click()
15       Set Option1.value = false
16       Set Option2.value = true
17       Set Option3.value = false
18     End Subprogram
19   Bottom option button:
20     name = Option3
21     caption = "Enter scores for test 3"
22     value = false
23     Subprogram Option3.Click()
24       Set Option1.value = false
25       Set Option2.value = false
26       Set Option3.value = true
27     End Subprogram
28   Left command button:
29     name = OKbutton
30     caption = "OK"
31     Subprogram OKbutton.Click()
32       If Option1.value == true Then
33         Set TestNum = 1
34       End If
35       If Option2.value == true Then
36         Set TestNum = 2
37       End If
38       If Option3.value == true Then
39         Set TestNum = 3
40       End If
41       Call EnterScores.Open
42       Call SelectTest.Close
43     End Subprogram
```

```
44  Right command button:
45    name = CancelButton
46    caption = "Cancel"
47    Subprogram CancelButton.Click()
48      Set Retrieve.visible = true
49      Call SelectTest.Close
50    End Subprogram
```

The EnterTestScores window

The EnterTestScores window contains two text boxes and a command button. The student names are displayed, one by one, in the upper text box. After each name is displayed, the user types the corresponding score in the lower text box and clicks the "Enter" button. When all student scores have been entered, this window closes automatically and the RetrieveGradeSheet window is displayed. The EnterTestScores window is shown in the Programming Challenges section at the end of this chapter, where you are asked to create a program that inputs test scores.

The ComputeTestAverages window

When the "compute test averages" option in the RetrieveGradeSheet window is activated by clicking the "OK" button in that window after this option button has been selected, the average score for each student is calculated and written to the Averages array. This pseudocode (which you are asked to provide as a Self Check exercise) is located in the "Compute Test Averages" StartUp method. The window itself is very simple. It consists of the message (label) "Average test scores have been computed!" and a single command button labeled "OK". When the latter is clicked, the window closes and the RetrieveGradeSheet window is reactivated.

Program Code

The program code is now written using the design as a guide. Even though this is not a procedural program, it still needs documentation. Header comments are used to help explain the general purpose of the program, each window, and the more complicated subprograms. Step comments are used to explain the purpose of certain variables, properties, and statements. Keep in mind the following points concerning the coding of this program:

- Some languages provide built-in class definitions for GUI objects, but they require you to write the code that creates these objects and adds them to the appropriate window. You may also have to, in code, specify an object's position, size, and many other attributes not mentioned in the pseudocode in this book.

- To display the contents of the "grades" file in a neat, readable fashion, the output produced in the DisplayGradeSheet window must be formatted. The names, test scores, and averages should line up in columns. This can be accomplished using the programming language's special print formatting statements.

Program Test

This program should be tested in a way similar to what we have previously done with pseudocode programs. Imagine that you are the instructor of a very small class (say, three students), and use the program to create the grade sheet, enter scores for each of the three tests, and compute the test averages. As always, you should test your program with both valid and invalid data. After all, you are creating a program for Professor Hirsch, who, while he may teach computer courses, may not always understand exactly how to enter data or what data is unacceptable. You need to make sure your program will not crash if Professor Hirsch (or any of the thousands of users who will buy the program after you become a well-paid software programmer) enters invalid data. Try entering zeros for all three test scores for one of the students (which could cause a division by zero in the computation of the average, depending on how the average function was written) or entering a word instead of a number for a test score.

After performing each of these tasks, display the grade sheet to check that the operation has been executed successfully. With a GUI interface, you need to consider design and appearance as well as functionality. As you perform the testing, examine each window and ask yourself if it could be improved in any way: Could it look better? Could it be made more intuitive? Could it be simplified?

Self Check for Section 11.5

For Self Check Questions 11.24–11.26 refer to the Grade Management Program developed in this section.

11.24 Draw a sketch of the RetrieveGradeSheet window.

11.25 Suppose that the (internal) name for the RetrieveGradeSheet window is "Retrieve", that the names of its option buttons are "Option1", "Option2", and "Option3", and that the name of its OK command button is "OKbutton".

a. Write a Click() procedure for "Option1" that causes it to acquire the bullet (and causes the other two option buttons to be bulletless).

b. Write a Click() procedure for "Okbutton" that hides the RetrieveGradeSheet window and opens the window named Display, SelectTest, or ComputeAverages, depending on the state of the option buttons.

11.26 The StartUp procedure for the ComputeAverages window uses the data in the Scores array to calculate the average test score for each student and writes this data to the Averages array. Write a subprogram called ComputeAverages.StartUp() that does this. Recall the following:

- The variable StudentCount holds the number of students in the class
- The array Scores has entries of the form Scores[testnum, studentnum]; for example, Scores[15, 2] holds the score of student 16 on test 3

11.6 Running With RAPTOR (Optional)

RAPTOR includes a way to create simple object-oriented programs with classes that have methods and attributes. You can create and instantiate objects and experiment with object-oriented programming in RAPTOR but you need to understand that this merely scratches the surface of an extremely complex and extensive subject.

Object-Oriented Mode

To use RAPTOR in OOP, you must select Object-oriented mode, as shown in Figure 11.10.

Figure 11.10 Object-oriented mode in RAPTOR

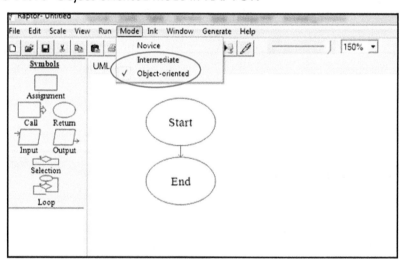

You will see two tabs: UML and main. RAPTOR uses a type of Unified Modeling Language to create the structure of an object-oriented program. The classes are created in the UML screen; therefore, click the UML tab. The button to add a new class is shown in Figure 11.11. Note that a new Return symbol has been added to the Symbols area.

Creating a Class

When you click the Add New Class button to add a new class, a Name box will appear. Enter a name for the Class, as shown in Figure 11.12.

In Figure 11.12, a Class named Cube has been created. Double-click inside the class (Cube) to add members (methods and attributes). In RAPTOR, note that attributes are called Fields. A new window opens to allow you to enter the members (see Figure 11.13).

Figure 11.11 Adding a new class in RAPTOR

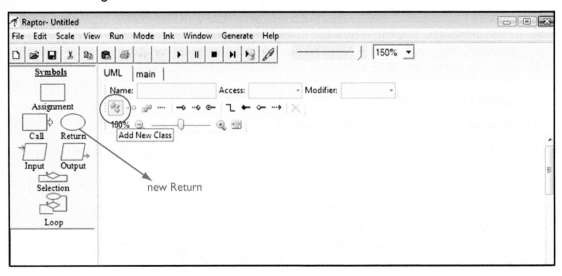

Figure 11.12 Entering a class name

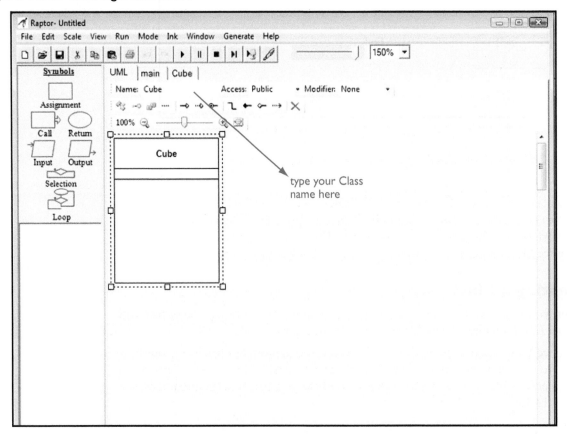

Figure 11.13 Adding members to a Class

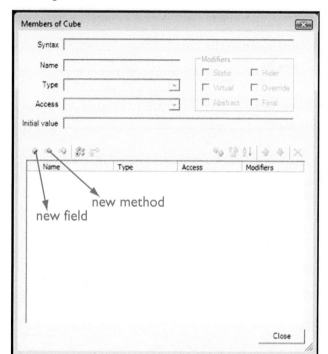

We will use an example to demonstrate the features of OOP mode and indicate how to use them in a program.

Example 11.10 **Using the Cube Class to Find the Volume of a Cube**

We will use RAPTOR Object-oriented mode to create a class named Cube that takes the value of a side of a cube and computes the cube's volume as we did in Example 11.1 earlier in this chapter. We need the following:

attributes: Side (Integer) and Volume (Integer)

methods: SetSide(), GetSide(), ComputeVolume(), and GetVolume()

Figure 11.14 shows the Class Cube and its members.

- Note the syntax for a Field (an attribute): A Field must be given a data type. The type of Side and Volume is int and, in this case, each field has an initial value of 1.
- Note the syntax for a Method. If the Method receives a value passed from main, you must include that parameter as follows:
  - The Method SetSide() is passed a value for the length of a side so the syntax for this Method is

    ```
    public void SetSide(int NewSide)
    ```

Figure 11.14 Creating the members of the Cube Class

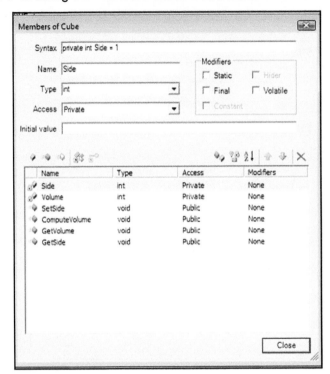

- The Method ComputeVolume() uses the value of the side of a cube to do its calculations so it needs one parameter, the integer variable Side. The syntax is

      public void ComputeVolume(int Side)

- The Method GetVolume() retrieves the value of the volume of the cube from ComputeVolume() so the syntax for this Method is

      public void GetVolume(int Volume)>

- The Method GetSide() does not need a parameter so the syntax is

      public void GetSide()

- At this point we do not need to worry about Type, Access, and Modifiers. We will leave their settings at the default values.

Once the Class has been created, a new tab is automatically added, with the name of the Class (see Figure 11.15).

Now the code for each of the Class's methods must be created. Click the Cube tab to see four new tabs—one for each Method, as shown in Figure 11.16.

Code the Methods

The Methods for this program are as follows: SetSide(NewSide),

    ComputeVolume(Side), GetVolume(Volume), and GetSide().

Figure 11.15 The new Cube Class

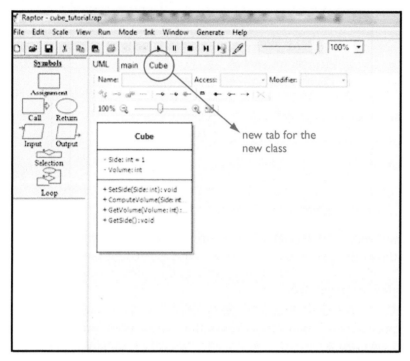

Figure 11.16 New tabs for each new Method of the Cube Class

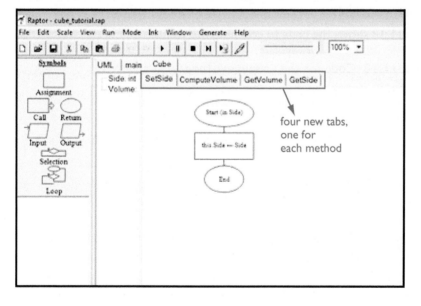

SetSide()Method: The SetSide() Method does one thing only. It sets the variable representing the side of a cube (Side) to the value passed from the main program using the parameter NewSide. This assignment is done using the **this** keyword. The code for this method is shown in Figure 11.17.

Figure 11.17 Code for the SetSide() Method

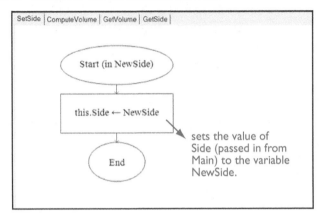

ComputeVolume(Side) **Method**: The ComputeVolume(Side) Method computes the volume of the cube. First, it must receive the value needed for the computation (Side). Then, it must do the computation by cubing the value. Finally, it needs to export this result when requested.

Let's take a moment to discuss the **this keyword** that is shown in Figure 11.17. Here it precedes the variable Side. While there are some differences in specific ways the this keyword is used in various languages, this normally refers to the current object, that is, the object whose method or property is being called. In Figure 11.17 this refers to the value of Side from the object of class Cube that will be passed in. The value of Side will be assigned to the variable NewSide, a value used in the SetSide() method.

Figure 11.18 shows the code to compute the volume.

Figure 11.18 Code for the ComputeVolume() Method

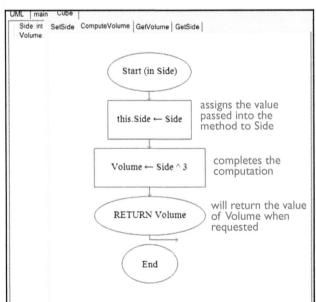

GetVolume(Volume**) Method:** The GetVolume(Volume) method retrieves the value of Volume when it is accessed and then returns it, as shown in Figure 11.19.

GetSide() Method: The GetSide() method retrieves the value of Side when it is accessed, as shown in Figure 11.20.

Figure 11.19 Code for the GetVolume() method

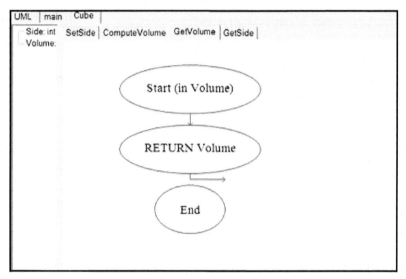

Figure 11.20 Code for the GetSide() method

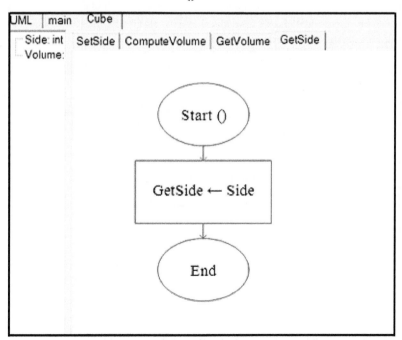

The `main` Program

Now the `main` program can be created. The program for this example is extremely simple; it will allow the user to enter a value for the side of a cube, compute the volume of that cube, and display the result. This is accomplished by instantiating (creating) an object of type `Cube`, which we will call `CubeOne`, and using the methods and attributes of `Cube`. Figure 11.21 shows how this is done the RAPTOR OOP way.

Inheritance and Polymorphism

Once you have mastered the basics: creating `Classes`, `Fields`, and `Methods`, and using dot notation in your program, you can use the OOP mode in RAPTOR to create and run more complicated programs. We will see how inheritance and polymorphism work in the Monster Evasion program, created next.

Figure 11.21 Code to input a side of a cube and output its volume

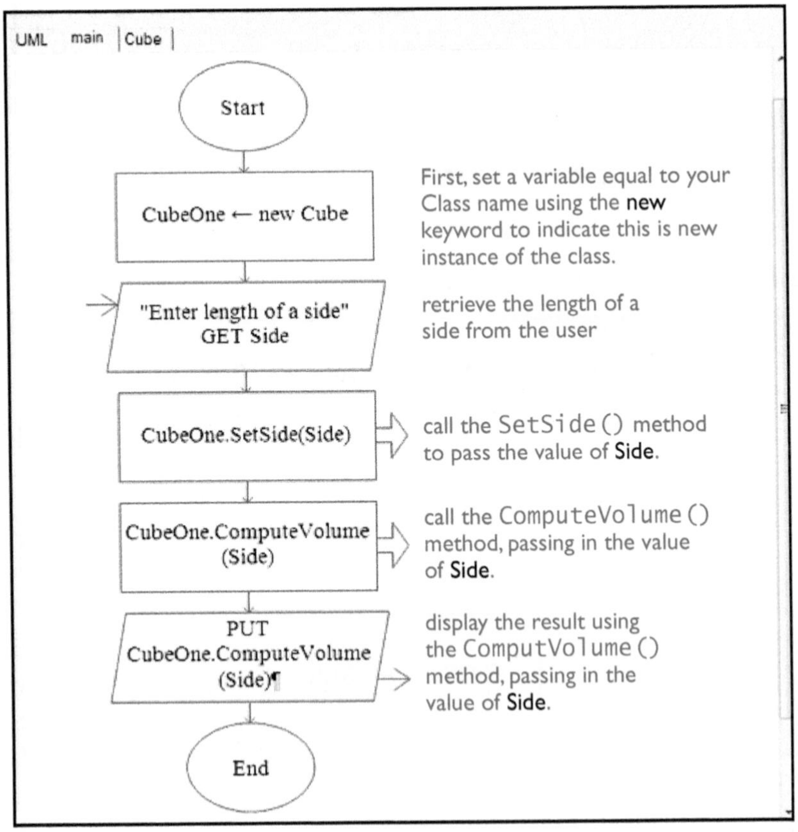

Run It: Monster Evasion

In this section, we will develop a short RAPTOR program that uses a parent class and two subclasses. We focus on creating the classes with their attributes (Fields) and methods to see how child classes inherit from the parent rather than focusing on complex programming logic. The program is designed to give you a taste of how OOP is used in a much larger software project such as creating an adventure game.

Problem Statement

Let's pretend we are developing an online adventure game. The players work their way through a forest where monsters lurk. We have been tasked with developing a module that forces the players to pick a direction to continue in the game. The players will meet their ends if any of three directions (north, south, west) are chosen and will only survive if the players choose to go east. A monster will be encountered if north, south, or west is chosen but the type of monster will depend on which direction is chosen. We need to create three monsters. However, because we understand that this little subprogram is part of a much bigger game program where many types of monsters may be utilized, we will use OOP concepts to develop a Monster class and allow two child classes to inherit from Monster while adding their own methods to make them different monster types.

Developing and Creating the Program

First, we need to determine the classes we need and their members. We already decided to have a Monster parent class and we will also include two child classes, which will be called Goblin and Harpie. For this program we will keep things simple; you can add more subclasses with more members to extend this program if you want.

For now, we will stick with only a few methods: to show the type of monster, the sound it makes, and the way it attacks. To demonstrate how inheritance and polymorphism work in a real program, we will allow the Goblin and Harpie child classes to inherit some methods from Monster but use their own methods for other things.

Before we begin to design the classes we'll give a very simplistic model of what this program will do, without any classes or OOP programming. It is shown in Figure 11.22.

Creating the Classes

To create this program, first open a new RAPTOR program and be sure to change the Mode to Object-oriented. Save the file with the filename monsters.rap. Now we can begin to create the classes and their methods. Click on the UML tab to start.

The Monster parent class

Create a new class named Monster and add four Methods. Each Method is created by clicking on the little pink diamond and entering the appropriate information. Our Monster class will have four methods, all of Type void, all with Public Access, and

Figure 11.22 General flowchart for the Monster Evasion Game

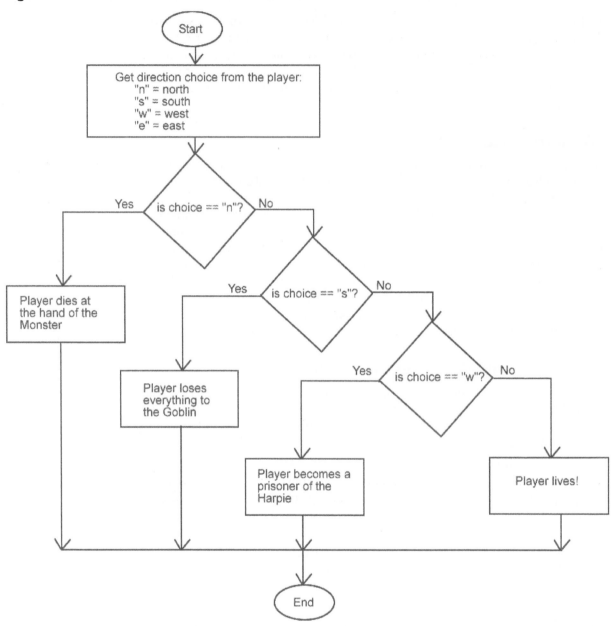

no Modifiers. At this introductory level, we do not need to concern ourselves with these options. The following Methods should be created:

- showMonsterType() will display the type of Monster in the program
- showMonsterStuff() will display information about an instance of Monster
- makeSound() will display a sound made by an instance of Monster
- Attack() will display the way this class of Monster attacks

When you are done, the Members of Monster window should look as shown:

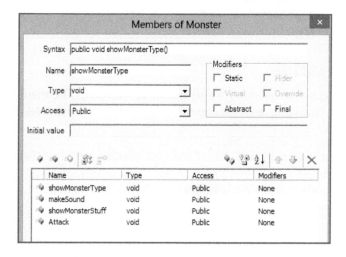

The Goblin child class

Create a new class named Goblin and add two Methods. The methods are of Type void, all with Public Access, and no Modifiers. The following Methods should be created:

- showMonsterType() will display the type of monster (a Goblin) in the program
- makeSound() will display a sound made by an instance of Goblin

The Goblin class will inherit the showMonsterStuff() and Attack() Methods from Monster but will use its own Methods for showMonsterType() (since it is a different type of monster) and makeSound() (since it makes a different sound). When you are done, the Members of Goblin window should look as shown:

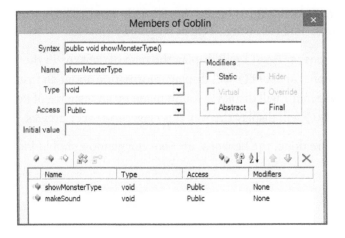

The Harpie child class

Create a new class named Harpie and add three Methods. The methods are of Type void, all with Public Access, and no Modifiers. The following Methods should be created:

- showMonsterType() will display the type of monster (a Harpie) in the program
- makeSound() will display a sound made by an instance of Harpie
- Attack() will display the way an instance of Harpie attacks

The Harpie class will inherit the showMonsterStuff() Method from Monster but will use its own Methods for showMonsterType() (since it is a different type of monster), makeSound() (since it makes a different sound), and Attack() (since it does not attack the same way as its parent class). When you are done, the Members of Harpie window should look as shown:

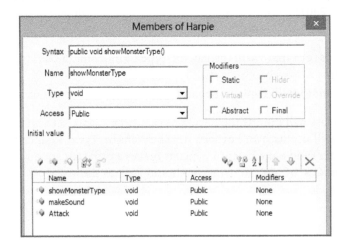

At this point your UML window should look as shown below. Use the New Association tool to show that the two child classes inherit from the parent class.

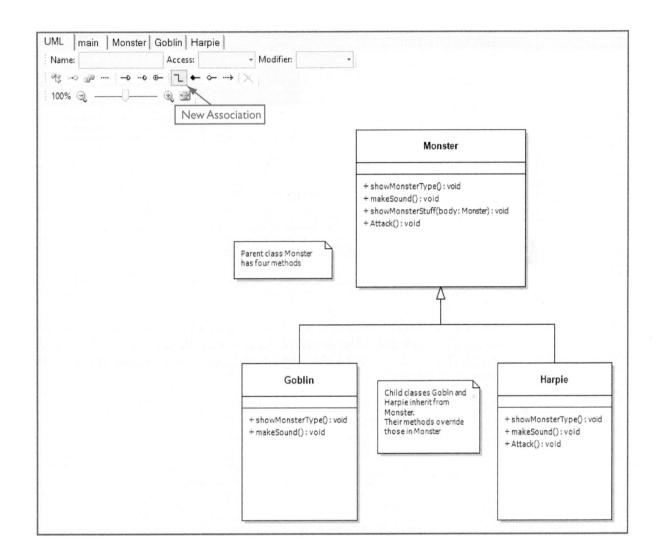

The main program

We can now begin creating the program. We need one String variable to hold the value of the player's choice of direction which we will call direction. Then we must create three class variables to hold an instance of each class object. We will call these oneMonster, oneGoblin, and oneHarpie. These variables are created in main as shown:

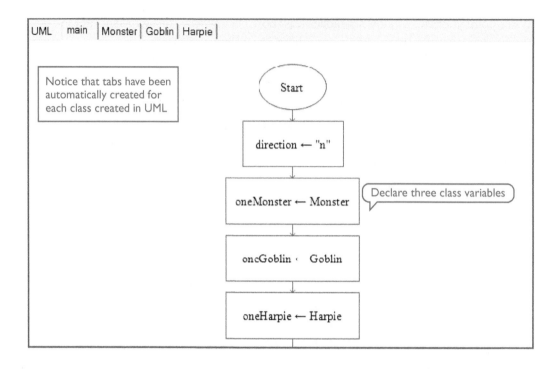

Now we will instantiate (create) a `Monster` object, a `Goblin` object, and a `Harpie` object. This code goes directly under the class variable declarations that we just created. To do this we set the class variable to an instance of the class using the `new` keyword, as shown:

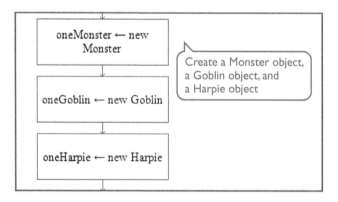

We'll use nested `Selection` symbols to create the program (see Figure 11.22 for the overall logic for this structure). The program will consist of a prompt for the player to enter a direction and, depending on the player's entry, information about one of the monsters will be displayed or, if the player is lucky, information about survival will be displayed. The following images display the `Output` boxes and `Calls` for each direction. You can, of course, create your own text for more interesting output. Then we will concentrate on what happens when each `Monster` object is called.

If the player chooses the northern route:

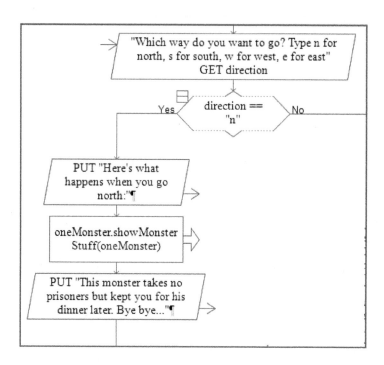

If the player chooses the southern route:

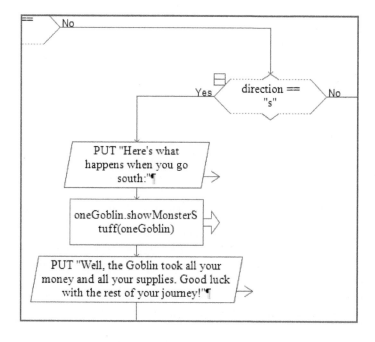

If the player chooses the western or eastern route:

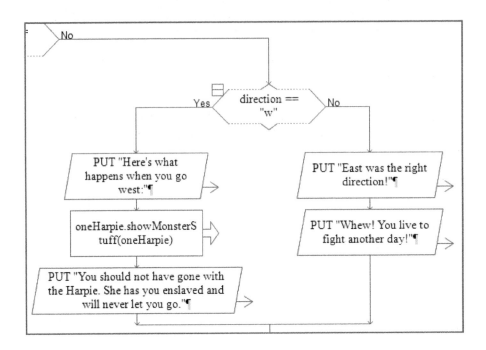

The entire selection structure in the main program is shown here:

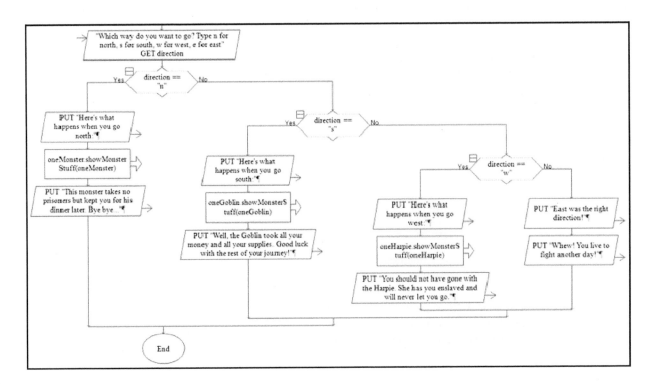

Using the Classes

This part can be somewhat difficult to understand. Therefore, we will discuss how the object-oriented aspects of this program work when each class is accessed.

A generic Monster object is called when the player chooses the northern route:

When the Call goes out to oneMonster.showMonsterStuff(oneMonster) the Monster class is accessed. If you click on the Monster subchart in RAPTOR, you will see that four new subcharts have been created, one for each Monster Method.

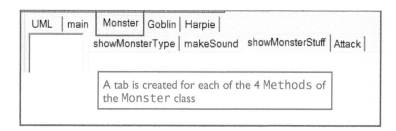

The Call is to the showMonsterStuff() Method so, if you click on that subchart you should create Calls to the three other Methods of the Monster class. In our program, we want to first display the type of monster so the first Call is to the showMonster-Type() method. But notice that showMonsterStuff has one parameter, which is named body. This parameter receives the argument that is sent in with the original Call. In the case of the northern route (the player enters "n"), the Call sends in oneMonster as its argument. Previously we have created oneMonster as an object of the Monster class. From now on, while the program is accessing Monster Methods, body refers to oneMonster. This why the Call to showMonsterType() uses dot notation and the following syntax to say, in effect, "apply the showMonsterType() method to oneMonster:

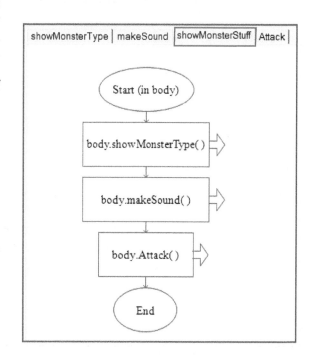

    body.showMonsterType()

We also want to display the sound this monster makes so the next Call is to the makeSound() Method, using body to identify the oneMonster instance of the Monster class. Similarly, we call the Attack() Method third to display how this monster will attack the player. The code for the showMonsterStuff() Method, therefore, is as shown to the right.

The next thing that happens in this program is that the `showMonsterType()` Method is accessed, once again, using `body` to identify the `oneMonster` object. This `Method`, in our simplified program will merely display a message about what this monster is. It is as shown:

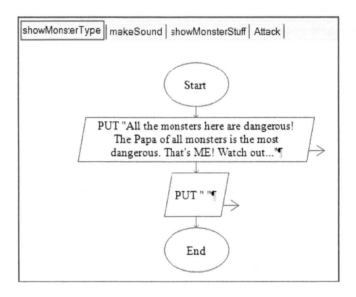

In this program, the `makeSound()` and `Attack()` Methods will also contain only text to be displayed on the screen. For the `Monster` class, the RAPTOR code for these methods is as shown:

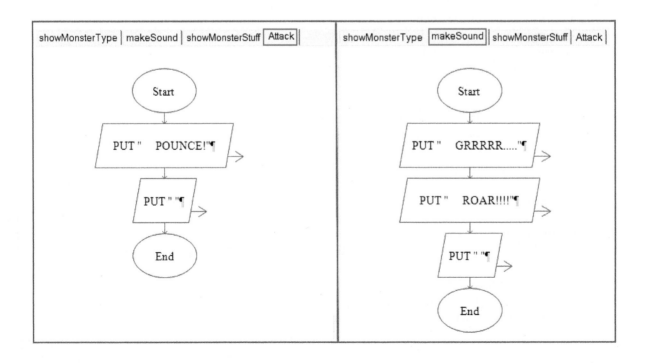

Thus, if the player chooses the northern route, the display will reflect everything we have programmed into the `Monster` `class` `Methods`. This will not be the case for any of the other routes.

A Goblin object is called when the player chooses the southern route

When the player enters "s" for the direction, after the initial output (see the "Yes" option in the `Selection` statement that checks for `direction == "s"`), a `Call` goes out to `oneGoblin.showMonsterStuff(oneGoblin)` and the `Monster` class is accessed once more. However, since `oneGoblin` has been defined as an object of the `Goblin` child class, the `oneGoblin` argument gets passed to the `body` parameter. Then the `Calls` to `showMonsterType()` and `makeSound()` in `showMonsterStuff()` now refer to `Goblin` `Methods`. If you click on the `Goblin` subchart in RAPTOR you will see that there are only two subcharts (`showMonsterType` and `makeSound`). This is because we created the `Goblin` child class with only two `Methods`. The `showMonsterStuff` subchart uses the `showMonsterType()` and `makeSound()` `Methods` of the `Goblin` class but uses the `Attack()` `Method` of the `Monster` class (since there is no `Attack()` method in `Goblin`).

The two `Methods` of `Goblin` have been coded as follows:

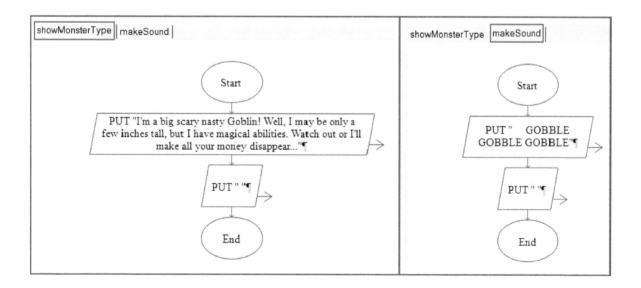

A Harpie object is called when the player chooses the western route

When the player enters "w" for the direction, after the initial output (see the "Yes" option in the `Selection` statement that checks for `direction == "w"`), a `Call` goes out to `oneHarpie.showMonsterStuff(oneHarpie)` and the `Monster` class is accessed again but, because `oneHarpie` has been defined as an object of the `Harpie` child class, the oneHarpie argument gets passed to the body parameter. Then the Calls to showMonsterType() and makeSound(), and Attack() in showMonsterStuff() now refer to Harpie Methods. If you click on the Harpie subchart in RAPTOR, you will see that this time there are three subcharts (showMonsterType, makeSound, and Attack). This is because we created the Harpie child class with three Methods. The showMonsterStuff subchart uses all three Harpie Methods when it receives a parameter, which is a Harpie object.

The Harpie Methods have been coded as follows:

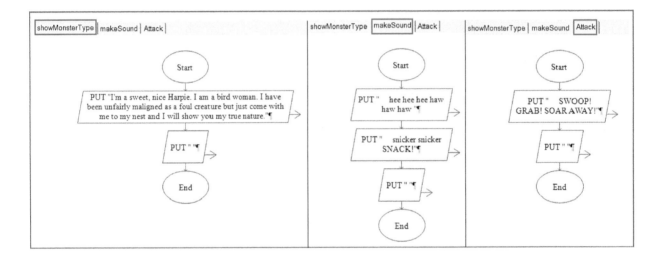

No object is called if the player chooses the eastern route

This program purposely does not include any error checking or validation so that the focus can remain on the use of classes, objects, and the new concepts of object-oriented programming introduced in this chapter. Thus, we must assume that the player enters valid data. Of course, if the player enters anything other than "n", "s", or "w" when prompted for direction, the last option will occur and, luckily for this player, he or she will not encounter a monster. It is up to you, if you create this program, to flesh it out with more attributes (Fields) for the monsters, error checking, and any other additions you care to make.

Check It Out

If you have created the program as given in this section, the following images show what the output should be in each circumstance.

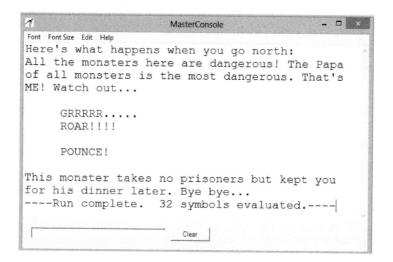

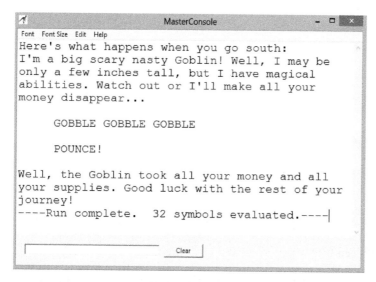

MasterConsole

Font   Font Size   Edit   Help

Here's what happens when you go west:
I'm a sweet, nice Harpie. I am a bird woman. I
have been unfairly maligned as a foul creature
but just come with me to my nest and I will
show you my true nature.

        hee hee hee haw haw haw
        snicker snicker SNACK!

        SWOOP! GRAB! SOAR AWAY!

You should not have gone with the Harpie. She
has you enslaved and will never let you go.
----Run complete.   34 symbols evaluated.----

Clear

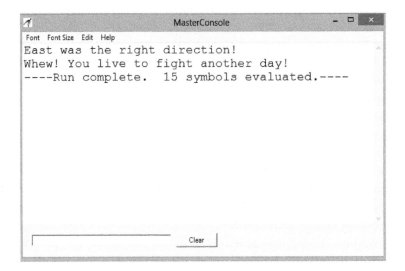

Chapter Review and Exercises

Key Terms

access methods
attribute
base class
check box
child or derived class
class (of objects)
command button
constructor
data hiding
default values
derived class
dot notation
drop-down list
dynamic behavior view
encapsulation
extends (as a derived class extends a
   parent class)
event
event handlers
event procedures
GUI
graphical user interface
inheritance

instance
instantiate (an object)
instantiation
label
list box
member
methods (of a class)
object
object-oriented programming (OOP)
option button
parent or base class
polymorphism
primitive data type
private (member)
procedural programming
protected (member)
public (member)
radio button
static structural view
text box
this keyword
Unified Modeling Language (UML)
window

Chapter Summary

In this chapter, we have discussed the following topics:

1. Classes and objects:
   - A class is a data type that defines a structure consisting of attributes (data) and methods (procedures).
   - An object is an instance of a class.
   - Classes follow a hierarchy in that a child (or derived) class can utilize the methods and attributes of parent (or base) classes. When a child class is declared, we say it extends the parent class.
   - Each class contains at least one constructor which is used to set default or other values to ensure validity.

2. Characteristics of an object-oriented programming language:
   - Encapsulation is the combining of data and operations on that data into a single package.
   - Inheritance is the ability to create a child (derived) class that automatically contains the attributes and methods of its parent (base) class.
   - Polymorphism is the ability to use several variations of a method with objects of different subclasses.

3. Object-oriented program design (specifically to analyze a problem):
   - Identify the classes to be used in the program.
   - Determine the attributes needed for these classes.
   - Determine the methods needed for these classes.
   - Determine the relationships among the classes.

4. Unified Modeling Language (UML) has been developed as an industry standard to aid in the creation of sophisticated, complex software.

5. Objects in a graphical user interface as follows:
   - `windows` act as containers for other objects.
   - `command buttons`, `check boxes`, `text boxes`, `option` (or `radio`) `buttons`, `list` (or `selection`) `boxes` are all objects.

6. A GUI object:
   - Properties (attributes) include `name`, `caption`, `value`, `enabled`/`disabled`, and so forth.
   - Methods include responding to a click and other events generated either by the user or the program.

7. Event-driven programming:
   - Respond to user or system events (actions).
   - Designed like an OOP program with the emphasis on the `windows` needed to solve a given problem.

Review Questions

Fill in the Blank

1. A(n) _____ is a data type that is made up of attributes and methods.

2. A(n) _____ is an instance of a class.

3. The property of OOP that refers to the incorporation of data and operations into a single unit is called _____.

4. The property of OOP that allows the creation of new classes based on existing ones is called _____.

5. The property of OOP that allows variations of a method to be applied to objects of different classes is called _____.

6. When a subclass is created based on an existing class, the original class is called the _____ or _____ and the new class is called the _____ or _____.

7. The _____ initializes an object's attributes and establishes the conditions that do not change in the class.

8. The industry standard for system modeling is _____.

9. The GUI object most commonly used to select a single option is a(n) _____ _____.

10. The GUI object most commonly used to allow the user to initiate an action is a _____ button.

True or False

11. T F One attribute of a command button object is its name.

12. T F The methods of an object are the operations that can be performed on that object's data.

13. T F Attributes are also known as subprograms, procedures, or functions.

14. T F Methods are also known as subprograms, procedures, or functions.

15. T F When contrasted to OOP, the approach to programming that uses top-down, modular program design is called procedural programming.

16. T F In designing an object-oriented program, the emphasis is placed on the procedures, rather than on the objects, needed to solve a given problem.

17. T F The attributes of objects that make up a GUI are also called properties.

18. T F All window components have the same attributes.

19. T F From a programming point of view, clicking a command button is considered an event.

20. T F The programming language supplies the code for the action that takes place when the user clicks a command button.

Short Answer

For Exercises 21–34 refer to the following pseudocode, which defines a class called Square *and its child class,* Rectangle.

```
Class Square
  Declare Protected Side, Area As Float
  Public Square()
    Set Side = 1.0
    Set Area = 1.0
  End Constructor
  Public Subprogram SetSide(NewSide)
    Set Side = NewSide
  End Subprogram
  Public Subprogram ComputeArea()
    Set Area = Side^2
  End Subprogram
  Public Function GetArea() As Float
    Set GetArea = Area
  End Function
  Public Function GetSide() As Float
    Set GetSide = Side
  End Function
End Class
Class Rectangle Extends Square
  Declare Private Height As Float
  Public Rectangle()
    Call Square()
    Set Height = 1.0
  End Constructor
  Public Subprogram SetHeight(NewHeight)
    Set Height = NewHeight
  End Subprogram
  Public Function GetHeight() As Float
    Set GetHeight = Height
  End Function
  Public Subprogram ComputeArea()
    Set Area = Side * Height
  End Subprogram
End Class
```

21. List the attributes of the class Square.

22. Give the names of the methods of the class Square.

23. Suppose Square1 is an object of the class Square and the statement

    ```
    Call Square1.ComputeArea()
    ```

    appears in the main program. Which formula for area is used in the execution of the subprogram ComputeArea()?

24. Suppose Rectangle1 is an object of the class Rectangle and the statement

    Call Rectangle1.ComputeArea()

    appears in the main program. Which formula for area is used in the execution of the subprogram ComputeArea()?

25. Create an instance of the class Square and reference it with the name MySquare.

For Exercises 26–28 refer to the object, MySquare, *created in Exercise 25 and the pseudocode given prior to Exercise 21.*

26. Write the statement that would be used in the main program to set the length of the side of MySquare equal to 20.

27. Write the statement that would be used in the main program to compute the area of MySquare.

28. Write the statement that would be used in the main program to display the area of MySquare.

29. List *all* attributes of an object in the class Rectangle.

30. List *all* methods of an object in the class Rectangle.

31. Create an instance of the class, Rectangle and reference it with the name MyRectangle.

For Exercises 32–34 refer to the object, MyRectangle, *created in Exercise 31 and the pseudocode given prior to Exercise 21.*

32. Write the statement that would be used in the main program to set the length of the side of MyRectangle equal to 15 and the height equal to 25.

33. Write the statement that would be used in the main program to compute the area of MyRectangle.

34. Write the statement that would be used in the main program to display the area of MyRectangle.

35. For the window shown in Figure 11.23 give the captions or labels for each of the following:
    a. text box(es)
    b. label object(s)

36. In the window shown in Figure 11.23 which option button is selected?

Figure 11.23 The window for Exercises 35 and 36

37. List three properties of a window.

38. List three properties common to command buttons, option buttons, and text boxes.

39. Write a subprogram called Abutton.Click() that sets the text in a text box named Text1 equal to "Hello" and grays out a command button named Bbutton.

40. Write a subprogram called OKbutton.Click() that opens a window named Window1 or a window named Window2, depending on whether option buttons named Option1 or Option2, respectively, contain a bullet.

41. Write a subprogram called Option1.Click() that places a bullet in an option button named Option1 and removes the bullet from an option button named Option2.

42. Write a subprogram called EnterButton.Click() that adds the number in a text box named NumberBox to a variable, Sum, and then clears the text box.

Programming Challenges

For Challenges 1 and 2, use pseudocode to write an object-oriented program that consists of a class definition and a main program to solve the given problem. RAPTOR can be used for Programming Challenges 1–4 but may require some advanced study of RAPTOR's OOP mode.

1. Write a program that inputs (from the user) the number of hours worked and hourly pay rate for employees and outputs their total pay. The program should process an arbitrary number of employees; the user will terminate input by entering 0 for hours worked and pay rate. Use a class called Worker with

   • Attributes: Hours, Rate, Total
   • Methods: ComputeTotal() and access methods (SetHours(), GetHours(), SetRate(), GetRate(), SetTotal(), and GetTotal()) for each of the attributes

2. Write a program that displays the income tax due in the state of Euphoria on a taxable income (in whole dollars) entered by the user, according to the tax table shown in Table 11.1.

Table 11.1 Tax table

| | Taxable Income | |
From	To	Tax Due
$0	$49,999	$0 + 5% of amount over $0
$50,000	$99,999	$2,500 + 7% of amount over $50,000
$100,000	...	$6,000 + 9% of amount over $100,000

The program should allow the user to enter a series of incomes, terminated by 0. Use a class called Tax, with attributes Income and TaxDue and methods that include ComputeTax() and access methods (SetIncome(), GetIncome(), SetTaxDue(), and GetTaxDue()) for each of the attributes.

3. Rewrite the two classes in the Parking Lot program of Section 11.2 to include an email attribute (`Email`) and its associated access methods (`SetEmail()` and `GetEmail()`). The `Email` attribute and access methods should be included in the `Person` class and available to the three derived classes, `Faculty`, `Staff`, and `Student`.

4. Everyone at OOPU gets assigned a college email account. The account is created using a simple formula. The email username is simply the person's first name and last name, separated by a dot. Then the OOPU domain name is appended with the @ sign. The OOPU domain name is `oopu.edu`. Rewrite the classes you created in Programming Challenge 3 to include a method to create an email address by using the `Name` attribute and concatenating it with the string "`@oopu.edu`" instead of having the user enter an email address.

   • The attribute you will need to add is `EmailAddress`.
   • The method you will need to add is `CreateEmail()`.
   • Some sample OOPU email addresses follow:
       • `Elizabeth.Drake@oopu.edu`
       • `Stewart.Venit@oopu.edu`
       • `Hermione.Crabbe@oopu.edu`

For Programming Challenges 5 and 6, use pseudocode to write an event-driven program according to the given specifications using the information covered in Section 11.4.

5. Using the `window` shown in Figure 11.24, write a temperature conversion program. To use this program, the user selects an option, types a temperature into the appropriate `text` box, and clicks the "`Convert`" command button. The corresponding temperature then appears in the other `text` box. Clicking the "`Done`" button should end the program.

   Use the following formulas for the conversions:
   • convert Fahrenheit to Celsius: `C = 5 * (F - 32) / 9`
   • convert Celsius to Fahrenheit: `F = 9 * C / 5 + 32`

Figure 11.24 The `window` for Programming Challenge 5

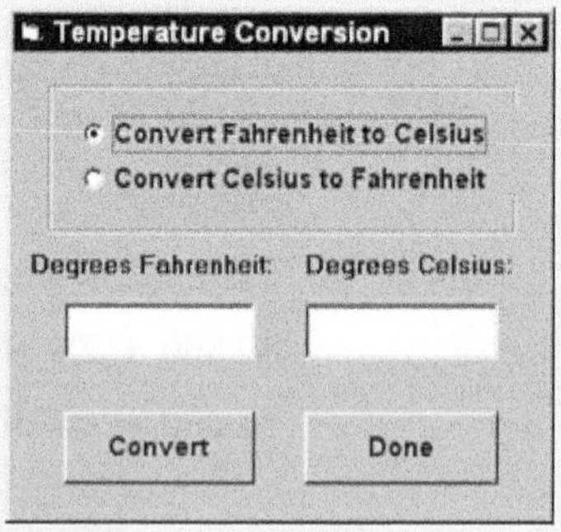

6. Write a program that displays the names of students in a certain class, one by one, and allows the user to enter a test score for the student displayed. The students' names and scores are contained in one-dimensional arrays called Names and Scores, respectively. Assume that both arrays have already been declared and that the Names array contains N entries.

The window for this program is shown in Figure 11.25. When the program starts, the first student's name is displayed in the upper text box. The user types the test score for that student in the lower text box and clicks the "Enter" button. This action assigns this value to the first element of the Scores array, displays the next name in the upper text box, and empties the lower text box so that the next score can be entered. When all the students' scores have been entered (and assigned to corresponding elements in Scores), the window closes automatically and the program terminates.

Figure 11.25 The window for Programming Challenge 6

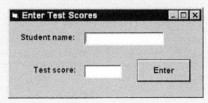

Study Skills

A.1 Achieving Success in the Course

Many students think programming courses are very difficult. There are new concepts to learn and at times the material can be confusing or intimidating. But learning programming can pay huge future dividends. You will gain skills that are useful in other courses and abilities that may lead to a rewarding career.

The following list includes ways to increase your chances for success in this course:

- **Attend every class and be on time.** Programming is difficult to learn if you miss even the occasional class. If you miss a class, borrow another student's notes and seek help in learning the material if necessary.

- **Ask questions.** Instructors welcome questions. If you have a question, it is likely that other students are confused by the same issue. If you don't ask for clarification of something that confuses you, you may not understand the rest of the lecture.

- **Take extensive notes.** At the very least, take down everything your instructor writes on the board or projects on the screen. Even if you get lost, keep writing. If you need help later you'll be able to point to specific places in your notes that need clarification. Your class notes will be invaluable as you review the material and prepare for tests.

- **Read the textbook.** The textbook is a valuable supplement to your instructor's lectures. As you read the textbook, work through the examples. The concrete process of solving problems instead of simply reading about them is invaluable. The examples summarize important points and provide the answers to many questions.

- **Before coming to class, read the section or sections that your instructor plans to cover in that lecture.** Even if you don't understand everything, keep reading. You will be surprised at how the material you read before class will make sense as your instructor covers that material.

- **Do the homework.** Homework helps you master the material or reveals that you need additional help.

- **Don't procrastinate.** Many instructors assign relatively complex programming projects with a generous schedule. Begin these projects as soon as possible so that you have ample time to get your questions answered and to deal with the inevitable problems that arise.

- **Study conscientiously.**   Tests provide a means for the instructor to evaluate your work and they give you a comprehensive review of the material.
- **Ask for help.**   It's important that you don't fall behind. In programming, each topic builds on previous ones. A topic covered today is a building block that may be crucial to understanding the rest of the course. If you don't understand something, get help as soon as possible from your instructor, a classmate, or a knowledgeable friend or family member.
- **Don't be shy!**   If you don't understand a specific point it's fairly certain that other students have the same question. Once one or two brave students ask questions, other students will be more comfortable about asking questions, which will make the entire class experience more valuable. Be brave!

A.2 Using the Textbook

Sometimes students try to get through a course without reading the required textbook. You're reading this page so you're obviously not one of them! Textbooks may seem intimidating, and to a generation raised with computers, not particularly user-friendly. On the other hand, students often print out material from online sources because they find it helpful to have explanations on paper as they work on the computer.

By using the textbook, you can jot down notes as appropriate, highlight important passages, and easily refer to concepts you may need to do the assignments. If you consistently read the textbook, you will know where things are in the book, and this will make it easy to find the information when you need it to complete homework for this and subsequent programming courses. Putting little post-a-notes on important pages is often helpful. Reading the textbook and carefully walking through the examples can greatly improve your chances of success in the course.

- Reading a textbook is not as easy as reading a magazine. You have to read a textbook more slowly and carefully than a novel or magazine. At first, some definitions, examples, or explanations might not make sense. You may have to read them several times until the idea is clear. And sometimes concepts will remain unclear despite rereading. Often, walking through an example that accompanies a concept will clarify it, but sometimes you will have to ask for help.
- As you read, highlight definitions, facts, explanations of statements, and other information that you think is important. This will help you review the material, especially when preparing for tests.
- Some students find that to grasp certain concepts, it's helpful first to read a relevant example and then go back, if necessary, to the explanation of the general concept. Discover if this approach works for you.
- After you finish reading a section in this textbook, try the Self Checks to see if you fully understand the concepts. If you have trouble with a particular exercise, return to the relevant explanation or example within the section for clarification.
- If your instructor is using RAPTOR in this course, it will be very helpful if you create the RAPTOR programs given in each section. Follow the

instructions in the chapter and test your programs. You should also try to create many of the examples throughout the book in RAPTOR. These will help you with assigned RAPTOR homework.

- Read the Key Terms and Chapter Summary to refresh your memory about the concepts covered in the chapter. To use the Key Terms to their best advantage, write your own definition for each of them.

- Answer the Review Questions at the end of the chapter even if they haven't been assigned. As with the Self Checks, the Review Questions will help you identify topics that are unclear.

- Use the textbook for reference purposes as well. If you've forgotten something or want more information about a certain topic, use the Index to locate the relevant material in the textbook.

A.3 Doing the Homework

One of the keys to success in any course, and especially in a programming course, is to complete the assigned homework on time. The only way you can really learn to program is by conscientiously doing the homework assignments and programming projects.

- Do your homework as soon as possible after the class in which it is assigned, while the corresponding material is still fresh in your mind.

- Do your homework where there are no distractions. It may seem less painful to do your homework in front of the TV or while listening to music, but you won't be able to concentrate as well, and even if you're able to complete an assignment, you won't gain as much from the learning process.

- If you can't answer a homework question, return to the relevant section in your notes or textbook. The answer is almost certainly there.

- If you get stuck on a programming problem, look for a similar problem in your notes or textbook. Often instructors choose homework problems that have the same basic structure as those covered in class or in the textbook.

- If you have trouble with a problem, it may be because you've forgotten or never really learned an earlier concept. You may have to review the relevant material. Many students are reluctant to do this, but it's worth the time and effort. If you don't get the concept correct now, in all likelihood it will cause you trouble in the future.

- If, after trying the prior suggestions, you still can't solve a problem, it's time to ask for help. Many instructors invite students to ask questions about the homework at the beginning of the next class. If so, avail yourself of the opportunity. There is no shame in asking your instructor (or anyone else) for help.

- Instructors have office hours specifically to help students. Make use of this time—it is for you! However, when you go to an instructor during office hours, be sure you have specific questions in mind. It is not helpful to simply say, "I don't understand the material." Your instructor has explained the concepts in a way he or she believes is clear. The authors of the textbook have written the material in a manner they believe will make it clear. But if something is still puzzling to you, you must be able to tell your instructor exactly what is giving you trouble.

- Organize your completed homework assignments in a separate notebook. They will be invaluable when preparing for tests.

A.4 Writing Programs

In this course and in future programming courses, you will write programs. Often students find that writing a suitable program to solve a given problem is a difficult and frustrating task. It is not a mechanical process, such as solving an algebraic equation. In algebra you can follow a simple step-by-step procedure. Although computer programs contain certain structures with specific steps, writing a program is a creative process. There are almost always several ways to solve a programming problem. Some are cumbersome; some are elegant. Eventually, you will find your own programming style, but the following suggestions will make the task of writing a program a little easier for you in the beginning:

- The first thing you must realize when you begin to create a program to solve a given problem is that there is no formula to follow! Often you can use pieces of code from other examples but you will almost always have to do some independent thinking. You can't just find the solution—you can find helpful ideas, but you will most likely have to do some creative thinking on your own. Keep this in mind at all times.
- Before you attempt to create a design for a program or write the program itself, be sure you are familiar with the concepts that are needed in its construction. Do you know the function of the statements that you'll have to use? Do you understand the concepts that have been recently introduced? Have you understood the examples that illustrate these statements and concepts? If you answer "no" to any of these questions you should return to the relevant part of your notes or textbook and reread the material.
- The closest thing there is to a step-by-step procedure for writing programs is the program development cycle. The first phase of this process tells you how to get started: look at the problem description and determine what you need to accomplish—the program's output. Then determine the given information—the program's input. Finally, and this is often the hard part, try to figure out what formulas or algorithms are needed to proceed from the given input to the desired output. This analysis will lead you to identify the three basic building blocks of your program—input, processing, and output.
- The input and output portions of the program are usually straightforward, but the processing part may be somewhat complicated. If so, follow the principle of modular programming and break it into pieces that are easier to handle.
- What do you do if you get stuck? (Most people *do* get stuck at one point or another.) Here are a couple of ways to get "unstuck." Try to find a similar

problem in your notes or textbook that has already been solved. Often, you can figure out how to solve a problem by relating it to one that you have seen before. If this doesn't work, ask your instructor, a classmate, or a friend for help (assuming that asking for help is allowed).

- Once you have written what you think is a suitable program, how can you tell if it works properly? In a course that uses an actual programming language, you could execute the program and check that it runs successfully, producing the desired results. In this course, you should *desk check* your program. Pretend that you are the computer and execute the statements one by one, supplying appropriate input data when needed, to see if everything works as planned. This is also a good way to test a program design regardless of whether you are writing pseudocode or writing a program in an actual programming language.

- If you are using RAPTOR for homework problems you can test your programs by running them. However, keep in mind that a program that works correctly with one set of data (input) may not work with all data. Make a list of possible input that might cause problems when the program is executed. Then run your program several times, trying all of these options for input. Your instructor will probably not only try to run your program; it is likely that he or she will try to *break* your program. For example, if you are writing a program that finds the average of several numbers, more often than not, your instructor will make sure you have taken the possibility of a division by zero error into account.

A.5 Preparing for Tests

In a programming course, the subject matter builds upon itself. As a result, topics are interrelated, making it difficult to cram for a test. Therefore, you should begin to prepare for tests at the beginning of the course rather than a week or night before the test. Plan to attend every class, be conscientious about doing the homework, and stay current with the course material. Nevertheless, even if you do all these things, in order to do well you must prepare for a test as follows:

- Be sure that you know what topics are included on the test. Don't get blind-sided by a question you weren't prepared for because you didn't realize the topic would be included.

- Know what materials, if any, you may use during the test. For example, will the test be open book? Will you be allowed to consult your notes, or will you have to memorize all the facts?

- As you prepare for a test, an effective first step is to review your notes and the relevant textbook sections. Create study sheets from pieces of notebook paper or study cards from index cards. Jot down definitions, statements, facts, and other information you'll need to know for the test. Even if you are not allowed to bring materials (books or notes) to a test, as you study, pretend that you are allowed to bring one sheet of paper with notes. Prepare this one sheet, as if you could bring it to the test. You may begin by writing as many notes as you think you need to do well on the test. Then rewrite the material as necessary so it will fit on a single sheet of paper. As you rewrite, you will be reviewing and organizing the required topics and you may find that, after completing the process, you don't even need the study sheet because you have learned all the material.

- Review the homework assignments that pertain to the upcoming test. Make sure you can work the assigned problems. Some instructor's pattern tests after the homework, but even if your instructor doesn't, checking homework is a good way to review the kinds of problems you may encounter on the test.

- Anticipate the kinds of problems that may appear in the test. What types of problems were covered in class and in the homework? Did your instructor emphasize particular kinds of problems? In previous exams, did your instructor use problems that appeared as examples in class, within the book, or in the homework?

- If the test covers topics that have appeared in previous tests or projects, be sure to review this material. If you have lost points in these earlier tests or projects, make sure that you understand your errors so that you don't make the same mistakes twice.

- If you are not allowed to use your notes or textbook during the test, with the help of your study sheets or study cards, memorize everything you might need to recall when you take the test.

A.6 More about Preparing for Tests

The following questions relate to preparing for tests. None of these questions has a simple answer.

- **Should I join (or form) a study group to prepare for a test?**   Many students find that studying in groups enables them to do better on tests. Students in the group can explain things that you don't understand, help you with problems that you can't solve, test you to see if you're ready for a test, and supply moral support. On the other hand, some students find that study groups are not an effective way to spend their limited time. You will have to decide if it's beneficial for you to study with a group. Most likely the answer will depend on how your personality and abilities mesh with those of the others in the group.

- **When should I start studying for an upcoming test?**   The answer depends primarily on how well you've been keeping up with the course material and how conscientiously you've been doing the homework assignments. You have to estimate how much review it will take to master the material covered on the test. If you're not completely comfortable with all the test topics, then don't wait until the night before the test to begin studying. Learning programming concepts requires a lot of time and effort.

- **Do I have to study for an "open book" test?**   Some programming instructors allow students to use the textbook during a test. This is a mixed blessing for students. On the plus side, if you forget something, you can look it up. However, each time you do, you use valuable time. Therefore, you should prepare for an open book test the same way you would for any test, including memorizing all necessary facts. And make sure that you have used the textbook often enough so you know where topics are discussed in the book. You can't afford the luxury of reading through a chapter to find a relevant concept during a test.

- **Do I prepare differently for the final exam?** Many programming courses have a comprehensive final exam—one that covers the complete course material. Preparing for (and taking) a final exam can be intimidating. Normally, a final exam covers a large amount of material and has a major impact on your course grade. Nevertheless, preparing for a final exam involves the same basic steps as preparing for a test: create study sheets or study cards while reviewing your notes and the relevant textbook sections; answer questions and solve problems for practice; anticipate the questions your instructor will ask; review the tests you've already taken; and memorize all necessary information. This will take time, so don't procrastinate. Allow the necessary time to prepare for the final exam. Keep in mind that final exams are usually longer, so your instructor may ask you to solve more complex problems than on previous tests.

A.7 Taking Tests

The most effective test-taking strategy is to conscientiously prepare for the test. However, there are many things you can do while taking a test that may improve your grade.

- Be on time! You may need to use every minute of the allotted time to complete the test.
- If you are not allowed to use your notes or textbook during the test, and you're not confident that you'll remember all of the facts that you've memorized, quickly write this information in the margins or on the back of the test paper as soon as you receive it.
- Unless the test is a very short one, quickly scan it to see what kinds of problems are included.
- If the test consists of different types of problems, such as short answer questions and programming problems, it's usually a good idea to get the short answers out of the way first. As a general rule, do the easy (or quick) problems first to build your confidence and then tackle the more difficult ones.
- Read the instructions carefully for each problem. Many errors occur simply because students don't answer the given question or solve the stated problem.
- If you don't know the answer to a question or how to solve a problem, place a mark next to it and move on to the next one. Return to these problems at the end of the test. Don't use a lot of valuable time trying to solve a problem that you are struggling with. You may end up not having time to answer other easier questions. Save the most difficult questions for last.

- If the test contains multiple choice or true/false questions (and if there is no penalty for guessing), don't leave blanks. If you're not sure of an answer, take your best guess, place a mark next to the question, and if you have time, return to it at the end of the test.

- When you complete the test, you will probably want to hand it in immediately. However, if there is time left, resist this temptation. Use the time to check your work. It's very common to make careless mistakes in a programming test, but you can catch many errors by going over your work before handing it in.

A.8 Overcoming Test Anxiety

Most students get a little nervous before and sometimes during a test. But when this nervousness becomes distress and interferes with your performance on a test—when it becomes test anxiety—you've got to deal with it or your grade may suffer. The following suggestions might help you overcome test anxiety:

- Thoroughly prepare for the test. In general, the more you prepare, the more confident and less anxious you will be.

- Remember that taking a test is different from doing homework. During a test you will be working under a time constraint, you may not be allowed to use your notes or textbook and problems will appear out of context.

- Study with a group. In addition to the other benefits of a study group, you will receive moral support by working with others.

- Get a good night's sleep prior to the exam and don't take the test on an empty stomach.

- Avoid last minute cramming.

- Allow plenty of time to get to the test. You don't want to be late or worry about the possibility of being late.

- Quickly scan the test for an overall picture, noticing the point values. Don't spend a lot of time on a question that is worth only a few points.

- Carefully read the instructions for and the content of each test problem. You can't get a problem right if you're actually answering a different question.

- If someone turns in his or her test early, don't panic. Don't worry about how others are doing—concentrate on your own test.

- Use the full allotted time. Nervousness can lead to mistakes, but you will catch many of them if you take the time to check your work before handing in the test.

- Some students find that it helps to take a small break—just for a few seconds—every once in a while during the test. Close your eyes and relax.

- If you have a test anxiety problem, your college may have certain resources available to help you. Check these out well in advance of the test.

The ASCII Character Set: Printable Characters

Decimal	Character	Description
32		Space
33	!	Exclamation point
34	"	Double quotes
35	#	Number sign
36	$	Dollar sign
37	%	Percent sign
38	&	Ampersand
39	'	Single quote
40	(	Opening parenthesis
41	)	Closing parenthesis
42	*	Asterisk
43	+	Plus sign
44	,	Comma
45	-	Minus sign - hyphen
46	.	Period
47	/	Slash
48	0	Zero
49	1	One
50	2	Two
51	3	Three
52	4	Four
53	5	Five
54	6	Six
55	7	Seven
56	8	Eight
57	9	Nine
58	:	Colon
59	;	Semicolon
60	<	Less than sign

Decimal	Character	Description
61	=	Equal sign
62	>	Greater than sign
63	?	Question mark
64	@	At symbol
65	A	Uppercase characters
66	B	
67	C	
68	D	
69	E	
70	F	
71	G	
72	H	
73	I	
74	J	
75	K	
76	L	
77	M	
78	N	
79	O	
80	P	
81	Q	
82	R	
83	S	
84	T	
85	U	
86	V	
87	W	
88	X	
89	Y	
90	Z	
91	[	Opening bracket
92	\	Backslash
93	]	Closing bracket
94	^	Caret - circumflex
95	_	Underscore
96	`	Grave accent

Decimal	Character	Description
97	a	Lowercase characters
98	b	
99	c	
100	d	
101	e	
102	f	
103	g	
104	h	
105	i	
106	j	
107	k	
108	l	
109	m	
110	n	
111	o	
112	p	
113	q	
114	r	
115	s	
116	t	
117	u	
118	v	
119	w	
120	x	
121	y	
122	z	
123	{	Opening brace
124	|	Vertical bar
125	}	Closing brace
126	~	Equivalency sign - tilde
127	[delete]	Delete

Appendix C

Answers to Self Checks

Chapter 0

Self Check 0.1

1. (a) a calculator cannot act independently on intermediate results

   (b) a programmable calculator cannot manipulate text; it cannot store such large amounts of data (other answers may apply)

2. (a) program   (b) ENIAC   (c) supercomputers   (d) Internet

3. True   4. False

5. False   6. False

7. (1) c   (2) a   (3) b

Self Check 0.2

8. (1) CPU   (2) RAM and ROM   (3) mass storage devices

   (4) input devices   (5) output devices

9. (a) The CPU is the brain of the computer. It receives program instructions, performs arithmetic and logical operations, and controls other computer components.

   (b) Mass storage devices store programs and data.

10. True   11. False

12. False

13. Answers will vary   14. Answers will vary

Self Check 0.3

15. Applications are programs used to enhance productivity.

    System software consists of programs used by the computer to control and maintain hardware, manage resources, and communicate with the user.

16. Answers will vary

    1. Word processors are used to create and format documents such as letters, essays, and the like.
    2. Spreadsheets are tables of values arranged in rows and columns, which allow you to manipulate the data in various ways. They are often used in businesses.

739

3. Web browsers are programs that allow the user to display web pages on a screen.

17. Machine languages, assembly languages, and high-level languages

18. Assembly language is faster, more powerful, and more efficient.

19. In a compiled language, the code is translated to machine-readable code at run time before the program executes, while in a scripting language, the code is interpreted as each line is executed.

20. Answers will vary

Chapter 1
Self Check 1.1

1. • understand the problem completely
   • devise a plan of action with step-by-step instructions
   • carry out the plan
   • review the results

2. Answers will vary

3. 1. analyze the problem
   2. design a program to solve the problem
   3. code the program
   4. test the program

4. The word *cycle* is used because we often have to return to previous steps as we discover flaws in subsequent steps.

Self Check 1.2

5. Input ⇔ Processing ⇔ Output

6. ```
   Write "Enter the temperature in degrees Fahrenheit: "
   Input Temperature
   ```

7. (a) amount invested, rate of interest, length of time

   (b) `Amount` = amount invested

   `Rate` = rate of interest

   `Time` = length of time invested

   (c) ```
       Write "Enter amount invested: "
           Input Amount
           Write "Enter the interest rate for this investment: "
           Input Rate
           Write "Enter the period of time, in months, that ↲
               this money was invested: "
       Input Time
       ```

8. (a) space not allowed

   (b) variable names cannot begin with a number

   (c) nothing is wrong but this name is really too long to be useful

   (d) nothing is wrong

Self Check 1.3

9. 35 degrees Celsius

10. (a) 12   (b) 11   (c) 12   (d) 12

11. `Number = 7`

12. (a) `Write Songs + "songs will cost $ " + DollarPrice`

    (b) `Write "The number of songs to be downloaded is " + Songs`
        `Write "The cost for this purchase in dollars is $ " + ↵`
        `DollarPrice`

13. `Write "Enter a temperature in degrees Fahrenheit: "`
    `Input DegreesF`

    Compute the temperature in degrees Celsius:
    `Set DegreesC = 5 * (DegreesF - 32)/9`
        `Write DegreesF + "degrees Fahrenheit is the same as "`
        `Write DegreesC + "degrees Celsius."`

Self Check 1.4

14. A `Character` variable can only hold a single character.

    A variable of `String` data type can hold as much text as desired.

15. 35   16. `JackieJ`

17. True   18. `step-by-step`

19. d   20. a

21. a   22. Answers will vary

23. False   24. Answers will vary

25. False

Chapter 2

Self Check 2.1

1. 5 is the base, 7 is the exponent

2. 1

3. (a) $6_{10} = 110_2$ (b) $38_{10} = 100110_2$ (c) $189_{10} = 10111101_2$

4. (a) $0010_2 = 2_{10}$ (b) $101010_2 = 42_{10}$ (c) $1111111_2 = 255_{10}$

Self Check 2.2

5. Because a 10, 11, 12, 13, 14, or 15 would require two places and this would put a 1 in the next column

6. (a) $10_2 = 2_{16}$ (b) $10_{10} = A_{16}$

7. (a) $64_{10} = 40_{16}$ (b) $159_{10} = 9F_{16}$ (c) $76458_{10} = 12AAA_{16}$

8. (a) $1110_2 = E_{16}$ (b) $1111111101000110_2 = FF46_{16}$

    (c) $0100101000110100_2 = 4A34_{16}$

9. Easy to read, 16 hexadecimal digits represent all possible combinations of 4 binary bits

Self Check 2.3

10. (a) 48_{10} = 00110000_2 (b) -39_{10} = 10100111_2 (c) -284_{10} = overflow
    (d) 0_{10} = 10000000_2 or 00000000_2

11. (a) 48_{10} = 00110000_2 (b) -39_{10} = 11011000_2 (c) -284_{10} = overflow
    (d) 0_{10} = 11111111_2 or 00000000_2

12. (a) 48_{10} = 00110000_2 (b) -39_{10} = 11011001_2 (c) -284_{10} = overflow
    (d) 0_{10} = 00000000_2

13. Only one way to represent 0

Self Check 2.4

14. (a) 0.5625_{10} = $.1001_2$ (b) 0.3125_{10} = 0.0101_2 (c) 5/8 = 0.1010_2

15. (a) 0.101_2 = 0.625_{10} (b) 0.11111_2 = 0.96875_{10}
    (c) 0.00001_2 = 0.03125_{10}

16. (a) $.515625_{10}$ = $.10001_2$ (b) $.125_{10}$ = $.001000_2$
    (c) $3/32_{10}$=$.09375$=000110_2

17. (a) 68.5_{10} = 1000100.1000_2 (b) 125.44_{10} = 1111101.0111_2
    (c) 99.99_{10} = 1100011.1111_2

Self Check 2.5

18. (a) $450,000$ = 4.5×10^5 (b) 0.000456789 = 4.56789×10^{-4}
    (c) $3,400,004,000$ = 0.3400004×10^{10}

19. (a) $123,000,000$ = 1.23E+8   (b) 0.0000003_{10} = 3.0E-7
    (c) 600_{10} = 6.0E+2

20. (a) $456,000$ = $.456 \times 10^6$ (b) 0.000456789 = $.456789 \times 10^{-3}$
    (c) $3,400,004,000$ = 0.3400004×10^{10}

21. (a) 111000 = $2^4 \times 1.1100$ (b) -1010101.0101_2 = $-2^6 \times 1.0101010101$
    (c) -101.101 = $-2^2 \times 1.01101$

22. (a) $2^3 \times 1.100100111$ = $01000001010010011100000000000000$
    (b) $-2^{12} \times 1.010101$ = $10111001101010100000000000000000$

23. (a) $4149C000_{16}$ (b) $B9AA0000_{16}$

Chapter 3

Self Check 3.1

1. 1. analyze the problem
   2. design a program to solve the problem
   3. code the program
   4. test the program

2. **Analyze the problem**: This phase entails identifying the desired results (output), determining the information needed (input), and figuring out the processes needed to get from input to output.

   Design a program to solve the problem: This phase entails creating a detailed description of the program to be created using either regular language or charts and models.

   Code the program: This phase includes translating the design into the syntax of the programming language that is being used.

   Test the program: This entails ensuring that the program is both free of errors and does what it is supposed to do.

3. (a) F   (b) T   (c) F

4. Input variable needed: weight in pounds = `pounds` → `Float`

   output variable needed: weight in kilograms = `kilos` → `Float`

   formula: `pounds = 2.2046 * kilos`

Self Check 3.2

5. Characteristics of a program module:
   - performs a single task
   - is self-contained and independent of other modules
   - is relatively short (usually not more than one page)

6. Benefits of modular design:
   1. program is easier to read
   2. program is easier to design, code and test, one module at a time
   3. can use one module in several places in a program or in several programs
   4. modules can be designed by different programmers

7. ```
Write "The item is: " + Item
Write
Write "The original price was: " + OriginalPrice
Write
Write "The discount rate is: " + DiscountRate + "%"
Write
Write "The sale price is $ " + SalePrice
Write
Write "The tax on this item is: " + Tax + "%"
Write
Write "The total price is $ " + TotalPrice
```

8. (a) `Set Doctor = "Dr. Miracle"`

   (b) `Write "My job here is done!"`
```

9.

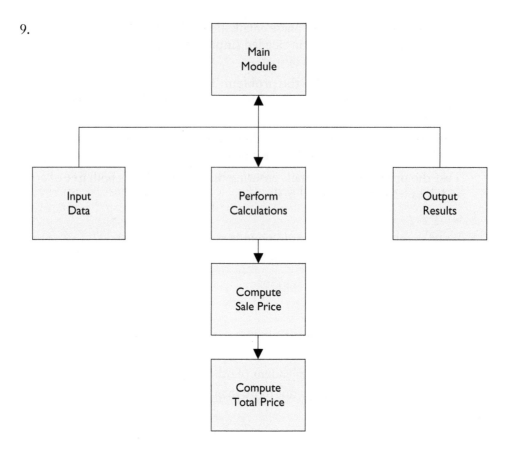

Self Check 3.3

10. **Header comments**: appear at the beginning of a program or module and provide general information about that program or module

   Step comments: also called inline comments and appear throughout the program to explain portions of the code

11. Tested

12. **Syntax errors** violate the programming language's rules for creating valid statements.

   Logic errors result from failing to use the proper combination of statements for a specific task.

13. Many possible answers. Here are a few:

   1. `DistanceTraveled` = 400 miles (or any positive number)

      `RateOfSpeed` = 40 mph (or any positive number)

   2. `DistanceTraveled` = 0 miles

      `RateOfSpeed` = 0 mph

   3. `DistanceTraveled` = -200 miles (or any negative number)

      `RateOfSpeed` = 40 mph (or any positive number)

    4. `DistanceTraveled` = 200 miles (or any positive number)

      `RateOfSpeed` = -40 mph (or any negative number)

Self Check 3.4

14. A **user's guide** is prepared for the lay person who is using the program and it explains how to use the program.

15. A **maintenance manual** is prepared for an expert to explain how the program works internally or why a certain type of code was used.

16. A **technical writer** prepares material for the lay person to use to understand how to use a program or piece of software. A technical writer must be experienced with computers and also able to communicate clearly in writing, for nonexperts.

17. **Design documentation** focuses on why a program was written in a certain way.

    Trade documentation is a comparison document that may suggest alternate ways to improve the program. It is a scientific publication and not a marketing publication.

Self Check 3.5

18. Principles of structured programming:
    1. follow the steps of the program development cycle
    2. design a program in a top-down modular fashion
    3. use comments to document the program

19.

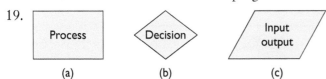

        (a)   (b)   (c)

20. control structures: sequence, selection (decision), and repetition (loops)

21. Good programming style is important because it makes a program more readable and easier to understand and debug, especially by others who may be working on the program or even by the programmer when he or she returns to that code at a later date.

22. 1. use descriptive variable names
    2. provide a welcome message for the user
    3. use a prompt before an input
    4. identify program output
    5. document all programs

Chapter 4

Self Check 4.1

1. single alternative, dual alternative, multiple alternative

2. (a) 5   (b) -1

     5

3. (a) 5   (b) 1

4. (a) If Number = 10, output is Yes

   If Number = -10, output is No

   (b)
```
        If Number > 0 Then
                Write "Yes"
        Else
                Write "No"
        End If
```

   (c)

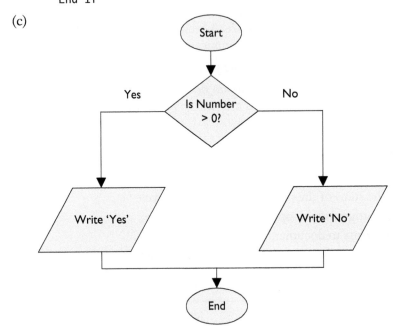

Self Check 4.2

5. (a) relational   (b) arithmetic   (c) logical

6. (a) T   (b) F

7. (a) T   (b) F   (c) T   (d) T

8. (a) T   (b) F   (c) F   (d) F

9.
```
Declare Number As Float
Write "Enter a whole number: "
Input Number
If (Number > 0) AND Number (< 100)
     Write "Correct"
End If
```

Self Check 4.3

10. (a) T   (b) T

11. (a) F   (b) F

12. (a) T   (b) F

13.
```
Declare S1, S2 As String
Write "Enter a string: "
Input S1
Write "Enter another string: "
Input S2
If S1 < S2 Then
    Write S1
Else
    Write S2
End If
```

Self Check 4.4

14. (a)
```
If x == 0 Then
     Write "Low"
End If
If (x == 1) OR (x == 2) Then
    Write "Medium"
End If
If (x > 2) AND (x <= 10) Then
    Write "High"
End If
```
(b)
```
If x == 0 Then
     Write "Low"
Else
    If (x == 1) OR (x == 2) Then
        Write "Medium"
    Else
        If (x > 2) AND (x <= 10) Then
            Write "High"
        End If
    End If
End If
```
(c)
```
Select Case of X
    Case 0:
        Write "Low"
        Break
    Case 1:
    Case 2:
        Write "Medium"
        Break
    Case 3:
    Case 4:
    Case 5:
    .
    .
    .
```

```
            Case 10:
                Write "High"
                Break
        End Case
15. If (Choice == "y") OR (Choice == "Y") Then
        Do YesAction
    Else
        If (Choice == "n") OR (Choice == "N") Then
            Do NoAction
        Else
            Write "Signing off! Goodbye"
        End If
    End If
```

Self Check 4.5

16. (a) 2   (b) 3

17.
```
If A < 0 Then
        Write "The square root of a negative number is undefined."
    Else
        If B == 0 Then
            Write "Division by zero is not allowed."
        Else
            Set C = Sqrt(A)/B
            Write C
        End If
    End If
```

18. (a) If the student did not take any exams, a division by zero error would occur.

    (b)
```
    Declare Average, TotalExamScore As Float
    Declare NumberExamsTaken As Integer
    Write "Enter the student's total exam score"
    Input TotalExamScore
    Write "How many exams did this student take?"
    Input NumberExamsTaken
    If NumberExamsTaken == 0 Then
            Write "An average cannot be computed."
    Else
            Set Average = TotalExamScore/NumberExamsTaken
            Write "The exam average for this student is " + Average
    End If
```

19. (a) T   (b) T

20.
```
    Declare Choice As Integer
    Write "To order a hamburger, enter 1"
    Write "To order a hot dog, enter 2"
    Write "To order a tuna salad sandwich, enter 3"
```

```
    Write "To quit the program, enter 4"
    Input Choice
```

Self Check 4.6

```
21. If EngineChoice =="S" Then
        Set EngineCost = 150
    Else
        If EngineChoice == "E" Then
            Set EngineCost = 475
        Else
            If EngineChoice == "D" Then
                Set EngineCost = 750
            End If
        End If
    End If
22. Call Base_Price module
    Base_Price module
    Declare BasePrice As Float
    Declare Choice As Character
    Write "Choose your model:"
    Write "To choose a 2-door model, enter X"
    Write "To choose a 4-door sedan, enter Y"
    Write "To choose an SUV, enter Z"
    Input BasePrice
    If Choice == "X" Then
        Set BasePrice = 20000
    Else
        If Choice == "Y" Then
            Set BasePrice = 25000
        Else
            If Choice == "Z" Then
                Set BasePrice = 28000
            End If
        End If
    End If
```

Chapter 5
Self Check 5.1

1. (a) 2   (b) 2
        4   4
                       6

2. In 2 years you will be 19
   In 3 years you will be 20

3. (a) T   (b) F   (c) F   (d) T   (e) F   (f) T

4. (a) T   (b) F   (c) F   (d) T   (e) T   (f) T

Self Check 5.2

5.

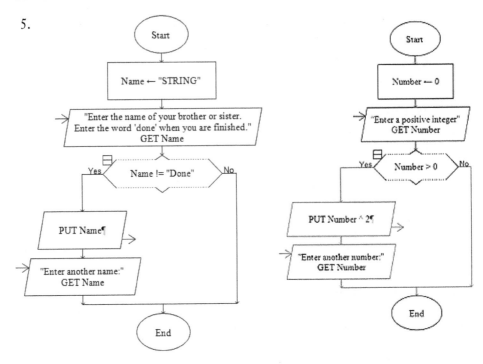

6. An input statement is missing inside the While loop or else, once entered, it will be an infinite loop since Number will never equal 0.

7. counter

8. True

9. True

10. False

11. (a) 6   3   (b) 10

      5   3   8

      4   3

      3   3

12.

```
Declare W As Integer              Declare W As Integer
Declare Count As Integer          Declare Count As Integer
Set Count = 1                     Set Count = 1
Set W = 2                         Set W = 2
Repeat                  OR        Do
    Write Count * W                   Write Count * W
    Set Count = Count + 1             Set Count = Count + 1
Until Count > 3                   While Count < 4
```

Self Check 5.3

13. (a) 3   3   (b) 10

        3   4   8

        3   5

14. (a)   3   (b) Hooray!

        5   Hooray!

        3   Hooray!

        4

        3

        3

15.
```
Declare Count As Integer
For (Count = 1; Count <= 3; Count++)
  Write Count * 10
End For
```

16.
```
Declare Number As Integer
Declare Name As String
For (Number = 1; Number <= 10; Number++)
  Input Name
  Write Name
End For
```

17.
```
Declare Number As Integer
Declare Name As String
Set Number = 1
Do
  Input Name
  Write Name
  Set Number = Number + 1
While Number <= 10
```

18.
```
Declare Beans, Count As Integer
Set Beans = 4
Set Count = Beans
While Count > 0
  Write "bean"
  Set Count = Count - 1
End While
```
Errors: Count >= 0 must be changed to Count > 0

       Count must be decremented

Self Check 5.4

19. ```
Declare MyCharacter As Character
Repeat
  Write "Enter any character: "
  Write "Enter * to quit."
  Input MyCharacter
Until MyCharacter == "*"
```

20. (a) ```
Declare Number As Float
    Write "Enter a number greater than 100: "
    Input Number
    While Number <= 100
      Write "Enter a number greater than 100: "
      Input Number
    End While
```

(b) ```
Declare Number As Float
    Repeat
      Write "Enter a number greater than 100: "
      Input Number
    Until Number > 100
```

21. (a) 5     (b) 4

22. (a) 3     (b) 786,942     (c) 4     (d) 8

23. (a) 11     (b) 0     (c) -7

24. ```
Declare Count As Integer
Declare Sum As Integer
Set Sum = 0
For (Count = 1; Count < 101; Count++)
  Set Sum = Sum + Count
End For
```

25. ```
Declare Count As Integer
Declare Sum As Integer
Declare Average As Float
Set Sum = 0
For (Count = 1; Count < 101; Count++)
  Set Sum = Sum + Count
End For
Set Average = Sum/Count
```

**Self Check 5.5**

26. X = 0     Cost = 10,000     X = 600     Cost = 107,200
Revenue = 0                              Revenue = 240,000
Profit = −10,000                         Profit = 132,800

27. NumRows = 8:                    NumRows = 7:
Spacing = 125                       Spacing = 142
Values of X:                        Values of X:
125, 250, 375, 500, 625, 750, 875, 1000     142, 284, 426, 568, 710, 852, 994
```

28.
```
Write "Enter the number of desired production levels:"
Write "It must be an integer greater than 0."
Input NumRows
While (NumRows != Int(NumRows)) AND (NumRows < 1)
  Write "Enter the number of desired production levels:"
  Write "It must be an integer greater than 0."
  Input NumRows
End While
```

29.
```
Declare X, Cost, Revenue, Profit As Integer
While X <= 1000
    Set Cost = 100000 + 12 * X
    Set Revenue = X * (1000 - X)
    Set Profit = Revenue - Cost
    Set Sum = Sum + Profit
    Write X + " " + Cost + " " + Revenue + " " + Profit
    Set X = X + Spacing
End While
```

Chapter 6

Self Check 6.1

1. After line 9 insert:
```
While Guess != Int(Guess)
  Write "Enter an integer value."
  Write "Guess the secret number: "
  Input Guess
End While
```

2. False 3. False

4. (a) True (b) False 5. (a) True (b) True

6. The Exit For statement needs to be inside the If-Then block, after Write "Good-bye". As it is written, the program will exit the For loop after the first iteration.

Self Check 6.2

7.
```
ItemCost → Float (verify numerical)
ItemTotal → Float (verify numerical)
Tax → Float (verify numerical)
Ship → Float (verify numerical)
Count → Integer
NumItems → Integer (verify numerical)
```

8. Display:
```
Your item total is $ 152.56
Shipping costs will be $ 0.00
The total amounts due, including sales tax, is $ 161.71
```

9.
```
Write "Enter your username: "
Input Username
If Length_Of(Username) > 15 Then
    Write "Your username cannot be more than 15 characters"
```

10.
```
Declare Amp As Character
Declare Hash As Character
Declare Count As Integer
For (Count = 1; Count < 11; Count++)
  Print Amp
End For
Print <NL>
For (Count = 1; Count < 11; Count++)
  Print Hash
End For
Print <NL>
For (Count = 1; Count < 11; Count++)
  Print Amp
End For
```

11.
```
Do
    Write "Enter a number: "
    Input Number
    If Number > 0
      Set Inverse = 1/Number
    Else
      If Number == 0
        Set Inverse = 0
      Else
        Set Inverse = (-1)/Number
      End If
    End If
    Write Inverse
    Set Count = Count + 1
While Count <= 5
```

Self Check 6.3

12. (a) {0, 1, 2, 3}   (b) {3, 4}   (c) {-2, -1, 0, 1, 2}

13.
```
Declare Count As Integer
Declare Number As Integer
For (Count = 1; Count <= 100; Count++)
  Set Number = Floor(Random * 11) + 10
  Write Number
End For
```

14.
```
Declare RandNum As Integer
Declare NumRolls As Integer
Declare Count As Integer
Write "Enter number of rolls: "
Input NumRolls
For (Count = 1; Count <= NumRolls; Count++)
  RandNum = Floor(Random * 2) + 1
```

```
        Write "Die # " + Count + " = " + RandNum
    End For
```

15. (a) from line 8:
```
If Guess < Given Then
    Write "You're too low."
Else
    If Guess > Given Then
        Write "You're too high."
        Else
            Write "Congratulations!"
    End If
End If
```
(b) from line 8:
```
Select Case Of Guess
    Case (Guess < Given):
        Write "You're too low."
        Break
    Case (Guess > Given):
        Write "You're too high."
        Break
    Case (Guess == Given):
        Write "Congratulations!"
        Break
    Default
        Write "Cannot process your guess."
End Case
```

16. Truly random: needs an equal probability of any number to be chosen at any time

    Pseudorandom: uses a seed value to generate a "random" number. The seed is fed into an algorithm.

Self Check 6.4

17. | 2 | 2 |
      |---|---|
      | 2 | 3 |
      | 3 | 2 |
      | 3 | 3 |
      | 4 | 2 |
      | 4 | 3 |

18.   1
      1
      1
      7
      7
      7

19.

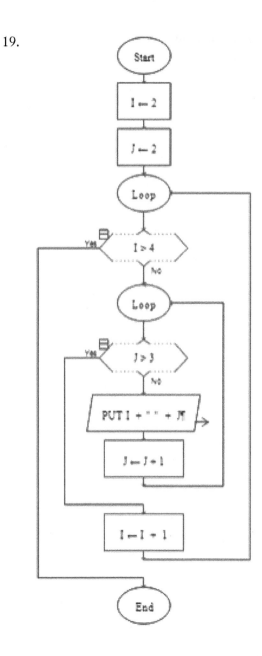

20. Write "Enter the length of a side of the square: "
    Input Side
    If Int(Side) != Side Then
        Write "Please enter an integer value"
        Input Side
    End If

21. Note: changes to code from Ex. 5.17 are in blue:

```
Declare Count1, Count2 As Integer
Declare Symbol As Character
Declare Side As Integer
Declare Width As Integer
Declare Length As Integer
Declare Choice As Character
Write "Choose a symbol (any character from the keyboard): "
Input Symbol
Write "Enter s for square or r for rectangle:"
Input Choice
If Choice == "s" Then
  Write "Enter the length of a side of the square: "
  Input Side
  Set Count1 = 1
  Set Count2 = 1
  While Count1 <= Side
    While Count2 <= Side
      Print Symbol
      Set Count2 = Count2 + 1
    End While (Count2)
    Print <NL>
    Set Count2 = 1
    Set Count1 = Count1 + 1
  End While(Count1)
Else
  If Choice == "r" Then
    Write "Enter the width of the rectangle:"
    Input Width
    Write "Enter the length of the rectangle:"
    Input Length
    Set Count1 = 1
    Set Count2 = 1
    While Count1 <= Length
      While Count2 <= Width
        Print Symbol
        Set Count2 = Count2 + 1
      End While (Count2)
      Print <NL>
      Set Count2 = 1
      Set Count1 = Count1 + 1
    End While(Count1)
  Else
    Write "Invalid entry"
  End If
End If
```

22.
```
Declare MyNumber As Integer
Repeat
  Repeat
    Write "Enter an integer between 0 and 10: "
    Input MyNumber
  Until MyNumber == Int(MyNumber)
Until (MyNumber > 0) AND (MyNumber < 10)
```

23. Change line 3 to read:
```
For (Count1 = 1; Count1 <= (Y + 1); Count++)
```

24. Same as before except Z-column will now be:
```
        ...,    Z = 5
        ...,    Z = 6
        ...,    Z = 7
Pass Number 2
        ...,    Z = 6
        ...,    Z = 7
        ...,    Z = 8
```

Self Check 6.5

25. {9, 10, 11, 12, 13}

26. {−1, 0, 1, 2, 3, 4, 5, 6, 7}

27. High = 45, Low = 41

28. Delete (+ LowRange)

29. Note: changes are in blue:
```
Declare Count As Integer
Set Count = 1
Write "I'm thinking of a whole number"
Write "between " + LowRange + " and " + HighRange
Write "Can you guess the number?"
Write "You have " + NumGuess + " chances to guess."
Input Guess
If Guess == Given Then
    Write "Wow! You won on the first try!"
Else
   While (Count <= NumGuess OR Guess != Given)
     While (Int(Guess) != Guess)
         Write "You must guess a whole number."
         Write "Guess again: "
         Input Guess
     End While
     Select Case of Guess
       Case < Given:
         Write "Your guess is too low. Guess again: "
         Break
       Case > Given:
         Write "Your guess is too high. Guess again: "
         Break
       Case Given:
         Write "Congratulations! You win!"
         Break
```

```
      End Case
    Set Count = Count + 1
    End While
  End If
```

30. Note: added code is in blue:

```
Write "The game normally allows a player 20 guesses."
Write "Do you want to change the number of guesses allowed?"
Write "Type 'y' for yes or 'n' for no."
Input Response
While Response != "y" OR Response != "n"
  Write "I don't understand your response."
  Write "Please enter 'y' for yes or 'n' for no."
  Input Response
End While
If Response == "y" Then
  Write "Enter the number of guesses you want to allow: "
  Input NumGuess
  While (Int(NumGuess) != NumGuess) OR (NumGuess < 1)
    Write "You must enter a whole number greater than 0."
    Write "Try again: "
    Input NumGuess
  End While
End If
```

Chapter 7

Self Check 7.1

1. Note: changes are in blue:

```
Declare Rain[12] As Float
Declare Sum As Float
Declare Average As Float
Declare K As Integer
Set Sum = 0
For (K = 1; K <= 12; K++)
  Write "Enter rainfall for month " + K
  Input Rain[K - 1]
  Set Sum = Sum + Rain[K - 1]
End For
Set Average = Sum/12
For (K = 1; K <= 12; K++)
  Write "Rainfall for Month " + K + " is " + Rain[K - 1]
End For
Write "The average monthly rainfall is " + Average
```

2. Note: changes are in blue:

```
Declare Rain[12] As Float
Declare Sum As Float
Declare Average As Float
Declare K As Integer
Set K = 0
```

```
Set Sum = 0
While K < 12
  Write "Enter rainfall for month " + (K + 1)
  Input Rain[K]
  Set Sum = Sum + Rain[K]
  Set K = K + 1
End While
Set Average = Sum/12
Set K = 0
While K < 12
  Write "Rainfall for Month " + (K + 1) + " is " + Rain[K]
  Set K = K + 1
End While
Write "The average monthly rainfall is " + Average
```

3. 10   4. F
    1   0
    2   0

5. The array name is not consistent with the array inside the loop. The fix:

   Declare X[10] → fix this line

6.
```
Declare Numbers[20]
For (I = 0; I <= 19; I++)
    Input Numbers[I]
End For(I)
For (J = 19; I >= 0; J--)
    Write Numbers[J]
End For(J)
```

7. It is much easier and more efficient to manipulate an array than a collection of simple variables and it uses less variable names.

8.
```
Declare Numbers[20]
For (I = 0; I <= 19; I++)
    Input Numbers[I]
End For(I)
For (J = 19; I >= 0; J--)
    Write Numbers[J]
End For(J)
```

Self Check 7.2

9&10.
```
Declare Rain[12], Snow[12] As Float
Declare SumRain, SumSnow As Float
Declare AvgRain, AvgSnow As Float
Declare K As Integer
Set SumRain = 0
Set SumSnow = 0
For (K = 1; K <= 12; K++)
```

```
       Write "Enter rainfall for month " + (K)
       Input Rain[K - 1]
       Write "Enter snowfall for month " + (K)
       Input Snow[K - 1]
       Set SumRain = SumRain + Rain[K - 1]
       Set SumSnow = SumSnow + Snow[K - 1]
     End For
     Set AvgRain = SumRain/12
     Set AvgSnow = SumSnow/12
     For (K = 1; K <= 12; K++)
       Write "month " + K +": Snowfall: " + Snow[K - 1] + ", ↵
             Rainfall: " + Rain[K - 1]
     End For
     Write "The average monthly rainfall is " + AvgRain
     Write "The average monthly snowfall is " + AvgSnow
```

11. Customers' names, addresses, phone numbers or members at a gym tracking their names and progress in terms of weight, times spent on machines, etc. Answers will vary

12. F

13. Names, addresses, emails, number bought, payment method, etc.

14. Inventory: item name, number on hand, price, etc.

Self Check 7.3

15. F

16.
```
    Set Date = " "
    Write "Enter the year of your birth in the form XXXX:"
    Input Date
    While (Length_Of(Date) != 4)
      Write "Enter the year of your birth in the form XXXX:"
      Input Date
    End While
```

17.
```
    Set Name[] = "Whoever"
    Set First = Name[0]
    Set Lgth = Length_Of(Name)
    Set Last = Name[Lgth - 1]
    Write "First character is " + First
    Write "Last character is " + Last
```

18.
```
    Declare String1[25] Of Characters
    Declare String2[25] Of Characters
    Write "Enter any combination of up to 25 characters: "
    Input String1
    For (K = 0; K <= Length(String1); K++)
        Set String2[K] = String1[K]
    End For
```

Self Check 7.4

19. `Declare A[4, 9]` → has 4 * 9 or 36 storage locations

   `Declare Left[10], Right[10, 10]` → Left has 10 storage locations and Right has 10 * 10 or 100 storage locations so, in total, there are 110 storage locations

20. (a) `Fog[0, 1] = 10`   `Fog[1, 2] = 35`

   (b) `15 = Fog[0, 2]`   `25 = Fog[1,0]`

21. 1 1 3   22. 60

23.
```
Declare Name[25] As String
Declare Inventory[25, 4] As Integer
Declare Num As Integer
Set Num = 0
For (Count = 0; Count < 25; Count++)
  Write "Enter the item's name:"
  Input Name[Count}
  Write "Enter item's ID number, number on hand in gold, number ↵
         on hand in silver, number on hand in stainless steel:"
  While Num < 4
    Input Inventory[Count, Num]
    Set Num = Num + 1
  End While(Num)
  Set Num = 0
End For(Count)
Write Max
```

Self Check 7.5

24. Added code is in blue:
```
Declare cols, rows, colCount, rowCount As Integer
Declare Magic[4, 4] As Integer
Set cols = 4
Set rows = 4
Set colCount = 0
Set rowCount = 0
While rowCount < rows
  While colCount < cols
    Write "Enter the value of the cell in row " ↵
          + (rowCount + 1) + ", column "+ (colCount + 1)
    Input Magic[rowCount, colCount]
    If Magic[rowCount, colCount] != floor(Magic[rowCount, ↵
      colCount]) Then
      Write "Please enter a positive integer: "
      Input Magic[rowCount, colCount]
    End If
    Set colCount = colCount + 1
    Write Magic[rowCount, colCount]
  End While(colCount)
```

```
    Set rowCount = rowCount + 1
    Set colCount = 0
  End While(rowCount)
```

25. Added code is in blue:

```
Declare SumCount, SumOne As Integer
Declare Flag As Boolean
Set SumCount = 0
Set SumOne = 0
Set colCount = 0
Set Flag = 0
While colCount < cols
  Set SumOne = SumOne + Magic[SumCount,colCount]
  Set colCount = colCount + 1
End While(colCount)
Write "The sum to be checked is: " + SumOne
Call Check_row_sums
If Flag == 0 Then
  Call Check_column_sums
  If Flag == 0 Then
    Call Check_diag_sums
  End If
End If
```

26. The following is given for the row sum code. It is almost identical for the column and diagonal sums.

```
Set rowCount = 0
While rowCount < rows OR Flag == 0
  Set NewSum = 0
  Set colCount = 0
  While colCount < cols OR Flag == 0
    Set NewSum = NewSum + Magic[rowCount,colCount]
    Set colCount = colCount + 1
  End While(colCount)
  If NewSum != OneSum Then
    Set Flag = 1
    Write "This sum on row number " + rowCount + " does not ⏎
          match the sum we are checking"
    Write "The value is " + NewSum
  End If
  Set rowCount = rowCount + 1
End While(rowCount)
```

27. In the Enter_info module, the value of cols and rows should be set to 6

28. In the Enter_info module, add the code in blue:

```
Declare cols, rows, colCount, rowCount, N As Integer
Declare Magic[4, 4] As Integer
Write "How big do you want your magic square? Enter an integer ⏎
      value, greater than 1:"
```

```
Input N
Set cols = N
Set rows = N
Set colCount = 0
Set rowCount = 0
Etc...
```

Chapter 8

Self Check 8.1

1. Answers will vary   2. False

3.
```
Declare Client[100] As String
Set nameKey = "Grokofiev"
Set Index = 0
Set Found = 0
While (Found == 0) AND (Index < 100)
  If Client[Index] == nameKey Then
    Set Found = 1
  End If
  Set Index = Index + 1
End While
If Found == 0 Then
  Write "This client is found"
Else
  Write "This client is not in this list"
```

4.
```
Declare Client[100] As String
Declare DateSeen[100] As String
Set nameKey = "Grokofiev"
Set Index = 0
Set Found = 0
While (Found == 0) AND (Index < 100)
  If Client[Index] == nameKey Then
    Set Found = 1
  End If
  Set Index = Index + 1
End While
If Found == 0 Then
  Write Client[Index] + "was last seen on " + DateSeen [Index]
Else
  Write "Client " + Client[Index] + " is not in this list"
```

Self Check 8.2

5.
```
My bird has green feathers.
My cat is black.
```

6. X = "Y", Y = "X" , Z = "X"

7. False   8.   2

9.
```
Declare Client [100] As String
Declare Count As Integer
Set Count = 100
Declare Flag As Integer
Declare K As Integer
Declare OneScore As Float
Declare Temp As Float
Set Flag = 0
While Flag == 0
      Set Flag = 1
      Set K = 0
      While K <= (Count - 2)
         If Client[K] > Client[K + 1] Then
               Set Temp = Client[K]
               Set Client[K] = Client[K + 1]
               Set Client[K + 1] = Temp
               Set Flag = 0
         End If
         Set K = K + 1
      End While(K)
End While(Flag)
```

Self Check 8.3

10. True   11. False

12.
```
Set Low = 0
Set High = N
Set Found = 0
Set Index = Int(N/2)
While (Found == 0) AND (Low <= High)
      If Key < Array[Index] Then
            Set High = Index - 1
            Set Index = Int((High + Low)/2)
      Else
            If Key > Array[Index] Then
                  Set Low = Index + 1
                  Set Index = Int((High + Low)/2)
            Else
                  Set Found = 1
            End If
      End If
End While
```

13. Assume "Reilly" is entered on line 7

Change lines 26-28 to:
```
Set ExamAvg = (Exam1[Index] + Exam2[Index] + Exam3[Index] ↵
                  + 2 * Final[Index])/5
Write "Exam Average is " + ExamAvg
```

Self Check 8.4

14. `False`   15.   `False`

16. Answers will vary

17.
```
Set Count = 0
   While (Count < 200)
      If (Ages[Count] < 17) Then
         Set Seventeen = Seventeen + 1
      Else
         If (Ages[Count] < 23 Then
            Set Twentytwo = Twentytwo + 1
         Else
            If (Ages[Count] < 31) Then
               Set Thirty = Thirty + 1
            Else
               If (Ages[Count < 46) Then
                  Set Fortyfive = Fortyfive + 1
               Else
                  Set Old = Old + 1
               End If(Fortyfive)
            End If(Thirty)
         End If(Twentytwo)
      End If (Seventeen)
      Set Count = Count + 1
   End While
   Write "Number of students younger than 17: " + Seventeen
   Write "Number of students between 17-22: " + Twentytwo
   Write "Number of students between 23-30: " + Thirty
   Write "Number of students between 31-45: " + Fortyfive
   Write "Number of students older than 45: " + Old
```

Self Check 8.5

18. (a) `import: Count, Names, Scores, Averages`
       `export: nothing`

    (b)
```
Subprogram Display_Student_Record(Count, Names, Scores, Averages)
   Declare K As Integer
   Declare Student As String
   Write "Enter the name of the student you want to see: "
   Input Student
   For (K = 0; K<= Count; K++)
      If Name[K] == Student Then
         Write "The record for" + Name[K] + "is:"
         Write "Test 1: " + Scores[0,K]
         Write "Test 2: " + Scores[1,K]
         Write "Test 3: " + Scores[2,K]
         Write "Test average is: " + Averages[K]
      End If
   End For
End Subprogram
```

19. (a) import: `Count, Names, Scores, Averages`
       export: `Scores, Averages`

    (b) `Subprogram Change_Test_Score(Count, Names, Scores As Ref, Averages ⏎`
         `                            As Ref)`

20. Must change the limits on number above and number below a bit to ensure that some scores are not counted twice. Change lines 59 – 69 to:

```
For (K = 0; K < StudentCount; K++)
  If Final[K] > Ceiling(ClassAvg) Then
    Set NumAbove = NumAbove + 1
  Else
    If Final[K] < Floor(ClassAvg) Then
      Set NumBelow = NumBelow + 1
    Else
      Set NumAvg = NumAvg + 1
    End If
  End If
End For
```

Chapter 9

Self Check 9.1

1.

2. Name and Age

3. Voter and VoterAge

4. Nothing

5.
```
Main
    Declare YourName As String
    Write "Enter your name: "
    Input YourName
    Call Display_Name(YourName)
    Call Display_Name(YourName)
    Call Display_Name(YourName)
End Main
Subprogram Display_Name(String Name)
    Write Name
End Subprogram
```

6. 3   2   1

7. (a) replace Num3 with A, Num2 with B, and Num3 with C   (b) no changes

Self Check 9.2

8. 3   2   1   9. Same as Question 8
   4   5   6
   6   2   3

10. (a)   (b)

    3   2   1   3   2   1
    4   5   6   4   5   6
    1   2   3   6   5   4

11. MARTY and jojo   12. (a) 1   (b) 0

Self Check 9.3

13. (a) 2   (b) 3

14. (a) 0   (b) 4   (c) "0.1"   (d) -32 and N = 1

15. 71

16. (a) `Function Area(L,W) As Float`
         `    Set Area = L * W`
         `End Function`

    (b) `Declare MyArea As Float`
         `Declare Length As Float`
         `Declare Width As Float`
         `Set Length = 5`
         `Set Width = 3`
         `Set MyArea = Area(Length, Width)`

17. Added code is in blue:

```
Main
  Declare TripGal[10] As Float
  Set Count = 0
  While Count < 10
    Write "Enter a description of this trip: "
    Input Name
    Set TripName[Count] = Name
    Write "How many miles did you drive? "
    Input Miles
    Set TripMiles[Count] = Miles
    Write "How many gallons of gas did you use this trip?"
    Input Gallons
    Set TripGal[Count] = Gallons
    Set TripMPG[Count] = Answer(Miles, Gallons)
    Set Count = Count + 1
  End While(Count)
  Set K = 0
```

```
        Write "Trip Name \t Miles Traveled \t MPG ⏎
                              \t  Gallons Used"
        While K < 10
          Write TripName[K] + "\t" + TripMiles[K] + "\t" + ⏎
                              TripMPG[K] + TripGal[K]
        Set K = K + 1
        End While(K)
      End Program
      Function Answer(Num1, Num2) As Float
        Set Answer = Num1/Num2
      End Function
```

18.
```
    Main
      Declare Exam As Float
      Declare Count As Integer
      Declare Sum As Float
      Declare Average As Float
      Set Sum = 0
      Set Count = 1
      While Count < 4
        Write "Enter one exam grade: "
        Input Exam
        Set Sum = Sum + Exam
        Set Count = Count + 1
      End While
      Set Average = Answer(Sum, Count - 1)
      Write "Exam average is: " + Average
    End Program
    Function Answer(Num1, Num2) As Float
      Set Answer = Num1/Num2
    End Function
```

Self Check 9.4

19. N = N * (N - 1)
20.
```
    Main
      Declare N, NFactorial As Integer
      Write "When you enter a positive integer, this program ⏎
            will compute:"
      Write "N! = 1 x 2 x 3 x  . . .  x N"
      Call InputN(N)
      Set NFactorial = Factorial(N)
      Call OutputResult(N, NFactorial)
    End Program
    Subprogram InputN(N As Ref)
      Declare Num As Real
      Write "Enter a positive integer."
      Input Num
      While (Num < 1) OR (Int(Num) != Num)
```

```
        Write "The number entered must be a positive integer."
        Write "Please reenter."
        Input Num
      End While
      Set N = Num
    End Subprogram
    Function Factorial(N) As Integer
      If N == 1 Then
        Set Factorial = 1
      Else
        Set Factorial = N * Factorial(N - 1)
      End If
    End Function
    Subprogram OutputResult(N, NFactorial)
      Write N + "! = " + NFactorial
    End Subprogram
```

21. Calling Factorial(N) with N = 3

If Execution Is Here	Value of N	Value of Factorial
Start of execution of first call to Factorial	3	Undefined
Start of execution of second call to Factorial	2	Undefined
Start of execution of third call to Factorial	1	1
End of execution of third call to Factorial	1	1
End of execution of second call to Factorial	2	2
End of execution of first call to Factorial	3	6

22.
```
    Declare N, NFactorial As Integer
    Declare Num As Float
    Repeat
      Write "Enter a positive integer."
      Input Num
    Until (Num > 0) AND (Int(Num) = Num)
    Set N = Num
    Declare Product, K As Integer
    Set Product = 1
    For (K = 1; K <= N; K++)
      Set Product = Product * K
    End For
    Set NFactorial = Product
    Write N, "! = ", NFactorial
```

Self Check 9.5

23. (a)
```
Function Positive(x)
    If x >= 0 Then
        Set Positive = true
    Else
        Set Positive = false
End Function
```

(b) Add the function to:

In the Initial_bmi() subprogram: after lines 5, 7, and 10

In the Fitness_goals() subprogram: after lines 4, 6, 8, 10, 16

In the Progress() subprogram: after lines 6, 9, 12, 15

24. (a)
```
Function Zero(x)
    If x == 0 Then
        Set Zero = false
    Else
        Set Zero = true
End Function
```

(b)
```
Function Quotient(x, y)
    Call Zero(y)
    If Zero == false Then
        Set Quotient = 0
    Else
        Set Quotient = x/y
End Function
```

Chapter 10

Self Check 10.1

1. (a) A text file is a file that consists only of standard keyboard characters

   (b) Text files are easier to create, can be displayed on screen or printed without any special software, and are universal (can be viewed on almost any computer).

2. Sequential file: stored in sequence. Each record in a sequential file must be read in sequence so, to read the 9th record, you must read records 1–8 first

   Direct-access file: These can be directly accessed, like a track on a CD

3.
```
Declare Name As String
Open "employee" for Input As EmployeeFile
While NOT EOF(EmployeeFile)
   Read EmployeeFile, Name
   Write Name
End While
Close EmployeeFile
```

```
4. Declare Name As String
   Open "employee" for Output As EmployeeFile
   Write "Enter an employee's name: "
   Write "Enter * when done."
   Input Name
   While Name != "*"
     Write EmployeeFile, Name
     Write "Enter an employee's name: "
     Write "Enter * when done."
     Input Name
     End While
   Close EmployeeFile
```

Self Check 10.2

```
5. Open "payroll" for Input As PayFile
   Open "scratch" for Output As TempFile
   While NOT EOF(PayFile)
     Read PayFile, Number, Name, Rate
     If Number != 138 Then
       Write TempFile, Number, Name, Rate
     End If
   End While
   Close PayFile, TempFile
   Open "payroll" for Output As TargetFile
   Open "scratch" for Input As SourceFile
   While NOT EOF(SourceFile)
     Read SourceFile, Number, Name, Rate
     Write TargetFile, Number, Name, Rate
   End While
   Close SourceFile, TargetFile

6. Open "payroll" for Input As PayFile
   Open "scratch" for Output As TempFile
   While NOT EOF(PayFile)
     Read PayFile, Number, Name, Rate
     If Number = 456 Then
       Write TempFile, Number, Name, 789
     Else
       Write TempFile, Number, Name, Rate
     End If
   End While
   Close PayFile, TempFile
   Open "payroll" for Output As TargetFile
   Copy "scratch" file onto "payroll" as in Self Check 5 (above)

7. Open "payroll" for Input As PayFile
   Open "scratch" for Output As TempFile
   Declare Inserted As Integer
   Set Inserted = 0
```

```
While (NOT EOF(PayFile)) AND (Inserted == 0)
  Read PayFile, Number, Name, Rate
  If Number == 167 Then
    Write TempFile, 167, "C. Jones", 8.50
    Set Inserted = 1
  End If
  Write TempFile, Number, Name, Rate
End While
If Inserted == 0 Then
  Write TempFile, 167, "C. Jones", 8.50
End If
While NOT EOF(PayFile)
  Read PayFile, Number, Name, Rate
  Write TempFile, Number, Name, Rate
End While
Close PayFile, TempFile
Copy "scratch" file onto "payroll" as in Self Check 5 (above)
```

8. (1) "Cornswaller" , 77

   Lines executed: $1-13, 17-22$

   Lines skipped: $14-16$

   (2) "Throckmorton", 67

   Lines executed: $1-13, 17-22$

   Lines skipped: $14-16$

   (3) "Zigler", 88

   Lines executed: $1-7, 12-22$

   Lines skipped: 8 - 11

9. Would use arrays because easier to manipulate. Answers will vary.

Self Check 10.3

10. (a) T   (b) T   (c) T

11. Neither record is written to the new file since the conditions on lines 18 and 22 only write the contents of these files while the records are not 0. The ending record (0, "0", 0.0) is written in line 26.

12. On line 10, the check is made to see if the record of payroll1 is less than payroll2. If it is, the payroll1 record is written to the new file. If not, the payroll2 record is written. Therefore, if two records are identical, the payroll1 record is skipped and the payroll2 record is written, ensuring that identical records are only written once.

13. Change line 10 to:
```
If Number1 > Number2 Then
```

Self Check 10.4

14&15.
```
Write "Harvey's Hardware Company"
    Write "          Monthly Sales"
```

```
        Write " Store number", "Salesperson", "Sales", "Month", "Year"
        Declare Month As String
        Declare Year As String
        Read DataFile, Store, Salesperson, Sales
        Write "Enter the date for the sales by " + Salesperson
        Write "Enter Month: "
        Input Month
        Write "Enter Year: "
        Input Year
```

16. First value of `PreviousStore` is 1

    Last value of `PreviousStore` is 3

17. `no changes`

Self Check 10.5

18. You would just have the welcome message, the word `Customer:` and the column headings. The amount due would be 0 and no parts would be listed.

19.
```
Repeat
    Set OrderNums[OrderCount] = Num
    Set OrderAmts[OrderCount] = Amt
    Set OrderCount = OrderCount + 1
    Write "Enter part number, quantity desired"
    Write "Enter 0, 0 when done"
    Input Num, Amt
Until Num = 0
```

20.
```
Main module
    Declare Names[100] Of Characters
    Declare Numbers[100] Of Float
    Declare Prices[100] Of Float
    Declare OrderNums[50] Of Integers
    Declare OrderAmts[50] Of Integers
    Declare ListCount As Integer
    Declare OrderCount As Integer
    Declare Customer As String
    Call Welcome Message module
    Call Input Data module
    Call Sort Parts Order module
    Call Print Invoice module
End Program

Welcome Message module
    Write "THE LEGENDARY LAWNMOWER COMPANY"
    Write "      Invoice Preparer"
    Write "This program will help you prepare an invoice ⏎
        for your customers."
    Write "You will be prompted for information about a ⏎
        customer and the parts and quantities ordered ⏎
        by that customer."
```

```
Write "An invoice will then be printed showing the parts ↵
      ordered, the prices, and part numbers as well as the ↵
      total cost for each part and total amount due."
```

Chapter 11
Self Check 11.1

1. Data and the operations on data (attributes and methods)

2. A class is like a data type. An object is an instance of this data type. The class defines the structure of the object.

3. Public class members are accessible to modules outside of the class.

   Private class members are protected because they are inaccessible to calls from outside the class.

4. Examples will vary. Data hiding maintains the security of the object's data. The data cannot be altered except by using one of the object's methods. This would be valuable when writing a game. It also helps shield the inner workings of the object from the programmer. The object's interface with the outside programming world (their methods) is made public but the way a method gets its job done and the variables with which it works are kept private.

5.
```
Class InAndOut
    Declare Private Value As Float
    // constructor
    Public InAndOut()
      Set Value = 1.0
    End Constructor
    Public Subprogram SetValue(Float NewValue)
      Set Value = NewValue
    End Subprogram
    Public Subprogram GetValue() As Float
       Return NewValue
    End Subprogram
End Class
```

6. A constructor is used to set or use default values for the instantiation of its class object. A constructor is like a model or a plan for constructing an object of its class type.

Self Check 11.2

7. procedural

8. (a) encapsulation   (b) inheritance   (c) polymorphism

9. derived or child . . . base or parent

10. • Rectangle would use the Get and Set methods for Side(height) from Shape and would need OtherSide(length) and ComputeArea(side*length)

    • Circle would need new Get and Set methods for Radius and ComputeArea(radius*radius*3.14)

    • Triangle would use Get and Set methods from Shape(height) and would need Get and Set methods for Base and ComputeArea (0.5*base*height).

Nine new methods are needed plus those in the parent class.

```
Class Rectangle Extends Shape
  Declare Private Length As Float
  Public Rectangle()
    Shape()  // call to parent constructor
    Set Length = 1.0
  End Constructor
  Public Subprogram GetLength() As Float
    Return Length
  End Subprogram
  Public Subprogram SetLength(Float NewLength)
    Set Length = NewLength
  End Subprogram
  Public Subprogram ComputeArea() As Float
    Return Length*Side
  End Subprogram
End Class

Class Circle Extends Shape
  Declare Private Radius As Float
  Public Circle()
    Shape()  // call to parent constructor
    Set Radius = 1.0
    Set Pi = 3.14
  End Constructor
  Public Subprogram GetRadius() As Float
    Return Radius
  End Subprogram
  Public Subprogram SetRadius(Float NewRadius)
    Set Radius = NewRadius
  End Subprogram
  Public Subprogram ComputeArea() As Float
    Return Pi * Radius * Radius
  End Subprogram
End Class

Class Triangle Extends Shape
  Declare Private Base As Float
  Public Base()
    Shape()  // call to parent constructor
    Set Base = 1.0
  End Constructor
  Public Subprogram GetBase() As Float
    Return Base
  End Subprogram
  Public Subprogram SetBase(Float NewBase)
    Set Base = NewBase
  End Subprogram
```

```
Public Subprogram ComputeArea() As Float
   Return .05 * Base * Side
End Subprogram
End Class
```

11. Inheritance occurs when a class is derived from another class, thereby making the new class a child or derived class. This means it will "inherit" or be allowed access to the members of the base (parent) class.

Self Check 11.3

12. • Identify the classes to be used
    • Determine the attributes needed
    • Determine the methods needed
    • Determine the relationships among classes

13. Extendibility is the ability to recycle

14. A modeling language contains a standard set of symbols that includes ways to arrange those symbols to model parts of an object-oriented software design or system design.

15. Functional requirements view

    Static structural view

    Dynamic behavior view

16. Answers may vary. UMLs help organize and contain a huge system design, create lines of communication between varying languages, allow designers to see one part of the system at a time, and more

Self Check 11.4

17. (a) `text box`   (b) `command button`   (c) `option (radio) button`

18. (a) `window: name, height`   (b) `text box: text, position`

    (c) `option button: caption, enabled` (all have other properties which are also correct, these are a few)

19. `Set OKbutton.caption = "OK"`

    `Set OKbutton.enabled = false`

20. (a) `true`   (b) `false`

21. `Change`

22. (a) Change lines 12 and 13 in the `Area Calculator` program to:
```
12   Set InputBox,text = "0"
13   Set OutputBox.text = "0"
```

    (b) Change the `CalculateButton.Click()` subprogram to:
```
If Val(InputBox.text) < 0 Then
  Set OutputBox.text = "Invalid input"
Else
  Set OutputBox.text = Val(InputBox.text)^2
```

23. (c) Determine which `windows` are needed

Self Check 11.5

24. Answers will vary

25. (a) Subprogram Option1.Click()
```
        Set Option1.value = true
        Set Option2.value = false
        Set Option3.value = false
    End Subprogram
```

(b) Subprogram OKbutton.Click()
```
        If (Option1.value == true) Then
          Call Display.Open
          Else If (Option2.value == true) Then
            Call SelectTest.Open
            Else If (Option3.value == true) Then
              Call ComputeAverages.Open
            End If
          End If
        End If
        Set Retrieve.visible = false
    End Subprogram
```

26. Subprogram ComputeAverages.StartUp()
```
    Declare J As Integer
    Declare Average As Float
    For (J = 0; J < StudentCount; J++)
      Set StudAvg = (Scores[0, J] + Scores[1, J] + ↵
                    Scores[2, J])/3
      Set Averages[J] = StudAvg
    End For
  End Subprogram
```

Index